Using WordStar®

2nd Edition

Steve Ditlea

Que® Corporation
Carmel, Indiana

Using WordStar®, 2nd Edition

Library of Congress Catalog No.: 88-61158
ISBN 0-88022-361-8

92 91 90 89 88 8 7 6 5 4 3 2 1

Interpretation of the printing code: the rightmost double-digit number is the year of the book's printing; the rightmost single-digit number, the number of the book's printing. For example, a printing code of 88-1 shows that the first printing of the book occurred in 1988.

Using WordStar, 2nd Edition, is based on WordStar Professional Release 5.0 and the earlier Release 4.0.

About the Author

Steve Ditlea is a free-lance journalist whose columns on Artificial Intelligence and Arts appear in *Omni* magazine. He has written about the personal computer field since 1978—specializing in word processing developments and applications. Since 1981, he has been a WordStar user on a dozen different computer models.

As an independent consultant, Mr. Ditlea has tutored computer beginners in WordStar's basics and taught business professionals to master its advanced features. He served as a tester for MicroPro International's latest version of WordStar—Release 5—prior to its publication.

This rewritten and updated version of the best-selling *Using WordStar* (for Release 4) is Mr. Ditlea's fourth book to be entirely composed with WordStar.

Publishing Manager

Scott N. Flanders

Senior Editor

Lloyd J. Short

Editors

Sandra Blackthorn
Jeannine Freudenberger
Elizabeth A. Hoger
Gregory Robertson
Steven Wiggins

Technical Editor

George Beinhorn

Editorial Assistant

Debra S. Reahard

Indexer

Connie Tewmey

Book Design and Production

Dan Armstrong
Cheryl English
Lori A. Lyons
Jennifer Matthews
Cindy Phipps
Joe Ramon
Dennis Sheehan
M. Louise Shinault
Peter Tocco

Composed in Garamond and OCRB
by Cromer Graphics

Screen reproductions in this book were created by means of the InSet program from INSET Systems Inc., Danbury, CT.

Contents at a Glance

Table of Contents

II Intermediate WordStar

Acknowledgments

The author wants to thank the following persons for their help in the development of *Using WordStar*, 2nd Edition.

Seymour Rubinstein and Rob Barnaby for creating the most popular word processing program in the world.

Peter Mierau, Walter Feigenson, and Leon Williams, President of MicroPro International, for help with the original edition of this book.

Cheryl Hanley, Product Manager for WordStar Professional Release 5, for assistance beyond the call of duty. Adrienne Bachleda, Dave Cannon, Laurie Fagundes, Jim Schair, and all the members of MicroPro International's technical support staff for imparting their knowledge of Release 5.

Jan Marciano of EPSON America, Inc., for the use of an Epson Equity II+ 10 MHz computer and high-speed LQ-850 printer to increase efficiency during the writing of this edition.

The 40,000 buyers of the first edition of *Using WordStar*. This second edition is a tribute to your confidence.

The millions of WordStar users who have kept WordStar thriving for nearly a decade.

Trademark Acknowledgments

Que Corporation has made every effort to supply trademark information about company names, products, and services mentioned in this book. Trademarks indicated below were derived from various sources. Que Corporation cannot attest to the accuracy of this information.

Brown Bag Software is a registered trademark, and PC-Outline is a trademark of Telemarketing Resources.

COMPAQ is a registered trademark of COMPAQ Computer Corporation.

CompuServe is a registered trademark, and VIDTEX is a trademark of CompuServe Incorporated.

CP/M is a registered trademark of Digital Research, Inc.

dBASE, dBASE II, dBASE III, and MultiMate are registered trademarks, and MultiMate Advantage and dBASE III Plus are trademarks of Ashton-Tate Corporation.

DEC is a registered trademark of Digital Equipment Corporation.

Dow Jones News Retrieval Service is a registered trademark of Dow Jones and Company.

EasyLink is a service mark of Western Union Telegraph Company.

Epson FX-80 and MX-80 are trademarks of EPSON America.

EPSON is a registered trademark of Seiko Epson Corporation.

Hayes Smartmodem 2400 is a trademark of Hayes Microcomputer Products, Inc.

Hewlett-Packard, HP, LaserJet, and LaserJet II are registered trademarks of Hewlett-Packard Co.

IBM is a registered trademark, and IBM Personal System/2, Systems Applications Architecture, OS/2, and DisplayWrite are trademarks of International Business Machines Corporation.

InSet is a trademark of INSET Systems, Inc.

Lotus, 1-2-3, and Symphony are registered trademarks of Lotus Development Corporation.

Mace Utilities is a registered trademark of Paul Mace Software.

Macintosh is a trademark of Apple Computer, Inc.

MCI Mail is a registered service mark of MCI Communications Corporation.

MicroPro, MicroPro International Corporation, MailMerge, TelMerge, WordStar Professional, WordStar, WordStar 2000, WordMaster, and CorrectStar are registered trademarks, and Advanced Page Preview, MailList, Easy, and ProFinder are trademarks of MicroPro International Corporation.

Microsoft, Microsoft Word, and MS-DOS are registered trademarks of Microsoft Corporation.

NewWord is a registered trademark of Newstar Software, Inc.

Norton Utilities is a trademark of Peter Norton Computing.

ONTYME is a registered trademark of McDonnell Douglas Corporation.

PFS: Professional Write is a registered trademark of Software Publishing Corporation.

PostScript is a registered trademark of Adobe Systems Incorporated.

ProKey is a trademark of RoseSoft, Inc.

Quattro, SideKick, SideKick Plus, Sprint, and SuperKey are registered trademarks of Borland International, Inc.

SAMNA Word is a trademark of SAMNA Corporation.

The Source is a service mark of Source Telecomputing Corporation.

Star Exchange is a trademark of Systems Compatibility Corporation.

Volkswriter is a registered trademark of Lifetree Software, Inc.

WANG is a registered trademark of Wang Laboratories, Inc.

Word Finder is a trademark of Microlytics, Inc.

WordPerfect is a registered trademark of WordPerfect Corporation.

Conventions Used in This Book

A number of conventions are used in *Using WordStar* to help you better understand the book.

1. Direct Quotations of words that appear on the screen are spelled as they appear on-screen and are printed in a `special typeface`. Text that the user should enter from the keyboard appears in *italic*. DOS commands the user enters are shown in lowercase italic because it is not necessary to type them in uppercase.

2. Throughout the text, Enter is used instead of Return to refer to the ↵ key on the keyboard.

3. Commands issued with the Ctrl key generally are represented by the caret (^) symbol. To invoke a Ctrl-letter command, you press and hold the Ctrl key while you next press the letter key. For example, the command Ctrl-E or ^E means that you press and hold the Ctrl key while you next press the E key. Other hyphenated key combinations, such as Alt-F10, are performed in the same manner.

4. If a command involves multiple keystrokes, such as Ctrl-KD or ^KD, you press and hold the Ctrl key while you next press the K key; then you release both keys and press the D key by itself.

Introduction

WordStar® is aptly named. It has been the star performer among personal computer word processing programs since its debut nearly 10 years ago (an eternity in the computer era). Rival software packages may outsell WordStar for a while, but no word processor comes close to WordStar's worldwide popularity. More buyers have chosen WordStar than any other word processing program. Countless business documents, reports, and published books have been created with it. Renowned authors, including William F. Buckley, Jr., Arthur C. Clarke, and James Clavell, use WordStar to facilitate their writing.

The latest version of this favorite, WordStar Professional Release 5, is designed to please loyalists and novices alike. For WordStar diehards—after enduring WordStar's scant program improvements as other software packages surged ahead in capabilities—WordStar Release 5 means no longer having to say you're sorry. WordStar is again one of the fastest and most versatile word processors on the market. With claims of more than 300 new features rendering the program fully competitive with its rivals, program publisher MicroPro® International has preserved WordStar's earlier commands (and menus). This powerful text-management tool retains the look and feel of the software classic known by millions of users. For new users, WordStar Release 5 includes an added set of beginners' menus—ending WordStar's reputation for being difficult to learn.

In spite of its success, WordStar often has been misunderstood (in part due to confusion with WordStar® 2000, a MicroPro International product that has little in common with it). Saddled with the reputation of being complicated, WordStar is, in fact, one of the most logically designed word processing packages on the market. While recent releases of WordStar's challengers, Microsoft® Word and WordPerfect®, have added major inconsistencies in design and commands, WordStar Release 5 continues the elegance of its well-known command structure. Based on methodically chosen key locations and keystrokes, WordStar's commands have little of the arbitrariness of its rivals. Nor do the commands suffer from the capricious terminology used by XyWrite™, another WordStar competitor among professional writers. Once you grasp WordStar's common-sense approach to word processing, you learn the program easily.

Unfortunately, even veteran users find themselves intimidated by WordStar's wealth of options. Learning WordStar's nearly 250 separate commands certainly can be daunting. Nevertheless, the commands for creating a simple document, such as a memo, total two dozen and can be learned in an hour. With its new pull-down menus of task-oriented commands, WordStar is ideal for a beginner's word processing needs. Text on-screen closely resembles what the text will look like in finished form, complete with line spacing and page breaks. Editing, inserting, and moving text are accomplished quickly with easily found keyboard commands—usually using fewer keystrokes than needed in rival programs. WordStar's search-and-replace function remains among the fastest and most powerful around.

As your familiarity with this software grows, so does WordStar's usefulness, thanks to its wide array of features. The program's varied commands place few limitations on composing, polishing, formatting, and printing text. Like training wheels on a bicycle, WordStar's pull-down menus can be removed and other functions reset as a user becomes more proficient. Thus unencumbered, WordStar becomes a swift, responsive word processor, ideal for intermediate and advanced applications.

WordStar Release 5 includes everything you need to produce professional-looking documents, from single-page correspondence to complex reports—including simple desktop publishing functions. Suppose, for example, that you must create a report incorporating information from a Lotus® 1-2-3® spreadsheet. The report must be footnoted and indexed. Your finished document should be impeccably spelled, without any redundant or inappropriate words. In addition, to aid in presentation, you must use boxed charts and snaking newspaper-style columns of text, and you may want to print everything on a professional-quality laser printer with a variety of type fonts or on a color printer using several colors.

WordStar Release 5 lets you accomplish all this with ease. During editing of a document, WordStar can display another file in an on-screen window, record annotations by various readers, and sort lists of information into alphabetical order. As you edit, changes in line length are automatically reformatted—a feature missing from WordStar until now. Supplementary programs included in the WordStar Release 5 package add to WordStar's functionality: PC-Outline™ provides complete control over outline formats; MailList™ helps generate and manage mailing lists; ProFinder™ simplifies locating and manipulating files on a hard disk; and TelMerge® opens the way to telecommunicating with other computers, networks, and data services.

True, you will find functions available in competing word processing packages that even the latest version of WordStar cannot match on its own. These functions include displaying more than two files on-screen, integrating graphics into a document, creating forms for office use, comparing documents on disk, and converting WordStar files to other word processors' formats. Still, as an industry leader, WordStar has attracted add-on programs that will accomplish these tasks if you need them.

Most of WordStar's current features have been included in previous versions for computers using CP/M® and MS-DOS® operating system software. The most complete version of the program, WordStar Release 5 for MS-DOS machines (IBM® PC and PS/2™ compatible models), is the one on which this book is based. More than 35 new commands have been added; these and other changes in Release 5 are flagged throughout this book. If you are using an earlier version of WordStar, remember that not all functions mentioned here will work with your program.

Who Should Use This Book?

Newcomers to WordStar and experienced users alike can benefit from the information between these covers. WordStar's features tend to be underused as a result of its hefty manuals. Even with the improved menus and documentation of WordStar Release 5, it still may be difficult for beginners to get the program up and running and for proficient users to take complete advantage of this powerful software. Veterans of previous versions who would like to apply the new features in Release 5 also find themselves stymied by the organization and briefness of explanations in the program's reference guide.

Over the years, the lack of clear documentation has given rise to many books on how to run WordStar. Frustrated users may end up buying several titles, to no avail. Some books are elementary tutorials that introduce the software without exploring its full powers; others, intended as references for advanced users, contain major technical errors. Many books on the shelves still refer primarily to earlier versions of the program instead of to the greatly expanded WordStar Release 5.

If you are just learning to use WordStar, this book will take you through the basics with brief explanations, handy shortcuts, and cautionary tips so that you can avoid the frustrations that come with trying to master any new software. *Using WordStar*, 2nd Edition, contains a step-by-step tutorial, including WordStar's beginner-level menus, and practical applications of the program's features to help you easily adapt the program to your own needs.

Are you already using WordStar's basic features for your documents? Then you should peruse this book's intermediate and advanced sections to learn about your word processor's more powerful capabilities. When you need to master a specific function, use these pages as a reference guide: let the Table of Contents or Index direct you to the discussion of a particular topic.

If you are a veteran user of previous editions of WordStar, check the parts of this book noted in the book's margins as *new in Release 5*. With more changes than any earlier upgrade, WordStar's newest release includes improved ways of dealing with your word processing applications. You may find that some commands to which you have grown accustomed have either been modified or augmented by more powerful ones. The new or enhanced commands are listed at the back of *Using WordStar*, 2nd Edition, in Appendix A, a useful resource as you make the transition to this software's latest version. All users will want to detach the command reference card inserted on the inside back cover and keep it handy.

If you are considering a first purchase of word processing software or are thinking of switching from another program, this book can help you decide whether WordStar Release 5 is the package for your needs. Defectors to other programs may find this recent release good reason to return to the most widely used word processor on earth (if you ever need help, there's bound to be a WordStar user nearby). If WordStar proves to be the right choice, this book can give you a head start on running useful applications.

An Overview of WordStar

Personal computer software is such a recent development that recounting the history of a particular program may seem trivial. For a classic like WordStar, however, a brief look at its origins and development will help you better understand the program's design and current implementation.

Even computer experts tend to forget how many innovations were pioneered by WordStar—features now taken for granted in most word processing programs for personal computers. Over the years, WordStar's firsts have included the following:

- Flexible composing and editing of text
- Accurate on-screen formatting
- Automatic page breaks
- Hyphenation help
- Automatic backup files
- Professional printing capabilities
- Optional menu and help screens
- A disk-based tutorial
- Easy resetting and customization of features
- Mail merging for form letters
- Phonetic spelling correction

Many of WordStar's original features—such as on-screen line spacing and saving of backup files—remain rare among today's word processors. Another rare feature is the logical placement of commands on a computer's letter keys; this WordStar feature has kept the program well suited for both the hunt-and-peck and the touch typist. More than 100 of WordStar's features can be turned off or modified at will during editing, and the program code can be customized to an extent unknown among rival word processors.

WordStar's enduring character results from the constraints under which the program was originally designed. In the days before inexpensive memory and standardized keyboards, the program had to deliver maximum utility with a minimum of program code and without exotic keystroke combinations. Though totally rewritten, WordStar's latest release is so compactly programmed that it can still be used with minimal internal memory (384K) on dual floppy computer systems—another rarity among recent word processors.

Compatibility was an essential design factor in the program's earliest versions: all of WordStar's commands had to be available on a variety of personal computer keyboards. The solution for on-screen editing was using the Control (Ctrl) and letter keys pressed in combination to differentiate commands from text characters. In addition, for print-time formatting, dot command codes satisfied the needs of those accustomed to such commands in mainframe computer editing software. Later, when the IBM PC keyboard became a standard, arrow and function key command options were added to WordStar.

The program's features reflect the personalities of WordStar's original designers. For example, WordStar starts with right-justification on (text is displayed and printed with the right margin aligned). Justification is one of the first features that experienced users turn off because it makes a printout look as if it were produced on a computer—hardly desirable for personalized correspondence. However, that's precisely why MicroPro International founder Seymour Rubinstein wanted justification on: to impress would-be computer users.

The notion that microcomputers could displace typewriters, dedicated word processors, and minicomputer systems was farfetched before Rubinstein's professional-quality word processing software came along. At a time when personal computers were still largely the domain of hobbyists, Rubinstein had the idea that all the benefits of expensive, dedicated word processing systems could be offered to the general public on reasonably priced microcomputer systems. Together with chief programmer Rob Barnaby, Rubinstein set out to improve on his company's first text editor, WordMaster®—a tool for programmers.

WordStar was announced in June, 1979, for computers using CP/M, an operating system that was then prevalent. Soon after, MicroPro began shipping the first in a succession of WordStar releases. The different editions (with release dates) included the following:

Release	*Date*	*Description*
0.88	July, 1979	A partial implementation
1.0	March, 1980	The first complete version
2.0	June, 1980	MailMerge® option
2.26	September, 1981	Optional spelling checker
3.0	June, 1982	First MS-DOS version, column mode
3.3	April, 1983	Improved install program
3.31	September, 1984	Improved color installation

3.4	September, 1984	United Kingdom and Canadian version
4.0	February, 1987	Undo, math, macros, thesaurus

Over the years, WordStar became the closest thing to a universal word processor. Available in American, British, French, French-Canadian, Dutch, Finnish, German, Italian, Spanish, and Swedish versions, WordStar has sold more than 3 million copies. At least an equal number of illegal bootleg copies (which helped spread WordStar's popularity) are in circulation. MicroPro International never used anti-piracy protection schemes to restrict copying of the program. By MicroPro's estimates, as many as 10 million people worldwide are "WordStar literate."

In 28 countries, WordStar is nearly as ubiquitous as another American classic—Coca-Cola. In fact, MicroPro's marketing of WordStar has paralleled the Coca-Cola Company's treatment of its best-selling soft drink. Just as New Coke was introduced to counter a competitive threat, MicroPro concocted WordStar 2000. The perceived competition was high-end word processing software (though the original WordStar had all the power needed to hold its own). Unlike the original Coca-Cola, the original WordStar was not to be discontinued. Still, MicroPro neglected its flagship product as the company brought new programs to market.

As with Coke, public clamor led to management's renewed support of its lead product. When MicroPro launched its first major upgrade to WordStar in three years—Release 4—it was essentially an already existing WordStar alternative, a program written to correct many of the best-seller's weaknesses. Eighteen months later, when the same design team produced the most recent version of WordStar—Release 5—one of the names considered for the product was WordStar Classic (shades of Coca-Cola!).

About WordStar Professional Release 5

In 1983, three former MicroPro International employees decided to create a better WordStar. Among them was programmer Peter Mierau, who wrote software with similar commands but used different program code in order to avoid copyright violations. The program, NewWord®, was introduced for CP/M and then MS-DOS computers. An upgrade, NewWord 3, came out in late 1985 and was greeted with rave reviews that called it "the program WordStar should have been." A further upgrade was in the works when MicroPro bought NewWord and its parent company for $3.1 million. A modified version of the NewWord upgrade became WordStar Release 4 in 1987.

Back at MicroPro's offices in San Rafael, California, Mierau and associates, under the supervision of Development Vice President Dave Cannon, set to work on a definitive update of WordStar: WordStar Professional Release 5. Personal computers were changing; IBM had discontinued its original PC line of computers in favor of more powerful systems, and laser printers were becoming affordable to all serious word processor users. Taking advantage of new hardware, WordStar Release 5 still would have to work on minimal configurations of IBM PC compatibles. Veteran users were asked for their wish lists of features. MicroPro International Chief Executive Officer Leon Williams campaigned on behalf of beginners for the addition of pull-down menus like those that had made his firm's Easy™ word processor and rival PFS®: Professional Write so easy to learn.

While retaining WordStar's classic commands, WordStar Release 5 had to be changed in one fundamental aspect. The characteristic WordStar disk file format, maintained in previous versions, would have to be modified to accommodate footnotes, endnotes, and annotations. WordStar Release 5 would read files created with earlier editions of the program; a conversion printer file could be used to produce disk files compatible with these earlier versions. At the same time, accompanying programs for the WordStar Release 5 package were being carefully evaluated. The result is the most versatile WordStar version to date.

Many of WordStar's previous limitations have been remedied in this newest version. Among the improvements in WordStar Release 5 are the following:

- Windows for editing two files at a time
- Automatic text realignment during editing
- Pull-down menus for beginning users
- Multipage preview of document on-screen
- Speed Write mode for quickly opening a document
- Cursor shape control
- Ruler line absolute measurement, active marker
- Input information from 1-2-3 files
- Automatic paragraph numbering
- Word count within a block
- Text sorting within a block
- Newspaper-style snaking text columns
- Consolidated page layout settings
- Tab settings retained with documents

- Automatically numbered footnotes and endnotes
- Printed annotations and hidden comments in documents
- Odd/even page printing of headers/footers
- Printer changes from within a document
- Font control on laser printers
- Downloading of soft fonts
- Support for PostScript® printers
- Color printing instructions for up to 16 colors
- Integrated thesaurus, including word definitions
- Thesaurus, spelling dictionaries in more compact files
- Document outlining with memory-resident program
- Mailing list management utility
- Telecommunications program included
- File and disk directory management utility

With this upgrade, MicroPro International is serving notice that its classic program can more than hold its own. WordStar Release 5's efficient command keystrokes, rapid response, full laser printer support, wide compatibility on MS-DOS computers, and well-known user interface make the program a logical alternative to any PC-compatible word processing software. For example, sales leader WordPerfect's already arcane commands (usually requiring more keystrokes than WordStar's) became even more complex in its latest upgrade, also numbered 5. To match WordStar's speed in the most recent release of Word, Microsoft's designers had to retreat from their program's slow graphical orientation by adding a character-oriented mode (WordStar's approach all along). A previous best-selling word processor, MultiMate®, has been far surpassed by WordStar's formatting and printing options, and IBM's DisplayWrite™ has grown increasingly incompatible with all but 100 percent IBM-compatible computers. As for XyWrite, it remains a cult favorite without the support of add-on products, books, and so on, ensured by WordStar's large user base.

WordStar Release 5's improved help menus for beginners make it as easy to learn as any of the simple but limited word processors on the market, including MicroPro's own Easy and Software Publishing's PFS: Professional Write. WordStar's advantage is that it has the capacity to accommodate a user's growing word processing needs. Everyday office or personal applications can benefit from WordStar Release 5's enhancements. More sophisticated functions—including outlining, mailing list management, and telecommunications—also are supported. All these upgrades make WordStar a sounder choice than ever for word processor beginning, intermediate, and advanced users.

An Overview of This Book

Using WordStar, 2nd Edition, follows the progression in which most users master this software's functions. Newcomers to word processing and veterans of other programs will want to start with the quick tour, using WordStar Release 5's pull-down menus as a guide. Entering, editing, and printing the sample text in this tutorial will expose you to the range of WordStar basics. Detailed explanations follow the tutorial. After completing the tutorial, you should be using WordStar for your own simple word processing needs within a few hours.

Feedback from readers of the first edition of *Using WordStar* has resulted in a different organization of information for intermediate and advanced users. Once they have learned WordStar's fundamentals, it seems, most users want to advance at their own pace. Instead of a keystroke-by-keystroke tutorial for more expert functions, this book offers a reference-style explanation of each program feature and applies it in a specific example. All of WordStar's commands are examined in order of increasing sophistication. Utilities and other programs included in the WordStar Release 5 package are included where appropriate.

Along with practical applications of WordStar functions, you will be shown short-cuts not in WordStar's documentation—shortcuts that will benefit even the most experienced user. If you have never gone beyond WordStar basics (perhaps because of confusing or inadequate documentation), you will find many pointers for improving your productivity. If you are already familiar with the functions discussed in a chapter, you may still find timesaving tips.

When upgrading from a previous version of WordStar, you should browse through this book's early pages to learn about additions to the program's most-often-used commands. The middle part of this volume can serve as a refresher for editing, formatting, and printing commands. The later chapters, especially those describing how to customize WordStar and run it with compatible and noncompatible software, will help any user expand the program's convenience and functionality.

The first part of the book is mainly for beginners. Chapter 1 takes you on a quick tour of WordStar Release 5 with a step-by-step tutorial. Chapter 2 covers the fundamentals of creating a working copy of WordStar and installing it to work with your particular computer system. Chapter 3 details the basic WordStar functions for creating a document: starting the program, and entering, saving, and printing text.

The middle section of this book deals with the remaining commands for everyday word processing applications. Chapter 4 describes all the important commands used during writing; it covers such features as tab settings, underlining, and centering text. Chapter 5 explains the range of commands for editing and polishing a document. Chapter 6 adds the formatting features you can use to make sure that your documents print exactly as needed. Chapter 7 discusses the use of WordStar's options during printing and ways to tailor printing for particular applications.

Advanced WordStar features and associated programs' enhancements of WordStar Release 5 are the subject of the book's last section. Chapter 8 introduces the program's merge-printing functions for form letters and its mailing list management and telecommunications utilities. Chapter 9 shows how to use WordStar's shorthand feature and how to combine functions to improve productivity. Chapter 10 offers instruction in correcting spelling and retrieving synonyms with WordStar's spelling checker and electronic thesaurus functions, as well as indexing, table of contents generation, and file locating. Chapter 11 covers how to use the WSCHANGE program to customize settings for individual needs. Chapter 12 explores the use of add-on software designed to complement WordStar, and techniques for using WordStar with noncompatible programs.

Appendix A summarizes the new or amended commands in WordStar Release 5. Appendix B is a list of printers on the WordStar Release 5 Printer Selection Menu. Appendix C is a list of ASCII characters and the IBM extended character set. An index rounds out this book's reference materials.

A supplemental reference feature found in this book is a command reference card for WordStar Release 5. By keeping this card on hand, you can quickly locate the command you need for your application. The card includes brief descriptions of each of WordStar's Opening Menu commands, Ctrl-letter commands, dot commands, function-key commands, shorthand commands, and more.

One last note about this book: *Using WordStar*, 2nd Edition, was entirely composed, edited, and configured for typesetting with WordStar. Virtually all Que® Corporation books, including those about other word processing programs, are typeset from WordStar document files. Because of the program's popularity, such files are a widespread standard within the typesetting industry, yet another reason for choosing WordStar. Although relatively few WordStar owners will want to use the program in this way, this book serves as one more reminder of WordStar's power and versatility.

Part I

Beginning with WordStar

The first part of this book includes all the information needed to begin using WordStar for simple word processing. The emphasis is on basic features that you can apply quickly after opening the program package—even if you have no prior experience with a computer or with a word processing program.

In Part I you learn how to prepare WordStar for use with your computer system; start the program; and compose, edit, and print text. With this knowledge, you can produce a brief memo or letter. You may find the functions described in this first section sufficient for your word processing needs, though exploring the full range of WordStar capabilities detailed later in this book will enhance your efficiency and improve the presentation of your documents.

While Part I is intended primarily for WordStar beginners, veterans of previous versions of the program may benefit from seeing WordStar Release 5's new pull-down menus and other changes in WordStar's screens, as well as from taking a refresher course in elementary word processing functions. You should install the program properly for your computer's display and printer. These steps are detailed in Chapter 2.

The three chapters in Part I cover the following fundamental topics:

- Chapter 1 leads you through a quick overview of WordStar Release 5's most-used features with an easily followed tutorial. The emphasis is on hands-on experience, with detailed explanations left to the following chapters.
- Chapter 2 discusses the procedure for creating a working copy of WordStar (including the use of the MS-DOS operating system), copying program files, and installing the program to fit your equipment.
- Chapter 3 details how to start WordStar, use the keyboard, understand basic screen displays, enter text, edit, save a file, and print a document. The features and terminology explained in this chapter are essential to everyday applications of the program.

Interspersed throughout Part I are handy pointers, shortcuts, and procedures to ease you into using WordStar.

1

A Quick Tour of WordStar

If you are like most personal computer users, you will want to try your new program straight out of the package. Because the magnetic disks on which the software is stored can be damaged easily, however, WordStar's publisher recommends that first you make copies of these disks and then install the program to suit your computer's configuration. The procedure for doing this with WordStar Release 5 is described in Chapter 2.

Nonetheless, for anyone who is curious or impatient, the half hour or more it takes to copy and install WordStar can seem like an eternity. Because a simpler generic installation will work with almost any computer for which the program was designed, you can take a quick preview of WordStar Release 5 before getting down to the process of creating a working copy for your specific system and word processing needs.

This chapter provides brief installation and practice sessions: Quick Starts similar to those featured in other recent Que Corporation books. By following the keystroke-by-keystroke procedure in the following pages, you will have some immediate experience of how WordStar works. This quick tour is hardly a complete rundown of WordStar Release 5's features. Nonetheless, the preview includes commands for typing, editing, saving, and printing a document. After you complete this chapter's exercise in creating a one-page memo, you will know enough to compose simple WordStar documents.

If you are new to computers, you need to know a few definitions. A *document* is any text formatted with a word processor—in this case, WordStar. A document displayed on-screen is actually a series of electrical pulses stored in your computer's memory chips, where they can be rearranged easily. When you are satisfied with what you have edited, the document can be stored as a *file* on a magnetic disk (either a removable *floppy* or a fixed *hard disk*) and then printed on paper, the *hard copy* version of text you are accustomed to handling. That's all the computer terminology you need for now. Further concepts, explanations, and reference information are provided in later chapters.

Experienced users of earlier WordStar versions will be familiar with the functions in this chapter's quick tour. You still may want to follow along, because commands new to WordStar Release 5 may improve your efficiency in starting and ending a work session. In addition, before configuring the program to advanced help levels, you can get a feel for WordStar's new pull-down menus. This experience is especially helpful if you will be instructing others in the use of this program.

Again, this chapter's tour of WordStar is meant only as a quick, one-time introduction to the program. Before using WordStar for anything but this elementary tutorial, you must copy your software and install it, as explained in Chapter 2.

Quick Start 1: Preparing To Use WordStar

This preliminary Quick Start session is necessary before you can begin your tour of WordStar. Because the program is supplied on floppy disks that cannot be modified or added to, you must create a copy of the principal files on a suitable disk and perform an elementary installation (if you are using a copy of WordStar that has been installed, just follow the procedure for starting your computer; then skip to Quick Start 2). The steps are kept to a minimum here, with explanations given in later chapters. The basic steps are the following:

- Turning on your computer and loading its start-up software
- Readying a disk for storage
- Copying essential WordStar files
- Making a simple installation of WordStar

As noted in the Introduction, this book assumes that you are using WordStar Release 5 on a computer system running MS-DOS (Version 2.0 or later). Your primary floppy disk drive is referred to as drive A. A second floppy drive below or to the right of it is called drive B. If you have a hard disk drive, it is designated drive C. If your program or equipment differs from this scheme, you should substitute appropriate designations.

Starting Your Computer

To start a computer with floppy disk drives, follow these steps:

1. Insert into drive A the DOS disk (sometimes called the start-up disk) supplied with your computer.
2. Press your computer's power switch into the On position. (Also, make sure that your monitor is turned on.)

3. If your screen displays a request for the date, press the keyboard's Enter key (often labeled with the ↵ symbol). If this message is followed by a request for the time, press Enter again.

4. The screen should display the following, called a *prompt*:

```
A>
```

To start a computer system with a hard disk on which MS-DOS has been installed (formatting a hard disk and installing MS-DOS is beyond the scope of this book; consult your operating system and hard disk manuals to do so), follow these directions:

1. With no disk in drive A, press your computer's power switch into the On position. (Also, make sure that your monitor is turned on.)

2. If the screen displays a request for the date, press the keyboard's Enter key (often labeled with the ↵ symbol). If this prompt is followed by a request for the time, press Enter again.

3. Your screen should display

```
C>
```

Now that your computer's start-up software is loaded, you're ready for the next step in preparing to use WordStar.

Readying a Disk for Storage

Before copying WordStar program files you must prepare the disk on which they will be stored. This procedure differs according to whether you use a floppy disk or a hard disk for this purpose.

On a computer with two floppy disk drives, follow these steps:

1. With your DOS disk in drive A, place a blank disk in drive B.

2. At the A> prompt, type *format b:/s* (in upper- or lowercase letters) and press Enter. On-screen you see the following message:

```
Insert new diskette in drive B:
and strike ENTER when ready
```

3. Press the Enter key. The following message appears:

```
Formatting...
```

4. Soon a message indicates that formatting is complete. After a few more seconds, the display shows the amount of disk space available, along with the following question:

```
Format another (Y/N)?
```

5. Press N for no, and A> appears again.
6. Now type *copy command.com b:* and press Enter. After a few moments, a message indicates that one file has been copied. A> appears below the message.
7. Type *b:*, then press Enter. You see B> on the screen.
8. Remove the DOS disk from drive A.

On a computer system with a hard disk, you do not need to format a disk, but you must create a directory to store your WordStar files. Follow these steps:

1. At the C> prompt, type *cd* and press Enter. C> reappears on the next line.
2. Type *md \ws5* and press Enter. C> is displayed on the next line.
3. Type *cd \ws5* and press Enter. C> appears.

Copying Essential WordStar Files

The WordStar package includes a variety of program and supporting files. You will copy only the files necessary to take you through a quick introduction to WordStar (follow the directions in Chapter 2 for making more complete copies). When handling any disk supplied in the program package, avoid touching its magnetic surface or placing it near heat or a magnetic field.

The procedure for copying WordStar is the same for floppy disk and hard disk systems, if you have followed the previous steps. Follow this procedure:

1. Insert into drive A the disk labeled

   WordStar Professional Program (5 1/4-inch disk)

   or

   WordStar Professional Program/Installation (3 1/2-inch disk)

2. Type *copy a:ws.exe* and press Enter. After a few moments, a message indicates that a file has been copied.
3. Now type *copy a:wsmgs.ovr* and press Enter. Again a message shows that a file has been copied.
4. Type *copy a:wshelp.ovr* and press Enter. A message appears on-screen to notify you that this file has been copied.
5. Type *copy a:drivert.ovr* and press Enter. The message that a file has been copied appears again.
6. Finally, type *copy a:draft.pdf* and press Enter. When the message shows that the file has been copied, you have completed the transfer of essential WordStar files.

7. Remove the WordStar program disk from drive A and return it to its original package.
8. Type *a:* then press Enter to display `A>` before continuing with installation of the copy of WordStar you have just made.

Making a Simple Installation of WordStar

WordStar Release 5 is preset to work with the most basic computer system, but you still must specify which disk drives you have and add a special file to the disk from which you start the program. To do this, you run a special program included with the program package. Follow these steps:

1. Insert into drive A the disk labeled

   WordStar Professional Installation Customization (5 1/4-inch disk)

   or

   WordStar Professional Program/Installation (3 1/2-inch disk)

2. Type *winstall* and press Enter to load the installation program. The screen displays a message requesting the name of the file to be installed. To end the program and exit to the DOS prompt at any time, press ^C.
3. On a floppy disk system, type *b:ws* and press Enter.

   On a hard disk system, type *c:ws* and press Enter.

   Another message asks for the name of the file to hold the installed WordStar.

4. On a floppy disk system, type *b:ws* and press Enter.

   On a hard disk system, type *c:ws* and press Enter.

   Your screen displays the Main Installation Menu (see fig. 1.1).

5. Press D to select the Computer option. The next display is the Computer Menu.
6. On a system with a hard disk, press A for the option indicating the disk drives on your computer. A screen for specifying these options appears. When asked whether you want to change the current setting, press Y. After the prompt requesting a drive letter, press C. Typing this letter establishes drive C as the default drive, which is where program files are stored. When asked whether this is a floppy drive, press N and then Enter. For the next drive requested, press A. At the prompt asking whether this is

Fig. 1.1. *WordStar's Main Installation Menu.*

```
                        Main Installation Menu

A  Console...........................Choose your monitor.

B  Printer...........................Choose your printer.

C  Default printer...................Choose a default printer.

D  Computer..........................Choose operating system and disk
                                     drives on your computer.  Check the
                                     CONFIG.SYS and AUTOEXEC.BAT files.

E  Dictionaries......................Specify location of the dictionaries.

F  Help level........................Specify pull-down or classic menus.

X  Finished with installation.

Enter your menu selection...          ? = Help
                                      For detailed changes, run WSCHANGE.
```

a floppy drive, press Y, then Enter. Press Enter again. When asked whether you want to change your setting, press N.

The display returns to the Computer Menu.

7. On both floppy and hard disk systems, to add a file essential to WordStar's proper functioning, press C at the Computer Menu.

   A screen titled `Check CONFIG.SYS Menu` is displayed.

8. At the prompt asking whether you want CONFIG.SYS checked, press Y.

9. An added prompt appears with a request for the letter of the disk drive used to start WordStar. On a floppy disk system, press B.

   On a system with a hard disk, press C.

   A message appears indicating that a CONFIG.SYS file has been added. If your CONFIG.SYS file is already present and contains the statements required by WordStar Release 5, the message `Your CONFIG.SYS is already correct` is displayed.

10. Press Enter to return to the Computer Menu.

11. Press D for the `Check AUTOEXEC.BAT` option. This displays a screen headed `Check AUTOEXEC.BAT File`. Press Y at the prompt asking whether this file should be checked. At the prompt asking for the letter of the drive used to start WordStar, press B on a floppy disk system, or press C on a hard disk system. After inserting needed information in the special start-up file, the screen returns to the Computer Menu.

12. Press X to display the Main Installation Menu. At the menu, press X to indicate the end of this quick installation.

13. Press Y to complete installation.

    When this operation is finished, `A>` is displayed.

14. Remove the WordStar installation disk from drive A and return it to its original package.

15. On a floppy disk system, remove the disk from drive B and place it in drive A.

16. Your computer now needs to be restarted because the installation program has altered the CONFIG.SYS and AUTOEXEC.BAT files with settings WordStar Release 5 needs to have available to DOS. To restart your computer, hold down the keys marked Ctrl, Alt, and Del. This command also clears your screen.

    On a floppy disk system, `A` appears.

    On a hard disk system, `C` appears.

The preceding installation should be sufficient for all systems running WordStar Release 5. If your computer has only 384K of memory, you can run the following quick tour of WordStar; in case of problems, you may have to restart the program after installing WordStar for a 384K system. Installing WordStar Release 5 for a 384K system is explained in Chapter 2.

You are now ready to try out WordStar for yourself.

Quick Start 2: Creating a WordStar Document

In this Quick Start session you can learn some of the essential techniques for using WordStar. Several procedures introduced here may later be simplified, combined, or automated. The basic stages, however, remain the same, including:

- Running the WordStar program
- Starting a document
- Typing and modifying text on-screen
- Using pull-down menus
- Saving a file
- Printing a document
- Exiting WordStar

Remember that this quick tour applies specifically to WordStar Release 5. Nevertheless, you can refer to it if you have a previous version of the program; features such as the Speed Write command and pull-down help menus are not available, but most other essential commands are similar.

Starting WordStar

With your computer running and an installed version of WordStar at hand, you can now start using your word processing program.

To start WordStar on a computer with two floppy disk drives, follow these steps:

1. With the installed copy of WordStar in drive A and `A>` on-screen, type *ws* (using either upper- or lowercase letters) and press Enter.
2. The drive with WordStar in it spins and loads the program into memory. The on-screen prompt is replaced by WordStar's preliminary displays: a copyright notice followed by the Opening screen.

To start WordStar on a computer with a hard disk drive, follow these steps:

1. With the installed copy of WordStar on your hard disk and `C>` on-screen, go to the directory containing the program by typing *cd \ws5* and pressing Enter. `C>` appears again.
2. Type *ws* and press Enter.
3. The hard disk spins and loads WordStar into memory. The on-screen prompt is replaced by the word processor's preliminary displays: first a copyright notice, then WordStar's Opening screen.

WordStar Release 5's Opening screen, shown in figure 1.2, is seen at the beginning and end of virtually every work session with an unmodified version of this program. This screen is like a theatrical curtain, appearing before and after WordStar's main event—editing text.

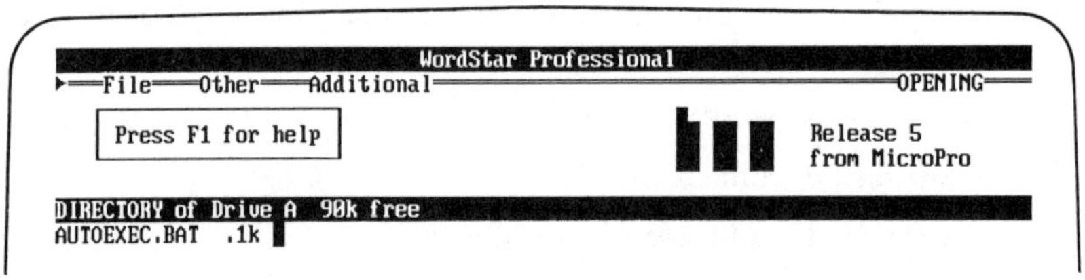
WordStar Professional
File Other Additional OPENING
Press F1 for help
Release 5
from MicroPro
DIRECTORY of Drive A 90k free
AUTOEXEC.BAT .1k

Fig. 1.2.
WordStar's Opening Menu.

In addition to the edition of WordStar and its publisher's logo, the Opening Menu lists the contents of the current disk. Near the top of the screen is a menu bar of available command menus and directions for obtaining help during a WordStar session.

While working with WordStar, you can receive help at the touch of a key. This feature is known as on-screen help. The key for obtaining help is always the same, as indicated on the Opening screen.

To use on-screen help, follow these directions:

1. Press the key labeled F1 on your keyboard (F1 is one of the function keys at the far left or across the top of the keyboard).
2. Read the information in the box that appears on-screen (see fig. 1.3). In this case, the help message explains WordStar's opening commands and menus.

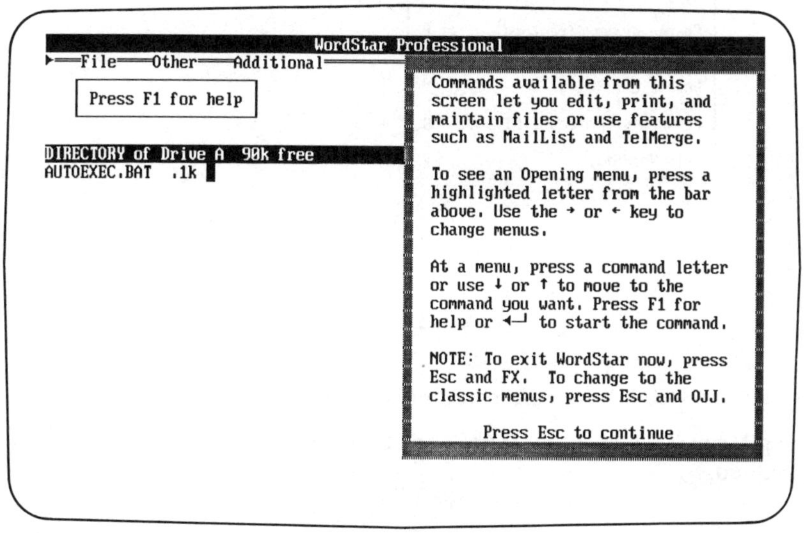
WordStar Professional
File Other Additional
Press F1 for help
DIRECTORY of Drive A 90k free
AUTOEXEC.BAT .1k
Commands available from this screen let you edit, print, and maintain files or use features such as MailList and TelMerge.
To see an Opening menu, press a highlighted letter from the bar above. Use the → or ← key to change menus.
At a menu, press a command letter or use ↓ or ↑ to move to the command you want. Press F1 for help or ↵ to start the command.
NOTE: To exit WordStar now, press Esc and FX. To change to the classic menus, press Esc and OJJ.
Press Esc to continue

Fig. 1.3.

The Opening Menu help message.

3. To remove help information from the screen, press the Escape key (the key labeled Esc at the upper left corner of the numeric keypad or at the far left of the top row). The display returns to its previous content.

When you are in doubt during a session with WordStar, remember that help is as close as the F1 key.

Starting a New Document

From the Opening Menu, you can begin creating a new document by doing the following:

1. Press Enter.

2. The Opening Menu displays a pull-down menu of WordStar file commands (see fig. 1.4). Highlighted is the Speed Write command, used for quickly starting a document.

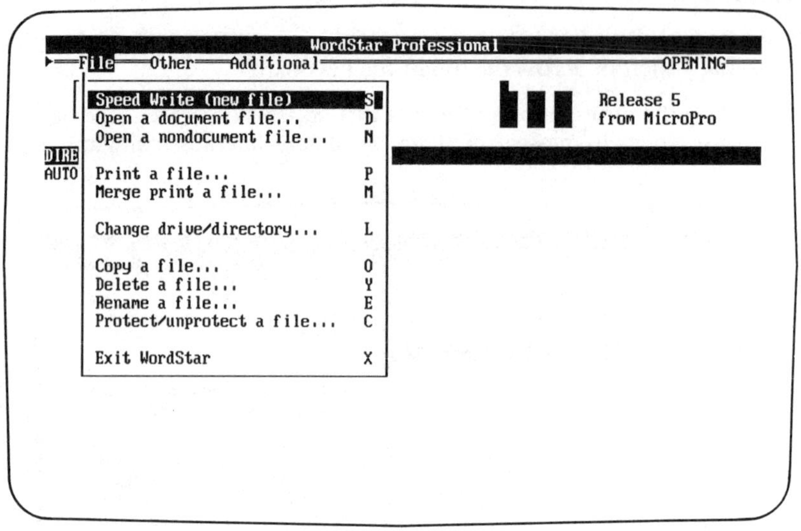
WordStar Professional
File Other Additional OPENING
Speed Write (new file) S
Open a document file... D
Open a nondocument file... N
Print a file... P
Merge print a file... M
Change drive/directory... L
Copy a file... O
Delete a file... Y
Rename a file... E
Protect/unprotect a file... C
Exit WordStar X
Release 5
from MicroPro
DIRE
AUTO

Fig. 1.4.
The pull-down File menu at the Opening Menu.

3. To select the Speed Write command, press Enter.

The Opening Menu is replaced by WordStar's Edit screen, on which text is composed and edited.

Typing and Editing Text

WordStar's Edit screen, shown in figure 1.5, is the equivalent of the paper in a typewriter. The top of the Edit screen includes three lines of information about the status of text entry functions, menu listings, and margins. (This Quick Start assumes that WordStar's margins are preset at `0.0"` and `6.40"` and that the notation `RgtJust` appears at the top right of the screen. If any of these have been changed, your text and cursor position will differ from the example that follows.) The Edit screen information lines are explained in Chapter 3.

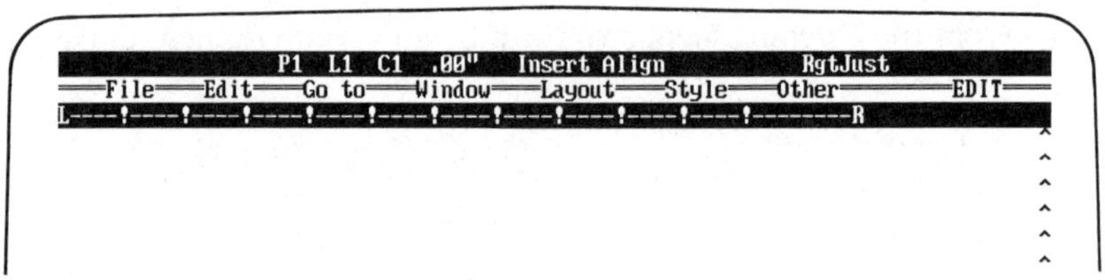
P1 L1 C1 .00" Insert Align RgtJust
File Edit Go to Window Layout Style Other EDIT

Fig. 1.5.
WordStar Release 5's Edit Menu.

From WordStar's Edit screen, pressing the letter or number keys on the keyboard displays the corresponding characters on-screen. Touch typists feel at home with WordStar; the characters you type appear on-screen as fast as you can press the keys.

To experience certain aspects of WordStar text entry, type a memo for a fictitious company that manufactures "widgets." You will type the following memo in several steps:

```
To: Production and Marketing Departments

From: John Doe

Re: New Products

As  you know, the mainstay of our company has been  the  standard
widget,  the best in the business. Because of  increased  foreign
competition, however, we have been losing market share, and sales
have  leveled off. The New Products Committee has spent the  last
six  months  studying the introduction of new  widget  models  to
regain our dominant position in the industry.

We have concluded that a premium widget using improved  materials
would  give  us  the edge we need. In addition,  a  super  widget
incorporating  advanced features would create a  high-end  market
and  lucrative  profit margins. Specifications for  new  products
are attached. Please submit a sample letter outlining pricing  to
our  customers  and a report on how we can best  market  our  new
product line.

cc:  F. Arouet
     S. Clemens
     R. Penniman
     E. Souse
```

If you make a mistake as you type, you can erase it by pressing the Backspace key (located to the right of the number and symbol keys on your keyboard). Later in the chapter, you will learn other ways to correct your on-screen copy. For now, follow these steps:

1. Type the first line—the memo's destination—as follows:

   To: Production and Marketing Departments

   As you type, a character is entered at the position of the flashing line or rectangle on-screen, which is called the *cursor*. The cursor advances to the following space as you type each character. On the status line at the top of the screen, the cursor position is measured by column number, `C`, and in inches, ". On the third line from the top, the cursor position is also indicated by a marker that advances as you type.

2. At the end of the word `Departments`, press Enter (the equivalent of a carriage return on a typewriter). The cursor returns to the first column of the next line.

   WordStar places a flag character (<) in the flag column at the right edge of the screen and moves the cursor to the left margin of the next line. The status line registers the cursor's new location as page 1, line 2, column 1, at 0 inches (`P1 L2 C1 .00"`).

3. To skip a line, as in the memo, press Enter.
4. Type the second line of the memo as follows:

   From: John Doe

5. At the end of the word `Doe`, press Enter.
6. To skip a line, press Enter again.
7. Type the third line of the memo as follows:

   Re: New Products

8. After `Products`, press Enter.
9. Press Enter to skip a line.
10. Compare your screen to the one shown in figure 1.6.

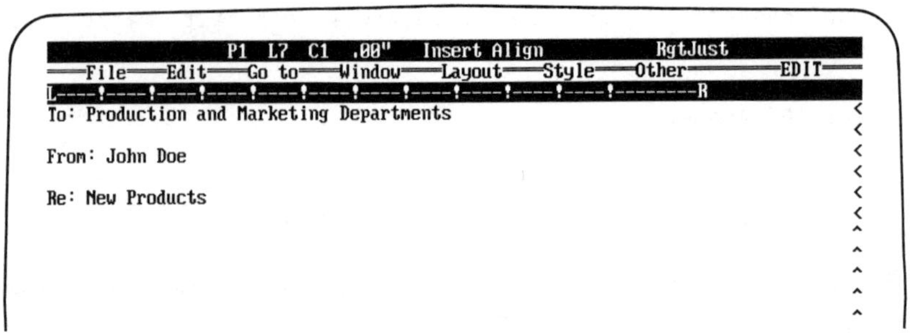
P1 L7 C1 .00" Insert Align RgtJust
File Edit Go to Window Layout Style Other EDIT
To: Production and Marketing Departments
From: John Doe
Re: New Products

Fig. 1.6.
The Enter key pressed after each of the first lines of the memo.

To enter the text of the first paragraph, follow these steps:

1. Type the first paragraph of the memo. While typing, don't press Enter at the end of a line. WordStar wraps the first line after `standard` and the second line after `foreign`. This word wrap function remains in effect as you continue typing text. As you type, WordStar places your text so that all the words at the right margin are aligned. This is known as *right justification*, hence the `RgtJust` at the top of the screen.

2. At the end of the paragraph, press Enter twice.
3. Compare the text you have typed so far to figure 1.7.

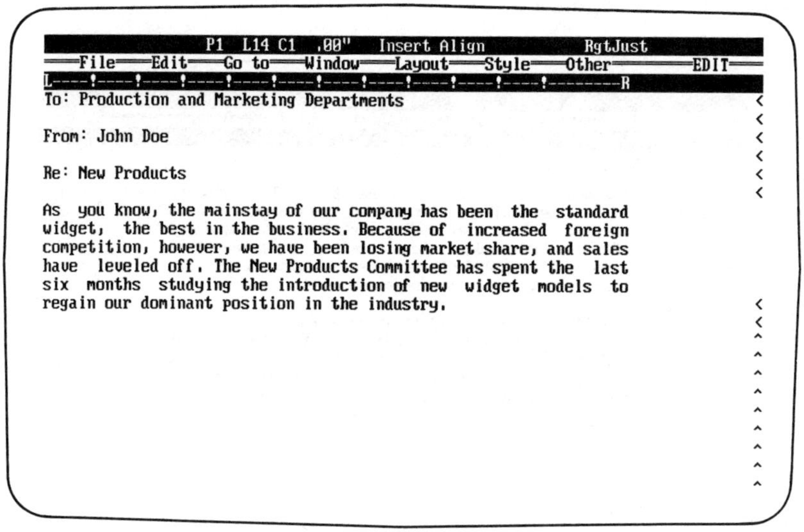
P1 L14 C1 .00" Insert Align RgtJust
File Edit Go to Window Layout Style Other EDIT
L----!----!----!----!----!----!----!----!----!--------R
To: Production and Marketing Departments
From: John Doe
Re: New Products
As you know, the mainstay of our company has been the standard
widget, the best in the business. Because of increased foreign
competition, however, we have been losing market share, and sales
have leveled off. The New Products Committee has spent the last
six months studying the introduction of new widget models to
regain our dominant position in the industry.

Fig. 1.7.
WordStar's justification of text.

Now follow these steps:

1. Type the memo's second paragraph. As you type, the words wrap after the first line in the second paragraph, text on the screen moves upward, and a blank line appears at the bottom. The first line of the memo disappears. This movement of text is known as WordStar's *scrolling* feature. The text continues to scroll upward as you type.
2. Press Enter twice after you finish the second paragraph.

Follow these steps to finish the memo:

1. Type *cc:*
2. After the colon, press the space bar twice, so that the cursor is even with the first exclamation point in the ruler line (column 6 on the status line). The ruler line consists of hyphens and exclamation points and is located at the top of the screen. (The ruler line is explained in Chapter 3.)
3. Type the first name on the list and press Enter.
4. Press the Tab key, located at the left side of the keyboard, so that you can type the next name directly under the first. When the Tab key is pressed, a tab symbol (►) appears on-screen. Each press of the Tab key moves the cursor in line with the next exclamation point on the ruler line.

5. Type the remaining names, continuing to use Enter and Tab. After typing the last name on the distribution list, press Enter once.

   The first two lines of the memo are now out of view. Your screen should resemble the one in figure 1.8.

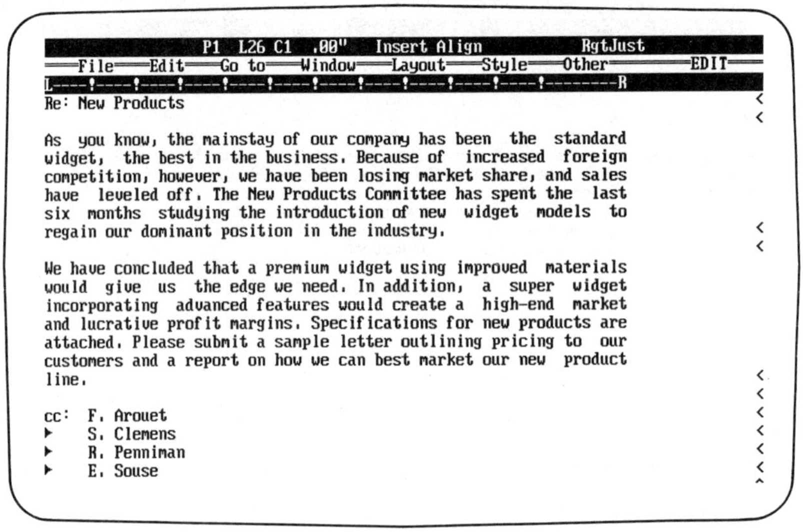
P1 L26 C1 .00" Insert Align RgtJust
File Edit Go to Window Layout Style Other EDIT
Re: New Products
As you know, the mainstay of our company has been the standard widget, the best in the business. Because of increased foreign competition, however, we have been losing market share, and sales have leveled off. The New Products Committee has spent the last six months studying the introduction of new widget models to regain our dominant position in the industry.
We have concluded that a premium widget using improved materials would give us the edge we need. In addition, a super widget incorporating advanced features would create a high-end market and lucrative profit margins. Specifications for new products are attached. Please submit a sample letter outlining pricing to our customers and a report on how we can best market our new product line.
cc: F. Arouet
S. Clemens
R. Penniman
E. Souse

Fig. 1.8.

Scrolled text on the WordStar screen.

When editing text on-screen, you must be able to move the cursor to make changes. Before editing the memo you typed, you need to learn how to use the cursor-movement commands.

WordStar offers two ways to move the cursor: Ctrl-letter combination keys and the arrow keys. Many of WordStar's commands consist of pressing the Ctrl key located at the left or at the bottom of your keyboard; often designated by the caret symbol (^) at the same time as a letter key. The arrow keys are on the numeric keypad on the right side of the keyboard (for these arrow keys to be active, the Num Lock feature must be turned off). They are also duplicated in a separate cluster on newer keyboards.

The arrow keys are more readily found and remembered, but Ctrl-letter combination commands let your fingers stay within the main section of the keyboard. Touch typists immediately appreciate the benefits of Ctrl-letter combinations; other users soon recognize their efficiency.

Follow these steps to practice both cursor-movement methods:

1. With your cursor at the bottom left corner of the screen, press ^E (press the Ctrl key and hold it down as you press the E key). Next, try pressing the up-arrow key to move the cursor up one line (if an arrow key on the numeric keypad doesn't work, press the Num Lock key).

The keyboard on IBM PCs, PS/2s, and compatibles has an *automatic repeat* feature. It repeats a character or command as long as the key or combination of keys is held down. Keep ^E or the up-arrow pressed down to move the cursor upward through the second paragraph of the memo. Stop when the cursor reaches the paragraph's first line.

2. Press ^D (or the right-arrow key) and then ^F (or Ctrl-right arrow) to move the cursor to the right. At the right end of a line, the cursor jumps down to the beginning of the next line and continues moving along the line. Now press ^S (or the left-arrow key) and then ^A (or Ctrl-left arrow) to bring the cursor left across a line. Notice that at the left edge of a line, the cursor moves backward to the right end of the line above and then continues across.

3. When the cursor moves beyond the beginning of the second paragraph, the text on-screen scrolls downward. Using Ctrl-letter commands or arrow keys, bring the cursor to the last line of the memo's first paragraph so that you can make changes.

When you edit text, you usually perform two tasks: erase text and type substitute copy. These tasks are examined in turn. Be sure that WordStar is in insert mode, with the word `Insert` at the top of the screen. If it isn't, press the Ins key on the numeric keypad (if the Ins key is inactive, press the Num Lock key atop the numeric keypad).

WordStar features several commands for erasing different amounts of text. Try the most common erase commands to edit the sample memo. Follow these steps:

1. Move the cursor to the `p` in `position` in the last line of the first paragraph.
2. Use ^G to delete the word a letter at a time. Also delete the space after the word.
3. Press ^T to delete each of the last three words in the sentence.
4. Press ^Y to delete the rest of the line.

   Note that one hard carriage return (<) is also deleted.

The second paragraph of the memo moves up on the screen to fill the void left by the deleted line. Try some other erase commands to edit the memo further. Follow these steps:

1. Press the Backspace key several times until the cursor moves left and erases `to`.
2. Press ^A several times or hold down the left-arrow key to move the cursor to the `t` in `the`.
3. Press the Del key at the bottom of the numeric keypad (Num Lock must be off), or the Delete key in the cluster of labeled keys on newer keyboards, to eliminate `the` and the space after it, one character at a time.

4. Press the F6 function key (at the left side or top of your keyboard) to delete the word to the right. The result is the same as pressing ^T.

5. To erase `of` and the space after it, hold down the Ctrl key and press the Backspace key three times.

6. Press the F5 function key to delete the remaining words on the line—the same as ^Y.

Occasionally, you might delete text by mistake and want to restore it. Your last deletion can be returned to the screen with WordStar's *Undo* function. You can choose a Ctrl-letter key combination or a function key to restore deleted text.

To restore the line just deleted, do the following:

1. Press ^U once. The text you erased reappears on-screen, with the first character at the cursor position.

2. Press F2. A string of text like the erased text appears at the cursor. You can restore only the most recent deletion.

3. Press ^Y to remove the text you restored. After deletions are complete, the last sentence in the first paragraph ends with the words `studying new widget models.`

4. Use ^F several times to move the cursor to the end of the sentence; then type a period.

5. Press Enter to insert a line between the two paragraphs.

You now have a less wordy business memo.

So far, you have erased text. Now it is time to correct the memo. The widget company's communications style sheet requires that its product names be capitalized. Follow these steps:

1. Use the Ctrl cursor-movement commands (^S, ^E, ^D, and ^X) or the arrow keys to move the cursor to the `s` in `standard`.

2. Delete the lowercase s by pressing ^G. The remaining letters on the line move left one space. You may see your line of text shift after this or other erasures. The shift in text is due to a WordStar feature called automatic realigning, which is explained below.

3. Type an uppercase *S*. The remaining characters move to the right to make room for the S.

In insert mode, you used two keystrokes to change a single letter. When overtype (also called overstrike) mode is on, you type only the correct character to make a similar change. Follow these steps:

1. Press ^V to turn off insert mode.

   The word `Insert` should disappear from the status line.

2. Press ^F twice to move the cursor to the `w` in `widget` in the second line.
3. Type an uppercase *W*, and the product name is corrected.
4. Use the cursor-movement keys to bring the cursor to the first line of the second paragraph.
5. Type over and replace the lowercase initial letters in `premium widget` with uppercase letters. Do the same for `super widget`.

Without separate deletions, you have corrected the product names to `Premium Widget` and `Super Widget`.

Overtype mode is well suited for secretarial or editorial use when many small corrections are necessary. But the correction must be the same length as the text you are replacing. If the correct copy is longer, you may find yourself typing over text you don't want to change.

With overtype mode turned on, make the following changes to your memo:

1. Bring the cursor to the first `i` in `incorporating` in the second paragraph.
2. Type the words *including even more* and watch the last letters replace the beginning of the word `advanced`.
3. To restore the missing letters, turn insert mode on by pressing ^V, and then type the characters in `advanced` that were eliminated when you were in overtype mode.

After you finish typing, notice that the end of the line extends beyond the right margin briefly. WordStar then rearranges the text so that the right margin is realigned. This is known as *automatic realigning* or *reformatting*.

Finish editing the memo to see a few examples of how adding and correcting text results in reformatting. Follow these steps:

1. Move the cursor to the third line of the second paragraph, to the `h` in `high-end`.
2. Type *profitable*.

   As you type, watch the words `high-end market` extend beyond the right margin and then move to the next line as they are word wrapped.
3. Place the cursor after the word `market` and press ^T.
4. Press ^T enough times to delete the words from the cursor to the end of the sentence.
5. Move the cursor to the beginning of the word `submit` and type *study these specifications and*

WordStar realigns your text after a change disrupts the right margin.

The memo's main text should now appear as in figure 1.9.

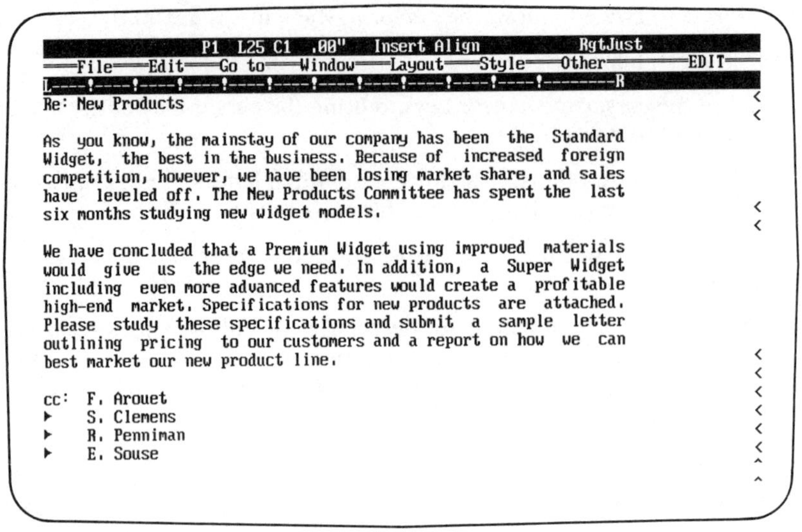
P1 L25 C1 .00" Insert Align RgtJust
File Edit Go to Window Layout Style Other EDIT
Re: New Products
As you know, the mainstay of our company has been the Standard Widget, the best in the business. Because of increased foreign competition, however, we have been losing market share, and sales have leveled off. The New Products Committee has spent the last six months studying new widget models.
We have concluded that a Premium Widget using improved materials would give us the edge we need. In addition, a Super Widget including even more advanced features would create a profitable high-end market. Specifications for new products are attached. Please study these specifications and submit a sample letter outlining pricing to our customers and a report on how we can best market our new product line.
cc: F. Arouet
S. Clemens
R. Penniman
E. Souse

Fig. 1.9.
Sample text after erasures and insertions.

After typing and editing a document with WordStar, you now know the most-used functions in the program. Next is a quick tour of some of WordStar's other powerful editing features.

Viewing Pull-Down Menus

Like the pull-down menu encountered briefly when starting a document, other listings of WordStar capabilities are accessible with a few keystrokes during editing. You can view these menus by doing the following:

1. Hold down the Alt key (on the bottom row of the keyboard) while pressing the space bar. The cursor and a triangular prompt appear on the *menu bar*, the second line from the top of the screen. Seven categories of functions are on the menu bar.

2. Press the right-arrow key. The first pull-down menu appears on-screen, partially covering your text. This File menu, shown in figure 1.10, lists commands for saving, printing, and other actions relating to WordStar documents (*files*). The commands on this menu are described in Chapters 4 and 6.

3. Press the right-arrow key again. The next pull-down menu lists useful editing commands (see fig. 1.11). You have already used the three at the top: Undo, Delete Word, and Delete Line. Others listed manipulate blocks of text for greater efficiency during editing. The commands on this menu are fully explained in Chapters 6 and 7.

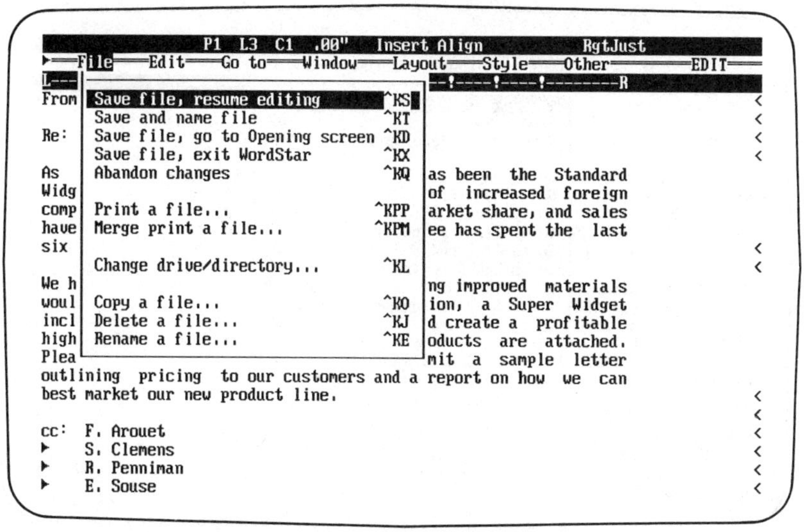
P1 L3 C1 .00" Insert Align RgtJust
File Edit Go to Window Layout Style Other EDIT
Save file, resume editing ^KS
Save and name file ^KT
Save file, go to Opening screen ^KD
Save file, exit WordStar ^KX
Abandon changes ^KQ
Print a file... ^KPP
Merge print a file... ^KPM
Change drive/directory... ^KL
Copy a file... ^KO
Delete a file... ^KJ
Rename a file... ^KE
outlining pricing to our customers and a report on how we can
best market our new product line.
cc: F. Arouet
S. Clemens
R. Penniman
E. Souse

Fig. 1.10. *The pull-down File menu at the Edit Menu.*

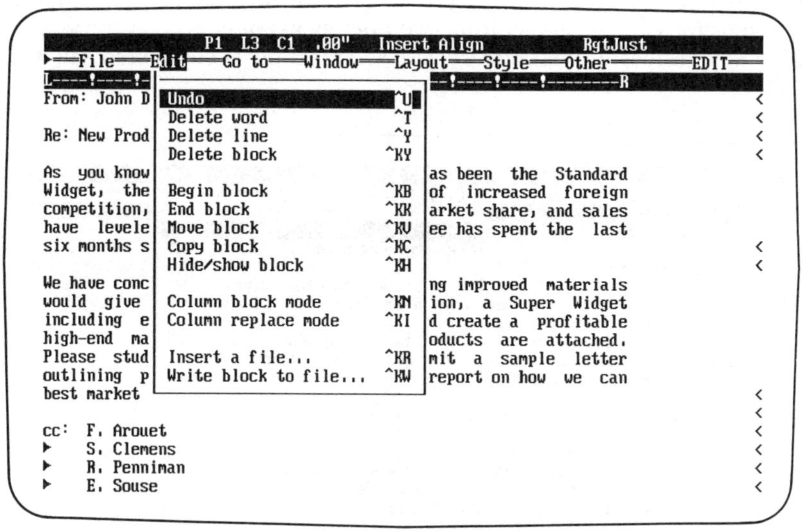
P1 L3 C1 .00" Insert Align RgtJust
File Edit Go to Window Layout Style Other EDIT
Undo ^U
Delete word ^T
Delete line ^Y
Delete block ^KY
Begin block ^KB
End block ^KK
Move block ^KV
Copy block ^KC
Hide/show block ^KH
Column block mode ^KN
Column replace mode ^KI
Insert a file... ^KR
Write block to file... ^KW
cc: F. Arouet
S. Clemens
R. Penniman
E. Souse

Fig. 1.11. *The pull-down Edit menu.*

4. Press Alt-G (hold down the Alt key while pressing the G key). You can view any of the menus indicated on the menu bar by pressing Alt and the first initial of the desired listing (or you can press the right-arrow key, as before, to advance through pull-down menus on-screen). The Go To menu (see fig. 1.12) on the display includes handy ways to move the cursor to a specific text, a chosen page, or the beginning or end of a document. The commands shown here are also discussed in Chapter 6.

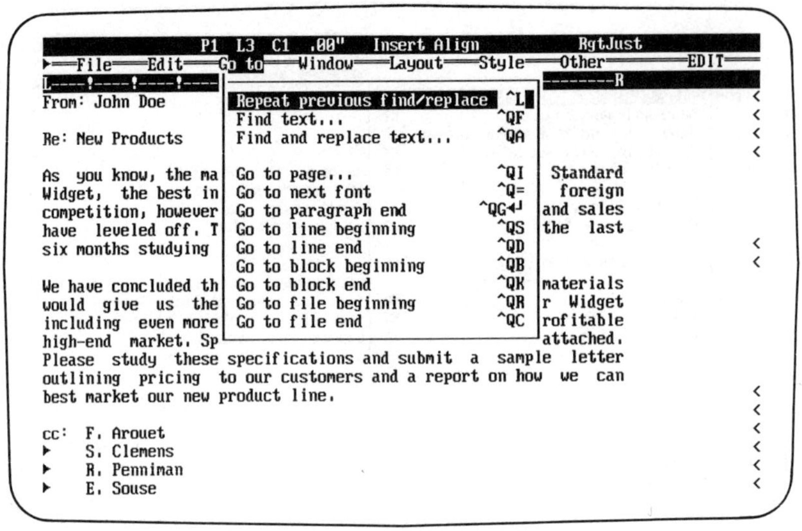
P1 L3 C1 .00" Insert Align RgtJust
File Edit Go to Window Layout Style Other EDIT
From: John Doe
Re: New Products
As you know, the ma
Widget, the best in
competition, however
have leveled off. T
six months studying
We have concluded th
would give us the
including even more
high-end market. Sp
Repeat previous find/replace ^L
Find text... ^QF
Find and replace text... ^QA
Go to page... ^QI
Go to next font ^Q=
Go to paragraph end ^QG
Go to line beginning ^QS
Go to line end ^QD
Go to block beginning ^QB
Go to block end ^QK
Go to file beginning ^QR
Go to file end ^QC
Standard
foreign
and sales
the last
materials
r Widget
rofitable
attached.
Please study these specifications and submit a sample letter
outlining pricing to our customers and a report on how we can
best market our new product line.
cc: F. Arouet
S. Clemens
R. Penniman
E. Souse

Fig. 1.12.

The pull-down Go To menu.

5. Press Alt-W (or the right-arrow key). The Window menu (see fig. 1.13) lists commands for viewing and editing two documents on-screen at the same time, a new feature in WordStar Release 5. This topic is covered in full in Chapter 6.

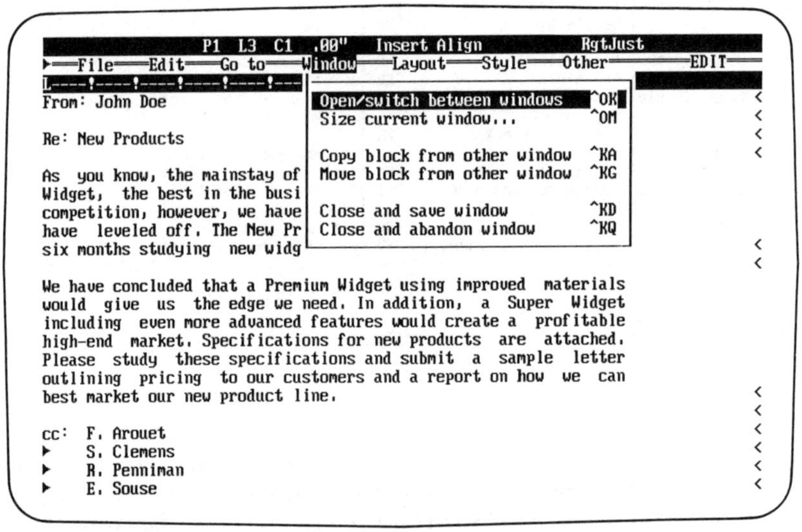
P1 L3 C1 .00" Insert Align RgtJust
File Edit Go to Window Layout Style Other EDIT
From: John Doe
Re: New Products
As you know, the mainstay of
Widget, the best in the busi
competition, however, we have
have leveled off. The New Pr
six months studying new widg
Open/switch between windows ^OK
Size current window... ^OM
Copy block from other window ^KA
Move block from other window ^KG
Close and save window ^KD
Close and abandon window ^KQ
We have concluded that a Premium Widget using improved materials
would give us the edge we need. In addition, a Super Widget
including even more advanced features would create a profitable
high-end market. Specifications for new products are attached.
Please study these specifications and submit a sample letter
outlining pricing to our customers and a report on how we can
best market our new product line.
cc: F. Arouet
S. Clemens
R. Penniman
E. Souse

Fig. 1.13.

The pull-down Window menu.

6. Press Alt-L. This displays the Layout menu (see fig. 1.14). The Layout commands control the appearance of a document on-screen and when printed. These enhancements to the presentation of your text are detailed in Chapters 5 and 7.

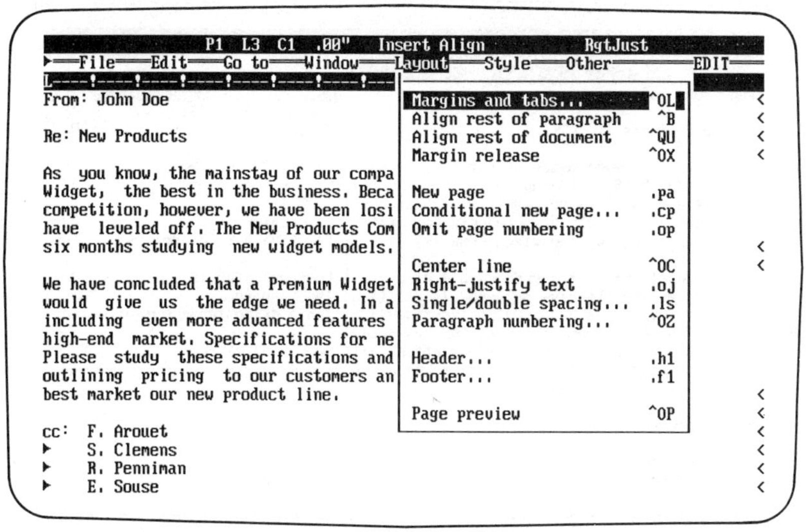
P1 L3 C1 .00" Insert Align RgtJust
File Edit Go to Window Layout Style Other EDIT
From: John Doe
Re: New Products
As you know, the mainstay of our compa
Widget, the best in the business. Beca
competition, however, we have been losi
have leveled off. The New Products Com
six months studying new widget models.
We have concluded that a Premium Widget
would give us the edge we need. In a
including even more advanced features
high-end market. Specifications for ne
Please study these specifications and
outlining pricing to our customers an
best market our new product line.
cc: F. Arouet
S. Clemens
R. Penniman
E. Souse
Margins and tabs... ^OL
Align rest of paragraph ^B
Align rest of document ^QU
Margin release ^OX
New page .pa
Conditional new page... .cp
Omit page numbering .op
Center line ^OC
Right-justify text .oj
Single/double spacing... .ls
Paragraph numbering... ^OZ
Header... .h1
Footer... .f1
Page preview ^OP

Fig. 1.14.

The pull-down Layout menu.

7. Press Alt-S. The Style menu (see fig. 1.15) shows commands for invoking common print style variations such as boldface, underline, and italics. Explanations of these often-used functions are in Chapters 5 and 8.

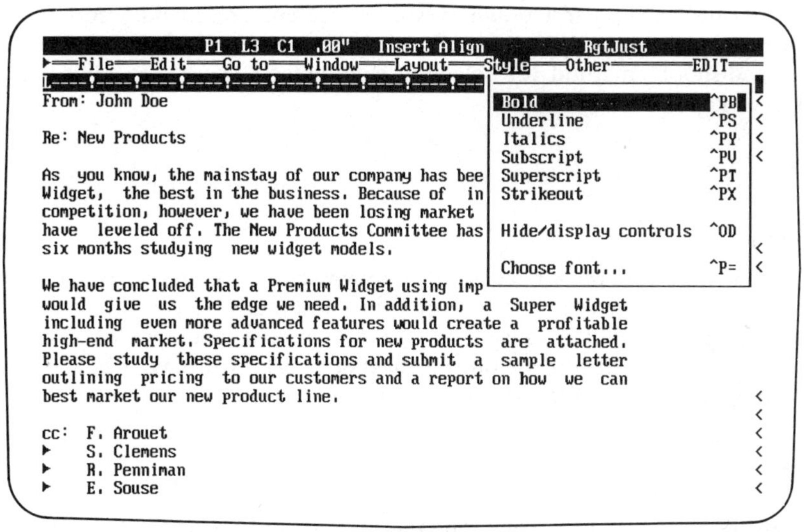
P1 L3 C1 .00" Insert Align RgtJust
File Edit Go to Window Layout Style Other EDIT
From: John Doe
Re: New Products
As you know, the mainstay of our company has bee
Widget, the best in the business. Because of in
competition, however, we have been losing market
have leveled off. The New Products Committee has
six months studying new widget models.
We have concluded that a Premium Widget using imp
would give us the edge we need. In addition, a Super Widget
including even more advanced features would create a profitable
high-end market. Specifications for new products are attached.
Please study these specifications and submit a sample letter
outlining pricing to our customers and a report on how we can
best market our new product line.
cc: F. Arouet
S. Clemens
R. Penniman
E. Souse
Bold ^PB
Underline ^PS
Italics ^PY
Subscript ^PV
Superscript ^PT
Strikeout ^PX
Hide/display controls ^OD
Choose font... ^P=

Fig. 1.15.

The pull-down Style menu.

8. Press Alt-O. The Other menu (see fig. 1.16) provides commands for time-saving features like the spelling checker, the thesaurus, and the on-screen calculator. These functions are examined in Chapters 7, 9, and 10.

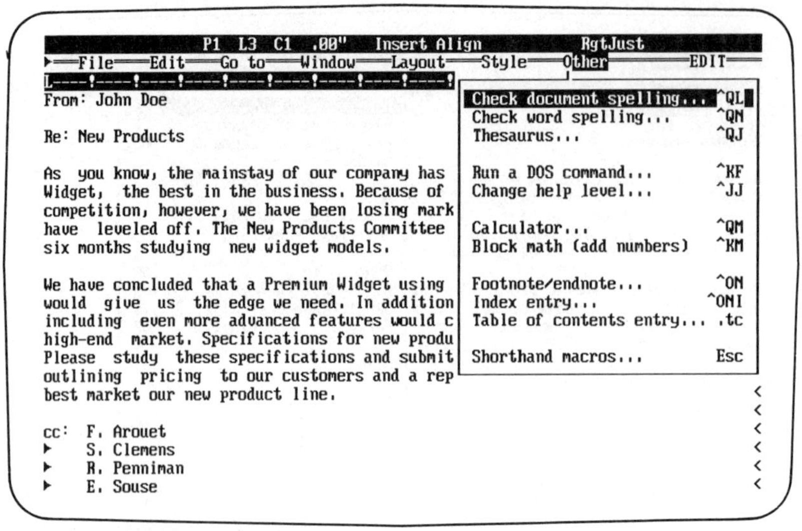
P1 L3 C1 .00" Insert Align RgtJust
File Edit Go to Window Layout Style Other EDIT
From: John Doe
Re: New Products
As you know, the mainstay of our company has
Widget, the best in the business. Because of
competition, however, we have been losing mark
have leveled off. The New Products Committee
six months studying new widget models.
We have concluded that a Premium Widget using
would give us the edge we need. In addition
including even more advanced features would c
high-end market. Specifications for new produ
Please study these specifications and submit
outlining pricing to our customers and a rep
best market our new product line.
cc: F. Arouet
S. Clemens
R. Penniman
E. Souse
Check document spelling... ^QL
Check word spelling... ^QN
Thesaurus... ^QJ
Run a DOS command... ^KF
Change help level... ^JJ
Calculator... ^QM
Block math (add numbers) ^KM
Footnote/endnote... ^ON
Index entry... ^ONI
Table of contents entry... .tc
Shorthand macros... Esc

Fig. 1.16.
The pull-down Other menu.

9. Press the Esc key and the pull-down menu disappears. You can eliminate any of the pull-down menus by pressing the Esc key.

On the pull-down menus, invoke a command simply by moving the highlight to the desired line (using the up- and down-cursor movement commands) and then pressing Enter. (If you want help with any highlighted command, press the F1 key.) This "point-and-shoot" method for selecting a command is used to save your document to disk.

Saving a File

So far, the memo you have created exists only on your screen and in the computer's temporary memory. If you were to turn off your computer's power switch now, everything in memory would be erased, and your document would be lost. That's why you must save your document onto a magnetic disk. WordStar has several commands for saving under different circumstances.

For the simplest way to save your memo file, follow these steps:

1. Press Alt-F to display the File menu. The first line is highlighted.
2. Press the down-arrow key twice. The highlighted line lists this command:

   `Save file, go to Opening screen ^KD`

3. Press Enter. On-screen you see a box containing the words `SAVE AS` (see fig. 1.17). The words `FILE (none)`, indicate that the file that will store your document on disk is as yet unnamed. To save a file, you must name it. This

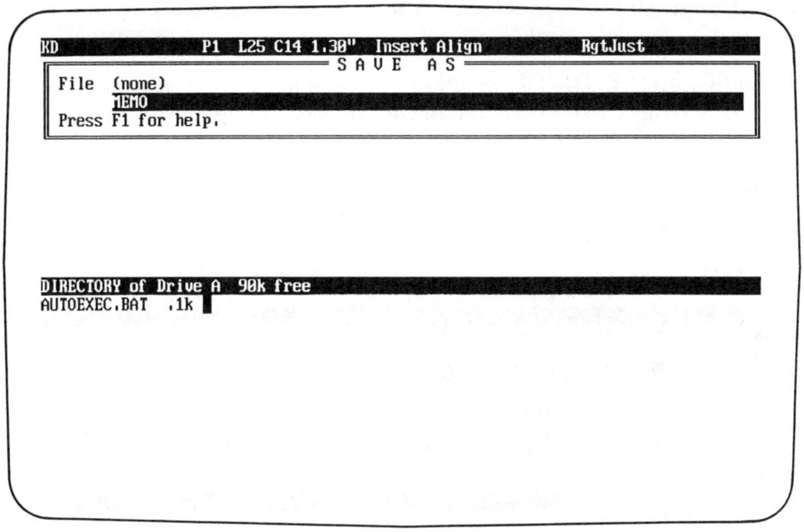
KD P1 L25 C14 1.30" Insert Align RgtJust
SAVE AS
File (none)
MEMO
Press F1 for help.
DIRECTORY of Drive A 90k free
AUTOEXEC.BAT .1k

Fig. 1.17.

Naming a file to be saved.

permits later retrieval. To name your file, type *memo*. The letters appear on the highlighted line.

4. Press Enter. The content of the on-screen box is replaced by the word:

   ```
   Saving...
   ```

   Your disk drive spins as the document is saved to disk. After the drive stops, the Opening Menu is displayed. Beneath the highlighted directory line is the name of the document you saved and closed—`MEMO`.

You now have a complete copy of your document's contents saved on a magnetic disk. To put the document on paper you must use WordStar's print function.

Printing Text

Before you begin to print a document, make sure that your printer is ready. Be sure that the printer is properly connected to your computer. The printer's power switch should be in the On position and its power indicator light should be on. Most printers also have an indicator light labeled READY or ON LINE; it should be on also. In addition, make sure that you have inserted the paper correctly. (Consult your printer manual if you are not sure about proper setup.)

To print your memo, follow these steps:

1. At the Opening Menu, press Enter. This displays the File menu (see fig. 1.4). The Opening Menu has command descriptions similar to those on the Edit screen's File menu (see fig. 1.10), but Opening Menu commands use a single letter and do not require you to press the Ctrl key. Also, you can invoke

these commands either by moving the highlight bar and pressing Enter or by just pressing the letter indicated.

2. To print a file, press P. The File menu disappears; in its place appears the Print Menu (see fig. 1.18). The name of the file to print appears near the top.

3. Press F10.

   Printing starts immediately.

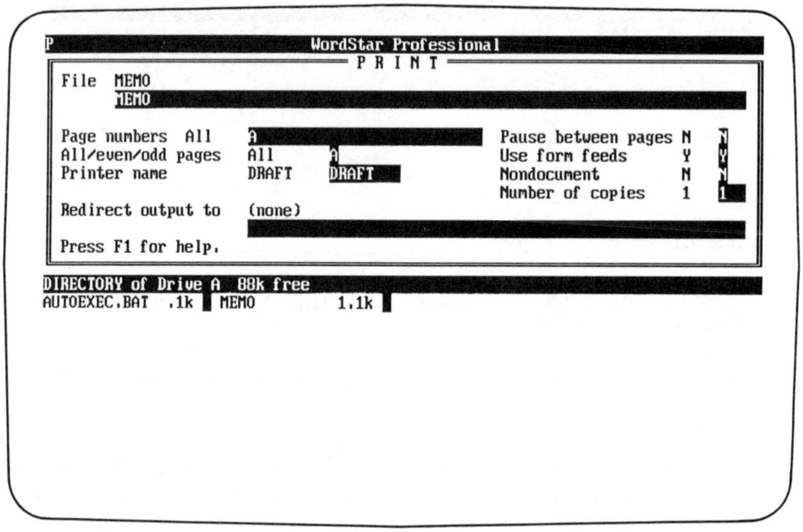
WordStar Professional
P R I N T
File MEMO
MEMO
Page numbers All
All/even/odd pages All
Printer name DRAFT
DRAFT
Redirect output to (none)
Press F1 for help.
Pause between pages N
Use form feeds Y
Nondocument N
Number of copies 1
DIRECTORY of Drive A 88k free
AUTOEXEC.BAT .1k
MEMO 1.1k

Fig. 1.18.
WordStar Release 5's Print Menu.

If your memo does not start printing, check again to see whether the printer is turned on and properly set up. If the memo still does not print, you may have installed WordStar incorrectly for your printer. Try installing the printer again. Printer settings are discussed in Chapter 7.

When the printer is finished, the Opening Menu is displayed again.

After your document is printed, look at it. You should see an exact replica of what appeared on-screen, complete with right-justification and identical positioning of the text.

Exiting WordStar

To bring this WordStar session to a close, press Enter. The File Menu appears. Select the Exit WordStar command by pressing X. The screen goes blank and displays the DOS prompt. From the DOS prompt, you can start another program.

Now that you have an overview of WordStar Release 5, continue to the next chapter to make a complete installation of the program.

2

Installing WordStar

Before you can use WordStar on your computer system, you must create a working copy installed for your particular display, disk drive configuration, and printer. Follow the steps in this chapter to tailor your word processor to your specific requirements, even if you worked with the simplified installation in the last chapter.

The WordStar Release 5 package contains 12 5 1/4-inch disks (or 6 3 1/2-inch disks) with program and supplementary files. On a large capacity hard disk, you can fit as many of these files as you need to create your *working copy disk* of WordStar. On a dual floppy disk system with limited capacity, you must choose those features and utility functions that are most important to your needs.

Make copies of the original WordStar disks and store the originals in a safe place. If your working copy and your original disks become damaged, you may find yourself unable to use the software you bought. If you register your copy of WordStar with MicroPro International, the publisher will replace faulty disks during the warranty period, but this takes time.

This chapter details the complete procedure for creating an installed copy of WordStar. The steps include the following:

- Loading MS-DOS
- Using MS-DOS to format a disk and copy files
- Deciding which files to include in your working copy
- Installing WordStar with the WINSTALL program

Beginners and experienced users alike can benefit from reading this chapter. Many veteran users of WordStar are ignorant of MS-DOS basics. If you are not familiar with these essential functions, you should learn about the basic functions of your computer's operating system (see the following section), formatting a disk, reading a disk directory, and copying files.

If you already know how to use MS-DOS to copy disk files, you can go directly to this chapter's middle section, which includes recommendations for creating working copies of WordStar on a standard 5 1/4-inch floppy disk, a 3 1/2-inch microfloppy disk, a high-density 5 1/4-inch or 3 1/2-inch disk, and a hard disk. After copying the necessary files from your original disks, you can proceed with installation, explained in the *Installing WordStar* section of this chapter.

Using DOS Functions

The following section introduces your computer's disk operating system (DOS). You must use DOS functions to start your computer and to make copies of the files on your WordStar disks. DOS controls computer operations that involve information storage on a magnetic disk, whether the disk is a removable floppy disk or a hard disk. Most IBM PCs, PS/2s, and compatibles use a version of MS-DOS or PC DOS, which are virtually identical. If you use the newer OS/2™ operating system on a PS/2 or compatible, you can run WordStar as an MS-DOS application (see your OS/2 manual for details).

Even experienced WordStar users may not be aware of DOS when working with their word processor, but WordStar needs DOS in order to function. The operating system allocates space on a disk, keeps track of what is stored there, makes copies of this information, and handles other record-keeping chores. To use WordStar properly, you need to know about three essential DOS functions: formatting a disk, reading a disk directory, and copying files.

Loading DOS

Before your computer can run any applications program—including WordStar—you must load the DOS program. Chapter 4 demonstrates a procedure for automatically starting DOS along with WordStar. For now, you can load DOS separately by following these steps:

1. Place the DOS disk supplied with your computer in drive A (the left, or on some machines, the upper, disk drive). Close the disk drive's door or handle.

2. Turn on your computer.

   When you turn on the computer, drive A starts and loads DOS into memory (if DOS is not in drive A, the computer seeks DOS in drive B, and then C; if you have a hard disk, designated C, with MS-DOS installed on it, DOS loads from it automatically). The drive's indicator light goes on as the DOS information is read. After a few seconds, your screen displays something similar to this:

```
Current date is 1-01-1980
Enter new date:
```

3. Type the correct date, separating with hyphens the numbers for the day, month, and year. Then press Enter. (If you don't want your files date-stamped, skip the instructions in step 3 by pressing Enter.)

   Your screen displays something similar to the following:

   ```
   Current time is 0:01:55
   Enter new time:
   ```

4. Type the correct time, using 24-hour clock notation, and then press Enter. For example, 3:30 in the afternoon would be entered as *15:30*.

   All documents stored on disk are now tagged with date and time information. (If you prefer not to tag your documents with the correct time, you can skip this step by pressing Enter.)

   The DOS prompt `A>` appears on-screen.

   The prompt indicates that DOS has been loaded into the computer's memory and is ready for use. Drive A is now the logged drive. That is, information can be read from or recorded to disks in drive A. (***Note:*** On most hard disk systems, DOS starts with C as the logged drive.)

Changing the logged drive is easy: at the DOS prompt, simply type the letter of the desired drive followed by a colon (:), and then press Enter. On dual floppy disk systems, the second drive is B. On hard disk drive systems, the hard disk is usually drive C. You can type the letter for the new drive in upper- or lowercase; DOS recognizes either. (All DOS commands may be in either upper- or lowercase.) The screen displays the new logged drive in the DOS prompt.

Formatting a Disk

Before you can store information on a disk, its surface must be magnetically partitioned or *formatted*. If you try to record data on an unformatted disk, the computer's screen displays an error message. With MS-DOS, this message is

```
General Failure error reading drive
```

The command for formatting a disk is FORMAT, a space, the letter designating the drive in which you have inserted the disk to be formatted, and a colon. To format a floppy disk in drive B, for instance, you would type *format b:*.

To format a floppy disk on a two disk drive system, use the following procedure:

1. With your computer turned on and DOS loaded from the disk in drive A, place a blank disk in drive B.

2. At the `A>` prompt, type *format b:* and press Enter. A message on-screen indicates that the disk to be formatted should be in drive B.

   Be sure that you have placed a ***blank*** disk in the indicated drive. If you insert a disk containing information, that information is erased during formatting.

3. Press Enter.

   The following message appears:

   ```
   Formatting...
   ```

   The disk drive indicator light goes on. After about a minute, a message indicates that formatting is complete. Seconds later, the display shows the number of bytes of disk space available. (One byte is equivalent to a single text character.) A screen message asks

   ```
   Format another (Y/N)?
   ```

4. Press Y, then Enter, if you want to format more disks. If not, press N. Press Enter and `A>` appears again.

To format a floppy disk on a computer system with a hard disk, follow these steps:

1. Be sure that your computer is on and that `C>` is displayed. Place a blank floppy disk in drive A.

2. At the `C>` prompt, type *format a:*. Be sure that you specify drive A.

   Warning: Issuing a command to format drive C, the hard disk, erases all the information you have stored on it.

   Press Enter. A message on-screen indicates that the floppy disk to be formatted should be in drive A.

3. Press Enter.

   The following message is displayed:

   ```
   Formatting...
   ```

   The disk drive indicator light goes on. After formatting, the display shows the disk space available. A screen message asks

   ```
   Format another (Y/N)?
   ```

4. Press Y, then Enter, if you want to format more disks. If not, press N. Press Enter and `C>` appears again.

To make a self-starting copy of WordStar on a floppy disk, you need a specially formatted disk that contains an additional portion of the DOS program. The process is essentially the same as formatting a disk, but you must type *format b:/s* (or *format a:/s* with a hard disk system). After formatting is complete, the screen informs you that the system has been transferred.

You must copy the DOS file COMMAND.COM onto your start-up disk by typing *copy command.com*, the target disk drive letter, a colon, and then pressing Enter. For more information on copying files, see the *Copying Files* section of this chapter.

For users of newer computer models with high-density floppy disk drives, it may be necessary sometimes to format disks capable of being read by older systems with lower density drives. To do so, you must type *format b:/4* (or *format a:/4*). The rest of the procedure remains the same.

Reading a Disk Directory

The information on a disk is stored in separate files that can be called up by name. Both programs and documents are written as files, the electronic equivalents of individual file folders bearing name labels. Names of files on a disk are stored in a listing or directory.

To find out what files a disk contains, you use the DOS command DIR. (As with all MS-DOS commands, you must press Enter after you type *dir* in order to execute the command.) After you issue a DIR command, the screen displays the file names, their lengths measured in kilobytes, the date and time each file was stored on disk, and the remaining amount of storage space (in kilobytes). *Kilobytes* (thousands of bytes) are represented by the letter K; two kilobytes equal roughly a page of text. *Megabytes* (millions of bytes) are represented by the letter M.

In this section, you learn how to read the directory on the disks supplied with your WordStar Release 5 program. The standard WordStar Release 5 package contains 12 5 1/4-inch floppy disks: the Program Disk, the Installation/Customization Disk, the Advanced Page Preview™ Disk, Printer Data Disk 1 and Printer Data Disk 2, the PostScript Files/Font Utility Disk, the Spelling Dictionary/Thesaurus Disk, the Definitions Disk, the ProFinder Disk, the MailList/TelMerge/PC-Outline Disk, the Advanced Customization Disk, and the Tutors Disk. When supplied on 3 1/2-inch microfloppy disks, WordStar comes with only six disks, which combine the same files.

These disks contain almost 200 different files, including program files; printer installation files; format previewing files; dictionary files for the spelling checker and thesaurus; utility programs files for outlining, information retrieval, telecommunications, and mailing list management; files for training; information files; and files for customizing WordStar.

To display a directory of Program Disk files, follow these steps:

1. Be sure that your computer is turned on and that `A>` is displayed. (If the DOS prompt shows a different logged drive, type *a:* and press Enter.)

2. Insert the Program Disk into drive A.

3. Type *dir* and press Enter.

You see the directory listing move up the screen, ending as shown in figure 2.1.

Fig. 2.1.

A part of the directory of the WordStar Program Disk in drive A.

```
$INDEX   OVR     3712   8-18-88   5:00p
$TOC     OVR     1408   8-18-88   5:00p
DRIVERA  OVR     3328   8-18-88   5:00p
DRIVERN  OVR     7936   8-18-88   5:00p
DRIVERT  OVR     2816   8-18-88   5:00p
WSHELP   OVR    40352   8-18-88   5:00p
WSHYPH   OVR    28892   8-18-88   5:00p
WSMSGS   OVR    21346   8-18-88   5:00p
WSSHORT  OVR      512   8-18-88   5:00p
WSSPELL  OVR    32896   8-18-88   5:00p
WSTHES   OVR    17190   8-18-88   5:00p
WSINDEX  XCL     1536   8-18-88   5:00p
RULER    DOC     1024   8-18-88   5:00p
TABLE    DOC     1024   8-18-88   5:00p
DIARY    DOC     3712   8-18-88   5:00p
TEXT     DOC     5760   8-18-88   5:00p
WINDOW   DOC      384   8-18-88   5:00p
ASCII    PDF      956   8-18-88   5:00p
DRAFT    PDF      938   8-18-88   5:00p
WS4      PDF      427   8-18-88   5:00p
PRINT    TST     9856   8-18-88   5:00p
BOX               512   8-18-88   5:00p
        24 File(s)     10240 bytes free

A>
```

You can read the directory of any of the WordStar disks in the same way you read the Program Disk directory.

Table 2.1 lists all the files on the WordStar Release 5 5 1/4-inch distribution disks, gives the length of each file, and describes the function of each file. (On each 3 1/2-inch distribution disk you will find files from two 5 1/4-inch disks.)

Table 2.1
Files on the WordStar Release 5 Distribution Disks

Name		*Size (bytes)*	*Function*
Program Disk			
WS	EXE	155136	Main WordStar program file
PECHO	EXE	540	Printer driver test file
$INDEX	OVR	3712	Index function program file
$TOC	OVR	1408	Table of contents program file
DRIVERA	OVR	3328	Special function printer driver
DRIVERN	OVR	7936	Printer driver for most printers
DRIVERT	OVR	2816	Printer driver for draft, special printers

Table 2.1—*Continued*

Name		*Size (bytes)*	*Function*
WSHELP	OVR	40352	Help messages
WSHYPH	OVR	28892	Hyphenation dictionary
WSMSGS	OVR	21346	WordStar messages and menus
WSSHORT	OVR	512	Expandable shorthand keyboard macro file
WSSPELL	OVR	32896	Spelling checker program file
WSTHES	OVR	17190	Thesaurus program file
WSINDEX	XCL	1536	Expandable index word exception list
RULER	DOC	1024	Sample file used in WordStar manual
TABLE	DOC	1024	Sample file used in WordStar manual
DIARY	DOC	3712	Sample file used in WordStar manual
TEXT	DOC	5760	Sample file used in WordStar manual
WINDOW	DOC	384	Sample file used in WordStar manual
ASCII	PDF	956	File for converting WS5 documents to ASCII
DRAFT	PDF	938	File for running generic printer driver
WS4	PDF	427	File for converting WS5 documents to WS4
PRINT	TST	9856	Printer text file
BOX		512	File used to facilitate box drawing
Installation/Customization Disk			
WINSTALL	EXE	1485	WordStar installation program
WSCHANGE	EXE	1485	WordStar customization program
PRCHANGE	EXE	164314	Printer customization program
PRCHANGE	HLP	17164	Printer customization messages

Table 2.1—*Continued*

Name		*Size (bytes)*	*Function*
INSTALL	OVR	39917	WordStar installation messages
WSCHANGE	OVR	46293	WordStar customization messages
CHANGE	OVR	76819	WordStar customization code
TABLES2	OVR	6120	Customization formatting file
DISPFONT	OVR	3134	Fonts for screen displays
Advanced Page Preview Disk			
PREVIEW	OVR	43792	Preview function program file
PREVIEW	MSG	8704	Preview function messages
FONTID	CTL	2560	Font identification file
NPSHLV1	WSF	17800	Formatting, font information files
NPSHLV2	WSF	20705	Formatting, font information files
NPSHLV3	WSF	17382	Formatting, font information files
NPSHLV4	WSF	20150	Formatting, font information files
NPSTMS1	WSF	18567	Formatting, font information files
NPSTMS2	WSF	19933	Formatting, font information files
NPSTMS3	WSF	18771	Formatting, font information files
NPSTMS4	WSF	20310	Formatting, font information files
PSHLV1	WSF	19996	Formatting, font information files
PSHLV2	WSF	22573	Formatting, font information files
PSHLV3	WSF	19388	Formatting, font information files
PSTMS1	WSF	21292	Formatting, font information files
PSTMS2	WSF	23865	Formatting, font information files
PSTMS3	WSF	20857	Formatting, font information files
Printer Data Disk 1			
INDEX	DTB	27648	Printer information index file
DB00	DTB	41602	Printer information data file
DB02	DTB	55211	Printer information data file

Table 2.1—*Continued*

Name		*Size (bytes)*	*Function*
DB01	DTB	98638	Printer information data file
DB04	DTB	97340	Printer information data file
Printer Data Disk 2			
INDEX	DTC	27648	Printer information index file
DB00	DTC	37847	Printer information data file
DB02	DTC	55087	Printer information data file
DB01	DTC	165432	Printer information data file
DB04	DTC	72536	Printer information data file
PostScript Files/Font Utility Disk			
LSRFONTS	EXE	123243	Laser font modification program
COURI	AFM	9909	Font information file
COURIB	AFM	9986	Font information file
COURIBO	AFM	9983	Font information file
COURIO	AFM	9963	Font information file
HELVE	AFM	12162	Font information file
HELVEB	AFM	12099	Font information file
HELVEBO	AFM	12158	Font information file
HELVEO	AFM	12138	Font information file
TIMESB	AFM	12415	Font information file
TIMESBI	AFM	12319	Font information file
TIMESI	AFM	12428	Font information file
TIMESR	AFM	12288	Font information file
DRIVERPS	OVR	6656	Printer driver for PostScript printers
BORDER	PS	389	PostScript description file
BOX	PS	1010	PostScript description file
EHANDLER	PS	2818	PostScript description file

Table 2.1—*Continued*

Name		*Size (bytes)*	*Function*
LETTER	PS	1439	PostScript description file
LOGO	PS	1371	PostScript description file
SETDTR	PS	198	PostScript description file
WSPROL	PS	4385	PostScript description file
WSPROL2	PS	4844	PostScript description file
PSHLV4	WSF	22011	Font description file
PSTMS4	WSF	23250	Font description file
Spelling Dictionary/Thesaurus Disk			
MAIN	DCT	126848	Expandable spelling dictionary
PERSONAL	DCT	128	Spelling dictionary file
THES	DCT	100674	Thesaurus dictionary file
Definitions Disk			
DEFN	DCT	250219	Thesaurus definition file
ProFinder Disk			
EXTLIST	PF	69	File finder external list format
USERSYN	PF	274	File finder synonym format
USERMENU	PF	620	File finder user menu format
QUITMENU	PF	128	File finder quit menu format
PF	EXE	164563	File finder program file
PFINST	EXE	51998	File finder installation program
PF	HLP	27922	File finder help messages
MailList/TelMerge/PC-Outline Disk			
WSLIST	COM	64000	Mail list program file
WSLIST	OVR	7228	Mail list messages file
INVNTORY	DEF	2048	Inventory list definition file
WSLIST	DEF	2304	Mail list format definition file
INVNTORY	DTA	128	Inventory list data file

Table 2.1—*Continued*

Name		*Size (bytes)*	*Function*
INVNTORY	NDX	128	Inventory list index file
WSLIST	DTA	128	Mail list data file
WSLIST	NDX	128	Mail list index file
INVNTORY	DOT	443	Inventory variables for merge printing
MAILLIST	DOT	435	Mail list variables for merge printing
ENVELOPE	LST	896	Special format printing instructions
HP-ENV	LST	1152	Special format printing instructions
HP-ENVMM	LST	768	Special format printing instructions
HP-LAB3	LST	3328	Special format printing instructions
HP2-ENV	LST	1152	Special format printing instructions
HP2-ENVM	LST	768	Special format printing instructions
INVNTORY	LST	1408	Inventory report printing instructions
LABEL	LST	256	Special format printing instructions
LABEL3	LST	256	Special format printing instructions
LABELXL	LST	256	Special format printing instructions
LSRLABL3	LST	3072	Special format printing instructions
PHONE	LST	896	Phone list format printing instructions
PROOF	LST	1280	Mail list report printing instructions
ROLODEX	LST	256	Rolodex format printing instructions
LABEL3A		2560	Formatting data file
LABELA		1280	Formatting data file
LABELXLA		1792	Formatting data file
ROLODEXA		1536	Formatting data file
SHOLABEL		1024	Formatting data file
SHOLABL3		2944	Formatting data file
SHOLABLX		1152	Formatting data file

Table 2.1—*Continued*

Name		*Size (bytes)*	*Function*
SHOROLDX		1152	Formatting data file
TELMERGE	EXE	67321	Telecommunications program file
TELMERGE	SYS	11008	Modifiable TelMerge system file
PCO	EXE	69856	Outliner program file
GOODCLK	COM	50	Resets time in outliner program
KEYSET	COM	1256	Keyboard customizing program
SAMPBLOC	PCO	2464	Outliner sample used in manual
SAMPCREA	PCO	2481	Outliner sample used in manual
SAMPDIVD	PCO	1726	Outliner sample used in manual
SAMPFIND	PCO	3487	Outliner sample used in manual
SAMPHIDE	PCO	2483	Outliner sample used in manual
SAMPMARK	PCO	3054	Outliner sample used in manual
SAMPMENU	PCO	2812	Outliner sample used in manual
SAMPMOVE	PCO	1888	Outliner sample used in manual
SAMPPLAC	PCO	2491	Outliner sample used in manual
SAMPSORT	PCO	2984	Outliner sample used in manual
SAMPSTYL	PCO	3018	Outliner sample used in manual
PCODAISY	PRN	703	Outliner printer driver
PCOIBM	PRN	1026	Outliner printer driver
PCOSTAN	PRN	705	Outliner printer driver
Advanced Customization Disk			
README	COM	29212	Late-breaking information program file
README	TXT	65644	Late-breaking information text
PDFEDIT	EXE	72163	Printer font customization program
MOVEPRN	EXE	19697	Customizing print program
SWITCH	COM	571	Change fonts utility
PATCH	LST	95872	Customizing patch information listing

Table 2.1—*Continued*

Name		*Size (bytes)*	*Function*
WS3KEYS	PAT	1792	Settings for WS3 keyboard compatibility
384K	PAT	128	Settings for 384K internal memory
HELP	PNF	33477	Printer font customization file
PDF	PNF	21712	Printer font customization file
FNT	PNF	10955	Printer font customization file
Tutors Disk			
WSTUTORA	BAT	213	Tutorial start-up file
WSTUTORB	BAT	213	Tutorial start-up file
WSTUTORC	BAT	232	Tutorial start-up file
SHOW	EXE	36352	Tutorial display program
WSTSETUP	SHO	4829	Tutorial setup file
WSTMENU	SHO	4224	Tutorial menu file
WST1	SHO	15447	Tutorial data file
WST1B	SHO	22338	Tutorial data file
WST2	SHO	22656	Tutorial data file
WST3	SHO	20112	Tutorial data file
WST4	SHO	20845	Tutorial data file
WST5	SHO	24192	Tutorial data file
WST6	SHO	13952	Tutorial data file
WST6B	SHO	17536	Tutorial data file
WST7	SHO	22656	Tutorial data file
WST7B	SHO	20210	Tutorial data file
WSTS	CMP	9764	Tutorial data file
WST1	CMP	11772	Tutorial data file
WST1E	CMP	4258	Tutorial data file
WST2	CMP	5906	Tutorial data file
WST2B	CMP	6844	Tutorial data file

Table 2.1—*Continued*

Name		*Size (bytes)*	*Function*
WST3	CMP	8884	Tutorial data file
WST4	CMP	8658	Tutorial data file
WST5	CMP	9644	Tutorial data file
WST6	CMP	11010	Tutorial data file
WST7B	CMP	8408	Tutorial data file
DOC	2	384	Tutorial sample file
DOC1	3	512	Tutorial sample file
DOC2	3	362	Tutorial sample file
DOC	4	768	Tutorial sample file
DOC	5	384	Tutorial sample file
DOC	6	384	Tutorial sample file
DOC	7	768	Tutorial sample file
A	WST	1	Tutorial start-up
B	WST	1	Tutorial start-up
C	WST	1	Tutorial start-up

Copying Files

Among the most used DOS functions is the copying of files on disk. You can apply the DOS command COPY to make archival copies of the WordStar distribution disks, a working copy of WordStar, or duplicate copies of document files you have created—for safekeeping.

The syntax for the COPY command in MS-DOS is straightforward: COPY, followed by a space, the name of the file to be duplicated, another space, and the letter and colon designating the drive that holds the disk to which the file should be copied. (If you have a single disk drive system, you use the DOS DISKCOPY command instead of COPY, as noted in what follows.)

The command line below illustrates the use of the COPY command to copy the file WS.EXE, the principal WordStar program file, from drive A to drive B. After the `A>` prompt, type

copy ws.exe b:

The file name—WS.EXE—is in two parts: a file name of up to eight characters, and an optional three-letter extension. File name and extension are separated by a period (.).

When you use the COPY command, you can type the name of a file to be copied, or you can designate one or more file names by using a wild card. DOS provides two wild cards: ? and *. The question mark can replace any one character in a file name, and the asterisk can replace any character or series of characters.

For example, suppose that you want to copy all the files on the Program Disk that are directly involved with WordStar functions. These file names begin with the letters WS. After the A> prompt, type

copy ws.* b:*

DOS would copy all these files to drive B:

WS.EXE
WSHELP.OVR
WSHYPH.OVR
WSMSGS.OVR
WSSHORT.OVR
WSSPELL.OVR
WSTHES.OVR
WSINDEX.XCL

To copy all the files on a disk regardless of file name, you can use the asterisk wild card for both parts of the file name. After the A> prompt, type *copy *.* b:*.

Follow the steps below to copy the WordStar distribution disk files on your system. (For a single disk drive, follow the instructions for a two floppy disk system, substituting ***diskcopy*** for the *copy *.** command.)

With a two floppy disk system, for archival copies, follow these steps:

1. Turn on your computer. A> is displayed.
2. Place the disk to be copied in drive A and place a blank, formatted disk in drive B.
3. Type *copy *.* B:* and press Enter.

   File names appear on-screen as each file is copied. When finished, DOS displays the number of files copied, and A> reappears.

Before copying files to a large capacity hard disk, you should be familiar with the basic organization of this device. Because a hard disk may hold thousands of files, DOS can divide files into directories and subdirectories. These divisions are like drawers or partitions in a filing cabinet.

On a hard disk system, the WordStar Release 5 program is preset to operate in a directory called \WS5. (The backslash tells DOS that WS5 is a directory.) If you have not already done so, create this directory on your hard disk by following these steps:

1. Turn on your computer. `C>` is displayed.

   Note: These instructions assume that your system's hard disk is drive C and that the floppy disk drive is A. If this is not the case, substitute the correct letters.

2. Type *md \ws5* and press Enter.

   DOS creates the directory \WS5.

Now copy the files from the WordStar Program Disk to your hard disk by following these steps:

1. Turn on your computer. `C>` is displayed.
2. Insert the WordStar Program Disk into drive A.
3. Type *copy a:*.* c:\ws5*

   DOS copies the files from the disk in drive A to the hard disk.

To verify that the files are on the hard disk, you need to change from the original directory to the \WS5 directory and issue the DIR command. To change the directory, type *cd \ws5*. Now type *dir* and press Enter. The screen displays the directory for \WS5.

The preceding discussion introduced the minimum needed to copy files to your hard disk. As you use WordStar, you will want to know more about directories and about maximizing the capabilities of your hard disk. For more information, consult your DOS manual. Chris DeVoney's Que books, *Using PC DOS* and *MS-DOS User's Guide*, and *Managing Your Hard Disk*, by Don Berliner with Chris DeVoney, are helpful.

Making Copies of WordStar

This section provides instructions for making copies of WordStar on various systems. First, you learn how to duplicate the WordStar disks. You can archive these duplicate disks as backups along with your original WordStar disks. Next, you learn how to make a working copy of WordStar so that the program files fit on one disk (or the smallest number of disks possible) most efficiently. If you have a hard disk, you can make a working copy simply by copying all the WordStar files onto it.

Duplicating the WordStar Disks

To create backup copies of WordStar's disks, duplicate each disk, labeling copies the same as the originals. This section gives step-by-step instructions for the procedure.

Duplicating the WordStar Disks on 360K, 5 1/4-Inch Disks

On a dual floppy disk system, duplicate the WordStar disks on 360K, 5 1/4-inch disks by following these steps:

1. Format 11 disks (you needn't make a duplicate of the Tutors Disk). Follow the instructions in the *Formatting a Disk* section earlier in this chapter to prepare your disks. Label each of the formatted disks as follows:

   WordStar Program Disk—Backup Copy

   Installation/Customization Disk—Backup Copy

   Spelling Dictionary/Thesaurus Disk—Backup Copy

   Definitions Disk—Backup Copy

   Printer Data Disk 1—Backup Copy

   Printer Data Disk 2—Backup Copy

   Advanced Page Preview Disk—Backup Copy

   PostScript Files/Font Utility Disk—Backup Copy (only for laser printer users)

   ProFinder Disk—Backup Copy

   MailList/TelMerge/PC-Outline Disk—Backup Copy

   Advanced Customization Disk—Backup Copy

2. Make certain that DOS is loaded and `A>` is on-screen. Place the original WordStar Program Disk in drive A and the blank disk labeled WordStar Program Disk—Backup Copy in drive B. To copy the WordStar program files to your working disk, type *copy *.* b:* and press Enter.

   When copying is complete, the DOS prompt appears again.

3. Following the directions given in step 2, duplicate each of the other 10 principal disks in the WordStar Release 5 package. The original disk should be placed in drive A, and the backup disk should be placed in drive B.

Duplicating the WordStar Disks on 3 1/2-Inch Disks or High-Density 5 1/4-Inch Disks

On a dual floppy disk system, duplicate the WordStar disks on 3 1/2-inch micro-floppy disks or high-density 5 1/4-inch disks by following these steps:

1. Format six disks (you needn't make a duplicate of the Tutors Disk). Follow the instructions in the *Formatting a Disk* section earlier in this chapter. Label each of the formatted disks as follows:

    Program/Installation Disk—Backup Copy

    Printer Data Disk—Backup Copy

    Definitions/Thesaurus Disk—Backup Copy

    Advanced Page Preview/Advanced Customization Disk—Backup Copy

    ProFinder/MailList/TelMerge/PC-Outline Disk—Backup Copy

    PostScript Files/Font Utility Disk—Backup Copy (only for laser printer users)

2. With DOS loaded and `A>` on-screen, place the 3 1/2-inch WordStar Program/ Installation Disk in drive A (if copying from 5 1/4-inch disks, the WordStar Program Disk) and the blank disk labeled WordStar Program/Installation Disk—Backup Copy in drive B. To copy the WordStar program files to your backup disk, type *copy *.* b:* and press Enter. When copying is complete, the DOS prompt again appears. (Now, if copying from 5 1/4-inch distribution disks, copy the contents of the Installation Disk onto the WordStar Program/Installation Disk in drive B.)

3. Following the directions given in step 2, duplicate each of the other WordStar Release 5 disks. Remember, the original disk should be placed in drive A, and the backup copy should be placed in drive B.

Duplicating the WordStar Disks on a Hard Disk System

Before you copy the files to your hard disk, make backup copies by following the instructions given earlier in this chapter for duplicating the WordStar disks on a dual floppy disk system.

If you have only one floppy disk drive along with your hard disk, you must follow these extra steps to overcome the lack of floppy-to-floppy copying capability:

1. Create a temporary directory on your hard disk for copying files from the WordStar distribution disks. With `C>` on-screen, type *md \temp* and press Enter. Move into the new directory by typing *cd \temp* and pressing Enter.

2. Place into drive A the first distribution disk to be copied. Type *copy a:*.** and press Enter.
3. When all the files on the distribution disk have been copied, replace the disk in drive A with the corresponding backup disk. Type *copy *.* a:* and press Enter.
4. Once these files have been duplicated onto the backup disk, erase them from the hard disk by typing *del *.** and pressing Enter, followed by typing *y* when asked by the prompt on-screen whether you are sure. Repeat this procedure until you have made backups of all the disks supplied in the WordStar package.
5. Type *rd \temp* to remove the temporary directory. If you want, you can omit this step to retain a convenient temporary directory for duplicating files onto floppy disks.

You should have floppy disk copies of the original WordStar disks, even though you will have a copy of the program on the hard disk. After you have created duplicate disks, you can copy your program files to the hard disk as described later in this chapter.

Making a Working Copy of WordStar Release 5

A hard disk can hold all the files on the WordStar Release 5 package disks. (***Note:*** If you are upgrading from a previous WordStar version, make a backup copy of the earlier program files that are on your hard disk and store them in a safe place for possible future reference. Delete those files from your hard disk.)

If your system has a high-density, 5 1/4-inch or 3 1/2-inch disk drive, you can include on a single disk all the WordStar files you need for most word processing functions. If your computer uses standard 3 1/2-inch microfloppy disks, you can fit at least 720K of files on your WordStar working disk, enough for the most often used WordStar files.

Deciding what to include on your working copy of WordStar is more difficult, however, if your computer has standard 5 1/4-inch disk drives. Standard 5 1/4-inch floppy disks can store files totaling no more than 360K. You may have to choose one set of files for your working copy and keep other files on separate disks.

Table 2.2 shows groups of files you can use on your working copy for various functions, along with the amount of disk space required to store each file.

Table 2.2
Basic WordStar Working Copy Disk Files (by Function)

File Name	*Kilobytes of Disk Space Required*
(SYSTEM TRACKS)	67
COMMAND.COM	26 (MS-DOS version 3.3)
Basic WordStar Files	
WS.EXE	152
WSMSGS.OVR	20
DRAFT.PDF	1
DRIVERT.OVR	2
WSHELP.OVR	39
Additional Basic Function Files	
WSSHORT.OVR	0.5
WSINDEX.XCL	1.5
$INDEX.OVR	3
$TOC.OVR	1
DRIVERA.OVR	3
DRIVERN.OVR	8
DRIVERPS.OVR	6
WSHYPH.OVR	27
Advanced Page Preview Files	
PREVIEW.OVR	43
PREVIEW.MSG	8
FONTID.CTL	2
*.WSF	300
Spelling Dictionary Files	
WSSPELL.OVR	31
MAIN.DCT	124
PERSONAL.DCT	0.1
Thesaurus Files	
WSTHES.OVR	16
THES.DCT	98
DEFN.DCT	244
Text Locating Files	
PF.EXE	160
PFINST.EXE	49
PF.HLP	25

Table 2.2—*Continued*

File Name	*Kilobytes of Disk Space Required*
Outliner File	
PCO.EXE	77
Telecommunications Files	
TELMERGE.EXE	68
TELMERGE.SYS	10
Mailing List Files	
WSLIST.COM	63
WSLIST.OVR	6
WSLIST.DEF	2
WSLIST.DTA	0.1
WSLIST.NDX	0.1

A working copy of WordStar must contain four files: WS.EXE, WSMSGS.OVR, one printer driver file, and a printer description file (PDF) for a specific printer. For a generic installation, you can use DRIVERT.OVR and DRAFT.PDF files (with the file extension PDF, chosen during installation with the WINSTALL program). As you can see in table 2.2, these files occupy about 175K of disk space, with another 39K for help messages in the WSHELP.OVR file. For a self-starting working copy of WordStar you also need the system tracks and DOS file COMMAND.COM (disk space for these files depends on your DOS version; for version 3.3 they total 33K). On a standard 5 1/4-inch disk, about 100K of storage space is left for other functions. If you choose to install a dot-matrix, daisywheel, or simple laser printer, you need the DRIVERN.OVR file (7K). For special disk-oriented printer description files, the DRIVERA.OVR file (3K) is also needed. For PostScript laser printers, the DRIVERPS.OVR file (6K) is a must.

To avoid swapping disks on standard 5 1/4-inch floppy drives, you need all your program and supporting files on one disk. Choose the functions that are most important for your applications to occupy the remaining space on your working copy. Some features require negligible amounts of space. For example, WordStar's shorthand function relies on the expandable file WSSHORT.OVR, beginning at a mere 0.5K, and indexing requires the $INDEX.OVR (3K) and the WSINDEX.XCL file, which starts at 1.5K. Other add-on features require larger files: the WSHYPH.OVR file for automatic hyphenation occupies 26K, while outlining requires the 77K PCO.EXE file.

In some cases, a single additional function can take up most of the remaining space on a standard 5 1/4-inch disk. For instance, the spelling checker requires WSSPELL.OVR, MAIN.DCT, and PERSONAL.DCT files, leaving little room on the disk for adding to your personal dictionary—and no space for the word definition file DEFN.DCT or any additional WordStar functions. If the synonyms in an electronic thesaurus are important to you, the necessary WSTHES.OVR and THES.DCT files on your disk leave no room for definitions or other functions.

If you need more add-on functions than fit on a standard 5 1/4-inch disk, you should consider a two disk solution. In the case of spelling and thesaurus features, you can place either the WSSPELL.OVR or the WSTHES.OVR file, or both, on the working copy disk in drive A, and put dictionary files on a disk to be placed in drive B or to be swapped with the disk in drive A. During installation with the WINSTALL program, explained later in this chapter, you can specify where your dictionary files are to be stored. If you have at least 512K of internal memory, another possibility is to create a boot disk with DOS tracks and the COMMAND.COM file and programs that are normally loaded before the WordStar WS.EXE file and remain resident in memory. These might include the file finder PF.EXE, the outliner PCO.EXE, or the telecommunications program TELMERGE.EXE, or some combination of the three. A second disk is then substituted in drive A for the boot disk in order to load WordStar's essential program files.

With so many possibilities due to the modest capacity of standard floppy disks, you probably will want to create a working copy of WordStar with only essential files, then add to or modify it as you learn to use additional functions. With larger capacity 3 1/2-inch disks or high-density 5 1/4-inch disks, you are less constrained in selecting functions to include on your working copy of WordStar.

Installation, information, and tutorial files are used only occasionally, so you do not need these files with your working copy of WordStar. Only on a hard disk system can you include all the files supplied in the WordStar package, although you still may want to be selective in your choices. With more than 4M of files supplied with WordStar Release 5, you may find your hard disk filling up faster than you expected—noticeably slowing down performance.

When you make your working copy of WordStar, use backup copies of the disks, not the original ones supplied with the package. This avoids possible damage to your original disks due to mishandling. Remember, after you make your working copy of WordStar, you still must install it for your computer. Installation instructions are covered in the last section of this chapter.

Making a Working Copy on 360K, 5 1/4-Inch Disks

You need to complete the steps in this section if your computer has two 360K, 5 1/4-inch disk drives.

1. Label one blank, formatted disk as follows:

   WordStar Working Copy Disk

2. Make certain that the DOS disk is in drive A and that A> is displayed on-screen. Insert into drive B the blank disk labeled WordStar Working Copy Disk and add the system files to it by typing *sys b:* and pressing Enter. Then, to copy COMMAND.COM to drive B, type *copy command.com b:* and press Enter.

3. Replace the disk in drive A with your WordStar Program—Backup Disk. To copy the WordStar program and associated files to your working disk, type these commands as follows and press Enter. Wait for copying of the files to be completed, then type the next command.

   copy ws.exe b: (copies WordStar's main program file)
   copy wsh.* b:* (copies help and hyphenation files)
   copy wsmsgs.ovr b: (copies WordStar messages)
   copy wsshort.ovr b: (copies shorthand function file)
   copy dri.* b:* (copies principal printer drivers)
   *copy *.pdf b:* (copies useful printer description files)

Note: These steps are only one method for putting a working copy of WordStar on standard 5 1/4-inch floppy disks. For alternative setups, see sections of this book detailing WordStar add-on functions.

Making a Working Copy on 720K, 3 1/2-Inch Disks

If your computer system has two standard 3 1/2-inch microfloppy drives, follow these steps to copy files from the disks supplied with the 3 1/2-inch disk WordStar Release 5 package. If you have an IBM PS/2 or compatible computer with a 1.44M disk drive, make your working copy by following the instructions for high-density floppy disks given in the next section.

1. Label two blank, formatted disks as follows:

   WordStar Working Copy Disk

   WordStar Dictionary Disk

2. Make certain that the DOS disk is in drive A and that A> is on-screen. Insert into drive B the blank disk labeled WordStar Working Copy and add the system files to it by typing *sys b:* and pressing Enter. Then, to copy COMMAND.COM to drive B, type *copy command.com b:* and press Enter.

3. Remove the disk from drive A and replace it with your backup copy of the WordStar Program/Installation Disk. To copy the files needed from the backup disk, type *copy *.* b:* and press Enter. When copying is complete, A> appears.

4. Replace the disks in drives A and B by putting the backup Thesaurus/Definitions Disk in drive A and the blank disk labeled Spelling Dictionary/Thesaurus/Definitions Disk in drive B. To copy the files, type *copy *.* b:* and press Enter. After copying is finished, `A>` reappears. You now have a working copy of the Dictionary Disk in drive B.

Note: These steps are only one method for putting a working copy of WordStar on 720K, 3 1/2-inch microfloppy disks. For other setups, see sections of this book detailing WordStar add-on functions.

Making a Working Copy on a High-Density Floppy Disk

If your two floppy disk computer system includes at least one high-density floppy disk drive (either 5 1/4-inch or 3 1/2-inch) with at least a 1.2M capacity, you can create a working copy of WordStar on just one disk with all the files needed for most word processing applications. Assuming that drive A is the high-density drive (if not, substitute the correct letter), follow these instructions:

1. Label one blank, formatted disk as follows:

   WordStar Working Copy Disk

2. With the DOS disk in drive B and `B>` on-screen, insert into drive A the WordStar Working Copy Disk and add the system file to it by typing *sys a:* and pressing Enter. Then, to copy COMMAND.COM to drive A, type *copy command.com a:* and press Enter.

3. Replace the DOS disk in drive B with your backup copy of the WordStar Program Disk. To copy all the files, type *copy b:*.* a:* and press Enter. After copying is complete, `A>` is displayed.

4. Take the Program Disk out of drive B and insert your backup copy of the Spelling Dictionary/Thesaurus Disk. To copy all files, type *copy b:*.* a:* and press Enter.

5. After copying is complete and `A>` reappears, replace the Spelling Dictionary/Thesaurus Disk in drive B with your backup copy of the Definitions Disk. To copy its files, type *copy b:*.* a:* and press Enter.

6. With `A>` displayed again, repeat the copying procedure for the Advanced Page Preview Disk: place your backup copy of that disk in drive B and type *copy b:*.* a:* and press Enter.

When all files have been copied, you have the WordStar program, spelling checker, thesaurus, and a few other files on a single high-density disk.

Note: You may want to substitute other files to invoke WordStar add-on functions that are more important to your applications, as described in later sections of this book.

Making a Working Copy on a Hard Disk

A computer system with a hard disk drive can store all the files in the WordStar Release 5 package, but you should be selective about which files you put on disk—too many files can slow down response time. Choose the functions you need, then add extra files for other features as you need them.

The following instructions assume that drive C is a hard disk and drive A is a floppy disk; if not, substitute the correct letters. These steps are based on transferring files from 5 1/4-inch distribution disks. If you are copying from 3 1/2-inch microfloppies, you can consolidate the copy commands for only half as many disks. Follow these steps:

1. Turn on your computer. `C>` appears on-screen. If you haven't created a directory called WS5 for your WordStar Release 5 files, type *md \ws5* and press Enter.

2. To log onto this directory, type *cd \ws5* and press Enter. WordStar Release 5 is set to work with the WS5 directory. If you want to use a different directory name for your program files, run the WSCHANGE program (see Chapter 11).

3. To copy the files in the WordStar package, begin by inserting into drive A your backup copy of the Program Disk. Type *copy a:*.* c:* and press Enter. (You can type *del *.doc* and press Enter to eliminate five unessential sample files.)

4. After copying is complete and `C>` is displayed again, remove the Program Disk from drive A and replace it with your backup copy of the Installation/Customization Disk. Type *copy a:*.* c:* and press Enter.

5. After file copying is finished and `C>` returns to the screen, replace the Installation/Customization Disk with your backup copy of the Spelling Dictionary/Thesaurus Disk. Type *copy a:*.* c:* and press Enter.

6. After the files on that disk are copied, replace the Spelling Dictionary/Thesaurus Disk with your backup copy of the Definitions Disk and repeat the copy procedure.

7. When `C>` reappears, remove the Definitions Disk and place Printer Data Disk 1 in drive A. Type *copy a:*.* c:* and press Enter.

8. Once `C>` is displayed again, substitute Printer Data Disk 2 for Printer Data Disk 1 in drive A. Type *copy a:*.* c:* and press Enter.

9. With C> back on-screen, remove Printer Data Disk 2 from drive A and put the Advanced Page Preview Disk in its place. Again type *copy a:*.* c:* and press Enter.

Once you have completed copying this disk, you can invoke WordStar's basic and intermediate functions. If you are using a PostScript-driven laser printer, copy the files from the PostScript Files/Font Utility Disk. For useful add-ons, you can copy the files from the ProFinder and MailList/TelMerge/PC-Outline Disks, though these will add 75 files to your disk. Finally, for sophisticated users, you may want the files from the Advanced Customization Disk on your hard disk.

Installing WordStar

Before you use your working copy of WordStar, you must install (adjust) the program to work with your computer's monitor, printer, disk drives, memory, and operating system. WordStar Release 5 has two programs for adjusting the main word processing program. The first, WINSTALL, makes the basic modifications necessary to get WordStar up and running. More extensive alterations are the province of WSCHANGE, which covers many features that once could be modified only by manipulating WordStar's program code. Customizing your word processor with WSCHANGE is the subject of Chapter 11.

If you are familiar with installing WordStar Release 4, you will find several additions to WINSTALL in Release 5 that make it easier to customize WordStar immediately without running WSCHANGE. The new options include more printer choices and the selection of screen color settings and help level. Complete instructions for the installation of WordStar Release 5 are provided in the sections that follow.

Loading the Installation Program

To load the installation program, complete the following steps (using your system's disk drive designations):

1. Turn on your computer and load DOS.
2. On a two floppy disk system, place the WordStar Installation Disk in drive A and your Working Copy Disk in drive B.

   On a hard disk system, change to the proper subdirectory (for example, type *cd \ws5*) and proceed (your files will be put in that subdirectory on drive C).
3. Type ***winstall*** and press Enter to load the installation program.

The screen displays a copyright notice and a prompt asking for the name of the file you want to install.

4. On a two floppy disk system, type *b:ws* and press Enter.

   On a hard disk system, type *ws* and press Enter.

   Another screen message appears, indicating that pressing Enter will assign WS as the name of the file to hold the installed WordStar. If you prefer to avoid errors, you can type *ws* as the name for the installed version of WordStar.

5. On a two floppy disk system, type *b:ws* and press Enter.

   On a hard disk system, type *ws* and press Enter (see fig. 2.2).

```
WINSTALL  11 Aug 88
Copyright (C) 1983, 1988 MicroPro International Corporation.
All rights reserved

IBM PC Compatible PC-DOS/MS-DOS Version


To install WordStar, type ws and press ←┘.  WS

To name the file ws, press ←┘.  WS


Note:  The uninstalled WordStar is called WS.  If you've renamed
the file, type the new name and press ←┘.

If you wish to name your WordStar file something else, type that
name and press ←┘.  At the end of the installation procedure,
you'll have a version of WordStar saved in a file with this name.
Be sure to type this name to start WordStar.
```

Fig. 2.2.

The WordStar file designated for installation.

Adjusting WordStar to Your System

Your computer loads the WordStar installation program file and then displays the Main Installation Menu (see fig. 2.3). To make a selection, type the letter to the left of the menu item. Each selection calls up another menu. For an orderly installation, select each letter in turn. (***Note:*** In this phase of the installation, you don't need to press Enter.) In order to run any of the installation programs (WINSTALL, WSCHANGE, PRCHANGE, LSRFONTS, or PDFEDIT), the TABLES2.OVR file, located on the Installation/Customization Disk, must be in the same directory as each installation program.

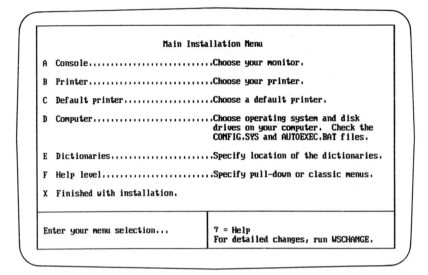

Fig. 2.3.
WordStar's Main Installation Menu.

```
                        Main Installation Menu

A  Console...........................Choose your monitor.

B  Printer...........................Choose your printer.

C  Default printer...................Choose a default printer.

D  Computer..........................Choose operating system and disk
                                     drives on your computer.  Check the
                                     CONFIG.SYS and AUTOEXEC.BAT files.

E  Dictionaries......................Specify location of the dictionaries.

F  Help level........................Specify pull-down or classic menus.

X  Finished with installation.

Enter your menu selection...         ? = Help
                                     For detailed changes, run WSCHANGE.
```

If you make a mistake during installation, you can start over or change a selection after you're finished. To exit the installation program, press ^C.

Specifying Screen Characteristics

In order to work properly, WordStar must be adjusted to fit the technical characteristics of your computer display. At the Main Installation Menu, press A to select Console. The screen displays the Console Menu (see fig. 2.4), which indicates WordStar's current setting and four function choices.

Press A again, and you see Monitor Selection Menu #1 (see fig. 2.5). Pressing 2 on this menu brings up Monitor Selection Menu #2 (see fig. 2.6).

If your computer monitor is monochrome and 100 percent IBM compatible, press A at Monitor Selection Menu #1.

For a 100 percent IBM compatible computer with a Color Graphics Adapter (CGA), you should choose B.

With a system that is not fully compatible or a color display that shows screen noise (*snow*) when you use WordStar, press C. (Selecting C slows the display perceptibly.)

If your system has an enhanced graphics adapter (EGA) permitting a higher resolution display with 43 lines of text, you can put nearly twice as many lines on the WordStar screen by selecting D.

```
                         Console Menu

WordStar is currently installed for:  IBM PC Compatible

A  Monitor Selection Menu
B  Underlining text
C  Soft space and soft tab display character
D  Video attributes

X  Finished with this menu


Enter your menu selection...     ? = Help
                                 For detailed changes, run WSCHANGE.
```

Fig. 2.4.
The Console Menu.

```
                   Monitor Selection Menu #1

A  IBM Compatible using video RAM directly.  (Fastest way to display
   characters on 100% IBM compatible machines.)

B  IBM Compatible using CGA video RAM directly.  (Removes most "snow" from
   screen but is slower.  Used for 100% IBM compatible machines only.)

C  IBM Compatible using ROM BIOS calls only.  (Removes all "snow" from screen
   but is slowest.  Also used for less than 100% IBM compatible machines.)

D  Use IBM EGA to display 43 lines in WordStar.  Restore to 25 lines
   when finished with WordStar.

2  Monitor Selection Menu #2
X  Finished with this menu

Enter your menu selection...     ? = Help
                                 For detailed changes, run WSCHANGE.
```

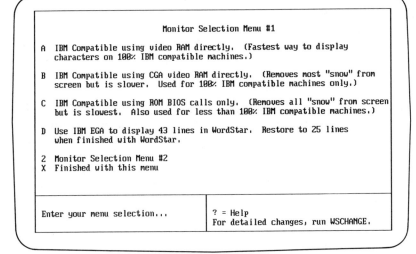

Fig. 2.5.
Monitor Selection Menu #1.

With the latest in display standards, the Video Graphics Array (VGA), WordStar can display a screen with 50 lines of text— almost a full page. For this setting, press 2 to display Monitor Selection Menu #2 and then press A.

If you press A, B, or C on a Monitor Selection Menu, a message asks whether you want to clear the screen once you exit WordStar. Press Y. Doing this or pressing D or X (to leave the monitor choice unchanged) returns you to the Console Menu.

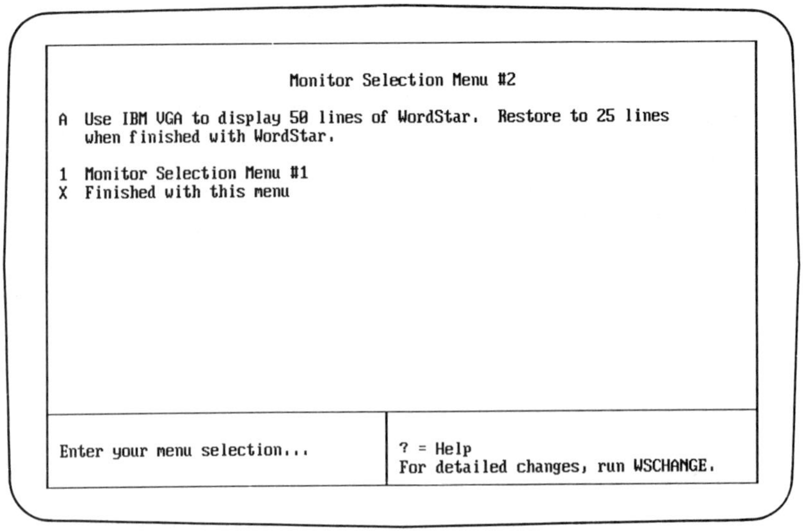
Monitor Selection Menu #2
A Use IBM VGA to display 50 lines of WordStar. Restore to 25 lines
when finished with WordStar.
1 Monitor Selection Menu #1
X Finished with this menu
Enter your menu selection...
? = Help
For detailed changes, run WSCHANGE.

Fig. 2.6. *Monitor Selection Menu #2.*

From the Console Menu, select B to view the options for displaying underlining on-screen. The Underlining Text Menu shows how underlined text is currently displayed. WordStar is initially set to indicate such text as underlined on a monochrome monitor and as blue on a color monitor. If this setting is satisfactory, select A on this menu. If you prefer underlined text to appear as white (on a color monitor) or highlighted (on a monochrome monitor), press B. Choose option C if you want underlining to be shown as *reverse video*—dark letters on a light background. Pressing X returns you to the Console Menu.

The Console Menu's next function is one that most users do not need to invoke. WordStar inserts soft spaces or soft tabs to set off text that is indented or otherwise formatted in nonstandard ways. These spaces and tabs normally are displayed as blanks, like those that result from pressing the space bar. If you choose, however, soft spaces can be shown with dots in them and soft tabs with tab symbols (►). To set this feature, press C. The screen text shows that the soft space character display is now OFF. Press A if you want to turn on the display. Press X to return to the Console Menu.

WordStar Release 5 is preset to display all text in monochrome—regular intensity letters against a dark background. If you have a color monitor, you can choose WordStar's default colors. Pressing D on the Console Menu displays the Video Attributes Menu. To set WordStar to display menus in white letters on a blue background, and the status line, ruler line, and directory headings in white letters on a red background, press A. (Text to be edited remains monochrome, with underline, subscript, superscript, and italics in various colors.) Display colors can be further customized by following instructions for the WSCHANGE program (see Chapter 11). For a monochrome display, press B. If you prefer to restore the default monochrome setting, press C at the Video Attributes Menu. Pressing X brings back the Console Menu.

Press X again to display the Main Installation Menu on-screen.

Specifying a Printer

Among WordStar Release 5's major changes is a new printer installation program, accessed through WINSTALL, to create a driver or printer description file for any of more than 100 listed printer models. In addition, the printer program can customize printer description files or create generic files for printers not specifically named. The customization procedures are detailed in Chapter 11 as part of the functions accessed with the WSCHANGE program. (For more information on printers and printing, see Chapter 7.)

If you followed the Quick Start installation in Chapter 1, you already have used the general-purpose printer description file DRAFT.PDF. This is sufficient for the simplest of printers with functions like underline and boldface, but advanced features like variable character width or proportional spacing are not supported. For these, you need to select the printer driver file appropriate for your specific printer and use it in conjunction with the DRIVERN.OVR printer driver. In addition, WordStar is set to work with one printer attached to your computer's parallel port: LPT1. If you are using another connector port or a serial printer, you can change this setting during printer installation.

To designate your system's printer, start from the Main Installation Menu. Press B for Printer. This loads the PRCHANGE.EXE printer installation program—a process that may take several seconds. The PRCHANGE.EXE file must be present on the same disk as WINSTALL; the PRCHANGE.HLP message file must also be on the same disk and directory. First you see a screen, followed by the printer installation program's Printer Type Menu, for selecting between laser printers and all other printers.

Notice that the bottom third of the Printer Installation screen displays standard directions that remain throughout the program. These include the Esc key to take you back to the previous menu; the arrow, Home, and End keys to move the highlighting in the menu area; and the Enter key (represented by an angled arrow) to select a highlighted option.

Press Enter to choose the currently highlighted selection—laser printers—if you have this kind of unit. On a floppy disk system, a message instructs you to replace the Installation/Customization Disk with one of the two Printer Data Disks. (When searching through the lists you may have to substitute the second Printer Data Disk.) Once you have replaced it, press Enter. On-screen you see the Printer Selection Menu with the names of 15 laser printer models (see fig. 2.7).

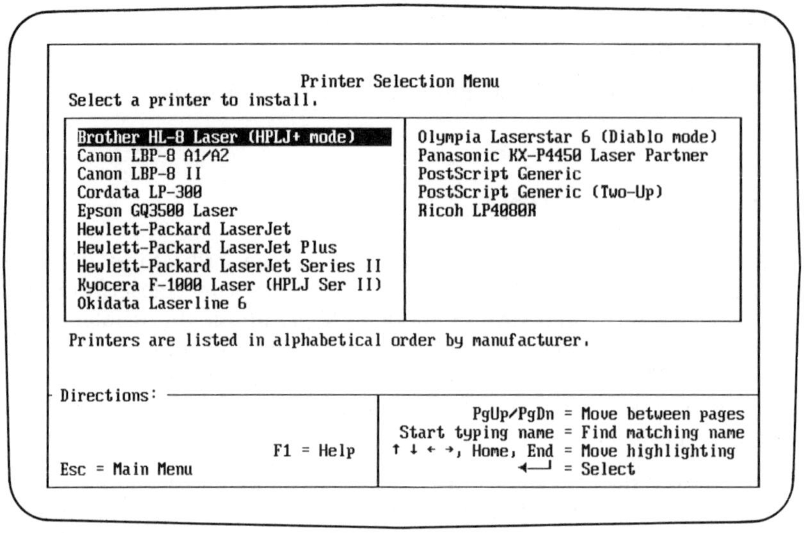
Printer Selection Menu
Select a printer to install.
Brother HL-8 Laser (HPLJ+ mode)
Canon LBP-8 A1/A2
Canon LBP-8 II
Cordata LP-300
Epson GQ3500 Laser
Hewlett-Packard LaserJet
Hewlett-Packard LaserJet Plus
Hewlett-Packard LaserJet Series II
Kyocera F-1000 Laser (HPLJ Ser II)
Okidata Laserline 6
Olympia Laserstar 6 (Diablo mode)
Panasonic KX-P4450 Laser Partner
PostScript Generic
PostScript Generic (Two-Up)
Ricoh LP4080R
Printers are listed in alphabetical order by manufacturer.
Directions:
F1 = Help
Esc = Main Menu
PgUp/PgDn = Move between pages
Start typing name = Find matching name
↑ ↓ ← →, Home, End = Move highlighting
↵ = Select

Fig. 2.7.

The Printer Selection Menu for laser printers.

For other types of printers, at the Printer Type Menu, move the highlight to `All other printers` and press Enter. This displays another Printer Selection Menu with its first page of alphabetized listings (see fig. 2.8). Beneath the listings and to the right, you note that this is page 1 of 5. Try to find your printer model among those listed here.

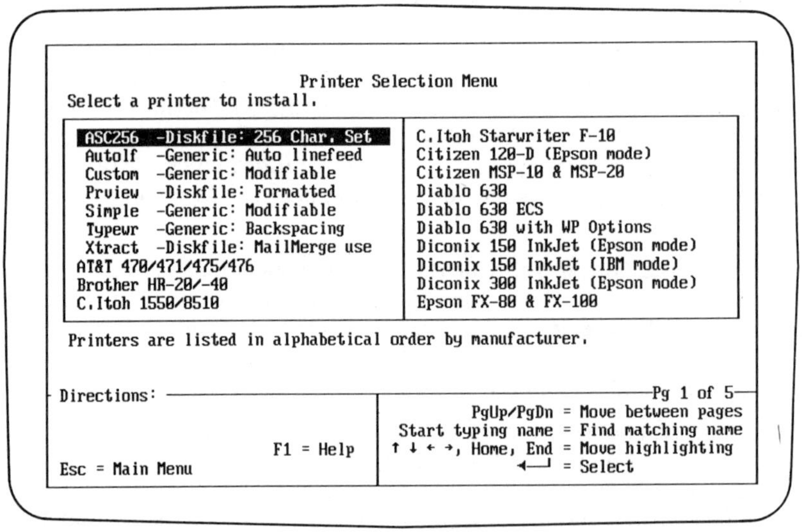
Printer Selection Menu
Select a printer to install.
ASC256 -Diskfile: 256 Char. Set
Autolf -Generic: Auto linefeed
Custom -Generic: Modifiable
Prview -Diskfile: Formatted
Simple -Generic: Modifiable
Typewr -Generic: Backspacing
Xtract -Diskfile: MailMerge use
AT&T 470/471/475/476
Brother HR-20/-40
C.Itoh 1550/8510
C.Itoh Starwriter F-10
Citizen 120-D (Epson mode)
Citizen MSP-10 & MSP-20
Diablo 630
Diablo 630 ECS
Diablo 630 with WP Options
Diconix 150 InkJet (Epson mode)
Diconix 150 InkJet (IBM mode)
Diconix 300 InkJet (Epson mode)
Epson FX-80 & FX-100
Printers are listed in alphabetical order by manufacturer.
Directions:
Pg 1 of 5
F1 = Help
Esc = Main Menu
PgUp/PgDn = Move between pages
Start typing name = Find matching name
↑ ↓ ← →, Home, End = Move highlighting
↵ = Select

Fig. 2.8.

The Printer Selection Menu, Page 1 of 5.

If you can't find your printer on the Printer Selection Menu's first page, you can try either of two ways to search for it. Pressing the PgDn key brings up the next page of printer listings (see fig. 2.9). Each time you press PgDn you advance to the next page of listings (see fig. 2.10). Pressing the PgUp key returns to the previous page of printer models. As indicated in the on-screen directions, you can also start typing the name of your printer and the listing advances to the matching manufacturer and model.

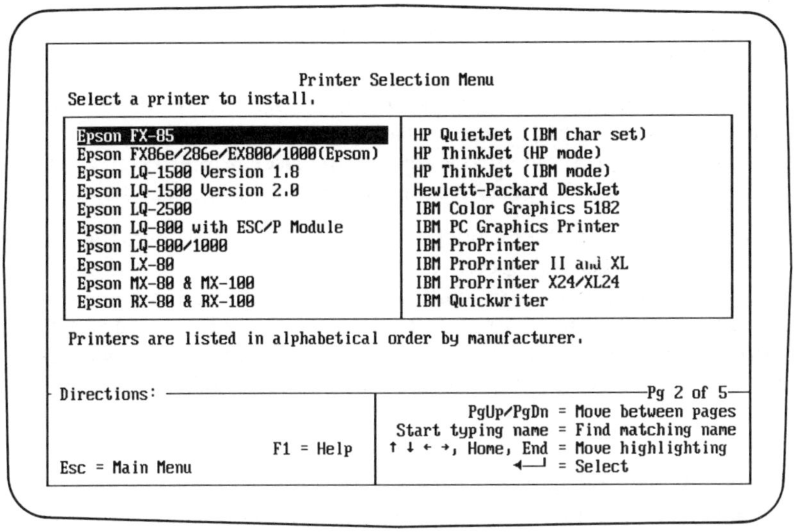
Printer Selection Menu
Select a printer to install.
Epson FX-85
Epson FX86e/286e/EX800/1000(Epson)
Epson LQ-1500 Version 1.0
Epson LQ-1500 Version 2.0
Epson LQ-2500
Epson LQ-800 with ESC/P Module
Epson LQ-800/1000
Epson LX-80
Epson MX-80 & MX-100
Epson RX-80 & RX-100
HP QuietJet (IBM char set)
HP ThinkJet (HP mode)
HP ThinkJet (IBM mode)
Hewlett-Packard DeskJet
IBM Color Graphics 5182
IBM PC Graphics Printer
IBM ProPrinter
IBM ProPrinter II and XL
IBM ProPrinter X24/XL24
IBM Quickwriter
Printers are listed in alphabetical order by manufacturer.
Directions:
Pg 2 of 5
PgUp/PgDn = Move between pages
Start typing name = Find matching name
F1 = Help
↑ ↓ ← →, Home, End = Move highlighting
Esc = Main Menu
↵ = Select

Fig. 2.9.
The Printer Selection Menu, Page 2 of 5.

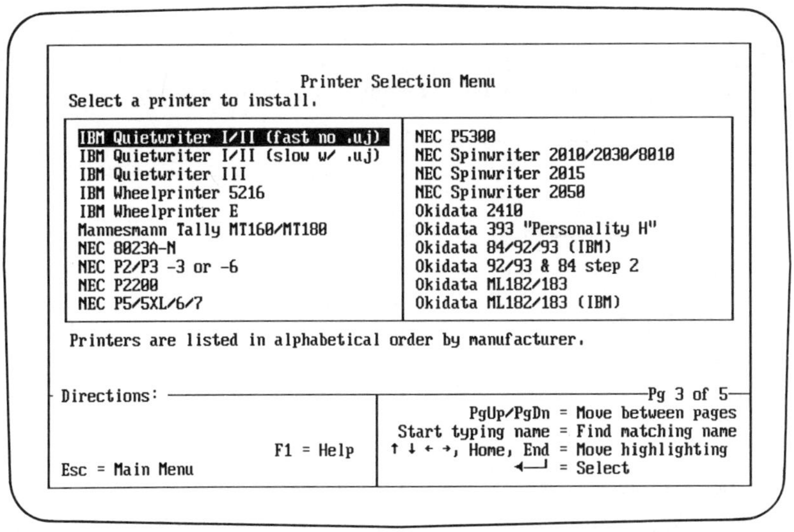
Printer Selection Menu
Select a printer to install.
IBM Quietwriter I/II (fast no .uj)
IBM Quietwriter I/II (slow w/ .uj)
IBM Quietwriter III
IBM Wheelprinter 5216
IBM Wheelprinter E
Mannesmann Tally MT160/MT180
NEC 8023A-M
NEC P2/P3 -3 or -6
NEC P2200
NEC P5/5XL/6/7
NEC P5300
NEC Spinwriter 2010/2030/8010
NEC Spinwriter 2015
NEC Spinwriter 2050
Okidata 2410
Okidata 393 "Personality H"
Okidata 84/92/93 (IBM)
Okidata 92/93 & 84 step 2
Okidata ML182/183
Okidata ML182/183 (IBM)
Printers are listed in alphabetical order by manufacturer.
Directions:
Pg 3 of 5
PgUp/PgDn = Move between pages
Start typing name = Find matching name
F1 = Help
↑ ↓ ← →, Home, End = Move highlighting
Esc = Main Menu
↵ = Select

Fig. 2.10.
The Printer Selection Menu, Page 3 of 5.

In the unlikely event that your printer is not among the dozens of models included in the WordStar Release 5 printer database, another of the printers listed is likely to work. Check your printer manual for information on what standard printer your model emulates. For example, many dot-matrix printers are compatible with Epson® models. If you have a dot-matrix printer that is not listed, press E to view the listing of the Epson models and then select the one your printer emulates by moving the highlighting (with the down-arrow key).

Assorted daisywheel printers work like Diablo models. To choose one of these settings, press D for the listing of these printers and highlight the correct one by pressing the appropriate arrow keys.

Various laser printers accept commands like those recognized by the Hewlett-Packard® LaserJet™. To pick this option, select the LaserJet or LaserJet II™ by highlighting it with the appropriate arrow keys on the laser printer Printer Selection Menu and pressing Enter. For other laser printer installations, see Chapter 7.

If you still are not sure which printer model corresponds to your printer, check the manual for your printer's general specifications and choose one of the generic settings on the first page of lists, such as `Auto-line feeding printer`, `Backspacing printer (typewriter)`, or `Non-backspacing printer`. These printer description files require the DRIVERA.OVR driver file on the WordStar program disk and directory when printing is invoked. To take advantage of nongeneric features, check the discussion of customized and nonstandard printer types in Chapter 7.

After you have highlighted the name of your printer model on the Printer Selection Menu, press Enter to create a PDF. Your disk drive goes into operation and after a few seconds you see the Installed Printer Menu (see fig. 2.11). (If you are using a floppy disk system, you may be prompted to replace the Printer Data Disk with the Installation Disk.) The Installed Printer Menu lists the name of the printer you just selected and requests that you type a name for its PDF. Simply type the model number or name, using no more than eight characters, and press Enter.

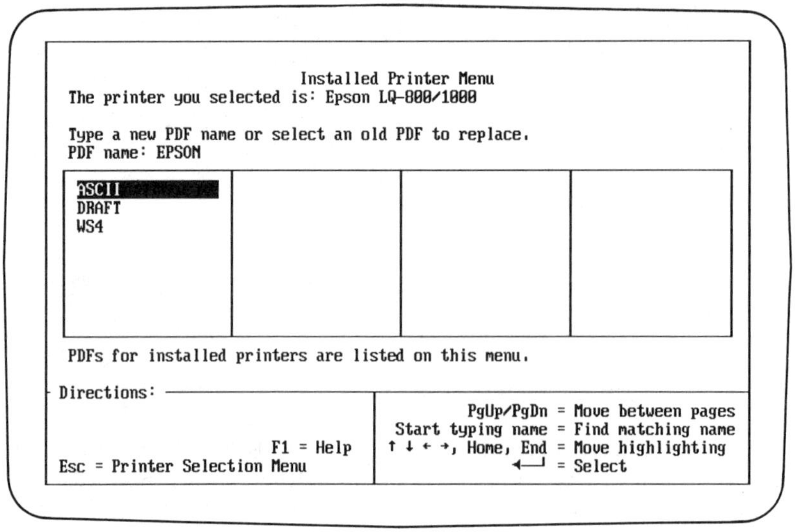
Installed Printer Menu
The printer you selected is: Epson LQ-800/1000
Type a new PDF name or select an old PDF to replace.
PDF name: EPSON
ASCII
DRAFT
WS4
PDFs for installed printers are listed on this menu.
Directions:
F1 = Help
Esc = Printer Selection Menu
PgUp/PgDn = Move between pages
Start typing name = Find matching name
↑ ↓ ← →, Home, End = Move highlighting
↵ = Select

Fig. 2.11.
The Installed Printer Menu.

The next display is the Additional Installation Menu (see fig. 2.12). In most cases, you can just press the Esc key to return to the printer installation main menu—in this case, the WINSTALL Main Installation Menu.

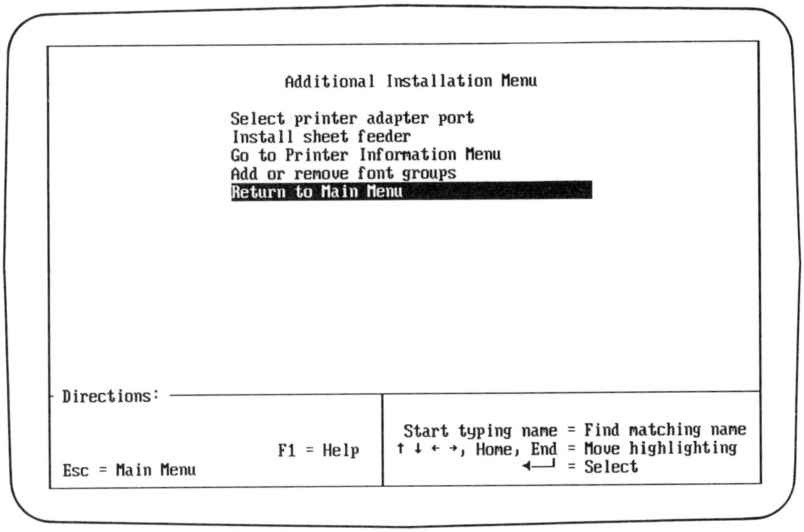
Additional Installation Menu
Select printer adapter port
Install sheet feeder
Go to Printer Information Menu
Add or remove font groups
Return to Main Menu
Directions:
F1 = Help
Esc = Main Menu
Start typing name = Find matching name
↑ ↓ ← →, Home, End = Move highlighting
↵ = Select

Fig. 2.12.
The Additional Installation Menu.

If your printer is connected to a port other than the main parallel port LPT1, or if you have a serial printer, at the Additional Installation Menu press the arrow key to move the highlight to the Select Printer Adapter Port option and press Enter. You see the Change Printer Adapter Port list (see fig. 2.13). By moving the highlight with the arrow keys you can designate parallel ports PRN, LPT1 (the same as PRN), LPT2, or LPT3; serial ports COM1 or COM2; or a user-defined disk drive or other output device. Pressing Enter saves your choice and returns the display to the Additional Installation Menu. Press the Esc key twice for the Main Installation Menu.

Further customization of printer description file settings is discussed in Chapters 7 and 12. If you will be using more than one printer you can repeat the printer installation procedure to select another printer description file; be sure to assign a second connector port to it.

The WordStar Release 5 Main Installation Menu has another new option concerning printer installation: `C Default printer`. With a one printer system, you can skip this selection, because WordStar automatically uses the one you installed (unless you specify another choice at print time). If you installed more than one printer, you must now designate the one to which WordStar defaults when printing. Press C and you see the Default Printer Selection Menu (see fig. 2.14). From the listed printers, including those you installed and several generic printer drivers, select the letter for the one to be your default printer. After typing this choice, the printer name appears as the current printer near the top of the menu. When you are satisfied with your choice, press X to return to the Main Installation Menu.

Fig. 2.13.

The Change Printer Adapter Port list.

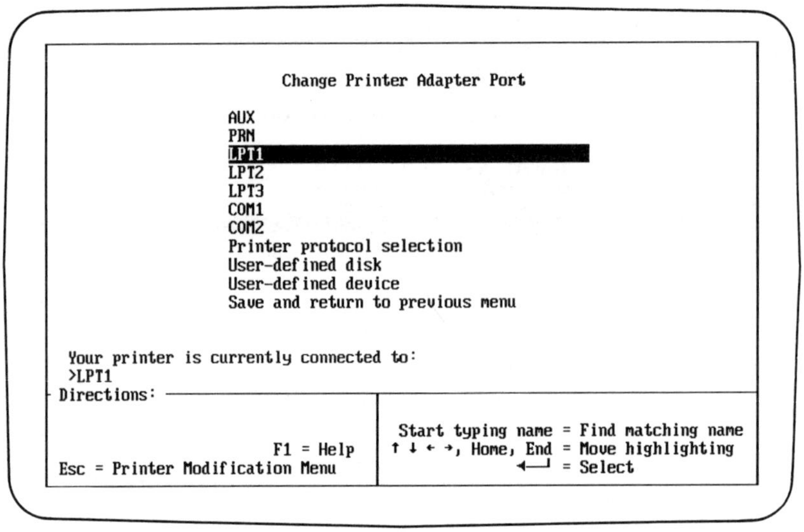
Change Printer Adapter Port
AUX
PRN
LPT1
LPT2
LPT3
COM1
COM2
Printer protocol selection
User-defined disk
User-defined device
Save and return to previous menu
Your printer is currently connected to:
>LPT1
Directions:
F1 = Help
Esc = Printer Modification Menu
Start typing name = Find matching name
↑ ↓ ← →, Home, End = Move highlighting
↵ = Select

Fig. 2.14.

The Default Printer Selection Menu.

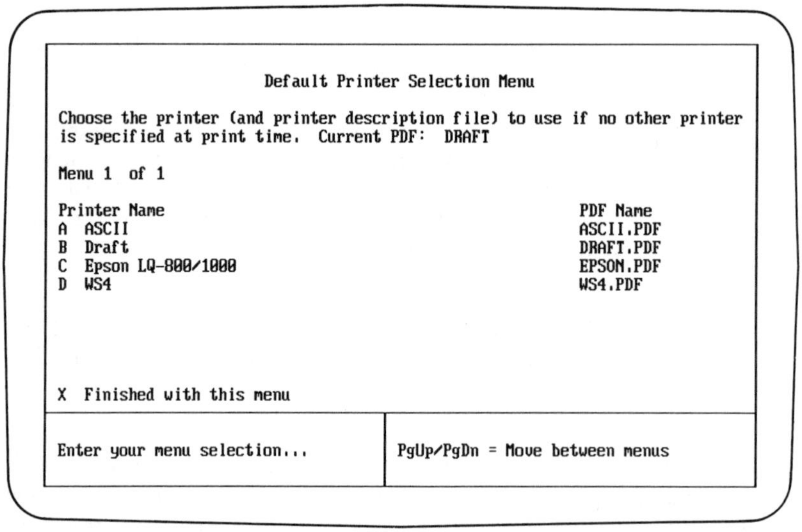
Default Printer Selection Menu
Choose the printer (and printer description file) to use if no other printer is specified at print time. Current PDF: DRAFT
Menu 1 of 1
Printer Name
PDF Name
A ASCII
ASCII.PDF
B Draft
DRAFT.PDF
C Epson LQ-800/1000
EPSON.PDF
D WS4
WS4.PDF
X Finished with this menu
Enter your menu selection...
PgUp/PgDn = Move between menus

Specifying Computer Characteristics

Unless you already followed the Quick Start installation in Chapter 1, you must install WordStar Release 5 to recognize your computer system's disk drive and MS-DOS configuration. From the Main Installation Menu, press D to display the Computer Menu (see fig. 2.15).

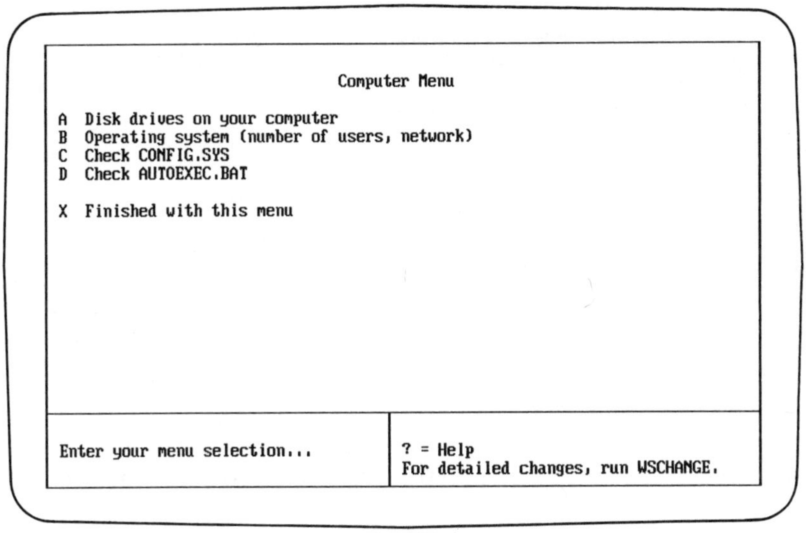
Computer Menu
A Disk drives on your computer
B Operating system (number of users, network)
C Check CONFIG.SYS
D Check AUTOEXEC.BAT
X Finished with this menu
Enter your menu selection...
? = Help
For detailed changes, run WSCHANGE.

Fig. 2.15.
The Computer Menu.

The WINSTALL Computer Menu lists four characteristics relating to your system's DOS configuration. Press A, and the display shows the letter designations of the disk drives the system can recognize—any floppy disk drive from A to Z. An asterisk indicates that program files are to be located on drive A. This setting is suitable for a standard two floppy disk system.

If you have a system with a hard disk or if you need to change the current setting to designate a different set of letters for your disk drives, press Y. The screen looks like that shown in figure 2.16.

Type the letter of the drive on which WordStar's program files are to be stored. For a hard disk system, the drive is customarily C. You are asked whether this default drive is for floppy disks; if so, press Y. If the default drive is a hard disk drive, select N and press Enter. Type the letters of all other drives in your system and indicate whether each is a floppy drive or a hard drive. Press Enter, and your choices for valid drives are displayed. An on-screen question asks whether you want to change this setting. Press N to leave the setting unchanged and to return to the Computer Menu.

Select the Operating System option on the Computer Menu if you are using WordStar on a multiuser system or local area network. Press B, and the Operating

```
                    Disk Drives on Your Computer Menu

These are the current valid disk drives.

    Hard:

   Floppy: A* B C D E F G H I J K L M N O P Q R S T U V W X Y Z

  Do you want to change this? (Y/N) Y

Tell WordStar what drives you have on your computer.  After you
specify each drive letter, you will be asked if it's a floppy disk
drive.

Press a drive letter (A-Z, or Press ◄┘ when done)...
```

Fig. 2.16.
The screen for changing WordStar's disk drive setting.

System Menu appears. Press B again, and the screen message poses the following question:

```
If 2 people try to edit the same document, should the second
user be able to browse through it (without making changes)?
(Y/N)
```

Choose the proper setting for shared file access by pressing Y or N. The Computer Menu returns to the screen.

The Computer Menu's third option deals with the way the program uses the computer's internal memory, called random access memory (RAM). With MS-DOS, such memory can be allocated to eight separate temporary files.

For WordStar Release 5 to work correctly, the statement FILES = 20 must be issued to DOS. This can be done easily with the CONFIG.SYS file with which the program is started (booted). The installation program can check to see whether such a file exists, and if it does not, it can create one. Press C at the Computer Menu. This selection brings up the Check CONFIG.SYS Menu (see fig. 2.17). Press Y for verification of this file. A message instructs you to insert the boot disk and to specify which drive contains the disk. After you insert the boot disk, type the appropriate letter and the installation program checks the CONFIG.SYS file's contents. You see a message indicating that the CONFIG.SYS file has been added.

Another addition to the installation procedure is due to WordStar Release 5's need for a PATH statement, indicating the location of the main WordStar program file, in the boot-up file AUTOEXEC.BAT (for more on AUTOEXEC.BAT, see Chapter 4). The installation program can check to see whether such a file exists and, if it does not, can create one. Pressing D at the Computer Menu displays a screen headed

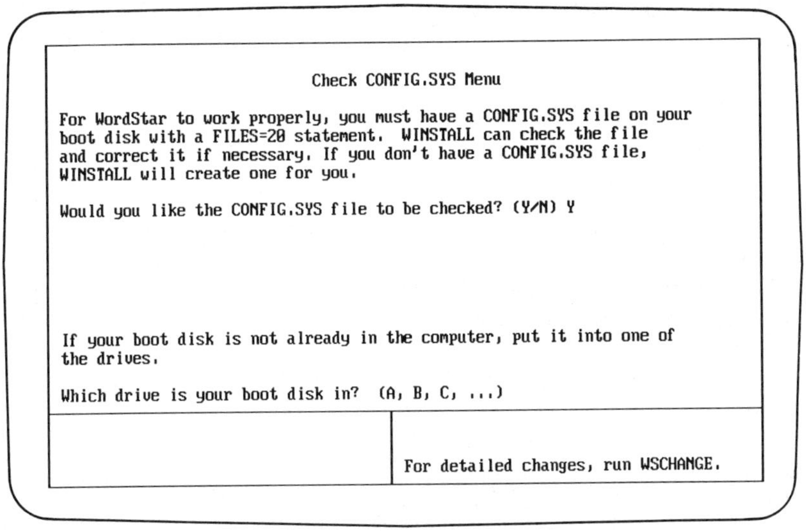
Check CONFIG.SYS Menu
For WordStar to work properly, you must have a CONFIG.SYS file on your boot disk with a FILES=20 statement. WINSTALL can check the file and correct it if necessary. If you don't have a CONFIG.SYS file, WINSTALL will create one for you.
Would you like the CONFIG.SYS file to be checked? (Y/N) Y
If your boot disk is not already in the computer, put it into one of the drives.
Which drive is your boot disk in? (A, B, C, ...)
For detailed changes, run WSCHANGE.

Fig. 2.17.
The message asking if you want the CONFIG.SYS file checked.

`Check AUTOEXEC.BAT File`. Press Y to verify or create an AUTOEXEC.BAT file. A message instructs you to insert the boot disk and to specify which drive contains the disk. Type the appropriate letter, and the installation program checks for AUTOEXEC.BAT's contents. If there is no AUTOEXEC.BAT file, you see a message indicating that the AUTOEXEC.BAT file has been added.

Press any key to return to the Computer Menu. Press X to display the Main Installation Menu.

Specifying the Dictionary's Location

If your computer uses standard 5 1/4-inch disks, the Dictionary Disk is probably separate from your WordStar working copy disk. To run a spelling check or to find synonyms with the thesaurus, you need to change disks, and WordStar needs to know the location of the Dictionary Disk. The Main Installation Menu's Dictionaries selection is used to specify the disk on which the spelling and thesaurus dictionaries are to be stored.

Note that the installation program deals only with the location of the MAIN.DCT and THES.DCT files. If the PERSONAL.DCT file is not on the same disk, the spelling checker function should be reset with the WSCHANGE program, as indicated in Chapter 11.

Press D to display the Dictionaries Menu (see fig. 2.18). The provision for swapping disks for a separate Dictionary Disk is currently off. To turn on the provision for floppy disks, press A. The new setting is displayed on-screen.

For a high-density floppy disk (1.2M or more) or a hard disk, the choice is B. When you are finished making the Dictionaries Menu selection, press X to display the Main Installation Menu.

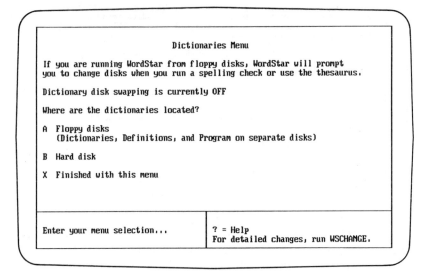

Fig. 2.18.
WordStar's spelling and thesaurus dictionaries being specified.

```
                         Dictionaries Menu

If you are running WordStar from floppy disks, WordStar will prompt
you to change disks when you run a spelling check or use the thesaurus.

Dictionary disk swapping is currently OFF

Where are the dictionaries located?

A  Floppy disks
   (Dictionaries, Definitions, and Program on separate disks)

B  Hard disk

X  Finished with this menu

Enter your menu selection...       ? = Help
                                   For detailed changes, run WSCHANGE.
```

Specifying the Help Level

WordStar Release 5 has a new series of pull-down menus meant for first-time users. WordStar is preset to display these when on-screen prompts are selected. Classic help menus that remain stationary at the top of the screen, familiar from previous versions, are also available. If you have used an earlier version of WordStar but have not advanced beyond the novice stage, you probably will want to invoke the installation option for the classic help menus. Intermediate or advanced users who reset WordStar Release 5 to help level 2, 1, or 0 can do so here or when starting a work session by using the F1 key or ^J.

To change the WordStar Release 5 Help Menu default, at the Main Installation Menu press F. This displays the Pull-Down or Classic Help Level Menu (see fig. 2.19). For the classic menus, press B. At the resulting classic Help Level Menu, you can select the help level to which you are accustomed: A for help level 3 and all its menus; B for help level 2 and fewer menus; C or D for expert levels 1 or 0 with few prompts and menus. Press X when finished with this menu.

If you want to reset WordStar for pull-down menus, you can press A at the Pull-down or Classic Help Level Menu. When you are satisfied with your choice, press X to return to the Main Installation Menu.

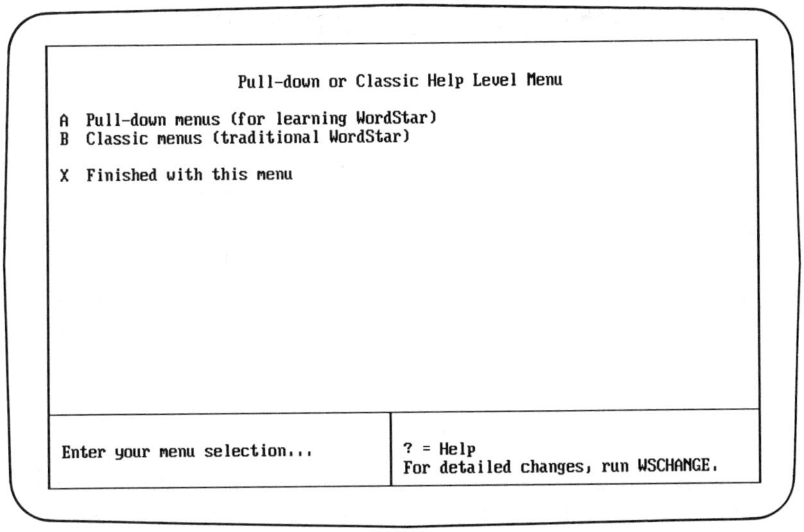
Pull-down or Classic Help Level Menu
A Pull-down menus (for learning WordStar)
B Classic menus (traditional WordStar)
X Finished with this menu
Enter your menu selection...
? = Help
For detailed changes, run WSCHANGE.

Fig. 2.19. *Selecting new pull-down or classic help menus.*

Completing the Installation Process

After you go through the different options, press X at the Main Installation Menu. You see a screen summing up the installation selections you made (see fig. 2.20).

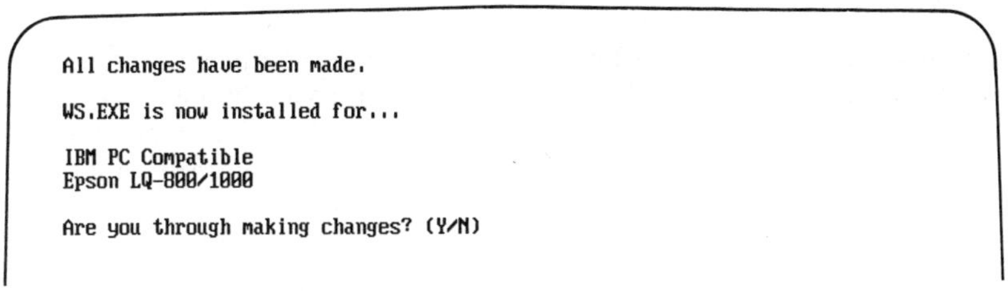
All changes have been made.
WS.EXE is now installed for...
IBM PC Compatible
Epson LQ-800/1000
Are you through making changes? (Y/N)

Fig. 2.20. *Completed WordStar installation selections displayed.*

You still can return to the Main Installation Menu to make further changes by pressing N. If you are satisfied with the installation choices you made, press Y to store the newly installed WordStar on disk. When the disk drive stops running and the operation is complete, `A>` or `C>` is displayed.

If you have a computer with less than 512K of memory, you will have to run one more installation procedure before starting to use WordStar. If you have sufficient RAM memory in your computer, you can proceed to Chapter 3.

Installing WordStar for a Computer with Less than 512K of Memory

While WordStar can work with a minimum of 384K of memory, it comes configured for systems with 512K. To adapt the unmodified WordStar to a system with 384K to 496K, you must follow an auxiliary installation procedure involving the WSCHANGE program. The WSCHANGE customization program is covered in detail in Chapter 11. For this installation, just follow the steps outlined here:

1. From the Advanced Customization Disk copy the 384K.PAT file to the disk and directory storing the Installation/Customization Disk files. These should also include the files WSCHANGE.EXE, WSCHANGE.OVR, CHANGE.OVR, and TABLES2.OVR.
2. Start the WSCHANGE program as you did the WINSTALL program, with disks in the same locations, then type *wschange*. As with WINSTALL, the screen asks for the name of the WordStar program to be installed—usually WS. Type this and press Enter, then press Enter again or type the name of the program file to store the installed WordStar version (usually WS) and press Enter.
3. From the WSCHANGE Main Installation Menu press E for the Patching option.
4. At the Patching Menu, choose A for the Auto-Patcher Menu.
5. Once at the Auto-Patcher Menu, type *384k.pat* and press Enter. This modifies the WordStar program to work in less than 512K of memory.
6. To complete installation, press Enter, then press X three times to return to the Main Installation Menu and to indicate that you have completed all changes for the moment. Press Y to store the special installation you have just made. With the exception of Advanced Page Preview and running the Tutors Disk, WordStar can perform virtually all the tasks available with 512K or more of memory.

To use your installed WordStar, restart your computer with the procedure outlined in Chapter 3.

3

Introducing WordStar's Basics

Who says WordStar is difficult to learn? If you followed the quick tour presented in Chapter 1, you know that WordStar Release 5's classic keyboard commands and new pull-down menus make this word processor easy to start and operate. As you may have seen, anyone can learn enough of WordStar's basic commands to write, edit, and print a brief memo within an hour of being introduced to the program. This chapter gives you details of the fundamental procedures for running a typical word processing session.

The essential terminology and commands covered in this chapter are sufficient for you to operate WordStar from turn-on to printout. Some users never go beyond these and a few other commands. Other users spend months comfortably at this level before assimilating more of the program's features. You can invoke most of this chapter's commands with just one keystroke or one Ctrl-letter key combination.

This chapter begins by giving you elementary instructions for invoking WordStar on a floppy disk system and on a hard disk system. Then the most frequently used displays and operations are explained in depth, and the features that are new to WordStar Release 5 are identified.

Here are some of the basics covered in this chapter:

- Using the keyboard
- Invoking help and setting the help level
- Understanding WordStar's Opening and Edit screens
- Entering, editing, saving, and printing text

If you have used previous versions of WordStar, you will be familiar with most of the commands covered here. Turn through the pages of this chapter and look for the *new in Release 5* icons to learn about menu changes, an easier way to save files, and—most important—the use of automatic reformatting of text during editing.

The point of this chapter is for you to learn to control a document's contents and appearance by using a small number of convenient keystrokes. The payoff is that you will be able to easily use WordStar to compose and revise the notes, briefs, minutes, precis, memos, proposals, synopses, and other short documents that are essential to written communication.

The functions included here are basic, but they may not always be the most efficient. Powerful features that you use to move the cursor, edit text, and format text, as well as to preview and print typeset-quality documents, are the subjects of Part II of this book.

Starting WordStar

The simplest way for you to start WordStar, though not the most effortless, is to load DOS separately before you invoke WordStar manually. As with most MS-DOS-based computer software, typing the appropriate program file name is all you need to start WordStar.

Typing *ws* at the DOS prompt and pressing Enter are sufficient for you to load the main WordStar program file WS.EXE and start WordStar. Pressing a few keys hardly seems complicated, but a one-time procedure explained in Chapter 4 makes even those keystrokes superfluous. After you create a self-starting version of WordStar, turning on your computer's power switch will be enough to get your word processor running. If you prefer manual start-up, you still can use any of eight options to the WS command, as explained in the next chapter. In the meantime, here's how to start WordStar on any floppy disk or hard disk system.

Invoking WordStar on a Floppy Disk System

WordStar runs on computer systems equipped with drives for 5 1/4-inch or 3 1/2-inch floppy disks. These removable disks remain the most widely used means of storing program and document files for safekeeping away from your computer.

To start WordStar on a system with two floppy disk drives, follow these steps:

1. With your computer turned off, place your working copy of WordStar into drive A and place a blank, formatted disk for storing documents into drive B.

2. Turn on your computer's power. The copy of DOS that you have placed on your working copy of WordStar loads from the disk into the computer's memory. On the screen, you see the following DOS prompt:

   ```
   A>
   ```

3. To start WordStar, type *ws* and press Enter.

   DOS loads the program from your working copy disk into your computer's memory.

When you use WordStar on a floppy disk system, the standard procedure is to store your working copy of the program and your document files on separate disks. This procedure is recommended because the disk that holds your working copy of WordStar may have little space left for document files. In addition, organizing your documents is easier because you can use separate disks for different subjects or tasks.

If your system has just a single floppy disk drive with a low-capacity 5 1/4-inch disk, remove your working copy disk from the drive and replace the disk with your document disk. If your working copy is on a disk that is capable of storing 720K or more, you have sufficient room for documents; leave your working copy of WordStar in the drive.

Invoking WordStar on a Hard Disk System

A computer system equipped with a hard disk is ideal for running WordStar. Hard disks perform disk recording and playback operations faster than floppy disks. The most modest hard disk also provides ample storage for all the files supplied with WordStar Release 5 along with years' worth of document files, which you can access without having to swap disks.

To start WordStar on a hard disk system, follow these steps:

1. Turn on your computer to load DOS from the hard disk. On the screen, you see the following DOS prompt:

   ```
   C>
   ```

2. To bring up the directory containing WordStar, type *cd \ws5* and press Enter.

   Starting a session with the command for changing to the directory that holds your copy of WordStar Release 5 is a good practice and ensures that program files will be accessible.

3. At the DOS prompt, type *ws* and press Enter.

   The WordStar program file is loaded from your hard disk into your computer's memory.

When using WordStar on a hard disk system, you can store your working copy of the program and your document files in the same DOS directory. To organize your documents on disk, you also can create separate subdirectories for different subjects or tasks. Among the subdirectory designations you may find handy are \DOC for active documents, \BAK for archival files, and \COR for continuing correspondence, as well as other abbreviations for projects or book-length manuscripts.

If this is the first time you are using WordStar on your hard disk, you may want to add a subdirectory reserved for document files. To do so, before starting WordStar, open a new subdirectory from the WS5 directory. At the DOS prompt, type *mkdir \ws5\doc*.

Then press the Enter key. When the DOS prompt returns, type *ws* and press Enter to run WordStar.

Understanding WordStar's Opening Displays

Each WordStar working session begins with the program's Opening display, which appears on-screen almost as soon as your word processor starts loading. With WordStar Release 5, users for the first time can choose among Opening screens, based on new pull-down menus or the program's classic boxed menus. What you choose depends on whether you are a first-time or an experienced user.

The Copyright Screen

As WordStar is being loaded, you see MicroPro's copyright notice for various parts of the WordStar program package. This screen (see fig. 3.1) also displays the WordStar program's release number and a reminder of the computer and printer models for which the program was installed.

After you use WordStar for a while, you may find that the copyright screen is an annoyance. The amount of time this screen remains displayed is known as "the long delay." You can shorten the delay to a split second by customizing WordStar with the WSCHANGE program. For details, see Chapter 11.

While WordStar continues to load, the copyright screen is soon replaced by one or another of the program's Opening menus.

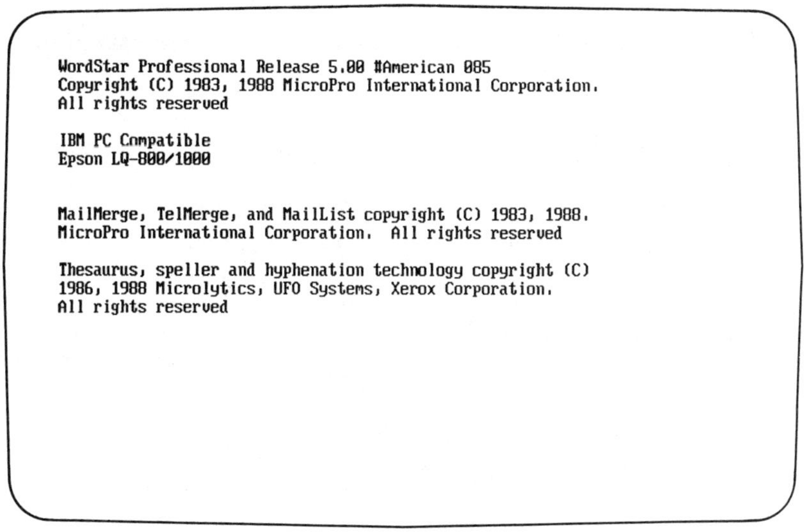
WordStar Professional Release 5.00 #American 085
Copyright (C) 1983, 1988 MicroPro International Corporation.
All rights reserved
IBM PC Compatible
Epson LQ-800/1000
MailMerge, TelMerge, and MailList copyright (C) 1983, 1988.
MicroPro International Corporation. All rights reserved
Thesaurus, speller and hyphenation technology copyright (C)
1986, 1988 Microlytics, UFO Systems, Xerox Corporation.
All rights reserved

Fig. 3.1.

The WordStar Release 5 copyright screen.

The Opening Screens

An unmodified copy of WordStar Release 5 automatically displays the Opening screen shown in figure 3.2. This Opening screen is the first of the menus displayed when WordStar is set for help level 4, the new release's help default. Designed for beginners and occasional users, this Opening screen is less cluttered than WordStar's classic Opening Menu. But you must use at least one extra keystroke to invoke most of the functions traditionally accessed from the Opening Menu.

Each of the principal commands available from this Opening Menu pulls down another menu of functions. You can use letter keys or left- and right-arrow keys to indicate choices. The pull-down Opening commands are listed in table 3.1.

Table 3.1
Pull-Down Opening Menu Commands

Command	*Function*
F	Pulls down File menu
O	Pulls down Other menu
A	Pulls down Additional menu
Left- or Right-arrow key	Pulls down the next menu
F1	Pulls down on-line help message

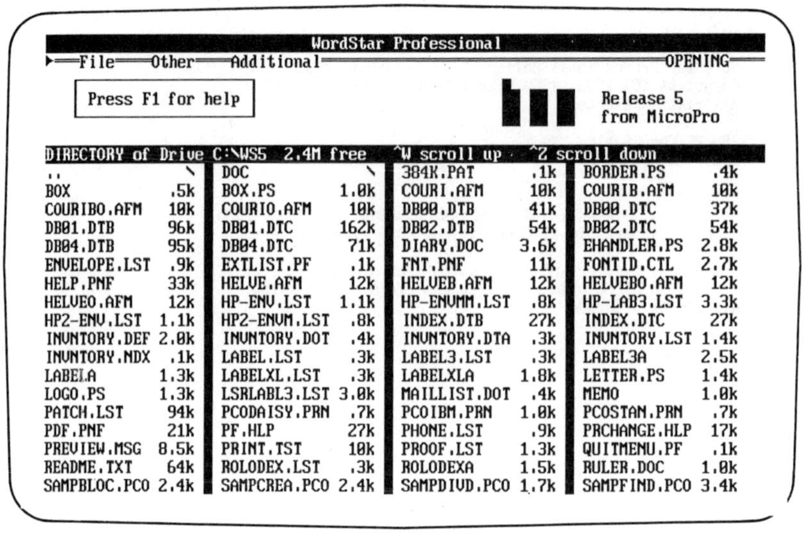
WordStar Professional
File Other Additional OPENING
Press F1 for help
Release 5
from MicroPro
DIRECTORY of Drive C:\WS5 2.4M free ^W scroll up ^Z scroll down
.. \ DOC \ 384K.PAT .1k BORDER.PS .4k
BOX .5k BOX.PS 1.0k COURI.AFM 10k COURIB.AFM 10k
COURIBO.AFM 10k COURIO.AFM 10k DB00.DTB 41k DB00.DTC 37k
DB01.DTB 96k DB01.DTC 162k DB02.DTB 54k DB02.DTC 54k
DB04.DTB 95k DB04.DTC 71k DIARY.DOC 3.6k EHANDLER.PS 2.8k
ENVELOPE.LST .9k EXTLIST.PF .1k FNT.PNF 11k FONTID.CTL 2.7k
HELP.PNF 33k HELVE.AFM 12k HELVEB.AFM 12k HELVEBO.AFM 12k
HELVEO.AFM 12k HP-ENV.LST 1.1k HP-ENVMM.LST .8k HP-LAB3.LST 3.3k
HP2-ENV.LST 1.1k HP2-ENVM.LST .8k INDEX.DTB 27k INDEX.DTC 27k
INVNTORY.DEF 2.0k INVNTORY.DOT .4k INVNTORY.DTA .3k INVNTORY.LST 1.4k
INVNTORY.NDX .1k LABEL.LST .3k LABEL3.LST .3k LABEL3A 2.5k
LABELA 1.3k LABELXL.LST .3k LABELXLA 1.0k LETTER.PS 1.4k
LOGO.PS 1.3k LSRLABL3.LST 3.0k MAILLIST.DOT .4k MEMO 1.0k
PATCH.LST 94k PCODAISY.PRN .7k PCOIBM.PRN 1.0k PCOSTAN.PRN .7k
PDF.PNF 21k PF.HLP 27k PHONE.LST .9k PRCHANGE.HLP 17k
PREVIEW.MSG 8.5k PRINT.TST 10k PROOF.LST 1.3k QUITMENU.PF .1k
README.TXT 64k ROLODEX.LST .3k ROLODEXA 1.5k RULER.DOC 1.0k
SAMPBLOC.PCO 2.4k SAMPCREA.PCO 2.4k SAMPDIVD.PCO 1.7k SAMPFIND.PCO 3.4k

Fig. 3.2.
A WordStar Release 5 Opening screen.

The three pull-down menus you can choose from this Opening screen are actually continuations of the Opening display. You invoke commands listed on these secondary menus by typing the letters indicated beside a function or by pressing the up- and down-arrow keys to highlight a selection and then pressing Enter. Any pull-down menu can be pulled back up and out of sight when you press the Esc key or the space bar. In general, using the letter commands is most efficient and is the procedure emphasized throughout this book.

Pressing F (or the right-arrow key) at the Opening Menu displays the pull-down File menu, illustrated in figure 3.3. This listing contains more than half the functions on the classic Opening Menu—11 commands for such essentials as opening and printing files and exiting from WordStar.

Pressing O at the Opening Menu pulls down the pull-down Other menu (see fig. 3.4). This menu includes six miscellaneous functions that are part of WordStar. These functions range from indexing and macros to resetting the help level.

Pressing A at the Opening Menu reveals the pull-down Additional menu (see fig. 3.5). The selections on this menu are limited to two add-on functions to WordStar that require auxiliary programs included in the Release 5 package: MailList and TelMerge.

New users and occasional users will find that only a few of the functions on the pull-down menus are essential for simple word processing. Sequences for invoking essential commands from the Opening Menu are presented in table 3.2. The initial letter you press to pull down the menu is included in the table. Other commands on the pull-down menus are discussed in Chapters 4, 9, and 10.

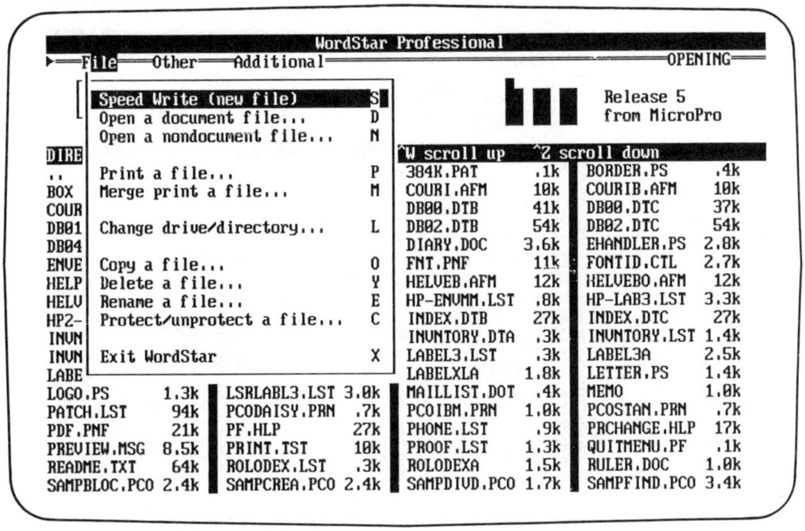
WordStar Professional
File Other Additional OPENING
Speed Write (new file) S
Open a document file... D
Open a nondocument file... N
Print a file... P
Merge print a file... M
Change drive/directory... L
Copy a file... O
Delete a file... Y
Rename a file... E
Protect/unprotect a file... C
Exit WordStar X
Release 5
from MicroPro
^W scroll up ^Z scroll down
384K.PAT .1k
BORDER.PS .4k
COURI.AFM 10k
COURIB.AFM 10k
DB00.DTB 41k
DB00.DTC 37k
DB02.DTB 54k
DB02.DTC 54k
DIARY.DOC 3.6k
EHANDLER.PS 2.8k
FNT.PNF 11k
FONTID.CTL 2.7k
HELVEB.AFM 12k
HELVEBO.AFM 12k
HP-ENVMM.LST .8k
HP-LAB3.LST 3.3k
INDEX.DTB 27k
INDEX.DTC 27k
INVNTORY.DTA .3k
INVNTORY.LST 1.4k
LABEL3.LST .3k
LABEL3A 2.5k
LABELXLA 1.8k
LETTER.PS 1.4k
LOGO.PS 1.3k
LSRLABL3.LST 3.0k
MAILLIST.DOT .4k
MEMO 1.0k
PATCH.LST 94k
PCODAISY.PRN .7k
PCOIBM.PRN 1.0k
PCOSTAN.PRN .7k
PDF.PNF 21k
PF.HLP 27k
PHONE.LST .9k
PRCHANGE.HLP 17k
PREVIEW.MSG 8.5k
PRINT.TST 10k
PROOF.LST 1.3k
QUITMENU.PF .1k
README.TXT 64k
ROLODEX.LST .3k
ROLODEXA 1.5k
RULER.DOC 1.0k
SAMPBLOC.PCO 2.4k
SAMPCREA.PCO 2.4k
SAMPDIVD.PCO 1.7k
SAMPFIND.PCO 3.4k

Fig. 3.3.
The pull-down File menu from the Opening screen.

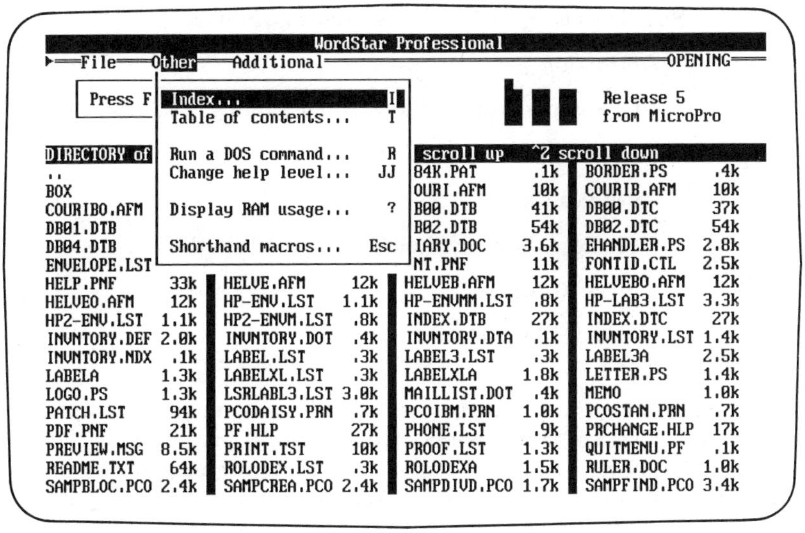
WordStar Professional
File Other Additional OPENING
Index... I
Table of contents... T
Run a DOS command... R
Change help level... JJ
Display RAM usage... ?
Shorthand macros... Esc
Release 5
from MicroPro
scroll up ^Z scroll down
BOX
COURIBO.AFM
DB01.DTB
DB04.DTB
ENVELOPE.LST
HELP.PNF 33k
HELVE.AFM 12k
HELVEB.AFM 12k
HELVEBO.AFM 12k
HELVEO.AFM 12k
HP-ENV.LST 1.1k
HP-ENVMM.LST .8k
HP-LAB3.LST 3.3k
HP2-ENV.LST 1.1k
HP2-ENVM.LST .8k
INDEX.DTB 27k
INDEX.DTC 27k
INVNTORY.DEF 2.0k
INVNTORY.DOT .4k
INVNTORY.DTA .1k
INVNTORY.LST 1.4k
INVNTORY.NDX .1k
LABEL.LST .3k
LABEL3.LST .3k
LABEL3A 2.5k
LABELA 1.3k
LABELXL.LST .3k
LABELXLA 1.8k
LETTER.PS 1.4k
LOGO.PS 1.3k
LSRLABL3.LST 3.0k
MAILLIST.DOT .4k
MEMO 1.0k
PATCH.LST 94k
PCODAISY.PRN .7k
PCOIBM.PRN 1.0k
PCOSTAN.PRN .7k
PDF.PNF 21k
PF.HLP 27k
PHONE.LST .9k
PRCHANGE.HLP 17k
PREVIEW.MSG 8.5k
PRINT.TST 10k
PROOF.LST 1.3k
QUITMENU.PF .1k
README.TXT 64k
ROLODEX.LST .3k
ROLODEXA 1.5k
RULER.DOC 1.0k
SAMPBLOC.PCO 2.4k
SAMPCREA.PCO 2.4k
SAMPDIVD.PCO 1.7k
SAMPFIND.PCO 3.4k

Fig. 3.4.
The pull-down Other menu from the Opening screen.

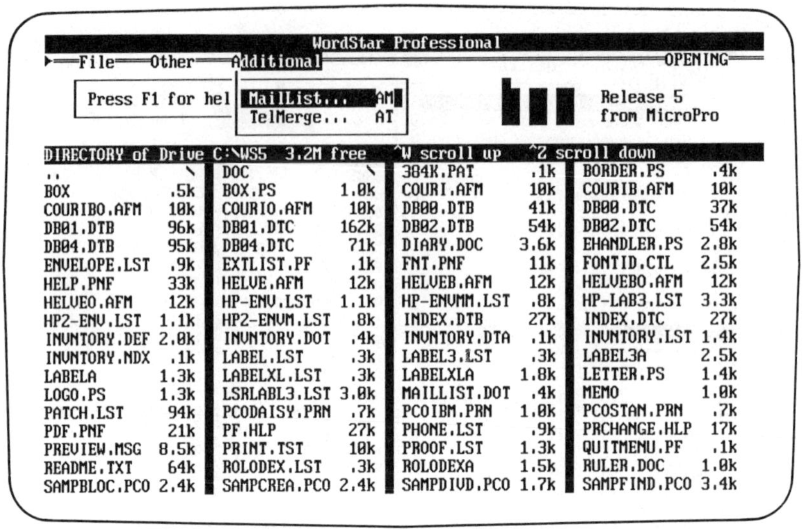
WordStar Professional
File Other Additional OPENING
Press F1 for hel
MailList... AM
TelMerge... AT
Release 5
from MicroPro
DIRECTORY of Drive C:\WS5 3.2M free ^W scroll up ^Z scroll down
.. \
BOX .5k
COURIBO.AFM 10k
DB01.DTB 96k
DB04.DTB 95k
ENVELOPE.LST .9k
HELP.PNF 33k
HELVEO.AFM 12k
HP2-ENV.LST 1.1k
INVNTORY.DEF 2.0k
INVNTORY.NDX .1k
LABELA 1.3k
LOGO.PS 1.3k
PATCH.LST 94k
PDF.PNF 21k
PREVIEW.MSG 8.5k
README.TXT 64k
SAMPBLOC.PCO 2.4k
DOC \
BOX.PS 1.0k
COURIO.AFM 10k
DB01.DTC 162k
DB04.DTC 71k
EXTLIST.PF .1k
HELVE.AFM 12k
HP-ENV.LST 1.1k
HP2-ENVM.LST .8k
INVNTORY.DOT .4k
LABEL.LST .3k
LABELXL.LST .3k
LSRLABL3.LST 3.0k
PCODAISY.PRN .7k
PF.HLP 27k
PRINT.TST 10k
ROLODEX.LST .3k
SAMPCREA.PCO 2.4k
384K.PAT .1k
COURI.AFM 10k
DB00.DTB 41k
DB02.DTB 54k
DIARY.DOC 3.6k
FNT.PNF 11k
HELVEB.AFM 12k
HP-ENVMM.LST .8k
INDEX.DTB 27k
INVNTORY.DTA .1k
LABEL3.LST .3k
LABELXLA 1.0k
MAILLIST.DOT .4k
PCOIBM.PRN 1.0k
PHONE.LST .9k
PROOF.LST 1.3k
ROLODEXA 1.5k
SAMPDIVD.PCO 1.7k
BORDER.PS .4k
COURIB.AFM 10k
DB00.DTC 37k
DB02.DTC 54k
EHANDLER.PS 2.0k
FONTID.CTL 2.5k
HELVEBO.AFM 12k
HP-LAB3.LST 3.3k
INDEX.DTC 27k
INVNTORY.LST 1.4k
LABEL3A 2.5k
LETTER.PS 1.4k
MEMO 1.0k
PCOSTAN.PRN .7k
PRCHANGE.HLP 17k
QUITMENU.PF .1k
RULER.DOC 1.0k
SAMPFIND.PCO 3.4k

Fig. 3.5.

The pull-down Additional menu from the Opening screen.

Table 3.2
Pull-Down Opening Command Sequences

Command	*Function*
FS	Opens a document file without naming
FD	Opens a document file by name
FP	Prints a file
FL	Changes the logged disk drive or file path
FX	Exits WordStar
OJJ	Changes help level

MicroPro says that among the advantages of the pull-down menus is compatibility with the new SAA (Systems Applications Architecture™) presentation standard, which is expected to bring similar interfaces to a variety of programs for PC- and PS/2-compatible computers. According to WordStar's publisher, the pull-down menus also were tested for maximum ease of use by new users. Unfortunately, by splitting up the commands listed in the classic Opening Menu, this interface scheme is less obvious than it could be. This scheme also adds keystrokes to some of WordStar's most often used commands.

If you have used WordStar before, you probably will opt for the classic-style Opening Menu, also available in Release 5. If you are a newcomer who wants greater efficiency by saving keystrokes and having prompts readily available, you also may want to change to the classic Opening Menu. To display this menu rather than the pull-down menus, you must reset WordStar's help level to 3 or less. You can do so by running the WINSTALL program (see Chapter 2), by running the WSCHANGE program (see Chapter 11) outside of WordStar, or by changing the help level temporarily during a work session (explained shortly).

At help level 3, 2, 1, or 0, WordStar displays a single Opening Menu screen (see fig. 3.6). In two columns and occupying the top two-thirds of the screen, this menu includes the commands and functions listed in the three separate pull-down menus.

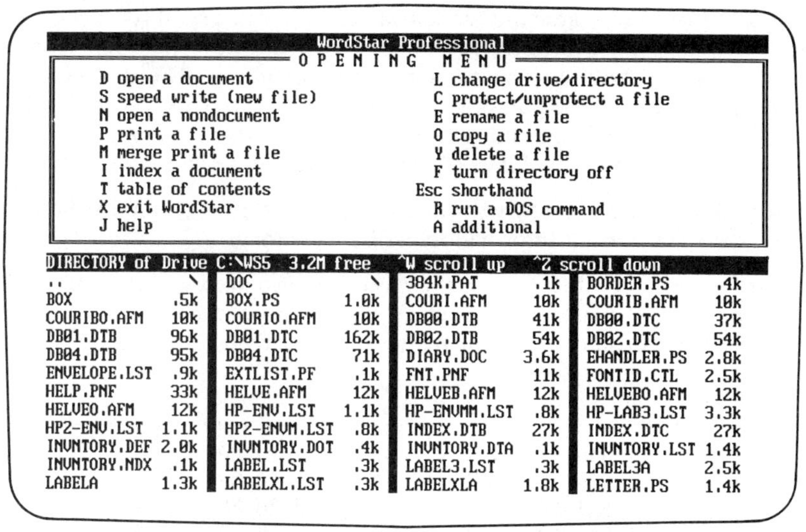
WordStar Professional
OPENING MENU
D open a document
S speed write (new file)
N open a nondocument
P print a file
M merge print a file
I index a document
T table of contents
X exit WordStar
J help
L change drive/directory
C protect/unprotect a file
E rename a file
O copy a file
Y delete a file
F turn directory off
Esc shorthand
R run a DOS command
A additional
DIRECTORY of Drive C:\WS5 3.2M free ^W scroll up ^Z scroll down
.. \
BOX .5k
COURIBO.AFM 10k
DB01.DTB 96k
DB04.DTB 95k
ENVELOPE.LST .9k
HELP.PNF 33k
HELVEO.AFM 12k
HP2-ENV.LST 1.1k
INVNTORY.DEF 2.0k
INVNTORY.NDX .1k
LABELA 1.3k
DOC \
BOX.PS 1.0k
COURIO.AFM 10k
DB01.DTC 162k
DB04.DTC 71k
EXTLIST.PF .1k
HELVE.AFM 12k
HP-ENV.LST 1.1k
HP2-ENVM.LST .8k
INVNTORY.DOT .4k
LABEL.LST .3k
LABELXL.LST .3k
384K.PAT .1k
COURI.AFM 10k
DB00.DTB 41k
DB02.DTB 54k
DIARY.DOC 3.6k
FNT.PNF 11k
HELVEB.AFM 12k
HP-ENVMM.LST .8k
INDEX.DTB 27k
INVNTORY.DTA .1k
LABEL3.LST .3k
LABELXLA 1.8k
BORDER.PS .4k
COURIB.AFM 10k
DB00.DTC 37k
DB02.DTC 54k
EHANDLER.PS 2.8k
FONTID.CTL 2.5k
HELVEBO.AFM 12k
HP-LAB3.LST 3.3k
INDEX.DTC 27k
INVNTORY.LST 1.4k
LABEL3A 2.5k
LETTER.PS 1.4k

Fig. 3.6.
WordStar's classic Opening Menu screen.

Among the choices on the classic Opening Menu are options for manipulating files and for performing system housekeeping chores. You activate each command by pressing the appropriate letter on the menu. As on the pull-down menus, only a handful of commands are fundamental to most word processing sessions. Table 3.3 lists the essential Opening Menu commands along with descriptions of their functions. Other commands on the classic Opening Menu are explored in Chapters 4, 9, and 10.

Table 3.3
Classic Opening Menu Commands

Command	*Function*
S	Opens a document file without naming
D	Opens a document file by name
P	Prints a file
L	Changes the logged disk drive or file path

Table 3.3—*Continued*

Command	*Function*
X	Exits WordStar
J or F1	Displays on-line help message
JJ or F1F1	Changes help level

Veterans of previous WordStar versions will spot two changes in Release 5's classic-style Opening Menu. The S command (which was used to run a spelling check with CorrectStar® in versions previous to Release 4) is now the way you open a document "on the fly," without having to name the document. The A command accesses the same choices as the pull-down Additional menu (see fig. 3.5). All other commands for opening or maintaining files remain the same. (As with previous versions, you don't need to press Enter after using Opening Menu commands.)

On both the pull-down Opening screen and the classic Opening Menu, the bottom of the screen shows important information: a disk directory.

The WordStar file directory differs from the directory displayed with the DOS DIR command (see fig. 3.7). WordStar's directory display does not include date and time, but the display can show more file names on the screen.

Fig. 3.7.
The directory displayed after you use the DOS DIR command.

```
$INDEX   OVR     3712  8-18-88  5:00p
$TOC     OVR     1408  8-18-88  5:00p
DRIVERA  OVR     3328  8-18-88  5:00p
DRIVERN  OVR     7936  8-18-88  5:00p
DRIVERT  OVR     2816  8-18-88  5:00p
WSHELP   OVR    40352  8-18-88  5:00p
WSHYPH   OVR    28892  8-18-88  5:00p
WSMSGS   OVR    21346  8-18-88  5:00p
WSSHORT  OVR      512  8-18-88  5:00p
WSSPELL  OVR    32896  8-18-88  5:00p
WSTHES   OVR    17190  8-18-88  5:00p
WSINDEX  XCL     1536  8-18-88  5:00p
RULER    DOC     1024  8-18-88  5:00p
TABLE    DOC     1024  8-18-88  5:00p
DIARY    DOC     3712  8-18-88  5:00p
TEXT     DOC     5760  8-18-88  5:00p
WINDOW   DOC      384  8-18-88  5:00p
ASCII    PDF      956  8-18-88  5:00p
DRAFT    PDF      938  8-18-88  5:00p
WS4      PDF      427  8-18-88  5:00p
PRINT    TST     9856  8-18-88  5:00p
BOX               512  8-18-88  5:00p
        24 File(s)      10240 bytes free

A>
```

The WordStar Directory Display

WordStar displays a file directory for the current disk drive (and subdirectory) at the bottom of the Opening Menu, as well as whenever a file-oriented function is invoked.

Document files are listed in the WordStar disk directory by alphabetized DOS name and size abbreviation (K = 1,024 characters, roughly 2K per page of text). File names are displayed four to a line, with more names on-screen than in a DOS file directory. The amount of storage still free on disk also is noted (M = 1,024K).

Although present on disk and occupying storage space, any files with the extensions EXE, COM, OVR, A, or B—all associated with various program functions—are excluded from WordStar's directory listing. File names to be excluded from directories can be modified with WSCHANGE (see Chapter 11).

The WordStar directory display in Release 5 differs from previous versions by listing names followed by file length. When displaying the less cluttered pull-down Opening menu in Release 5, the WordStar directory can include at least 20 more names on-screen than with the classic Opening screen. On the other hand, the directory display is partly obscured whenever the File menu is pulled down.

The Help Screens

WordStar includes a series of screens to help you find your way around the program. These help screens include menus of commands and explanations of features. Having pioneered on-screen help in word processing programs, MicroPro International continues to elaborate on WordStar's built-in help system.

With Release 5, WordStar's help feature is at last fully context sensitive: specific help is now available for every command listed on every menu. MicroPro International says that more than 200 help messages exist, and most of them are completely rewritten. Actually, two sets of help screens are in WordStar Release 5: pull-down and classic-style boxed messages.

The pull-down help message from the Opening screen (see fig. 3.8) exemplifies the new style of screens available at help level 4. This message includes information that is similar to the help message displayed from the classic Opening Menu at help level 3 or less. The classic-style help menu is illustrated in figure 3.9.

Due to the optional nature of WordStar Release 5's help screens (you also can turn off these screens to save disk space by using a WSCHANGE procedure explained in Chapter 11), several alternative ways are available for you to invoke help. With the addition of a fourth help level, changing the default help setting also becomes an essential option.

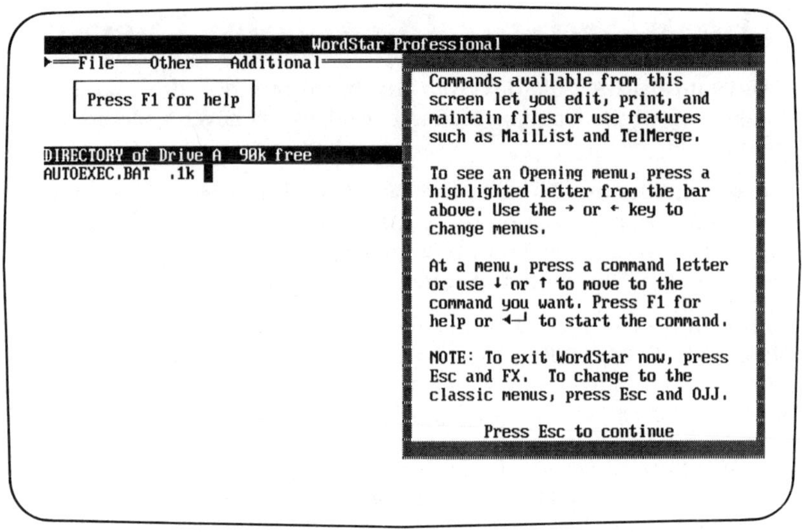
WordStar Professional
File Other Additional
Press F1 for help
DIRECTORY of Drive A 90k free
AUTOEXEC.BAT .1k
Commands available from this screen let you edit, print, and maintain files or use features such as MailList and TelMerge.
To see an Opening menu, press a highlighted letter from the bar above. Use the → or ← key to change menus.
At a menu, press a command letter or use ↓ or ↑ to move to the command you want. Press F1 for help or ←┘ to start the command.
NOTE: To exit WordStar now, press Esc and FX. To change to the classic menus, press Esc and OJJ.
Press Esc to continue

Fig. 3.8.
A pull-down help message from the Opening screen.

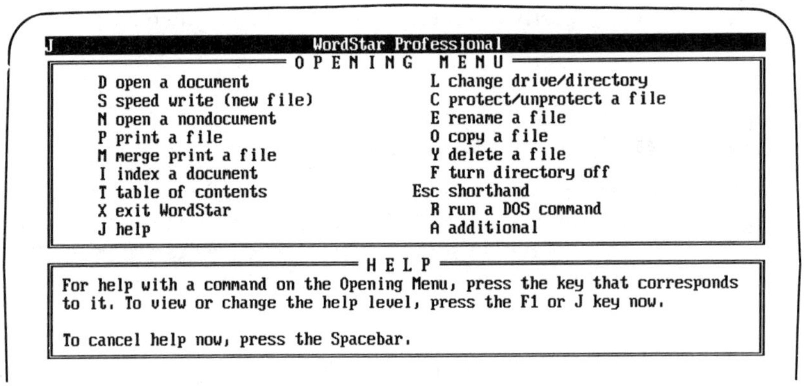
J
WordStar Professional
O P E N I N G M E N U
D open a document
S speed write (new file)
N open a nondocument
P print a file
M merge print a file
I index a document
T table of contents
X exit WordStar
J help
L change drive/directory
C protect/unprotect a file
E rename a file
O copy a file
Y delete a file
F turn directory off
Esc shorthand
R run a DOS command
A additional
H E L P
For help with a command on the Opening Menu, press the key that corresponds to it. To view or change the help level, press the F1 or J key now.
To cancel help now, press the Spacebar.

Fig. 3.9.
WordStar's help message at the classic Opening Menu.

Invoking Help

Whatever level of help you set for WordStar, you usually will receive succinct, easy-to-read help explanations by pressing one or two keys. When in doubt, press the F1 function key. Although it is not indicated on most menus, this function key is reserved for invoking help throughout WordStar. In addition, using the central keyboard commands ^J or J can invoke the same help messages under specific circumstances.

5

With an unmodified copy of WordStar Release 5 or one reset to help level 4, the pull-down Opening screen includes the following listing at the upper left corner of the screen:

```
Press F1 for help
```

Pressing F1 actually issues the command ^J; you can use both F1 and ^J interchangeably to invoke help throughout this pull-down style installation of Release 5. When issued at the Opening screen, F1 or ^J displays a pull-down explanation of the Opening commands (refer back to fig. 3.8). If invoked at a pull-down menu, the help message explains the highlighted command.

When set at help level 3 or lower for classic menus, the Opening Menu includes a help command at the bottom of the left column:

```
J help
```

At the Opening Menu, pressing the F1 function key is equivalent to pressing J. Pressing either J or F1 displays the WordStar classic-style help message, which explains how to issue Opening Menu commands (see fig. 3.9). From this help screen, pressing the letter for a command displays help information on any of the Opening Menu's choices. At the Edit screen, pressing F1 still invokes help. Following F1, you type the letter for the command you want explained.

You always can uninvoke help. To remove a help message from your screen, press the Esc key.

In effect, either Opening screen is the first of WordStar's help screens. Whether pull-down or classic, this first layer of help screens cannot be turned off after you are familiar with the program. As you become adept at using WordStar, you will find that waiting even a second or two for help screens to appear slows your word processing tasks. You will want to turn off more and more of these messages until, eventually, you will use the program with nearly all the help screens turned off.

Setting the Help Level

You can reset WordStar's help level at any time during a work session. To change the help level, you usually press J or F1 two times, depending on where you are in the program.

If you have an unmodified copy of WordStar Release 5 or one reset to help level 4, the command for resetting the help level is listed on the pull-down Other menu, accessed when you press O at the Opening screen. The Other menu (see fig. 3.4) includes the following listing:

```
Change help level...      JJ
```

From the Opening screen, pressing O and then JJ (O is one of the extra keystrokes you must use due to the pull-down style installation of WordStar Release 5) displays a screen with the heading HELP LEVEL (see fig. 3.10). Pressing 4, 3, 2, 1, or 0 resets WordStar to the desired level; the different levels apply to first-time or experienced users.

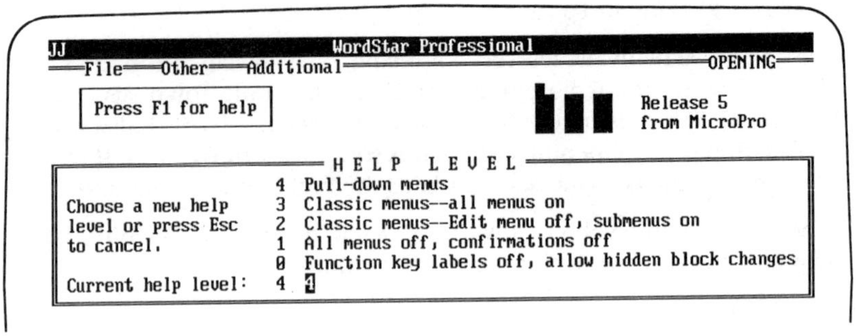
JJ
WordStar Professional
File Other Additional
OPENING
Press F1 for help
Release 5
from MicroPro
HELP LEVEL
4 Pull-down menus
Choose a new help level or press Esc to cancel.
3 Classic menus--all menus on
2 Classic menus--Edit menu off, submenus on
1 All menus off, confirmations off
0 Function key labels off, allow hidden block changes
Current help level: 4

Fig. 3.10.

The Help Level dialog box with pull-down menus.

If your copy of WordStar is set at help level 3 or lower, the classic Opening Menu includes the J help command. Press J or the F1 function key once to display the help message shown in figure 3.9. Pressing J or F1 again brings up the Help Level dialog box shown in figure 3.11. This box is essentially the same as the one shown in the pull-down style of menus (see fig. 3.10). Thus, from the classic Opening Menu, press either JJ or F1 F1 to display the Help Level dialog box options. Again, press 4, 3, 2, 1, or 0 to set help to the level you want.

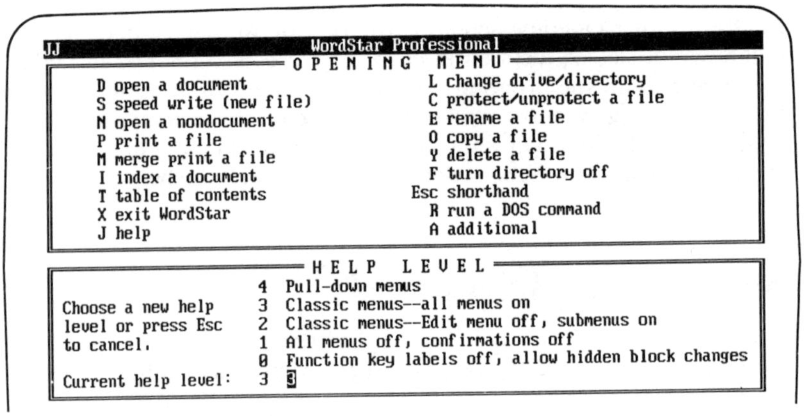
JJ
WordStar Professional
OPENING MENU
D open a document
S speed write (new file)
N open a nondocument
P print a file
M merge print a file
I index a document
T table of contents
X exit WordStar
J help
L change drive/directory
C protect/unprotect a file
E rename a file
O copy a file
Y delete a file
F turn directory off
Esc shorthand
R run a DOS command
A additional
HELP LEVEL
4 Pull-down menus
Choose a new help level or press Esc to cancel.
3 Classic menus--all menus on
2 Classic menus--Edit menu off, submenus on
1 All menus off, confirmations off
0 Function key labels off, allow hidden block changes
Current help level: 3

Fig. 3.11.

The Help Level dialog box with classic menus.

During editing, you can change the help level by pressing ^J^J or F1 F1. This repeated command displays a help-level screen that is similar to the ones you see from the Opening displays.

Once you are at a help-level screen, you can retain the current setting by pressing Enter or Esc.

WordStar Release 5 offers five levels of assistance, as summarized in table 3.4. The unmodified WordStar program always sets the help level at 4 for first-time and occasional users.

Table 3.4
WordStar Help Levels

Level	*Menus*
4	Pull-down menus
3	All classic menus, including Edit
2	Classic menus for multiple-keystroke commands
1	Classic Opening Menu, few prompts
0	Classic Opening Menu, no prompts

Help level 4, providing pull-down menus throughout, can be navigated easily (though not most efficiently) by WordStar beginners. The editing screen is uncluttered and not helpful.

At level 3, beginners actually get the most on-screen help. The classic Edit Menu is especially helpful; all single-keystroke control commands are shown, along with function key commands. Prompts guard against accidental erasures and loss of files.

When using help level 2, intermediate WordStar users no longer see the classic Edit Menu, opening up a third of the screen for more text. Two-keystroke command sequences still elicit informative classic menus.

Help level 1, for intermediate and expert users, displays only the most essential program information. Except for the Opening Menu, none of the classic menus is shown unless requested.

Help level 0, tamed in Release 5, is now a useful alternative for expert users. Level 0 no longer eliminates the status line at the top of the editing screen (it did in Release 4). With no function key assignments at the bottom of the screen, this level still gives you the least cluttered of WordStar editing screens. This level does require you to use caution, however, because hidden blocks can be deleted accidentally.

5

In addition to the commands for resetting the WordStar help level during a work session, remember that Release 5 includes two procedures for setting the default help level so that your working copy always starts out at the correct level. You can use the WINSTALL installation program (see Chapter 2) or the WSCHANGE customization program (explained in Chapter 11).

Getting To Know the Keyboard

Before creating a document with WordStar, you need to be familiar with your keyboard's layout. This book uses for primary references the original IBM PC keyboard and the IBM Enhanced Keyboard, standard on recent PC and PS/2 compatibles. The original keyboard, standard for IBM PCs and compatibles, is shown in figure 3.12. An illustration of the IBM Personal Computer AT keyboard is shown in figure 3.13. The IBM Enhanced Keyboard is shown in figure 3.14.

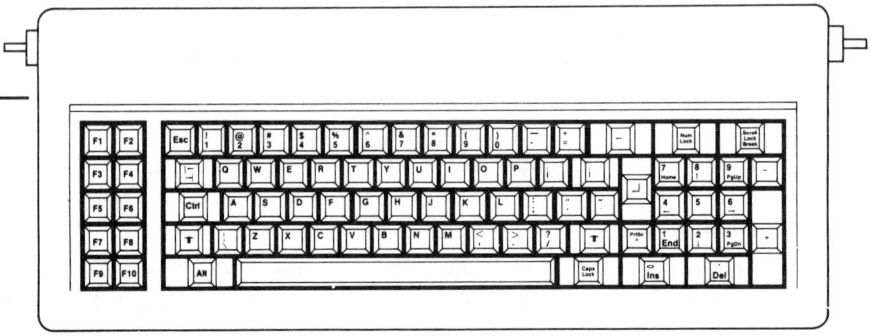
F1 F2 F3 F4 F5 F6 F7 F8 F9 F10
Esc Q W E R T Y U I O P
Ctrl A S D F G H J K L
Z X C V B N M
Alt Caps Lock
Num Lock Scroll Lock Break
Home PgUp End PgDn Ins Del PrtSc

Fig. 3.12.
The IBM PC keyboard.

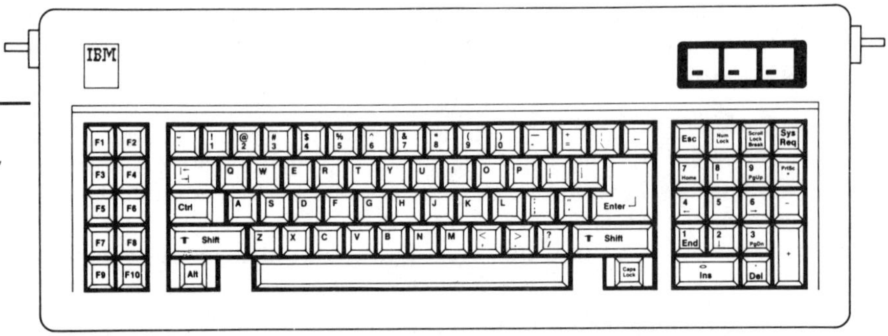
IBM
F1 F2 F3 F4 F5 F6 F7 F8 F9 F10
Q W E R T Y U I O P
Ctrl A S D F G H J K L Enter
Shift Z X C V B N M Shift
Alt Caps Lock
Esc Num Lock Scroll Lock Break Sys Req
Home PgUp PrtSc End PgDn Ins Del

Fig. 3.13.
The IBM Personal Computer AT keyboard.

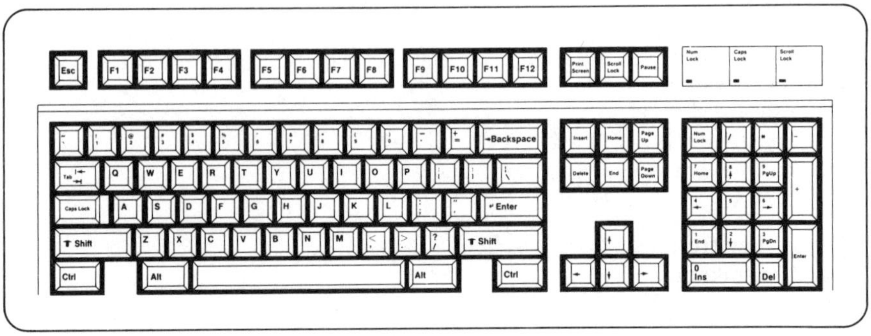
Esc F1 F2 F3 F4 F5 F6 F7 F8 F9 F10 F11 F12
Print Screen Scroll Lock Pause
Num Lock Caps Lock Scroll Lock
Backspace
Tab Q W E R T Y U I O P
Caps Lock A S D F G H J K L Enter
Shift Z X C V B N M Shift
Ctrl Alt Alt Ctrl
Insert Home Page Up
Delete End Page Down
Num Lock Home PgUp End PgDn Ins Del Enter

Fig. 3.14.
The IBM Enhanced Keyboard.

The computer keyboard is divided into three sections: the alphanumeric keyboard in the center, the numeric keypad on the right, and the function key section on the left or in the top row.

The Alphanumeric Keyboard

All text characters composed with WordStar and all commands available from either of the Opening menus are entered with the alphanumeric keys in the center of the keyboard. These are the same keys you use on any typewriter to enter letters, numbers, and punctuation. Most WordStar editing commands also are entered with these keys. Several keys on the alphanumeric keyboard serve unique functions; these keys are Shift, space bar, Enter, Backspace, and Tab. WordStar also uses keys that are not commonly found on a typewriter: Ctrl, Esc, and Alt.

The Shift key—sometimes designated by an upward-pointing arrow— changes the center section of the keyboard to uppercase letters and characters. The Shift key also allows you to enter numbers, using the numeric keypad on the right (equivalent of a temporary Num Lock). Press the Shift key before or at the same time as a letter or number key.

The space bar at the bottom of the keyboard adds spaces, as does the space bar on a typewriter keyboard. The space bar also is used in Release 5 to advance through pull-down menus.

You use the Enter (or Return) key, to the right of the alphabetical keys, to indicate the end of a paragraph of text or to insert a blank line. The Enter key also signals the computer to execute a command.

With the Backspace key (above the Enter key and marked by a left-pointing arrow), you can move back through text, deleting a character at a time—"destructive" backspacing.

You use the Tab key (bearing left and right arrows), located to the left of the letter keys, to advance the cursor along a line in preset increments.

The Ctrl key, located above the left Shift key on the IBM PC and original AT keyboards (and below the Shift key on the Enhanced Keyboard), is one of the most important keys used in WordStar. From within a document, most WordStar commands are executed when you press and hold down the Ctrl key while pressing a letter key.

The caret symbol (^) is often used to denote a Ctrl-letter combination. (Do not confuse this symbol with the caret on the Shift-6 key at the top of the keyboard.) For example, Ctrl-A or ^A means that you press and hold down the Ctrl key while you press A.

The Esc key frequently is used to exit from a command or function that has been issued mistakenly. On the IBM PC keyboard, the Esc key is located on the left, above the Tab key; on the IBM Enhanced Keyboard, Esc is at the left of the row of function keys; on the AT keyboard, it is at the top left corner of the numeric keypad.

In WordStar Release 5, the Esc key is limited essentially to two functions: exiting from a screen or invoking the program's "shorthand" macro function for recording keystrokes so that they can be reentered automatically. In Release 5, you no longer use the Esc key to change defaults when setting margins, to accelerate a search-and-replace operation, or to skip settings options when printing.

The Alt key, located directly below the Shift key on the IBM PC and the original AT keyboards (and on both sides of the space bar on the Enhanced Keyboard), is similar to the Ctrl and Shift keys in that Alt is always pressed along with another key. The Alt key is used to display nonstandard keyboard characters on-screen. Various Alt-key combinations in Release 5 display pull-down menus or activate add-on functions during editing.

The Numeric Keypad

At the right of the keyboard is the numeric keypad. At the center of the numeric keypad is a cluster of nine numeric keys, four of which also are marked with directional arrows. The numeric keypad serves double duty. The primary duty is for cursor movement. However, the numeric keys also can be used to enter numbers when either the Caps Lock key or Num Lock key has been pressed. On the IBM Enhanced Keyboard, dedicated arrow keys also are available, clustered beside the numeric keypad.

While editing a document, you can use the arrow keys to move the cursor up, down, right, or left in the text (although Ctrl-letter commands can do the same thing from the alphanumeric keyboard). Similarly, you can use the numeric keys labeled Home, End, PgUp, and PgDn to move the cursor by greater increments within a document. On the IBM Enhanced Keyboard, the Home, End, PgUp, and PgDn keys are duplicated as a cluster of dedicated keys to the left of the numeric keypad. (For more information on these keys, see *Moving the Cursor Quickly* in Chapter 5.)

Also on the numeric keypad are the PrtSc, Ins, and Del keys (these keys are duplicated as dedicated keys on the IBM Enhanced Keyboard).

The PrtSc key is a handy feature on the keyboard. Press and hold down the Shift key while you press the PrtSc key to print the contents of the current screen display. However, note that this command does not produce a printed document in its final formatted form.

In WordStar Release 5, you use the Ins key to switch back and forth between insert and overtype modes. And you use the Del key to erase the character at the cursor.

The Function Keys

On the left side of the keyboard (on the IBM PC and original AT keyboards) are the function keys: 10 keys labeled F1 to F10. On the Enhanced Keyboard, 12 function keys are located above the top row of number keys.

In Release 5, the function keys are assigned the same commands as in Release 4—a total of 40 writing and editing features that you can call up by pressing a single function key or a function key combined with the Ctrl, Shift, or Alt key. WordStar's preset assignments are explained in table 3.5. If some of the preset assignments of these keys aren't useful in your word processing application, or if you prefer commands assigned in a previous WordStar version, you can reassign the function keys easily with the WSCHANGE program. (For more information on how to customize function key commands, see Chapter 11.)

Table 3.5
WordStar's Function Key Assignments

Function Key	*Operation*
F1	Gets on-line help
F2	Restores the last erasure or cancels an operation
F3	Toggles underline on/off
F4	Toggles boldface on/off
F5	Deletes one line at the cursor
F6	Deletes one word to the right of the cursor
F7	Aligns a paragraph and returns the cursor to its previous position
F8	Embeds ruler line into text
F9	Saves a file and resumes editing
F10	Saves a file and exits to the Opening Menu
Shift-F1	Toggles the print display on/off
Shift-F2	Centers text
Shift-F3	Checks the spelling in the rest of file
Shift-F4	Checks the spelling of a word at the cursor
Shift-F5	Deletes a block of text
Shift-F6	Toggles block display
Shift-F7	Moves a block of text
Shift-F8	Copies a block of text

Table 3.5—*Continued*

Function Key	*Operation*
Shift-F9	Marks the beginning of a block of text
Shift-F10	Marks the end of a block of text
Ctrl-F1	Finds a character string in a document
Ctrl-F2	Finds and replaces a character string
Ctrl-F3	Repeats a find operation
Ctrl-F4	Finds a page by number in a document
Ctrl-F5	Sets the left margin at the column you specify
Ctrl-F6	Sets the right margin at the column you specify
Ctrl-F7	Sets the paragraph margin
Ctrl-F8	Inserts a page break
Ctrl-F9	Moves the cursor to the left end of a line
Ctrl-F10	Moves the cursor to the right end of a line
Alt-F1	Draws a vertical line character
Alt-F2	Draws a horizontal line character
Alt-F3	Draws an upper-left corner character
Alt-F4	Draws an upper-right corner character
Alt-F5	Draws a lower-left corner character
Alt-F6	Draws a lower-right corner character
Alt-F7	Draws an upper line intersection character
Alt-F8	Draws a lower line intersection character
Alt-F9	Draws a left line intersection character
Alt-F10	Draws a right line intersection character

Creating a Document

To compose and edit text with WordStar, you must start by opening a document file. In the latest version of WordStar, a new command opens a document file without your having to name the file until it is saved. You still can start a document in the classic manner: the first time a document file is created, you assign a name to it before going to the Edit screen. The file name designates how the document will be identified when stored on disk.

If you want the document you create to be saved on a disk or in a hard disk subdirectory other than the one from which WordStar is loaded, you can either precede file names with disk letters, colons, and directory paths, or you can change the logged drive or directory. Do the same if a document you want to edit is on a different disk drive or in another directory. Once you set the storage location for your document, you can proceed with your choice of commands for opening the document on-screen.

Changing the Logged Drive or Directory

When you start WordStar, the Opening screen displays the file directory for the drive (and subdirectory) from which the command to run the program was issued (see figs. 3.2 and 3.6). WordStar will save files on the same drive and directory unless you instruct otherwise. This designated drive/file path is called the *logged drive*.

With WordStar Release 5 at help level 4, pressing F at the Opening screen displays the pull-down menu of File commands. Midway down its listings is the following function:

```
Change drive/directory...    L
```

To reset the logged storage area for WordStar, press F and then L at the Opening screen; a box headed with the word LOG is displayed (see fig. 3.15). In the space below the line listing `Drive/directory` in the LOG display, you can type a drive letter and a colon and, optionally, a backslash (\ ) followed by a new subdirectory path. Pressing Enter establishes the new logged setting.

When WordStar is set for classic menus, at help level 3 or less, the Opening Menu's top right column shows this option:

```
L change drive/directory
```

Pressing L from the classic Opening Menu directly displays the same Log dialog box obtained from the pull-down menus at help level 4 (see fig. 3.15). Here, too, you can type a new drive letter, followed by a colon, a backslash (\ ), and a new subdirectory path. Pressing Enter saves the new logged setting.

When you are at help level 4 and are editing, you can change the logged drive and directory by pressing Alt-F for the pull-down File menu and invoking the listed

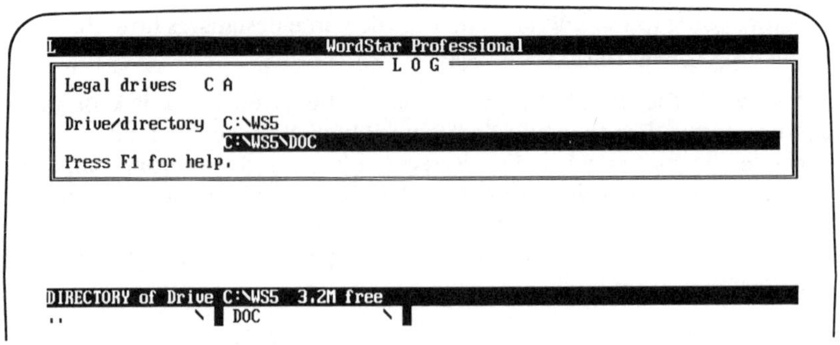
WordStar Professional
L O G
Legal drives C A
Drive/directory C:\WS5
C:\WS5\DOC
Press F1 for help.
DIRECTORY of Drive C:\WS5 3.2M free
.. \ DOC \

Fig. 3.15.
The screen for changing WordStar's logged disk drive.

command ^KL. At any help level, simply press ^KL from the Edit screen. This command sequence displays the Log dialog box, in which you are prompted to type a drive and directory path.

When changing the logged drive on a two floppy disk system started with WordStar in drive A, you usually type *b:* to make drive B the one that will contain your document files. On a hard disk system, you may type *c:\ws5\doc* or a similar file path to log onto a directory created earlier for your document files.

After you type the new logged drive name and press Enter, the designated drive spins to inform WordStar of its contents and the display returns to the Opening screen. Now this Opening screen's disk directory lists the new file path and the names of the files stored there, along with the amount of remaining disk space.

While in the Log dialog box, you can leave the current file path unchanged by pressing the Esc key or by using either of the Undo commands: ^U or F2.

Unlike the preceding version of WordStar, Release 5 does not include on-screen instructions for editing what you type at the prompt. If you make a mistake in typing the logged drive and directory, you can use the Backspace key to delete any mistakes you make before you press Enter. Or you can use the editing commands described in a later section of this chapter.

Responding to WordStar Prompts

WordStar Release 5 displays dialog-box prompts whenever a user's answer is required for a function to be completed; responses run the gamut from file paths and file names to page measurements and font selections. Adapted from Macintosh® styles of displays, the uncluttered dialog box replaces the more informational prompts of WordStar Release 4.

Responses to dialog boxes can be up to 80 characters long when typed. Or you can supply responses by highlighting a file name in the directory if such information is called for. Any response can be saved, canceled, erased, or edited with many of the same commands you use for editing text.

The essential commands that you issue while responding to WordStar prompts are summarized in table 3.6.

Table 3.6
Commands for Responding to WordStar Prompts

Command	*Function*
Enter or ^K or F10	Signals that a response is complete
Esc or ^U or F2	Cancels a response
^R	Repeats a response
Tab or Shift-Tab	Moves the cursor through response fields
^X or down-arrow	Moves the cursor into directory
^E or up-arrow	Moves the cursor back out of directory
^S or left-arrow	Moves the cursor left one character at a time
^D or right-arrow	Moves the cursor right one character at a time
Backspace or Del or ^G	Deletes a typed response one character at a time
^T	Deletes a typed response one word at a time
^Y	Deletes completely a typed response

The first listing, invoked with the Enter key or ^K or F10, confirms a typed response. Press any of these keys to indicate that an answer is to be read by WordStar.

Pressing Esc or ^U or F2 halts the current function and returns to the previous screen. You also use these commands to undo or interrupt functions throughout WordStar.

Another useful command, ^R, repeats your last response to a WordStar prompt. This command writes the file name on-screen. This feature comes in handy when you need to open the same file a number of times in succession.

When a dialog box has several fields for responses, you can press Tab or Shift-Tab to move the cursor forward or backward from field to field.

Pressing ^X or the down-arrow key moves the cursor into a directory where you can select as a response one of the subdirectories or files indicated on the logged drive. Pressing ^E or the up-arrow key moves the the cursor back to the prompt line where you can type a response.

The next pair of commands—^S (or left-arrow) and ^D (or right-arrow)—are for cursor movement within a response. The text of the response is not altered.

The deletion commands—Backspace, Del, ^G, ^T, and ^Y—are the same as those you use when editing text. All these commands are explained later in this and the next chapter.

Opening a Document File

Most WordStar applications involve the creation and storage of text as document files. Like paper documents, WordStar document files include full text and formatting; unlike paper pages, WordStar document files are continuous and limited in theory only by your computer's disk capacity. A slightly different file, without formatting and printing codes, is created when you open a nondocument file (see Chapter 4).

For the first time since WordStar's introduction, its disk file format for documents has been significantly changed. With Release 5, a WordStar document file includes formatting information encoded at the beginning of the file. Although the information is not seen on-screen, the loss of such file header information could make recovering a stored document difficult. Over the years, among WordStar's most appreciated characteristics has been the ruggedness of document files on disk—in part because of the lack of header information subject to loss from normal disk wear and tear. Only time will tell whether the new document format proves as solid, so caution is recommended in the form of file backups. (For more information on WordStar Release 5's document file format, see Chapter 12.)

Another major change in WordStar Release 5 is a choice of commands for opening a document file: a new Speed Write function for starting a new document without naming it or the classic procedure of naming a file before going to the Edit screen.

Starting a new document file quickly, without interrupting your creative flow to type file names, is the purpose of WordStar Release 5's Speed Write command—appropriately invoked when you press the S key. With this feature, you can use just one or two keystrokes to go directly from the Opening display to WordStar's editing screen. Speed Write is useful for such things as quick notes, brainstorms, or addenda—whenever you want to type first and take the time to name the file later.

If WordStar is set at help level 4, pressing F at the Opening screen displays the pull-down File menu. The top line of the File menu lists the following function:

```
Speed Write (new file)     S
```

From the Opening Menu, pressing F and then S is the complete sequence for quick starting a new document.

A key design decision in WordStar Release 5 was to have the File menu option and the Speed Write command first among possible selections, allowing you to invoke these options as defaults by just pressing Enter twice. Whether you press the letter keys F and S or press Enter twice, the Opening screen is replaced by the Edit screen—complete with pull-down menus. Later in this chapter, more information is presented about this screen, where all text entry and editing take place.

At help level 3 or less, WordStar's classic Opening Menu displays a new command in the second line of the left column:

```
S speed write (new file)
```

From the Opening Menu, pressing S starts a new document and displays the classic Edit Menu (at help level 3) or the editing screen (at help level 2 or less).

Regardless of the help level or menu, when you save your Speed-Write-created document to disk at the end of the work session, you are prompted to name the document. The name must conform to DOS conventions for file designations, as explained shortly. Options for saving files are discussed at the end of this chapter.

Opening and Naming a Document File

Even with the new Speed Write function, the most frequently used command in WordStar is the one for opening a document file by name. Every time you edit an existing document, you must invoke this command from the Opening display—in addition to using this classic procedure for naming a new document as it is opened.

With pull-down menus (at help level 4), pressing F at the Opening screen displays the File menu. The second listing on that menu follows:

```
Open a document file...  D
```

Pressing F and then D at the Opening screen invokes a document to be named before you begin composing or editing. Pressing the F and D keys displays a dialog box labeled DOCUMENT (see fig. 3.16). Here you can type the name of a new document you want to open or an existing file you want to read and revise.

When using WordStar's classic menus (at help level 3 or less), you will see the following command listing at the top of the Opening Menu's left column:

```
D open a document
```

Pressing D at the Opening Menu displays the Document dialog box. In this dialog box, you indicate a file name for the document you want to open.

In the Document dialog box, you can type a file name and press Enter. WordStar checks the disk directory. At help levels 3 and 2, if the name is not already in use, a second dialog box appears with this prompt:

D
WordStar Professional
DOCUMENT
File (none)
Press F1 for help.
DIRECTORY of Drive C:\WS5\DOC 3.2M free
..

Fig. 3.16.
The prompt for naming a WordStar document file to be opened.

```
Can't find that file. Create a new one (Y/N)?
```

If you press Y, the WordStar editing screen is displayed (this screen is explained later in this chapter).

Whatever the help level, you don't have to type the name of the file if you are opening a file that already has been created. WordStar provides a convenient way for you to designate file names with the cursor. As previously noted, when WordStar asks you to specify a file, and the file directory is displayed on the same screen, you can move the cursor to the directory by pressing ^X or the down-arrow key. You then can use the arrow keys or the ^S, ^E, ^D, and ^X keys to move the cursor within the directory to the appropriate file name. When you press the Enter or Esc key, the file name is entered in the space where you would have typed the name.

To open a new document file successfully with the D command (or to save a document that you began with the Speed Write function), you must observe the conventions for naming DOS files. If you do not observe these conventions, you will obtain an error message when you indicate the would-be name and press Enter.

Naming a File

WordStar accepts the same kinds of file names as DOS does. That is, a document file can be assigned a name of up to eight letters or digits. This name can be followed (without spaces) by an extension—a period and up to three characters. You can use the extension to designate the file's category. For example, the extension EXE on the file name WS.EXE (the principal WordStar program file) denotes an executable program file. The extension DOC often is used for a document file. Upper- or lowercase letters can be used interchangeably.

Here are examples of valid names for WordStar files:

FILENAME
A
1-23-87
december.86
ASSETS.DOC
REPORT.NEW

On the other hand, because they don't observe the proper form, the following names are not valid WordStar file names:

FILENAMES	The name has too many characters.
"A"	Quotation marks cannot be used in file names.
1/23/87	/ is not an admissible character.
december,86	A comma cannot be used in file names.
ASSETS.FILE	The extension is too long but will be truncated by WordStar to ASSETS.FIL.
REPORTNEW	The period before the extension is missing.

In general, give your files names that make the documents easy to recognize. Because you cannot examine the contents of your files in WordStar without opening the files, try to assign descriptive names. If you will be opening a file often, give it a short name that is easy to type. For documents you use every day, why not use a single character designation? Variations on a file can be indicated with an apostrophe (') or an appropriate extension.

Understanding WordStar's Editing Screen

The editing screen is WordStar's work surface, where text entry, editing, and formatting take place. Here text is easily typed, erased, unerased, replaced, moved, and improved. The editing screen is the part of WordStar you see most.

With the addition of pull-down menus, WordStar Release 5 features four possible views of the editing screen. All these views include two lines of essential information about the document being composed and edited. Depending on the help-level setting, more space is devoted to on-screen help with commands available for manipulating text—with a corresponding narrowing of space available for the text itself.

At help level 4 with its pull-down menus, when you begin to work on a document, the editing screen looks like the one shown in figure 3.17. With the exception of level 0, this level gives you the least cluttered editing screen. You can receive help instantly, however, from any of seven pull-down menus; press and hold down the Alt key while pressing the appropriate letter on the menu bar.

Fig. 3.17.

The editing screen at help level 4 with pull-down menus.

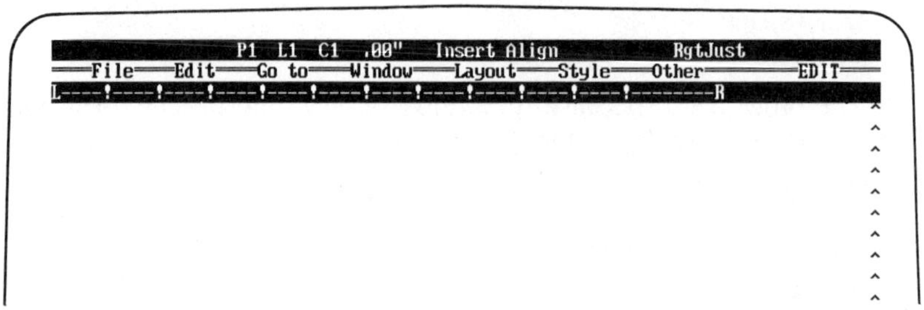
P1 L1 C1 .00" Insert Align RgtJust
File Edit Go to Window Layout Style Other EDIT

When WordStar is set at classic help level 3, the editing screen appears as shown in figure 3.18. This screen has room for only half the amount of text that is displayed at help level 4, but the screen features the Edit Menu, listing 22 single-keystroke commands and indicating access to other menus for more complex command sequences. Along with the two lines of function key commands indicated at the bottom of the screen, this variation on the editing screen displays the most information.

Fig. 3.18.

The WordStar editing screen at help level 3.

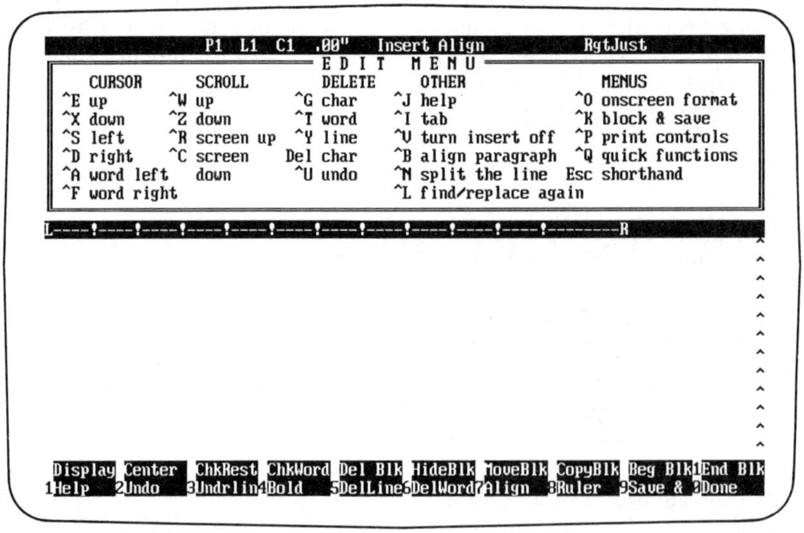
P1 L1 C1 .00" Insert Align RgtJust
E D I T M E N U
CURSOR SCROLL DELETE OTHER MENUS
^E up ^W up ^G char ^J help ^O onscreen format
^X down ^Z down ^T word ^I tab ^K block & save
^S left ^R screen up ^Y line ^V turn insert off ^P print controls
^D right ^C screen Del char ^B align paragraph ^Q quick functions
^A word left down ^U undo ^N split the line Esc shorthand
^F word right ^L find/replace again
Display Center ChkRest ChkWord Del Blk HideBlk MoveBlk CopyBlk Beg Blk End Blk
1Help 2Undo 3Undrlin 4Bold 5DelLine 6DelWord 7Align 8Ruler 9Save & 0Done

At help level 2 or 1, WordStar's editing screen looks like the one shown in figure 3.19. Without the Edit Menu, nine more lines of text are available on-screen.

If set at help level 0, the WordStar editing screen is at its sparsest. This version leaves the most lines on-screen for the text you are editing (see fig. 3.20). You must change the help level to display on-screen command help, so this screen works best if you're an expert user.

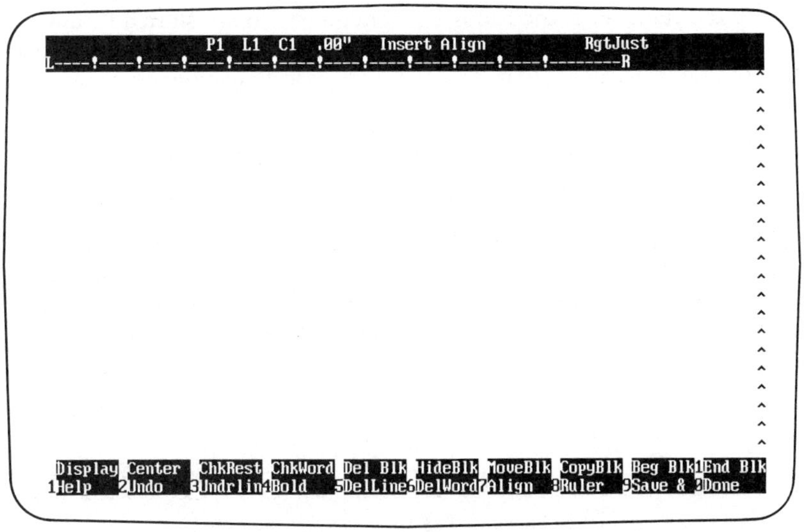
P1 L1 C1 .00" Insert Align RgtJust
Display Center ChkRest ChkWord Del Blk HideBlk MoveBlk CopyBlk Beg Blk End Blk
1Help 2Undo 3Undrlin 4Bold 5DelLine 6DelWord 7Align 8Ruler 9Save & 0Done

Fig. 3.19.

The WordStar editing screen at help level 2 or 1.

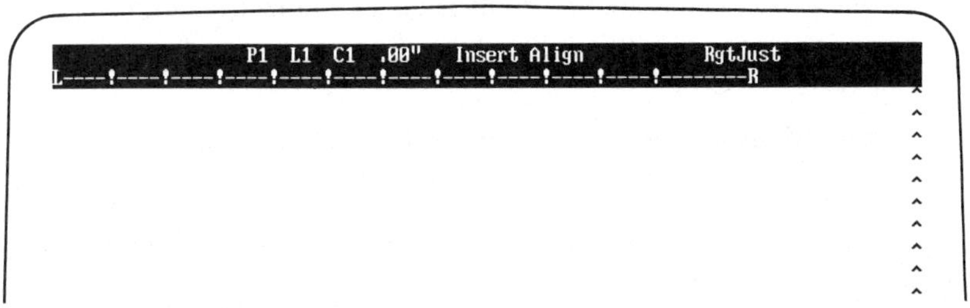
P1 L1 C1 .00" Insert Align RgtJust

Fig. 3.20.

The WordStar editing screen at help level 0.

From top to bottom, the editing screen shows document status information, a menu bar, editing commands, tab stops and line formatting, and function key labels (depending on the screen display you set). Each part of the editing screen is explained in the following sections.

The Status Line

At any help level, the WordStar *status line* is at the top of the editing screen. This line provides essential information on the status of a document at any moment during the editing process.

From left to right, the status line can show the letters for a command in progress; the name of the document you are creating (with the drive, directory, and subdirectory to which the file will be saved); and your place in the document by page, line, column number, and, for the first time, inches from the left margin.

On the right of the status line, the following functions also are shown if they are turned on: insert, align, document protect, and right-justification. If your document is other than single-spaced, that information is indicated at the far right of the status line.

On a hard disk system, the status line typically resembles the following:

```
C:\DOC\MEMO     P1 L1 C8 .70"  Insert    Align     RgtJust
```

Warnings also appear in the status line. For example, warnings appear when you reach the limit of dot commands WordStar can track during editing or when you are using a "LargeFile"—one close to the limit of your system's memory. While in operation, functions such as find-and-replace and printing display messages in the status line.

The Menu Bar and Pull-Down Menus

5

At help level 4, the editing screen's second line lists seven pull-down menus available for viewing. The menus are named by their generalized functions:

```
══File══Edit══Go to══Window══Layout══Style══Other══
```

You can pull down and display any of the menus listed on the menu bar by holding down Alt while pressing the initial letter of the desired menu. Alternatively, holding down Alt while pressing the space bar moves the highlight to the menu bar, where you can designate a menu by moving the highlight with the left- and right-arrow keys.

At the editing screen, pressing Alt-F displays the File menu (see fig. 3.21). This menu lists 11 commands for saving, printing, and other actions relating to WordStar files.

Pressing Alt-E pulls down the Edit menu (see fig. 3.22). This menu has 13 commands for deleting text and manipulating blocks of text for greater efficiency during editing. Details of these commands are given in Chapters 5 and 6.

Selecting Alt-G produces the pull-down Go To menu (see fig. 3.23). This menu lists a dozen commands for moving the cursor in useful increments. These commands are discussed in Chapter 5.

If you press Alt-W, the Window menu appears with its six command listings for viewing and editing two documents on-screen at the same time (see fig. 3.24). WordStar Release 5's new windowing feature is covered in full in Chapter 5.

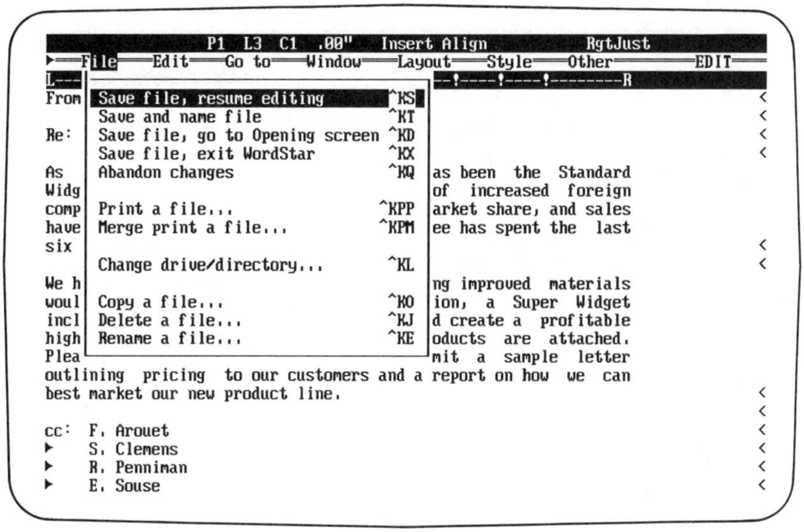
P1 L3 C1 .00" Insert Align RgtJust
File Edit Go to Window Layout Style Other EDIT
Save file, resume editing ^KS
Save and name file ^KT
Save file, go to Opening screen ^KD
Save file, exit WordStar ^KX
Abandon changes ^KQ
Print a file... ^KPP
Merge print a file... ^KPM
Change drive/directory... ^KL
Copy a file... ^KO
Delete a file... ^KJ
Rename a file... ^KE
outlining pricing to our customers and a report on how we can
best market our new product line.
cc: F. Arouet
S. Clemens
R. Penniman
E. Souse

Fig. 3.21.

The pull-down File menu from the editing screen.

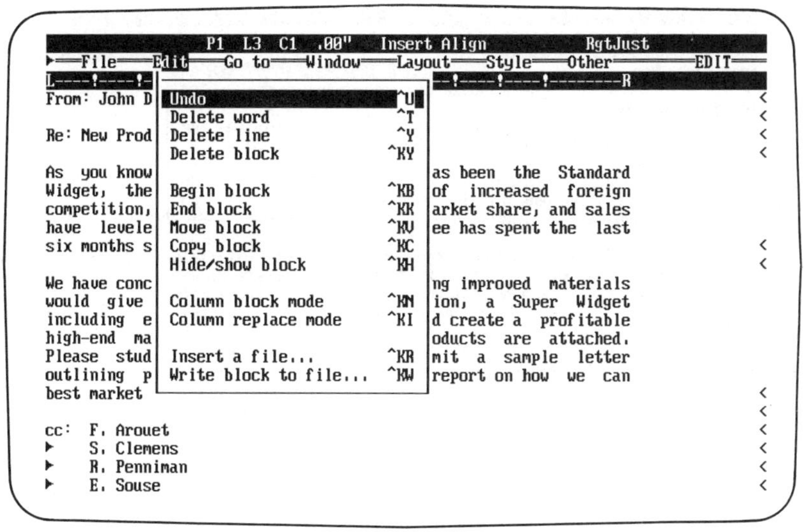
P1 L3 C1 .00" Insert Align RgtJust
File Edit Go to Window Layout Style Other EDIT
Undo ^U
Delete word ^T
Delete line ^Y
Delete block ^KY
Begin block ^KB
End block ^KK
Move block ^KV
Copy block ^KC
Hide/show block ^KH
Column block mode ^KN
Column replace mode ^KI
Insert a file... ^KR
Write block to file... ^KW
cc: F. Arouet
S. Clemens
R. Penniman
E. Souse

Fig. 3.22.

The pull-down Edit menu from the editing screen.

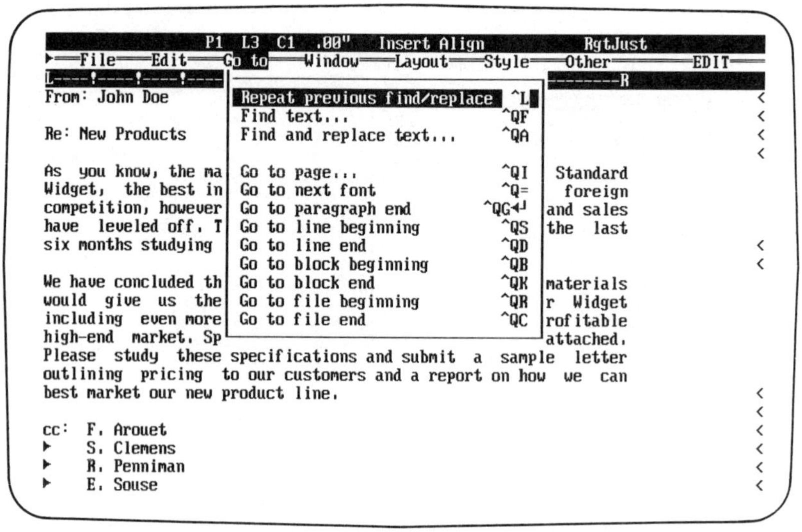
P1 L3 C1 .00" Insert Align RgtJust
File Edit Go to Window Layout Style Other EDIT
From: John Doe
Re: New Products
Repeat previous find/replace ^L
Find text... ^QF
Find and replace text... ^QA
Go to page... ^QI
Go to next font ^Q=
Go to paragraph end ^QG
Go to line beginning ^QS
Go to line end ^QD
Go to block beginning ^QB
Go to block end ^QK
Go to file beginning ^QR
Go to file end ^QC
Please study these specifications and submit a sample letter
outlining pricing to our customers and a report on how we can
best market our new product line.
cc: F. Arouet
S. Clemens
R. Penniman
E. Souse

Fig. 3.23.

The pull-down Go To menu from the editing screen.

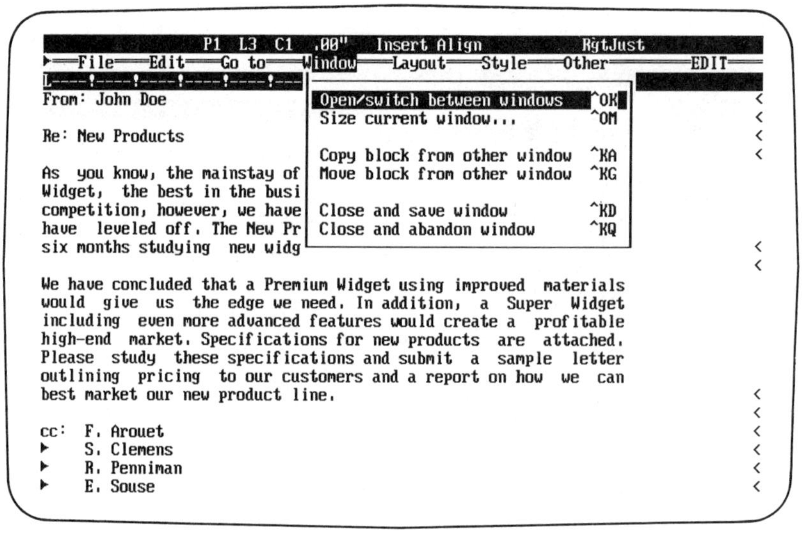
P1 L3 C1 .00" Insert Align RgtJust
File Edit Go to Window Layout Style Other EDIT
From: John Doe
Re: New Products
Open/switch between windows ^OK
Size current window... ^OM
Copy block from other window ^KA
Move block from other window ^KG
Close and save window ^KD
Close and abandon window ^KQ
We have concluded that a Premium Widget using improved materials
would give us the edge we need. In addition, a Super Widget
including even more advanced features would create a profitable
high-end market. Specifications for new products are attached.
Please study these specifications and submit a sample letter
outlining pricing to our customers and a report on how we can
best market our new product line.
cc: F. Arouet
S. Clemens
R. Penniman
E. Souse

Fig. 3.24.

The pull-down Window menu from the editing screen.

Pressing Alt-L displays the Layout menu (see fig. 3.25). The 14 Layout commands control the appearance of a document on-screen and when printed. These text enhancements are explained in Chapters 6 and 7.

Pressing Alt-S pulls down the Style menu (see fig. 3.26). This menu has eight commands for print style variations such as boldface, underline, and italic. For more information about these functions, see Chapters 4 and 7.

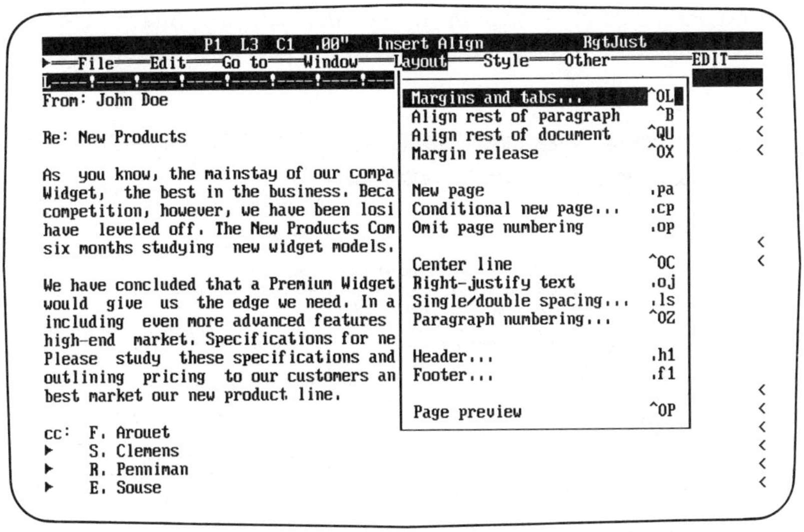
P1 L3 C1 .00" Insert Align RgtJust
File Edit Go to Window Layout Style Other EDIT
From: John Doe
Re: New Products
As you know, the mainstay of our compa
Widget, the best in the business. Beca
competition, however, we have been losi
have leveled off. The New Products Com
six months studying new widget models.
We have concluded that a Premium Widget
would give us the edge we need. In a
including even more advanced features
high-end market. Specifications for ne
Please study these specifications and
outlining pricing to our customers an
best market our new product line.
cc: F. Arouet
S. Clemens
R. Penniman
E. Souse
Margins and tabs... ^OL
Align rest of paragraph ^B
Align rest of document ^QU
Margin release ^OX
New page .pa
Conditional new page... .cp
Omit page numbering .op
Center line ^OC
Right-justify text .oj
Single/double spacing... .ls
Paragraph numbering... ^OZ
Header... .h1
Footer... .f1
Page preview ^OP

Fig. 3.25. *The pull-down Layout menu from the editing screen.*

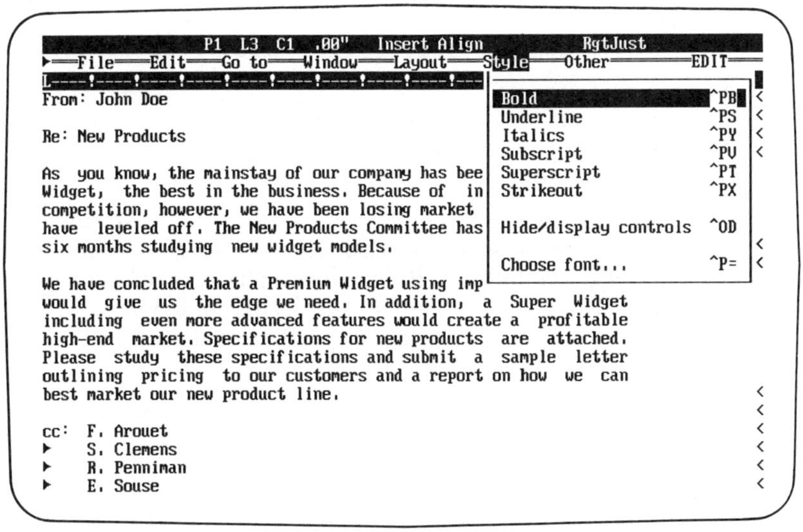
P1 L3 C1 .00" Insert Align RgtJust
File Edit Go to Window Layout Style Other EDIT
From: John Doe
Re: New Products
As you know, the mainstay of our company has bee
Widget, the best in the business. Because of in
competition, however, we have been losing market
have leveled off. The New Products Committee has
six months studying new widget models.
We have concluded that a Premium Widget using imp
would give us the edge we need. In addition, a Super Widget
including even more advanced features would create a profitable
high-end market. Specifications for new products are attached.
Please study these specifications and submit a sample letter
outlining pricing to our customers and a report on how we can
best market our new product line.
cc: F. Arouet
S. Clemens
R. Penniman
E. Souse
Bold ^PB
Underline ^PS
Italics ^PY
Subscript ^PV
Superscript ^PT
Strikeout ^PX
Hide/display controls ^OD
Choose font... ^P=

Fig. 3.26. *The pull-down Style menu from the editing screen.*

Selecting Alt-O produces the Other menu (see fig. 3.27). Among its 11 miscellaneous commands are those for the spelling checker, thesaurus, and on-screen calculator—functions examined in Chapters 6, 9, and 10.

Press the Esc key to eliminate any pull-down menus after you have viewed them.

You can issue a command listed on a pull-down menu by moving the highlight to the desired line, using the up- or down-arrow keys, and then pressing Enter. The point-and-shoot method for selecting a command often takes more keystrokes than the corresponding letter commands invoked manually. For this reason, letter commands are emphasized throughout this book.

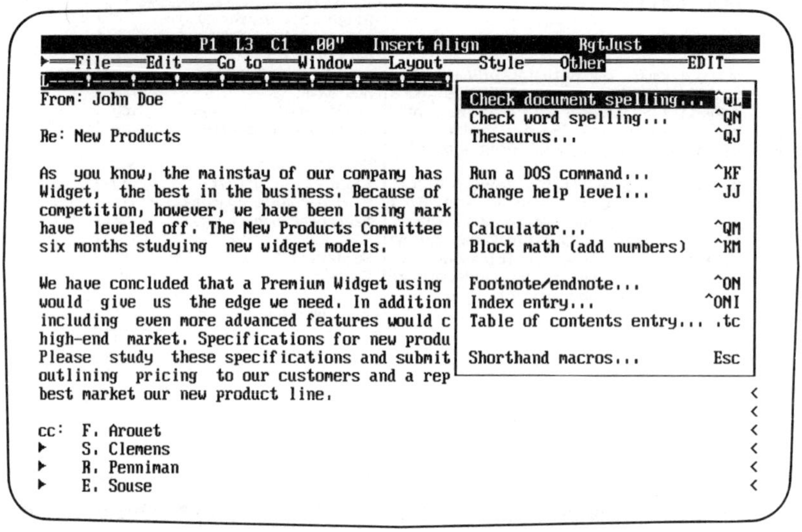
P1 L3 C1 .00" Insert Align RgtJust
File Edit Go to Window Layout Style Other EDIT
From: John Doe
Re: New Products
As you know, the mainstay of our company has
Widget, the best in the business. Because of
competition, however, we have been losing mark
have leveled off. The New Products Committee
six months studying new widget models.
We have concluded that a Premium Widget using
would give us the edge we need. In addition
including even more advanced features would c
high-end market. Specifications for new produ
Please study these specifications and submit
outlining pricing to our customers and a rep
best market our new product line.
cc: F. Arouet
S. Clemens
R. Penniman
E. Souse
Check document spelling... ^QL
Check word spelling... ^QN
Thesaurus... ^QJ
Run a DOS command... ^KF
Change help level... ^JJ
Calculator... ^QM
Block math (add numbers) ^KM
Footnote/endnote... ^ON
Index entry... ^ONI
Table of contents entry... .tc
Shorthand macros... Esc

Fig. 3.27.
The pull-down Other menu from the editing screen.

The Edit Menu

When WordStar is set at help level 3, the editing screen shows the classic Edit Menu (see fig. 3.18). The Edit Menu in WordStar Release 5 is essentially unchanged from the previous version. This boxed listing of 21 essential single-keystroke commands includes 17 often used functions not displayed in any of the pull-down menus. Also on the Edit Menu are the commands for bringing up help menus for more complex commands.

Remember that the caret symbol (^) in the menu represents the Ctrl key. Pressing Ctrl and holding it down while pressing the accompanying letter key invokes the listed command. The commands are arranged by function for easy reference: cursor, scroll, delete, other, and menus.

The Ruler Line

At every help level, WordStar's editing screen displays a line of hyphens and exclamation points—the *ruler line*. The ruler line provides essential information on how your text will be positioned or "formatted." The ruler line looks like this:

L----!----!----!----!----!----!----!----!----!----!--------R

The L shows the left margin setting, and the R shows the right margin setting. Each exclamation point (!) represents a tab setting. The hyphens (-) between the exclamation points fill out the ruler line; each hyphen represents a character space. Chapter 4 shows you how to modify margin settings for special formatting needs. You also can create new ruler lines on the fly while you compose a document, as explained in Chapter 5. For more lasting modifications to the ruler line, including its elimination from the screen, you can use the WSCHANGE program (see Chapter 11).

One of the most visible changes in WordStar Release 5 is the appearance of a "phantom" cursor, a highlighted cursor on the ruler line, moving parallel with the active cursor in the text area below it.

The Cursor

In the text area under the ruler line is a flashing line or rectangle on a blank expanse of screen. This flashing *cursor* indicates where your text will be entered. As you type, a character is entered at the cursor position, and the cursor advances to the next space.

The cursor also can move within your text to places where you want to make editing changes. The cursor cannot, however, advance beyond the point where you have entered text (or blank spaces). While you work on a document, the cursor is a guidepost for finding your way around. When in doubt, look for the flashing cursor.

In Release 5, WordStar users for the first time can change the shape of the cursor for better visibility. You can change the cursor's shape and alter the cursor's speed when moving by using the WSCHANGE program, as explained in Chapter 11.

The Function Key Labels

At help levels 3, 2, or 1, the bottom of the editing screen displays two lines of WordStar function key labels and corresponding numbers. These function key assignments are unchanged from the previous version of the program. Release 5's function key label display looks like this:

```
 Display Center ChkRest ChkWord Del Blk HideBlk MoveBlk CopyBlk Beg Blk1End Blk
1Help   2Undo  3Undrlin4Bold   5DelLine6DelWord7Align  8Ruler  9Save & 0Done
```

The numbers correspond to the 10 function keys on the left side (or the top edge) of the computer keyboard. The keys are labeled F1 through F10. (The IBM Enhanced Keyboard includes F11 and F12 keys, but WordStar doesn't address these keys.) When you press any single function key, you issue the applicable command listed on the bottom line. Pressing F1, for example, issues a Help command.

When you press and hold down the Shift key while you next press a function key, the combination invokes the applicable command shown on the upper line. By pressing a function key in combination with the Ctrl or Alt key, you can issue another 20 commands. The function keys used alone and in combination with the Shift, Ctrl, and Alt keys give you a total of 40 distinct commands. These commands are explained throughout the text as they are used in creating documents.

Note: If you prefer two more lines of document text on-screen, you can turn off the function key label display with the WSCHANGE program (see Chapter 11).

Typing a Document

WordStar was among the first programs to combine two essential word processing functions on-screen: text entry and formatting. Some of the latest and hottest word processing programs still don't offer this feature. In addition to showing what you type, WordStar indicates how the printed text will look—thanks to WordStar's on-screen formatting features, a few of which are summarized in this chapter.

WordStar is sometimes described as a WYSIWYG (what you see is what you get) word processor. With a few exceptions, noted in later chapters, WordStar prints what you see on its editing screen. This capability makes WordStar well suited for producing professional-looking copy.

Control Commands

You press the Ctrl key in combination with a letter key to issue most WordStar commands for editing a document. Although complex functions can require that you press the Ctrl key in combination with several other letters, most basic WordStar commands require that you press the Ctrl key and a single other letter.

The letter keys used in these Ctrl-single-letter commands are shown in figure 3.28. Notice that on the keyboard, the keys are grouped by function to make them easy to locate and use. Refer to this figure often as you learn WordStar's basic functions. The logic behind the placement of Ctrl-key assignments will help you learn these more quickly.

Strategically placed on the left-hand keyboard position are all the cursor- and screen-movement commands, including the S-E-D-X diamond of Ctrl-letter commands that work similarly to the arrow keys.

In the middle, between both hands' home positions, are the delete, insert, and realign commands.

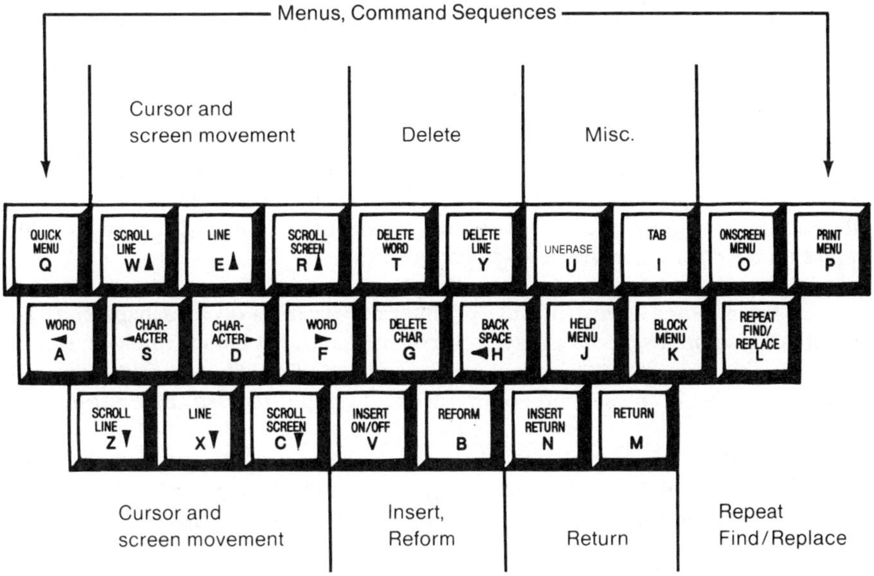
Menus, Command Sequences
Cursor and screen movement
Delete
Misc.
QUICK MENU Q
SCROLL LINE W
LINE E
SCROLL SCREEN R
DELETE WORD T
DELETE LINE Y
UNERASE U
TAB I
ONSCREEN MENU O
PRINT MENU P
WORD A
CHAR-ACTER S
CHAR-ACTER D
WORD F
DELETE CHAR G
BACK SPACE H
HELP MENU J
BLOCK MENU K
REPEAT FIND/ REPLACE L
SCROLL LINE Z
LINE X
SCROLL SCREEN C
INSERT ON/OFF V
REFORM B
INSERT RETURN N
RETURN M
Cursor and screen movement
Insert, Reform
Return
Repeat Find/Replace

Fig. 3.28. *WordStar's Ctrl-single-letter commands (courtesy MicroPro International).*

On the right-hand keyboard position are miscellaneous commands for unerase, carriage return, and other menus (at help levels 3 and 2).

Although the control-letter commands are optional with pull-down menus, using these combinations requires fewer keystrokes and less effort than using the point-and-shoot method of issuing commands. This more efficient method, therefore, is emphasized in this book.

The Enter Key

On an electric typewriter, when you finish entering text on a line and want to continue to the beginning of the next line, you press the Return key. The Enter (or Return) key on your computer's keyboard performs the same function. Press Enter to end a line or a paragraph or to add a blank line to your screen. This procedure produces a carriage return. (***Note:*** Because WordStar has a word wrap feature, you don't have to press the Enter key at the end of every line; see the "Word Wrap" section in this chapter.)

Pressing Enter while you are working on a WordStar document produces three actions:

1. A less-than symbol (<), called a *flag character*, appears at the right of the screen to indicate that Enter has been pressed.

2. The cursor jumps to the beginning of the next line.

3. The status line at the top of the screen shows the cursor in column 1 of the new line.

These actions are WordStar's equivalent of a simple carriage return on an electric typewriter.

WordStar has a Ctrl-letter command combination, not on any menu, that produces the same effect as pressing Enter. Pressing ^M also places a carriage return symbol in the rightmost or *flag column* on-screen, moves the cursor to the next line, and displays on the status line the new cursor position.

WordStar has another command that produces a variation on pressing Enter. This alternate command inserts a carriage return and leaves the cursor in place, moving any text to the right of the cursor down to the next line. On the Edit Menu, this command is listed in the second column from the right, toward the bottom:

```
^N split the line
```

Pressing ^N splits the line at the cursor location and leaves the cursor at its original position. In contrast, when you use Enter or ^M, the cursor moves to the next line.

Word Wrap

On a typewriter, you press a carriage return at the end of each line. In a WordStar document, however, you do not need to press Enter after every line of text. In fact, WordStar is set to fit your text between margins automatically as you type.

During text entry with WordStar, when the cursor goes beyond the right margin, any word that will not fit at the end of the line is automatically moved to the beginning of the next line. This feature is known as *word wrap*. As fast as you type, WordStar wraps your words back and forth across the screen like a continuous ribbon of text.

When a line is wrapped by WordStar, the flag column at the far right remains empty, without the symbol for a carriage return. The ribbon of text has been folded in what is called a soft carriage return. When text formatting is changed, WordStar's word wrap feature can reposition words onto other lines that end in soft carriage returns.

By contrast, when you press Enter, ^M, or ^N, you insert a hard carriage return that fixes the words of a line in place. Only after you remove the flag character (<) indicating a hard carriage return can the word at the end of a line be relocated by word wrap. (Removing a hard carriage return is explained later in this chapter.)

Auto-Align

An appreciated new feature, WordStar Release 5 automatically realigns text after editing has altered line lengths. This auto-align feature was commonplace in other word processors while WordStar users had to keep bashing away at a control command to reformat text between margins every time a line was edited.

Auto-align is essentially a retroactive word wrap, tidying up the screen after you disrupt the formatting of your document. Adding clarity and legibility to the editing process, auto-align is essential to efficient word processing.

WordStar's auto-align feature is especially convenient; proportional fonts' line and page breaks are fully supported. You can adjust the pause between a halt in typing and the realignment of text by using WSCHANGE (see Chapter 11).

Because auto-align can disrupt formatting of tables, scripts, and so on, you can turn off this feature by typing *^oa*. While auto-align is off, you still can invoke alignment with the ^B command (covered later in this chapter). Pressing ^OA again turns auto-align back on.

Justification

Text typed with an unmodified copy of WordStar is set to align evenly along the right margin. This feature is known as *right-justification*. To fit text into this format, WordStar varies spaces between words and places the ends of lines flush right. Typesetters do the same thing to justify text in books.

Justification can be useful for typeset-like laser printing. More often, however, justification is distracting for simple documents such as memos and correspondence. Chapter 4 shows how to turn off justification when you start a work session. You can turn off justification permanently with the WSCHANGE program, as explained in Chapter 11.

Scrolling

The movement of text upward or downward on the WordStar document screen is called *scrolling*. Think of WordStar text as being typed on a continuous roll of paper, with only a portion of the paper showing at any time. Your computerized document is the high-tech equivalent of the parchment scrolls used in antiquity. When the text you create exceeds the borders of the WordStar screen, a portion scrolls off the screen, but the text remains in your computer's memory. On the Edit Menu, WordStar offers the following commands for scrolling:

```
    SCROLL
^W  up
^Z  down
^R  screen up
^C  screen
    down
```

In addition to the commands for scrolling on the Edit Menu, WordStar has the following scrolling commands: Ctrl-PgUp, Ctrl-PgDn, PgUp, and PgDn. Table 3.7 lists WordStar's commands for scrolling, along with descriptions of their functions. For additional material about scrolling, see Chapter 5.

Table 3.7
Commands for Scrolling

Command	*Function*
^W or Ctrl-PgUp	Scrolls up one line
^Z or Ctrl-PgDn	Scrolls down one line
^R or PgUp	Scrolls up one screen
^C or PgDn	Scrolls down one screen

Editing a Document

Any text entered in a document can be modified easily in WordStar. Editing a document requires two kinds of WordStar commands: those for changing cursor location (to go to text you want to change) and those for erasing text. These functions are indispensable for any word processing application. In this section, you will learn the simple commands for cursor movement and text erasure on the Edit Menu. Chapter 5 discusses the full gamut of WordStar editing commands.

Moving the Cursor

The principal cursor-movement commands that follow are listed in the left column of the Edit Menu. In addition to moving the cursor during editing, these commands move the cursor in text you type at a prompt.

```
    CURSOR
^E  up
^X  down
^S  left
^D  right
```

```
^A word left
^F word right
```

The functions of each of these cursor-movement commands are described in table 3.8.

Table 3.8
Cursor-Movement Commands

Command	*Function*
^S or left-arrow	Moves the cursor one character to the left
^D or right-arrow	Moves the cursor one character to the right
^A or ^left-arrow	Moves the cursor to the first character of the word to the left
^F or ^right-arrow	Moves the cursor to the first character of the word to the right
^E or up-arrow	Moves the cursor one line up; moves the cursor back from the file directory to the Opening Menu
^X or down-arrow	Moves the cursor one line down; moves the cursor to the file directory from the Opening Menu

Look at the keyboard. Notice that the Ctrl-letter combinations for cursor commands are symmetrically grouped (see fig. 3.29). Cursor-movement commands are clustered in a logical manner around a "diamond" consisting of the S, E, D, and X keys. Each of these keys, respectively, corresponds to moving the cursor left, up, right, and down, like the points on a compass. The commands using the A and F keys flank the S-E-D-X diamond. These commands move the cursor a word at a time.

WordStar originated the S-E-D-X diamond as an alternative to arrow keys back when arrow keys were not yet standard on personal computer keyboards. Because of WordStar's popularity, the S-E-D-X diamond pattern has been used in many compatible programs.

On the IBM PC, AT, and Enhanced Keyboards, the arrow keys also move the cursor. The left-, up-, right-, and down-arrows provide the same cursor movement as the S-E-D-X diamond but without the use of the Ctrl key. Beginners may prefer using the arrow keys with their clearly indicated functions. As you become expert with WordStar, however, you probably will use the Ctrl commands for cursor movement, because these keys can be pressed while you keep your fingers within the main portion of the keyboard.

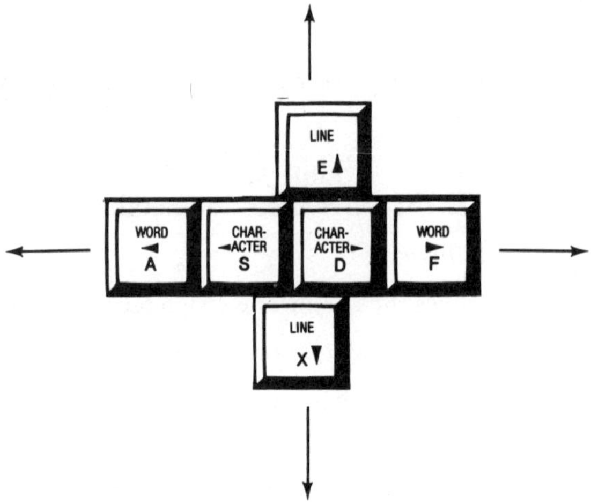
LINE
E
WORD
A
CHAR-
ACTER
S
CHAR-
ACTER
D
WORD
F
LINE
X

Fig. 3.29. WordStar's principal cursor-movement commands (courtesy MicroPro International).

An additional pair of arrow-key commands is available. Pressing Ctrl along with the left- or right-arrow key is the equivalent of pressing ^A or ^F, respectively. These Ctrl-arrow key commands move the cursor to the beginning of the next word left or right.

Deleting Text

Deleting desired amounts of text is the role of a word processor's delete functions. WordStar's commands for deleting text are displayed in the third column of the Edit Menu:

```
     DELETE
^G   char
^T   word
^Y   line
Del  char
^U   undo
```

At help level 4, the pull-down Edit menu (displayed when you press Alt-E from the editing screen) includes these three commands at the top of the menu:

```
Undo            ^U
Delete word     ^T
Delete line     ^Y
```

The delete commands, listed in table 3.9, eliminate a character, word, or line at a time. You use ^G to delete the character at the cursor. To delete a word or portion of a word from the cursor to the right, you use ^T. ^Y deletes the entire line where the cursor is located.

Table 3.9
Text Erasure Commands

Command	*Function*
^G or Del or Ctrl-Backspace	Erases one character at the cursor
^H or Backspace	Erases one character to the left
^T or F6	Erases one word to the right
^Y or F5	Erases one line at the cursor; erases answer to a prompt
^U or F2	Restores the last erasure; cancels an operation

Single character deletion can be invoked with any of five different commands, including ^H, which is not listed on the Edit menu, and the Backspace key; either command deletes a character to the left of the cursor. Pressing ^G, Ctrl-Backspace, or the Del key erases the character at the cursor. Together these commands add flexibility to editing with WordStar.

The function key assignments in WordStar Release 5 (see the section *The Function Key Labels*) include two basic erase commands. Pressing the F5 function key, labeled `5DelLine` at the bottom of the screen, erases an entire line, as does ^Y. Pressing F6 (`6DelWord`) removes the word to the right of the cursor, as does ^T.

To avoid moving your hand away from the home keys on the keyboard when deleting text, you can try using only the four letter-keys to the right of the cursor-movement diamond: G, H, T, or Y. These four main erase commands, at the center of the keyboard, delete a character at or to the left of the cursor and erase a word or a line. The commands are arranged in a square (see fig. 3.30). Keep in mind that the lower pair of keys (^G and ^H) erases the least amount of text (deletion of a single character), and the higher pair of keys (^T and ^Y) erases greater amounts of text (deletion of a word or line, respectively).

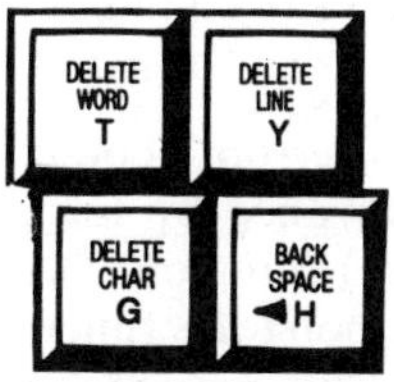
DELETE
WORD
T
DELETE
LINE
Y
DELETE
CHAR
G
BACK
SPACE
◄H

Fig. 3.30.
WordStar's principal delete commands (courtesy MicroPro International).

Note that any letter, number, or punctuation mark can be erased from the text area on-screen. For example, a flag character (<) that indicates a hard carriage return can be deleted like any character at the end of a line. With the cursor to the left of the flag character and between it and any preceding text, press ^G, Del, ^T, or ^Y (if you want to delete all the text on that line). From the line below the carriage return, press ^H or the Backspace key. In addition to erasing text on the editing screen, these commands operate on text typed in response to a WordStar prompt.

Warning: The proximity of ^T and ^Y can cause you to delete accidentally an entire line rather than a single word. The same hazard is posed by the proximity of the F6 and F5 keys. Fortunately, you can "unerase" such a mistaken use of ^Y or F5.

Unerasing Text

One of the most important functions in WordStar is the "unerase" command for restoring to the screen your single latest deletion, whether it is a word, line, or more. The command is listed at the top of the pull-down Edit menu at help level 4:

```
Undo            ^U
```

Also, listed at the bottom of the level 3 classic Edit Menu's DELETE column is the following command:

```
^U undo
```

This vital command is easy to remember. ^U undoes the latest erasure of a group of characters, whether you deleted them with ^T, ^Y, F6, or F5 (or other deletion commands that will be covered in Chapter 5). Single characters deleted with ^G, ^H, Del, or the Backspace key cannot be unerased in an unmodified copy of WordStar Release 5. (You can restore single character deletion, however, by modifying WordStar with the WSCHANGE program; see Chapter 11.)

You don't have to invoke ^U immediately after a deletion. At any time during editing, ^U restores whatever you deleted last and places the deleted material at the current cursor location. This feature allows you to use ^U as a quick way to move material around in a document: erase the material, move the cursor to the new location, and press ^U.

Unerase also has its own function key command—`2Undo`. Pressing the F2 function key is the single-key equivalent of ^U. You will be reaching often for F2.

Pressing ^U also serves as an "interrupt" command—used to stop or terminate a function that may have been invoked by mistake. When you are not editing a document, ^U retains this cancel function. Often, ^U will halt a WordStar command that is being executed. Among the functions the command stops are those that display a prompt. ^U also halts such operations as find and replace, hyphen help, spell checking, and printing. In many cases, a message on-screen notes that the function has been interrupted and that you must press Esc to continue.

Whenever you are faced with a problem caused by a mistakenly invoked WordStar command, press ^U or F2. This practice often will prevent further complications.

If the interrupt command does not work, try pressing the Esc key. As a last resort, if you cannot recover control of the keyboard and save your text to disk, you can press Ctrl-Alt-Del or turn off the power entirely and restart WordStar—with the loss of whatever work was added on-screen since the document was last saved.

Using Insert and Overtype

After you have deleted text in a document, you may need to make additions—to replace erasures or append new material. WordStar includes two ways of adding text: the insert and overtype modes.

The most common way to add text is simply to type the text at the cursor position. New characters are entered as the cursor travels across the line, pushing previous text to the right and then down to the next line as the line word-wraps. To add text in this way, WordStar's insert function must be on, as indicated by `Insert` on the status line at the top of the screen. As its name suggests, the insert mode allows you to include text within existing copy. The unmodified WordStar program always starts with insert mode turned on.

At certain times, on the other hand, deleting and then inserting text can be tedious. In such cases, you might want to put the cursor at the beginning of the text to be changed and—merging the delete and fill-in functions—type over existing copy. WordStar works this way in the overtype mode—replacing the character at the cursor with any character you type and advancing the cursor to the next character.

In the fourth column of the Edit Menu (at help level 3), the following listing is among the OTHER commands:

```
^V turn insert off
```

Press ^V and the `Insert` message disappears from the status line. Notice that the listing in the Edit Menu changes to the following:

```
^V turn insert on
```

Press ^V again and the `Insert` message reappears on the status line. Like many WordStar commands, ^V is a *toggle*. A toggle turns a feature on and off alternately as you press the keys. When WordStar's insert mode is off, the overtype feature is on, and vice-versa. Therefore, ^V acts as a toggle between insert and overtype modes.

The insert (Ins) key at the right of the keyboard produces the equivalent of a ^V command. You can use the Ins key as a convenient alternate toggle for insert and overtype modes.

New WordStar users may turn on overtype mode accidentally with ^V or Ins and then may be shocked to see that additions to a document are wiping out existing text. If this happens to you, simply check the status line to see whether insert mode is on. If not, press ^V or Ins.

Note: The Undo command (^U or F2) will not restore text that you have erased by overtyping.

Aligning a Paragraph

Although WordStar Release 5 features an auto-align function, existing text is not realigned if you change a document's margins, tabs, or other formatting settings. To refit such text into the on-screen margins, you must use the Align Paragraph command.

From the editing screen at help level 4, the pull-down Layout menu (displayed when you press Alt-L) includes the following command on its second line:

```
Align rest of paragraph        ^B
```

At help level 3 on the classic Edit Menu, the OTHER column shows this listing:

```
^B align paragraph
```

Pressing ^B reforms text from the cursor to the next carriage return, moving the cursor to the beginning of the next line. The ^B command is often invoked after editing operations that involve insertions; the command is located beside the ^V insert mode toggle (see fig. 3.31).

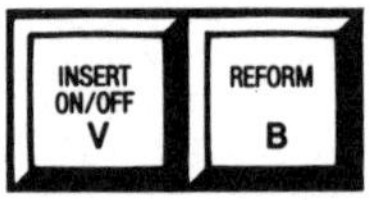
INSERT
ON/OFF
V
REFORM
B

Fig. 3.31.
WordStar's Reform and Insert command letter keys (courtesy MicroPro International).

Caution: Because of the proximity of ^B and ^V, pay close attention when you press either of these keys.

The Align command is assigned to one of the function keys, `7Align`. Pressing the F7 function key rewraps text from the cursor to the next hard carriage return and then, unlike ^B, automatically returns the cursor to its previous position. Not having to reposition the cursor after a realignment makes using F7 preferable to using ^B.

Saving a File

WordStar has several commands for saving a file onto disk so that you can retain a document after your computer's power is turned off. The save commands are essential commands during writing and editing, as well as when ending a word processing session. Frequent saving is a safeguard against losing work because of a power failure, an accidental erasure, or another misfortune. You should save your work at least once every 20 minutes during a word processing session with WordStar.

Warning: Never turn off your computer's power before saving the current document.

Release 5 introduces two improvements to saving a file with WordStar. You can save automatically at preselected time intervals on IBM AT-compatible computers by using the WSCHANGE program (see Chapter 11). WordStar also includes a command for saving a file under a new name—a useful option when you want to keep all the different versions or drafts of a document.

This chapter discusses four different save commands: saving and resuming, closing a document, closing a document and naming it, and closing a document and exiting from WordStar. Also included in the sections that follow is the command for quitting a document without saving. These varied commands are summarized in table 3.10.

Table 3.10
Save Commands

Command	*Function*
^KS or F9	Saves a file and returns the cursor to its position before the save
^KD or F10	Saves a file and displays the Opening screen
^KT	Saves a file under a new name and displays the Opening screen
^KQ	Quits a document without saving and displays the Opening screen
^KX	Saves a document; exits to DOS from WordStar

Saving a File and Resuming the Edit

While you work on a document, you will want to save its contents to disk periodically to make sure that none of your work is lost accidentally. The Save & Resume Edit command records the current version of a document to disk and allows you to resume a work session where you left off.

WordStar includes a simple function key command for invoking a save-and-resume operation: `9Save &`. Pressing F9 initiates a save to disk and a return to the editing screen.

As with other major functions, WordStar also provides a Ctrl-letter command for saving a file and resuming editing. But unlike almost all the other commands in this chapter, the save commands consist of Ctrl-letter sequences of multiple keystrokes.

To initiate a Ctrl-letter command that involves more than one letter key, you press the Ctrl key and hold it down while you press the first letter key; then you release those keys and press the following letter key alone.

At help level 4, WordStar's pull-down File menu (invoked when you press Alt-F from the editing screen) shows this as its topmost listing:

```
Save file, resume editing     ^KS
```

At help levels 3 and 2, the classic Block & Save Menu (displayed from the Edit Menu when you press ^K) includes the following listing under the SAVE commands at the left of the menu:

```
S save & resume
```

Don't forget that this S follows the ^K you already have pressed. Therefore, the complete sequence for saving a document while still editing is ^KS.

When you press ^KS or F9, the menu at the top of the screen is blanked out and replaced by a box with this word:

```
Saving...
```

Depending on the size of your document, saving to disk may be instantaneous or may take several seconds. After saving is complete, the screen displays the text you were editing with the cursor positioned as it was before you issued the save command.

Invoking ^KS saves the file you are editing under its current name, as noted in the upper left corner of the editing screen. If the file is not named (if it was opened with the Speed Write command), after pressing ^KS, you are prompted for a name by which the file should be saved. After typing an acceptable file name and pressing Enter, the save-and-resume function is completed.

Saving a File When Editing Is Complete

Once you have completed work on a WordStar document, you must close the file and save it to disk before you can proceed with other activities or turn off the computer. Ending a work session by saving a document to disk and returning to the Opening Menu is as basic as flipping a file folder closed.

In Release 5, WordStar users have a choice of closing and saving a document under its current name or closing and saving a document under a new name. The most frequently invoked function is the former—a classic save-when-done operation.

5

The simplest way you can invoke the save-when-done operation is with the single keystroke available with one of the the function key commands. The listing `0Done` at the bottom of the screen (at help level 3, 2, or 1) means that pressing the F10 function key (at any help level) closes a document when you have finished editing.

When at help level 4, WordStar's pull-down File menu (displayed when you press Alt-F from the editing screen) includes the following command on the third line from the top:

```
Save file, go to Opening screen    ^KD
```

With WordStar set at help level 3 or 2, the classic Block & Save Menu (invoked from the Edit Menu when you press ^K) lists this at the top of the SAVE commands at the left side of the menu:

```
D save
```

Because the D follows the ^K that you already have pressed, the full sequence for saving and closing a document file when you are done editing is ^KD.

Pressing ^KD saves the file you have finished editing under the name noted in the status line. If the file was opened with the Speed Write command and has no current name, the Save As dialog box prompts you for a name by which the file should be saved. Typing an acceptable file name and pressing Enter completes the save operation.

WordStar saves the edited document under its current name, while the previous version of this file on disk is renamed with a BAK extension as a backup file. Any previous backup file under that name is erased. After you execute the save-when-done command, WordStar's Opening display is back on-screen.

Saving and Naming a File

Closing a WordStar document and saving it under another name is a convenient feature for anyone concerned with keeping different document versions or drafts.

This save-as function is also ideal for using boilerplate files to generate individualized contracts, reports, or letters. By closing the changed file and saving it on disk along with the original version under another name, you can keep copies of all your documents.

With Release 5, WordStar users finally can open a document under one name and then change their minds and rename the document while saving to disk (without marking off the entire document as a block and saving it). Because a new file can be preceded by a letter and colon designating a different disk, this command is helpful when the logged disk is full and you want to save the edited document to another disk.

At help level 4, WordStar's pull-down File menu shows this command on the second line:

```
Save and name file        ^KT
```

At WordStar's help level 3 or 2, the classic Block & Save Menu includes the following command beside the Save command:

```
T save as
```

With ^K already pressed, the full sequence for saving and naming a document file is ^KT.

Pressing ^KT displays the Save As dialog box. This prompt displays an empty line where you type a file name by which the document should be saved and then press Enter. After completing the save-as operation, WordStar's Opening screen is displayed with both the original file name and the new file name on the disk directory.

Quitting a File without Saving

You sometimes will want to exit a document without saving and then return to the Opening display. For instance, you might want to open a document merely to look at its contents and not make any changes. Or you may open a document by mistake and want to close it quickly. At times, you might make a major mistake in revising a document; exiting without saving and then starting over may be the wisest choice in that case. The Quit command can prevent much frustration.

While at help level 4, the WordStar pull-down File menu displays this command on its fifth line:

```
Abandon changes      ^KQ
```

If set to help level 3, WordStar displays the classic Block & Save Menu, which has the following command on its fourth line:

```
Q abandon changes
```

When you press ^KQ and no changes have been made in your file, a box prompt will note that WordStar is abandoning the current file.

If you have made any changes since opening the document file or last saving it, a different message appears:

```
Changes have been made. Abandon anyway (Y/N)?
```

If you are certain that nothing you have changed in the document since you last saved is worth saving, press Y (for Yes). If you want to salvage part or all of your file, press N. You can save any part of the document by marking off the desired block with ^KB and ^KK and invoking the ^KW command to save the block to disk (for more on block saves, see Chapter 5).

Printing a Document

After you have saved a document to disk, you can initiate printing with WordStar in several ways. The method described here is the simplest. For other procedures, see Chapters 4, 7, and 8.

You invoke printing with an often-used command available from WordStar's Opening display.

At help level 4 with WordStar Release 5's pull-down menus, pressing F at the Opening screen displays the File menu, which shows the following command on the fourth line:

```
Print a file...      P
```

At WordStar help levels 3 through 0, the classic Opening Menu includes the following command in the menu's left column, on the third line:

```
P print a file
```

After you press F and then P or just P from the Opening screen, WordStar displays the Print dialog box. In this chapter, the only option you need to consider is the file name option near the top of the screen. The listed file name is that of the last document saved or printed during a word processing session; if no save or print operations have been invoked yet, the word `(none)` is shown. If you need to designate a different file name to be printed, you can type another name or point to the name in the directory below the Print box by using the arrow keys and then press Enter.

With WordStar Release 5, to accept the default choices and start printing immediately, you can press F10. Users of previous versions should note that pressing the Esc key, which used to accept defaults and start printing, now cancels the print operation. (Changing printing options is covered in Chapter 7.)

While WordStar is printing your file, the screen shows the Opening display. As the printer works, you can proceed with other WordStar tasks—opening another file for editing, if you want.

If you are finished using WordStar, you are ready to exit from the program. The procedure is described in the next section.

Exiting from WordStar

The WordStar program can be terminated while you keep the computer running so that you can load another program. Exiting from WordStar returns the computer screen to the DOS prompt—from which you can run DOS file commands or start another program by typing its file name.

5 With the pull-down menus at help level 4, pressing F from the Opening screen displays the File menu. At the bottom of this menu is the following listing:

```
Exit WordStar        X
```

From the pull-down Opening screen, pressing F and then X invokes the Exit command. Because of the layout of pull-down menus, an alternative way of invoking the exit function is available. Just press Enter at the Opening display, followed by X.

With the classic menus at help level 3 or less, the command for stopping WordStar is listed in the Opening Menu's left column, one line from the bottom:

```
X exit WordStar
```

Pressing X from the Opening Menu is sufficient to end the program and bring up the DOS prompt.

You don't have to be at the Opening display to exit from WordStar to DOS. When you have completed a work session on a document and want to leave WordStar directly, you can save the file on disk and exit to DOS by using one command. The command for saving a file and exiting from WordStar is issued when you use a keystroke sequence beginning with ^K.

When at help level 4, WordStar's pull-down File menu shows this command on the fourth line:

```
Save file, exit WordStar      ^KX
```

When at help level 3 or 2, the classic Block & Save Menu includes the following command on the third line of the SAVE column:

```
X save & exit
```

Because you already have pressed ^K, the full command—which can be issued from anywhere in a document—is ^KX.

Invoking ^KX is similar to saving a file with ^KD or ^KT and then pressing X at the Opening Menu. However, after a file has been saved with ^KX, the display bypasses the Opening Menu and goes directly to the DOS prompt.

Making Duplicate Copies of Files

Before you leave the computer, take a minute to do one more important task: duplicate your document files. The importance of making duplicate copies cannot be stressed enough to beginning and veteran users alike. WordStar always saves as a backup on the same disk the previous version of a file that has been edited, but this backup feature is not enough. (WordStar's classic file backup for saving documents is discussed in Chapter 5.)

After you lose a crucial document because of a damaged or misplaced disk, you surely will realize the importance of periodically making extra backups. So why wait for your first disaster? Routinely duplicating copies of document files after a word processing session will save you much frustration.

To copy your new document file, use the steps outlined in Chapter 2 for copying files onto a disk. Then store your disk in a safe place.

Part II

Intermediate WordStar

Part I of this book is meant to help beginners and former WordStar users get started with WordStar Release 5. The functions explained in Part I are essential for word processing, but they represent less than a quarter of WordStar's commands. Once you feel comfortable with the commands introduced in Chapters 1 and 3, you can begin mastering more powerful functions.

The middle section of this book covers the majority of built-in WordStar commands: those that increase your efficiency in starting the program and in entering, editing, formatting, and printing text. The functions explained in Part II can be essential in business, professional, and personal applications, including desktop publishing-style presentation of documents.

You can read Part II in sequence or consult it about features you need to use immediately. WordStar beginners and veterans alike can benefit from learning WordStar Release 5's improved printer control, new annotating functions, and the long-awaited window feature for editing two files at the same time. All regular users of WordStar should follow the steps in Chapter 4 for creating a DOS batch file to start the program automatically at a flick of the computer's power switch.

The four chapters of Part II detail the following intermediate-level topics:

- Chapter 4 covers functions for text entry, including variations on starting WordStar, file handling from the opening display, on-screen text formatting, and print enhancements. Step-by-step creation of an AUTOEXEC.BAT file is included.
- Chapter 5 explains file operations from the editing screen, block commands, window functions, quick cursor movement, find-and-replace, and hyphen-help. These features permit efficient editing of a document.
- Chapter 6 explores added formatting features, including column operations, ruler line changes, dot commands for page design, and WordStar Release 5's new note options. Also reviewed here are WordStar's math and sort functions.

- Chapter 7 presents all of WordStar Release 5's printing options, including new prompts, on-screen proportional spacing, font and color control, and easy selection of alternate printers. Greater laser printer control is one of the benefits.

Within the pages of Part II are numerous tips, warnings, and how-to's for adding to WordStar's usefulness. Sooner or later, you will need much of the information in this section.

4

Writing with WordStar

Chapter 3 covered enough commands for you to start using WordStar for simple word processing tasks. This chapter explains the remaining commands for entering text and commands for the simple formatting of text. You also learn to improve WordStar's performance during text entry by changing several initial program settings.

About two dozen commands are explained in this chapter. With these, you will be able to start WordStar more easily; handle files at the Opening Menu; and—during text entry—set margins, reset tabs, center text, and use other simple formatting and print-enhancement features. After you learn these commands, you will be able to create professional-looking documents.

Major topics covered in this chapter include the following:

- Options for starting WordStar
- Copying, deleting, and renaming files from the Opening display
- Setting on-screen margins, line spacing, and tabs
- Text underlining, boldface, subscript, and superscript

Veteran users of WordStar will find most of the functions discussed in these pages unchanged in Release 5. Among the changes in Release 5, however, are the new Margins & Tabs screen, tab enhancements, automatic paragraph numbering, pull-down menus, and minor changes to WordStar's classic menus.

Regardless of your expertise, you should take the time to make WordStar self-starting. Surprisingly, many otherwise expert computer users still don't take advantage of this handy shortcut. If your computer's primary application is word processing, having WordStar automatically appear on the screen after you flip on the power switch goes beyond mere convenience. By following the Quick Start instructions for creating a batch file, you can save time and effort every time you start your computer.

To illustrate the functions in this chapter, examples are provided in two sample documents: a brief pricing letter and a marketing report, both of which you can enter on your computer for practice. Even if you do not type these samples, study these examples so that you can put these operations to good use in your own word processing applications.

Chapter 5 covers WordStar's remaining editing commands to further enhance your documents. Advanced formatting features are explained in Chapter 6.

Starting WordStar

Chapter 3 showed you the easiest way to start WordStar, but the easiest may not be the best. Among other drawbacks, this method often requires extra keystrokes to change the logged disk drive or directory after the Opening Menu is displayed. By completing the proper steps, you can make typing *ws* to start WordStar superfluous, too.

The alternative start-up procedures discussed in this chapter will let you bring up WordStar with the correct logged drive, bypass the opening screens, and go directly into editing or printing a document, or have WordStar load itself automatically as soon as the power goes on. Use the method that proves to be best suited to your word processing needs and working habits.

Table 4.1 summarizes the commands for starting WordStar from the DOS prompt. Each of the commands described in the table is discussed in the sections that follow.

Table 4.1
Commands for Starting WordStar from the DOS Prompt

Command	*Function*
B: A:WS	Starts WordStar on a two floppy disk system with B as the logged drive
CD \WS5\DOC C:\WS5\WS	Starts WordStar on a hard disk system with DOC as the logged directory
WS FILENAME	Starts WordStar and opens a file
WS FILENAME /N	Starts WordStar and opens a nondocument file
WS FILENAME /D	Starts WordStar and opens a document file if default file mode is nondocument
WS /S	Starts WordStar and opens a Speed Write file
WS FILENAME /P	Starts WordStar and prints file
WS FILENAME /M	Starts WordStar and merge prints file

Table 4.1—*Continued*

Command	*Function*
WS FILENAME /P/X	Starts WordStar, prints a file, and exits to DOS
WS FILENAME /EM	Opens file and executes macro M
WS /[M	Starts WordStar and runs macro M from the Opening Menu

Starting WordStar Manually from DOS

One of the alternative start-up procedures lets you reset WordStar's logged disk drive and directory from the DOS prompt before you start the program. When WordStar starts up, the logged disk drive and directory are the same ones from which you give the command to start the program; you then need to change to the drive where the documents you create will be stored. By resetting the DOS letter prompt and directory (for hard disks), you can avoid having to change the logged disk drive setting after you begin a WordStar session.

As you learned in Chapter 2, changing the logged disk drive at the DOS prompt is easy: type a letter and a colon (:) for the new drive, and press Enter. To reset the file directory on a hard disk, you need to use the CD command followed by the name of the subdirectory in which your documents are stored.

If you are using a dual floppy drive system, changing the logged drive and starting WordStar manually from DOS is straightforward. Follow these steps:

1. Be sure that your computer is on and that `A>` is displayed.
2. To change to the subdirectory for WordStar documents, type *cd \ws5\doc* and press Enter.
3. Type *b:* and press Enter.

   The DOS prompt displays the new logged disk drive:

   ```
   B>
   ```

4. To start the WordStar program on the disk in drive A, type the command *a:ws* and press Enter.

   WordStar starts loading. You see the MicroPro copyright screen followed by WordStar's Opening Menu. Notice that the display includes the directory for drive B. You have started WordStar with the proper logged disk drive.

On a hard disk system, the manual procedure for logging and starting WordStar involves changing subdirectories at the DOS prompt. Follow these instructions:

1. Be sure that your computer is on and that `C>` is displayed.
2. To change to the subdirectory for WordStar documents, type *cd \ws5\doc* and press Enter.
3. To invoke WordStar, type *c:\ws5\ws* and press Enter.

   The program loads into your computer. The display shows the MicroPro copyright screen followed by WordStar's Opening Menu. The directory display is the one for C>\WS5\DOC. The proper logged disk drive for WordStar is now set.

An alternative start-up procedure applies to both floppy disk and hard disk installations: if you know the name of a document file, you can have WordStar go directly to that file, bypassing the Opening display entirely. To bypass this screen, type *ws* and follow the command with a space and the name of the file you want to open. For a dual floppy disk system, the form to follow looks like the following on-screen:

```
A>ws b:filename
```

For a hard disk system, after you are in the \WS5 directory, invoke WordStar using a command in the following form:

```
C>ws c:ws5\doc\filename
```

When you press Enter, WordStar loads and goes to the text of your document on the editing screen. ***Note:*** If the file you open is for a new document, the text area will be blank.

Typing an option character after the file name adds to the versatility of this method for loading WordStar. Depending on the option, WordStar can load and open a nondocument file, open a Speed Write file, print a file, merge print a file, exit WordStar, or run a shorthand macro's series of commands. A few of these options are new in WordStar Release 5, but all differ from previous releases in requiring a slash (/) before an option character.

The /N option opens the file you indicate as a nondocument file. The start-up command would look like the following on a dual floppy disk system:

```
A>ws b:filename /n
```

On a hard disk system the following would be the correct form:

```
C>ws c:\ws5\doc\filename /n
```

After typing either of these DOS command lines, press Enter to start WordStar and display the nondocument editing screen (shown in fig. 4.1). (If you reset WordStar's default to creating text in nondocument mode, a document file can be opened by substituting */d* for */n* in the previous examples.)

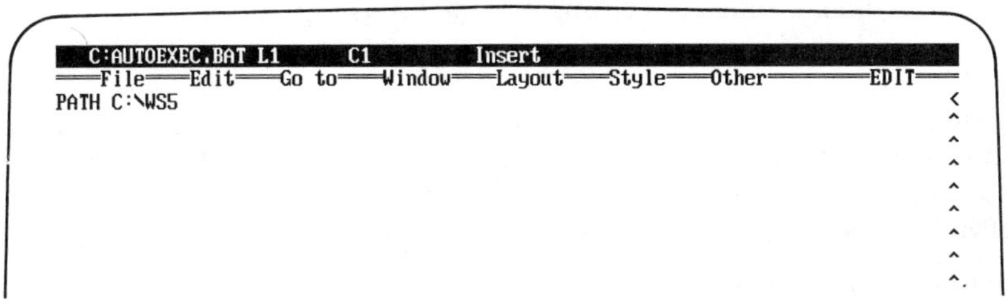
C:AUTOEXEC.BAT L1 C1 Insert
File Edit Go to Window Layout Style Other EDIT
PATH C:\WS5

Fig. 4.1.

The non-document screen at help level 4.

You can start WordStar Release 5's Speed Write function with the /S option. Because Speed Write opens a document without needing a name, you can begin typing almost immediately after issuing the WordStar start command and no file name. On a system with dual floppy disks, the following shows how the start-up command would look:

```
A>ws b: /s
```

The DOS command line for a hard disk would be the following:

```
C>ws c:\ws5\doc /s
```

Type one of these command sequences and press Enter; WordStar starts up in Speed Write mode (see Chapter 3).

Typing */p* after a file name and the start-up command loads the program and begins printing the designated document. On-screen, the command looks like the following for a floppy disk system:

```
A>ws b:filename /p
```

On a hard disk system, it looks something like the following:

```
C>ws c:\ws5\doc\filename /p
```

When you press Enter, WordStar is loaded and begins to print the file you have specified. If you substitute */m* for */p* in these examples, you invoke merge printing for your file. Adding the */x* option after */p* exits WordStar and returns the DOS prompt to the screen after your printing is done.

One of the new features in WordStar Release 5 awaiting discovery by users is the /[shorthand option when WordStar is started. When you call up a favorite shorthand macro, your start-up command can invoke a whole series of operations to be performed automatically on a document once the program begins. For example, by defining a shorthand character with the appropriate commands (see Chapter 9), you could have WordStar start up at a reformatted boilerplate letter on-screen with the current date inserted.

On a dual floppy disk system, a shorthand-invoking start looks like this (with [B as the shorthand character):

```
A>ws /[b
```

On a hard disk system, it looks something like the following:

```
C>ws /[b
```

If you want to start up WordStar with an open document and then invoke a shorthand sequence, the correct form uses a modifier of /E. For a dual floppy disk system, then, the WordStar start-up command looks like the following (with B as the shorthand character):

```
A> ws b:filename /eb
```

For a hard disk system, it looks something like this:

```
C>ws c:\ws\doc\filename /eb
```

These alternative manual procedures for starting WordStar still require numerous keystrokes before you can use the program. You can, however, make your copy of WordStar load automatically. The next section explains how to create a special file to invoke the start-up commands when you turn on your computer's power.

Using a Start-Up Batch File

With MS-DOS, you can create a file that contains DOS commands to be executed as soon as the computer is turned on and the operating system is loaded. This type of file is known as a *batch* file. Any DOS batch file that automatically executes commands when you start the computer is always called *AUTOEXEC.BAT*.

To make your working copy of WordStar self-starting, you can write a simple batch file that contains the commands normally used to start the program manually. Once this file is saved, you will never have to type these commands again to start WordStar. When the AUTOEXEC.BAT batch file is stored on the same floppy disk with the copy of DOS used to start WordStar or in the root directory of your hard disk, AUTOEXEC.BAT issues the start-up commands automatically.

Creating a file is almost the same in document and nondocument modes. Because a batch file does not need the formatting information ordinarily included in a document, you should create it in WordStar's nondocument mode. In nondocument mode, you open a file, write your text, and save the text with commands that are virtual duplicates of those used in document mode. The help menus available to you are also almost identical. The major difference in the modes is that the resulting nondocument file will be in a form DOS can read accurately.

Using Nondocument Mode

Nondocument mode in WordStar creates a special kind of file that has no formatting. These files conform to the ASCII standard for "plain-vanilla" text, readable by most MS-DOS programs. Although most often used by programmers, nondocument mode is also handy for other applications, including database files, mailing list files, and batch files.

At help level 4, pressing F from the Opening display pulls down the File menu. This menu lists the following command:

```
Open a nondocument file...    N
```

The full command sequence for opening a nondocument file is FN.

At help level 3 or lower, the command for starting a nondocument file is listed in the left column of the classic Opening Menu:

```
N open a nondocument
```

Press N at the classic Opening Menu to open a nondocument file.

At any help level, invoking nondocument mode displays a dialog box headed NONDOCUMENT. This box shows a prompt for `File` and a line below it for the name of the nondocument file you wish to open. This box is much like the one you see when you open a document file. To open a nondocument file, type the file name and press Enter.

Once you complete selection of a file, the nondocument screen is displayed. The nondocument screen at the different help levels (illustrated in figs. 4.1, 4.2, 4.3, and 4.4) appears as a modified version of the one seen in document mode.

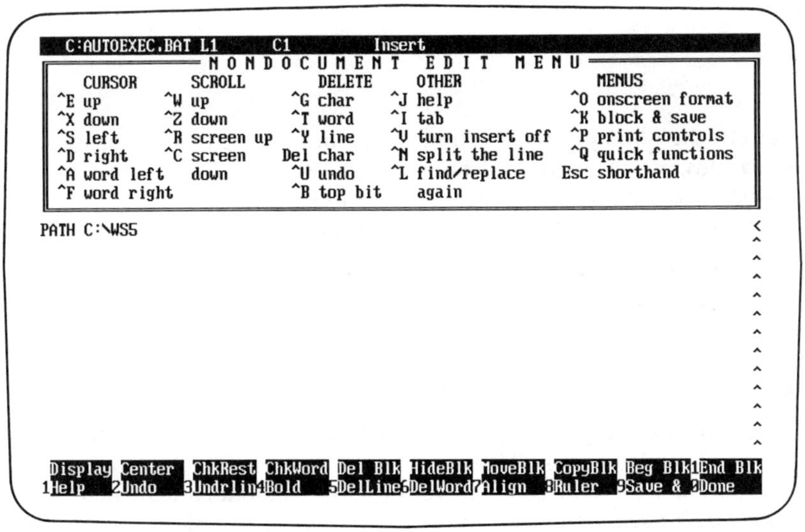
C:AUTOEXEC.BAT L1 C1 Insert
N O N D O C U M E N T E D I T M E N U
CURSOR SCROLL DELETE OTHER MENUS
^E up ^W up ^G char ^J help ^O onscreen format
^X down ^Z down ^T word ^I tab ^K block & save
^S left ^R screen up ^Y line ^V turn insert off ^P print controls
^D right ^C screen Del char ^N split the line ^Q quick functions
^A word left down ^U undo ^L find/replace Esc shorthand
^F word right ^B top bit again
PATH C:\WS5
Display Center ChkRest ChkWord Del Blk HideBlk MoveBlk CopyBlk Beg Blk End Blk
1Help 2Undo 3Undrlin 4Bold 5DelLine 6DelWord 7Align 8Ruler 9Save & 0Done

Fig. 4.2.

The nondocument screen and Nondocument Edit Menu at help level 3.

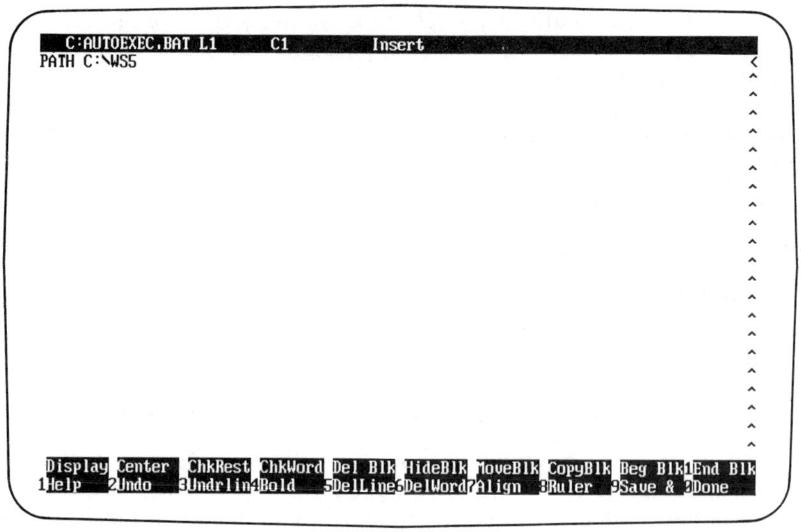
C:AUTOEXEC.BAT L1 C1 Insert
PATH C:\WS5
Display Center ChkRest ChkWord Del Blk HideBlk MoveBlk CopyBlk Beg Blk End Blk
1Help 2Undo 3Undrlin 4Bold 5DelLine 6DelWord 7Align 8Ruler 9Save & 0Done

Fig. 4.3.
The non-document screen at help levels 2 and 1.

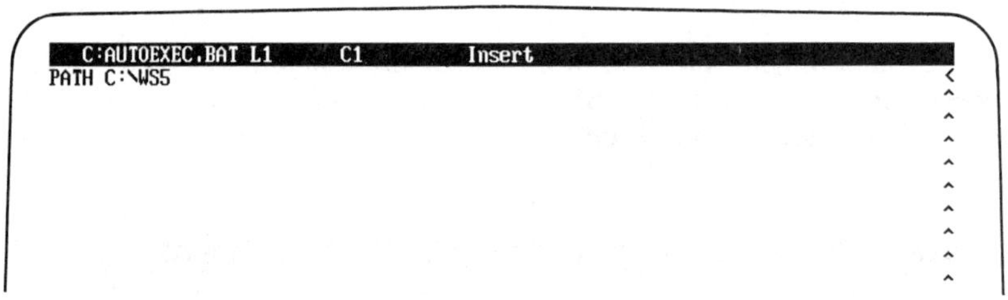
C:AUTOEXEC.BAT L1 C1 Insert
PATH C:\WS5

Fig. 4.4.
The non-document screen at help level 0.

At all help levels, the nondocument editing screen has no ruler line because such features as margins, word wrap, and justification are turned off. For a similar reason, the word `Align` does not appear on the status line. Also note that the status line displays no page information other than line (`L`) and column (`C`) numbers.

Among the formatting functions absent in nondocument mode are line spacing, centering, and automatic hyphenation. The menus available at each help level are abbreviated to show the remaining functions. Two commands are unique to nondocument mode: ^OI sets tab width and ^6 toggles on auto-indent (useful for programming in Pascal and other high-level computer languages).

For the nondocument editing screen, most WordStar document mode text entry, cursor movement, text deletion, block manipulation, and text finding functions are valid. When you compose and edit text in WordStar's nondocument mode, the keystrokes used are almost identical to those used in document mode.

For more information on using nondocument mode with merge printing files, see Chapter 8.

Quick Start 3: Making WordStar Self-Starting

This Quick Start is more than a brief learning exercise; it's a practical step toward using WordStar more efficiently. Follow the step-by-step instructions for either a floppy disk or hard disk system to make WordStar self-starting when you switch on your computer's power. The steps themselves are simple and include the following:

- Opening a nondocument file
- Typing DOS commands for starting WordStar
- Closing the nondocument batch file
- Restarting WordStar automatically

The nondocument file for starting WordStar automatically is named AUTOEXEC.BAT because of the DOS convention under which the file operates. In addition, this batch file should be on the same disk used to start DOS or on a hard disk's root directory. When you start your computer, the disk operating software will read each line of text in the file as though the text were being typed at the DOS prompt. In fact, you have already created a simple version of AUTOEXEC.BAT during installation of WordStar Release 5 (see Chapter 2). An unmodified version of this file contains the DOS statement PATH and the correct disk and directory for the WordStar program file.

A PATH statement allows WordStar to be started without specifying its directory, regardless of which directory currently may be logged. This makes it convenient to restart WordStar once it has been exited (with the computer still on) by simply typing *ws*.

To modify an AUTOEXEC batch file, making WordStar self-starting on a two floppy disk system, follow these steps:

1. To start WordStar, place your working copy disk (with the DOS system files and COMMAND.COM) in drive A and type *ws*.
2. With the pull-down menus at help level 4, from the Opening screen press Enter (or F) and then N to open a nondocument file.

   At help level 3 or below, from the classic Opening Menu, press N to create a nondocument file.
3. At the box prompt for the file name, type the batch file name preceded by the letter designating the drive and/or subdirectory from which DOS is loaded:

   A:*autoexec.bat*

   or

   C:\ *autoexec.bat*

4. Press Enter.

   The Nondocument editing screen appears with the contents of the AUTOEXEC.BAT file created during the installation procedure: a PATH statement for WordStar program files.

5. Move the cursor to the end of the line with the PATH statement and press Enter. From the second line, type the following two lines, pressing Enter after each line:

   b:
   a:ws

   These are the same commands you would type at the DOS prompt. The first changes the logged drive, and the second starts WordStar from drive A with B as the logged drive.

6. To close and save this file, at any help level press ^KD or the F10 function key.

   The AUTOEXEC.BAT file is stored on the disk in drive A, and the Opening display returns to the screen.

If you have a single floppy disk, you can make WordStar self-starting by following the previous sequence and omitting the B: command for changing drives.

For a hard disk drive system, the procedure for creating the AUTOEXEC batch file is as follows:

1. To start WordStar from the working copy on your hard disk, type *c:\ws5\ws*

2. With the pull-down menus at help level 4, from the Opening screen press Enter (or F) and then N to open a nondocument file.

   At help level 3 or below, from the Opening Menu, press N to create a nondocument file.

3. At the prompt for the file name, type the disk drive letter, a colon, and a backslash (\) for the root directory from which DOS is loaded, followed by the AUTOEXEC.BAT file name, as shown here:

   c:\autoexec.bat

4. Press Enter.

   The nondocument editing screen is displayed, showing the contents of the AUTOEXEC.BAT file created during the installation procedure: a PATH statement for WordStar program files.

5. Move the cursor to the end of the line with the PATH statement and press Enter. Type the following two lines, pressing Enter after each line:

   cd \ws5\doc
   ws

These are the same commands you would type at the DOS prompt. The first changes the logged drive and directory to a subdirectory called DOC, where your document files are stored (any directory name can be substituted). The second starts WordStar from anywhere on the hard disk, with DOC remaining as the logged directory.

6. To close and save the file, press ^KD or F10.

   The Opening display appears and the AUTOEXEC.BAT file is stored in the root directory of your hard disk.

Whether you have a floppy disk or a hard disk system, you can type any of the options for modifying the WordStar start-up so that it does not remain at the Opening display (see earlier section in this chapter). For example, you could add a \S Speed Write option to have WordStar come up with the editing screen displayed, or you might print the latest version of a document whenever you start a new work session by adding the file's name and the \P option.

You also should include in your AUTOEXEC.BAT file commands to load other software (usually memory-resident programs remaining in the background until needed) that must be invoked before WordStar. These could include the add-on programs packaged with WordStar Release 5, like PC-Outline and ProFinder. Commands for loading other memory-resident programs, like SideKick® and InSet®, should also be in your batch file, usually in a specified order. See Chapter 12 for details.

A batch file for a hard disk WordStar start-up (to the Speed Write editing screen), complete with memory-resident program commands, might look like the one shown in figure 4.5.

```
   C:AUTOEXEC.BAT L8      C17          Insert
SOUND ON
PATH C:\WS5
CD \INSET
INSET
CD \SIDEKICK
SKPLUS
CD \WS5
WS C:\WS5\DOC /S
```

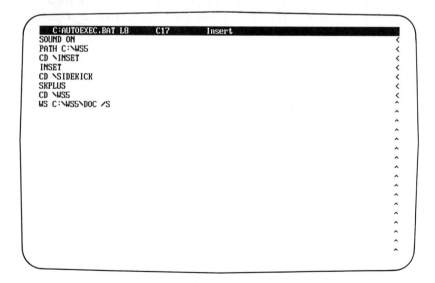

Fig. 4.5.

An advanced-level batch file for starting Wordstar.

Now that you have created and saved the batch file, you can watch it automatically start WordStar for you. Reset your computer by pressing Ctrl-Alt-Del (press Ctrl and Alt and hold them down while you press Del). Pressing this combination of keys, called a *warm boot*, suspends your computer's processing, clears its memory of programs and data, and starts DOS with the power still turned on.

When you press Ctrl-Alt-Del, the screen clears, and your computer emits a beep to indicate that the computer has been reset. Then DOS reloads and reads the contents of the AUTOEXEC batch file. You see the commands in the AUTOEXEC file displayed, followed by the WordStar copyright screen and the Opening screen with the directory for the appropriate logged disk drive.

Congratulations! You have just made WordStar self-starting.

Managing Your Files at the Opening Screen

If you worked through the tutorial in Chapter 1 or read about the basic functions in Chapter 3, you are now familiar with about a third of the WordStar commands available at the Opening display. The next section of this chapter covers the file management functions you can invoke from WordStar's starting screen. These include another third of the commands available at this point in the program.

File management—being able to find, rename, copy, delete, or protect your document files—is a vital part of most word processing applications. Some of these file functions also can be invoked during editing, but using them from the Opening display often saves time and avoids confusion.

At help level 4 in WordStar Release 5, you will find the half-dozen file functions covered in this chapter on the File and Other pull-down menus. Including the keystroke for pulling down the appropriate menu, these file management commands are summarized in table 4.2. Each of these commands is discussed in the sections that follow.

Table 4.2
Pull-Down Opening Screen Commands for Managing Your Files

Command	*Function*
FE	Renames a file
FO	Copies a file
FY	Deletes a file

Table 4.2—*Continued*

Command	*Function*
FC	Protects a file
OR	Runs a DOS command
O?	Checks memory usage

At help level 3 or lower, the classic Opening Menu lists the same file management functions and an extra one that can only be invoked from the classic menu—to toggle off a file directory listing. These Opening Menu file commands are summarized in table 4.3. Each command is detailed in the following pages.

Table 4.3
Opening Menu Commands for Managing Your Files

Command	*Function*
E	Renames a file
O	Copies a file
Y	Deletes a file
C	Protects a file
F	Toggles file directory off/on
R	Runs a DOS command
?	Checks memory usage

Regardless of the help level, several of these commands available from WordStar's Opening display perform file management functions that also can be handled with DOS commands. WordStar lets you perform these functions easily without exiting the program. If you need to invoke these file management functions from within a document, you can do so with the commands detailed at the beginning of Chapter 5.

Renaming Files

Changing a file name can be the handy solution to such frequent problems as misnamed, easily confused, or duplicated documents. You can substitute a new file name for an old one, without altering the file's contents, by using the REN command (typed in the following form: *ren oldname newname*) at the DOS prompt. More conveniently, you can rename a file from WordStar's Opening display.

At help level 4, pressing F from the pull-down Opening menu exposes the File menu, with the following listing near the bottom:

```
Rename a file...                E
```

The sequence for invoking the Rename a file command is FE.

On the classic Opening Menu, at help level 3 or below, the following function appears in the right-hand column on the third line:

```
E rename a file
```

Whether you press FE with the pull-down menus or press E in classic WordStar command style, the Opening display is replaced by a dialog box with separate lines for the current name of the file to be renamed and its new name—as illustrated in figure 4.6. This Rename dialog box replaces the two-part prompts in previous versions of WordStar.

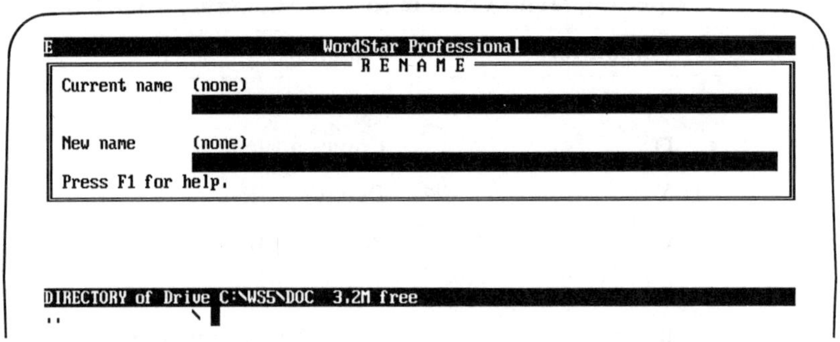
E
WordStar Professional
R E N A M E
Current name (none)
New name (none)
Press F1 for help.
DIRECTORY of Drive C:\WS5\DOC 3.2M free

Fig. 4.6.

The dialog box for renaming a file.

To complete the renaming operation, at the dialog box type the name of the file to be renamed or use ^X or the down-arrow key to move the cursor to the appropriate name in the file directory on-screen. Pressing Enter moves text entry to the next line. (***Note:*** If you type the name incorrectly, WordStar will indicate that the file cannot be found.) Use the Tab key or ^I to move between the current name and the new name boxes.

On the line for the new name, type the new characters to assign to the file. The name should conform to the rule for a DOS file name: up to eight characters long, with an optional extension of up to three characters set off by a period. In addition, you should choose a name that is not already in use by a file on your disk. If you choose the name of an existing file, WordStar displays a warning message and allows you to choose a different name.

When you press Enter, the Opening display reappears on-screen, and the directory below it shows the new file name but not the old one.

Copying Files

Copying a file is useful when you want to retain the original version of a document and edit a copy under a different name—or under the same name on another disk or in a different directory. Duplicating a file without a change in its text is done at the DOS prompt by typing *copy*, followed by a space, the name of the file to copy, followed by another space and the name of the new copy. You can also easily copy a file at WordStar's Opening display.

At help level 4, pressing F from the Opening display pulls down the File menu, which contains the following listing:

```
Copy a file...              O
```

The complete sequence for copying a file is FO.

At WordStar's help level 3 or lower, the classic Opening Menu includes this function in the right-hand column:

```
O copy a file
```

Invoking the COPY command replaces the Opening display with a dialog box for the name of the file to be copied and the name of the copy to be created, as seen in figure 4.7.

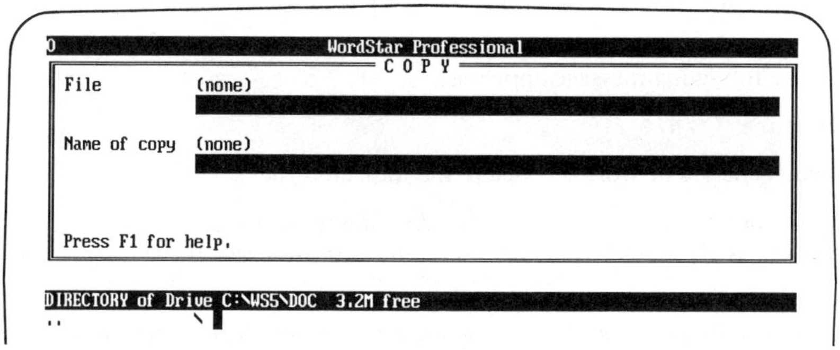
WordStar Professional
COPY
File (none)
Name of copy (none)
Press F1 for help.
DIRECTORY of Drive C:\WS5\DOC 3.2M free

Fig. 4.7.

The dialog box for copying a file.

At the Copy dialog box, type the name of the file to copy, or press ^X or the down-arrow key to highlight one of the file names in the directory below it. Press Enter or Tab, and the cursor moves to the line for the name of the file to contain the copy. The name you choose should not be the name of another file on disk. The name also must conform to the rules for file names. To copy the file to another disk or directory, the name must be preceded by the letter designating the other drive, a colon, and the file path. Pressing Enter completes the copy operation and returns the Opening display to the screen.

If you type the name of an existing file, WordStar will ask whether the new copy should replace the existing document. A Y answer replaces the old file with the new one. An N answer returns you to the Opening Menu.

Deleting Files

Deleting a file discards a stored document that you no longer plan to use, freeing up space for saving other files. (Deleted files are not permanently erased, but can often be restored with a program like the Norton Utilities™ from Peter Norton Computing or the Mace Utilities® from Paul Mace Software.) At the DOS prompt you can erase a file by typing *del* followed by a space and the name of the file to delete; then press Enter. Or you can quickly delete a file from WordStar's Opening display with a simple command.

When WordStar is set for pull-down menus at help level 4, pressing F from the Opening display shows the File menu, which lists the following function:

```
Delete a file...            Y
```

The complete sequence for erasing a file is FY.

When set at help level 3 or below, WordStar's classic Opening Menu shows the following in the right-hand column:

```
Y delete a file
```

With either file deletion command invoked from the Opening display, a dialog box headed DELETE appears on-screen with a line for the name of the file to be deleted. You can type the name of the file or use the arrow keys to highlight its name on the disk directory beneath the dialog box, and then press Enter.

At help levels 2, 3, and 4, after you enter the name of the file to be deleted and press Enter, the following message appears:

```
Are you sure (Y/N)?
```

Only after you type *y* will WordStar delete the indicated file.

The file delete command can be treacherous. As a matter of habit, before you erase a file, always check the name you type. You don't want to erase the wrong file by mistake.

To delete or not to delete a file? That question is not as simple as it may seem. On the one hand, eliminating files you no longer need is a good idea, especially when you are working with floppy disks that have limited capacity. If you try to save an edited file, and the disk in the logged drive has insufficient room, WordStar will indicate that the disk is full. A `disk full` error sometimes can result in the loss of your file. To avoid this catastrophe, you should delete excess files.

On the other hand, experienced word processor users swear that you often seem to need a file only after it has been deleted. Fortunately, a number of utility programs, such as the Norton Utilities or Mace Utilities, can restore files that were deleted under particular circumstances.

Protecting Files

To guard against accidental erasure or modification of a document, WordStar provides an important feature for protecting a file. In effect, by invoking the protection command, you lock a file into its current content, changeable only after you remove protection with the same command.

You can copy or read a protected file on the editing screen, but you can issue only a few valid commands, such as those for cursor movement. Commands for text insertion or deletion do not operate because the file cannot be modified until protection is removed. Such protection is often used for preserving final drafts of documents and storing files shared on a local area network.

At WordStar's help level 4, pressing F from the Opening display pulls down the File menu. The menu lists this function:

```
Protect/unprotect a file...  C
```

The full sequence for invoking file protection is FC.

At help level 3 or lower, the WordStar classic Opening Menu displays the following in the right-hand column:

```
C protect/unprotect a file
```

Whether you use pull-down or classic menus for invoking protection, you will next see a dialog box headed PROTECT, with a line for designating the file to be locked in. This file name can be typed or you can use the arrow keys to highlight a name on the directory on-screen. Then press Enter.

The following message appears below the Protect dialog box:

```
The file is currently not protected.  Protect it? (Y/N)
```

Press Y to indicate that you want to protect the file. WordStar executes the command, and the Opening display reappears on-screen.

When a protected file is opened onto the editing screen, `Prtect` appears on the status line. At help level 3, the Edit Menu has been replaced by the Protected Menu (see fig. 4.8). The Protected Menu lists commands for cursor movement and text display as well as some commands for miscellaneous functions. However, this menu lacks all commands that relate to text modification. If you press a letter key to enter text, your computer responds with a beep to indicate that the file is protected.

To remove protection from your document file, repeat the procedure: at the pull-down menu Opening screen press FC, or at the classic Opening Menu press C, designate the file name, and press Enter.

This time the following message partly covers the Protect dialog box:

```
The file is currently protected.  Unprotect it? (Y/N)
```

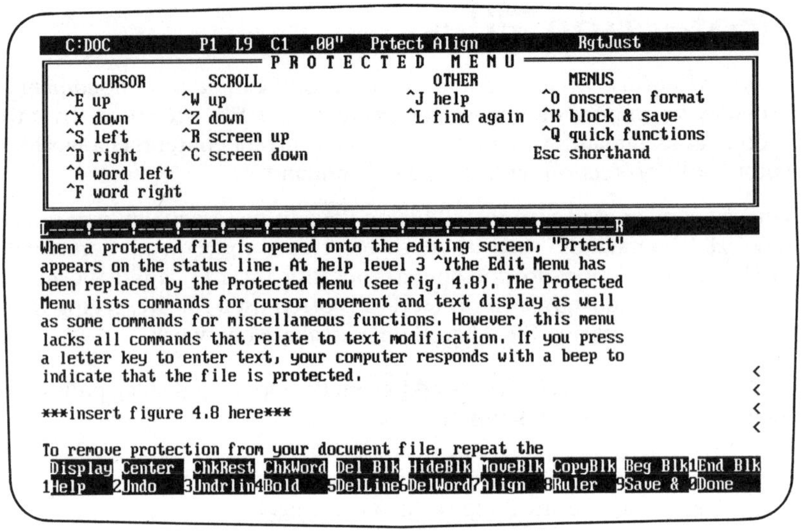
C:DOC P1 L9 C1 .00" Prtect Align RgtJust
PROTECTED MENU
CURSOR SCROLL OTHER MENUS
^E up ^W up ^J help ^O onscreen format
^X down ^Z down ^L find again ^K block & save
^S left ^R screen up ^Q quick functions
^D right ^C screen down Esc shorthand
^A word left
^F word right
When a protected file is opened onto the editing screen, "Prtect" appears on the status line. At help level 3 ^Ythe Edit Menu has been replaced by the Protected Menu (see fig. 4.8). The Protected Menu lists commands for cursor movement and text display as well as some commands for miscellaneous functions. However, this menu lacks all commands that relate to text modification. If you press a letter key to enter text, your computer responds with a beep to indicate that the file is protected.
insert figure 4.8 here
To remove protection from your document file, repeat the
Display Center ChkRest ChkWord Del Blk HideBlk MoveBlk CopyBlk Beg Blk End Blk
1Help 2Undo 3Undrlin 4Bold 5DelLine 6DelWord 7Align 8Ruler 9Save & 0Done

Fig. 4.8.

The Protected Menu.

Pressing Y removes protection from the file, allowing it to be edited again.

Incidentally, all of WordStar's automatic backup files (noted by the BAK file name extension) are protected, in keeping with their archival function. For more on WordStar backup files, see Chapter 5.

Toggling the File Directory

In the absence of a pull-down menu activated by pressing F, at help level 3 or lower the F key invokes a function of its own from the classic Opening Menu.

The right column of the Opening Menu lists the following command:

```
F turn directory off
```

Pressing F turns off the file directory. The directory disappears from the screen, and the Opening Menu then displays the following in place of its previous listing:

```
F turn directory on
```

The file directory command's description may obscure its usefulness. This command does more than simply turn the directory off and on. When you press F to turn on the file directory, WordStar lets you specify which files to display in the directory. The default is ????????.???; every file name and extension will be shown in the directory if you type *.* and press Enter. The dialog box for filtering out directory names is shown in figure 4.9.

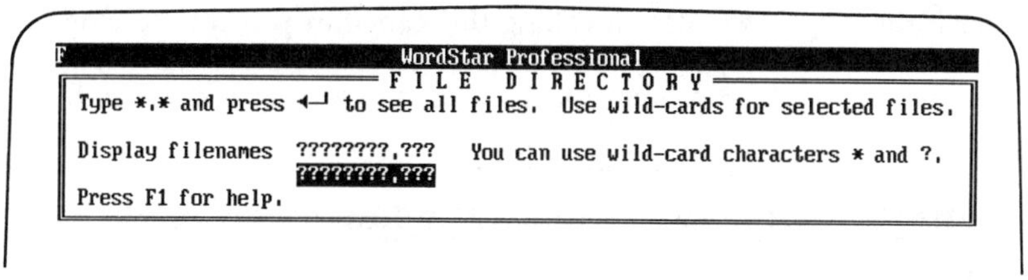
WordStar Professional
FILE DIRECTORY
Type *.* and press ↵ to see all files. Use wild-cards for selected files.
Display filenames ????????.??? You can use wild-card characters * and ?.
????????.???
Press F1 for help.

Fig. 4.9.
The dialog box for resetting the directory listing.

You can use wild card characters to display only certain file names. By typing parts of the file names you want listed, you limit what will be displayed. For example, if you type **.doc*, WordStar displays those files that have DOC as the extension. This feature is useful if your file directory is large and you want to locate a specific kind of file.

Although you may not have any reason to toggle off the WordStar directory displays, the file directory command has an important application for you if you have a dual floppy disk computer. When you decide to change the document disks in the logged drive, the directory will continue to display the contents of the original disk.

You could alter the directory by pressing L to change the logged disk, typing the letter for the same drive, and pressing Enter. The computer would read the directory of your new disk and display the file names on-screen. An alternative procedure is to press F twice: the first time you press F, the directory disappears. The second time, follow the F by typing *.* and pressing Enter to display the directory of all files on the new disk.

Running a DOS Command

You can accomplish other file-management tasks from the Opening screen by bringing up the DOS prompt—without having to exit from WordStar. For example, you can use the DOS directory command DIR to look up the date files were last saved (WordStar does not include this information in its directory display). Invoking a DOS command is also useful for running another program without having to end a WordStar session. Running a DOS command is easy once the DOS prompt is on-screen within WordStar.

If you have WordStar set at help level 4, the pull-down Other menu displayed by pressing O includes the following function:

```
Run a DOS command...   R
```

The full command for putting the DOS prompt on-screen in a dialog box is OR.

If set at help level 3 or below, WordStar's classic Opening Menu shows the following near the bottom of the right-hand column:

```
R run a DOS command
```

5

No matter what the help level, after invoking this function you see a dialog box with the word RUN at the top, as illustrated in figure 4.10. Under the message `Enter a DOS command`, the DOS prompt for the logged disk drive is displayed.

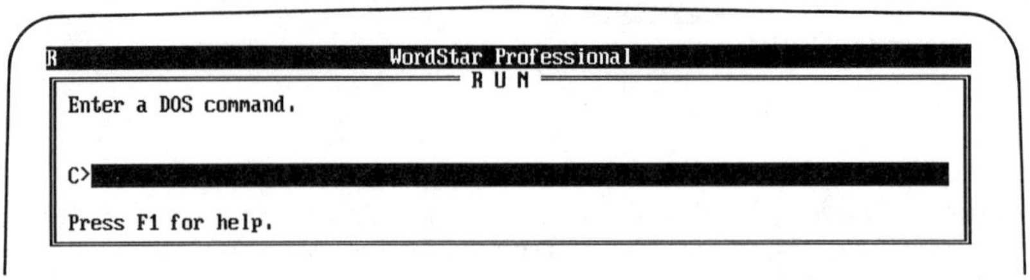
WordStar Professional
R U N
Enter a DOS command.
C>
Press F1 for help.

Fig. 4.10.
The dialog box for running a DOS command from WordStar.

At the Run dialog box, to issue a DOS command, simply type the command at the prompt and press Enter. After the DOS function is performed, a message on-screen tells you to press any key to return to WordStar. Press any key and the Opening display returns to the screen.

Among the advantages of running a DOS command is the option of using wild card characters to designate several files at a time for a file management operation—rather than the single file selections available with WordStar's commands. For example, you can type ***del* *.*bak*** to rid a disk of all its backup files, avoiding a possible disk full error on a floppy disk system. Another useful DOS command for hard disk users is COPY *.* A:, making copies of all the files in your current directory on a floppy disk in drive A—for archival purposes.

From WordStar's Run dialog box you can run another program—even a second copy of WordStar—if your computer has sufficient memory for both programs, the data documents you have created, and any other program modules you have loaded into memory. In general, computer systems with less than 512K of RAM will be hard-pressed to run another program in addition to WordStar.

Occasionally, after you have run a DOS command from WordStar, pressing a key will not return you to WordStar. You should be especially careful when you run a memory-resident program after you have invoked the `Run a DOS command` function. ***Note:*** Such a program can usurp WordStar's memory space, causing your system to ***crash***, or become unresponsive to keyboard input.

Checking Memory Usage

To avoid overloading your computer's internal memory, WordStar provides a handy way to check memory usage. The command for this useful function is a logical one: a question mark.

At WordStar's help level 4, pressing O from the Opening screen displays the Other menu. The menu shows the following command:

```
Display RAM usage...   ?
```

The full sequence to check on memory usage is O?.

At help level 3 or lower, the WordStar classic menus omit this function, but it is still valid. To find out how much RAM memory is being used when WordStar is running, press ? from the Opening Menu.

Once this feature is invoked, the screen displays a list of the programs and related files stored in memory, the amount of space occupied by each, the total space used, and remaining internal memory (see fig. 4.11).

Pressing the Esc key brings back the Opening Menu.

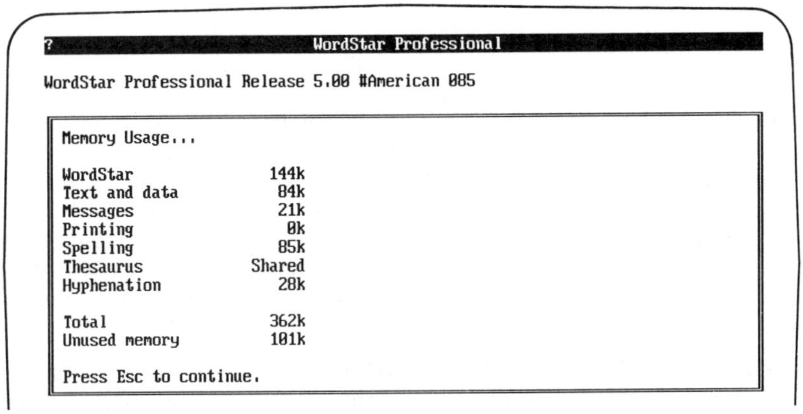
? WordStar Professional
WordStar Professional Release 5.00 #American 005
Memory Usage...
WordStar 144k
Text and data 84k
Messages 21k
Printing 0k
Spelling 85k
Thesaurus Shared
Hyphenation 28k
Total 362k
Unused memory 101k
Press Esc to continue.

Fig. 4.11.
A breakdown of WordStar memory usage.

Formatting Text On-Screen

When you type a document, certain formatting conventions render your copy more legible. Centered text, tab alignment, and indented paragraphs all help to set off material by differentiating it from plain margin-to-margin lines of copy. WordStar has a number of commands for formatting text on-screen so that the user sees how it will appear when printed.

The commands for formatting text on-screen are summarized in table 4.4. Each of these commands is discussed in the sections that follow.

Table 4.4
Commands for Formatting Text On-Screen

Command	*Function*
^OL	Resets left margin
^OR	Resets right margin
^OS	Resets line spacing
^OJ	Toggles justification on/off
.OP	Omits page numbering
^OC or Shift-F2	Centers text
^I or Tab	Moves cursor to next tab stop
^OI	Sets tab stop

Users of previous versions of WordStar will notice one of Release 5's most visible changes—inch measurements to define text formatting positions, often as an alternative to column numbers. Adjusting should be easy: at a standard ten characters or columns per inch, divide the number of characters by ten for their equivalent in inches, remembering to take into account changes in starting defaults. Thus the old left and right margin defaults of 1 and 65 are the same as WordStar Release 5's settings of 0.0″ and 6.4″. The change to inches was made to accommodate formatting of printer fonts in nonstandard sizes (see Chapter 7).

Several of the formatting functions described in this chapter, used to change WordStar's initial settings, can be invoked when you start a work session. The program's document defaults provide single-spaced lines up to 65 standard characters long with text justified at the right margin. These settings are those used most often for business documents. Many documents, however, use wider or narrower lines of text, double spacing, and ragged right (nonjustified) margins. WordStar's default settings can be modified temporarily with Ctrl-letter command sequences. (For more permanent alterations to WordStar, see Chapter 11.)

The unmodified WordStar program automatically prints page numbers—a feature you need to turn off at times for letters and one-page memos. Eliminating page numbering requires a special kind of command—a dot command—that appears on-screen but not in your printed document. The omit page numbering command is an example of the more than one hundred dot commands covered in Chapters 6, 7, 8, and 10.

Other on-screen formatting features, like tabs and centering, are useful for positioning text on a line during text entry. Most WordStar commands to format text or change default settings while working on a document consist of keystroke sequences that begin with ^O.

At help level 4, most of the formatting commands detailed in this chapter are listed on the pull-down Layout menu. Displayed by pressing Alt-L at the editing screen, the Layout menu is shown in figure 4.12. Almost half of the 14 commands on this menu are explained in this chapter.

At help levels 4, 3, or 2, pressing ^O displays the classic Onscreen Format Menu, shown here in figure 4.13.

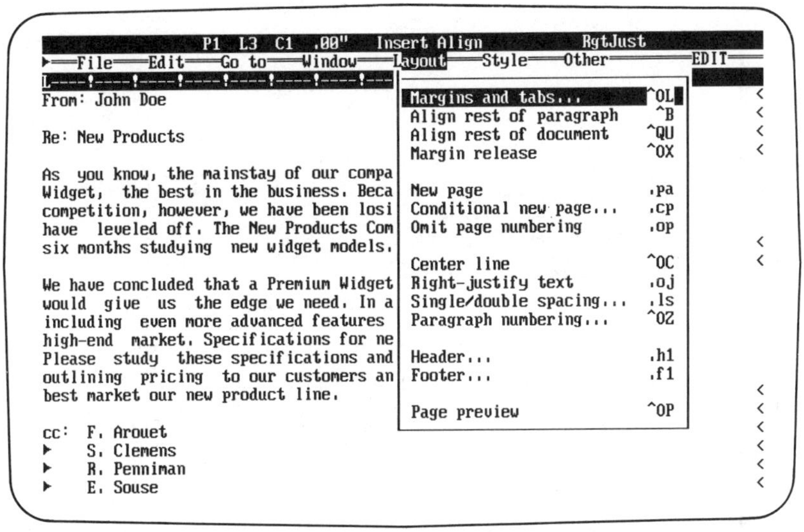
P1 L3 C1 .00" Insert Align RgtJust
File Edit Go to Window Layout Style Other EDIT
From: John Doe
Re: New Products
As you know, the mainstay of our compa
Widget, the best in the business. Beca
competition, however, we have been losi
have leveled off. The New Products Com
six months studying new widget models.
We have concluded that a Premium Widget
would give us the edge we need. In a
including even more advanced features
high-end market. Specifications for ne
Please study these specifications and
outlining pricing to our customers an
best market our new product line.
cc: F. Arouet
S. Clemens
R. Penniman
E. Souse
Margins and tabs... ^OL
Align rest of paragraph ^B
Align rest of document ^QU
Margin release ^OX
New page .pa
Conditional new page... .cp
Omit page numbering .op
Center line ^OC
Right-justify text .oj
Single/double spacing... .ls
Paragraph numbering... ^OZ
Header... .h1
Footer... .f1
Page preview ^OP

Fig. 4.12.

The Layout menu.

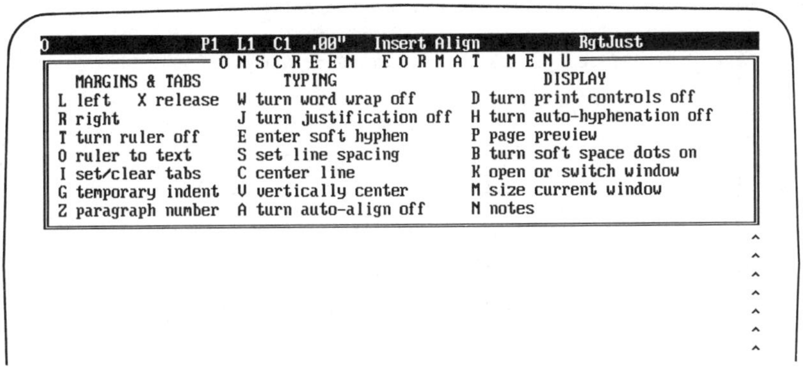
O P1 L1 C1 .00" Insert Align RgtJust
O N S C R E E N F O R M A T M E N U
MARGINS & TABS
L left X release
R right
T turn ruler off
O ruler to text
I set/clear tabs
G temporary indent
Z paragraph number
TYPING
W turn word wrap off
J turn justification off
E enter soft hyphen
S set line spacing
C center line
V vertically center
A turn auto-align off
DISPLAY
D turn print controls off
H turn auto-hyphenation off
P page preview
B turn soft space dots on
K open or switch window
M size current window
N notes

Fig. 4.13.

The Onscreen Format Menu.

The 22 commands listed on the Onscreen Format Menu in WordStar Release 5 are divided into three columns titled MARGINS & TABS, TYPING, and DISPLAY. To remind you that all these commands must be preceded by ^O, the top left corner of the menu displays an O.

Incidentally, pressing ^O in nondocument mode will not initiate on-screen formatting commands, because these commands do not apply to nondocument files. Instead, ^O sets tab widths in nondocument mode.

Examples of on-screen formatting features like centered text, tab alignment, and indented paragraphs, as well as line drawing, are provided in the pages that follow by referring to a sample document—the widget pricing letter requested in the memo typed in Chapter 1. The text of the pricing letter is shown in figure 4.14, including on-screen formatting familiar to any word processing user.

Fig. 4.14.
The sample pricing letter.

Widgets, Inc.

November 14, 1988

Richard Roe
Western Fastmart Co.
1313 Blueview Terrace
San Francisco, CA 94107

Dear Mr. Roe:

You are among the first to know about plans for extending our product line with a new and improved Premium Widget and a high-end Super Widget.

You will share our enthusiasm for these models when you see the figures below. The margins between wholesale and suggested list prices should provide you with ample profits. By placing an advance order now, you will be guaranteed the following prices:

Price	1-999 units	1000 or more	Sug. List
Premium Widget	$9.75	$7.95	$19.99
Super Widget	$12.95	$10.25	$29.99

Our local sales rep will be calling you soon with details on our introductory pricing structure.

Help us make the launch of these new Widgets the most mutually rewarding ever in our industry!

Sincerely,

You may type this sample letter, as indicated in the following sections, to demonstrate how changes in key WordStar format settings modify the appearance of a document.

Setting Margins

Margins define the boundaries for text on a page. Left and right margins set the location of the vertical edges of text. In WordStar Release 5, the default left and right margin settings are 0.0" and 6.5"—yielding a maximum of 65 characters per line (at 10 characters per inch). On the editing screen, the `L` at the beginning of the ruler line marks the left margin, and the `R` the right margin.

With WordStar Release 5's new inch notation (instead of previous versions' character or column numbers), the 6 1/2-inch line length is suitable for most report and manuscript formats on 8 1/2-by-11-inch paper. Individualized letterheads, notes, forms, and the like may require resetting the margins. To change these settings quickly, you can invoke either of two margin commands listed on WordStar menus.

At help level 4, from the editing screen press Alt-L for the pull-down Layout menu. At the top of this menu is the following command:

```
Margins and tabs...        ^OL
```

Because its new dialog box includes several formatting settings, WordStar Release 5 functionally combines resetting left and right margins, as well as tabs, with the same command, ^OL—though another margin command is also valid.

At help levels 4, 3, or 2, pressing ^O at the editing screen displays the classic Onscreen Format Menu, with the following two commands near the top of the MARGINS & TABS column:

```
L left
R right
```

Keep in mind that these command sequences begin with ^O. The complete commands for setting margins are ^OL for the left margin and ^OR for the right margin. In WordStar Release 5 these commands actually duplicate each other.

Regardless of how you invoke them, both margin reset commands display the same dialog box, headed MARGINS & TABS, shown in figure 4.15. Depending on the command, the cursor appears at either the left or right margin setting prompt, beside the current settings, expressed in inches.

You can set either side margin in WordStar Release 5 by typing inch measurements—between *0.0"* and *36.0"* for the left margin and between *0.0"* and *36.0"* for the right, with at least 0.2 inches between the two margins. Using a standard of 10 characters per inch, you can set lines as long as 360 characters. However, some printers won't print more than 160 characters across a line. Most business documents are 8 inches wide, with 6.5" of text between left and right margins. Once you have typed in a new value for a margin, pressing ^K or F10 changes the setting and displays a reset ruler line on the editing screen. Into your text WordStar Release 5 adds a dot command, either .LM or .RM, followed by a margin measurement (the command appears on-screen but is not printed) for the changed setting. You can also change margins by typing the proper dot command in your text, as noted in Chapter 6.

Veterans of previous WordStar versions can no longer use an old shortcut for changing the margin: pressing the Esc key with the cursor at the desired position for the new margin. Instead of this handy feature, pressing Esc at WordStar Release 5's MARGINS & TABS dialog box merely removes the box from the screen. The same dialog box makes it easy to change several settings at a time. When you have typed a new value for the left margin, for example, pressing Enter moves the cursor to the next line for the right margin. The Tab key, down-arrow key, or ^X also move the cursor to the next line of settings, first the left column of settings, then the right column, and then the line at bottom. Pressing Enter at the bottom line accepts all the settings in the dialog box and redisplays the editing menu. Pressing ^K or F10 anywhere in the menu accepts the current settings.

In the sample pricing letter, before typing text (or later) pressing ^OL or ^OR brings up the Margins & Tabs dialog box; the left margin would be reset to 0.7" and the right margin to 5.9" to match the letter's intended formatting. Pressing Enter until the cursor is at the line spacing setting allows this formatting default to be reset. You also could press ^K or the F10 function key to accept current settings and change the line spacing separately.

Setting Line Spacing

An unmodified copy of WordStar Release 5 single-spaces lines of text on-screen and on the printed version. Changing to double- or triple-spacing (with more white space between lines) to improve legibility is important when editing or printing some documents. If set for any spacing except single, the status line on the editing screen displays the abbreviation `LinSp-` followed by the spacing number.

From the editing screen at help level 4, pressing Alt-L pulls down the Layout menu, which lists this command:

```
Single/double spacing...   ^OS
```

Only single and double spacing are listed, but at all help levels, WordStar accepts spacing increments from 1 to 9.

From the Edit display at help levels 4, 3 or 2, invoking ^O displays the classic Onscreen Format Menu, including this function in the Typing column:

```
S set line spacing
```

The entire sequence for setting line spacing is ^OS.

Whatever the help level, in WordStar Release 5 the new Margins & Tabs dialog box (see fig. 4.15) includes a place to specify line spacing. Once you press ^OS, the Margins & Tabs box appears, with the cursor beside the line spacing notation. Typing the appropriate number from 1 to 9 (2 for double-spacing, 3 for triple-spacing, and so on) and pressing ^K or the F10 function key returns you to the editing screen, with the new line spacing noted at the upper-right corner. Also inserted on-screen in WordStar Release 5 is the .LS dot command for setting spacing. This can also be typed manually, as described in Chapter 6.

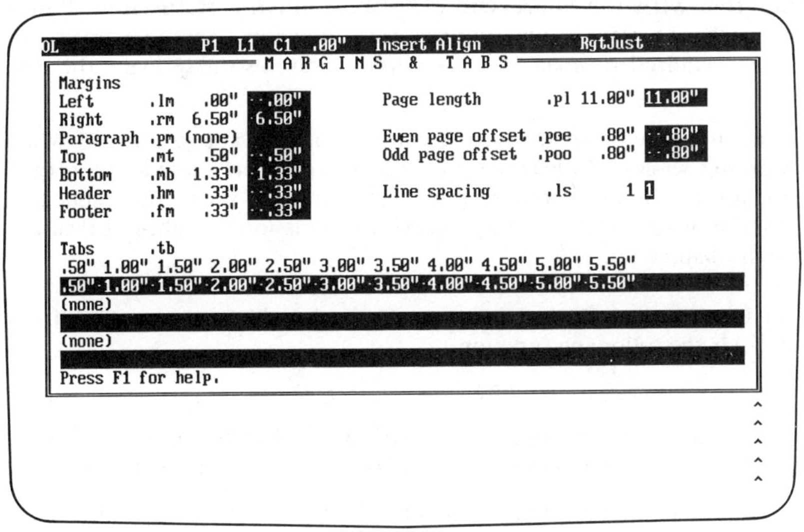

P1 L1 C1 .00" Insert Align RgtJust
MARGINS & TABS
Margins
Left .lm .00" .00"
Right .rm 6.50" 6.50"
Paragraph .pm (none)
Top .mt .50" .50"
Bottom .mb 1.33" 1.33"
Header .hm .33" .33"
Footer .fm .33" .33"
Page length .pl 11.00" 11.00"
Even page offset .poe .80" .80"
Odd page offset .poo .80" .80"
Line spacing .ls 1 1
Tabs .tb
.50" 1.00" 1.50" 2.00" 2.50" 3.00" 3.50" 4.00" 4.50" 5.00" 5.50"
.50" 1.00" 1.50" 2.00" 2.50" 3.00" 3.50" 4.00" 4.50" 5.00" 5.50"
(none)
(none)
Press F1 for help.

Fig. 4.15.

The dialog box for setting margins, tabs, and other on-screen formatting.

Notice that resetting line spacing alters the spacing between paragraphs. Unlike the last version of WordStar, Release 5 inserts an appropriate number of hard carriage return symbols (<) on the right edge of the screen at the end of a paragraph, adding a soft carriage return to fill out multiple spacing between lines. When you reformat text, auto-align preserves the extra soft return along with the hard returns. Although this provision can be confusing, it is meant to ease conversion of documents from multiple-spacing to single-spacing.

As an example of resetting line spacing, consider the sample pricing letter mentioned earlier in this chapter: it is short enough to look best with double-spaced text. To change WordStar's setting to double-space, press ^OS at the Edit display, type *2* at the prompt on the Margins & Tabs dialog box, and press ^K or the F10 function key. When the status line returns to the screen, the editing display shows the new spacing as `LinSp-2` and the .LS2 dot command interspersed in text right above the cursor.

Incidentally, if you usually create multispaced documents, you may want to alter the default line spacing of your WordStar working copy with the WSCHANGE program (see Chapter 11).

Turning Off Right-Justification

Right-justified text appears on-screen and prints out with all lines flush along the right margin. Right-justification is WordStar's default setting; when on, the editing screen notes this with the abbreviation `RgtJust` on the status line. Right-justification may have a place in typeset or laser-printed copy, but the extra spaces between words required to make the lines end evenly also may make the text difficult to read.

Right-justification is one WordStar setting you will often want to turn off when starting a working session. To leave evenly spaced words on a line and a ragged right margin, you can invoke another simple Ctrl-command formatting sequence. (The WSCHANGE program allows more permanent omission of right-justification, as explained in Chapter 11).

At help level 4, on the pull-down Layout menu (displayed by pressing Alt-L from the Edit screen) is the following function:

```
Right-justify text...     ^OJ
```

This same command toggles right-justification off when already on and on when it is turned off. This is depicted more specifically on WordStar's classic menus.

At help levels 4, 3, or 2, invoking ^O at the editing screen displays the classic Onscreen Format Menu, including this command in the Typing column:

```
J turn justification off
```

Remembering the initial Ctrl-character, when you press ^OJ at the editing screen you toggle the justification setting off—as confirmed by the elimination of the `RgtJust` message on the status line. WordStar Release 5 also inserts the dot command `.OJ OFF`. (For more on using this dot command, see Chapter 7.)

Once right-justification is off, pressing ^O at help level 4, 3, or 2 displays the classic Onscreen Format Menu with the following listing:

```
J turn justification on
```

If invoked again, the ^OJ command turns on justification, displays `RgtJust` at the status line, and inserts `.OJ ON` in your text.

Justification only works automatically on text as it is entered. If you change the justification setting and want to reformat existing text, you must press ^B or ^QU to realign your words.

In the sample pricing letter, turn off right-justification before you enter text by pressing ^OJ, eliminating the `RgtJust` prompt on the status line.

Omitting Page Numbers

WordStar automatically prints a page number at the bottom of each document page. This is useful for manuscripts, reports, and other business documents, but for many documents, including single-page correspondence, page numbering is best omitted.

Unlike other formatting changes discussed in this chapter, changing the page printing default does not involve pressing a sequence of Ctrl and letter keys.

Turning off page numbering requires a command that is embedded in your document. The command is typed as text but will not be printed, though it is saved with your document. Embedded commands always are preceded by a period and therefore are called *dot commands*. In WordStar Release 5, dot commands are automatically inserted when most on-screen formatting settings are changed. Dot commands used manually for advanced formatting and printing are discussed at length in Chapters 6 and 7.

At help level 4 with its pull-down menus, pressing Alt-L displays the Layout menu, which includes this dot command:

```
Omit page numbering       .op
```

If you move the highlighting to this line with the down-arrow key or the space bar and press Enter, the editing screen reappears with the dot command inserted in text.

At other help levels, the classic menus do not list this command. Yet at all help levels, the dot command for omitting page numbers, .OP, remains valid. This dot command may be typed at any point in the document, but must always begin in the first column.

Because omitting page numbers usually is meant for an entire document, a .OP command should be inserted as close to the beginning of a document file as possible.

To type the omit page numbering command, be sure that the cursor is positioned in the first column of the first line on the document screen. Type *.op*. (Dot commands can be entered in upper- or lowercase.) Then press Enter. At printing time, page numbers will be left off.

When the first character of text on a line is a period, the cursor stays outside the margin to allow correct entry of dot commands. For example, even though set at 0.7″ (the left margin of the sample pricing letter), a dot command would be entered on-screen beginning at 0.0″.

To omit page numbers in the sample letter, follow the instructions in this section and type *.op* at the beginning of the document.

Centering a Line of Text

Centering text horizontally on a line dramatically illustrates the difference between using a typewriter and using WordStar. To center text with a typewriter, you have to count characters in the text to be centered and calculate a position equidistant from both margins. To center text with WordStar, you simply invoke a command with two or three keystrokes, and the text is centered instantly.

At help level 4, typing Alt-L from the Edit screen pulls down the Layout menu. Among its listings is the following function:

```
Center line...              ^OC
```

At help levels 4, 3, or 2, invoking ^O at the editing screen displays the classic Onscreen Format Menu. On this menu, in the Typing column, is this command:

```
C center line
```

The complete sequence for centering a line of text horizontally is ^OC. You can position the cursor anywhere on the line of text to be centered, then press ^OC; text is repositioned immediately. WordStar ignores any spaces before or after your text when centering it.

In WordStar Release 5 (as in Release 4) you can use Shift-F2, exactly like ^OC, to center a line of text.

As with most ^O on-screen formatting commands, there is also a dot command for centering text—in this case more than one line at a time. The .OC dot command, new with WordStar Release 5, is detailed in Chapter 7. During merge printing, another dot command automatically centers text; for more on this, see Chapter 8.

In the sample pricing letter, you could center the top line of text, in lieu of letterhead. After you type the words *Widgets, Inc.*, press ^OC to center the line.

WordStar Release 5 includes a new command, one that centers text vertically on a page—inserting spaces where necessary to create even top and bottom margins from the cursor to the next page break. This vertical centering is another illustration of the difference between using a typewriter and using WordStar. Again, instead of counting spaces on the page and calculating a position equidistant from two margins, to center text with WordStar, you simply invoke an on-screen formatting command, and the text is centered instantly on the page.

At help levels 4, 3, or 2, pressing ^O at the editing screen displays the classic Onscreen Format Menu. Also on this menu is this command:

```
V vertically center
```

The complete sequence for vertically centering text is ^OV. You can position the cursor anywhere on the page; once you press ^OV, text below the cursor to the next page break is repositioned to midway between top and bottom within the remaining space on the page. WordStar inserts necessary blank spaces for formatting between the cursor and the text after it. WordStar ignores any blank lines between the cursor and text when centering vertically. If no page break command has been inserted, this function adds a .PA command in text. (For more on this dot command, see Chapter 7.)

Using Tabs

WordStar's tab stop function is handy for column entries or indenting text as it is typed. As on a typewriter, invoking the tab function advances the cursor to the next of several tab stops. WordStar indicates tab stops with exclamation points on the editing screen's ruler line.

In Release 5, WordStar's tab stops are preset at five-column intervals across the line—at 0.50″, 1.00″, 1.50″, 2.00″, 2.50″, 3.00″, 3.50″, 4.00″, 4.50″, 5.00″, and 5.50″. When you change the margin settings, the tab stops remain in place, although tabs outside the margins are temporarily eliminated.

When you press the Tab key or ^I, the cursor moves to the next tab setting to the right on a line. Pressing the Tab key when WordStar is in insert mode moves the cursor to the next tab stop, inserts hard spaces on the line, and pushes to the right any text in the way of the cursor. In overtype mode, on the other hand, the cursor jumps to the next tab setting without altering the text on the line.

New in WordStar Release 5 is the insertion of a tab symbol (►) on-screen to indicate a hard tab—one that is stored with the document and cannot be reset with auto-align. To avoid reformatting problems, when working with tabs you can turn off auto-align with a ^OA command. ***Note:*** Font size and proportional spacing may cause your text not to align correctly on-screen if it has tabs or is centered. If this is the case, a small arrow is displayed to the left of the text.

In the sample pricing letter, tab stops conveniently position the date at 4.00″. To move the cursor across the line to 4.00″, you could keep pressing the space bar, but using WordStar's tab feature is faster. To position the cursor, keep pressing either the Tab key or ^I to move the cursor through 1.00″, 1.50″, 2.00″, 2.50″, 3.00″, and 3.50″, to 4.00″. Then type the letter's date.

Changing WordStar's tab stop settings is invoked in WordStar Release 5 more efficiently than ever before with the new Margins & Tabs dialog box. In the following sections, you learn to reset regular tabs (to change tab stops) and set decimal tabs (for aligning numbers). Chapter 6 explains how to use paragraph tabs (to reset a left margin temporarily).

Resetting Regular Tabs

If WordStar's initial tab settings do not conform to your formatting needs, you can easily reset them. You can create your own ruler line by typing the appropriate dot command, a line of hyphens or other characters, including exclamation points for the tab spots, as explained in Chapter 6. In this chapter, you will use the simpler Margins & Tabs dialog box to reset tabs in a document.

With the streamlining of WordStar Release 5 functions listed on the pull-down menus, setting tab stops has no listed command of its own, sharing instead the ^OL command on the Layout menu (Margins and tabs). Nonetheless, from the editing screen at help levels 4, 3, or 2, pressing ^O displays the classic Onscreen Format Menu, with the following command in the Margins & Tabs column:

```
I set/clear tabs
```

To reset tab stops, the full command is ^OI (not ^I, which advances the cursor to the next tab). Using the ^OI command is preferable to the one indicated in the pull-down menus because ^OI brings up the Margins & Tabs dialog box (see fig. 4.15) with the cursor at the bottom line for tab stops.

On WordStar Release 5's Margins & Tabs dialog box, an unmodified copy of WordStar displays these tab stop settings: 0.50″, 1.00″, 1.50″, 2.00″, 2.50″, 3.00″, 3.50″, 4.00″, 4.50″, 5.00″, and 5.50″. You can edit, erase, or add to these tabs on the same line using WordStar's cursor movement and deletion commands (explained in Chapter 3).

No longer are you limited to changing each tab stop individually, as in previous WordStar versions. In WordStar Release 5, you can type column numbers (from 2 through 254) or inch measurements, ending with the inch sign (″—from 0.1″ to 25.3″), anywhere on the tab stop line. All tab stop numbers must be separated with spaces or commas.

When you finish typing tab stop numbers, press ^K or the F10 function key to return to the editing screen. Newly located exclamation points in the ruler line represent the new tab stops. WordStar Release 5 also inserts the .TB dot command in your text to indicate the new tab stops (for more on using this dot command, see Chapter 6).

Veterans of previous WordStar versions should note that the old ^ON tab erase function is no longer needed, so WordStar Release 5 has allocated the ^ON command for note functions (covered in Chapter 6). Also no longer operative is the shortcut of positioning the cursor in the column where you want to clear a tab and pressing Esc. (Esc now clears the dialog box.) Pressing A no longer clears all the tab settings as it did in earlier versions of WordStar.

The sample pricing letter provides a good example of using reset tab stops. To conform to the letter's pricing table caption format, WordStar's default tab stops would have to be replaced with stops at columns 10, 19, 33, and 50. To set new tab stops, press ^OI and, at the dialog box, type *10, 19, 33,* and *50*; or *0.9", 1.8", 3.2",* and *4.9"*, then press ^K or F10. With the new tab settings in place, pressing the Tab key (or ^I) moves the cursor to each tab stop where you can type the appropriate headings.

Setting Decimal Tabs

When you type tables with numbers and decimals, you can improve legibility by lining up the decimal points in columns. In WordStar, you can accomplish this alignment easily with decimal tab stops. When you type numbers at decimal tab stops, whole numbers are automatically placed to the left of the tab stop and numbers following the decimal point are entered to the right.

To set a decimal tab, you follow a procedure similar to that for setting regular tabs. After pressing ^OI from the editing screen, simply type a number sign (#) followed by the inch measurement desired for the decimal tab stop. Several decimal tab stops can be set at the same time, separated by commas or spaces. Regular and decimal stops can be intermixed on the same tab stop line. When number entry is complete, press ^K or F10 to accept the new decimal tabs and display the editing screen. The ruler line will display number signs at the decimal tab locations.

To use decimal tabs in the sample letter, the two lines of pricing figures should be typed at columns 24, 39, and 55 to match the formatting of the numbers in its table. To set decimal tabs, press ^OI, type *#2.3, #3.8, #5.4* and enter this setting by pressing ^K or F10. The decimal tab stops are indicated on the ruler line.

To complete use of the decimal tab stops in the sample pricing letter, press the Tab key (or ^I) to bring the cursor to the first decimal tab stop. If you type *$9*, these characters move to the left of the decimal stop. Then once a decimal point (.) is typed, further numbers are entered to the right of the decimal tab stop—like the decimal numbers .75. Pressing the Tab key or ^I moves the cursor to the next decimal tab stop for continued number entry.

If you need to switch from regular tabs to decimal tabs, or vice versa, you must reset the tab, delete the existing indents, and retab the text. The same procedure may be necessary if you insert or delete columns in a table with both types of tabs.

Drawing Lines and Boxes

Framing text in borders is helpful for setting off important contents in a report, letter, or chart. WordStar Release 5 lets you draw lines and boxes with special characters that are part of the extended character set on IBM PCs and compatible machines. To draw line or box characters, WordStar employs combinations of the Alt and function keys, as indicated in figure 4.16.

Fig. 4.16.
Line- and box-drawing characters (courtesy MicroPro International).

Alt-F1	│	Alt-F2	─
Alt-F3	┌	Alt-F4	┐
Alt-F5	└	Alt-F6	┘
Alt-F7	┬	Alt-F8	┴
Alt-F9	├	Alt-F10	┤

The combination of the Alt key and the F1 function key produces a vertical line; Alt-F2 gives you a horizontal line. Corners for a box are produced with Alt-F3, Alt-F4, Alt-F5, and Alt-F6. And various T-shaped line intersections are produced with Alt-F7, Alt-F8, Alt-F9, and Alt-F10.

The line and box characters produce continuous lines on-screen, but whether they will reproduce exactly that way on paper depends on your printer. Laser printers will duplicate what you see on-screen. On the other hand, if you have a dot matrix or a daisywheel printer, WordStar will have to substitute available characters to approximate the drawing characters.

Quick Start 4: Framing a Table

This Quick Start provides hands-on experience with line and box drawing, one of WordStar's most underused features. With a little practice, you can add to your documents' impact with the line drawing characters. Regardless of help level or type of system, this step-by-step set of instructions can lead you through the procedure for framing a table, applicable to all kinds of text. The functions used include the following:

- Drawing with line characters
- Inserting corner characters
- Toggling overtype and insert mode

If you have not already done so, you should start at the editing screen by typing the text of the table in the sample pricing letter—the seven lines from "Price" to

"Widget," using the margins and tabs indicated in previous examples in this chapter. Be sure to turn off auto-align (^OA) and right-justification (^OJ).

To draw the box in the sample letter, you use the Alt-function key combinations for vertical and horizontal lines as well as for corners. As you draw, you need to observe certain precautions so that you won't disrupt the formatted text you already have on-screen. Before beginning the steps that follow, be sure that WordStar is set in insert mode; the word `Insert` should be displayed on the status line.

1. Move the cursor to the line that contains column headings for the pricing table—the line that begins with the word `Price`.
2. To change the line spacing to single-space, press ^OS, type *1*, and press Enter.
3. Now press Enter to move the table down on-screen and to insert a blank line. To avoid producing any extraneous characters that might disrupt existing formatting, toggle off insert mode (turn on overtype) by pressing ^V. (`Insert` disappears from the status line.)
4. Press Alt-F3 to create the top left corner of the box.
5. To draw a horizontal line across the top border of the box, press Alt-F2 in every column through column 59. (Check the status line for the column number.)
6. To draw the top right corner of the box in column 60, press Alt-F4. Press Enter to bring the cursor to the beginning of the next line.
7. To draw a vertical line at the left border, press Alt-F1. Then move the cursor to column 60 and press Alt-F1 again to put a vertical line character at the right border. Press Enter to go to the next line. Repeat this step to draw vertical line characters on both sides of the next six lines of text.
8. Press Alt-F5 to place a corner at the lower left of the box.
9. To place a horizontal line along the bottom edge of the box, press Alt-F2 in columns 9 through 59.
10. To complete the box, draw a right bottom corner with Alt-F6.
11. Toggle insert mode back on with ^V. Press Enter to insert another blank line. The box is now finished on-screen.

To see a printout of this box, first save the document by pressing ^KD. Once at the Opening display, invoke printing of this file and your printer will produce a hard copy of the text.

Using Print Enhancements

In addition to the on-screen formatting features you have encountered so far, WordStar includes functions to enhance the appearance of printed documents. These functions are called print controls. Among WordStar's print-control features are underline, boldface, double strike, overprint, strikeout, subscripts, and superscripts.

Most of the commands for print controls act as toggles. You must use one command in front of text to turn on the effect you want and one command after the targeted text to turn off the effect. You should turn off special print effects before punctuation marks; otherwise, these items will also be printed with the enhancement.

The effects of print-control commands are not usually displayed on-screen. Instead of seeing what will actually appear in a printout (as you do with most WordStar features), you see on the computer screen the control characters that indicate the command for the intended print effect.

WordStar's print-control commands are summarized in table 4.5. Notice that all the print-control commands use keystroke sequences that start with ^P. Each of these commands is discussed in the sections that follow.

Table 4.5
Print-Control Commands

Command	*Function*
^PS or F3	Toggles underline on/off
^PB or F4	Toggles boldface on/off
^PD	Toggles double strike on/off
^PH	Overprints a character
^P ↵	Overprints a line
^PX	Toggles strikeout on/off
^PV	Toggles subscript on/off
^PT	Toggles superscript on/off
^OD or Shift-F1	Toggles print display on/off
^PC	Pauses printing

At help level 4, most of the principal print enhancement commands covered in this chapter are listed on the pull-down Style menu (see fig. 4.17). From the editing screen this menu is displayed by pressing Alt-S. All but one of the eight functions on this menu are detailed in the following pages. The Choose Font command is explained in Chapter 7.

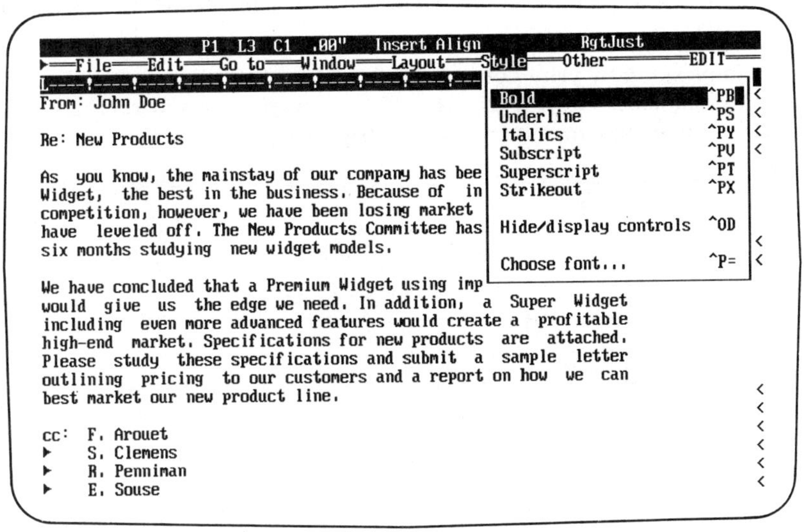
P1 L3 C1 .00" Insert Align RgtJust
File Edit Go to Window Layout Style Other EDIT
Bold ^PB
Underline ^PS
Italics ^PY
Subscript ^PV
Superscript ^PT
Strikeout ^PX
Hide/display controls ^OD
Choose font... ^P=
From: John Doe
Re: New Products
As you know, the mainstay of our company has bee
Widget, the best in the business. Because of in
competition, however, we have been losing market
have leveled off. The New Products Committee has
six months studying new widget models.
We have concluded that a Premium Widget using imp
would give us the edge we need. In addition, a Super Widget
including even more advanced features would create a profitable
high-end market. Specifications for new products are attached.
Please study these specifications and submit a sample letter
outlining pricing to our customers and a report on how we can
best market our new product line.
cc: F. Arouet
S. Clemens
R. Penniman
E. Souse

Fig. 4.17.

The pull-down Style menu.

At WordStar help levels 4, 3 or 2, for a more complete listing of available print-control commands, press ^P at the editing screen. The WordStar classic Print Controls Menu will be displayed on your screen. This menu is illustrated in figure 4.18.

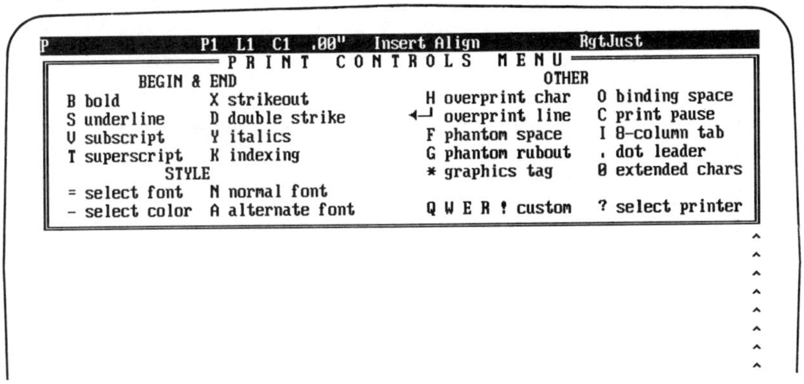
P P1 L1 C1 .00" Insert Align RgtJust
P R I N T C O N T R O L S M E N U
BEGIN & END
B bold X strikeout
S underline D double strike
V subscript Y italics
T superscript K indexing
STYLE
= select font N normal font
- select color A alternate font
OTHER
H overprint char O binding space
overprint line C print pause
F phantom space I 8-column tab
G phantom rubout . dot leader
* graphics tag 0 extended chars
Q W E R ! custom ? select printer

Fig. 4.18.

The Print Controls Menu.

In WordStar Release 5, 24 functions are listed in four columns on the Print Controls Menu. To use the commands in the columns labeled BEGIN & END, you must place a command before and after the text that the commands affect. Two more columns, labeled OTHER, list print commands that are not used in pairs. Remember that all the commands listed on the menu are preceded with ^P, as indicated by the P in the top left corner of the menu. Pressing the space bar clears this menu.

Note: Ten of the print-control commands on the classic Print Controls Menu are covered in this chapter. The other commands on this menu are discussed in Chapter 7.

To provide examples of how print controls work, the rest of this chapter refers to another sample document. Shown in figure 4.19 is a new products marketing plan, also requested in the sample memo created in Chapter 1.

Fig. 4.19.

The new products marketing plan.

Selling The Widget Lifestyle

Historically, Widgets, Inc. has led the industry with the Standard Widget, the best in the business. Our marketing approach was straightforward, touting the product's high quality.

With the New Products Committee's decision to introduce new widget models, our marketing will have to branch off in two directions: **brand recognition** and **product differentiation.**

After consulting demographic projections and focus group tests, we recommend the following unifying theme for all marketing efforts: "The Good Life--Widgets and You."

An institutional campaign will link the Widgets, Inc., name with the Good Life in famous resort areas. Putting our logo on ski chalets, rafts and sail boats in places like Mégève, the Grand Cañon, and Malmö will help spread the word. We may also start a graffiti campaign in these places with the likes of "~~Work~~--Widgets" to capture the youth market's attention.

At the same time, we will spend heavily on twin ad campaigns using the central theme for product differentiation. To emphasize the Premium Widget's improved materials, we will portray it in grueling environments like alpine blizzards and tropical H_2O.

On the other hand, the Super Widget campaign will stress the high-end market, with images of leisure and wealth. According to Fetzer in his 1984 study of consumer buying habits*, this should give us the most bang for our bucks.

As this marketing strategy is implemented, we welcome input from all concerned departments and individuals.

---

* Fritz F. Fetzer, "Snob Appeal and Sales Surges Among Tri-Lateral Consumers", Media Methods, March 1984.

As you can see, this sample marketing report includes examples of underline, boldface, subscript, and superscript, as well as other features explained in the following pages. To practice all the principal WordStar print-control commands once in text, you can type this brief document, as called for in the following pages. You may, however, prefer to apply these print enhancements directly to your own documents.

Using Underlining

Underlining is one of the most commonly used print-control effects. Underlining is indispensable in printed documents for emphasis, titles, or italics. Though underlining is actually seen on-screen only with a monochrome graphics adapter, WordStar's underlining begin and end markers are easy to spot and use on other displays.

When WordStar is used at help level 4, pressing Alt-S from the Edit screen pulls down the Style menu. On the second line of this menu's listings is the following command:

```
Underline                    ^PS
```

When at WordStar's help levels 4, 3, or 2, pressing ^P from the editing screen displays the classic Print Controls Menu. On this menu, also on the second line (of the leftmost BEGIN & END column) is this command:

```
S underline
```

From the editing screen, the complete command for initiating underlining is ^PS.

In addition, as with the previous version of WordStar, Release 5 assigns the underline command to function key F3. At help levels 3, 2, and 1, the editing screen's listing of function key commands at the bottom includes this: `3Undrlin`. Pressing F3 executes a ^PS combination.

When you use either ^PS or F3, remember to type the command before and after any characters you want to underline in your printout. The underline command itself appears on-screen as `^S`, but is not added to the character count or printed. If you forget to enter the command a second time to toggle off the print effect, the rest of your text will be underlined. Always use a second toggle command to turn off a BEGIN & END print effect.

WordStar displays on-screen highlighting for text that will be underlined in print. When you installed WordStar, you chose whether to have this highlighting appear as underlining, as a color, as brighter characters, or in reverse type. You can further customize the color attributed to underlining with either the WINSTALL or WSCHANGE programs, described in Chapter 2 and 11, respectively. The advantage of on-screen highlighting is that you can immediately see whether you have omitted the command to turn off underlining in the rest of your text.

Note that the underline command does not underscore spaces between words—unless you modify WordStar with the WSCHANGE program or use a dot command (see Chapter 6). For now, if you want to underline between words, you can type an underscore (the shifted hyphen key).

The sample report includes a title and a phrase to be underlined. When typing the title, start by pressing ^PS or F3, type the report's title, and turn off underlining after the title by pressing ^PS or F3 again. In the report's body copy, the phrase `the best in the business` should be underlined between words, as well. Preceding the phrase with ^PS or F3, as you type its text, enter underscores where you otherwise would include spaces between words; then press ^PS or F3 again to turn off underlining.

Using Boldface and Double Strike

Denser printing of text can stress the importance of selected words or phrases, making them stand out in a document. WordStar provides two print-control functions for such emphasized text: boldface and double strike. Boldface text is extremely dense, because the printer strikes three times to form each character. On letter-quality printers, the multistriking is slightly offset to broaden each character. Double strike is a lighter boldface function that has the print element strike each character twice.

Although boldface and double strike should be used sparingly, some people occasionally print entire documents in double strike to obtain printed characters that are darker. On dot-matrix printers, double strike can fill the gaps between dots to create more legible characters.

At help level 4, the pull-down Style menu (displayed by pressing Alt-S from the editing screen), features this function as the first of its listings:

```
Bold                        ^PB
```

At WordStar's help levels 4, 3, or 2, when you press ^P at the editing screen, the classic Print Controls Menu is displayed. On this menu are a pair of commands, on the first and second lines of the first and second columns—under the BEGIN & END heading:

```
B bold
            D double strike
```

The complete sequences for initiating the commands are ^PB for boldface and ^PD for double strike. (Though not indicated on the pull-down menus, the ^PD double strike command is a valid command at help level 4.)

WordStar Release 5's function key F4 also issues a ^PB command for boldface. You can press ^PB or F4 to execute the boldface command.

When you press ^PB (or F4), the symbol `^B` is displayed on-screen. Remember that commands for boldface and double strike are toggles that must be invoked twice—once to turn on the print effect and again to turn it off.

WordStar Release 5 highlights on-screen text to be printed in boldface or double-strike print. As with the underline feature, the on-screen highlight indicates whether you have included the second boldface or double-strike command to turn off the print effect. With the WSCHANGE program, you can assign different colors or intensities to the on-screen attributes for bold or double strike (see Chapter 11).

In the sample marketing report, the words `brand recognition` should be printed in boldface. To do so, press ^PB or F4 once before and again after you type the words. `^B` will appear on-screen where you have entered the boldface command, and the text between the print-control symbols will be highlighted. To invoke double strike printing of the marketing motto a few lines farther down, press ^PD before and after typing the words `"The Good Life-Widgets and You."` The commands appear on-screen as `^D` with the highlighted characters in-between.

Using Overprint

Printing two characters in the same space overcomes the limitations of standardized keyboard character sets. For instance, you can use this print effect to place an accent mark over a letter or to create a foreign character that your printer cannot normally produce from its character set.

WordStar has a ^P command sequence for instructing the printer to backspace and print a character over one that has just been printed. You must insert this overprint command in text just after the character that is to be printed over, then enter the accent or other character that is to overprint the letter. The overprint command is invoked just once to cause the printer to backspace and overprint the character with another strike of the print head. The ^P ↵ command overprints an entire line with another.

None of the pull-down menus in WordStar Release 5 lists a command for overprinting. On the classic Print Controls Menu, however, you will find a pair of useful overprint functions. At help levels 4, 3, or 2, press ^P from the editing screen to display the classic Print Control Menu. The top two listings in the menu's third column (headed OTHER) are the following:

```
H overprint char
↵ overprint line
```

The first command overprints a single character, but invoking the second command can overprint an entire line of text with the next line in a document. Taking into account the initial keystroke for the Print Controls Menu, the full sequence for the overprint command is ^PH; the combination for overprinting a line of text is ^P ↵ .

To overprint a character, type the first character, then press ^PH (a `^H` marker is displayed on-screen), followed by the character to print over it. For additional overprints of the same character you can press ^PH before each extra character. When overprinting for accents, umlauts, and so on, type the letter first, followed by pressing ^PH and then the appropriate symbol to place above it when printing.

To overprint a line with the next one, the two lines must be single-spaced. Press ^P at the end of the first line and then press Enter. ***Note:*** Don't hold down the Ctrl key while you press Enter, or else the second line may not begin printing at the left margin. A hyphen appears in the flag column at the far right side of the screen. End the second line by pressing Enter. When you print the document, the second line overprints the first on a single line.

The sample report includes overprinting examples in French, Spanish, and Swedish place names to be correctly printed using a standard English-language keyboard. To type these foreign names, instruct WordStar to overprint accent marks in Mégève by pressing ^PH and typing an apostrophe (′), and further in the word, pressing ^PH and a backward apostrophe (‘). Type the letter to be accented followed by ^PH and the accent mark. The same is true of the tilde (˜) in Cañon and the quotation marks (") used to broaden the o in Malmö. The symbol `^H` would appear on-screen between the characters to be overprinted.

Using Strikeout

A variation on overprinting is of special use in legal documents. This strikeout function consists of overprinting text with hyphens—a convention in marking legal text to be deleted while keeping it readable. Unlike the overprinting commands, the strikeout command is a toggle and must be used twice—to turn the effect on and off.

5

At WordStar's help level 4, the pull-down Style menu (to display, press Alt-S from the editing screen) includes the following function toward the bottom of its listings:

```
Strikeout            ^PX
```

At help levels 4, 3, or 2, pressing ^P at the editing screen brings up the classic Print Controls Menu. This menu features the same command at the top of the second BEGIN & END column:

```
X strikeout
```

Remember that the full command is actually ^PX. When you use the command, `^X` appears on-screen.

Like other BEGIN & END print-control commands in WordStar, text after the strikeout command is highlighted on-screen until you turn off the effect. (You can also adjust the color or shading of this highlighting with the WSCHANGE program; see Chapter 11.)

WordStar Release 5 includes a new dot command for changing the strikeout character from within a document. The command is .XX, followed by the new character. This feature is useful for double underlining: invoke the underscore character (.XX—) as the strikeout character and invoke print control commands for both underline (^PS) and strikeout (^PX).

As before, the strikeout character can be changed more permanently with the WSCHANGE program. For details see Chapter 11.

The fourth paragraph of the sample marketing report contains an example of the strikeout feature. To have the word `Work` struck out when the document is printed, press ^PX, type the word, and press ^PX again.

Using Subscript and Superscript

Printing subscripts and superscripts is essential for mathematical formulas, chemical symbols, footnotes, and other applications. WordStar uses ^P commands to print text below (subscript) or above (superscript) the line on which the command appears.

Note: Some printers won't accommodate a subscript or superscript in single-spaced text. With such printers, subscripts and superscripts will be positioned properly only with double-spaced text. Check your printer manual for information.

5

With the pull-down menus at help level 4, you can find the following print-control commands halfway down the Style menu (obtained by pressing Alt-S from the editing screen):

```
Subscript          ^PV
Superscript        ^PT
```

The classic Print Controls Menu, seen at help levels 4, 3, or 2 by pressing ^P at the editing screen, lists the subscript and superscript commands in the first column of the BEGIN & END commands:

```
V subscript
T superscript
```

The complete command sequences are ^PV for subscript and ^PT for superscript. On-screen, you see `^V` and `^T`. The subscript and superscript commands must be used before and after the characters to be printed below or above a line. Any characters typed after a subscript or superscript command are highlighted on-screen until the command is issued again to turn off the effect.

To set how far below or above the line a subscript or superscript appears when printed, you can specify the amount of printer roll with a dot command (see Chapter 7).

The sample marketing report contains examples of subscripts and superscripts. To print the symbol H2O correctly, you must print 2 as a subscript. Press ^PV, type *2*, and press ^PV again (putting ^V symbols on-screen and highlighting the 2).

In the next-to-last paragraph of the report, you would need to print an asterisk (*) as a superscript to call attention to an article citation at the end of the report. To do this, press ^PT, type the asterisk, and then press ^PT again. The ^T symbols and the highlighting or color attribute between them on-screen indicate that the asterisk will be printed above the line.

Toggling the Print-Control Command Display

Print-control commands distort the appearance of formatted text on-screen. Lines of text that include print-control commands often extend beyond the right margin on-screen. The commands themselves don't appear in a printout, and the document's formatting is not distorted on paper. However, the discrepancy can be distracting when you are formatting copy on-screen, particularly when you are working with tabular material.

So that you can see how your text will look when printed, you can turn off the display of WordStar print-control commands with an on-screen format function.

At help level 4, the pull-down Style menu (Alt-S from the editing screen) shows this listing:

```
Hide/display controls   ^OD
```

At help levels 4, 3, or 2, the classic Onscreen Format Menu (^O from the editing screen) includes the following at the top of the DISPLAY column:

```
D turn print controls off
```

The ^OD command is a toggle. The command turns off the display of print controls; if they are already turned off, ^OD returns the display to the screen.

At help levels 3, 2, and 1, the function key lines at the bottom of the screen show `Display` in the line for Shift-function key commands. At all levels, Shift-F1 acts as a toggle for the print-control display. Pressing this function key combination has the same effect as pressing ^OD.

If you typed the text of the sample report with all the print-control commands, the copy on your screen would look like the text shown in figure 4.20 (complete with formatting distortions).

```
                   ^SSelling The Widget Lifestyle^S
   Historicaly, Widgets, Inc. has led the industry with the
Standard Widget, ^Sthe_best_in_the_business^S. Our marketing approach
was straightforward, touting the product's high quality.
   With the New Products Committee's decision to introduce new
widget models, our marketing will have to branch off in two
directions: ^Bbrand recognition^B and ^Bproduct differentiation^B.
   After consulting demographic projections and focus group
tests, we recommend the following unifying theme for all
marketing efforts: "^DThe Good Life--Widgets and You^D."
   An institutional campaign will link the Widgets, Inc., name
with the Good Life in famous resort areas. Putting our logo on
ski chalets, rafts and sail boats in places like Me^H'g`^Heve, the
Grand Can^H~on, and Malmo^H" will help spread the word. We may also
start a graffiti campaign in these places with the likes of
"^XWork^X--Widgets" to capture the youth market's attention.
   At the same time, we will spend heavily on twin ad campaigns
using the central theme for product differentiation. To emphasize
the Premium Widget's improved materials, we will portray it in
grueling environments like alpine blizzards and tropical H^V2^VO.
   On the other hand, the Super Widget campaign will stress the
high-end market, with images of leisure and wealth. According to
Fetzer in his 1984 study of consumer buying habits^T*^T, this should
give us the most bang for our bucks.
    As this marketing strategy is implemented, we welcome input
from all concerned departments and individuals.
-----
^T*^T Fritz F. Fetzer, "Snob Appeal and Sales Surges Among Tri-
---------------------------------------------------------------------P
Lateral Consumers", ^SMedia_Methods^S, March 1984.
```

Fig. 4.20.
The sample marketing plan as it appears on-screen.

To see the report's actual formatting, press ^OD. The on-screen print-control commands disappear, and the report's format conforms to margin settings that otherwise appear when printed. To restore display of print-control commands, press ^OD.

Understanding the Page-Break Feature

One of WordStar's pioneering features was the display of page breaks, an on-screen indication of a page's limit. Page breaks are automatically shown as a line of hyphens ending with a P:

```
------------------------------------------------------------------------------------------------P
```

On a graphics screen the line is solid, not made up of hyphens. These characters do not appear in printed documents.

WordStar's preset page length of 66 lines allows 55 lines of text per page. On standard 8 1/2-by-11-inch paper, this page length includes a top margin of 3 lines and a bottom margin of 8 lines. (You can change the number of lines per page, as well as the top and bottom margins, either temporarily with the formatting commands detailed in Chapter 6 or permanently with the WSCHANGE program explained in Chapter 11.)

As in past versions, WordStar Release 5 inserts page breaks automatically when text exceeds the limits of page format settings. New with WordStar Release 5 are newspaper-style columns (see Chapter 6) and the display of page breaks only when the last column is filled. In such a case, the break is a "soft" page break, subject to reformatting if text is later extended or deleted. To insert "hard" page breaks that always start a new page, use the dot command .PA, as explained in Chapter 6.

If you typed the sample marketing report, pressing Enter twice at the end of the last paragraph of the report itself would display a page break because the text exceeds 55 lines. The status line at the top of the screen would show that the cursor is on page 2.

To see the effects of the sample report's print-control commands on paper, finish typing the citation to the footnote in the report and then save the document and print it. You should, however, know about one more print command if you do not have an automatic sheet feeder or continuous-feed paper.

Pausing a Print Job

Unless you issue a command to do otherwise, WordStar prints successive pages without stopping. This feature is a problem if you have to feed sheets of paper into your printer manually. WordStar provides a number of ways to stop printing temporarily. The easiest way inserts a print control command in a document at the point where you want the printer to stop printing. To stop printing between pages, answer yes to the `Pause between pages?` prompt on the Print Menu.

None of WordStar Release 5's pull-down menus includes the print pause function, but the classic Print Controls Menu still lists it. At help levels 4, 3, or 2, pressing ^P from the editing screen displays this classic menu, with the following function listed in the menu's last column (headed OTHER):

```
C print pause
```

The complete command sequence is ^PC. You can place this printing pause command in a document anywhere you want to stop your printer.

While printing a document, the printer stops when it encounters a ^PC command. The message `Print Wait` appears at the right of the screen. During this pause, you can put a new sheet of paper in the printer. To continue printing, press P. The Printing Menu appears. In the left column is the following command:

```
C continue after pausing
```

To resume printing, press C.

For most documents, including the sample report, you can enter the ^PC command immediately after each page break line on-screen. This placement gives you the opportunity to insert a new sheet of paper during the pause. After you press ^PC, the symbol ^C is displayed on-screen.

In the example of the sample marketing report, having entered all necessary print commands into its text, you would now save the document by pressing the save-and-done command: ^KD. Once back at the Opening display, you could print your document by pressing P, entering the file name *report* at the prompt, and pressing ^K or F10. When printing pauses, you would insert a new sheet of paper, press P, and then press C.

5

Editing with WordStar

Having learned about WordStar's simpler text-editing commands in Chapter 3, you can advance to features for maximizing text changes with a minimum of keystrokes. Once you are familiar with the WordStar commands introduced in this chapter, you can achieve greater efficiency in correcting and polishing text.

Good writing is often 90 percent good editing. Every thought, however brilliant, can benefit from refinement. The text-revision functions presented in this chapter give you the freedom and flexibility to rework and improve your material quickly and easily. Many of the examples of WordStar's text-editing facilities are based on the sample documents you created according to instructions in previous chapters.

This chapter covers about 50 commands, most of which you will find useful in your daily work. With these commands, you can perform the following time-saving functions:

- Manipulate disk files while editing a document
- Move, copy, erase, and save blocks of text
- Open and size an on-screen window and move text into it
- Send the cursor quickly to any location in a document
- Locate specified text and replace it automatically

If you have used previous releases of WordStar, you will appreciate the added commands indicated by the Release 5 icons. Among the new features are windowing for dual file editing; improved hyphenation; and the pull-down menus, which supplement WordStar's classic menus. You also will notice improved performance in the speed of scrolling and find-and-replace operations.

Both recent WordStar converts and veterans of previous versions commonly ignore many of the commands in this chapter—at a significant loss in efficiency when editing text. Not only knowing the editing functions but applying them with a minimum of keystrokes is the key to increased productivity.

Many commands mentioned in this chapter are used in combination for everyday word processing applications; you can streamline these commands by creating keystroke-saving shorthand macros—a process explained in Chapter 9. Also of help during editing are the spelling-checker and synonym-finding features discussed in Chapter 10.

Performing File Operations from within a Document

Among the commands introduced in Chapter 4 are single-letter Opening Menu commands that rename, copy, and delete files, and commands that print files and run DOS commands. These functions also can be performed from within a document. Without leaving the text you are editing, you can perform operations on other files. This section discusses these commands and an additional function that lets you incorporate other files into your text while you continue to edit.

All the command sequences discussed in the first part of this chapter begin with ^K (see table 5.1) and are listed on the Block & Save Menu (introduced at the end of Chapter 3).

Table 5.1
Commands for Performing File Operations from within a Document

Command	*Function*
^KL	Change logged drive/directory
^KE	Rename file
^KO	Copy file
^KJ	Delete file
^KF	Run DOS command
^KP	Print file
^KR	Insert file into document

5

These commands for file operations during editing are unchanged from the latest version of WordStar; but in Release 5, the prompts have been replaced by dialog boxes for specifying directory or file names. Many of these dialog boxes are identical to the ones displayed for file commands at the Opening screen.

While you are editing at help level 4, the pull-down File menu lists most of the available file-handling commands. Press Alt-F at the Edit screen to display this menu. The entire menu is devoted to the file functions, including one that has been split in two to provide a pair of options. Other important file operations are listed on the Edit menu, pulled down by pressing Alt-E, and the Other menu, invoked with Alt-O.

When you are using help level 4, 3, or 2, pressing ^K at the Edit screen displays the Block & Save Menu (see fig. 5.1). Notice that the Block & Save Menu lists under FILE all the file-handling commands available during editing.

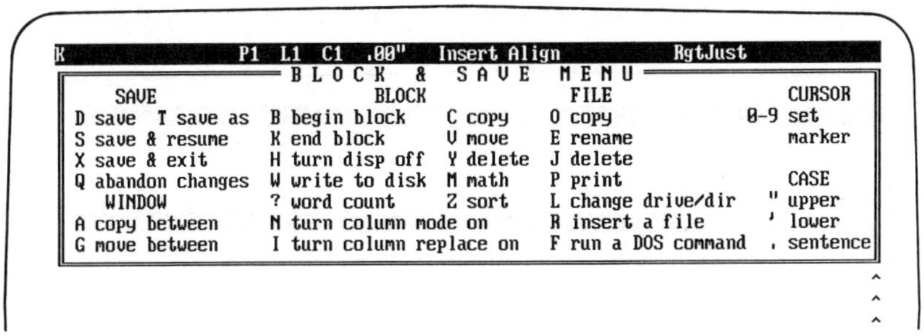
K P1 L1 C1 .00" Insert Align RgtJust
B L O C K & S A V E M E N U
SAVE
D save T save as
S save & resume
X save & exit
Q abandon changes
WINDOW
A copy between
G move between
BLOCK
B begin block C copy
K end block V move
H turn disp off Y delete
W write to disk M math
? word count Z sort
N turn column mode on
I turn column replace on
FILE
O copy
E rename
J delete
P print
L change drive/dir
R insert a file
F run a DOS command
CURSOR
0-9 set marker
CASE
" upper
' lower
. sentence

Fig. 5.1. *WordStar's commands for manipulating blocks of copy.*

The seven file operations on the Block & Save Menu may not be among the best known, but you should become familiar with them. These options help you avoid closing a document and interrupting your work for routine file handling. On floppy disk systems, some of these commands can save your work from loss during a disk-full error (see the end of this chapter). The commands for file handling while editing are detailed in the following pages.

Changing the Logged Drive or Directory

Changing WordStar's logged drive or directory is handy while you are editing a document. For instance, you may want to retrieve a file from a drive or directory other than the one that is currently logged. Or when starting your WordStar session, if you don't designate the correct logged drive (and directory on a hard disk), your document will not be saved to the proper location.

At help level 4, press Alt-F to pull down the File menu, where the following command is given:

```
Change drive/directory... ^KL
```

At help levels 4, 3, and 2, if you press ^K, you can see the classic Block & Save Menu. In the menu's FILE column, notice the following listing:

```
L change drive/dir
```

The letter L serves the same function on the Block & Save Menu as it does on the Opening Menu. From the document screen, the complete command is ^KL.

While editing a document, you press ^KL to display the Log dialog box, identical to the one you see when you press L at the Opening Menu. The Log box lists the letters that designate valid drives for your system, tells you the current logged drive and directory, and displays a line where you can enter a new logged drive (see fig. 5.2). If you want to change the logged drive, type the correct drive letter (and directory) and press Enter. If the current drive information is satisfactory, simply press Enter or Esc. (For more about using the Log dialog box, see Chapter 3.)

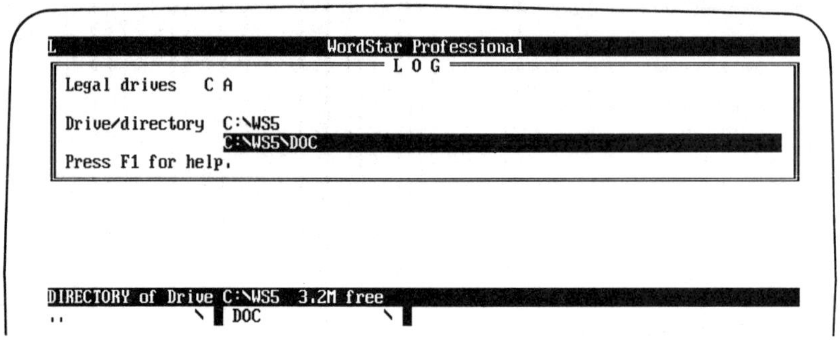
L
WordStar Professional
L O G
Legal drives C A
Drive/directory C:\WS5
C:\WS5\DOC
Press F1 for help.
DIRECTORY of Drive C:\WS5 3.2M free
.. \ DOC \

Fig. 5.2.
Dialog box for changing the logged drive and directory.

Renaming a File

While editing a document with WordStar, you may want to rename another document file. For instance, to save the current document under the same name as an existing file without losing the second file's content, you can rename the second file. With the file renaming command at the Edit screen, you cannot rename the document on which you are working, but you can rename another one stored on disk. To rename your document, you use the Save As command—^KT on the Block & Save menu (explained in Chapter 3).

If WordStar is set for help level 4, you find this listing on the File menu:

```
Rename a file...            ^KE
```

If WordStar is set for help level 4, 3, or 2, when you press ^K, you display the classic Block & Save Menu. The command for renaming a file is listed on the second line of the menu's FILE column, as follows:

```
E rename
```

This command performs the same function as the E command available at the Opening screen. From the Edit screen, the complete command sequence for renaming a file is ^KE.

When you press ^KE from the document screen, WordStar displays the message shown when you press E at the Opening Menu—the Rename dialog box. Below the box are listed the names of the files on the logged drive and directory. The box contains lines for entering the name of the file to be renamed and its new name (see fig. 5.3).

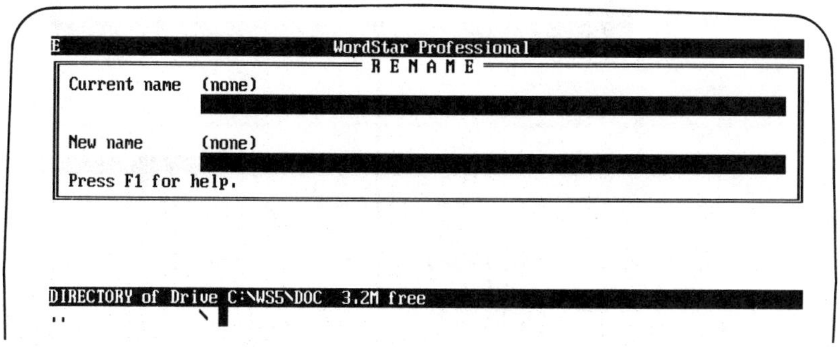

E
WordStar Professional
R E N A M E
Current name (none)
New name (none)
Press F1 for help.
DIRECTORY of Drive C:\WS5\DOC 3.2M free
..

Fig. 5.3.
Dialog box for renaming a file.

You type the name of the file to be renamed or point to it in the directory of files on-screen. Then press Enter to move the cursor to the line for a new name. After typing that name, press Enter to complete the process. For more on using the Rename box, see Chapter 4.

Copying a File

Making a duplicate of a file while you are editing another document can be useful for archival purposes. Having an extra copy is also important when you move a file to another disk or directory; a duplicate is good insurance in case of a disk failure or loss of a file.

At help level 4, the pull-down File menu shows the following command:

```
Copy a file...              ^KO
```

At help level 4, 3, or 2, the classic Block & Save Menu includes at the top of the menu's FILE column the function for copying a file from within a document:

```
O copy
```

The complete keystroke sequence for making a copy of a file from a document screen is ^KO.

When you invoke the Copy File command while editing, the on-screen display is the one you see when you press O at the classic Opening Menu: the Copy dialog box. As illustrated in figure 5.4, this box shows lines for the name of the file to copy and the copy's new name. You type the name of the file to be copied or use the arrow keys to point to the name in the file directory; then press Enter. The cursor moves to the line for the copy's name.

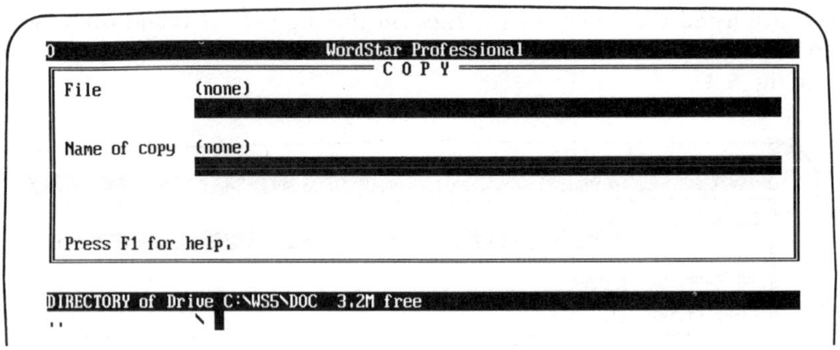
WordStar Professional
C O P Y
File (none)
Name of copy (none)
Press F1 for help.
DIRECTORY of Drive C:\WS5\DOC 3.2M free

Fig. 5.4.
Dialog box for copying a file.

The new file name must follow the rules for DOS file names. The new name should not be used by another file on disk, unless you want the new copy of your document to replace an existing file. After you have typed the new name, press Enter to complete the copy procedure. If you supply the name of a file that already exists on that directory, a message asks whether you want to replace the existing file with the new copy. If you want to do so, press Y.

Once a new file name is accepted, WordStar duplicates the original file, and the name of its copy is added to the directory.

Deleting a File

While you are working on a document, you may want to delete a file simply for disk housekeeping, or you may need to get rid of a file to avoid a disk-full error. This error occurs when you try to save a document on a disk that has insufficient space. Being able to delete files helps prevent losing all your work on a document. Avoiding a disk-full error is discussed in "Recovering from a Disk-Full Error" in this chapter.

At help level 4, pressing Alt-F from the Edit screen brings on the pull-down File menu, which includes this command:

```
Delete a file...          ^KJ
```

While at help level 4, 3, or 2, with the classic menus, pressing ^K at the Edit screen produces the Block & Save Menu, which lists the following command in its FILE column:

```
J delete
```

The full command sequence of ^KJ corresponds to the deletion command at the classic Opening Menu.

The prompt you see when you press ^KJ is identical to the one displayed when you press Y at the Opening Menu—the Delete dialog box, with its line for the name of the file to be erased. You can type the name or use the down and up cursor-movement commands to highlight the file name in the file directory on-screen; then press Enter. (You also can use wild-card characters to erase a group of files with one command.)

After you enter the file name, at help levels 3 and 2, a prompt asks whether you are sure about the deletion. Press Y, and the file is eliminated. The program then displays your document screen.

Running a DOS Command

Running a DOS command without exiting from the document you are editing is a convenience when you suddenly realize the need for a DOS file function or want to start a program from within WordStar. A command sequence that begins with ^K suspends editing and displays a dialog box with the DOS prompt, where you can type a command.

At help level 4, pulling down the Other menu by pressing Alt-O brings the following function listing on-screen:

```
Run a DOS command...      ^KF
```

At help level 4, 3, or 2, the Block & Save Menu shows this command in the FILE column:

```
F run a DOS command
```

After you press ^KF from within a document, you see the Run dialog box, which is the same as the one displayed when you select R from the Opening Menu (see fig. 5.5). This dialog box includes the DOS prompt, where you type the command to be executed. Press Enter to run the command. Once the operation is completed, press any key to return to the Edit screen.

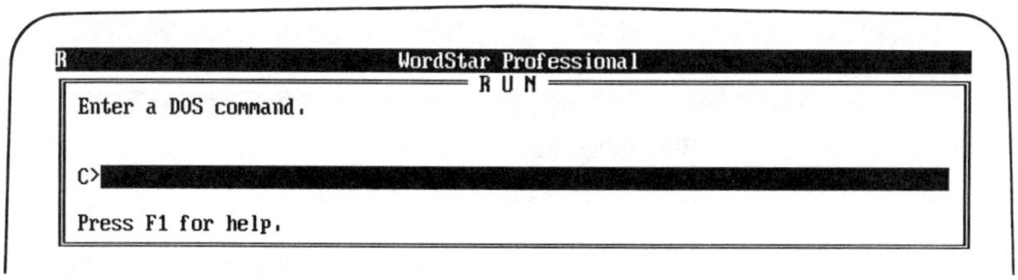
R
WordStar Professional
R U N
Enter a DOS command.
C>
Press F1 for help.

Fig. 5.5.
Dialog box for running a DOS command from a file.

A word of caution: Although pressing any key should return you to your document, occasionally, the procedure does not work properly. Problems arise particularly when you are trying to run another program. To guard against losing your work, save your document by pressing ^KS or F9 before you press ^KF.

Printing a File

One useful WordStar feature is the capability of printing a file stored on disk while you work on another document. Or if you save your current document to disk and resume editing, you can print the disk file of that document.

Do you have WordStar set at help level 4? Then you will find the following pair of printing commands on the File menu:

```
Print a file...           ^KPP
Merge print a file...     ^KPM
```

These commands—among the few three-stroke commands listed on the pull-down menus—represent the options available when the print command, ^KP, is invoked.

With WordStar set at help level 4, 3, or 2, press ^K from the Edit screen to display the classic Block & Save Menu. The fourth line on the menu's FILE column is

```
P print
```

This command is the same as the Print a File command at the Opening screen. The complete sequence for printing a file from the document screen is ^KP.

Before you print a file, make sure that your printer is turned on and that the paper is loaded. When you press ^KP to begin printing, Release 5 displays the following boxed prompt:

```
Print or merge print (P/M)?
```

Pressing P at this prompt is the equivalent of choosing P at the Opening screen. The Print dialog box is displayed (see fig. 5.6). After you specify the name of the file to be printed, you can accept the printing defaults and begin printing by pressing F10. The document you are editing returns to the screen while printing goes on. For more on printing, see Chapter 7.

Fig. 5.6.
The Print dialog box.

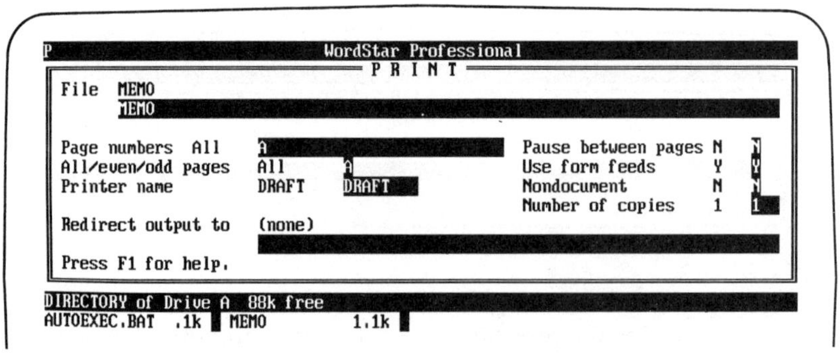
P
WordStar Professional
PRINT
File MEMO
MEMO
Page numbers All
All/even/odd pages All
Printer name DRAFT
DRAFT
Redirect output to (none)
Press F1 for help.
Pause between pages N
Use form feeds Y
Nondocument N
Number of copies 1
DIRECTORY of Drive A 88k free
AUTOEXEC.BAT .1k
MEMO 1.1k

Pressing M for merge printing invokes the same display as pressing M at the classic Opening Menu. To learn about merge printing, read Chapter 8.

Inserting a File into a Document

If you plan to learn only a few more WordStar features, be sure to master this: inserting a file stored on disk into a document you are editing. With this feature, you never have to retype frequently used text. Instead, you can add files of boilerplate copy to your document and then edit the document. You also can store useful letter or report formats as separate disk files and read the files into a new document.

With Release 5, WordStar's file-insertion function can read a range of 1-2-3, Symphony®, or Quattro® worksheet data directly into a document on the Edit screen. With this new feature, you can easily insert spreadsheet figures as well as text into a document.

At help level 4, the pull-down Edit menu (displayed by pressing Alt-E from the document screen) includes the following function:

```
Insert a file...          ^KR
```

At help level 4, 3, or 2, on the classic Block & Save Menu in the FILE column, you see

```
R insert a file
```

The full command sequence for inserting a file into your document is ^KR. The second half of the command is easily remembered as the way to *read* in text from outside a document.

When you invoke the Insert a File command, Release 5 displays a dialog box headed INSERT A FILE (see fig. 5.7). This box has a line for the name of the file to be inserted. As in other dialog boxes, you can type the name of a file or use the ^X or down-arrow key to move the cursor into the directory and highlight the file name; then press Enter. The Edit screen returns with the inserted file's contents starting at the cursor. The file on disk is not altered by the read operation.

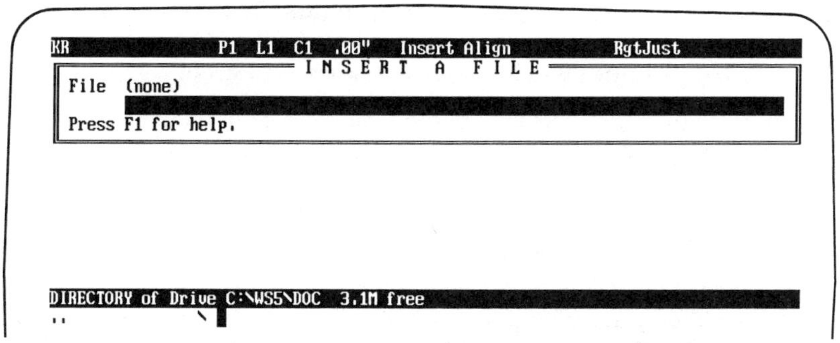
KR P1 L1 C1 .00" Insert Align RgtJust
INSERT A FILE
File (none)
Press F1 for help.
DIRECTORY of Drive C:\WS5\DOC 3.1M free
..

Fig. 5.7.
Dialog box for inserting a file into a document.

If you designate a file with the extension WKS—a spreadsheet file of the type created with 1-2-3, Symphony, or Quattro—another Release 5 dialog window appears. This dialog box has room for specifying a range of cells and displays a list of the range names in the worksheet. To insert just a portion of the worksheet into your document, enter a range of cells or the appropriate range name; then press Enter. To insert the entire worksheet, just press Enter.

Because any file imported with the ^KR command is inserted in your document at the cursor, be careful to place your cursor at the proper position in text before you invoke this function. When you read one file into another, text below the cursor in the current file is pushed downward to make room for the file you are inserting.

As an example of using the File Insert command, you can combine the sample documents created in previous chapters. At the Edit screen of an opened empty file, press ^KR; type the name of the file containing the sample pricing letter, LETTER; and press Enter. The text of the letter appears on-screen, beginning at the cursor position. With the cursor still at the beginning of the file, press ^KR again, type *memo*, and press Enter. The new text appears at the cursor, pushing down the text of the document LETTER.

Press ^KR once more, type *report* at the dialog box, and press Enter. This command reads in the text of the sample marketing report at the cursor. Your document now consists of the combined files REPORT, MEMO, and LETTER, in that order. You can easily rearrange the document by using the editing commands presented in the rest of this chapter.

Manipulating Blocks of Text

This section explains a set of WordStar commands for working with blocks of text in a document. You can cut and paste electronically—that is, cut out a block of copy and paste it at another location. WordStar lets you easily move, copy, delete, overlay, or save a text block to disk for later use.

A block of text can be a few characters or dozens of pages. Your computer's internal memory capacity determines the limit. If a block is too long for WordStar, the program displays an error message. With windows on-screen, WordStar can manipulate only one block at a time in each window, but blocks can be redefined and moved anywhere within a window as many times as desired.

Marking a block with beginning and ending markers and then using a block operation saves you from countless repetitive functions performed a character or a line at a time. If you are not familiar with WordStar's block commands, take the time to read the following information and apply it to your word processing applications for greater efficiency.

All the commands for block functions begin with ^K (see table 5.2). These seven commands are listed on the new pull-down Edit menu and on the classic Block & Save Menu in the BLOCK column. All but one of these commands can also be invoked by a Shift-function-key combination, listed in the on-screen function key listings at help levels 3, 2, and 1.

Table 5.2
Commands for Manipulating Blocks of Text

Command	*Function*
^KB or Shift-F9	Mark beginning of text block
^KK or Shift-F10	Mark end of text block
^KH or Shift-F6	Toggle block display on and off
^KV or Shift-F7	Move text block
^KC or Shift-F8	Copy text block
^KY or Shift-F5	Delete text block
^KW	Write (save) text block to disk

If you are familiar with WordStar Release 4, you will find little changed in Release 5's block commands. Nonetheless, the addition of a text window in WordStar adds to the versatility of the block commands. Window functions are introduced in the section following the discussion of classic block commands. For explanations of other block functions, including column and math features, see Chapter 6.

Marking a Block

When you perform a cut-and-paste operation on paper—like moving or removing a section of a document—you start by marking the text to be manipulated. In a WordStar block operation, you mark the beginning and end of a text block on-screen. You can set only one beginning and one end marker in a document or window at a time, but you can reset these markers whenever you need.

You can set either marker first, but a block operation cannot be performed unless both markers are displayed on-screen. The beginning marker must precede the end marker in the document.

Using WordStar with help at level 4, when you press Alt-E for the pull-down Edit screen, you see the following pair of functions:

```
Begin block          ^KB
End block            ^KK
```

Using WordStar at help level 4, 3, or 2, on the classic Block & Save Menu, you see these commands in the BLOCK column:

```
B begin block
K end block
```

The command sequences for marking a block are ^KB to mark the beginning and ^KK to mark the end. Many WordStar veterans use a simple reminder for these beginning and end markers, which often appear as `<B>` and `<K>` on-screen; the letters are the beginning and ending letters of the word *block*.

At help levels 3, 2, and 1, the top line of function-key labels lists Beg Blk for F9 and End Blk for F10. These keys are function-key equivalents of the block beginning and end commands. Shift-F9 issues a ^KB, and Shift-F10 enters a ^KK.

To mark the beginning of a block, place the cursor at the desired location in a document and press ^KB or Shift-F9. The `<B>` beginning marker appears. Highlighting appears in the far right (flag) column on-screen.

To mark the end of a block, move the cursor to the appropriate place in your text and press ^KK or Shift-F10. If you mark the end of a block before you mark the beginning, the end marker appears on-screen as `<K>`.

After beginning and end markers are placed in the correct order, the defined block of text is shown in reverse video (on most monitors). That is, text and background intensities or colors are reversed. Unlike previous versions of WordStar, Release 5 shows the flag column in reverse video from beginning to end of the block.

If the beginning and end markers are in reverse order when you issue a block command, the program displays the following message in a dialog box:

```
End of the block is at or before start of block.

Press Esc to continue.
```

When this message appears, press Esc, and then use the block-marker commands to define the block correctly.

When you need to perform a block operation on an entire paragraph, place the end marker at the start of the line that follows the paragraph so that the carriage return is included in the block. You can, however, place beginning and end markers anywhere in a document, including in the middle of a line or word.

Beginning and end marker commands are toggles: you can clear block markers by repeating the ^KB (or Shift-F9) and ^KK (or Shift-F10) commands. You also can clear block markers by using the command explained in the following section. You cannot, however, have more than one beginning marker and one end marker in a document or a window.

Hiding and Redisplaying Block Markers

After you have marked a text block, the markers and reverse video remain until you mark another block in the same window or hide the markers. When invoking block operations, you need to see the beginning and end markers; but you can hide block markers for a less cluttered screen when reviewing text on the Edit screen. The same command sequence acts as a toggle, turning display on and off.

At help level 4, the pull-down Edit menu shows this command:

```
Hide/show block          ^KH
```

At help level 4, 3, or 2, the classic Block & Save Menu lists the following function in the left column of BLOCK commands:

```
H display on
```

The complete command is ^KH. Issuing the command makes block markers and reverse video disappear from the screen and changes the menu description to

```
H display off
```

Giving the command a second time toggles on block display.

WordStar Release 5 also assigns this task to a function-key combination. The notation HideBlk, which is given for F6 on the top function-key line on-screen at help levels 3, 2, and 1, means that pressing Shift-F6 at any help level produces the same effect as pressing ^KH.

At all help levels except level 0, block-operation commands are not executed after a block is hidden. If you try to move a hidden block, this error message is displayed:

```
Hidden block. Press ^KH and try again.

Press Esc to continue.
```

If you see this message, follow its instructions. To perform a block operation, you must press Esc and then toggle the block marker display back on by pressing ^KH.

An important warning: At help level 0, invoking ^KH to hide a block does not disable the block operation. Even though block markers and reverse video are not displayed, you can execute a block command—and sometimes produce an undesired result, such as deletion of an entire block. To avoid this problem, relocate the beginning marker below the end marker, making impossible the accidental execution of a block operation.

Moving a Block

Moving a block is WordStar's equivalent of a cut-and-paste operation on paper: removing a portion of text from one place and inserting it elsewhere in a document. Moving text is often the only way to reorganize a document you are editing. WordStar makes this procedure easy. After a block is marked, you place the cursor anywhere in the file or window in which you are working and move the marked text to that location with a ^K command sequence.

When the program is set at help level 4, the following command appears in the Edit menu:

```
Move block                ^KV
```

If WordStar is set at help level 4, 3, or 2, pressing ^K at the Edit screen shows the classic Block & Save Menu. In the second column of BLOCK commands, you see

```
V move
```

The full command for moving a block is ^KV. (Be careful not to press ^V, which turns on overtype mode; see Chapter 3).

If you prefer function-key commands, note that at help levels 3, 2, and 1, the top on-screen function-key line lists MoveBlk for F7. Pressing Shift-F7 moves a block just as ^KV does.

However you invoke the Move command, it relocates a marked block to begin at the location of the cursor. To use this block command, place the cursor at the appropriate spot in your document before issuing the Move command. In Release 5, the ^KV command applies to moving text only within an open text window. To move a block into text in another window, you must use a different command—^KG, explained later in this chapter.

Moving a block into the middle of your text may distort alignment. You may have to realign a paragraph with a ^B command or use commands like Backspace or ^H to fit the moved block into surrounding text.

Print-control commands within a block move with the block. When you use commands like ^KV to manipulate blocks, therefore, be sure that you do not split pairs of beginning and ending print controls (see Chapter 4). Otherwise, your printed document may not appear as you intended.

For an example of moving a text block, work with the combined sample document created earlier in this chapter. To move the text of the marketing report, for instance, you mark the beginning and end of that block with ^KB and ^KK (or Shift-F9 and Shift-F10), respectively. Use the cursor-movement commands to bring the cursor to the beginning of the line that follows the text of the sample pricing letter. Then press ^KV or Shift-F7. The text block is inserted below the cursor. Existing text is pushed down to make room for the moved block. Text that followed the moved block fills up the space left by that block.

Warning: If you plan to use Page Preview, you must reformat any block you have moved or copied by using ^B or ^QU. If you do not, your tabs may not be correct.

Copying a Block

WordStar offers a variation of the cut-and-paste operation: the equivalent of photocopying a block of text and placing the copy elsewhere in your document while leaving the original text unmoved. In WordStar, this operation is called copying a block. This function can be particularly useful when a document is composed of reworkings of the same text.

At help level 4, pulling down the Edit menu displays the following command directly beneath the Move Block command:

```
Copy block                ^KC
```

At help level 4, 3, or 2, the classic Block & Save Menu exhibits this listing at the top of the second column of BLOCK commands:

```
C copy
```

The full sequence for copying a block is ^KC. Don't confuse this command with the one to the right of it in the FILE column of the Block & Save Menu: ^KO. The ^KO command, as explained earlier in this chapter, is for copying a disk file.

At help levels 3, 2, and 1, the top function-key line in WordStar lists CopyBlk for F8. Shift-F8 is the equivalent of ^KC.

When you use the Copy Block command, a duplicate of the marked block appears at the cursor. The original block remains marked until you remove the markers. In Release 5, when windows are on-screen, you can use Copy Block only within the same window. For an explanation of the new command for copying a block from one window to another, ^KA, see the windowing section in this chapter 5

As an example of copying a block, you can use this function for the sample text marked in the example at the end of the preceding section. If you place the cursor on the line that follows the marked block and press ^KC or Shift-F8, the block's text appears again at the cursor. The lines of the original block are unchanged; you have inserted a copy of the block below itself.

Deleting a Block

An important variation of the cut-and-paste function is deleting a section of text and closing up the remaining text. Many a report on paper has been salvaged at the last minute by cutting out a block, squeezing text together, and hoping that nobody would see the cut lines on the photocopies. WordStar allows you to perform this operation automatically and seamlessly with a block command sequence that begins with ^K.

If WordStar is set at help level 4, displaying the pull-down Edit menu by pressing Alt-E from the Edit screen shows this function: 5

```
Delete block              ^KY
```

If WordStar is at help level 4, 3, or 2, the classic Block & Save Menu lists the following command in the second BLOCK column:

```
Y delete
```

The full sequence for deleting a block is ^KY. Don't press ^Y by mistake, or you may lose a line of text. (Deletion of either a line or block can be restored with the ^U Undo command.)

At help levels 3, 2, and 1, you also can check the on-screen function-key lines, where Del Blk appears for F5. Pressing Shift-F5 deletes a marked block, just as ^KY does.

After deletion, the cursor moves to the position of the block you have deleted. You can issue the ^KY or Shift-F5 command from anywhere in your text, even if the marked block is off-screen. Because the cursor does not need to be in or near the block you want to delete, you should use ^KY or Shift-F5 with caution. If not careful, you could accidentally eliminate a portion of a document that is not currently on-screen.

WordStar's Undo command, ^U, can restore a deleted block of up to 500 characters. (You can increase this limit with the WSCHANGE program; see Chapter 11.) You must unerase a block before you make the next deletion; otherwise, restoring a block may be impossible. If you try to delete a block that is larger than the undo limit, WordStar displays a warning message so that you can change your mind before completing an irreversible deletion.

If you followed the example in the preceding section, now you can use the block-deletion command to erase the original of the block you copied. This block is still highlighted. When you press ^KY or Shift-F5, the highlighted block immediately disappears, along with the beginning and end block markers.

Writing a Block to Disk

Being able to save a block of text in a separate disk file (without changing the document on-screen) can prove important for many word processing applications. While editing a letter, report, or manuscript, you may want to preserve some portion of your text for later comparison or as a document in its own right. On floppy disk systems, saving a block to disk can prove crucial to recovering from a disk-full error (see the end of this chapter).

5 In Release 5, WordStar's function for writing a block to disk includes a new option: adding text to the end of an existing disk file. This capability can increase your productivity when you are using material from several files in a single document.

At help level 4, the pull-down Edit menu exhibits the following function:

```
Write block to file...    ^KW
```

At help level 4, 3, or 2, the classic Block & Save Menu includes this command in the left BLOCK column:

```
W write to disk
```

The full command is ^KW. The second part of the command is the initial of its function: writing to a file.

As in other block commands, before you invoke this function, be sure that the appropriate text has been marked with beginning and end markers. In WordStar Release 5, when you press ^KW, a dialog box headed WRITE BLOCK appears. The dialog box has a line for designating the name of the file to store the block. If you type a new name and press Enter, the block is saved on disk under this file name, and you can resume editing. (The block you marked remains intact on-screen after the file has been written to disk.)

If you designate an existing file on disk (at help level 4 or 3), another boxed prompt comes on-screen, as illustrated in figure 5.8. The prompt's question— whether to overwrite or append the named file—has three possible answers: pressing Y substitutes the marked block's text for the disk file's current content; pressing A adds the block of text to the existing file and saves the combined file; pressing N returns the cursor to the WRITE BLOCK dialog box for a new file name.

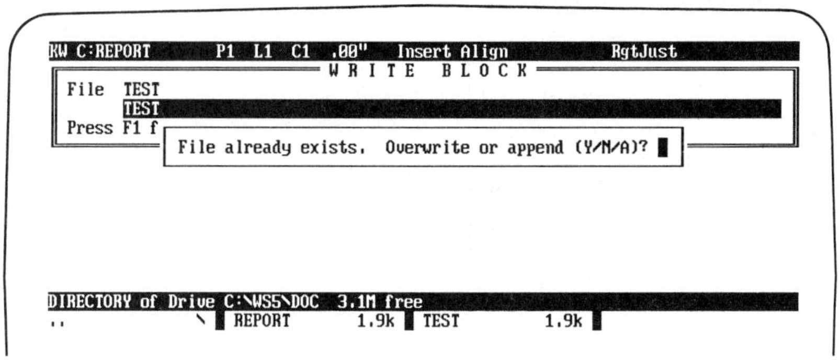
KW C:REPORT P1 L1 C1 .00" Insert Align RgtJust
W R I T E B L O C K
File TEST
TEST
Press F1 f
File already exists. Overwrite or append (Y/N/A)?
DIRECTORY of Drive C:\WS5\DOC 3.1M free
.. \ REPORT 1.9k TEST 1.9k

Fig. 5.8.
Screen for writing a block to an existing disk file.

After a block is written to disk and the Edit screen is redisplayed, the cursor moves to the beginning of the marked block. The block on-screen is not changed.

As an example of saving a block, use the document combining sample text (produced in previous sections of this chapter) and write to disk the text of your marketing report. First, you place beginning and end markers at appropriate places in the document by moving the cursor and using ^KB (or Shift-F9) and ^KK (or Shift-F10), respectively. The marked block is displayed in reverse video.

To save the marked block to disk, press ^KW. WordStar displays the Write Block dialog box, requesting the name of the file to hold the marked text for storage on disk. Type *test* and press Enter. The block is saved to disk under this name. When your document reappears on-screen, the marked block is unchanged.

Using Text Windows

5

One of the most important new features in WordStar Release 5 is windowing—the capability to display at the same time two documents or two portions of the same document. This feature is referred to as if you are opening a window into the second file, but in WordStar you actually split the screen horizontally with a second ruler line with text below it, or you can switch between entire screenfuls of text.

The significance of windows will be obvious to anyone who has ever needed to look up something in another file while editing a document, perhaps to refer to past correspondence, copy some technical language, or avoid duplicating text. By having two files on-screen, you have no more need for time-consuming closing and opening of files. Viewing two parts of the same document also provides greater editing efficiency; no more having to scroll back and forth in a document to compare two sections of the same file. With commands for moving or copying text between windows, the new functions enhance productivity when you are compiling and editing boilerplate, forms, lists, and other repetitive documents.

The functions for using text windows consist of four new commands—two on-screen sequences beginning with ^O and two block functions starting with ^K—and two Save commands with additional attributes (see table 5.3).

Table 5.3
Commands for Windows

Command	*Function*
^OK	Open/switch windows
^OM	Set current window size
^KA	Copy block from other window
^KG	Move block from other window
^KD	Close and save window
^KQ	Close and abandon window
^- (Ctrl-hyphen)	Make current window larger and other smaller by increments of one line

At help level 4, the pull-down Window menu groups all six commands for window functions (see fig. 5.9). To display the Window menu from the Edit screen, you press Alt-W. With the highlighting at the top listing on the menu, press Enter to open a window—a convenient shortcut. All other window commands can be invoked most efficiently by their Ctrl-letter combinations.

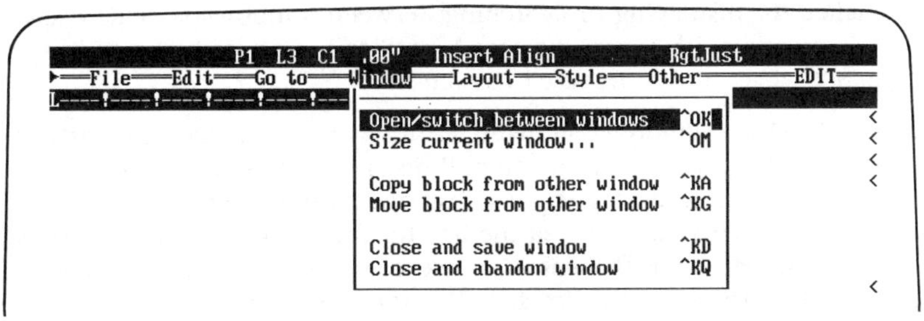
P1 L3 C1 .00" Insert Align RgtJust
File Edit Go to Window Layout Style Other EDIT
Open/switch between windows ^OK
Size current window... ^OM
Copy block from other window ^KA
Move block from other window ^KG
Close and save window ^KD
Close and abandon window ^KQ

Fig. 5.9.
The pull-down Window menu.

Four window commands are also listed on the classic menus, available at help levels 4, 3, and 2. The commands for opening and sizing a window are on the Onscreen Format Menu (displayed by pressing ^O at the Edit screen), and the Copy and Move between Window functions are included in the Block & Save Menu.

Some of WordStar's rivals boast of up to nine text windows, but MicroPro International claims that tests have shown that two windows are sufficient for most applications. If you need more than WordStar's two simultaneous screens, you can add one or more Notepad windows with the memory-resident program, SideKick® Plus from Borland International.

Because WordStar literally doubles access to on-screen text, both veterans and neophytes using WordStar's window commands are spared hundreds of hours of needless juggling of document files— if the windows' full potential is used. Handy window functions are detailed in the pages that follow.

Opening a Window

The process of opening a text window is similar to opening a document file. After naming a new or an existing file, you see a text display complete with ruler line. The cursor flashes in this text area. The command that opens a window also moves the cursor from one window to the other so that you can edit in either one.

You can open a window whenever you are editing a file. WordStar's default setting is for document format in a window. If you often work with nondocument files as well, you may want to use WSCHANGE to add a prompt asking whether a window should be a document or nondocument (see Chapter 11).

When you are using WordStar with help at level 4, the pull-down Window menu shows the following:

```
Open/switch between windows ^OK
```

When you are using WordStar at help level 4, 3, or 2, the classic Onscreen Format Menu includes this command in the DISPLAY column:

```
K open or switch window
```

The full sequence for displaying or switching between windows is ^OK. Okay—that's easy to remember. It's surprising that WordStar has never had a ^OK command before, but what an okay feature to assign it!

Once you issue the Open Window command, either by pressing ^OK or by pressing Enter with the highlight at the top of the pull-down Window menu, you see the same Document dialog box displayed when you open a document at the Opening screen (see fig. 5.10). With the cursor at the line for the name of the file to appear in the window, you can type the name or use cursor-movement commands to highlight one of the entries on the directory list; then press Enter.

D
WordStar Professional
DOCUMENT
File (none)
Press F1 for help.
DIRECTORY of Drive C:\WS5\DOC 3.2M free
..

Fig. 5.10.
Dialog box for opening a window.

If you designate the name of the file currently being edited, you see in the window the text as last saved to disk; for the most up-to-the-minute version of the file, you may want to press ^KS or F9—Save and Resume—before opening the window.

If you have not modified WordStar with WSCHANGE, after you specify the file name for the window and press Enter, WordStar splits the Edit screen in half, with the original document being edited at the top half and the new file at the bottom. At the left of the status line a 1 or 2 indicates which window is active, with the name of the current file you can move through and edit.

When the window first appears on-screen, the cursor is located at the beginning of text in the new window. All cursor-movement, text-entry, deletion, and formatting commands are now valid in the second window. To return the cursor to the original file being edited, you press ^OK again. Pressing ^OK alternates the cursor between windows.

Opening a window is easy using the sample documents from previous chapters. For instance, suppose that you are editing the sample pricing letter and want to see the sample memo at the same time. You press ^OK and at the dialog box type *memo* and press Enter. The screen is split in the middle with the letter at the top and the memo at the bottom, as shown in fig. 5.11. The cursor is in the bottom window—where text can be edited—until you press ^OK again and the cursor returns to the top window.

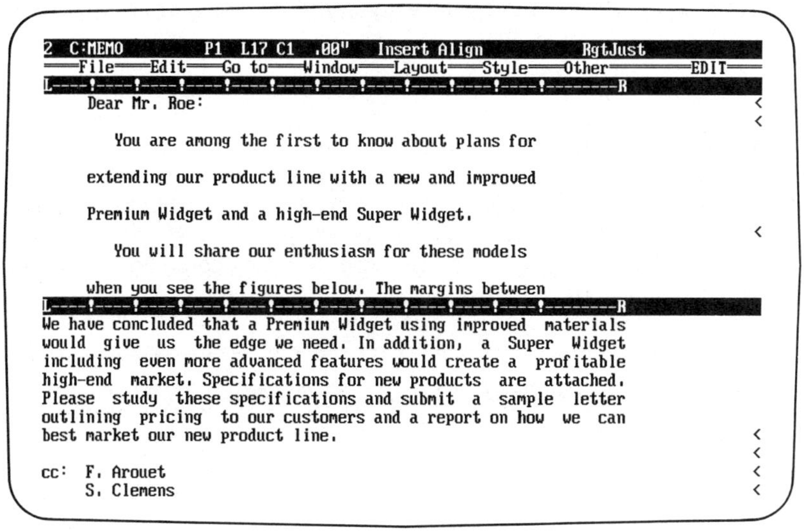

```
2 C:MEMO          P1  L17 C1  .00"   Insert Align          RgtJust
═══File═══Edit═══Go to═══Window═══Layout═══Style═══Other══════════EDIT═══
L----!----!----!----!----!----!----!----!----!----!--------R
     Dear Mr. Roe:                                                    <
                                                                      <
        You are among the first to know about plans for

     extending our product line with a new and improved

     Premium Widget and a high-end Super Widget.
                                                                      <
        You will share our enthusiasm for these models

     when you see the figures below. The margins between
L----!----!----!----!----!----!----!----!----!----!--------R
We have concluded that a Premium Widget using improved  materials
would  give  us  the edge we need. In addition,  a  Super  Widget
including  even more advanced features would create a  profitable
high-end  market. Specifications for new products  are  attached.
Please  study  these specifications and submit  a  sample  letter
outlining  pricing  to our customers and a report on how  we  can
best market our new product line.                                     <
                                                                      <
cc:  F. Arouet                                                        <
     S. Clemens                                                       <
```

Fig. 5.11.

WordStar's text windows.

Sizing a Window

If splitting the screen in half leaves too little room for your documents, another new command lets you reset the size of a window or show two separate screens of text.

You can change the size of a window to display more of one file than the other, or you can set the window so that full text areas of each file can be alternated on-screen. Resized windows lend themselves to applications such as a two- or three-line "notepad" at the bottom of the screen to jot thoughts and inspirations for saving on a separate file or an arrangement for flipping between full screens of the same file like pages in a book.

Resetting the size of a window may not be critical at help level 4 or 0, where standard text windows are 12 and 11 lines long, respectively; but at help level 3, with its Edit menu and function-key lines, text windows on-screen are only 7 and 6 lines long and could benefit from resizing. For "permanent" resetting of window size, you can use the WSCHANGE program, explained in Chapter 11. For resizing a window as you edit, WordStar provides a simple on-screen format command sequence starting with ^O.

At help level 4, the pull-down Window menu exhibits the following function:

```
Size current window...      ^OM
```

At help level 4, 3, or 2, the classic Onscreen Format Menu includes this command near the bottom of the column headed DISPLAY:

```
M size current window
```

The complete command is ^OM. The sizing command can be issued with the cursor anywhere in the window to be altered.

When you press ^OM, WordStar displays the Size Window dialog box, shown in figure 5.12. You use this box to specify the number of text lines for the window's length. Typing any number between 1 and 21 sets the window's size as soon as you press Enter. (Type any number between 1 and 40 with EGA color display or between 1 and 53 with VGA color, if one of these display options has been chosen with the WINSTALL or WSCHANGE program; see Chapter 2 or 11.) The result of resizing is seen immediately on the Edit screen; use the sizing command as needed to settle on the proper window length.

Fig. 5.12.

Dialog box for sizing a text window.

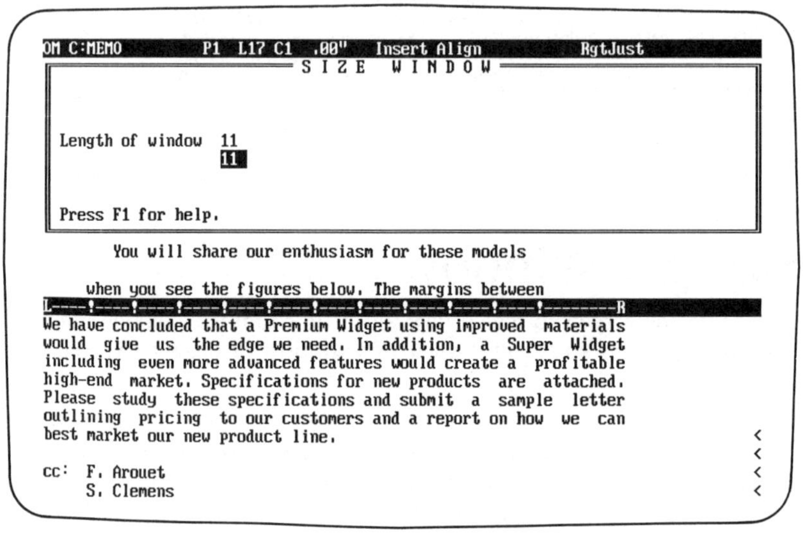
OM C:MEMO P1 L17 C1 .00" Insert Align RgtJust
S I Z E W I N D O W
Length of window 11
11
Press F1 for help.
You will share our enthusiasm for these models
when you see the figures below. The margins between
We have concluded that a Premium Widget using improved materials
would give us the edge we need. In addition, a Super Widget
including even more advanced features would create a profitable
high-end market. Specifications for new products are attached.
Please study these specifications and submit a sample letter
outlining pricing to our customers and a report on how we can
best market our new product line.
cc: F. Arouet
S. Clemens

If you type 0 or the number 22 or higher (41 or higher with EGA or 54 or higher with VGA graphics), the full text area on-screen is devoted to the current window. Pressing ^OK displays the content of the other window, also in the full text area. You can flip back and forth between windows with ^OK.

Tip: *You can use a shortcut to change the sizes of windows. Press ^- (Ctrl-hyphen) to make the current window larger and the other window smaller. Each time you press ^-, the current window gets one line larger and the other window gets one line smaller.*

In the example of the sample windowed documents—opened in the last section—you press ^OM from either window, type *0*, and press Enter to create full text windows. You page between them by pressing ^OK.

Using Window Block Commands

Copying or moving a block of text from one window to another makes it easy to combine portions of different files into your current document. Copying a block from the other window duplicates marked text at the cursor and leaves the original block intact. Moving a block from the other window transfers the block to the cursor location on the active Edit screen and deletes the block from the other file.

5

As noted earlier in this chapter, you can copy or move a block within the same window the way you copy or move in an ordinary document—by using the standard ^KC and ^KV commands. Two new window commands are also ^K block commands, but these commands bridge the gap between windows for easy transfer of selected text from one file to another.

If WordStar is set at help level 4, these commands are on the Window menu:

```
Copy block from other window  ^KA
Move block from other window  ^KG
```

At help level 4, 3, or 2, WordStar also displays these commands on the classic Block & Save Menu under the heading WINDOW:

```
A copy between
G move between
```

The complete command sequences for these block commands are ^KA to copy text between windows and ^KG to move text between windows.

In a manner similar to using other block commands, you first mark the beginning and end of the text to be manipulated with ^KB and ^KK commands, respectively. Then move the cursor to the other window by pressing ^OK. After you position the cursor where you want the block, press ^KA to duplicate the marked text or ^KG to transfer the marked block and erase it from the other window. Copying or moving text between windows is completed instantly.

You can have blocks marked in both windows on-screen. When you press either ^KA or ^KG, the function is applied to the marked block in the window opposite the one with the cursor. If the other window contains no block or one that is improperly marked, WordStar displays the applicable error message.

To demonstrate the use of window block commands with the sample documents previously put in windows, mark a block with beginning and end markers by using ^KB and ^KK, respectively; then move to the opposite window by pressing ^OK. Once you position the cursor, press ^KA or ^KG to copy or move the block between windows.

Closing a Window

When you have completed viewing or editing text in a window, you may want to close it to free up space on-screen. Once a work session is complete, you have to close a window before you can save the other document on which you are working. You have two ways of closing a window, both of them invoked with commands also used for closing a document: ^KQ and ^KD.

How you want to dispose of text in a window determines the appropriate command for closing a window. If you are merely viewing a document or have made changes but don't want to save them, you want to close the window and abandon its contents. If you have edited the text in the window and want to preserve this latest version, you need the Close and Save command. These functions may sound familiar because they are the same as the commands used to close and abandon or close and save a document, described in Chapter 3.

WordStar's pull-down menus at help level 4 include listings for the commands to close a window. These commands can be found on the Window menu:

```
Close and save window       ^KD
Close and abandon window    ^KQ
```

Although these commands' application to windows is not specifically listed on classic menus, pressing either ^KD or ^KQ invokes the window function at all help levels.

The functions for closing a window work the same way they do when they are used to close a document—except that after a window is closed, the Edit screen remains with a full text area showing the other document. Either window can be closed, regardless of which document was opened first.

When you use the Close and Save Window command, ^KD, in either window, the Saving box appears on-screen while the window's content is recorded on disk. Then you see the full editing display for the other document. If you issue the Close and Abandon Window command, ^KQ, and have not altered text in the window, you see the Abandoning box, followed by a full text area of the remaining document. If you have changed text in the window, before abandoning the document, WordStar displays the boxed prompt: `Changes have been made. Abandon anyway (Y/N)?` Press Y to complete the process of closing the window.

Moving through Text

The cursor-movement commands covered in Chapter 3 give you the basic ways of changing your position within a document. Basic cursor-movement commands, however, are inefficient for moving through more than a few lines of text. WordStar provides commands that let you move more quickly and precisely through text.

Moving through a document involves either changing the position of the cursor or scrolling the screen display. You have learned that a document is displayed like a continuous paper scroll, with the screen acting like a window onto a portion of the text. Cursor movement is the equivalent of repositioning a pointer in text; scrolling is like moving the text itself past your window.

The next sections elaborate on the scrolling functions introduced in Chapter 3 and explain the keystroke sequences for moving speedily through text. The quick cursor commands and the scrolling commands are summarized in table 5.4.

Table 5.4
Commands for Moving through Text

Command	*Function*
Quick Cursor Commands	
^QE or Home	Move cursor to top of screen
^QX or End	Move cursor to lower right corner of screen
^QS or Ctrl-F9	Move cursor to left end of line
^QD or Ctrl-F10	Move cursor to right end of line
^QR or ^Home	Move cursor to beginning of document
^QC or ^End	Move cursor to end of document
^QW	Scroll up continuously line-by-line
^QZ	Scroll down continuously line-by-line
^QP	Move cursor to preceding position
^QB	Move cursor to beginning of text block
^QK	Move cursor to end of text block
^QV	Move cursor to preceding position of beginning of text block
^K1 through ^K9	Mark places in document
^Q1 through ^Q9	Move cursor to marked places in document
Basic Scrolling Commands	
^W or ^PgUp	Scroll up one line
^R or PgUp	Scroll up one screen
^Z or ^PgDn	Scroll down one line
^C or PgDn	Scroll down one screen

About a third of these cursor and scrolling commands are listed in the pull-down menus at help level 4. They are listed on the Go To Menu (displayed by pressing Alt-G at the Edit screen.) All 18 functions are shown on the classic menus, mostly the Quick Menu (press ^Q during editing), and in the on-screen listings of function-key commands. All these menu and function-key commands are applicable at all help levels.

WordStar also includes functions for moving the cursor to specific places in your text—a designated character, character string, or a page. These and other Find commands are explained later in this chapter.

Moving the Cursor Quickly

To speed editing, WordStar provides powerful command sequences for moving through text quickly. Moving the cursor a character or a line at a time may be enough for short documents, but when a file fills the Edit screen and beyond, you need commands for moving in larger increments.

At help level 4, the pull-down Go To menu lists 12 functions for moving the cursor through text (see fig. 5.13). All but one of these functions are covered in this chapter.

Fig. 5.13.

The pull-down Go To menu.

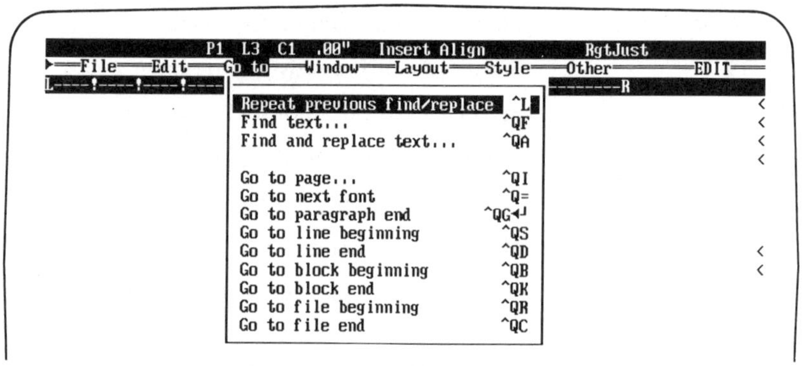
P1 L3 C1 .00" Insert Align RgtJust
File Edit Go to Window Layout Style Other EDIT
Repeat previous find/replace ^L
Find text... ^QF
Find and replace text... ^QA
Go to page... ^QI
Go to next font ^Q=
Go to paragraph end ^QG↵
Go to line beginning ^QS
Go to line end ^QD
Go to block beginning ^QB
Go to block end ^QK
Go to file beginning ^QR
Go to file end ^QC

At all help levels but 1 and 0, more "quick" commands, 30 in all, are listed on the classic Quick Menu (see fig. 5.14). All these commands are multiple-keystroke sequences that begin with ^Q. Most of the commands on the classic Quick Menu (except those in the SPELL column and the math functions) are described in this chapter.

After many alterations in previous versions, the quick movement commands were essentially unchanged between Release 4 and Release 5 (although some of their descriptions on the Quick Menu have been rewritten). A few quick movement commands have been slightly modified. The only completely new function—moving to a specific font—is explained in Chapter 7.

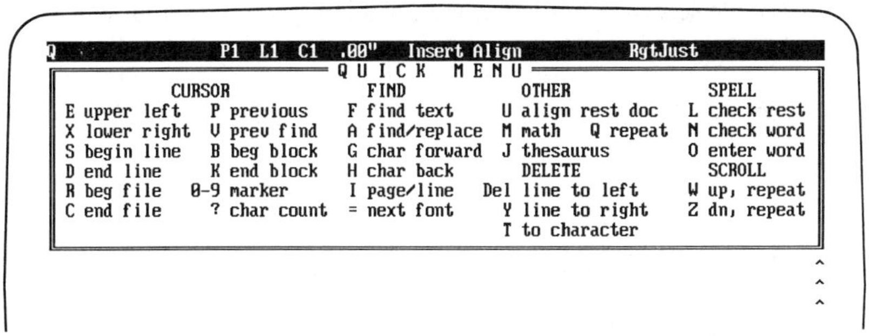
Q P1 L1 C1 .00" Insert Align RgtJust
QUICK MENU
CURSOR
FIND
OTHER
SPELL
E upper left P previous F find text U align rest doc L check rest
X lower right V prev find A find/replace M math Q repeat N check word
S begin line B beg block G char forward J thesaurus O enter word
D end line K end block H char back DELETE SCROLL
R beg file 0-9 marker I page/line Del line to left W up, repeat
C end file ? char count = next font Y line to right Z dn, repeat
T to character

Fig. 5.14. *WordStar's classic Quick Menu.*

Moving Quickly On-Screen

Several of the ^Q quick movement sequences amplify basic cursor-movement commands. Among these ^Q commands are sequences that jump the cursor to the beginning or end of a line and to the top or bottom of the screen.

When set at help level 4, WordStar Release 5 displays only two of these commands on the pull-down Go To menu:

```
Go to line beginning        ^QS
Go to line end              ^QD
```

All four of the amplified cursor-movement commands are listed in the left column of the Quick Menu, displayed at help levels 4, 3, and 2:

```
E upper left
X lower right
S begin line
D end line
```

^QE moves the cursor to column 1 of the top line on-screen. ^QX moves the cursor to the last column of the bottom line on-screen (unless the bottom line is blank, in which case the cursor ends up on the bottom line at the left edge of the screen). ^QS moves the cursor to the beginning of the line on which the cursor is located. And ^QD moves the cursor to the right of the last character of the line on which the cursor is located. You will recognize the preceding commands as the familiar ^S, ^E, ^D, ^X cursor-movement commands, with their functions augmented by ^Q.

Two keys on the numeric keypad also move the cursor to the top or bottom of the screen. Pressing the Home key has the same effect as pressing ^QE: the cursor moves to column 1 of the screen's top line. Pressing the End key is the same as pressing ^QX: the cursor moves to the screen's bottom text line.

WordStar also assigns to function keys the movement of the cursor to the beginning or end of a line. These assignments are not indicated on any menu. Ctrl-F9 moves the cursor to the beginning of a line, as does ^QS; and Ctrl-F10 moves the cursor to the right end of a line, as does ^QD.

For a quick tour of the screen edges, use these commands to do the following with any screenful of text. Press ^QD to move the cursor to the right edge of the current line; press ^QX (or End) to move the cursor to the screen's bottom right corner; press ^QS to move to the bottom left corner; and finally press ^QE (or Home) to move up to the top left corner.

Moving to the Beginning or End of a Document

During editing, being able to move the cursor directly to the beginning or end of a document is helpful for such tasks as checking a document's length (go to the end of the file and look at the status line) and reworking a title (move to the file's beginning).

The pull-down Go To menu at help level 4 shows these functions:

```
Go to file beginning        ^QR
Go to file end              ^QC
```

WordStar's classic Quick Menu also includes these commands for sending the cursor directly to either end of a file:

```
R beg file
C end file
```

The complete commands are ^QR to move the cursor to column 1 of a document's first line and ^QC to move the cursor to the last character of a document.

The letters for completing the command sequences should be familiar: they correspond to the single-letter commands ^R and ^C for scrolling up or down one screen at a time. When you precede these letters with ^Q, the commands move the cursor the entire length of a document.

You also can press the Ctrl key along with the Home and End keys to move to the beginning or end of a document, respectively. Pressing ^Home produces the same result as pressing ^QR: the cursor moves to the beginning of the document. And ^End is equivalent to ^QC: the cursor moves to the end of the document.

Moving to the beginning or end of a document may take a few seconds or more as the file is read from the disk where parts of the file are stored temporarily. The amount of time for this operation depends on the length of your document and your computer's memory capacity and hard disk access speed.

Returning the Cursor to Its Preceding Position

Returning the cursor to where it was before the execution of a cursor-movement command is another useful function made possible by a ^Q command sequence. This feature is available only immediately after you move the cursor or scroll the screen. After you enter or edit text, you no longer can return to the cursor's earlier position.

Although this function is not listed on any of the pull-down menus, the command for returning the cursor to its preceding position is shown at the top of the second column headed CURSOR on the classic Quick Menu:

```
P previous
```

The complete sequence is ∧QP.

The ^QP command sends the cursor to its last position before a cursor move, block operation, or window function. This command goes back only to the most recent move.

To see how convenient this command can be, in any document of a page or more, press ^C to scroll down a screen. Pressing ^QP returns the cursor instantly to its preceding position, one screen higher.

Moving to Block Markers

WordStar provides three commands for moving the cursor directly to the beginning, end, or original position of a marked block. This feature can be handy when you are editing a long document and frequently using block moves, copies, or deletions for large-scale revisions.

At help level 4, a pair of the commands are exhibited on the Go To menu:

```
Go to block beginning       ^QB
Go to block end             ^QK
```

All three block-related quick movement commands can be found in the second CURSOR column on the Quick Menu:

```
V prev find
B beg block
K end block
```

^QV places the cursor at the original position occupied by a marked block before the block was moved or copied. ^QB moves the cursor to the beginning marker of a block, and ^QK moves the cursor to a block's end marker. To better understand and remember these commands, recall the commands for marking the beginning of a block (^KB), marking the end of a block (^KK), and moving a block (^KV).

The block-related cursor-movement commands can be issued anywhere within a document during editing. These commands are applicable only to a block within the same window if a second text area is put on-screen.

As an example of using these block-related cursor-movement commands, mark with ^KB the beginning of a block anywhere in a document; then move the cursor down one screen by pressing ^C and place an end-of-block marker at the new cursor position by pressing ^KK. Press ^QB to move the cursor to the beginning of the block—the first highlighted character. Press ^QK to return the cursor to the end of the block. After pressing ^C again, you can perform a block operation by pressing ^KV to move the marked block to the new cursor position. Then press ^QV to send the cursor to the previous location of the beginning marker. Finally, press ^KV again to move the block back to where it was before you started this exercise.

Moving to Place Markers

Among WordStar's quick cursor-movement features are ^Q command sequences that move the cursor to any of as many as 10 markers in a document. Putting place markers in your text allows you to shift your attention during editing to other parts of a document and then resume work at a specified location.

A place marker consists of a character in reverse video. In this way, place markers resemble block markers. Place markers alter on-screen formatting, but they disappear when a file is closed and saved, and they are not printed. (You also can hide place markers and any block markers on-screen with the ^KH command.) You set place markers with a ^K command sequence. Movement to the markers involves a ^Q command sequence.

None of the new pull-down menus in Release 5 lists these commands, but you can find them on two classic menus: the Block & Save Menu and the Quick Menu. At help levels 4, 3, and 2, the Block & Save Menu displays this notation in the top right corner, labeled CURSOR:

```
0-9 set
    marker
```

Pressing ^K followed by a single-digit number sets a marker with that number at the cursor location. Once set, a place marker can be moved or removed with the same command.

Note: Your finger should not be on the Ctrl key when you press the number key; otherwise, the place marker will not appear on-screen.

At a press of ^Q, the classic Quick Menu appears with the following listing near the bottom of the second CURSOR column:

```
0-9 marker
```

Pressing ^Q and a single-digit number moves the cursor to the corresponding place marker. When using this command sequence, be sure that you release the Ctrl key before you press the number key.

For an example of using the place marker and movement commands, in any document, press ^K and then 1. This combination displays a 1 in reverse video at the cursor position. Then move the cursor down one screen by pressing ^C, place another marker at the new position with ^K and 2. To return to the first marker, press ^Q followed by a 1; then move back to the second marker with ^Q and 2.

Scrolling through Text

WordStar includes commands for scrolling the screen up or down in convenient increments. These scrolling functions, first introduced in Chapter 3, are invoked with combinations listed only on the classic Edit Menu. In the following sections, you also see how WordStar speeds the performance of two of the scrolling functions with commands listed on the classic Quick Menu.

At help level 3, the Edit Menu lists the scrolling commands in the SCROLL column:

```
^W up
^Z down
^R screen up
^C screen
   down
```

The scrolling commands are arranged according to the increments by which they move the text. The top two commands scroll the screen one line at a time. To scroll the screen up line-by-line, the command is ^W; to scroll the screen down line-by-line, the command is ^Z. The bottom two commands, ^R and ^C, scroll up and down one screen, respectively.

WordStar's scrolling commands can best be remembered by noticing their location on the keyboard. The commands are arranged in a square around the S-E-D-X cursor-movement diamond (see fig. 5.15).

Note that scrolling the screen up is the equivalent of moving text downward, and vice versa. When you scroll one line at a time, the cursor remains where positioned on a word or space. When the end of a paragraph reaches the upper or lower boundary of the screen, the cursor moves to the left edge of the screen, while the line the cursor was on moves beyond the limits of the screen.

Scrolling text one screen at a time actually moves text about 3/4 of a screen, leaving enough of an overlap for you to find your place in the document. When you scroll text one screen at a time, the cursor also moves. The cursor usually jumps to the beginning of a line, even though the original position may have been in the middle of a line.

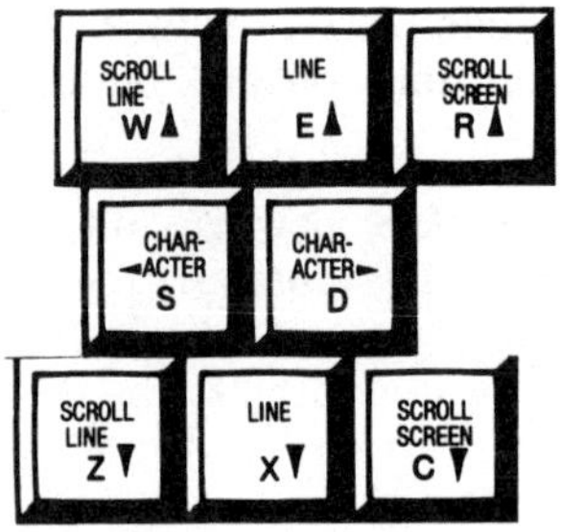
SCROLL LINE W
LINE E
SCROLL SCREEN R
CHAR-ACTER S
CHAR-ACTER D
SCROLL LINE Z
LINE X
SCROLL SCREEN C

Fig. 5.15.
WordStar's scrolling commands, surrounding the cursor-movement diamond (courtesy MicroPro International).

You can scroll up or down one screen at a time with the PgUp and PgDn keys (the equivalent of ^R and ^C). In combination with the Ctrl key, these keys also scroll text one line at a time: ^PgUp scrolls text up one line, as does ^W; and ^PgDn scrolls text down one line, as does ^Z.

An example of using the vertical scrolling commands to move through text can be performed with any document. First, press ^W (or ^PgUp) a few times to see the screen scroll up one line at a time—that is, the text moves downward. Then press ^Z (or ^PgDn) several times to scroll down several lines and watch the text move upward. Press ^R (or PgUp) to scroll up by one screen and press ^C (or PgDn) to scroll down by one screen, restoring the text display to what you saw before you pressed ^R.

By combining basic scrolling and cursor-movement commands, you can fine-tune the cursor's position on-screen. For documents of several pages or more, however, WordStar provides other commands for even more rapid movement.

Scrolling Continuously

Being able to scroll through text without keeping command keys pressed down is another useful WordStar feature; continuous-scrolling commands provide a handy way to advance a document for reading. You can issue command sequences to scroll continuously in either direction all the way through your text. Actually, the commands for scrolling one line at a time are amplified with a ^Q.

Neither continuous scroll function is listed on the new pull-down menus, but these commands can be seen in the SCROLL column of the classic Quick Menu:

```
W up, repeat
Z dn, repeat
```

^QW scrolls the screen up, and ^QZ scrolls the screen down. Remember that these commands are amplified versions of the single letter commands for scrolling one line at a time: ^W and ^Z.

You can adjust the speed of automatic scrolling by typing a number from 0 through 9 after you issue the command. The fastest rate is 0, and the slowest is 9. WordStar comes preset at 3 for a moderate rate of scrolling. The speed of the scrolling stays in effect as long as you are editing the current document. Opening another file resets the speed to the default of 3.

When the cursor reaches the beginning or end of a document, scrolling stops. You also can stop continuous scrolling by pressing ^U.

Want an example of the repeat scrolling commands? In any document of a page or more, press ^QZ, sending the screen scrolling downward line-by-line—in effect moving text up continuously at the default speed of 3. Typing 1 increases the rate of scrolling; typing 6 slows scrolling. You also can try pressing ^QW to scroll the screen up and the text down. To stop automatic scrolling, you press ^U.

Scrolling Horizontally

WordStar can scroll across a document horizontally in the same way the program scrolls vertically. This feature is handy for documents with lines wider than the 80 columns of text WordStar displays.

On an extended line, if you move the cursor to the right beyond column 80, the screen automatically scrolls 20 columns to the right. The text appears to shift 20 columns to the left. To scroll the screen and move the cursor to the extended part of the line, you use the same commands you use for moving the cursor quickly on-screen. When you press ^QD (or Ctrl-F10), the cursor goes to the end of the line, which can extend as far as column 255. Pressing ^QS (or Ctrl-F9) scrolls the screen to the left, returning the cursor to column 1.

For an example of scrolling the screen horizontally, create a line of text longer than 80 columns. With any document, first turn off WordStar's auto-align by pressing ^OA. Then place the cursor at the end of the first line of your document's body text and press ^T as many times as necessary to bring the next line of text up to the line the cursor is on. You will notice that the right edge of the screen displays a plus sign (+) to indicate that the line extends beyond the screen boundary. Pressing ^QD scrolls the screen to the right across the line. The text appears to move to the left. If this action is performed with the sample marketing report, the document looks something like figure 5.16. Pressing ^QS returns the cursor to the left edge of the line. To restore the text's original alignment, press ^B.

Finding Selected Text

At times while editing, you want to find specific words or phrases in a document and perhaps replace them. Most word processing programs can search for a string or sequence of characters. WordStar's find functions, as these commands are called, operate quickly—befitting Quick Menu commands.

Fig. 5.16.

The document screen after scrolling horizontally.

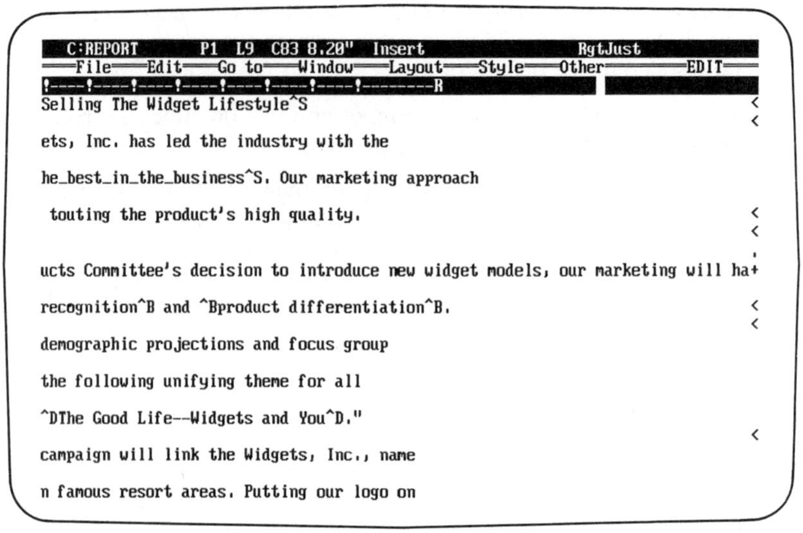
C:REPORT P1 L9 C83 8.20" Insert RgtJust
File Edit Go to Window Layout Style Other EDIT
Selling The Widget Lifestyle^S
ets, Inc. has led the industry with the
he_best_in_the_business^S. Our marketing approach
touting the product's high quality.
ucts Committee's decision to introduce new widget models, our marketing will ha+
recognition^B and ^Bproduct differentiation^B.
demographic projections and focus group
the following unifying theme for all
^DThe Good Life--Widgets and You^D."
campaign will link the Widgets, Inc., name
n famous resort areas. Putting our logo on

WordStar's Find command can locate strings up to 65 characters long, which is more than enough characters to narrow a search to a unique phrase in a document. After a simple Find command is given, WordStar searches the file forward from the cursor position, for the first occurrence of an exact string of characters. (You can modify a search with the options described in the next section.) Table 5.5 summarizes WordStar's commands for finding text.

Table 5.5
Commands for Finding Text

Command	*Function*
^QF or Ctrl-F1	Find character string in document
^L or Ctrl-F3	Repeat find operation
^QG	Find character forward in document
^QH	Find character backward in document
^QI or Ctrl-F4	Find page by number or line
^QA or Ctrl-F2	Find and replace character string in document

WordStar veterans will find these commands largely unchanged in Release 5. The one significant upgrade is the capability to move the cursor by page increments—an extension of the existing command for going to a numbered page. Each Find command is discussed in the following paragraphs.

The basic command for finding text is listed at help level 4 on the pull-down Go To menu:

```
Find text...            ^QF
```

The same command can be seen at help levels 4, 3, and 2 at the top of the FIND column in the Quick Menu:

```
F find text
```

The complete sequence for moving the cursor to a specified string of characters is ^QF.

WordStar also includes a function-key command to start a find operation, although the command is not listed on any menu. Ctrl-F1 performs the same task as ^QF.

When you press ^QF or Ctrl-F1, WordStar Release 5 displays a dialog box with the heading FIND (see fig. 5.17). This box displays a line where you enter the character string or phrase to be found. On the second line, you specify options for modifying the search. Below this line is a list of available options. Except for the new dialog box, the find function is unchanged from the preceding version of WordStar.

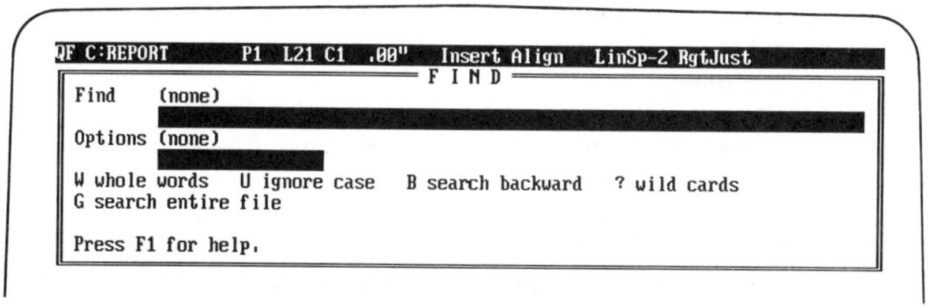
QF C:REPORT P1 L21 C1 .00" Insert Align LinSp-2 RgtJust
F I N D
Find (none)
Options (none)
W whole words U ignore case B search backward ? wild cards
G search entire file
Press F1 for help.

Fig. 5.17. *Dialog box for the Find command.*

When the Find dialog box appears, the cursor is in the line for the text to locate. Type the character string you want to find (up to 65 characters including spaces, control characters, and other special characters). WordStar searches for exactly what you type (unless you broaden the search with options). Be sure to include any capital letters, spaces, and punctuation marks in the phrase you want to find.

Among the characters you may want to find are print commands, such as ^PS (which appears on-screen as ^S and initiates underlining). Since WordStar Release 4, you can find any Ctrl-letter characters displayed in your text by using ^P, the literal command—indicating that the next character is to be accepted as indicated. To find the underline command, therefore, you press ^P^S, holding down the Ctrl key for both characters. To find a hard carriage return, you press ^P^M^P^J; this string represents the combination of a carriage return and a printer line feed. Two other find entries that may prove useful are ^P^- for locating soft hyphens at the end of a line and ^P^6 for finding soft hyphens in the middle of a line.

After you type the string to be found, you can press ^K or F10 to skip the choice of options and execute the find operation directly. (For veterans of previous WordStar versions, you can no longer use the Esc key to skip options and begin a search; in Release 5 pressing Esc cancels the Find command). At the top left of the screen, you see the word `Wait`. You may have to wait several seconds for WordStar to complete the search. The time required depends on your computer's internal memory and the amount of text between the cursor and the string to be found.

As in the last version of WordStar, the cursor always stops at the beginning of the string. The find function also recognizes character strings that begin on one line and continue past the carriage return to the next line or that begin on one page and continue past a page break.

If the character string you specify does not occur in your document exactly as entered, the following message appears on-screen:

```
Could not find:

Press Esc to continue.
```

The cursor is located at the end of your document. To return the cursor to the position from which you initiated the find operation, after you press Esc, press ^QP.

After you have found a word or phrase in your text, you can repeat the Find command to locate the next occurrence of the specified string without reissuing the Find command and string. This capability is helpful when you are correcting a recurring error in a document.

5

If you are using WordStar at help level 4, the command for repeating a find command is listed on the Go To menu:

```
Repeat previous find/replace  ^L
```

If WordStar is set for help level 3, the same command is exhibited on the classic Edit Menu in the OTHER column:

```
^L find/replace again
```

At all help levels, the ^L command advances the cursor to the next occurrence of the search string.

WordStar also offers a function-key sequence for repeating a find operation. The command Ctrl-F3 is the same as ^L.

After you have repeated a find operation, you can return the cursor to the last find with ^QV. You may want to set a place marker before you start a multiple find or replace operation; this technique allows you to use the corresponding Quick command to return to the marker.

Now, you can conduct a simple search through the sample customer letter drafted in Chapter 4. With the letter on the Edit screen, press ^QF to invoke the find function. Then type ***Mr. Roe*** as the character string to find, and press ^K or F10. The cursor advances to the words *Mr. Roe* in the salutation. If you repeat the search by pressing ^L, WordStar searches for other instances of Mr. Roe. Because these words do not occur again in your document, WordStar displays a message that the string cannot be found. Press the Esc key to resume editing. The cursor is now at the end of the file.

Using Find Options

Several options modify the Find command and enhance its power. When you are unsure of a spelling or capitalization or you don't know whether the character string occurs above or below the cursor location, you can use these search modifications to zero in on your target. The Find options, summarized in table 5.6, allow you to fine-tune any search operation and thereby save time and extra keystrokes.

Table 5.6
Find Command Options

Command	*Function*
W	Restrict search to whole words only
U	Ignore case of characters
B	Search backward
G	Search through whole file
?	Consider ? in search string as wild card

To select an option, press Enter after you type the character string to find. The cursor moves to the second line of the Find dialog box—where you can specify one or more options. You can type upper- or lowercase letters to correspond with the options. Type the letters with or without spaces between them; then press Enter. (If you decide not to choose any options, press ^K or F10, and WordStar performs a standard find operation.)

The effects of these Find options are easy to understand. Specifying W ensures that only whole words are recognized, even though your character string appears as a portion of another word. For example, unless you choose the W option, WordStar finds the word *market* in *marketing*. With U, the find operation ignores case. The search operation, for instance, does not exclude a word or phrase because you are not sure which letters should be capitalized. Selecting B instructs WordStar to search backward toward the beginning of the document. When you select the G option, the find operation starts at a document's beginning. When you use the G option with the B option to search backward, the search starts at the end of the document.

Entering ? at the options prompt instructs WordStar to consider any question marks in your string as wild cards that match any character in that position. For example, if you are unsure whether a name is spelled Smith or Smyth, type the search string as *Sm?th* and select the ? option. If you include a question mark in a string without selecting the ? option, the find operation looks for a string that includes a question mark.

One more Find option is not indicated in the on-screen message. If you type a whole number *n*, the find operation finds the *n*th occurrence of the specified string.

As an example of using the Find options, in the sample pricing letter, search for specific occurrences of the word *widget*. After the search for the string *Mr. Roe*, the cursor is at the end of the document. To find the second occurrence of the word *widget* without going back to the beginning of the file, you press ^QF to invoke the Find command, type *widget* and press Enter, and you are then at the `Options` line of the Find box. To search backward for the second occurrence of the whole word *widget* without regard to case, you type *b2wu* and press Enter. After a brief search, the cursor appears in the middle of the letter.

Using Special Find Functions

In addition to the standard find function, WordStar provides three specialized find operations for more efficient cursor movement to specific locations: a single character following the cursor, a single character preceding the cursor, or a specific page or line in your document.

Two of these commands are listed on the pull-down Go To menu at help level 4, although one is actually a variation of the other function, as follows:

```
Go to page...            ^QI

Go to paragraph end      ^QG↵
```

At all help levels but 1 and 0, the three special find functions are listed in the FIND column of the classic Quick Menu:

```
G char forward
H char back
I page/line
```

The full commands are ^QG to move forward to a character, ^QH to move backward to a character, and ^QI to find a page by number or increment.

WordStar also provides a function key that duplicates the command for finding a page by number. Pressing Ctrl-F4 produces the same effect as pressing ^QI.

To use any special find function, you follow this basic procedure. After you start the command, a dialog box appears on-screen. Specify the place where you want the cursor to appear. When the function is completed, the flashing cursor is relocated as designated.

When you press ^QG or ^QH, the box labeled GO TO includes the question `Go to what character?` As soon as you type a character, the cursor appears at that character's next occurrence, forward (^QG) or backward (^QH). You do not need to press Enter or Esc. The response at the Go To box can be a character, number, symbol, or punctuation mark. After you press ^QG, for example, typing a period (.) moves the cursor to the end of a sentence. Similarly, pressing ^QG and Enter sends the cursor to the hard carriage return at the end of the paragraph, as noted in the pull-down Go To menu.

When you press ^QI, the dialog box headed GO TO PAGE is displayed; it has a prompt area for the page number with room for up to four digits. After you type the page number, you press Enter to execute the command. When WordStar searches forward to find a page, the cursor jumps to the first line of the page. When the search moves backward, the cursor appears on the page's last line. In nondocument mode, ^QI searches for a specified line number rather than a page number.

In Release 5, the go-to-page feature also accepts incremental responses with a plus (+) or minus (−) sign. Typing + or − at the Go to Page dialog box moves the cursor, respectively, to the next or preceding page; typing a number after a plus or minus sign sends the cursor forward or backward that number of pages.

For examples of special Find commands in the sample marketing report from Chapter 4, start with the cursor at the beginning of the second paragraph of the document's body copy. Press ^QG and type *W* (for the next occurrence of an uppercase W, as in Widgets) in the Go To dialog box. The cursor moves down six lines to the next W. Pressing ^QH and typing *W* moves the cursor back up eight lines to the preceding occurrence of this character. Finally, to move the cursor to the top of page 1, you press ^QR.

Editing with Find and Replace

Among the handiest of editing features in any word processing program is the capability to replace a word or phrase with another, as many times as needed. This function, called find and replace, has saved hours of retyping proper names, updated statistics, or any repeated entries in reports, scripts, manuscripts, and other long documents.

WordStar's find-and-replace function is a variation of its standard Find command: finding one string and substituting another in its place. The Find and Replace command and its options are also similar to a simple Find command.

At help level 4, the pull-down Go To menu lists this function directly below the Find Text command:

```
Find and replace text...    ^QA
```

At help levels 4, 3, and 2, the classic Quick Menu lists the command in the FIND column:

```
A find/replace
```

The full command sequence is ^QA.

WordStar also includes a function-key combination for invoking this feature. Pressing Ctrl-F2 produces the same effect as pressing ^QA. Both key sequences start the find-and-replace function.

When you start a replace operation, WordStar Release 5 displays a dialog box titled FIND & REPLACE (see fig. 5.18). This box has space for you to enter the string to be found, the replacement string, and the options for altering the find-and-replace operation.

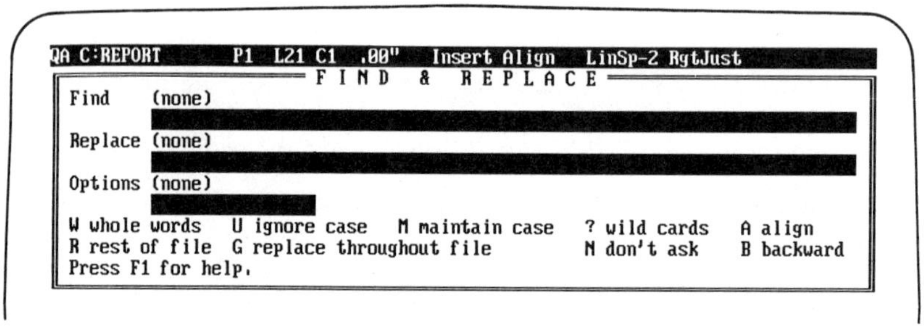
QA C:REPORT P1 L21 C1 .00" Insert Align LinSp-2 RgtJust
FIND & REPLACE
Find (none)
Replace (none)
Options (none)
W whole words U ignore case M maintain case ? wild cards A align
R rest of file G replace throughout file N don't ask B backward
Press F1 for help.

Fig. 5.18.
Dialog box for the Find and Replace command.

When the Find & Replace dialog box first appears, the cursor is in the line for `Find`. Here you can type the character string you want to find, observing the same conventions as for a simple find operation. Press Enter to advance the cursor to the line for the character string to replace the first. After typing this string, you can skip any options by pressing ^K or F10.

The standard find-and-replace function searches forward one time for the exact string of characters to replace. The cursor appears at the first occurrence of the string to be found, and another cursor flashes at the top right of the screen beside a confirmation message: `Replace Y/N`. Pressing Y completes the substitution. If you press N, the text remains unchanged.

After you indicate your choice, you can edit at the cursor, press ^L to invoke another find-and-replace operation, or press ^QP to go back to the position where ^QA was issued.

For an example of finding and replacing, use this function to search for the word *widget* in the sample memo (created in Chapter 1) and substitute *Widget*, as per the fictitious Widgets, Inc. corporate style manual. To start the operation, you press ^QA, and at the Find & Replace box, type *widget*. Press Enter, and at the `Replace` line, type *Widget* and press ^K. When the cursor appears at the word, press Y; and *Widget* is substituted for *widget*.

In this case, the replacement string is the same length as the original string. If the replacement string is shorter or longer, you have to press ^B to realign your paragraph, or you can use one of the Find and Replace options discussed in the next section.

Using Find and Replace Options

As noted, an unmodified Find and Replace searches forward one time for an exact string to replace. WordStar allows you to select any of several options for increased flexibility. Some of these options work in the same way as the Find command options; others are unique to the find and replace function. Table 5.7 summarizes the find and replace function's options.

Table 5.7
Find and Replace Options

Command	*Function*
W	Restrict search to whole words only
U	Ignore case of characters
M	Maintain case of characters
B	Search backward
G	Search globally through entire file
?	Consider ? in search string as wild card
A	Align paragraph after replacement
R	Search through the rest of a file
N	Suppress confirmation prompts

Of the nine options, four operate exactly like their counterparts in the Find options: W to recognize whole words only; U to ignore case in the search string; B to search backward through a document; and ? to treat a question mark in the search string as a wild card.

The other options are easy to remember once you understand their effects. The A option automatically aligns a paragraph when the replacement string is longer or shorter than the original string. Pressing ^B to align a paragraph is therefore no longer necessary. The R option causes WordStar to search through the rest of document—that is, the portion from the cursor position onward. The M option retains the same case when replacing the Find string with another; invoking M causes WordStar to ignore the U option.

Two of the Find and Replace options work differently than they do in find operations. The G option causes WordStar to search globally for every instance of the search string throughout the entire file, from the beginning or end of a document. This option frees you from pressing ^L to continue the search-and-replace operation. WordStar pauses for confirmation before replacing a string unless you choose the N option—don't ask!

The Find and Replace command also has a number option. Typing a whole number *n* instructs WordStar to find the next *n* occurrences of the string for possible replacement. For example, you can type *10* at the options prompt to locate the next 10 occurrences of a word or phrase in your document.

If you select options for multiple substitutions without confirmations to halt the process, when you press Enter, the substitutions continue automatically throughout the document. In Release 5, pressing the space bar after Enter makes the replacement occur much faster—in your computer's memory but not immediately on-screen. Only when the find-and-replace operation is complete do you see a prompt box instructing you to press Esc to continue editing.

For an example of how the Find and Replace options work in the sample memo, continue finding and replacing the word *widget* with *Widget*. To invoke the find and replace operation, you press ^QA, and at the first prompt in the dialog box type *widget*; then press Enter. For the replacement string, type *Widget* and press Enter. To complete the replacements of *widget*, you type *wugn* at the options prompt and press Enter. These options replace the whole word, find both upper- and lowercase, search globally, and replace the word without asking for confirmation.

Using Other Quick Menu Commands

Previous sections of this chapter have covered ^Q command sequences for moving through and editing text. Three other editing functions invoked with ^Q combinations are summarized in table 5.8. One of these commands is listed on the pull-down Other menu at level 4, and all three are included on the classic Quick Menu, viewed at help level 4, 3, or 2. Learning to use these miscellaneous ^Q sequence commands can add to your efficiency in using WordStar.

In addition to a function for repeating any command, WordStar has a feature that repeats realignment of the paragraphs in a file. Another quick command produces a character count for a document. (As for other commands on the Quick Menu, WordStar's built-in calculator and math capabilities are covered, along with column math, in Chapter 6.)

Table 5.8
Other Quick Menu Commands

Command	*Function*
^QQ	Repeat a command
^QU	Realign paragraphs
^Q?	Display character count

Using the Repeat Function

At times, you want to repeat the entry of a character or repeat a single-stroke command. For instance, you may want to enter many hyphens or issue repeated commands to move the cursor. WordStar includes a command sequence that automatically repeats whatever follows the command. This repeat command begins with ^Q.

This useful function is not listed on any of the new pull-down menus, but it is included in the OTHER column of the classic Quick Menu (displayed by pressing ^Q at the Edit screen):

```
Q repeat
```

The full Repeat command is ^QQ.

When you use the Repeat command, the keystroke following the command is repeated until you press another key—preferably the space bar. If you intend to repeat a command that uses a combination of the Ctrl key and a letter key, be sure to hold down the Ctrl key as you invoke the command. Otherwise, the letter itself appears on-screen. You can vary the speed of the repetition by pressing a number key after the repetition begins. Entering 0 produces the fastest repetition; 9, the slowest. The default speed is 3.

You can try using the Repeat command, for instance, to move the cursor forward word by word though any document. With the cursor at the beginning of the document, press ^QQ^F, sending the cursor through the text, stopping at the first letter of each word from left to right. Also try slowing the rate of movement by pressing 9, and speeding the process by pressing 1.

Realigning a Document

To align all the paragraphs in a file, you can use the Repeat function with the ^B command. By issuing the command sequence ^QQ^B, you can realign an entire document after a change in margins or other formatting operations. WordStar provides another ^Q command sequence to invoke the same task much faster and with only two keystrokes.

At help level 4, this specialized command can be found on the pull-down Layout menu (displayed by pressing Alt-L while editing), shown as follows:

```
Align rest of document    ^QU
```

This function is also listed at the top of the classic Quick Menu's OTHER column:

```
U align rest doc
```

The complete command is ^QU.

When you press ^QU, WordStar aligns the paragraph at the cursor to fit the margins. The cursor pauses briefly after the carriage return and then continues as the program aligns the following paragraphs until every one in the document is aligned. To stop the alignment process, press ^U.

As an example of applying this function, you can realign the memo created in Chapter 1. The memo is formatted with its lines flush right. To reformat, place the cursor at the beginning of the document, and press ^OJ to turn off justification; then press ^QU for realignment of the document's paragraphs. The cursor advances through your text as WordStar reformats.

Realigning paragraphs is straightforward when text consists of relatively short words. When you realign text with many longer words, WordStar helps you with hyphenation. This feature is discussed in the section of this chapter on auto-hyphenation.

Getting a Character Count

WordStar includes a Quick Menu command for displaying a character count. (This command is not included on any pull-down menu.) This function, which counts the characters from the beginning of an open document to the cursor position, is useful when you edit a document to fit a precise character count.

The command, which is another ^Q sequence, is listed in the CURSOR column of the classic Quick Menu:

```
? char count
```

When you press ^Q?, a message box with the following appears near the top of the screen:

```
Byte count at cursor:

Press Esc to continue.
```

The actual number of bytes is displayed on the first line of the message. Each byte is the equivalent of a character.

WordStar veterans should note that instead of an exact character count, as in previous versions, Release 5 counts all bytes of information in a file—including special codes at the beginning of WordStar's new file structure. This information adds 128 bytes to any file. When you are figuring the character count up to the cursor, subtract 128 from the byte count. Remember also that spaces and punctuation are included in this count.

WordStar Release 5 also includes a function for counting words and characters in a marked block, as explained in Chapter 6. When no block is marked, the count is for the entire file.

To get a character count, move the cursor to the end of any document. Then press ^Q?. The number of character bytes is displayed at the top of the screen. Pressing the Esc key lets you continue editing.

Reformatting Paragraphs: Additional Functions

When you edit and realign text, a long word may be moved to another line. This realignment may leave a large gap at the right side of a line, or if the text is justified, the realignment may leave large spaces between words. To avoid this situation, a WordStar feature automatically detects long words, splits them, and inserts hyphens where needed.

The hyphenation help feature in WordStar Release 4 relied on an unsophisticated method: the program flagged any words that would leave a gap of more than five characters and hyphenated those words at the margin, regardless of syllable breaks. To provide more accurate hyphenation, Release 5 uses grammatical rules for word breaks. These rules are contained in the file WSHYPH.OVR, which must be on your working copy of WordStar for this feature to work. Auto-hyphenation is set to be activated whenever a word would leave a gap of five characters or more. The program splits and hyphenates the word correctly. (The five-character limit can be reset with the WSCHANGE program, see Chapter 11.) The hyphenation commands are summarized in table 5.9.

Table 5.9
WordStar's Hyphenation Commands

Command	*Function*
^OH	Toggle hyphen help off/on
^OE	Insert soft hyphen

Using Auto-Hyphenation

The default setting for the hyphenation feature is a major difference between WordStar Release 4 and Release 5. The earlier release came preset with hyphen help turned off; Release 5 starts with auto-hyphenation turned on. Many users will want to turn off hyphenation when starting a work session. (You can turn off auto-hyphenation permanently with WSCHANGE.)

None of the new pull-down menus lists hyphenation functions, but the classic Onscreen Format Menu includes the auto-hyphenation toggle command in the DISPLAY column:

```
H turn auto-hyphenation off
```

The complete command sequence for toggling hyphen help either on or off is ^OH. Press this combination when WordStar starts up and auto-hyphenation is turned off. You will see the corresponding change in the classic Onscreen Format Menu:

```
H turn auto-hyphenation on
```

Issuing the ^OH command again turns on the automatic hyphenation feature.

With ^OH toggled on, auto-hyphenation is activated when you realign a paragraph. While WordStar is reformatting, the cursor stops briefly at the right margin of a line where a word of more than five characters is about to be split. WordStar breaks the word between syllables and inserts a hyphen at the right margin, wrapping the second part of the word to the next line.

Users of previous versions of WordStar will notice that Release 5 does not display a Hyphen Help Menu with the hyphenation feature. Because the word breaks are more accurate than before, confirmation is no longer needed before the program inserts hyphens, one reason the function is called auto-hyphenation.

Any hyphen inserted by auto-hyphenation is known as a soft hyphen—a conditional mark that is printed only if the word occurs at the end of a line. During realignment, a soft hyphen moved away from the right margin is represented on-screen by an equal sign (=). (You can alter this character choice with WSCHANGE.)

In contrast, hyphens you type in text are called hard hyphens because they print regardless of formatting considerations. When WordStar's hyphen help function scans a word to be divided, hard hyphens are recognized as characters.

With text that is extensively edited and realigned, soft hyphens may clutter your copy and disrupt formatting, although those hyphens will not be printed. To see your document without soft hyphens, you can invoke the ^OD command, which toggles block markers off the screen. Pressing ^OD also turns off the display of soft hyphens, although they remain active in case of reformatting. Pressing ^OD again puts soft hyphens back on-screen.

Inserting Soft Hyphens

Whether auto-hyphenation is turned on or off, you can indicate ahead of time possible breaks in words by inserting soft hyphens—in unusual or foreign words, for instance. During reformatting, those soft hyphens are used to create automatic word breaks at the right margin.

Although not on any pull-down menu, the command for placing soft hyphens in text can be found in the TYPING column on the classic Onscreen Format Menu:

```
E enter soft hyphen
```

The full command is ^OE.

In Release 5, inserting a soft hyphen at the beginning of a word by pressing ^OE marks the word so that it will not be split by auto-hyphenation, even if the word contains a hard hyphen. The entire word remains on one line, regardless of formatting.

Using Quick Erase Commands

In addition to augmenting cursor-movement and scrolling functions, pressing ^Q before several other commands can enhance WordStar editing functions. Three single-keystroke erase commands are modified when preceded with ^Q. Unlike cursor-movement and scrolling commands that have their actions incrementally increased, ^Q delete functions provide variations on the single-letter erase commands.

Not found on any pull-down menu, the commands are listed in the DELETE column of the classic Quick Menu:

```
Del line to left
  Y line to right
  T to character
```

The full commands are, respectively, ^Q-Del, ^QY, and ^QT. Each command erases useful amounts of text, as summarized in table 5.10.

Table 5.10
Quick Erase Commands

Command	*Function*
^Q-Del	Delete text from cursor left to beginning of line
^QY	Delete text from cursor right to end of line
^QT	Delete text from cursor forward to specified character

When you erase part of a line with ^Q-Del, the cursor and the remaining portion of the line are pulled all the way to the left and auto-align reformats the paragraph as soon as you start typing or move from the line. Erasing part of a line to the right of the cursor with ^QY also triggers auto-align if the cursor is moved. Both the ^QY and ^Q-Del commands are executed immediately.

Pressing ^QT displays a boxed prompt:

```
Delete forward to what character?
```

After you type a character, text through that point is deleted. The designated character can be a letter, number, symbol, or punctuation mark. For example, by typing a period (.) as the designated character, you can use the ^QT command as an easy way to erase text through the end of a sentence.

As with other erase functions in WordStar Release 5, your last deletion with ^QY, ^Q-Del, or ^QT can be restored at the cursor by pressing ^U or F2.

For an example of each of these quick deletion functions, you can use any open document. Starting with the cursor at the beginning of a line, type two lines of random characters that can be erased; end the second line with a single period (.). Move the cursor to the middle of the first line of random characters. Press ^Q-Del; the text to the left of the cursor disappears. Pressing ^QY then erases the remaining characters on the line. Pressing ^QT and typing a period (.) deletes the rest of your expendable text.

Understanding WordStar's Backup Files

From the first version, WordStar has had an important safeguard against losing important text during or after editing. The program's backup file-saving feature helps you avoid aggravation when you accidentally erase or damage a document file. If you save any document more than once, WordStar renames the version currently on disk as a backup copy with the file extension BAK. When a backup file already exists, WordStar replaces that file with the latest backup version.

In Release 5, WordStar adds another kind of automatic backup feature—periodically saving the current contents of a document to disk. (This function works only on IBM AT and compatible computers.) You set the time between save operations with the WSCHANGE program (see Chapter 11.)

WordStar does not allow a BAK file to be edited unless you rename the file. You can, however, read a backup file in protected mode. (In protected mode, the notation `Prtect` replaces `Insert` on the status line.) If you try to type characters, the computer beeps to indicate that nothing in the file can be changed in protected mode (see Chapter 4).

To edit a backup file, you first must rename it with the E command at the Opening Menu. The new file name should not include a BAK extension. Usually, if the file was accidentally deleted, you simply use the original name of the file. Text in a BAK file can be edited when read into a document with a ^KR command.

During editing, WordStar creates several temporary files, one of which eventually is saved on disk as a copy of your document and replaces the current disk version, which becomes the backup file. In the earliest releases of WordStar, one temporary file was created with the extension $$$; beginning with Release 4, as many as three separate temporary files are created and stored on disk.

When you open a document (or nondocument) file with Release 5, WordStar creates two temporary disk files using the file name and the extensions A and B. If the space a document requires exceeds the amount of internal memory, beginning sections of the document are then saved in the B file. When you later return to the beginning of a file, portions in internal memory are saved in the A file. During block operations, a third temporary file with the extension C may be created. When you save a document, the contents of the A file are read into the B file, which now contains all your edited document, and the B file is saved under the document's file name. After this procedure is completed, the previous version of the file on disk is renamed with the BAK extension.

A WordStar error is possible due to this temporary file scheme. The error can occur if you don't properly close a file, but abandon it in the midst of editing. This error may occur, for instance, if you experience a power outage or if you turn off your computer. The temporary files remain on disk, but you cannot see their names on the file directory when you start a new session; file names with extensions A, B, and C are not displayed. Even though the name of your file appears on the directory (and you haven't protected the file), if you try to reopen the file you were working on before the power went off, you may see a boxed message indicating that the file is being edited and asking whether you would like to view it as a protected file. The options at this point are typing Y for Yes or N for No.

To recover from this error, press N to return to the Opening Menu. You can use the E command on the menu to rename the temporary files into readable ones without their A or B extensions. This procedure recovers work that would otherwise be lost.

If you have saved your work and not changed the document since, you can delete the temporary files. Press R to run a DOS command, and at the DOS prompt type *del *.$** (a command that uses the wild-card character to delete all temporary files). Then press Enter. Press any key to return to the Opening display.

Recovering from a Disk-Full Error

When your disk space is limited, you may encounter another kind of error caused by WordStar's backup files. Because of its design, the program requires adequate space on disk for the original file, its backup file, and any temporary files created during editing. Available disk space, therefore, must be at least twice as large as a document before you can successfully save the file to disk.

If disk space is limited during a save operation, portions of the backup file are erased to make room for the file you are saving. If insufficient space remains on disk, you cannot save your current document file—a situation known as a disk-full error.

If you try to save a file, and not enough room is available on your disk even after you have erased the file's backup file, Release 5 displays the following boxed message:

```
File error. The disk may be full, or there was disk write
error, or CONFIG.SYS on your boot (system) disk lacks the
line FILES=20.

Press Esc to continue.
```

If you encounter a disk-full error, press Esc to regain control of the keyboard. You can use ^KJ to erase excess disk files. If you have no expendable files, you can use the copy command (^KO) to move files onto another disk and then erase those files from your logged disk. After you have freed sufficient space, you can save your current document.

As an alternative procedure, you can try saving portions of your document separately with the block command ^KW. Then you can erase those portions from the document in order to shorten the file to be saved. Later, after clearing enough disk space to accommodate a longer file, you can rejoin these short files.

Even when you are mindful of your disk's contents, you sometimes will be unable to avoid a disk-full error, particularly when you work with long files on a floppy disk system. For this reason, restricting file size to 25 pages on a 5 1/4-inch floppy disk system is a good idea. You always can combine files or print them in sequence later.

6

Using WordStar's Page Formatting Features

Whether you prepare documents for commerce, education, or communication, your text's appearance on the page determines its clarity and impact. Using WordStar's wide array of formatting features in your word processing can greatly enhance your documents' appeal. In Chapter 4, you worked with WordStar's simpler formatting commands. This chapter introduces the functions you can use to control page layout.

Some of the functions in this chapter change how your text appears on-screen; the effect of other functions can be seen only when a document is printed. Two complementary sets of commands are used: Ctrl-letter combinations and dot commands. Both are seen on the Edit screen but not on paper—even though their action may change considerably the way your pages look in print. WordStar includes a preview function to let you see on-screen exactly how a document will look before you print it.

With the commands explained in this chapter, you can perform many kinds of format operations, including

- Using text in columns and calculating numbers in columns
- Creating a simple outline
- Adding annotations, comments, endnotes, and footnotes
- Selecting ruler lines to create multiple formats
- Laying out headers, footers, and custom page numbering

If you are fluent in an earlier version of WordStar, you will appreciate the numerous additions to the layout functions in Release 5. Such long-awaited features as text sorting, snaking columns, paragraph numbering, note options, and style guides are marked with Release 5 icons in this chapter. Release 5's improved preview mode, which displays on-screen the effects of formatting commands before printing, has been hailed as the most advanced of its kind among word processing programs for PC- and PS/2-compatible computers.

The WordStar commands discussed here deal with page layout and its associated functions, but the commands covered in this chapter do not depend on printer-specific capabilities. Printer-related dot commands are explained fully in the next chapter. You may use many of the functions in this chapter so habitually that you will want to incorporate the functions as shorthand macros (explained in Chapter 9). You also might want to change page design permanently by using the WSCHANGE program to reset WordStar (described in Chapter 11).

Manipulating Columns of Text and Numbers

To edit listings, itineraries, numerical data, financial results, and other information presented in tabular form, the block commands presented in Chapter 5 have serious limitations. Those standard block commands are designed for use on portions of lines or all the text between the left and right margins. Electronic cut-and-paste operations with such block commands can ruin the formatting of text columns. To edit columns, you need special functions that preserve column formatting while moving, copying, deleting, and making other block operations.

WordStar's column mode and related block commands make editing and reformatting tabular material easy. For example, column moves are as simple as other cut-and-paste operations, thanks to the column replace function. Related block commands can convert text to all upper- or all lowercase letters and can total columns of numbers.

Veterans of earlier releases will applaud WordStar's added sentence conversion function, which converts upper- and lowercase letters to conform to standard sentence style. Release 5 users also will appreciate the new feature for alphabetical or numerical sorting of text—most often applied to columnar listings. Incidentally, to avoid disrupting the page format when you invoke many of these functions, you may want to turn off Release 5's auto-align feature by pressing ^OA.

Table 6.1 lists WordStar's column mode commands and related block commands. Each of these commands is discussed in the following sections.

Table 6.1
WordStar's Column Mode Commands and Related Block Commands

Command	*Description*
^KN	Toggles column mode
^KI	Toggles column replace
^K'	Converts text block to lowercase
^K"	Converts text block to uppercase
^K.	Converts a block to sentence style
^KZ	Sorts lines in a text block
^KM	Totals a column of numbers

Of the column-related functions detailed in this chapter, only three are listed on WordStar's new pull-down menus: ^KN and ^KI are on the Edit menu (displayed by pressing Alt-E while editing), and ^KM is on the Other menu (press Alt-O).

At help levels 4, 3, and 2, all seven column features appear on the classic Block & Save Menu. From within a document, you access this menu by pressing ^K. Four of the commands are near the bottom of the BLOCK columns, and the other three occupy a corner at the bottom right of the menu, the CASE column.

To learn how to use these column-oriented ^K commands for editing text and calculating columns of numbers, you can type a sample document called AD-BUDGT, a budget summary for shooting television ads for Widgets, Inc. (see fig. 6.1). Creating this document will introduce you to the commands you will use to produce your own documents containing tabular information. The double-spaced, unjustified sample document includes tabular material at WordStar's preset tabs at 1 inch, 3 inches, 4 inches, 4.5 inches, and 5 inches, as shown here:

If you type this brief sample document exactly as you see it here, you will be ready to try the examples that follow.

Using Column Mode

A column of text is defined by left and right edges at boundaries other than the page margins. Standard text blocks do not preserve these boundaries. When you edit columns, you should use WordStar's column mode—retaining the left and right edges of a block as well as its upper and lower limits.

At help level 4, the command for invoking column mode is displayed on the pull-down Edit menu (press Alt-E while editing), as follows:

5

```
Column block mode          ^KN
```

Fig. 6.1.
The advertising budget document.

To: All concerned

From: Cost Accounting Office, Marketing and Communications

Super Widgets TV Ad Campaign--Estimated Shooting Budget

As requested, here is the bottom line on the television ad campaign launching Super Widgets. More detailed break-downs are available to authorized bidders.

Lengths	Title	Location	Days	Crew	Total Budget
15", 30"	"Old Boy"	England	3	5	1,037,206
15", 60"	"Palace Gossip"	Spain	4	10	1,994,921
30", 60"	"Inside Trader"	Monaco	3	6	1,345,236
30", 60"	"Civilization"	Egypt	5	17	2,882,476
Totals					

At all help levels except 1 and 0, the same command is listed two lines from the bottom of the classic Block & Save Menu (shown by pressing ^K at the Edit screen):

```
N turn column mode on
```

The command for setting column mode is a toggle. Pressing ^KN once turns on this feature, changing the listing on the Block & Save Menu to

```
N turn column mode off
```

Pressing ^KN again turns off the feature.

When column mode is on, the word `Column` appears at the right of the status line (where `RgtJust` also appears). When you mark a block, the beginning and end markers indicate the top left and bottom right corners of the block. The column between the markers is in reverse video. The end marker must be below and to the right of the beginning marker. If not, when you try to invoke a column block function, an on-screen message informs you of the error in marker location.

Column mode does not change the way you enter text. This mode lets you perform all the standard block operations on a marked column—moving, copying, and deleting—while preserving the column's left and right boundaries. These operations can disrupt the formatting of existing text (to minimize problems, turn off auto-align with ^OA). For example, when you move a marked column, the block is pushed to the right at the location where you insert it, and the space from where you moved the column is collapsed. Therefore, check both locations after you move a column. And as with earlier WordStar releases, carriage returns within a marked column remain in place if you move or delete the block.

You can use all the block commands in column mode. For instance, pressing ^KW saves a marked column directly to disk, and pressing ^U or F2 restores a deleted column block, just as with standard blocks.

When you use column mode, you should keep in mind some of its potential hazards. Be particularly cautious when the operation involves print-control commands, embedded dot commands, or an imported file. Each of these traps is discussed in the following paragraphs.

If you separate a pair of print-control commands when you manipulate columns, you might produce unintended print effects throughout your document. Therefore, be sure to check print-control commands after you use column commands.

Moving or deleting a column in column mode excludes the dot commands embedded in the text. To preserve intended layout modifications, you may have to move the dot commands to the new location in your text.

When you use ^KR to insert a file in column mode, the program scans the imported file to see whether this file also is formatted in columns. If it is, WordStar inserts the file at the cursor. If text in an imported file is not formatted in columns (with lines of equal length), the following boxed error message appears on-screen:

```
That file is not a column (line lengths vary).  You can...

     1.  Insert the entire file.

     2.  Insert the file up to the point where it starts to
         vary.

     3.  Insert the file up to the point where it starts to
         vary and highlight it (for easy deletion).

Which option (1/2/3) ?
```

The options are similar to those in WordStar Release 4, although the corresponding keyboard entries are different in Release 5. Pressing 1 inserts the whole file at the cursor regardless of format. Pressing 2 reads in only the part of the file in column format. Pressing 3 inserts the import file's text to the point where it stops being formatted in column mode, marking the inserted text as a block for easy moving or deleting.

To learn to use column mode, you can try moving the first column of information to the right of the second column in the sample advertising budget. After typing the document, press ^KN to turn on column mode (also make sure that the word `Align` is not on the status line; if it is, press ^OA). Then define the first column of the sample document. Move the cursor to the first letter in `Lengths` and press ^KB or Shift-F9; move the cursor to the end of the last `60"`, and press ^KK or Shift-F10. The column is displayed in reverse video, as shown in figure 6.2.

Next, move the cursor to where you want the column moved: to the top line of the tabular material at column 19, between `Title` and `Location` (`C19` appears in the status line). Press ^KV, relocating the top left corner of the marked column at the cursor, as in figure 6.3.

Fig. 6.2.

A column marked and ready to be moved.

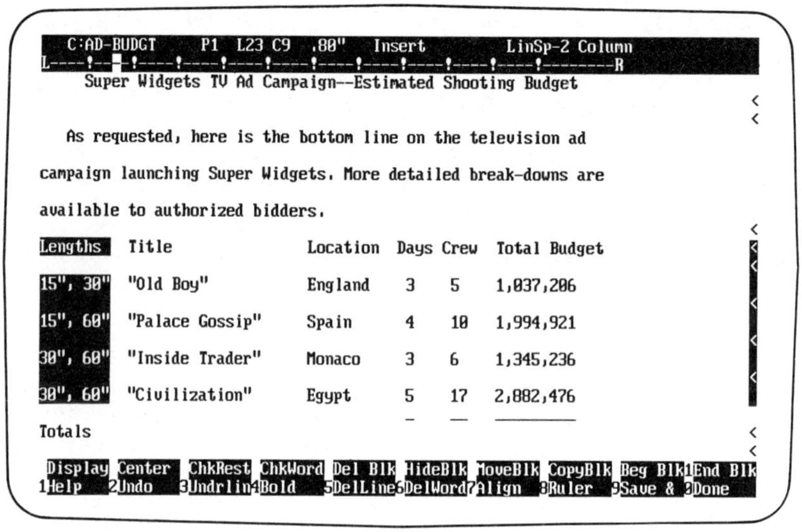
C:AD-BUDGT P1 L23 C9 .80" Insert LinSp-2 Column
Super Widgets TV Ad Campaign--Estimated Shooting Budget
As requested, here is the bottom line on the television ad
campaign launching Super Widgets. More detailed break-downs are
available to authorized bidders.
Lengths Title Location Days Crew Total Budget
15", 30" "Old Boy" England 3 5 1,037,206
15", 60" "Palace Gossip" Spain 4 10 1,994,921
30", 60" "Inside Trader" Monaco 3 6 1,345,236
30", 60" "Civilization" Egypt 5 17 2,082,476
Totals
Display Center ChkRest ChkWord Del Blk HideBlk MoveBlk CopyBlk Beg Blk End Blk
1Help 2Undo 3Undrlin 4Bold 5DelLine 6DelWord 7Align 8Ruler 9Save & 0Done

Fig. 6.3.

A block of text moved in column mode.

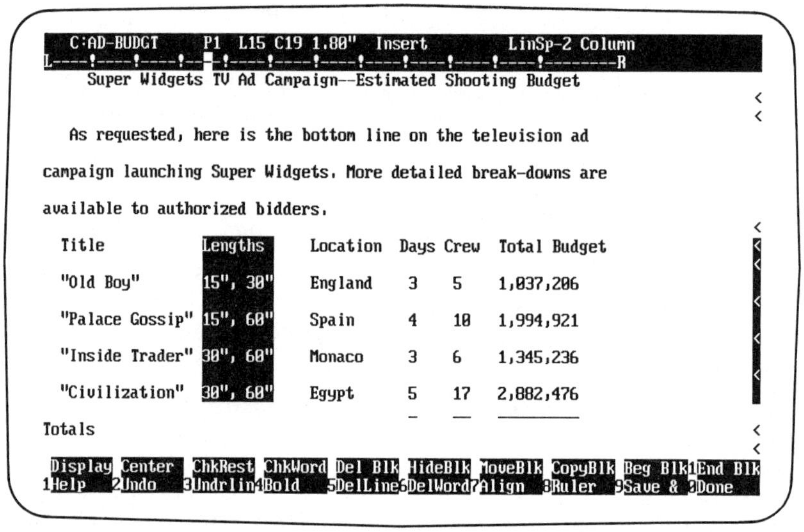
C:AD-BUDGT P1 L15 C19 1.80" Insert LinSp-2 Column
Super Widgets TV Ad Campaign--Estimated Shooting Budget
As requested, here is the bottom line on the television ad
campaign launching Super Widgets. More detailed break-downs are
available to authorized bidders.
Title Lengths Location Days Crew Total Budget
"Old Boy" 15", 30" England 3 5 1,037,206
"Palace Gossip" 15", 60" Spain 4 10 1,994,921
"Inside Trader" 30", 60" Monaco 3 6 1,345,236
"Civilization" 30", 60" Egypt 5 17 2,082,476
Totals
Display Center ChkRest ChkWord Del Blk HideBlk MoveBlk CopyBlk Beg Blk End Blk
1Help 2Undo 3Undrlin 4Bold 5DelLine 6DelWord 7Align 8Ruler 9Save & 0Done

Because the Lengths and Title columns simply changed places within the same section of text, column formatting was preserved. However, moving a column elsewhere within the document would wreak havoc with formatting.

Using Column Replace

To make column cut-and-paste operations easier, WordStar includes a command for inserting a column that replaces existing text without disrupting formatting. This column replacement function is the column equivalent of overtype mode (see Chapter 3).

At help level 4, this feature is shown on the pull-down Edit menu, directly below the Column Block Mode command, like this:

```
Column replace mode      ^KI
```

At help levels 4, 3, and 2, this command appears on the Block & Save Menu:

```
I turn column replace on
```

The full command is ^KI. Like the Column Block Mode command, this command is a toggle. Pressing ^KI turns on column replace; pressing ^KI again turns off this mode.

When you turn on column replace, WordStar displays `ColRepl` on the right side of the status line. Column replace functions only when column mode is on. When both modes are on, you can perform block operations such as cutting and pasting on columns. Column replace causes a moved, copied, or inserted block to take the place of text at the cursor. If you move or delete a column, WordStar inserts spaces into the remaining text to maintain its formatting.

With column replace turned on, you also can use either the ^U or F2 Undo command to restore the text that a moved, copied, or inserted column replaced. The program treats the replaced text as if you had deleted it with an erasing command. By pressing ^U or F2, you can return the text on-screen at the cursor. By combining a column-replace operation with unerase, you can swap columns of text.

In previous versions of WordStar, you needed to apply both column mode and column replace to juggle columns into the style used in newsletters: the last line of the left-hand column continues to the first line of the right-hand column. In Release 5, WordStar makes invoking *snaking columns* easy with a set of new dot commands, which are discussed later in this chapter.

You can move columns of data in the sample advertising budget document using column replace. To switch the columns headed Days and Crew, press ^KI to toggle on column replace (making sure that you have already invoked column mode with ^KN). To mark the Days column, press ^KB or Shift-F9 at the beginning of the `Days` heading. Then move the cursor three spaces past the 5 at the bottom of the column, and press ^KK or Shift-F10. The column is displayed in reverse video. Move the cursor to the beginning of the `Crew` heading, and press ^KV. The Days column replaces the Crew column, as shown in figure 6.4.

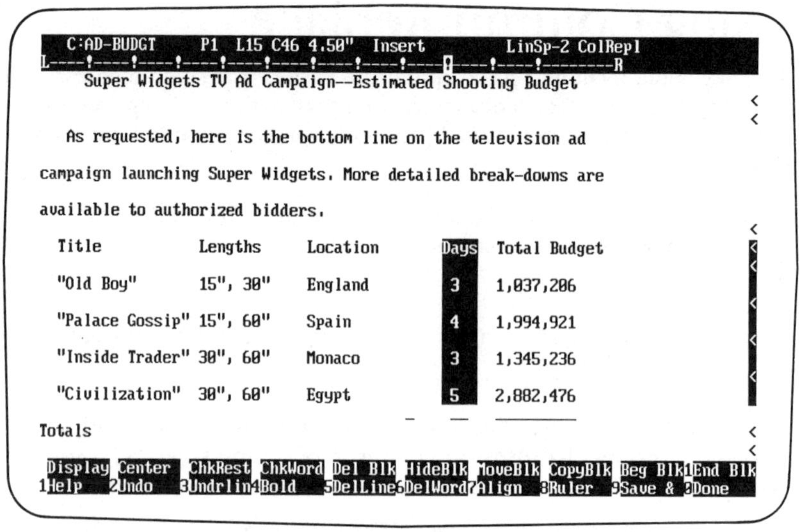
C:AD-BUDGT P1 L15 C46 4.50" Insert LinSp-2 ColRepl
Super Widgets TV Ad Campaign--Estimated Shooting Budget
As requested, here is the bottom line on the television ad
campaign launching Super Widgets. More detailed break-downs are
available to authorized bidders.
Title Lengths Location Days Total Budget
"Old Boy" 15", 30" England 3 1,037,206
"Palace Gossip" 15", 60" Spain 4 1,994,921
"Inside Trader" 30", 60" Monaco 3 1,345,236
"Civilization" 30", 60" Egypt 5 2,882,476
Totals
Display Center ChkRest ChkWord Del Blk HideBlk MoveBlk CopyBlk Beg Blk End Blk
1Help 2Undo 3Undrlin 4Bold 5DelLine 6DelWord 7Align 8Ruler 9Save & 0Done

Fig. 6.4.

The Crew *column replaced by the* Days *column.*

To insert the Crew column where the Days column was, move the cursor to column 41 on the first line of the tabular material, and press ^U. Your document should look like figure 6.5.

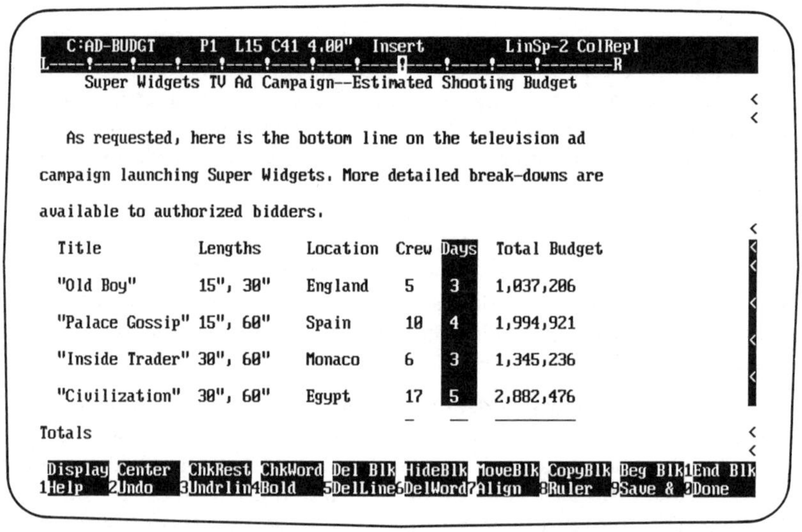
C:AD-BUDGT P1 L15 C41 4.00" Insert LinSp-2 ColRepl
Super Widgets TV Ad Campaign--Estimated Shooting Budget
As requested, here is the bottom line on the television ad
campaign launching Super Widgets. More detailed break-downs are
available to authorized bidders.
Title Lengths Location Crew Days Total Budget
"Old Boy" 15", 30" England 5 3 1,037,206
"Palace Gossip" 15", 60" Spain 10 4 1,994,921
"Inside Trader" 30", 60" Monaco 6 3 1,345,236
"Civilization" 30", 60" Egypt 17 5 2,882,476
Totals
Display Center ChkRest ChkWord Del Blk HideBlk MoveBlk CopyBlk Beg Blk End Blk
1Help 2Undo 3Undrlin 4Bold 5DelLine 6DelWord 7Align 8Ruler 9Save & 0Done

Fig. 6.5.

The unerase function used to restore the Crew *column.*

Using Case Conversion

WordStar features a set of block commands that transform the letters in a block to all uppercase, all lowercase, or sentence style (uppercase only after periods or other terminal punctuation). Case conversion is useful for programmers who write programming languages in all uppercase (such as BASIC) or in all lowercase (such as Pascal). Sentence-style case conversion is helpful for making the all-uppercase text in telex messages more readable.

Although the new WordStar pull-down menus do not include the case conversion functions, the classic Block & Save Menu for the first time lists these commands in a separate column, labeled CASE:

```
" upper
' lower
. sentnce
```

Including the ^K keystroke, the full sequences for these commands at all help levels are ^K" to convert all marked text to uppercase, ^K' to change all text in a block to lowercase, and ^K. to invoke sentence style.

Before invoking any of these block conversion functions, you must define a block of text with begin and end markers (using ^KB or Shift-F9 and ^KK or Shift-F10). The block can be a standard block or a block in column mode. When you issue a case conversion command, remember to release the Ctrl key before you press the ', ", or . key; otherwise, WordStar will not enter the second part of the command. As soon as you press ^K', K", or ^K., the marked text is converted.

Sentence-style conversion is a new feature in WordStar Release 5. This command scans a marked block for terminal punctuation (periods followed by a space, exclamation points, and question marks) and capitalizes the next letter. Then this command converts all text to lowercase except the letters after terminal punctuation. The letter *I* remains uppercase whenever spaces surround it—as for the personal pronoun *I*.

You can use the case conversion commands on the titles of the commercials in the sample AD-BUDGT document. First, check the status line to verify that you are in column mode (if not, press ^KN). Then, move the cursor to the beginning of `"Old Boy"` in the Title column, and press ^KB or Shift-F9 to place a begin marker there. To mark the end of the column, move the cursor to the end of `"Civilization"` and press ^KK or Shift-F10. Press ^K' to convert the characters in the marked block to lowercase, as in figure 6.6.

Next, press ^K., converting the titles within the block to sentence-style text, with initial uppercase on the first line, as illustrated in figure 6.7.

Fig. 6.6.

A block converted to lowercase.

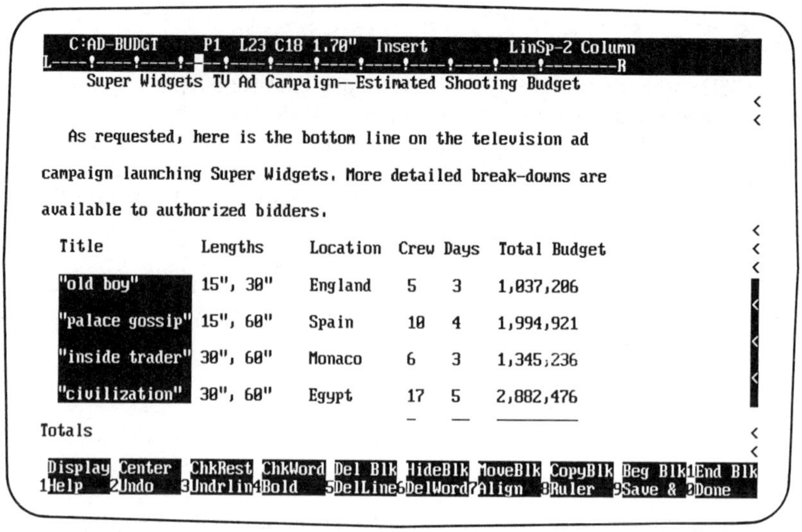
C:AD-BUDGT P1 L23 C18 1.70" Insert LinSp-2 Column
Super Widgets TV Ad Campaign--Estimated Shooting Budget
As requested, here is the bottom line on the television ad
campaign launching Super Widgets. More detailed break-downs are
available to authorized bidders.
Title Lengths Location Crew Days Total Budget
"old boy" 15", 30" England 5 3 1,037,206
"palace gossip" 15", 60" Spain 10 4 1,994,921
"inside trader" 30", 60" Monaco 6 3 1,345,236
"civilization" 30", 60" Egypt 17 5 2,882,476
Totals
Display Center ChkRest ChkWord Del Blk HideBlk MoveBlk CopyBlk Beg Blk End Blk
1Help 2Undo 3Undrlin 4Bold 5DelLine 6DelWord 7Align 8Ruler 9Save & 0Done

Fig. 6.7.

A block converted to sentence-style text.

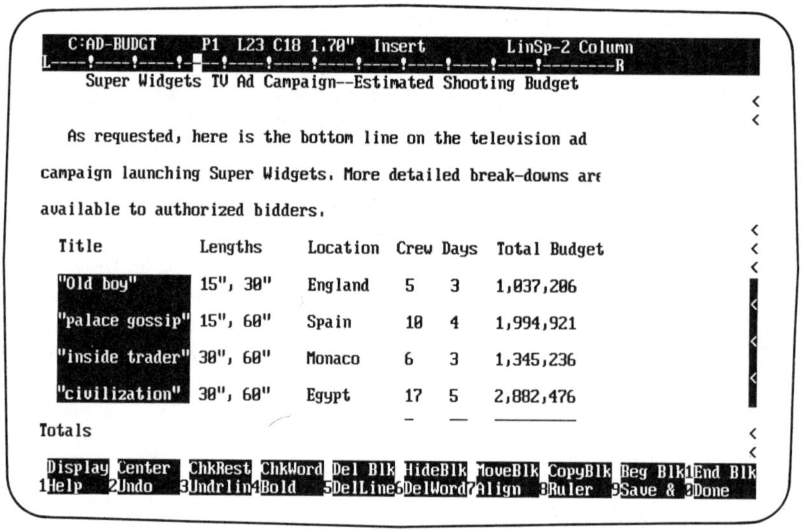
C:AD-BUDGT P1 L23 C18 1.70" Insert LinSp-2 Column
Super Widgets TV Ad Campaign--Estimated Shooting Budget
As requested, here is the bottom line on the television ad
campaign launching Super Widgets. More detailed break-downs are
available to authorized bidders.
Title Lengths Location Crew Days Total Budget
"Old boy" 15", 30" England 5 3 1,037,206
"palace gossip" 15", 60" Spain 10 4 1,994,921
"inside trader" 30", 60" Monaco 6 3 1,345,236
"civilization" 30", 60" Egypt 17 5 2,882,476
Totals
Display Center ChkRest ChkWord Del Blk HideBlk MoveBlk CopyBlk Beg Blk End Blk
1Help 2Undo 3Undrlin 4Bold 5DelLine 6DelWord 7Align 8Ruler 9Save & 0Done

Finally, press ^K" to convert the marked text to all uppercase, as shown in figure 6.8.

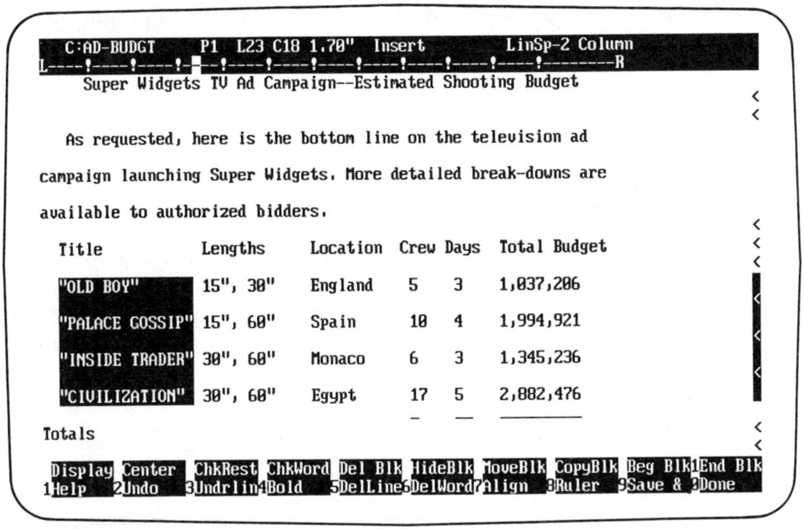
C:AD-BUDGT P1 L23 C18 1.70" Insert LinSp-2 Column
Super Widgets TV Ad Campaign--Estimated Shooting Budget
As requested, here is the bottom line on the television ad
campaign launching Super Widgets. More detailed break-downs are
available to authorized bidders.
Title Lengths Location Crew Days Total Budget
"OLD BOY" 15", 30" England 5 3 1,037,206
"PALACE GOSSIP" 15", 60" Spain 10 4 1,994,921
"INSIDE TRADER" 30", 60" Monaco 6 3 1,345,236
"CIVILIZATION" 30", 60" Egypt 17 5 2,882,476
Totals
Display Center ChkRest ChkWord Del Blk HideBlk MoveBlk CopyBlk Beg Blk End Blk
1Help 2Undo 3Undrlin 4Bold 5DelLine 6DelWord 7Align 8Ruler 9Save & 0Done

Fig. 6.8.
A block converted to uppercase.

Sorting a Text Block

Do you need to put the ad titles in alphabetical order or their budgets in numerical order? You could do a lot of swapping with the cut-and-paste block functions, or you could use a new WordStar feature to sort your text quickly.

Putting a list into alphabetical or numerical order can come in handy if you maintain address listings, account records, inventory rosters, or similar files. Although other word processing programs have had sorting capabilities, only recently has WordStar added this feature to its block functions.

The new pull-down menus have no listing for sorting text, but in Release 5 the classic Block & Save Menu shows this function in the second BLOCK column:

```
Z sort
```

At help level 4, 3, and 2, the complete command sequence for sorting text is ^KZ.

When you invoke the Sort command for a marked block, Release 5 displays a prompt box with the following prompt:

```
Sort into ascending or descending order (A/D)?
```

If you press A, each line in the marked block is rearranged in ascending order, either numerical (from 0 up) or alphabetical (from A to Z). If you press D, the sort order is descending, either down to 0 or from Z to A. When scanning a block for sorting, WordStar considers text in the following order of importance: spaces (least important), symbols, numbers, and letters (most important). You can change this order of importance with the WSCHANGE program (see Chapter 11).

When column mode is on, the sort function applies to the highlighted text between the begin and end markers. If column mode is off, sorting refers to all the characters on a line. Whether column mode is on or off, a sort operation keeps the entire line together when the first word is sorted.

To sort mailing lists, especially ones with pages of data and many fields of information, the MailList feature included in Release 5 is more efficient than the sort command. For an explanation of MailList, see Chapter 8.

For an example of using alphabetical and numerical sorts, you can change the order of the commercials listed in the sample ad budget document. With auto-align off and column mode on, mark as a column block the budget figures in the tabular material. First, move the cursor to the 1 in `1,037,206`, and press ^KB; then move the cursor after the 6 in `2,882,476`, and press ^KK. Press ^KZ, and type *a* at the prompt box to sort the budget figures in ascending order. The entire lines are sorted along with the budget numbers, as illustrated in figure 6.9.

Fig. 6.9.
Text sorted in ascending numerical order.

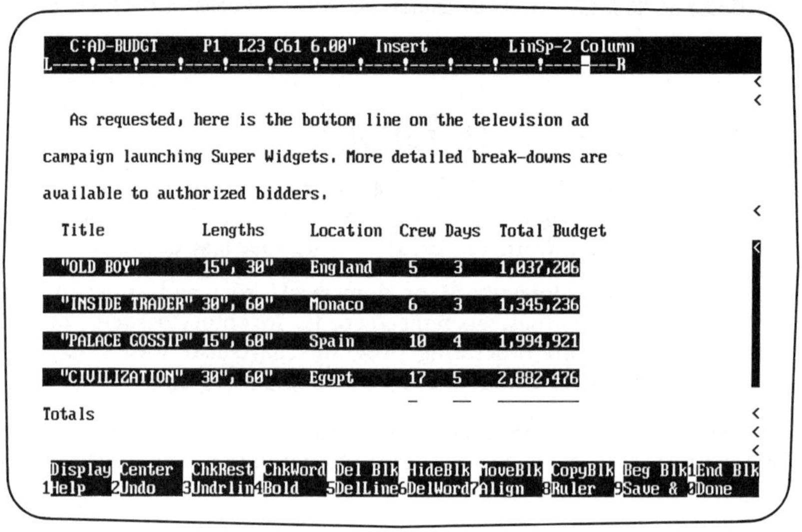
C:AD-BUDGT P1 L23 C61 6.00" Insert LinSp-2 Column
As requested, here is the bottom line on the television ad
campaign launching Super Widgets. More detailed break-downs are
available to authorized bidders.
Title Lengths Location Crew Days Total Budget
"OLD BOY" 15", 30" England 5 3 1,037,206
"INSIDE TRADER" 30", 60" Monaco 6 3 1,345,236
"PALACE GOSSIP" 15", 60" Spain 10 4 1,994,921
"CIVILIZATION" 30", 60" Egypt 17 5 2,882,476
Totals
Display Center ChkRest ChkWord Del Blk HideBlk MoveBlk CopyBlk Beg Blk End Blk
1Help 2Undo 3Undrlin 4Bold 5DelLine 6DelWord 7Align 8Ruler 9Save & 0Done

To sort alphabetically in standard block mode, turn off column mode by pressing ^KN. Then redefine the block, placing a begin block marker before `"OLD BOY"`. Press ^KZ and type *a* at the prompt, sorting the commercial titles and their accompanying information in ascending alphabetical order. Figure 6.10 shows the result.

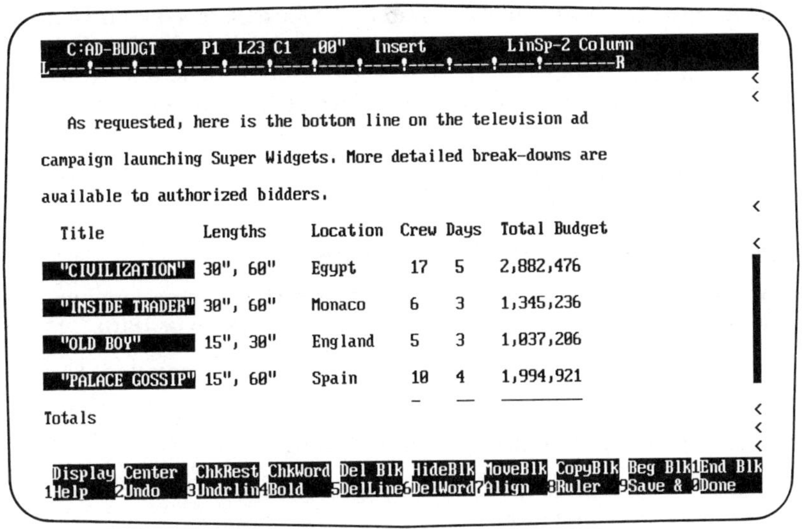
C:AD-BUDGT P1 L23 C1 .00" Insert LinSp-2 Column
As requested, here is the bottom line on the television ad
campaign launching Super Widgets. More detailed break-downs are
available to authorized bidders.
Title Lengths Location Crew Days Total Budget
"CIVILIZATION" 30", 60" Egypt 17 5 2,882,476
"INSIDE TRADER" 30", 60" Monaco 6 3 1,345,236
"OLD BOY" 15", 30" England 5 3 1,037,206
"PALACE GOSSIP" 15", 60" Spain 10 4 1,994,921
Totals
Display Center ChkRest ChkWord Del Blk HideBlk MoveBlk CopyBlk Beg Blk End Blk
1Help 2Undo 3Undrlin 4Bold 5DelLine 6DelWord 7Align 8Ruler 9Save & 0Done

Fig. 6.10.
Text sorted in ascending alphabetical order.

Using Column Math

In addition to its text-oriented functions, WordStar also integrates math capabilities. As a result, you can perform math operations within a document without running another program. WordStar actually includes two separate math features: a block operation for adding and subtracting the numbers in marked text, and an on-screen calculator (discussed in the next section).

At help level 4, the pull-down Other menu (displayed by pressing Alt-O while editing) shows the following command:

```
Block math (add numbers)    ^KM
```

At all help levels except 1 and 0, you can find this command in the BLOCK column of the Block & Save Menu:

```
M math
```

When you mark a block and press ^KM, WordStar totals the numbers in the block and displays the result in a box showing this prompt:

```
Sum of the numbers in the block is:

Press Esc to continue.
```

After the program displays the result of a math calculation, press Esc to return to the Document screen.

Notice that the marked block can be a standard block or in column mode. In addition, numbers in the block do not need to be decimal-aligned. ^KM also works horizontally, totaling all numbers in a marked block on a single line. WordStar's block math function obeys the following rules when it scans the contents of a block:

- Any set of numerals (0 through 9) enclosed by spaces, parentheses, or other non-numeric characters is read as a number.
- A period preceding a numeral is read as a decimal point.
- A hyphen before a numeral, or parentheses surrounding a number, cause that amount to be subtracted—for example, 18 –6 or 18(6).
- Numerals surrounding an *e* are interpreted as scientific notation. For example, 2e16 on-screen means 2×10^{16}.
- No number can be more than 30 numerals long.
- Results have 12-numeral precision. Longer results are rounded and shown in scientific notation.
- Dollar amounts are displayed with two numerals to the right of the decimal point and with commas every three places to the left of the decimal point.

After WordStar calculates a total, you can insert the total at the cursor by pressing Esc and then either the equal sign (=) for standard number format or the dollar sign ($) for dollar amount format. Don't hold down the Esc key when you press the equal sign or the dollar sign; pressing Esc shows the Shorthand Menu. For now, when this menu appears, simply press the correct key to enter the results of a column total.

If you want to use different amounts to perform quick "what if" calculations, block math is inefficient. You would have to change the text repeatedly, and you could only add or subtract.

WordStar's block math feature thus has strengths and weaknesses. The feature is fast, practical, and designed for frequent application in a document. However, the function does not handle multiplication, division, or other vital mathematical calculations. You can accomplish these common operations by using the other WordStar math function, which is explained in the following section of this chapter.

To try block math, total the columns of numbers in the AD-BUDGT sample document. With column mode on (if not, press ^KN), follow these steps:

1. Mark the numbers in the Days column with properly placed ^KB and ^KK commands.
2. Press ^KM to add the numbers in the Days column, displaying a prompt box with the result: 15. Press Esc to return to the Document screen.

3. Position your cursor on the `Totals` line at the bottom of the Days column. Press Esc and the equal sign (=), entering the result of the calculation. The total number of shooting days (15) appears in the appropriate place on-screen.

4. Total the numbers in the Crew and Total Budget columns. Designate each column in turn with begin and end markers. Then total each column by pressing ^KM.

5. In the `Totals` line at the bottom of the Crew column, enter the total (38) by pressing Esc and then the equal sign (=). At the bottom of the Total Budget column, enter the total (7,259,839.00) by pressing Esc and then the dollar sign ($).

Using Calculator Math

For a wider range of math operations, WordStar also features a 14-function calculator that you can access by using a ^Q command sequence.

With WordStar at help level 4, the pull-down Other menu shows this command:

```
Calculator...          ^QM
```

When WordStar is at help level 4, 3, or 2, pressing ^Q calls up the classic Quick Menu. The menu's OTHER column lists this command:

```
M math
```

The full sequence for the command is ^QM, a logical abbreviation for "quick math." Pressing ^QM from the Document screen displays the Math Menu, which includes instructions, operator characters, and available math functions (see fig. 6.11).

When the calculator's Math Menu is displayed, you can type an equation. When you press Enter, WordStar solves the equation and displays the answer in the menu next to the words `Last result`. You can press ^R to restore the preceding equation to the screen. Pressing ^U clears the calculator and returns the editing display.

The calculator math function calculates any equation written in standard algebraic notation. As indicated on the Math Menu, the arithmetic operators perform the following functions when placed between numbers in an equation:

+	Addition
−	Subtraction
*	Multiplication

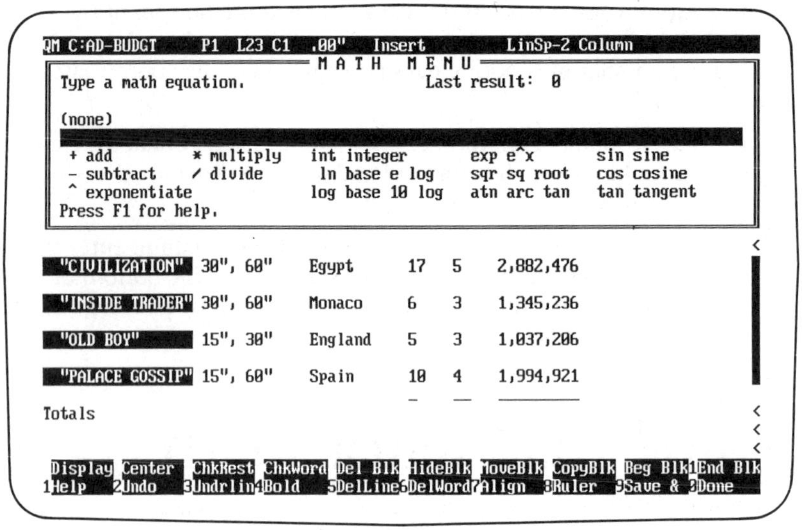
QM C:AD-BUDGT P1 L23 C1 .00" Insert LinSp-2 Column
M A T H M E N U
Type a math equation. Last result: 0
(none)
+ add * multiply int integer exp e^x sin sine
- subtract / divide ln base e log sqr sq root cos cosine
^ exponentiate log base 10 log atn arc tan tan tangent
Press F1 for help.
"CIVILIZATION" 30", 60" Egypt 17 5 2,882,476
"INSIDE TRADER" 30", 60" Monaco 6 3 1,345,236
"OLD BOY" 15", 30" England 5 3 1,037,206
"PALACE GOSSIP" 15", 60" Spain 10 4 1,994,921
Totals
Display Center ChkRest ChkWord Del Blk HideBlk MoveBlk CopyBlk Beg Blk End Blk
1Help 2Undo 3Undrlin 4Bold 5DelLine 6DelWord 7Align 8Ruler 9Save & 0Done

Fig. 6.11.

The WordStar calculator function's Math Menu.

/ Division

^ Exponentiation (raising a number to the power of the number after the symbol)

You can use these arithmetic operators in various combinations. When more than one operator is used in an equation, the WordStar calculator performs exponentiation first, then multiplication and division, and then addition and subtraction.

You can change the order of operations to be performed by enclosing in parentheses operations to be completed first. When parentheses are *nested* (placed within each other), the calculator executes the operation in the innermost set of parentheses and then moves outward. Nesting is limited to 32 sets of parentheses.

The other functions in the Math Menu involve an operator abbreviation and a variable amount entered in parentheses. These functions include the quadratic and logarithmic functions shown in table 6.2.

Table 6.2
WordStar's Quadratic and Logarithmic Functions

Function	*Description*
int( )	Removes the part of a number to the right of its decimal point
ln( )	Calculates the natural base-e logarithm of the number in parentheses
log( )	Calculates the base-10 logarithm of the number in parentheses

Table 6.2—*Continued*

Function	*Description*
exp( )	Raises e—2.71828182846—to the power in parentheses
sqr( )	Computes the square root of the number in parentheses

The WordStar calculator also incorporates the trigonometric functions shown in table 6.3.

Table 6.3
WordStar's Trigonometric Functions

Function	*Description*
atn( )	Computes the arctangent of the angle expressed in degrees within the parentheses
sin( )	Computes the sine of the angular amount in parentheses
cos( )	Computes the cosine of an angle in parentheses
tan( )	Computes the tangent for the angle in parentheses

Equations typed in the Math Menu theoretically are limited in length only by the width of the screen. Too many nested operations, however, can cause an error (indicated by an error message), as can calculations involving numbers that are too large or too small for the calculator to handle. Instead of trying to get the calculator to compute a long equation, you should split operations into simpler parts. Also keep in mind the span of numbers that the calculator can handle: the range is from 1^{-63} (a decimal point followed by 62 zeros and a 1) to 1^{63} (a 1 followed by 63 zeros).

After you type and calculate an equation, you can insert the result in your document at the cursor by pressing Esc and then either the equal sign (=) for standard number format, or the dollar sign ($) for dollar amount format. An additional function, Esc and #, inserts at the cursor the last equation solved by the calculator.

For an example of using the calculator, you can try a "what if" analysis of the total budget figure in the sample AD-BUDGT document. Display the calculator's Math Menu by pressing ^QM. Compute the change after a 10 percent reduction in the budget total: type *7,259,839*.9* and press Enter. The solution, 6533856.1, appears next to the `Last result` prompt. Then recalculate the same equation for .8, which is a 20 percent reduction. Edit the equation for the new value .8 instead of .9, and press Enter. The result, 5807871.2, appears after the prompt.

You can use this method to test the results of different values in your calculations. If you want to insert the result in your text, remember that you can press either Esc and = or Esc and $ to enter your last result.

5

WordStar Release 5 includes one more block command, which counts the words and characters in a marked block or, if no block is specified, in an entire document file. Although not specified on any pull-down menu, the command for counting words is on the classic Block & Save Menu, at help levels 4, 3, or 2:

```
? word count
```

Pressing ^K? during editing displays a box on-screen with prompts indicating the number of words and the number of bytes (or characters). If you marked a block with beginning and end markers, these totals are for the block. If no block is marked, these totals are for the entire file.

If you have followed the order of this book, you have encountered all of WordStar's ^K block and column commands. A few remaining on-screen format commands—the ^O sequences—are useful for quickly changing margins and for formatting text and notes as you write or edit. These commands are discussed in the sections that follow.

Creating an Outline

One of the advantages of word processing on a computer is that you can easily format indent-style outlines. This kind of multiple-margin outlining—taught in high-school English classes—allows you to create heads, subheads, and lower-level subheads that can clarify the organization of topics and ideas on-screen and on paper.

5

With Release 5, the WordStar Professional package now includes an auxiliary program, PC-Outline, that provides specialized block and display operations for streamlining the creation and manipulation of an outline. To learn about this useful memory-resident program, see Chapter 12.

Although the main WordStar program's functions for manipulating outline-formatted text are not as advanced as PC-Outline's capabilities, your word processing software has several commands of its own to aid in formatting simple outlines or any other multiple-indent applications.

If you have a floppy disk drive system, the size of the PC-Outline program may make its use prohibitive—leaving WordStar's main program as the sole source of outlining help. If you have a hard disk drive, you still may find WordStar's built-in functions, including Release 5's new paragraph numbering feature, sufficient for your needs.

The commands for indenting and reformatting text to create an outline are, appropriately, on-screen format command sequences beginning with ^O. Table 6.4 lists these commands.

Table 6.4
Commands for Outlining

Command	*Description*
^OG	Indents to the next tab stop
^OX	Toggles margin release
^OZ	Numbers paragraphs
^OB	Toggles soft-space dot display

Two of these commands—^OX and ^OZ—are listed on the pull-down Layout menu, but all four are on the classic Onscreen Format Menu.

An outline for a Super Widgets TV commercial illustrates the outline formatting possibilities of WordStar's built-in commands. As you create the sample outline in stages, you can experiment with commands for changing margins and reformatting text. The result is a document that looks like figure 6.12.

```
                    "INSIDE TRADER"

                        Outline


The story meeting on 10/25/88, attended by Allen Konigsberg,
Cherilyn Sarkisian, and Paul Rubenfeld, resulted in this outline
for 30" and 60" TV spots:

 1    Campaign to stress leisure and wealth, according to memo.
      1.1  Location: Monaco. Scenes of casino gaming tables.
      1.2  Actors: A tuxedo-clad man, 39, and his evening-
           gowned female companion, 26.
           1.2.1 Man like Redford in "The Great Gatsby."
           1.2.2 Woman like Christie Brinkley.
           1.2.3 Props. Backgammon board, tasteful jewelry.
 2    Inside trader scenario.
      2.1  Man wins at backgammon. Tells woman: "I only bet on
           sure things!"
      2.2  Woman smiles seductively: "Is that how you made your
           fortune on Wall Street?"
      2.3  Man grins: "A little inside information never hurt."
           2.3.1 He should be sympathetic.
           2.3.2 She should be admiring.
 3    The Super Widget pitch.
      3.1  Woman: "Like you were saying about Super Widgets?"
      3.2  Man looking about: "Not so loud--or it won't be
           inside information anymore."
```

Fig. 6.12.
The ad outline.

Using Temporary Indent

When you need to present information that has different levels of importance, as in an outline, you can use a temporary indent to set off paragraphs from the left margin. WordStar's temporary indent function moves the left margin for text being typed to the next tab stop. Text is indented through the end of the paragraph.

None of the new pull-down menus lists this command, but you can find it on the classic Onscreen Format Menu (displayed by pressing ^O). Near the bottom of the MARGINS & TABS column is this listing:

```
G temporary indent
```

The complete command for a temporary indent at the Document screen is ^OG.

When you press ^OG, the left margin advances to the next tab stop when you begin typing. If you use the program's preset tabs, ^OG indents the text five spaces, moving the left margin from column 1 to column 6. Pressing ^OG again indents the text five more spaces to the next tab setting to the right, and so on. These increments are well suited for multilevel outlines.

WordStar's display indicates the indent with a V on the ruler line. This temporary left margin remains in effect until you press Enter to end a paragraph or ^B, the Align Paragraph command. With the temporary indent no longer set, the left margin is restored.

As an example of using the Temporary Indent command, you can type the first half of the sample ad outline. Start by opening a document file and pressing ^OJ to turn off right-justification. Then type and center the title and subtitle, and enter the introductory paragraph within WordStar's default margins.

To create multilevel indents for the outline itself, use ^OG commands. The outline has indents at columns 6, 11, and 16. To enter the outline, press ^OG once, setting the temporary indent at column 6. Type the first line of the outline, omitting the line number (you will learn how to use automatic numbering later in this chapter). Press Enter to return to the original left margin. Press ^OG twice (do not press Enter until the next heading), indenting the subheads at column 11, and type the two headings at the second level. Press ^OG three times to set the temporary indent for the third level of headings at column 16. Type the outline, using the temporary indent at column 16, until you get to the second main heading: *Inside trader scenario*.

This outline uses three different increments of indentation. If you reset the margin to the middle-level heading indent, then lower-level subheads are only one ^OG command away. To type headings at the least indented level, however, you must have a simple WordStar command that releases the margins and allows the cursor to move to the left: the Margin Release Command.

Using Temporary Margin Release

When you write or edit, you may find that writing text outside the left or right margin is useful for comments. That added text can be printed if there is enough room on the paper. WordStar has a command that temporarily allows the cursor to move outside the margins. The command also is useful if you outline from an intermediate level of indentation.

At help level 4, the pull-down Layout menu (shown by pressing Alt-L during editing) includes this listing:

```
Margin release           ^OX
```

At all help levels but 1 and 0, the Onscreen Format Menu displays the following command in the MARGINS & TABS column:

```
X release
```

The complete command for temporary margin release within a document is ^OX.

After you press ^OX, the left margin is temporarily reset at column 1, the right margin is removed, and word wrap is turned off. As long as the temporary margin release is in effect, `Mar-Rel` is displayed on the status line. The temporary margin release stays in effect until you either press Enter to end a paragraph, move the cursor between the margins or to another line, or toggle off the feature by issuing another ^OX command. No preset tab stops outside the margins are shown, although they are in effect when margin release is turned on.

In the sample ad outline, the Margin Release command and a reactivated tab setting can be used to help finish typing the commercial outline:

1. Reset the left margin to column 11 by pressing ^OL, typing *1.0*, and pressing Enter.

   This new margin setting conforms to formatting for the outline's secondary headings. To type headings to the left of that margin, you need to issue the Margin Release command: ^OX.

2. To enter the line ***Inside trader scenario***, press ^OX, move the cursor to column 1 of the same line, and press Tab to move the cursor to the preset tab at column 6. Type the line, and press Enter to end the temporary margin release.

3. Type the three subheads from the current margin (line numbers will be added in the next section).

4. Type the two lowest-level subheads by pressing ^OG twice. Press Enter after each line.

5. To enter the line ***The Super Widget pitch***, use the ^OX command. Then type the last three lines from the current margin.

Numbering Paragraphs

Automatic paragraph numbering is a handy feature for typing legal documents or draft proposals, as well as for outlining documents. The standard form for such paragraph designation is to assign a single numeral to principal headings, two numerals separated by a period for second-level headings, three numerals separated by periods for third-level headings, and so on.

WordStar includes an automatic paragraph numbering function for the first time in Release 5. This function keeps track of paragraph numbers and levels throughout a document, and can insert the appropriate numbers at the cursor wherever invoked.

At help level 4, this command appears on the pull-down Layout menu:

```
Paragraph numbering...     ^OZ
```

If WordStar is at help level 4, 3, or 2, the classic Onscreen Format Menu (called up during editing by pressing ^O) includes the following listing in the MARGINS & TABS column:

```
Z paragraph number
```

The complete command for WordStar's paragraph numbering feature is ^OZ.

With the cursor where you want to number a paragraph, pressing ^OZ displays the Paragraph Number dialog box, as shown in figure 6.13. This dialog box includes the current available number for a paragraph (starting with 1) and three commands for accepting or adjusting the number's value.

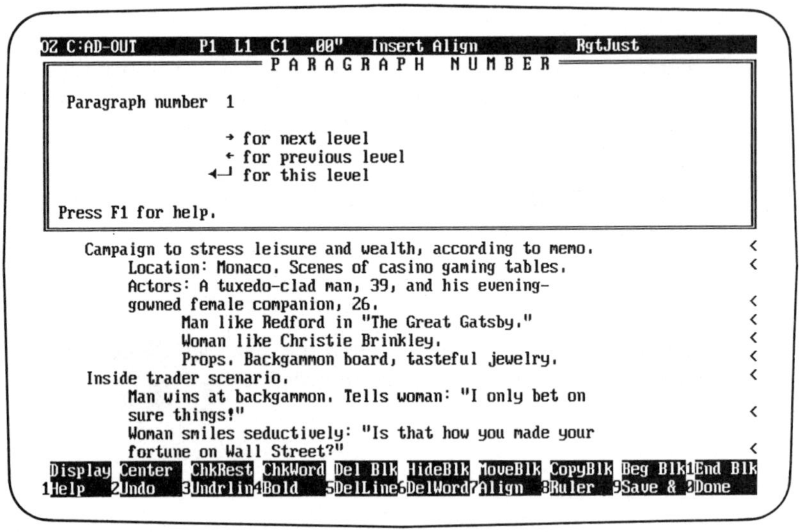
OZ C:AD-OUT P1 L1 C1 .00" Insert Align RgtJust
PARAGRAPH NUMBER
Paragraph number 1
→ for next level
← for previous level
↵ for this level
Press F1 for help.
Campaign to stress leisure and wealth, according to memo.
Location: Monaco. Scenes of casino gaming tables.
Actors: A tuxedo-clad man, 39, and his evening-
gowned female companion, 26.
Man like Redford in "The Great Gatsby."
Woman like Christie Brinkley.
Props. Backgammon board, tasteful jewelry.
Inside trader scenario.
Man wins at backgammon. Tells woman: "I only bet on
sure things!"
Woman smiles seductively: "Is that how you made your
fortune on Wall Street?"
Display Center ChkRest ChkWord Del Blk HideBlk MoveBlk CopyBlk Beg Blk End Blk
1Help 2Undo 3Undrlin 4Bold 5DelLine 6DelWord 7Align 8Ruler 9Save & 0Done

Fig. 6.13.
The Paragraph Number dialog box.

From the Paragraph Number dialog box, pressing Enter (noted by < in the box) inserts the current number at the cursor. Each time you press the right-arrow key (or ^D), the number in the dialog box changes down one heading level. For instance, the paragraph number 2.1 changes to 2.1.1 if you press the right-arrow key once and to 2.1.1.1 if you press the key twice. The left-arrow key (or ^S) revises the number in the box up one level; thus you can change 2.1.1 to 2.2 by pressing the left-arrow key once and to 3 by pressing the key twice. Pressing Enter inserts the chosen number into your document.

The paragraph numbers that WordStar Release 5 inserts are not standard text but command tags similar to the print control symbols you see on-screen. The numbers will print with your document, even though they cannot be edited like standard characters. You can delete a paragraph number with the usual deletion commands, but to change a number you must place the cursor on it, press ^OZ, and specify a new number. When a number is deleted or changed, WordStar automatically renumbers all the paragraphs after the number.

WordStar's default paragraph numbering system offers eight levels of numerals, starting with the number 1. You can alter the program's default numbering system by modifying the WSCHANGE program (see Chapter 11). You can redefine the numbering system for the document you are working on by inserting a dot command at column 1 where needed. (For more about using dot commands, see the latter sections of this chapter.)

Use the same dot command to specify either a starting number or a paragraph numbering scheme different from WordStar's default setting: .P#. To specify a different starting number, simply type the number after the dot command—for example, *.p# 5*. You can alter the numbering scheme itself to include upper- and lowercase letters or Roman numerals by inserting the .P# command followed by the following symbols: a 9 wherever numerals should appear, a Z where uppercase letters should appear, a z for lowercase letters, and an I or i for upper- or lowercase Roman numerals, respectively. Separate these symbols by appropriate periods to indicate different heading levels—for example, .P# z.9.i. To change to letter format, you must put a comma before the format character, such as .p#,Z.9.z.

To change both the starting number and the numbering scheme, you can type the appropriate characters with a single dot command, with the starting number followed by a comma. Therefore, to invoke a numbering system starting with B, then B.1 at the next level, and B.1.a at the next level, you would type *.p# B,Z.9.z*. Any other characters (brackets, parentheses, and so on) included after the .P# command will be printed along with the paragraph numbers. If your printer is capable of reproducing the IBM extended character set, you can even include the paragraph symbol (¶) or the section symbol (§) by invoking Alt-20 or Alt-21, respectively, as explained in Chapter 7.

A related dot command for automatically printing line numbers in a document is described in the next chapter.

You can use paragraph numbers to complete the sample ad outline. To insert the paragraph numbers without disrupting the existing text,

1. Switch off auto-align by pressing ^OA.
2. Restore the original left margin by pressing ^OL and typing *0*. Press ^K or F10 to return to your document.
3. Move the cursor to column 2 in the first outline heading, press ^OZ, and press Enter to insert a *1* at the appropriate place in the document. (Press ^G to delete the empty spaces to bring the text to its proper position.)
4. Move the cursor to column 6 of the next line, press ^OZ, and press the right-arrow key to change heading level (to 1.1). Press Enter to insert this number. Press ^G to delete the excess empty spaces.
5. Move the cursor to the next line at column 6, press ^OZ, and press Enter to place the number *1.2* at the cursor. Press ^G to delete the excess empty spaces.
6. Move the cursor down two lines to the next heading level, and position the cursor at column 11. Press ^OZ, the right-arrow key, and then Enter to insert the number *1.2.1*. Press ^G to delete any extra empty spaces.
7. Following the commands in the Paragraph Number dialog box, change levels up and down to number the rest of the ad outline.

Displaying Soft Spaces

Beginning with Release 4, WordStar includes a display option that makes indents more distinctive. The program can place "soft space" dots on-screen from column 1 up to any indented text. (The dots are not printed.) Purists who seek the exact look and feel of earlier WordStar releases may be disturbed by the sight of the dots on-screen. After the feature is toggled on, however, you may find that the dots actually enhance the look of on-screen outlines.

Although not on any pull-down menu, the command for toggling the soft-space display is on the classic Onscreen Format Menu. If you press ^O at help level 4, 3, or 2, you can see the command in the column headed DISPLAY:

```
B turn soft space dots on
```

From the Edit screen, ^OB is the full command for toggling on soft-space dots. Pressing ^OB again suppresses them.

When you installed WordStar Release 5 with the WINSTALL program (see Chapter 2), you had the option of displaying soft-space dots. If you retained the program's initial display-off setting, your first use of ^OB turns on the soft-space dots. To change the default setting for the soft-space display, you can run WINSTALL again or use the WSCHANGE program (see Chapter 11).

You can turn on soft-space dots in the sample outline. Press ^OB; you will see dots fill the left side of the screen and make the different levels of the outline more distinguishable (see fig. 6.14). To turn off soft-space dots, press ^OB again.

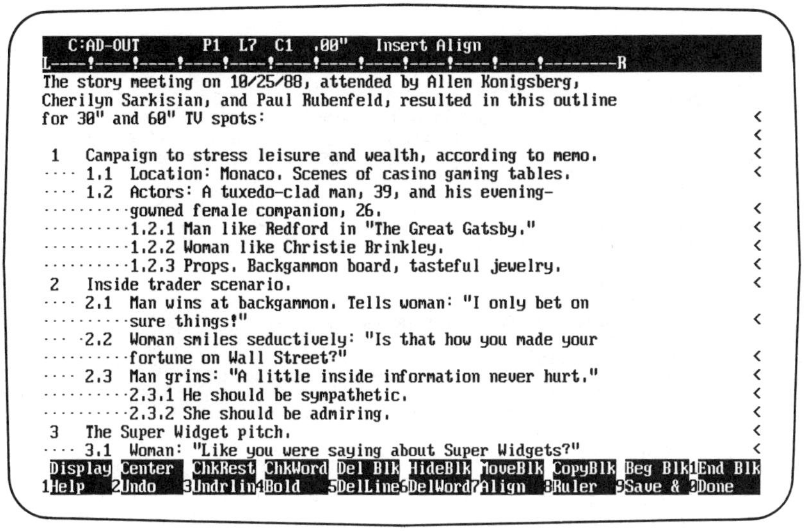
```
 C:AD-OUT       P1  L7  C1  .00"   Insert Align
L----!----!----!----!----!----!----!----!----!----!----!-------R
The story meeting on 10/25/88, attended by Allen Konigsberg,
Cherilyn Sarkisian, and Paul Rubenfeld, resulted in this outline
for 30" and 60" TV spots:                                           <
                                                                    <
 1   Campaign to stress leisure and wealth, according to memo.      <
···· 1.1  Location: Monaco. Scenes of casino gaming tables.          <
···· 1.2  Actors: A tuxedo-clad man, 39, and his evening-
··········gowned female companion, 26.                              <
··········1.2.1 Man like Redford in "The Great Gatsby."             <
··········1.2.2 Woman like Christie Brinkley.                       <
··········1.2.3 Props. Backgammon board, tasteful jewelry.          <
 2   Inside trader scenario.                                        <
···· 2.1  Man wins at backgammon. Tells woman: "I only bet on
··········sure things!"                                             <
··· ·2.2  Woman smiles seductively: "Is that how you made your
··········fortune on Wall Street?"                                  <
···· 2.3  Man grins: "A little inside information never hurt."      <
··········2.3.1 He should be sympathetic.                           <
··········2.3.2 She should be admiring.                             <
 3   The Super Widget pitch.                                        <
···· 3.1  Woman: "Like you were saying about Super Widgets?"        <
Display Center ChkRest ChkWord Del Blk HideBlk MoveBlk CopyBlk Beg Blk End Blk
1Help  2Undo  3Undrlin 4Bold  5DelLine 6DelWord 7Align 8Ruler 9Save & 0Done
```

Fig. 6.14.

Soft spaces displayed in a document.

Using Note Functions

In reports, manuscripts, and academic papers, notes are essential for clarifying points, citing information, or attributing sources outside the main body of text. As word processing programs have evolved, they have incorporated features for automating the numbering and formatting chores involved with creating notes in documents.

After lagging behind its rivals and offering no automated note functions in previous versions, WordStar now includes one of the most versatile of such features. In Release 5, footnotes, endnotes, annotations, and comments are easy to create, edit, and print. Release 5 can handle numbering and formatting for all four types of notes in a single document.

At level 4, the pull-down Other menu lists the following command:

```
Footnote/endnote...          ^ON
```

At help levels 4, 3, and 2, pressing ^O while editing brings up the classic Onscreen Format Menu, with this listing in the DISPLAY column:

```
N notes
```

Including the keystroke for the classic menu, the complete command is ^ON.

When you press ^ON within an open document file, you will see the Notes Menu, as illustrated in figure 6.15. This menu includes 10 commands relating to note functions.

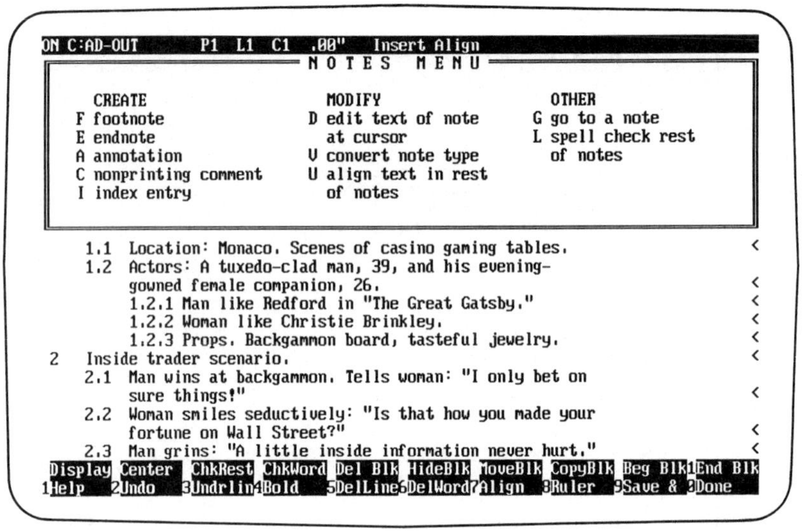
ON C:AD-OUT P1 L1 C1 .00" Insert Align
NOTES MENU
CREATE
F footnote
E endnote
A annotation
C nonprinting comment
I index entry
MODIFY
D edit text of note
at cursor
V convert note type
U align text in rest
of notes
OTHER
G go to a note
L spell check rest
of notes
1.1 Location: Monaco. Scenes of casino gaming tables.
1.2 Actors: A tuxedo-clad man, 39, and his evening-
gowned female companion, 26.
1.2.1 Man like Redford in "The Great Gatsby."
1.2.2 Woman like Christie Brinkley.
1.2.3 Props. Backgammon board, tasteful jewelry.
2 Inside trader scenario.
2.1 Man wins at backgammon. Tells woman: "I only bet on
sure things!"
2.2 Woman smiles seductively: "Is that how you made your
fortune on Wall Street?"
2.3 Man grins: "A little inside information never hurt."
Display Center ChkRest ChkWord Del Blk HideBlk MoveBlk CopyBlk Beg Blk End Blk
1Help 2Undo 3Undrlin 4Bold 5DelLine 6DelWord 7Align 8Ruler 9Save & 0Done

Fig. 6.15.
WordStar's Notes Menu.

Two of the commands on the Notes Menu—those for indexing and checking spelling—are discussed in Chapter 10. The remaining choices on the Notes Menu are summarized in table 6.5.

Table 6.5
WordStar's Note Functions (from the Notes Menu)

Function	*Description*
F	Creates a footnote (to be printed at the bottom of a page)
E	Creates an endnote (to be printed at the end of a document)
A	Creates an annotation (to be printed at the bottom of a page)
C	Creates a comment to be shown on-screen but not printed
G	Moves the cursor to a specified note
D	Displays the full text of a note for editing
U	Aligns the text in all notes to conform to the formatting altered with WSCHANGE
V	Converts a designated note to another type

The text of any one note can occupy up to 40K of text—more than 15 pages. After you enter a note and turn on screen display, the first 15 characters are shown as a tag within brackets in your document, to remind you of the note's content. When you issue ^OD to turn off on-screen marker display, only the note's reference number or symbol is shown in your text (comments are not referenced).

WordStar's note functions automatically maintain numbering for referenced notes. Each time you add a new note to a document, its correct number is listed according to the note's sequence. If you delete or reposition some notes, WordStar appropriately adjusts their reference characters.

When you print a document, WordStar handles the notes for you. References to notes are printed in superscript. The different kinds of notes are positioned correctly: footnotes and annotations at the bottoms of pages, and endnotes at the end of the document. References to notes are printed in the same font as their surrounding text. The notes are printed in the default font, unless you change the font within the note or reset the font with the WSCHANGE program. With WSCHANGE, you also can customize notes' default margins, line spacing, page positioning, and other formatting details (see Chapter 11).

Creating Footnotes and Endnotes

WordStar automatically references two kinds of notes: footnotes and endnotes. As their names indicate, *footnotes* are printed at the bottom of the page, and *endnotes* on the last page of a document.

On Release 5's Notes Menu, displayed by pressing ^ON, you will see the following listings in the CREATE column: 5

```
F footnote

E endnote
```

From the Edit screen, the complete command sequences are ^ONF to create a footnote and ^ONE to create an endnote.

The procedures for creating a footnote and endnote are similar. Move the cursor to where the note's reference is to appear in a document. Press ^ONF or ^ONE. A window with the current reference number or letter opens at the bottom of the screen for the note's text; the word `FOOTNOTE` or `ENDNOTE` appears in the status line at the top of the screen. Next, type and edit the content of your note in this window as you would in an ordinary window. If the note's text exceeds the space in the window, the note scrolls up as with standard text. Each note can occupy approximately 15 pages. Save the text by pressing the Save command, ^KD.

If screen display of command tags is on, the first 15 characters of the note are shown between brackets. If you toggle off on-screen display by invoking ^OD, only the note's reference number or symbol appears on-screen.

When you print a document, WordStar automatically superscripts the reference characters in the text. Footnotes are printed at the bottom of the page, separated from the main text by a line of hyphens. If a footnote is too long to fit at the bottom of a page, it continues into the next page's footnote section (unless the footnote starts on the last page of document text, in which case the footnote continues onto the top of the next page). At least three lines of main text are printed on each page until the end of a document.

WordStar normally assigns alphabetical reference sequences to footnotes and numerical references to endnotes, automatically revising the references when notes are deleted or moved. However, you can change the sequencing for footnotes or endnotes with appropriate dot commands. For footnotes the command .F# specifies the beginning value for references; the equivalent command for endnotes is .E#. When you type these commands at column 1 at the beginning of a document, you can follow them with an upper- or lowercase *A* (or another letter) for alphabetical references, a *1* (or another numeral) for numeric references, or any symbol (which will be used in increasing multiples) for note references in your text. However, if you want to use symbols as references to notes, you must change the note reference characters in WSCHANGE.

Another dot command, .PE, causes endnotes to print elsewhere in a document than after the main text. For instance, a single document file might consist of several chapters; typing *.pe* at the end of a chapter causes endnotes for a chapter to print at that location.

You can add a footnote and an endnote to your sample outline. First, place the cursor after the date in the first line of body text. Press ^ONF to place a footnote reference at this point; the footnote window opens at the bottom of the screen. Type the text of the footnote in the window: *Postponed from the original date of 10/20/88.* Press ^KD to close the window and save its contents. Move the cursor after the words `TV spots` in the third line. Press ^ONE, opening an endnote window. Type the endnote text in the window: *Ad lengths tentative, subject to change.* Press ^KD to save the endnote's text.

On-screen, you see brackets containing the first 15 characters of the footnote and endnote where entered. Pressing ^OD replaces these highlighted tags with reference characters in your text: *A* for the footnote and *1* for the endnote.

Creating Comments and Annotations

WordStar's note feature also includes two kinds of notes that are not automatically numbered: annotations and comments. An *annotation* is a note printed at the bottom of a page, but unlike a footnote an annotation can apply to several references in your text. *Comments* are notes that appear on-screen but are not printed, making them useful in a document that must be revised or edited.

On the new WordStar Notes Menu, which appears when you press ^ON, the following listings can be found in the CREATE column:

```
A annotation

C nonprinting comment
```

During editing, the full sequences for these functions are ^ONA to create an annotation and ^ONC to create a nonprinting comment.

To place one of these notes in your document, you put the cursor where the note's reference is to be inserted, call up the Notes Menu, and select the kind of note to create. Although the process of opening a window for the note (typing its content and closing the window with ^KD) is similar to the way footnotes and endnotes are created, the processes contain some differences because annotations and comments are not automatically numbered.

When you issue ^ONA for an annotation, you see a dialog box headed ANNOTATION MARK with a prompt for the annotation mark to be used to refer to an annotation in your text. This mark can be any character or combination of characters that will distinguish your annotation from other kinds of notes. After you type the mark and press Enter, a window with the annotation mark appears at the bottom of the screen, and the word `ANNOTATION` appears in the status line. What you type in this window will be printed at the bottom of the document page. After you press ^KD to save your annotation and close the window, if you invoke ^ONA on the same page and type the annotation mark again, the same mark and (if you want) a second note will be referenced.

When you invoke ^ONC, a comment window without a reference mark appears on-screen because this note will not be printed with your document. The word `COMMENT` appears in the status line at the top of the display. After you type your comment, you can close the window and save the comment by pressing ^KD.

The same 40K, 15-page limits to a note's text apply to both annotations and comments. With on-screen command tags turned on, each note's first 15 characters are shown within brackets. If you press ^OD to toggle off the display tags, annotation marks appear on-screen; comments are completely hidden.

You can add such notes to your sample outline. For an annotation after the word `actors` in paragraph 1.2, place the cursor there and press ^ONA. Type an asterisk (*) at the prompt, press Enter, and type into the window the annotation text: *Casting subject to C.E.O. approval.* Then save the annotation by pressing ^KD. You can refer to this annotation again by pressing ^ONA and typing the same mark after the words `Man` and `Woman` at paragraphs 1.2.1 and 1.2.2.

To add a comment, move the cursor directly after the word `seductively` in paragraph 2.2, press ^ONC to display a comment window, and type *Is this word going to offend anyone?* Then press ^KD to save the comment. After you type both notes, brackets appear on-screen where you entered the notes, containing the first 15 characters of each note. Pressing ^OD displays only the annotation marks in place of the tags.

If you print the sample outline, the endnotes, footnotes, annotations, and their reference characters (in superscript) will print as intended. Comments are not printed.

Opening and Finding Notes

Because notes in WordStar are coded differently from regular text, to open an existing note for viewing or editing you must place the cursor at its on-screen tag and invoke a command from the Notes Menu. Another option on the Notes Menu lets you find and display a note from anywhere in a document by the note's reference character or a character string within the note.

5

On the Notes Menu is this command in the MODIFY column:

```
D edit text of note
  at cursor
```

If you move your cursor to a note's opening bracket in a document (or to its reference tag if on-screen display has been toggled off), pressing ^OND reopens the note window at the bottom of the screen, where you can read and edit the note's full text. You can use all of WordStar's standard editing commands to modify this text. When you are finished editing a note, you can save the new version and close the note window by pressing ^KD. To leave the content of the window unchanged even after editing its text, you can use the Abandon Changes command, ^KQ.

To open a note and view its text, you must place the cursor directly on the note's reference tag or its opening bracket. If the cursor is not properly placed, instead of the note's text you will see the following error message:

```
Cursor is not on a note.

Press Esc to continue.
```

You can press Esc, reposition the cursor, and invoke ^OND. Or you can press Esc and invoke a Notes Menu option that does not require you to accurately position the cursor. In the OTHER column of the Notes Menu is this listing:

```
G go to a note
```

From anywhere in a document, pressing ^ONG displays the Go To Note dialog box, shown in figure 6.16. This dialog box asks for the kind of note you want to open and lists single-letter responses for each of the four kinds of notes and a fifth option, N, for any note.

After you type a letter in the Go To Note dialog box and press Enter, WordStar displays another dialog box on-screen, the Find Note dialog box (see fig. 6.17). This box resembles the Find dialog box (covered in Chapter 5), with one line for characters to find and a second line for search options.

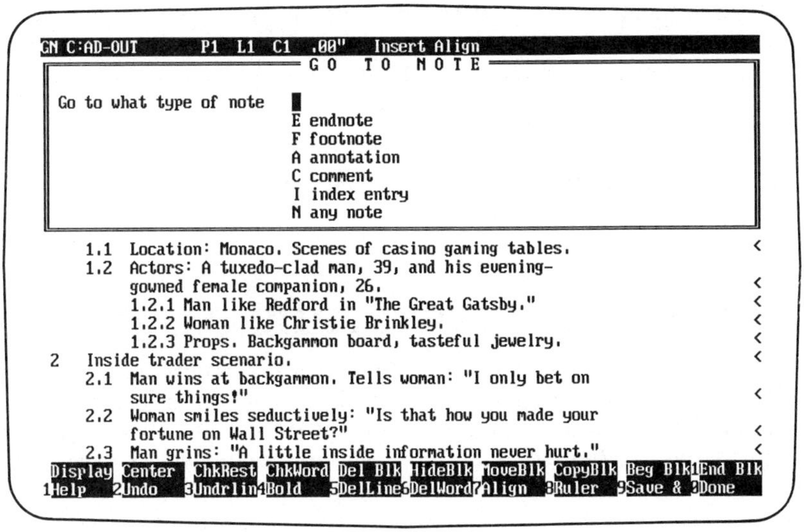
GN C:AD-OUT P1 L1 C1 .00" Insert Align
G O T O N O T E
Go to what type of note
E endnote
F footnote
A annotation
C comment
I index entry
N any note
1.1 Location: Monaco. Scenes of casino gaming tables.
1.2 Actors: A tuxedo-clad man, 39, and his evening-
gowned female companion, 26.
1.2.1 Man like Redford in "The Great Gatsby."
1.2.2 Woman like Christie Brinkley.
1.2.3 Props. Backgammon board, tasteful jewelry.
2 Inside trader scenario.
2.1 Man wins at backgammon. Tells woman: "I only bet on
sure things!"
2.2 Woman smiles seductively: "Is that how you made your
fortune on Wall Street?"
2.3 Man grins: "A little inside information never hurt."
Display Center ChkRest ChkWord Del Blk HideBlk MoveBlk CopyBlk Beg Blk End Blk
1Help 2Undo 3Undrlin 4Bold 5DelLine 6DelWord 7Align 8Ruler 9Save & 0Done

Fig. 6.16.

Specifying the kind of note to be found.

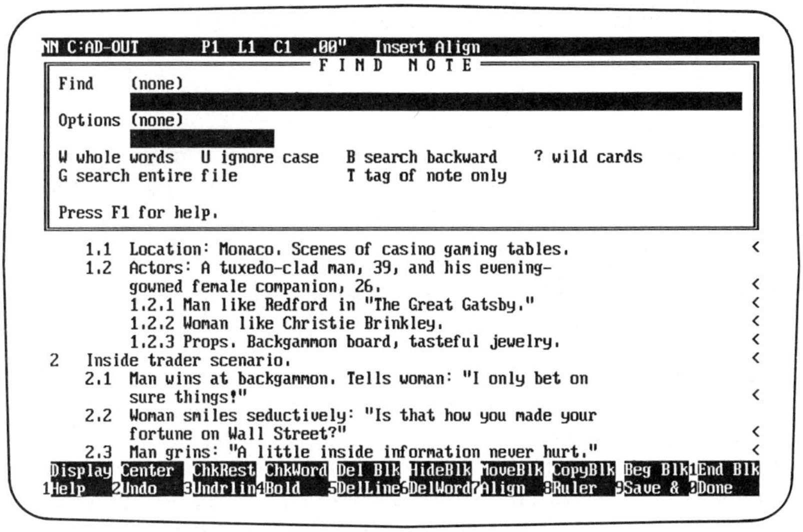
NN C:AD-OUT P1 L1 C1 .00" Insert Align
F I N D N O T E
Find (none)
Options (none)
W whole words U ignore case B search backward ? wild cards
G search entire file T tag of note only
Press F1 for help.
1.1 Location: Monaco. Scenes of casino gaming tables.
1.2 Actors: A tuxedo-clad man, 39, and his evening-
gowned female companion, 26.
1.2.1 Man like Redford in "The Great Gatsby."
1.2.2 Woman like Christie Brinkley.
1.2.3 Props. Backgammon board, tasteful jewelry.
2 Inside trader scenario.
2.1 Man wins at backgammon. Tells woman: "I only bet on
sure things!"
2.2 Woman smiles seductively: "Is that how you made your
fortune on Wall Street?"
2.3 Man grins: "A little inside information never hurt."
Display Center ChkRest ChkWord Del Blk HideBlk MoveBlk CopyBlk Beg Blk End Blk
1Help 2Undo 3Undrlin 4Bold 5DelLine 6DelWord 7Align 8Ruler 9Save & 0Done

Fig. 6.17.

The Find Note dialog box.

In the first prompt line of the Find Note dialog box, you can type a character string unique to the note you want to open, or simply type its reference character; then press Enter. In the second prompt line, you can type any or all of the options for modifying the search. All these options but one are the same ones available in a regular find operation. The option unique to the Find Note box is T, which indicates that the character(s) in the `Find` line apply only to the note's reference tag. After you type the options, press Enter to start the find operation. The designated note's text is displayed in a window at the bottom of the screen.

You do not have to open a note to delete its contents. You can remove a note simply by deleting its reference tag. Any notes of the same kind that follow the deleted note are renumbered automatically. If you want to restore a note that has just been deleted, you can issue the Undo command ^U or F2.

Footnote and endnote text can be edited, but the reference characters (numbers, letters, symbols) assigned to the notes cannot be edited. Editing these characters disrupts sequencing.

Formatting and Converting Notes

WordStar's note feature includes two handy functions for modifying notes you have created, regardless of their category. One of these functions can reformat all later notes to conform to margin changes made in WSCHANGE. Another command converts any note into a different kind of note, without forcing you to reenter it. Both these functions can spare you from entering numerous keystrokes when altering notes.

5

On WordStar's Notes Menu, the MODIFY column lists this option:

```
U align text in rest
  of notes
```

WSCHANGE can be used to set alternative formatting for notes. If you set such a format, you can realign all notes to fit this format by returning to the Edit screen and pressing ^ONU. You will see each of the subsequent note windows open onscreen, and its text realigned automatically, until the operation is complete.

Also in the Notes Menu's MODIFY column is this listing:

```
V convert note type
```

When you position the cursor on a note's reference character and press ^ONV, the Convert Note dialog box appears, with a prompt asking you the kind of note to which you want to convert the current note. Listed as options are letters for each of the four kinds of note: E for endnote, F for footnote, A for annotation, and C for comment. Typing one of these letters and pressing Enter completes the conversion, including appropriate renumbering. (If you are converting to an annotation, you will see the Annotation Mark dialog box, into which you type a designator character and press Enter).

Instead of converting each note individually, you can use a dot command, .CV, to print all the notes of one type in a document as another type, complete with correct numbering. Type this command at column 1 at the beginning of your document, and follow it with the letter of the kind of note to convert (E, F, A, or C). Then type a greater-than sign (>), and the letter of the kind of note to which this note should be converted. For instance, to print all footnotes as endnotes you enter the command *.cv f>e*; to print all comments as endnotes you type *.cv c>e*.

Using Ruler Lines To Change Formats

The *ruler line* above the text on the WordStar screen establishes and displays settings for the left and right margins, and regular and decimal tab stops for the text that follows the ruler line. The ruler line always appears near the top of the screen and also as the divider when a window is opened. However, you can move the ruler line in and out of a document's text area, changing the format of the text that follows. This capability is handy for altering margin and tab settings at one time, instead of having to change settings separately. Such ruler-line operations make switching between formats within a document easy. For highly structured documents, ruler-line functions greatly simplify multiple formatting.

5

Inserting and substituting ruler lines in text has been made progressively easier with each new version of WordStar. Release 5 retains previous ruler line commands and adds an important new feature: the capability to invoke predefined ruler lines stored by the program. In addition to a standard ruler line with default margins and tabs, WordStar comes with two preset ruler lines, one with margins indented for quoted material and another suitable for outlines; seven more ruler lines can be formatted and stored with the WSCHANGE program (see Chapter 11). You can add any of these ruler lines with a dot command also used for defining a ruler line in text.

The ruler-line commands are not listed on any of WordStar's new pull-down menus, but they are in the classic Onscreen Format Menu and in the dot-command help listings (shown at all levels but 4 by pressing F1. or ^J. and Enter during editing). The ruler-line functions are summarized in table 6.6.

Table 6.6
Ruler-Line Commands

Command	*Description*
^OT	Toggles ruler line display
^OF	Copies ruler line from text
^OO or F8	Embeds current ruler line into text
.RR	Embeds typed ruler line in text
.RR *n*	Embeds stored ruler line in text

Incidentally, if you create or edit different script types or other multiple-format documents, you can define more than the ten ruler lines in WordStar. You can create single-line documents stored as separate files on disk and then insert them into text, or you can program ruler lines as shorthand macros (see Chapter 9).

To demonstrate the use of different ruler lines in a document for changing margin settings, you can type (in stages) a sample page of a script for Widget, Inc.'s new TV ad campaign. Even if you don't type the examples in the next several sections, you can apply the ruler line functions to composing complex formats such as the script shown in figure 6.18.

Fig. 6.18.

The script for the commercial.

```
                              "INSIDE TRADER"

                                30" Script

Revision 7A--11/14/88

EXT. CASINO - MONACO - DAY
Stepping out of Rolls-Royce an elderly WOMAN and a distinguished-
looking elderly MAN head for casino entrance.

                                  WOMAN
     (Dressed like a color-blind Ruth Gordon. Speaks loudly
     as if she is deaf, or a little daft.)

               Oh my, I feel awfully guilty having
               this fling with an insane traitor.

                                   MAN
     (Could pass for Don Ameche in spats. Speaks in a slow
     Southern drawl.)

               That was inside trader, m'a'm.

INT. CASINO - MONACO - DAY
The MAN and WOMAN watch the roulette wheel as it stops on his
number. A pile of chips is pushed across the table toward them.
The MAN reaches into his pocket and tosses a Super Widget to the
croupier as a tip. There are appreciative murmurs all around.

                                  WOMAN
     (She speaks up, even more boisterous than before.)

               There's one thing I'm sure of!

                                   MAN
               What's that?

                                  WOMAN
               You know your Super Widgets.

                                   MAN
               You can say that again.

                                  WOMAN
               You know your Super Widgets!

Note: This script must still be approved by corporate
     communications, our marketing consultants and network
     standards and practices.
```

This sample script uses different margin formats invoked with Ctrl-letter combinations or dot commands, with several of their functions duplicating or complementing each other. These ruler-line commands are discussed in the following sections.

Toggling the Ruler-Line Display

WordStar's ruler line controls margins and tabs for typing and editing document text (there is no ruler line in nondocument mode). However, the ruler line does not have to be displayed to activate these formatting functions or for its margin and tab settings to be altered. Toggling off the ruler-line display frees an additional line for text on-screen.

WordStar's classic Onscreen Format Menu lists the command for ruler-line display in the column headed MARGINS & TABS:

```
T turn ruler off
```

The complete sequence for toggling the ruler line off is ^OT. After you issue this command, the menu shows this listing:

```
T turn ruler on
```

Pressing ^OT turns on the ruler line again.

When you press ^OT the first time, the ruler line disappears from the top of the screen. The text moves up to fill the void, displaying an extra line of text. For an uncluttered WordStar Document screen that displays only text, you can reset the program to turn off ruler-line display, hide the status line, and remove function-key lines. You can make all these changes to the program with WSCHANGE, as explained in Chapter 11.

For an example of ruler-line display toggle, you can open a document file for the sample script shown in figure 6.18. The Document screen appears, with the preset WordStar ruler line near the screen's top edge. Pressing ^OT clears the ruler line. Pressing Tab several times demonstrates that the preset tabs are still set even though the ruler line is off-screen. Pressing ^OT displays the ruler line again.

Changing a Ruler Line

When you switch formats within a document, you may need to change all the current margin and tab settings. Instead of altering these settings individually in the Margins & Tabs dialog box in Release 5, you can perform the process more efficiently with a command for changing all ruler-line information at once—conforming with a line you create on-screen. You can type an alternate ruler line within the text area and use a ^O format command to substitute that line for the current ruler line above your text.

The command for creating a ruler from a line in the text area is not on any menu in Release 5. You issue this command by pressing ^OF. When you invoke the ^OF command, the ruler line assumes the characteristics of the line of text where the cursor is located. If that line consists of text in your document, ^OF changes the left and right margin settings in the active ruler line to match the line's margins.

For greater control over ruler-line formatting, you can type characters that invoke specific margin and tab functions when the ^OF command transfers them into the active ruler line. The characters you can type and their function when in the ruler line are listed in table 6.7. Any other characters are translated as hyphens on the ruler line.

Table 6.7
Ruler-Line Characters

Character	*Description*
L	Sets left margin
R	Sets right margin
P	Sets paragraph margin
!	Sets tab stops
#	Sets decimal tab stops
-	Erases tab stop in current ruler line

By typing the appropriate combination of hyphens, number signs, and exclamation points, you can create an entire replacement ruler line within a document. Adding markers for the left margin (L) and the right margin (R) is optional, because WordStar automatically reads the beginning and end characters of a text line as margin limits in the ruler line. The paragraph margin (P) is an indent that applies to the first line of each paragraph.

For an example of ruler-line substitution, you can type part of the sample Widgets TV script. First, type the title, subtitle, dateline, and first three lines of the script, using the default ruler line. With the cursor on the line that begins with `(Dressed like . . .`, type a special format for script descriptions by moving the cursor to column 6 and then typing the line and two extra spaces to move the cursor to column 59. Press ^OF to transfer this line's margins to the ruler line on-screen. Continue typing the description of the WOMAN in the script; the words wrap to conform to the new margins.

You would achieve the same effect on the ruler line by typing a line of random characters from column 6 to column 59 and invoking ^OF. (Remember that hyphens, exclamation points, and number signs are reproduced in the ruler line.) Before you change the ruler line again, you can save the current ruler line for later use. Transferring the ruler line from the top of the screen to the document area is the function of complementary on-screen format commands described in the following section.

Embedding a Ruler Line

WordStar includes a simple means of copying the current ruler line directly into document text—the opposite of the preceding function for copying the ruler line from a line of text. The Onscreen Format Menu command that lets you place the ruler line anywhere within a document also adds a related dot command, ensuring that the embedded ruler line will be active, formatting everything below it. (This embedded ruler line is not printed.)

Although the format command for embedding the current ruler line within a document is not included on any pull-down menu, it is listed in the MARGINS & TABS column of the Onscreen Format Menu in help levels 4, 3, and 2:

```
O ruler to text
```

The complete command for duplicating the current ruler line within a document is ^OO.

The important Ruler to Text command has also been allocated a single-stroke function-key command. On the bottom line of the Edit screen at help level 3 or 2, you see `8Ruler`; pressing the F8 key invokes the same function as the ^OO command.

When you press ^OO or F8, the ruler line is duplicated as a line of hyphens, exclamation points, and other characters at the cursor. Distinguishing this line from ordinary text is the .RR dot command at the beginning of the line, automatically inserted so that the line affects formatting as a ruler line would. This dot command is described on the sixth screen of dot-command help as follows (for more on dot-command help, see the next part of this chapter):

```
.rr text              Start embedded ruler line
```

Like any dot command, a .RR command must start at column 1 to be recognized by WordStar. Therefore, to ensure that the dot command is active, you should place the cursor at column 1 when you use ^OO. The line's formatting stays in effect until the next time you issue a command that alters ruler-line parameters. When you embed the ruler line at the start of a document before saving it, you ensure the preservation of formatting whenever you open the file.

In addition to being automatically inserted, the .RR command can be typed along with the hyphens, exclamation points, number signs, and L and R margin markers. To set a left margin at column 1 (0″), type a hyphen directly after .RR; do not use an *L*. For a left margin at column 2 or 3 (.1″ or .2″), due to the space occupied by the dot command, you need to invoke an overprinted line, using ^P ↵ after .RR; then type *L* at the proper location on the next line.

The embedded version of a ruler line, complete with the .RR command, can be stored for later use by saving the line as a block to disk or programming the line as a shorthand macro. When read into a document, the stored ruler line will govern the document's line format. Inserting different ruler lines stored on disk is one way to make formatting changes in a document.

With Release 5, you also can use the .RR command to insert a preset ruler line stored as part of WordStar, a handy feature that is discussed in the following section.

For an example of embedding the ruler line in text, continue typing the sample script for the Widgets, Inc. TV commercial. For the shortest line format in the script (indicating dialogue), type the first line of the WOMAN's dialogue, starting at column 16 and ending at column 50. To make this line's margins a ruler line, press ^OF. Move the cursor to column 1, and press ^OO to embed the ruler line in your document's text, preceded by the .RR command. When typed, the second line of the WOMAN's dialogue will conform to the embedded ruler line's margins. To use this same format later for dialogue, mark the ruler line with begin and end block markers, and save it to disk by pressing ^KW and naming this file something easily remembered, such as DIA for "Dialogue."

To type the next two formats for the MAN's reply in the script, mark the embedded description ruler line and copy it above where you type the MAN's description. Then read in the DIA file for the dialogue format where you enter the MAN's words.

Using Preset Ruler Lines

Many word processing programs include predefined formats for common applications, allowing complex formatting settings for a new document to be set with just a few keystrokes. Sometimes many of the formats included are inappropriate for most users.

With Release 5, WordStar now provides up to 10 ruler lines that can set formatting in a document with a simple dot command followed by a single numeral. Called *paragraph style guides*, only three of these ruler lines come with WordStar. The other seven style guides can be set for your own needs with the WSCHANGE program (see Chapter 11).

The dot command for invoking a preset ruler line is a variation on the command for embedding a ruler line in text. On the sixth screen of dot-command help menus is the following option:

```
.rr n                  Insert preformatted ruler line 0-9
```

By typing *.rr n* (replacing the *n* with a single-digit number from 0 to 9) as needed in a file, you can set margins and tabs that conform to the corresponding preset ruler line, which appears above (not embedded in) your on-screen text. Table 6.8 lists the available paragraph style guides supplied with WordStar.

Table 6.8
Paragraph Style Guides

Number	*Kind of Style Guide*
0	Default ruler line—standard margins and tabs
1	Quoted material or script description ruler line—left and right margins indented 1/2 inch
2	Outline ruler line; 1/2-inch hanging indent
3-9	User-defined ruler lines

Style guide 0 can be used to restore standard formatting in a document after margin and tab settings have been altered. Style guide 1 is useful when you need to offset text at the left and right sides for emphasis. For a paragraph where all the lines after the first are indented, you can use style guide 2. If you often use other formats, you should set the other style guides with the WSCHANGE program.

As an example of using preset ruler lines, finish typing the sample script. Invoke the standard ruler line by typing *.rr 0* at column 1, and enter the text for the location and action of the second scene. Set the appropriate style guide for the description of the WOMAN by typing *.rr 1* at column 1. Continue typing the script, copying the ruler line for dialogue from elsewhere in the document. Finally, set the format for the note at the bottom of the script by typing *.rr 2*.

Once finished, your document on-screen should look like the one in figure 6.19, with embedded ruler lines and paragraph style guides controlling formatting (although they won't print).

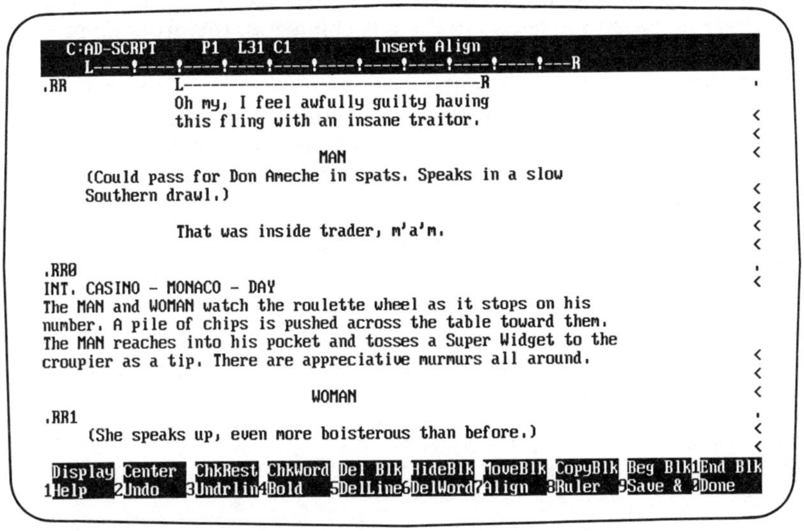

C:AD-SCRPT P1 L31 C1 Insert Align
.RR
Oh my, I feel awfully guilty having
this fling with an insane traitor.
MAN
(Could pass for Don Ameche in spats. Speaks in a slow
Southern drawl.)
That was inside trader, m'a'm.
.RR0
INT. CASINO - MONACO - DAY
The MAN and WOMAN watch the roulette wheel as it stops on his
number. A pile of chips is pushed across the table toward them.
The MAN reaches into his pocket and tosses a Super Widget to the
croupier as a tip. There are appreciative murmurs all around.
WOMAN
.RR1
(She speaks up, even more boisterous than before.)
Display Center ChkRest ChkWord Del Blk HideBlk MoveBlk CopyBlk Beg Blk End Blk
1Help 2Undo 3Undrlin 4Bold 5DelLine 6DelWord 7Align 8Ruler 9Save & 0Done

Fig. 6.19.
Embedded and preset ruler lines in a multiple-format page.

The commands for embedding typed or preset ruler lines are among dozens of WordStar's powerful dot commands. The next major section of this chapter is devoted to dot commands for formatting documents.

Designing a Page Format with Dot Commands

In addition to its print-control commands, WordStar features a full set of dot commands for formatting, print refining, merge printing, indexing, and generating tables of contents. Non-formatting dot commands are covered in later chapters.

To issue a dot command, enter a period (a dot) in column 1; a two-character command code; often, other information; and finally a carriage return. Formatting dot commands don't appear in the printed document; however, their effects are obvious on-screen. WordStar Release 5 includes a "baker's dozen" of new dot commands—in addition to modifications to 14 dot commands from previous WordStar releases. Also new in Release 5 are control-command combinations and dialog boxes that automatically add formatting dot commands to a document.

A dot command can be entered on any line in a document. To be effective, however, some commands must be at the beginning of a document or page. When you enter such dot commands properly, WordStar displays a 1 in the flag column on the right edge of the screen.

In early versions of WordStar, if you typed a period in column 1, a question mark was displayed in the flag column to indicate that you had to complete the dot command. After you typed the letters in the dot command, the program scanned them to see whether they were correct. In Release 5, the program also operates this way, if the line on which you type the dot command is not blank—that is, as long as a caret (^) is not displayed in the flag column. The program checks for errors in a dot command only when the flag column has either a soft carriage return (the edge remains blank) or a hard carriage return (designated by a < in the flag column).

If the program doesn't recognize a dot command you have entered, the question mark remains in the flag column. If a recognizable command works only during printing, a colon (:) is displayed in the flag column. A correctly typed dot command that affects on-screen formatting and printing anywhere within a document produces a period (.) in the flag column. A one (1) in the flag column indicates a dot command that works best on line 1 of a page.

Dot commands can be typed in upper- or lowercase letters. They must begin at the far left side of a line. When you reformat text, check that a dot command hasn't been inadvertently moved to the middle of the text. (***Note:*** Changing the left margin ordinarily does not move a dot command.)

Information required by a dot command consists of two characters of text, a number, or the word *on* or *off*. Data can be separated from the two-letter dot-command code by a space, but the space isn't necessary. When a required number is not entered, WordStar reverts to the default setting or assumes a value of zero.

WordStar tracks dot commands that alter margins, page length, or other formatting settings, and displays their effects on-screen as the cursor moves through the document. Release 5 stores in memory as many as 2,000 dot-command characters per document—a four-fold increase over the preceding version of the program. If more dot commands are used in a file, the prompt `Dot-Limit` appears in the status line and the display may be incorrect, although the document will print correctly. (You can increase the dot-command limit with the WSCHANGE program; see Chapter 11.)

WordStar displays the on-screen effects of most dot commands setting page appearance. About three dozen dot commands that define the layout of documents can be edited on-screen. Because the effects are displayed, you don't need to run a test printout. The dot commands for adjusting a document's appearance (which should be familiar to WordStar veterans) have been augmented by several functions that cover the full range of page parameters and column layouts. The page layout features controlled by dot commands are summarized in figure 6.20.

By using appropriate dot commands to specify layout settings at the beginning of a WordStar document, you can regulate the document's presentation throughout its successive pages. If you want to change a formatting element within the document, simply embed the proper dot command wherever necessary.

Accessing Dot-Command Help

In Release 5, WordStar's on-line help for dot commands has been entirely rewritten. At all help levels except 4, you can access this help by pressing either ^J or the F1 key. The first help screen that appears on-screen offers more specialized help options, including the following:

```
For help with dot commands, type a period (.).
```

When you press the complete sequence for dot-command help—^J. or F1.—WordStar displays an introductory screen, shown in figure 6.21. After this introductory screen, six screens listing the dot commands and their definitions are displayed in turn when you press Enter. (Pressing Esc cancels the help screens.)

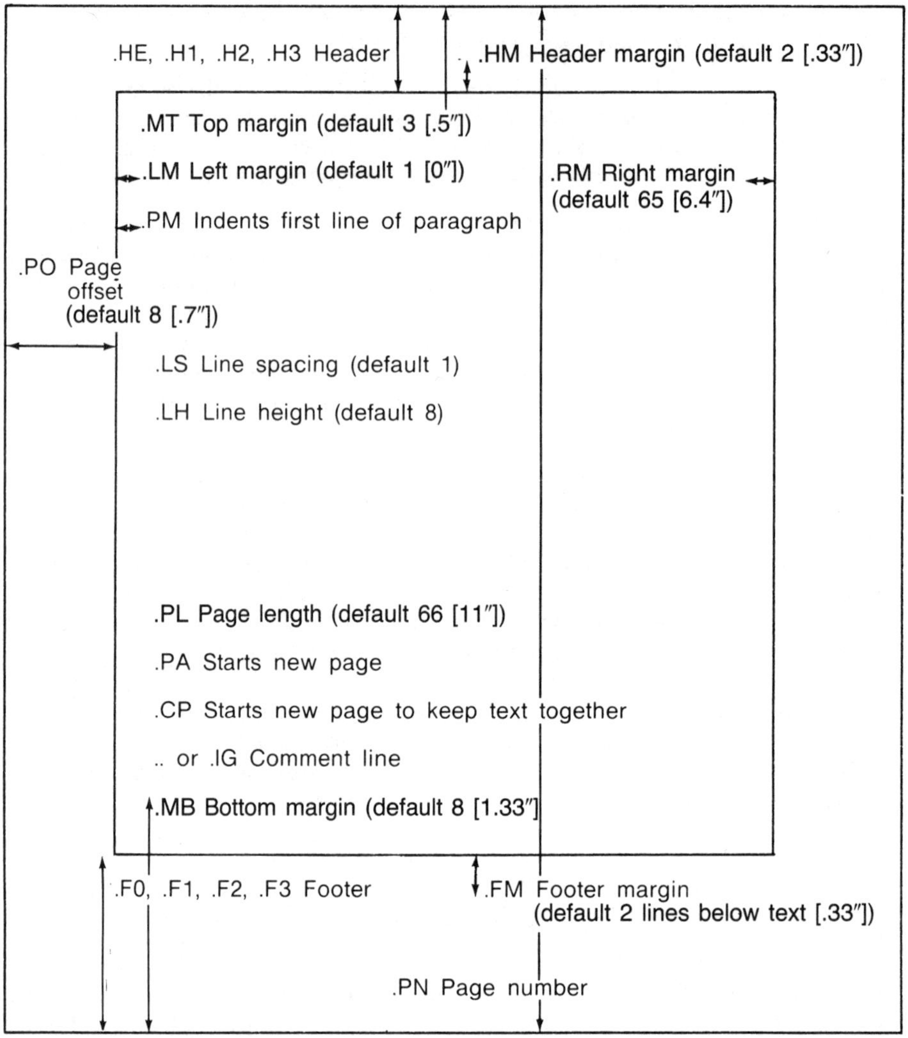
.HE, .H1, .H2, .H3 Header
.HM Header margin (default 2 [.33″])
.MT Top margin (default 3 [.5″])
.LM Left margin (default 1 [0″])
.RM Right margin
(default 65 [6.4″])
.PM Indents first line of paragraph
.PO Page
offset
(default 8 [.7″])
.LS Line spacing (default 1)
.LH Line height (default 8)
.PL Page length (default 66 [11″])
.PA Starts new page
.CP Starts new page to keep text together
.. or .IG Comment line
.MB Bottom margin (default 8 [1.33″]
.F0, .F1, .F2, .F3 Footer
.FM Footer margin
(default 2 lines below text [.33″])
.PN Page number

Fig. 6.20.
Page-layout features set with WordStar dot commands.

In Release 5, WordStar's dot-command help screens list commands alphabetically, with merge-print commands given a screen of their own. Although these changes are improvements over the help screens in Release 4, dot-command help is still not context sensitive. You can't access a specific listing directly; you must flip through the screens to reach the information you need.

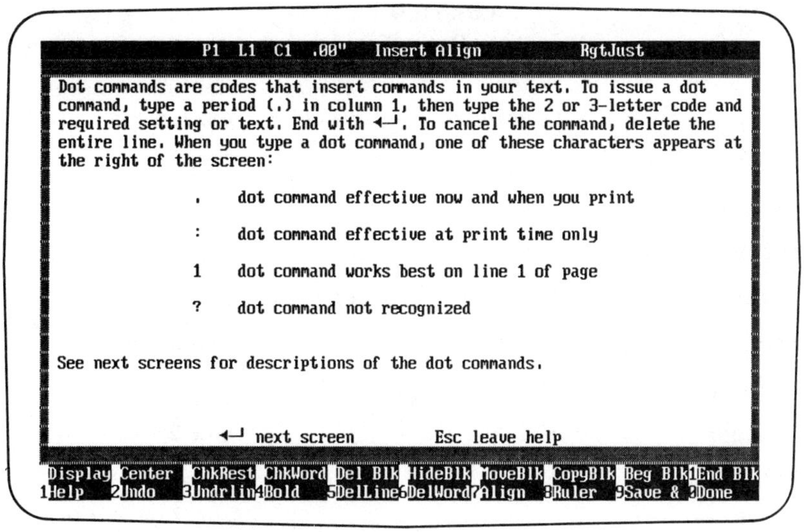
P1 L1 C1 .00" Insert Align RgtJust
Dot commands are codes that insert commands in your text. To issue a dot command, type a period (.) in column 1, then type the 2 or 3-letter code and required setting or text. End with ↵. To cancel the command, delete the entire line. When you type a dot command, one of these characters appears at the right of the screen:
. dot command effective now and when you print
: dot command effective at print time only
1 dot command works best on line 1 of page
? dot command not recognized
See next screens for descriptions of the dot commands.
↵ next screen Esc leave help
Display Center ChkRest ChkWord Del Blk HideBlk MoveBlk CopyBlk Beg Blk End Blk
1Help 2Undo 3Undrlin 4Bold 5DelLine 6DelWord 7Align 8Ruler 9Save & 0Done

Fig. 6.21.
WordStar's introductory dot-command help screen.

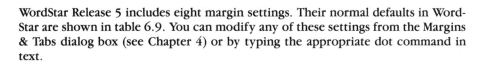

Setting Page Margins

When the text area of a document is printed, the text occupies the center of a page, similar to a picture in a frame. The frame in this case is the white space around the text. As shown in figure 6.20, you can precisely position the central text area on paper by adjusting WordStar's margin settings.

WordStar's default format settings always have been well suited for general use in report or manuscript pages. With these default settings, you can position your text symmetrically and have enough space at the bottom for page numbers. In Release 5 for the first time, WordStar's margins can be expressed in inches as well as in column and line numbers, making it easier to measure them on paper and set them for on-screen formatting. When you type inch measurements, remember to include the inch indicator ("), or WordStar will read the numbers as column designations. (In WordStar the double quotation mark indicates inches.)

WordStar Release 5 includes eight margin settings. Their normal defaults in WordStar are shown in table 6.9. You can modify any of these settings from the Margins & Tabs dialog box (see Chapter 4) or by typing the appropriate dot command in text.

Table 6.9
WordStar Page Margins

Margin	*Dot Command*	*Default Setting*	*Column or Line Equivalent*
Left margin	.LM	0.0″	Column 1
Right margin	.RM	6.4″	Column 65
Top margin	.MT	.5″	Line 3
Bottom margin	.MB	1.33″	Line 8
Page offset	.PO	.7″	Column 8
Header margin	.HM	.33″	Line 2
Footer margin	.FM	.33″	Line 2
Paragraph margin	.PM	Off	

Header and footer margins are discussed later in this chapter.

The remaining margin dot commands are covered in this section. These commands should be familiar to users of the preceding version of WordStar, although the commands' flexibility has been increased in Release 5.

The WordStar margin dot commands are shown on the third and fourth screens of dot-command help screens in Release 5. If you press ^J. or F1. and then Enter three times, you will see a screen of the dot commands that begin with the letters *I* to *O* (see fig. 6.22).

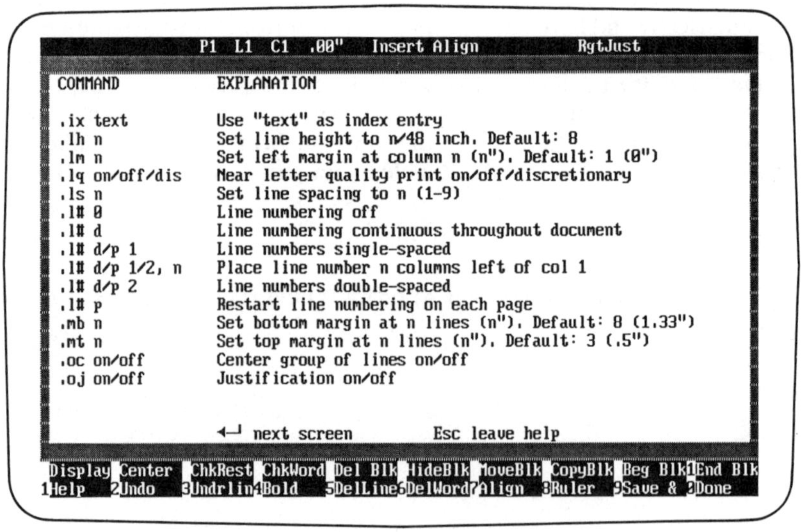
P1 L1 C1 .00" Insert Align RgtJust
COMMAND EXPLANATION
.ix text Use "text" as index entry
.lh n Set line height to n/48 inch. Default: 8
.lm n Set left margin at column n (n"). Default: 1 (0")
.lq on/off/dis Near letter quality print on/off/discretionary
.ls n Set line spacing to n (1-9)
.l# 0 Line numbering off
.l# d Line numbering continuous throughout document
.l# d/p 1 Line numbers single-spaced
.l# d/p 1/2, n Place line number n columns left of col 1
.l# d/p 2 Line numbers double-spaced
.l# p Restart line numbering on each page
.mb n Set bottom margin at n lines (n"). Default: 8 (1.33")
.mt n Set top margin at n lines (n"). Default: 3 (.5")
.oc on/off Center group of lines on/off
.oj on/off Justification on/off
next screen Esc leave help
Display Center ChkRest ChkWord Del Blk HideBlk MoveBlk CopyBlk Beg Blk End Blk
1Help 2Undo 3Undrlin 4Bold 5DelLine 6DelWord 7Align 8Ruler 9Save & 0Done

Fig. 6.22.
WordStar's third screen of dot-command help listings.

The dot commands on this screen include the formatting commands for the left, bottom, and top margins. These commands are listed as follows:

```
.lm n    Set left margin at column n (n"). Default: 1 (0")

.mb n    Set bottom margin at n lines (n"). Default: 8 (1.33")

.mt n    Set top margin at n lines (n"). Default: 3 (.5")
```

The remaining margin dot commands covered in this section are shown on the fourth dot-command help screen. To view this screen from the current (third) screen, you can simply press Enter. The dot commands on the fourth screen begin with the letters *O* to *R*, as illustrated in figure 6.23.

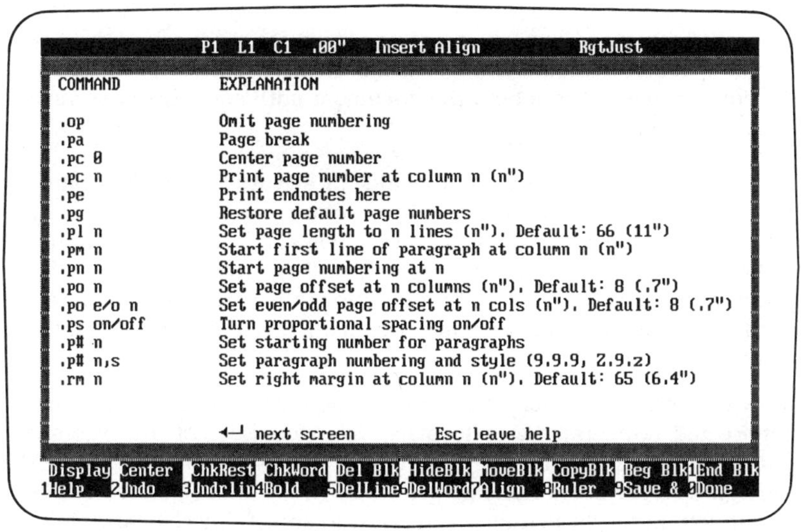
P1 L1 C1 .00" Insert Align RgtJust
COMMAND EXPLANATION
.op Omit page numbering
.pa Page break
.pc 0 Center page number
.pc n Print page number at column n (n")
.pe Print endnotes here
.pg Restore default page numbers
.pl n Set page length to n lines (n"). Default: 66 (11")
.pm n Start first line of paragraph at column n (n")
.pn n Start page numbering at n
.po n Set page offset at n columns (n"). Default: 8 (.7")
.po e/o n Set even/odd page offset at n cols (n"). Default: 8 (.7")
.ps on/off Turn proportional spacing on/off
.p# n Set starting number for paragraphs
.p# n,s Set paragraph numbering and style (9.9.9, Z.9.z)
.rm n Set right margin at column n (n"). Default: 65 (6.4")
next screen Esc leave help
Display Center ChkRest ChkWord Del Blk HideBlk MoveBlk CopyBlk Beg Blk End Blk
1Help 2Undo 3Undrlin 4Bold 5DelLine 6DelWord 7Align 8Ruler 9Save & 0Done

Fig. 6.23.
WordStar's fourth screen of dot-command help listings.

Among the dot commands on the fourth screen of help listings are the commands for the paragraph margin, the page offset, and the right margin. Their listings are shown like this:

```
.pm n       Start first line of paragraph at column n (n")

.po n       Set page offset at n columns (n"). Default 8 (.7")

.po e/o n   Set even/odd page offset at n cols (n"). Default 8 (.7")

.rm n       Set right margin at column n (n"). Default 65 (6.4")
```

WordStar also includes function-key combinations for three of the margin commands, letting you quickly insert a left-, right-, or paragraph-margin dot command and a hard carriage return on the line where the cursor is positioned (any text moves down one line). Ctrl-F5 inserts .LM at the left edge of the screen; Ctrl-F6 inserts .RM, also at the left edge. In either case, you must type the column number of the new left or right margin after the command and press Enter. If a number is not specified, the margins revert to columns 1 and 65. The Ctrl-F7 command inserts the .PM 6 command for a paragraph margin at column 6. If you change the number, you change its setting.

The left- and right-margin dot commands, .LM and .RM, are the counterparts of the ^OL and ^OR commands explained in Chapter 4. In Release 5, left- and right-margin dot commands can be followed by the column number of the new margin or by the distance in inches (indicated by ") for the new margin's position. Like ^OL and ^OR, maximum settings for .LM and .RM are 360 and 361 (35.9" and 36") respectively, although few printers accommodate these settings. For most applications, you will keep margins within the 1-through-65 (0"-through-6.5") range of WordStar's defaults.

When a .LM or .RM command appears in text, the ruler line at the top of the screen conforms to the specified margin setting. The margins are reset from the line that contains the dot command throughout the document until another dot command that resets the margin appears.

A further enhancement to margin dot commands in Release 5 is the capability of changing margins by incremental as well as by absolute measurements. When you follow the dot command by a plus (+) or minus (−) sign and an inch measurement, you move the margin setting forward or backward by that distance from its preceding setting. Thus, typing *.lm +1"* would move the margin one inch to the right. Using this procedure, all indented material maintains its relative relationship to the changed margin.

To indent only the first line of each paragraph throughout a document, as in many standard report and correspondence formats, you can use .PM, the Paragraph Margin command. A number after the command specifies the column where the paragraph margin is to be set (a number with the inch symbol sets the margin in inches). As with left and right margins, you also can specify incremental changes from a previous paragraph margin with a plus or minus sign and the proper inch measurement. When you set a paragraph margin to a number lower than the left margin, the result is a ***hanging indent***, with the first line of each paragraph extending farther left than the rest of the text. Hanging indents are useful for outlines and numbered lists.

When the .PM dot command is used in a document, the letter P appears on the ruler line, indicating where the first line of every paragraph will be indented. The paragraph margin and its ruler-line symbol remain in effect until you embed another .PM command in the text. If the dot command is not followed by a number, the command acts as a toggle: omitting paragraph indents from the line where the command appears until the next occurrence of .PM in the document. When you use .PM, you must reformat the paragraph by pressing ^B or ^QU.

Another dot command for controlling your text's positioning on the page, .PO, adjusts the amount of white space between the left edge of the paper and the position where column 1 of the text area is printed. This setting (known as the *page offset*) and the left margin determine where text lines begin on paper.

When using the .PO dot command for page offset, you can type a column number or an inch measurement (with the inch sign) to indicate the distance between the left edge of a page and the left edge of the text area. This offset usually stays close to the default setting of 8 (.7″). For instance, if you intend to bind pages at the left edge of the paper, an appropriate page-offset setting is 10 or 12 (1″ or 1.2″).

As displayed on the fourth screen of dot-command listings (refer to fig. 6.23), in addition to the dot command for page offset used in earlier WordStar releases, Release 5 provides for different page offset settings on even- and odd-numbered pages. By typing *e* or *o* before the offset setting, you can compensate for space differences in the margins of facing pages to accommodate the binding in reports and books. In bound formats, even-numbered pages require smaller page offsets (leaving more room for the binding on the right side of the page), and odd-numbered pages require larger offsets (leaving extra space on the left). Typically, you might type *.poe .5″* and *.poo 1″* for a page offset of 1/2 inch on even pages and 1 inch on odd-numbered pages.

A .PO command embedded in a document shows no effect on-screen. WordStar adds the page offsets when you print your document. To have the page offset revert to the default setting, you simply embed *.po* in the document and don't type a number after it.

In addition to these horizontal margin settings, you also can control the vertical characteristics of a page with two WordStar dot commands. The commands' codes represent the functions they invoke: .MT for margin top, and .MB for margin bottom. Like other margin commands, these must be followed by either an inch measurement (with the inch sign) or a line number, indicating the distance from the top edge of the page to the top margin or from the bottom edge to the bottom margin. The default top margin is 3 lines (.5″), and the default bottom margin is 8 lines (1.33″). In general, top- and bottom-margin settings remain in the single-digit range (under 12 lines or 2″).

Inserting top- and bottom-margin dot commands at the beginning of a document sets the size of the frame of white space above and below the text in your printed documents. Increasing the top or bottom margin decreases the amount of text per page. You can toggle on and off the default margin setting's effect by embedding another .MT or .MB command without a number beside it.

Although top and bottom margins are not directly displayed during editing, they help determine where a page will break on-screen as well as on paper. With an unmodified copy of WordStar, on a standard 8 1/2-inch-by-11-inch page the default top margin (1/2 inch) and bottom margin (1 1/3 inches) leave enough space for 11 inches minus 1.83 inches (.5 inch plus 1.33 inches), or 9.17 inches of text. With the default line height, that leaves room for 55 lines of text per standard page.

Remember that in Release 5 you can set all of WordStar's page margins at one time in the Margins & Tabs dialog box (see Chapter 4), which inserts the corresponding dot commands in your text. For more permanent alterations of the page margins you can use the WSCHANGE program, as detailed in Chapter 11.

For an example of using the margin-setting dot commands, you could combine all the sample ad documents shown in this chapter as one document. Use the ^KR command to insert into a single document the sample ad budget, the outline, and the script, in that order. Next, modify the margins for this composite document by typing the following column of formatting dot commands at the beginning of the document file:

.LM 6

.RM 60

.PM 9

.MT 7

.MB 12

.PO 12

Each dot command must begin at column 1 and occupy a separate line that ends with a carriage return. Type dot commands in either upper- or lowercase, with numbers following commands directly or separated by a space. In this example, both the left and right margins (.LM and .RM) are indented by five columns, leaving more white space around the text when printed; the paragraph margin, set by .PM, invokes the often-used three-space indentation; both the top and bottom margins (.MT and .MB) are moved in by four lines; and in order that these pages can be stapled together, the page offset (.PO) on the left edge of the page is increased.

Setting Page Length

An unmodified copy of WordStar is preset for a standard-sized 8 1/2-inch-by-11-inch manuscript page. Such a page spans a total of 66 lines, including top and bottom margins and 55 lines of text, at a line height of 6 lines per inch. What if you type on legal-sized 14-inch-long paper (with a total of 84 lines)? Or do you want to use shorter paper or envelopes? You can alter the WordStar page length default with the WSCHANGE program (see Chapter 11). Or you can adjust the total line length of a page with a WordStar dot command.

The command for setting page length is on the fourth screen of dot-command help listings, illustrated in figure 6.23. The Page Length command is noted as follows:

```
.pl n      Set page length to n lines (n"). Default: 66 (11")
```

You can remember this dot command by the initials of the formatting feature it sets: .PL for page length. In Release 5, the command must be followed by a designation for the length of the page, either the number of lines at a rate of 6 lines per inch, or the page length in inches (with the inch sign). The default page length is 66 lines (11"). Other common settings are 25 lines (4.2") for standard business envelopes and 84 lines (14") for legal-sized paper.

Embedding a .PL command at the beginning of a document influences the amount of text displayed and printed on a page. The number of document lines printed per page equals the page length minus the top- and bottom-margin settings. Therefore, a change in the page-length setting alters the amount of text per page. After you set the page length with .PL, page breaks in the text—both on-screen and on paper—reflect the change. If you want to reset the page length to the default setting, type *.pl* without a number.

To apply the page-length dot command, you can print the combined ad document created in the preceding section on legal-sized paper. On 14-inch paper, you can print 65 lines of text (along with 19 lines of top and bottom margin space) on a page by typing *.pl 84* at the beginning of the file.

Line height is only one of the characteristics of text lines that can be reset with dot commands. All page-length settings described in this section are based on WordStar's default setting for line height: six lines per inch.

Setting Line Characteristics

5

Among WordStar's formatting options are three dot commands for modifying the appearance of text lines on-screen and on the printed page. Two of these commands were in previous versions of WordStar: the command that sets the unit of space between lines and the one that determine the number of units between lines. In addition, Release 5 provides a new command for printing line numbers at the left margin—a useful feature for legal and draft documents.

The WordStar default line height of six lines per inch is standard for a single-spaced typed document. The distance is measured from the bottom of a line of text to the bottom of the next line. If you place a WordStar dot command at the beginning of a document, you can reset the line height throughout the document for more or less space between the lines.

The dot command for altering the line-height setting is included on the third screen of the dot-command help listings (refer to fig. 6.22). The help screen defines this command:

```
.lh n                Sets line height at n/48 inch. Default: 8
```

This command is easy to remember: .LH for line height. Although you normally insert the .LH dot command at the beginning of a page or document, you can use the command anywhere in a document to alter line height.

The number following the .LH command is calibrated in 48ths of an inch. (If a printer does not move in 1/48-inch increments, the WordStar printer driver compensates by using closer increments.) The default line height of 6 lines per inch is equivalent to an interval of 8/48 of an inch, or a line-height setting of 8. Settings can range from 2 to 255, but the most useful line height numbers are shown in table 6.10.

Table 6.10
Line Height Settings

Dot Command	*Lines Per Inch*
.LH 6	8
.LH 7	6.8
.LH 8	6
.LH 10	4.8
.LH 12	4
.LH 16	3
.LH 24	2

According to this list, the line height setting .LH 16 produces half as many lines of text as the program default, .LH 8. Therefore, specifying *.lh 16* is one method for producing double-spaced text, although you will not see double-spacing on-screen. Using a .LH command to reset line height does adjust page length (according to the number of lines) and the resulting page breaks, on-screen and on paper. You should take care to adjust the page-length setting to fit your paper size if you change the line height.

WordStar's dot command for setting line spacing in a document and seeing the spacing on-screen is the same one inserted when you issue ^OS (see Chapter 4). This dot command is displayed on the third screen of dot-command help listings (refer to fig. 6.22). Among the formatting features listed is this one:

```
.ls n          Sets line spacing to n (1-9)
```

The number after the dot command represents single-, double-, triple-, or other spacing. The numbers are the same as those used for ^OS: 1 for single-spacing, 2 for double-spacing, and so on through 9. When you embed the .LS command in a document, any text you type, from that line until the next .LS command or the end of the file, conforms to the new line spacing on-screen. To reformat existing text with the new spacing, you must press ^B or ^QU.

If you use the .LS command to double- or triple-space text on-screen, this text will occupy much more space on disk than if you change line height for a similar effect at print time, because the blank lines on-screen are stored as part of the file. When working with large files, you may prefer to change line spacing in your printed document by invoking the space-saving ^OS command. Regardless of the method you use, the correct spacing will be shown by WordStar's page preview feature (discussed later in this chapter).

WordStar Release 5 includes a versatile feature for numbering lines of text in a document when printed. Options are available for continuous numbering throughout a document, for restarting numbers on each page, for single- or double-spaced line numbering, and for positioning the numbers by column. The numbers are not shown on-screen.

The many settings for line numbering are covered on the third screen of dot-command help listings (refer to fig. 6.22). Six lines of information are devoted to this command—more than for any other dot command:

```
.l# 0             Line numbering off
.l# d             Line numbering continuous throughout document
.l# d/p 1         Line numbers single-spaced
.l# d/p 1/2, n    Place line number n columns left of col 1
.l# d/p 2         Line numbers double-spaced
.l# p             Restart line numbering on each page
```

The .L# dot command should be typed at column 1 of the line above the first line you want to number. After the dot command, the options for the style, spacing, and column location should follow, in that order. Finally, press Enter to add a hard carriage return.

The style choices for line numbering are D to have continuous numbers throughout a document or P to have numbering start over at the beginning of each page. If one of these letters is not entered after .L#, line numbering starts over on each page. The spacing options for line numbers are 1 for single-spacing or 2 for double-spacing. Omitting a number for spacing or typing *0* after *.l#* turns off line numbering.

You specify the column location where line numbers will be printed by typing a comma and the number of columns to the left of column 1. The default setting for line numbers is 3, placing them in column 4. If a document's page offset is too small to provide space for line numbers, WordStar increases the offset to accommodate them. For laser printers unable to print the edges of a page, you may need to reset the numbering option.

Combining the options after .L# can invoke line numbering in the appropriate configuration for any document. These same options can be reset permanently with the WSCHANGE program.

As examples of using dot commands to modify line characteristics, you can set formats for different sections of the combined ad document assembled previously. For printing continuous line numbering throughout the document, single-spaced and at column 3, type *.l# d1,2* at column 1 above any text; then press Enter. To print the outline section with wider spacing between lines, enter *.lh 12* at column 1 of the line before the beginning of the outline, and press Enter. (A setting of 12 is equivalent to 1 1/2-line spacing.) Next, type *.lh* after the end of the outline to restore the default line height, and press Enter again. To leave room for corrections, reset the line spacing for the document's script section for double-spacing by moving the cursor to the beginning of the script section, typing *.ls 2* at column 1, and pressing Enter. Finally, press ^QU to realign the text below WordStar's .LS command.

Setting Tabbed or Snaking Columns

With Release 5, WordStar now includes two kinds of column formats for different applications. ***Tabbed columns***, covered in Chapter 4, have text entered in rows, for charts, tables, and other listings; for the first time, WordStar provides dot commands for entering tabs in addition to the control commands used in previous versions. Also new in Release 5 are ***snaking columns***, with text continuing from the bottom of one column to the top of the next—the kind used for newspapers, newsletters, and other publishing-style documents. This section discusses dot commands for both column formats.

The dot command for setting tabs is displayed on the fifth screen of Release 5's dot-command help listings. At all help levels but 4, if you press ^J. or F1. from the Edit screen and then Enter five times, you will see listings for the dot commands that start with the letters *R* to *X* (see fig. 6.24).

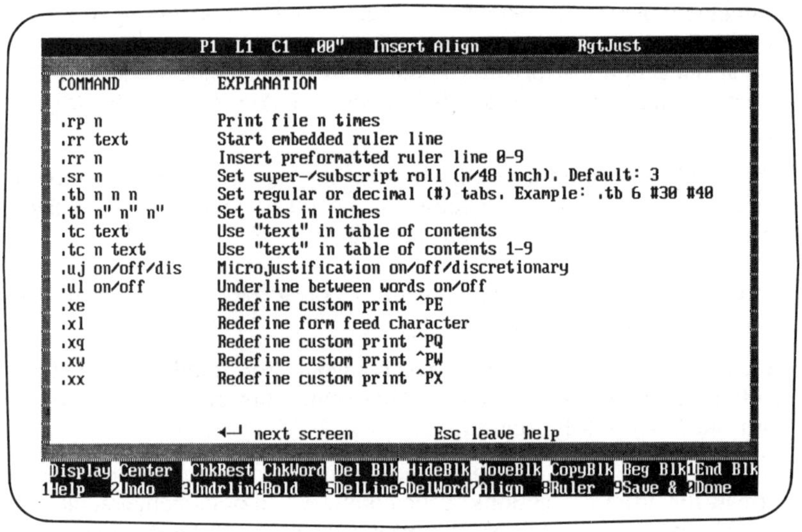
P1 L1 C1 .00" Insert Align RgtJust
COMMAND EXPLANATION
.rp n Print file n times
.rr text Start embedded ruler line
.rr n Insert preformatted ruler line 0-9
.sr n Set super-/subscript roll (n/48 inch). Default: 3
.tb n n n Set regular or decimal (#) tabs. Example: .tb 6 #30 #40
.tb n" n" n" Set tabs in inches
.tc text Use "text" in table of contents
.tc n text Use "text" in table of contents 1-9
.uj on/off/dis Microjustification on/off/discretionary
.ul on/off Underline between words on/off
.xe Redefine custom print ^PE
.xl Redefine form feed character
.xq Redefine custom print ^PQ
.xw Redefine custom print ^PW
.xx Redefine custom print ^PX
next screen Esc leave help
Display Center ChkRest ChkWord Del Blk HideBlk MoveBlk CopyBlk Beg Blk End Blk
1Help 2Undo 3Undrlin 4Bold 5DelLine 6DelWord 7Align 8Ruler 9Save & 0Done

Fig. 6.24.
WordStar's fifth screen of dot-command help listings.

On this screen of listings are two lines noting variations on the tab dot command:

```
.tb n n n       Set regular or decimal (#) tabs. Example: .tb 6 #30 #40

.tb n" n" n"    Set tabs in inches
```

As noted in the help listings, you can set tabs manually by typing *.tb* at column 1 followed by column numbers or inch measurements (indicated by inch signs) for regular tabs. For decimal tabs, precede these numbers by the number sign (#). These dot commands are the same ones inserted in text by setting tabs from the Margins & Tabs dialog box when invoked with ^OI. Tabs are used to format columns and rows of text as detailed in Chapter 4.

The dot commands for snaking columns are on the first screen of Release 5's dot-command help listings. To view this screen, at any help level except 4 you can press ^J. or F1. from the Edit screen and then Enter. Dot commands on this first screen are those that start with the letters *A* to *E*, as shown in figure 6.25.

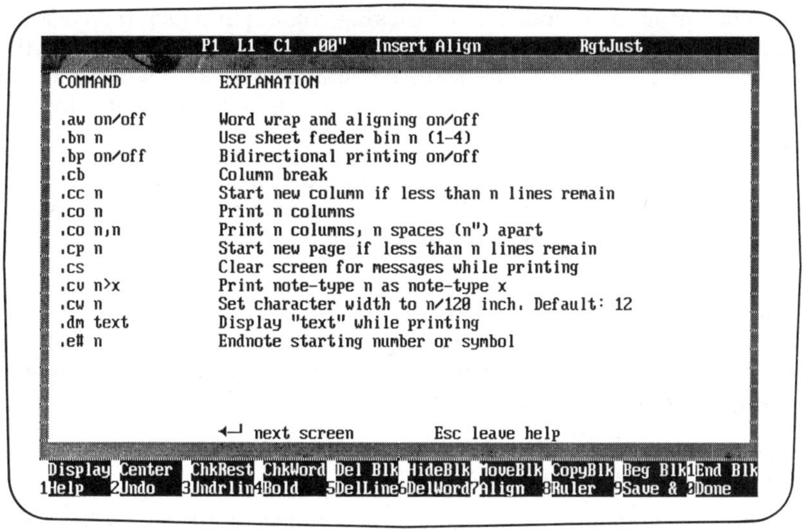
P1 L1 C1 .00" Insert Align RgtJust
COMMAND EXPLANATION
.aw on/off Word wrap and aligning on/off
.bn n Use sheet feeder bin n (1-4)
.bp on/off Bidirectional printing on/off
.cb Column break
.cc n Start new column if less than n lines remain
.co n Print n columns
.co n,n Print n columns, n spaces (n") apart
.cp n Start new page if less than n lines remain
.cs Clear screen for messages while printing
.cv n>x Print note-type n as note-type x
.cw n Set character width to n/120 inch. Default: 12
.dm text Display "text" while printing
.e# n Endnote starting number or symbol
next screen Esc leave help
Display Center ChkRest ChkWord Del Blk HideBlk MoveBlk CopyBlk Beg Blk End Blk
1Help 2Undo 3Undrlin 4Bold 5DelLine 6DelWord 7Align 8Ruler 9Save & 0Done

Fig. 6.25.
WordStar's first screen of dot-command help listings.

The dot commands for column functions are grouped together on this screen, as follows:

```
.cb         Column break

.cc n       Start new column if less than n lines remain

.co n       Print n columns

.co n,n     Print n columns, n spaces (n") apart
```

To print snaking columns, type the dot command *.co* followed by the number of columns you want to have appear side by side on the page. You can type any number from 2 to 8, for up to eight columns of text. Typing a comma and a number for column spacing or a measurement in inches designates the amount of separation you want between columns. To turn off snaking columns and resume standard page layout, type *.co* or *.co 1* at the start of the next page.

After you enter the snaking-column dot command, the left edge of the screen displays special markers: groups of three hyphens, or "bars," at each line. Any column you type will be as wide as the margins in the current ruler line (tab settings in the ruler line are also in effect). For columns to fit on the page when printed, you may have to adjust your margins before invoking snaking-column mode. Newspaper-style columns are not displayed next to each other on-screen. To view such column formatting the way it will be printed, you should use the preview function described later in this chapter.

After you complete the first page-long snaking column of text, a column break is displayed on-screen. This break is a double line across the screen, with a `C` in the flag column on the right. Text below this column break will wrap into the column to the right when printed. To indicate the snaking column in which the cursor is currently located, the markers at the left of the screen are two across for the second column, three across for the third column, and so on. When the last column of text fills a page, WordStar starts a new page (noted in the status line).

When you edit snaking-column text, column breaks adjust automatically. To keep several lines together in one column regardless of the break, you can invoke a conditional break by typing *.cc* above the lines, along with the number of lines to be grouped together. To start a new column before the end of a page, you can force a break by typing *.cb*.

When you use snaking columns, any footnotes included in your text are automatically printed as endnotes. If you need to change snaking columns back to standard page layout, delete the .CO dot command and any .CC and .CB commands embedded in the document; then realign the text.

Entering a .CO command on a page where snaking columns are already in effect starts a new page with the new column format.

After a page break, you must reset the number of columns on the page with a .CO command before adding text in the new column format, or else a blank page is inserted before the next text format when printing.

To apply an example of snaking columns, reopen the memo typed in the Chapter 1 Quick Start. With this document on-screen, change the right margin to 30 by typing the dot command *.rm 30* at column 1 of the first line and pressing Enter. Then realign the document by pressing ^QU. Move the cursor to the top of the document, and enter the dot command for formatting two snaking columns four spaces apart; type *.co 2,4* and press Enter. The column indicator characters appear at the left of the screen. To see the columns break, move the cursor to the bottom of the first page, showing the column-break separator illustrated in figure 6.26. To view how this document will look when printed, use the page preview feature described later in this chapter.

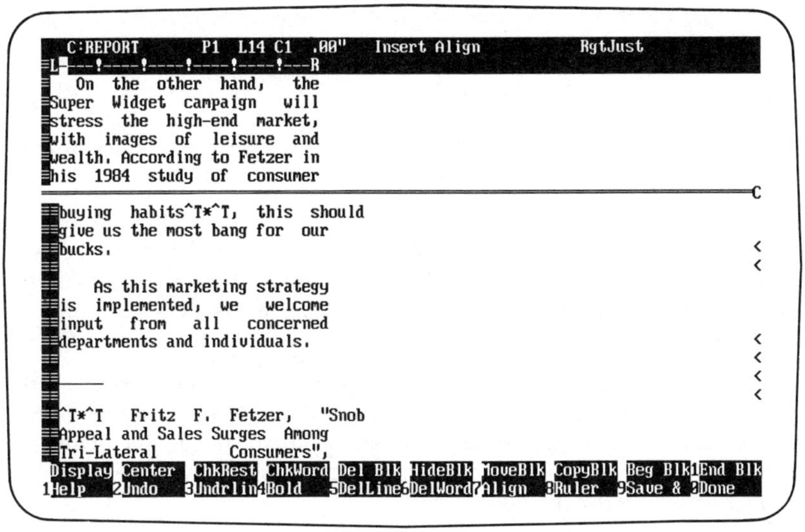
C:REPORT P1 L14 C1 .00" Insert Align RgtJust
On the other hand, the
Super Widget campaign will
stress the high-end market,
with images of leisure and
wealth. According to Fetzer in
his 1984 study of consumer
buying habits^T*^T, this should
give us the most bang for our
bucks.
As this marketing strategy
is implemented, we welcome
input from all concerned
departments and individuals.
^T*^T Fritz F. Fetzer, "Snob
Appeal and Sales Surges Among
Tri-Lateral Consumers",
Display Center ChkRest ChkWord Del Blk HideBlk MoveBlk CopyBlk Beg Blk End Blk
1Help 2Undo 3Undrlin 4Bold 5DelLine 6DelWord 7Align 8Ruler 9Save & 0Done

Fig. 6.26.
Snaking columns in WordStar.

Using Page-Break Commands

As with snaking columns, sometimes you want to break a page of standard text at a different line than where the page break normally occurs. This practice sometimes avoids dangling-text imbalances called *widows* and *orphans*. Or you might want to print a complete table on a page regardless of where the page breaks. Commands for automatically or conditionally starting a new page have been in WordStar's arsenal of dot commands for a long time.

In WordStar Release 5, at help level 4 the commands for page breaks are among the few dot commands listed on a pull-down menu—in this case on the Layout menu. In this menu you will see these command lines:

```
New page                          .pa

Conditional new page...           .cp
```

At Release 5's other help levels, the dot commands for page breaks are on the first and fourth screens of the dot-command help listings (refer to figs. 6.25 and 6.23). The commands' descriptions appear as follows:

```
.cp n          Start new page if less than n lines remain

.pa            Page break
```

The .PA command needs no number after it. The .CP command, however, is usually followed by the number of lines that must be kept intact on a page. After the two commands are embedded in text, their major difference is that .PA always produces a page break at the next line. However, .CP is triggered only when the number you type beside it is greater than the number of lines remaining on a page, according to WordStar's page length and margin settings.

Whenever WordStar encounters a .PA command, the next line on-screen indicates a page break by displaying a row of hyphens and a `P` at the right edge of the screen. When WordStar reads a .PA command during printing, the program issues instructions to the printer to move the paper to a new page.

To invoke a conditional page break with the .CP command, embed the command above the first line of the section of text that must be kept intact. The number you type after .CP should include the subsequent group of lines. If fewer lines than that number remain on the page, the program displays a page break on-screen directly beneath the .CP command and prints the group of lines on the following page.

For examples of the page-break commands' use, apply them to key sections of the sample ad documents combined earlier in this chapter. To ensure that page breaks occur after the budget and outline sections, move the cursor to the line below the last line of each of these sections, type *.pa*, and press Enter. A page-break line appears on the line below the .PA command.

To guarantee that the text lines in your budget table and in the ad outline remain intact regardless of page breaks, place conditional page breaks before these sections. Move the cursor to the line above the column headings in the table (`Title`, `Lengths`, and so on), type *.cp 11*, and press Enter. Move the cursor to the line above `1 Campaign to stress leisure . . .` in the outline section, type *.cp 19*, and press Enter. Your document breaks into separate pages for each section, despite other formatting changes.

Using Page-Numbering Options

WordStar Release 5 is preset to print page numbers at the bottom of each page (at column 28) starting with page 1 and continuing to the end of the file. These page-numbering settings can be reconfigured with dot commands. The defaults can be changed more permanently with the WSCHANGE program (see Chapter 11).

If you use separate files for sections of a long document, you may want the page numbers to follow successively in each file. Any change in page numbering with dot commands is immediately reflected in the status line. In addition, you can use the ^QI command to access a numbered page on-screen (see Chapter 5).

In Release 5 the command for renumbering pages is on the fourth screen of dot-command help listings (refer to fig. 6.23). In the middle of the screen is the following command:

```
.pn n         Start page numbering at n
```

This dot command is easy to remember by the initials of its function: .PN for page number. The number following the command should be no more than 3 numerals long to appear completely on the status line—although WordStar accurately tracks page numbers up to 65,536. For page numbers greater than 999, WordStar displays an asterisk and the last two digits of the number on the status line. For example, 12,034 would be displayed as `*34`.

As soon as you enter the .PN command and an appropriate number to reset the page number, the new setting is reflected in the status line for the rest of the document. If no number is typed after the .PN command, page numbering begins at 0 at that position.

Three other WordStar dot commands also affect page numbering. One of these commands is listed at help level 4 on the pull-down Layout menu, like this:

```
Omit page numbering        .op
```

All three of these page-numbering dot commands (and a variation) are listed on the fourth screen of dot-command help listings (refer to fig. 6.23). Among the commands listed on this screen are the following:

```
.op            Omit page numbering

.pc 0          Center page number

.pc n          Print page number at column n (n")

.pg            Restore default page numbers
```

The .OP command, discussed in Chapter 4, is easy to remember: .OP omits page numbers. This command suppresses page numbering in the printed document; however, the status line on-screen continues to track page numbering. To specify the column number or the location in inches (noted by the inch sign) where you want the page numbers printed, type the .PC command with an appropriate number; in a new variation of this command, typing *0* centers page numbers between the current margins. After you embed an .OP command, use the .PG dot command to restore the printing of page numbers.

5

These auxiliary page-number dot commands take effect only when you print the document. When you edit, they don't change anything on-screen. They all can be overridden or replaced by header or footer commands (see this chapter's *Using Headers and Footers* section).

Veterans of early WordStar versions will find that printouts of documents created with those versions will appear different in Release 5 because of its default for the page-numbering column—28 instead of the 33 default in versions before Release 4. Typing *.pc 33* at the beginning of a document file preserves the appearance of printed documents created with early releases.

You can use the page-numbering dot commands to change the default settings in the combined sample ad document. With the cursor at the beginning of the document, type *.pn 10* and press Enter to start page numbering at 10, for continuation from a preceding file that ends on page 9. At column 1 on the next line, type *.pc 33* to cause page numbers to be printed at column 33, as in early WordStar releases. To omit page numbers in the document's outline section, move the cursor to the start of the outline, type *.op*, and press Enter. To restore page numbering after the outline, move the cursor to the line below the outline, type *.pg*, and press Enter.

You now have encountered all the major dot commands for the layout of document pages. Two more sets of dot commands affect the appearance of special text in a document. As an alternative to the new WordStar comment function, one set of commands inserts text in a file for on-screen notes and comments but doesn't print them. The other set of commands prints lines of text on every page of a document, above or below the text area, although you type the extra lines in the file only one time.

Using Comment Lines

Instead of using Release 5's new Notes feature, which obscures all but the first 15 characters of a comment on-screen (see *Using Note Functions* in this chapter), you may prefer to insert entire comment lines in your document without printing them. Editorial notations, last-minute addenda, document history, and other material can be fully displayed in a document file and not appear in printouts, thanks to two dot commands that act identically. These useful comment-line commands, which have been a part of WordStar for several years, tend to be overlooked by many users.

In Release 5, the comment-line commands appear on the second screen of dot-command help listings. At any help level except 4, pressing ^J. or F1. while editing and then pressing Enter twice displays the screen of dot commands that start with the letters *F* to *I*, as shown in figure 6.27.

On the second screen of dot-command listings, the following two commands are specified:

```
.ig text      Display "text" as nonprinting comment

..  text      Same as .ig
```

Both these dot commands perform the same function: they instruct the program to ignore the text on that line when the document is printed. These comment-line commands can be placed at column 1 of any line in a document. With an .IG or .. command embedded at the beginning of a line, the text can continue beyond the right margin to a length of 255 characters, although multiple comment lines should be used so that you can read comments within current screen limits.

As examples of embedding comments with dot commands in the combined ad document, insert comment lines at the beginning of the text. Move the cursor to column 1, and type the following:

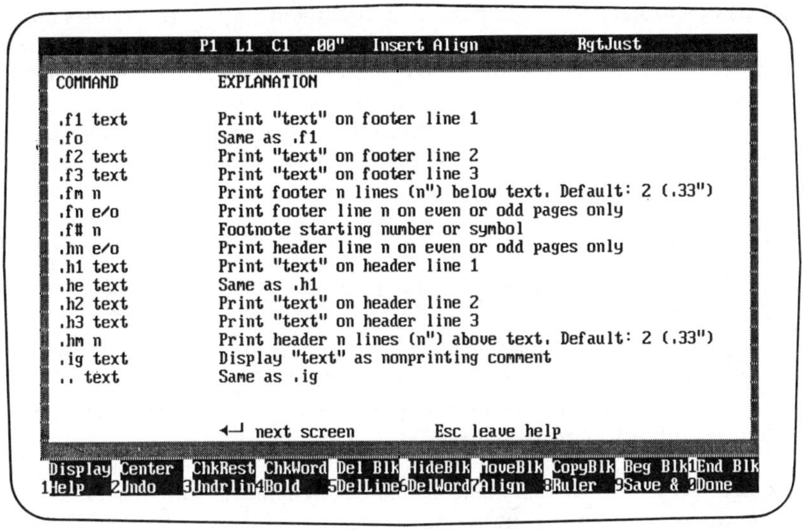
P1 L1 C1 .00" Insert Align RgtJust
COMMAND EXPLANATION
.f1 text Print "text" on footer line 1
.fo Same as .f1
.f2 text Print "text" on footer line 2
.f3 text Print "text" on footer line 3
.fm n Print footer n lines (n") below text. Default: 2 (.33")
.fn e/o Print footer line n on even or odd pages only
.f# n Footnote starting number or symbol
.hn e/o Print header line n on even or odd pages only
.h1 text Print "text" on header line 1
.he text Same as .h1
.h2 text Print "text" on header line 2
.h3 text Print "text" on header line 3
.hm n Print header n lines (n") above text. Default: 2 (.33")
.ig text Display "text" as nonprinting comment
.. text Same as .ig
next screen Esc leave help
Display Center ChkRest ChkWord Del Blk HideBlk MoveBlk CopyBlk Beg Blk End Blk
1Help 2Undo 3Undrlin 4Bold 5DelLine 6DelWord 7Align 8Ruler 9Save & 0Done

Fig. 6.27.
WordStar's second screen of dot-command help listings.

.IG Documents related to Super Widgets launch TV ads

Press Enter, and on the next two lines type this text:

.. Store file through end of campaign

.. --Bill

These annotations will not be printed, nor will they affect the on-screen line counts on the status line.

Using Headers and Footers

Printing lines of text at the top or bottom of each page in a document can be helpful for identifying the title, the author, or the draft version for multipage printouts. Among WordStar's pioneering features was the capability of printing single-line headers and footers automatically throughout documents, later expanded to three lines each for headers and footers.

The latest WordStar release expands the versatility of header and footer dot commands with the capability of easily specifying different text for odd- and even-numbered pages, as in book-style pagination (in the preceding version of the program such a function required an awkward print control command). A maximum of 100 characters can be printed in either a header or footer; however, you can increase this limit with the WSCHANGE program (see Chapter 11).

To print headers or footers on every page of a document, type a dot command at the beginning of your file. Then type the text of the header or footer after the dot command. WordStar is preset to enter page numbers automatically as a footer; when you enter a dot command to set a footer, the default page numbering is disabled. Headers and footers are printed within the top and bottom margins of the page, but they are not counted as lines of text when you calculate the height of body text.

Setting Headers and Footers

The text of headers or footers will be printed on each page of a document from the page where you enter the dot commands through the end of your text. The commands for headers and footers should appear at the beginning of any document in which you intend to print them.

5

In WordStar Release 5, two of the dot commands for headers and footers are at help level 4 on the pull-down Layout menu:

```
Header...              .h1
Footer...              .f1
```

Information about header and footer functions occupies most of the second screen of dot-command help listings available at all help levels but 4 (refer to fig. 6.27). Commands for setting headers or footers require that you type text after them and then press Enter. The dot-command help screen lists these header and footer commands:

```
.f1 text   Print "text" on footer line 1
.fo        Same as .f1
.f2 text   Print "text" on footer line 2
.f3 text   Print "text" on footer line 3
.fm n      Print footer n lines (n") below text. Default: 2 (.33")
.fn e/o    Print footer line n on even or odd pages only
.f# n      Footnote starting number or symbol
.hn e/o    Print header n on even or odd pages only
.h1 text   Print "text" on header line 1
.he text   Same as .h1
.h2 text   Print "text" on header line 2
.h3 text   Print "text" on header line 3
.hm n      Print header n lines (n") above text. Default: 2 (.33")
```

Header and footer commands are toggles. Using the same dot command without text turns off header or footer printing. When header and footer text is printed, text (including spaces) starts at the left margin on the line that contains the dot command. When one space (or none) appears between a dot command and its text, the document's header or footer begins at column 1. When two spaces appear, header or footer text begins at column 2, and so on.

Page numbers can be inserted automatically in a header or footer by typing a number sign (#) in the dot-command line. For example, to print *Page 1* and subsequent numbers in a header, you type *.h1 Page #*. To position the header material in the top right corner, you place the appropriate number of spaces between the dot command and *Page #*. To actually print a number sign (#), you must precede it with a backslash (\) in the dot-command text. For example, the command *.fo Revision \#2* prints as *Revision #2*. To print a backslash in header or footer text, you must type two backslashes (\ \).

To add simple headers and footers to the combined ad document used previously, move the cursor to the beginning of the report and type these two header lines:

.H1 Super Widgets Campaign

.H2 11/31/88

Remember to press Enter after each line. Then add a footer line for page numbers to be printed as text and digits by typing the following command at column 1, immediately after the .H2 command (remember to press Enter):

.F1 Page #

When you print this document, each page will have the header text you entered and will be numbered at the bottom as *Page 1*, *Page 2*, and so forth.

Even after such modest additions, you can see how manipulating header and footer lines can enhance the presentation of multipage documents. WordStar includes several features for further control of header and footer appearance. These are discussed in the next section.

Formatting Headers and Footers

In addition to the dot commands for creating headers and footers detailed in the preceding section, WordStar includes several functions for enhancing their format when printed. By invoking combinations of these features, you can tailor header and footer text to fit your word processing applications.

Two dot commands set the number of blank lines between a header or footer and the main text of a document. These header and footer margin commands are listed in table 6.9: .HM and .FM. You can remember these dot commands by the functions they invoke: .HM for header margin and .FM for footer margin. Both commands must be accompanied by the number of lines or inches (with the inch sign) between the body of the text and the last header line or the first footer line.

The total number of header lines and header margin lines (or their equivalent in inches) must be less than or equal to the top margin setting. Similarly, total footer lines and footer margin lines (or inch equivalents) must be less than or equal to the bottom margin setting. If header or footer line totals are greater than the margin settings, formatting is disrupted by text that "creeps" beyond the page boundaries.

Caution: WordStar's default settings for a top margin of 3 (.5″) and a header margin of 2 (.33″) leave room for only one line (.17″) of header text. To make room for multiple-line headers, you can alter WordStar's settings with either the header-margin dot command .HM 0 (for 0 lines between header and text) or the top-margin dot command .MT 5 (to widen the top margin 5 more lines). Just as you can modify most other page-layout parameters, header and footer margins can be modified permanently with the WSCHANGE program (see Chapter 11).

If you want to leave an extra blank line between two lines of text in a header or a footer, instead of typing text after a .H2 or .F2 command, just press the space bar twice and press Enter.

5

When you print a document that will be reproduced with book-style pagination, Release 5's new dot command can alternate formats for left and right headers or footers. As noted in the preceding section's listing, typing *e* or *o* directly after the appropriate dot command will cause the text that follows to print on only even (left-hand) or odd (right-hand) pages. For instance, typing *.hee Title* and *.heo Chapter* will cause the word *Title* to print only on left-hand pages and *Chapter* to print only on right-hand pages, as in a standard book-style format.

If you place print-control commands such as ^PS for underlining or ^PB for boldface in the header or footer command lines, the program recognizes those commands. Although the effects of the print-control commands are not displayed on-screen, the control codes (^S or ^B) are entered, and the header or footer text reflects the enhancement when printed. Print-control commands inserted in header or footer text do not modify the printing of body text, nor do print controls in the rest of the document alter the header and footer text. Header codes must be entered at line 1, or else the settings take effect on the next page.

Header and footer text is printed consistently throughout a document, retaining the same line height and font you set—even if you change these settings later within a document. In header or footer text, the first line sets line height and other formatting parameters for the second and third lines as well.

For examples of header and footer formatting options, set the header in your combined ad document to print in boldface. Precede the text in the header line at the top of your document by pressing ^PB (^B on-screen). Create alternate footer formats by typing *.f1 o* so that page numbers appear only on odd-numbered pages.

You have used WordStar's range of advanced formatting features on the sample documents presented in this chapter. When combining functions, you can easily lose track of the effects produced when you print your documents. The print-control commands and the dot commands that don't show their effects on-screen during editing can cause confusion. A test printout can demonstrate a document's final appearance, but an improved function in Release 5 saves time and paper, and makes previewing a document's appearance on-screen easier and more accurate with WordStar than with most word processing programs.

Using Page Preview

An invaluable function in any word processing program is the capability of previewing the appearance of a document on-screen before printing. Earlier versions of WordStar had only limited previewing capability, with on-screen format commands: the ^OD command to hide print-control commands and restore accurate line formatting, and the ^OP command to suppress dot-command display while maintaining most of these commands' on-screen effects. But neither of these preview functions could show the actual results of header and footer commands, italicized print, font changes, and other essential print effects.

With Release 5, WordStar's preview feature has not only caught up with competing word processing programs, but it has surpassed them. WordStar's publisher, MicroPro International, is so proud of the new preview function that the company has coined the name *Advanced Page Preview* and is claiming it as a trademark. Observers of the personal computer industry agree that this may well be the most advanced preview function currently available on IBM PC- and PS/2-compatible computers. The preview command remains the same as in earlier releases, but not its on-screen effect.

To show exactly what will appear on a printed page, WordStar's new preview feature translates characters and their formatting attributes into an accurate graphic representation on-screen. That's why this feature requires a computer system with graphics hardware—both a graphics adapter (CGA, EGA, or VGA) and a corresponding monitor. Unfortunately, systems equipped with a monochrome adapter and screen cannot take advantage of this feature. Depending on your graphics equipment, WordStar can now preview as many as 144 pages of text on-screen at one time. Most users will prefer to see one or two pages on-screen at a time, with the option of "zooming" in on just a portion of a page for greater detail.

Advanced Page Preview shows almost all on-screen formatting, including underline, italic, fonts, and notes (endnotes are not reproduced).

Because WordStar and the Advanced Page Preview together require 640K of memory, you cannot preview a page unless you have full random-access memory—free of any memory-resident programs such as PC-Outline.

To run Advanced Page Preview, the following files (all on the Advanced Page Preview disk) must be on the same disk and directory as the WS.EXE WordStar program file: PREVIEW.OVR (preview function program file), PREVIEW.MSG (preview messages), FONTID.CTL (font identification), and several font-display generating files with the file extension WSF. The Advanced Page Preview disk includes 14

WSF files. However, if you have WordStar on a floppy disk system, you may have room for only a few WSF files. If you have limited disk space for storing WSF files, you may want to load NPSHLV1.WSF and NPSHLV2.WSF. On a hard disk system you can copy several or all of the Advanced Page Preview WSF files.

When selecting WSF files to include with WordStar, you can identify the files according to their beginning letters: PS indicates proportional fonts, NPS indicates non-proportional fonts, HLV represents Helvetica-style sans serif fonts, and TMS indicates Times Roman-like serif fonts. Numbers in the WSF file names mean the following: 1 is for normal fonts, 2 is for italic, 3 is for bold, and 4 is for bold italic.

After you load the proper files, Advanced Page Preview can be started at any time from the Edit screen.

5

At help level 4, Release 5's pull-down Layout menu shows the command for invoking the preview feature:

```
Page preview                    ^OP
```

At help level 4, 3, or 2, the command for starting the preview feature appears on the Onscreen Format Menu in the column labeled DISPLAY, as follows:

```
P page preview
```

5

The full command sequence for advanced page preview is ^OP. Pressing ^OP clears the screen immediately, but depending on the speed and memory capacity of your computer and the complexity of your document, you may have to wait several seconds before your text is shown on-screen.

Release 5 includes another way to start Advanced Page Preview: pressing Alt-1 while editing performs the same function as pressing ^OP. Once invoked, the preview display shows the entire current page on about two-thirds of the full screen, with a line of available commands above the display, as illustrated in figure 6.28.

Pressing the initial for any of the four commands at the top of the Preview screen displays a pull-down menu with two to seven possible actions. In turn, any of these menu choices can be selected by the point-and-shoot method of moving the cursor with the up- or down-arrow keys and pressing Enter, or by simply typing the initial letter of your choice. The principal preview commands and their pull-down menu listings are summarized in table 6.11.

Table 6.11
Page Preview Commands and Choices

Command	*Choices*
Go To	Specified page First page Last page Next page Previous page

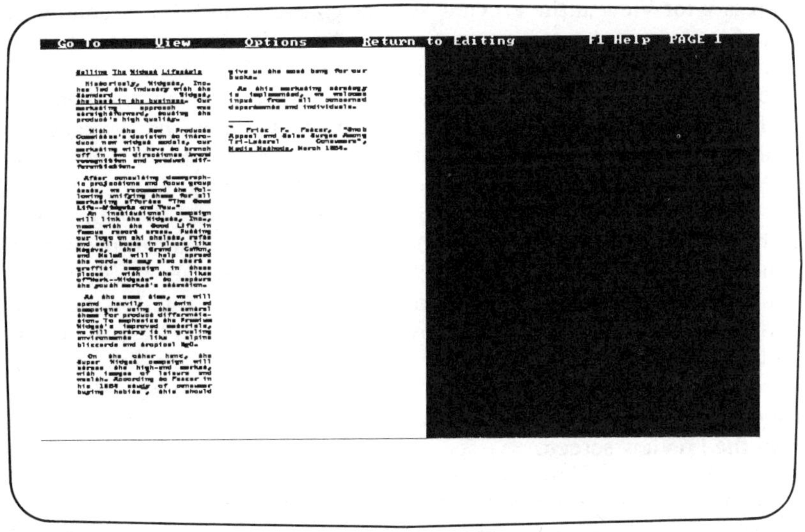
Go To
View
Options
Return to Editing
F1 Help
PAGE 1

Fig. 6.28.
The Entire Page display with WordStar's Advanced Page Preview function.

View	Entire page Facing pages Multiple pages Thumbnail display 2X zoom 4X zoom Adjust window
Options	Automatic scan Scan Range. . . Grid display On/off
Return to Editing	Original page Current page

Page preview commands can be used to select which pages to display on-screen, the amount of text shown (from part of a page to dozens of pages), options for scanning through text, and where in the document to return to editing.

The page in your document from which you invoke the preview function is the one shown on-screen; its page number is indicated at the top right of the screen. Pressing G for Go To displays a pull-down menu with five choices. If you press S, you can designate a page to be previewed by number. The four other menu listings are for strategic page choices: F to move to the first page in the document, L to move to the last page, N for the next page after the current one, and P for the preceding page. These same pages can be chosen directly from the Preview screen by pressing the Home or End keys for the first or last pages of the document; pressing PgDn or PgUp keys moves to the next or previous pages.

When you press V for View at the Preview screen, you see a pull-down menu with seven choices for the amount of text to display. The Entire Page view is the one shown when you invoke the Preview command. Pressing F for Facing Pages puts two pages on-screen, as if you were looking at a book open to those pages. Selecting M for Multiple Pages displays four pages on a CGA monitor, six pages on an EGA monitor, or 10 pages on a VGA monitor. Press T for Thumbnail Display and you can see 10 pages with a CGA, 18 pages with an EGA (see fig. 6.29), 32 pages with a VGA, or 144 pages on a high-resolution display. Of course, the more pages on-screen, the less detail you can see. For close-ups of a page, you can press 2 for 2X Zoom, showing about half a page complete with legible fonts (see fig. 6.30). For an even closer view, press 4 for 4X Zoom. To select a specific area within the page, press A for Adjust Window and use the arrow keys or the numeric keypad keys to move a window around a miniature view of the page; pressing Enter returns to the close-up view of that section of the page. Whichever view you choose, pressing + or – lets you increase or decrease the magnification of a page or set of pages directly from the Preview screen.

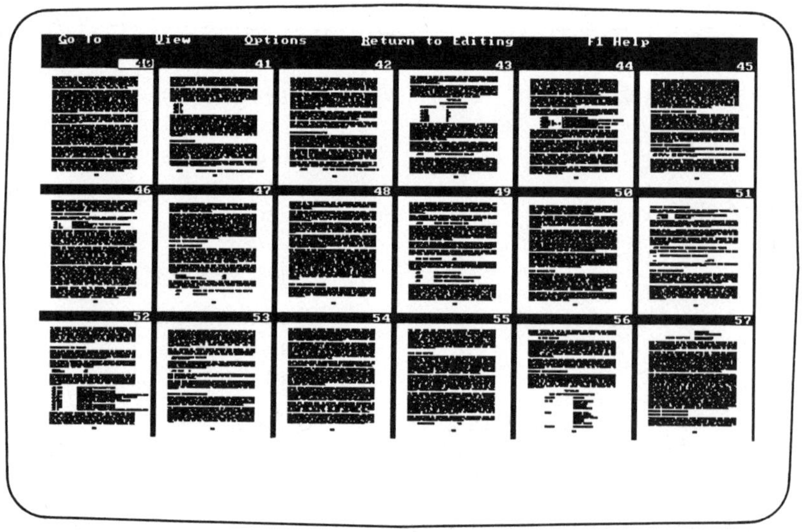
Go To
View
Options
Return to Editing
F1 Help
40
41
42
43
44
45
46
47
48
49
50
51
52
53
54
55
56
57

Fig. 6.29.
The Thumbnail Display with WordStar's Advanced Page Preview function on an EGA monitor.

Pressing O for Options provides three useful choices. Select A to scan forward through the pages of your document until you press Esc. Press S to specify a beginning and end page between which to scan. Press G to superimpose a grid on-screen so that you can check text alignment.

While previewing a document, you cannot edit the material on-screen. To change what you see or to save the document to disk, you first must go back to the Edit screen. Pressing R for Return to Editing displays two possibilities. Press O, and the Edit screen will show the page you were on before invoking page preview; press C to edit the page currently shown or highlighted on the Preview screen. These same choices can be made directly from the preview display by pressing Alt-1 or Esc to edit the page currently on-screen, or Alt-2 to return to editing your original page.

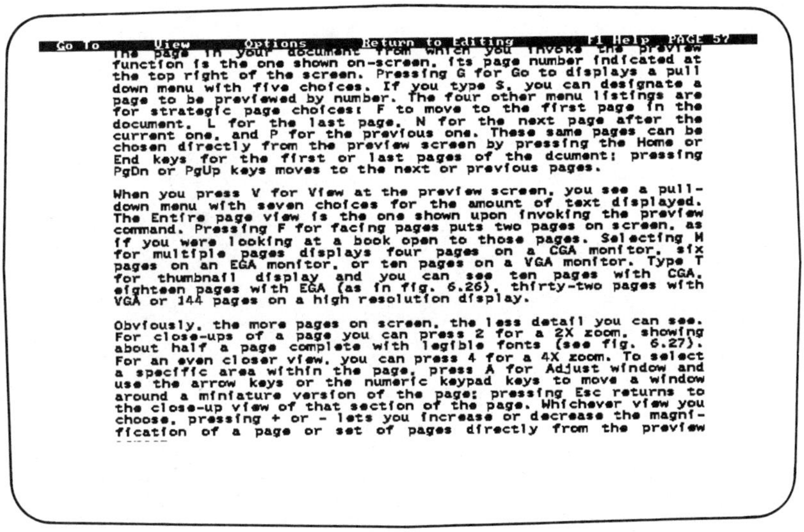
Go To View Options Return to Editing F1 Help PAGE 57
The page in your document from which you invoke the preview function is the one shown on-screen. its page number indicated at the top right of the screen. Pressing G for Go to displays a pull down menu with five choices. If you type S, you can designate a page to be previewed by number. The four other menu listings are for strategic page choices: F to move to the first page in the document. L for the last page. N for the next page after the current one, and P for the previous one. These same pages can be chosen directly from the preview screen by pressing the Home or End keys for the first or last pages of the dcument; pressing PgDn or PgUp keys moves to the next or previous pages.
When you press V for View at the preview screen, you see a pull-down menu with seven choices for the amount of text displayed. The Entire page view is the one shown upon invoking the preview command. Pressing F for facing pages puts two pages on screen, as if you were looking at a book open to those pages. Selecting M for multiple pages displays four pages on a CGA monitor, six pages on an EGA monitor, or ten pages on a VGA monitor. Type T for thumbnail display and you can see ten pages with CGA, eighteen pages with EGA (as in fig. 6.26), thirty-two pages with VGA or 144 pages on a high resolution display.
Obviously, the more pages on screen, the less detail you can see. For close-ups of a page you can press 2 for a 2X zoom, showing about half a page complete with legible fonts (see fig. 6.27). For an even closer view, you can press 4 for a 4X zoom. To select a specific area within the page, press A for Adjust window and use the arrow keys or the numeric keypad keys to move a window around a miniature version of the page; pressing Esc returns to the close-up view of that section of the page. Whichever view you choose, pressing + or - lets you increase or decrease the magnification of a page or set of pages directly from the preview

Fig. 6.30.

The 2X Zoom display with WordStar's Advanced Page Preview function.

For an example of page preview, invoke this feature for the snaking-column-formatted document (refer to fig. 6.26). To see how the document will print, simply press ^OP from the Edit screen. The Preview screen looks like the one shown in figure 6.31. Pressing Alt-2 returns you to the Edit screen.

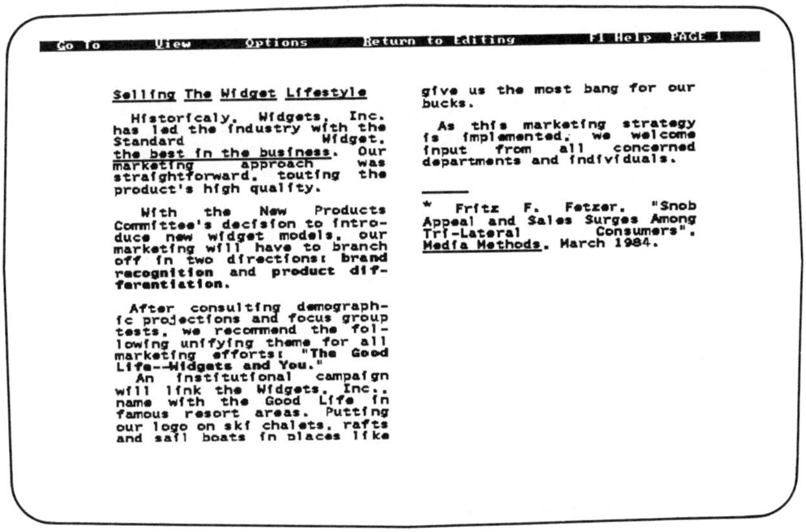
Go To View Options Return to Editing F1 Help PAGE 1
Selling The Widget Lifestyle
Historicaly, Widgets, Inc. has led the industry with the Standard Widget, the best in the business. Our marketing approach was straightforward, touting the product's high quality.
With the New Products Committee's decision to introduce new widget models, our marketing will have to branch off in two directions: brand recognition and product differentiation.
After consulting demographic projections and focus group tests, we recommend the following unifying theme for all marketing efforts: "The Good Life--Widgets and You."
An institutional campaign will link the Widgets, Inc., name with the Good Life in famous resort areas. Putting our logo on ski chalets, rafts and sail boats in places like
give us the most bang for our bucks.
As this marketing strategy is implemented, we welcome input from all concerned departments and individuals.
* Fritz F. Fetzer. "Snob Appeal and Sales Surges Among Tri-Lateral Consumers". Media Methods. March 1984.

Fig. 6.31.

The WordStar Advanced Page Preview function used on snaking columns.

7

Using WordStar's Printing Options

Of all WordStar's features, printing has evolved the most over the life of the program. In less than a decade WordStar has gone from printer output to simple draft printers to full support for the latest laser printers with multiple fonts, the PostScript document description language, and even color. Whether you use a dot-matrix, daisywheel, or laser printer, WordStar provides a full complement of options for tailoring the printing process to your system.

Until now, this book has bypassed printing choices when printing a document. This chapter describes all of WordStar's printing options, control commands for invoking special functions, and dot commands that change printer settings. You learn another three dozen WordStar commands—about equally divided between Ctrl-letter commands and dot commands. Some commands invoke tasks that any printer can carry out; other commands invoke functions available only on certain printers.

You learn how to do the following:

- Designate a printer, multiple copies, pauses, page numbers
- Invoke special printer description files for custom output
- Specify fonts and colors to give greater impact to documents
- Use extended characters for symbols and foreign languages

Veterans of earlier WordStar releases will appreciate the complete overhaul of printing possibilities in WordStar Release 5. It includes a new printing options dialog box as well as seven innovative print control commands for full mastery over font selection, color printing, invoking the IBM extended character set, and other vital functions. In place of earlier versions' printer drivers, WordStar Release 5 uses four basic drivers and printer description files (PDFs) that modify a printer driver to support particular printer features. More than 100 PDFs are included in the WordStar Release 5 package, and 100 more are available from MicroPro upon request, giving unprecedented control over a vast array of printers.

Selectively applying the commands in this chapter enhances any printing application. The commands discussed in this chapter relate to individual printouts. Merge printing for applications such as multiple mailings is covered in Chapter 8. You can also program printer adjustments into WordStar with WSCHANGE, as noted in Chapter 11. The commands described in the following sections give you greater control of documents at print time.

Using Print-Time Options

Whichever method you use to invoke document printing—selecting Print a File on the pull-down File Menu at help level 4 from the Opening display, pressing P at the Opening Menu at other help levels, or pressing ^KP within a document—WordStar provides useful print-time options for printing your document.

In previous versions of WordStar, options for controlling a print run were shown one at a time as a series of prompts after you entered the name of the document to be printed. Veteran users and newcomers will benefit from seeing all these choices at once in the new Print dialog box, with space for typing responses to eight different print-time options. The Print dialog box was seen by anyone following Quick Start 2 in Chapter 1 and is shown in figure 7.1. Before, it was used only to enter the name of the file to be printed. In this chapter you learn how to use the options in the Print dialog box.

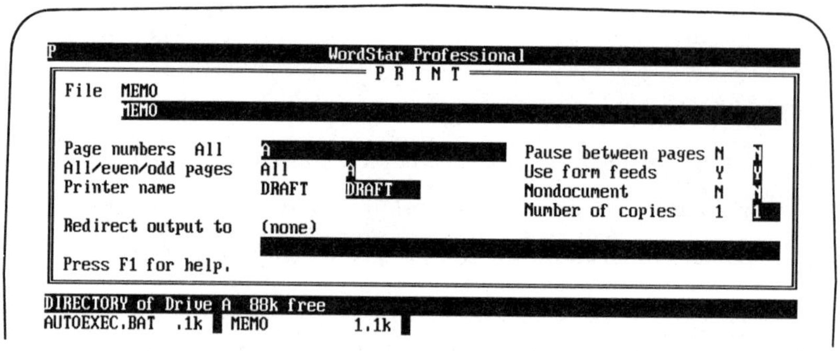
WordStar Professional
P R I N T
File MEMO
MEMO
Page numbers All
All/even/odd pages All
Printer name DRAFT DRAFT
Redirect output to (none)
Press F1 for help.
Pause between pages N
Use form feeds Y
Nondocument N
Number of copies 1
DIRECTORY of Drive A 88k free
AUTOEXEC.BAT .1k
MEMO 1.1k

Fig. 7.1.
The Print dialog box.

WordStar veterans will find the order of printing choices changed from earlier releases. Added to the options are functions that let you print even- or odd-numbered pages of a document and redirect printer output. Being able to view all print-time options on one display, along with the added selections, makes printing with WordStar easier than ever.

The options in the dialog box can be accessed after you specify the name of the file to print or accept the default (the last file printed) and press Enter. If you press ^K or the F10 key without changing any of the listed responses, WordStar uses all the options' default settings. You can reset any of the options in the dialog box by moving the cursor to the desired setting with the up- and down-arrow keys and typing a new response. Pressing Enter to accept a default advances the cursor through the options in the print-time options box as well. If you make a mistake, you can use WordStar's deletion commands to remove a response, then retype it. Unlike previous WordStar editions, in WordStar Release 5 pressing Esc while at the print-time options cancels printing and returns you to where printing was invoked. To start printing from the Print dialog box, the correct command is ^K or F10.

In several cases, functions covered by the printing options can be invoked in an alternative manner, by placing in a document a print-control or dot command to be executed at print time. Such commands within a document guarantee that a desired option is applied and allow you to bypass on-screen print options.

Specifying Pages To Print

Selecting specific amounts of text to be printed, from an entire document to individual pages or sets of pages, is essential to efficient use of any word processor. WordStar Release 5 makes it simple to specify which pages you want to print.

5

In WordStar Release 5, the first modifiable printing option combines what were two separate page options in earlier program versions. The cursor flashes at the `Page numbers` prompt, replacing previous starting and ending page number options. The complete prompt for this setting is the following:

```
Page numbers    All      A
```

WordStar is preset to print all the pages of a designated file—starting with page 1 or the first numbered page if you have specified different page numbers with a .PN dot command (see Chapter 6) and continuing through to the last page in the file. Typing a numerical response at the `Page numbers` prompt limits printing only to the pages you list.

You can type a single page number or specify several individual pages by separating their numbers with commas. You can specify a range of pages to be printed by typing the first page number, a hyphen, and the last page number. You can combine ranges and individual pages. For example, typing *3-7,9,12* instructs WordStar to print pages 3 through 7, 9, and 12.

If you specify a page number more than a few pages from the beginning of a document, you notice a pause before printing starts as WordStar finds the desired page. Typing a number greater than the final document page number results in printing that continues through the last page.

If you mistakenly type a character or symbol other than a number and press Enter, WordStar displays this error message:

```
Enter page numbers.  Example:  3,5-7,17,20-22

Press Esc to continue.
```

To resume selection of pages to print, press Esc and type an appropriate number or set of numbers.

With WordStar Release 5, the option of printing only even- or odd-numbered pages has its own prompt. After indicating the page numbers to be printed and pressing Enter, advance the cursor in the Print dialog box to the next line, where you see the following option, new in this version of WordStar:

```
All/even/odd pages   All       A
```

The default setting for printing all designated pages can be changed easily. Pressing E results in only even-numbered pages being printed; pressing O specifies that only odd-numbered pages are printed.

Practice specifying pages to be printed by using the combined AD document created and modified in Chapter 6. Set the combined document's page numbering to start with page 10. You can print the following pages by typing *11-13* at the `Page numbers` prompt and pressing Enter. To limit printing to the odd-numbered pages, press O at the `All/even/odd pages` prompt and then press Enter.

Pausing between Document Pages

Being able to pause printing between pages of a document is indispensable if you use single sheets of paper rather than continuous-feed (or fanfold) paper. As explained in Chapter 4, one way to pause printing is to invoke the control command ^PC. For long documents, however, you should select the pause option when you invoke printing.

In an unmodified copy of WordStar Release 5, the Print dialog box prompt for pausing printing, including defaults, is the following:

```
Pause between pages N   N
```

Yes and No are the only possible settings. If you press Enter without typing a response, WordStar does not pause between pages during printing. Pressing another key before you press Enter displays the following error message:

```
Please enter Y for yes or N for no.

Press Esc to continue.
```

Pressing the appropriate key after the Esc key sets the option to pause after each page or to print the document without stopping.

If you choose to pause printing, WordStar halts printer operation after the last line of a page. To resume printing, press P (at help level 4, FP) and then C to continue.

Try the Pause Between Pages option for the combined AD document. At the prompt, press Y and then Enter. After printing starts, WordStar pauses at the end of each page. To restart printing, press P, then C.

Using Form Feeds and Line Feeds

In word processing operations, a form feed is a special character that instructs the printer to advance to the top of the next page. WordStar should send a form feed to the printer when page lengths vary in a document or when you use a laser printer or a sheet feeder. Check your printer's manual to be sure that it recognizes form feeds.

In WordStar Release 5, the prompt for invoking form feeds is as follows:

```
Use form feeds Y    Y
```

Respond to the `Use form feeds` prompt by pressing Y or N, then Enter.

The default setting, Yes, is accepted if you type nothing before you press Enter. If you respond No to the form-feed prompt, WordStar uses a line feed; this is a series of characters that WordStar usually uses to end a line. Line feeds are described later in this section.

Pressing a key other than Y or N before pressing Enter displays this message:

```
Please enter Y for yes or N for no.

Press Esc to continue.
```

Pressing either key after Esc replaces the character at the prompt, setting the option for issuing or omitting form feeds.

Another way to invoke form feeds is by placing a control command sequence at the points in a document where the printer should advance to the top of the next page. In WordStar Release 5, the command sequence is not listed on any of the menus. As in previous versions, however, the form-feed print-control command is ^PL.

Wherever a document should be advanced to the next page during printing, press ^PL. You can enter the command anywhere on a line. Where you type *^pl*, you see `^L` followed by a dotted line that looks like a page break symbol, with an F in the far right column to indicate a form feed:

```
^L -------------------------------------------------------------F
```

Any printer that recognizes form feeds automatically begins a new page at a form-feed print-control character. In effect, ^PL is the equivalent of a .PA page-break command, although no footer or page number is printed on the page following the ^PL command.

For printers that require a form-feed code different from the one in WordStar's PDF, WordStar Release 5 includes the special dot command .XL. This command, followed by code specified in your printer manual, redefines the form-feed command ^PL or the feeds issued automatically by answering Y to the `Use form feeds` prompt.

On occasion, you may want to issue line feeds from somewhere within a document to advance the printer carriage. This print-time function is easy to invoke if you plan ahead. A line feed advances the print head to the same column on the next line, instead of to column 1 as in the case of a carriage return.

Though not listed on any of WordStar's menus, typing *^pj* in the text produces a line feed at print time. ^PJ splits the line (sending the right side to column 1 on the next line) and places a J at the flag column on the right side of the screen. If a printer acknowledges line feeds, as most do, an embedded ^PJ advances the print head to the next line and resumes printing in the column after the one containing the line-feed character.

For examples of invoking form feeds in the sample AD document, place ^PL print commands in the text itself or wait until print time, and at the `Use form feeds` prompt, press Y, then Enter. For a line feed in your document, type *^pj* on page 1 to end the first paragraph of the memo; you see the line split and a `J` appears on right side of the screen. When printing your document, WordStar invokes a line feed to set off the table that follows.

Printing a Nondocument File

Because a nondocument file has no need for special formatting effects, it can be printed literally without regard to dot commands or other print controls.

The prompt for printing a nondocument file is as follows:

```
Nondocument    N  N
```

Pressing Y prints a nondocument file with WordStar's default settings for page formatting, including margin limits and page breaks. If you are printing a document file and press Y, WordStar reproduces all the dot commands in the file without executing them. If you do not want to apply this option, press N or Enter.

In the sample AD document, you can put on paper a record of the dot commands used to format the file. Press Y at the nondocument prompt and your file prints with all dot commands showing.

Printing Multiple Copies

Printing more than one copy of text at a time, without having to invoke the print command for each copy, enhances your efficiency when using WordStar. When you set a single option at print time, you can produce duplicate copies of a document as easily as making copies with a copying machine.

The Print dialog box option for multiple copies is as follows:

```
Number of copies     1   1
```

Typing a number at the `Number of copies` prompt and pressing Enter sets your print run for that many copies of the pages previously designated. The default setting is 1. The space at the cursor for this option allows up to 999 copies to be specified.

If you press another character instead of a number and then press Enter, WordStar displays this error message:

```
Only numbers are valid.

Press Esc to continue.
```

After pressing Esc, you can type the appropriate number of copies to be printed.

WordStar also provides a dot command that you can use from within a document to specify multiple copies at print time. Early releases of WordStar included this command in the optional MailMerge module. WordStar Release 4 and WordStar Release 5 include the command as part of the main program.

The dot command for printing multiple copies is on the fifth screen of dot-command help listings after the introductory screen. At all help levels, except 4, this fifth screen is displayed by pressing ^J or F1 and a period (.) from within a document (see fig. 7.2). The command for printing multiple copies is listed as follows:

```
.rp n              Print file n times
```

To repeat printing of a document, type *.rp* at the beginning of your text, starting in column 1, followed by a space and the number of copies to be printed.

Early releases of WordStar recognized .RP only if it was used with a data file for merge printing. In WordStar Release 5, this command should *not* be used with a merge printing data file. To produce multiple copies when merge printing data files, the `Number of copies` option should be used at print time.

Try printing multiple copies of a document by using the combined AD document created earlier. Type *.rp* at the beginning of the file and press Enter to obtain two copies. You can use the multiple-copy option instead simply by typing *2* at the `Number of copies` prompt.

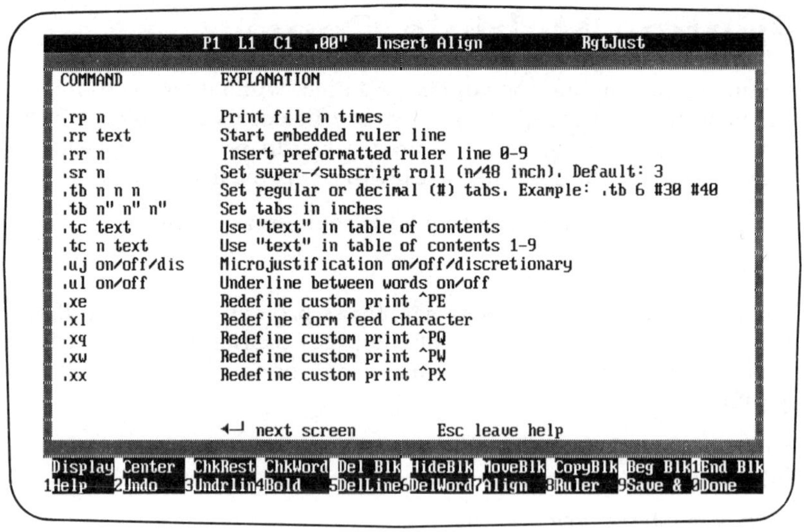
P1 L1 C1 .00" Insert Align RgtJust
COMMAND EXPLANATION
.rp n Print file n times
.rr text Start embedded ruler line
.rr n Insert preformatted ruler line 0-9
.sr n Set super-/subscript roll (n/48 inch). Default: 3
.tb n n n Set regular or decimal (#) tabs. Example: .tb 6 #30 #40
.tb n" n" n" Set tabs in inches
.tc text Use "text" in table of contents
.tc n text Use "text" in table of contents 1-9
.uj on/off/dis Microjustification on/off/discretionary
.ul on/off Underline between words on/off
.xe Redefine custom print ^PE
.xl Redefine form feed character
.xq Redefine custom print ^PQ
.xw Redefine custom print ^PW
.xx Redefine custom print ^PX
next screen Esc leave help
Display Center ChkRest ChkWord Del Blk HideBlk MoveBlk CopyBlk Beg Blk End Blk
1Help 2Undo 3Undrlin 4Bold 5DelLine 6DelWord 7Align 8Ruler 9Save & 0Done

Fig. 7.2.
Screen showing dot command for printing multiple copies.

Designating a Printer

Most WordStar users have systems with one printer, designated the default printer during installation (see Chapter 2). If you replace your printer with another model, the default printer can be reset with WSCHANGE—as noted in Chapter 11. However, if you use more than one printer with your system, or if you print a WordStar Release 5 file created on a system with another printer, you can designate a different printer and its associated PDF, either with a print-time option or during editing of a document.

In previous versions of WordStar, printer drivers were invoked only when a file was to be printed. With WordStar Release 5, every document file includes at its beginning a code for the name of the PDF with which it is meant to be used. This PDF is usually the default set for your system during installation and must be reset if you use a different printer model.

In the Print dialog box, the printer selection prompt is as follows:

```
Printer name          DRAFT     DRAFT
```

If you installed a specific printer model as the default printer, that name appears here in the Print dialog box. When the cursor is at this prompt, the contents of the directory at the bottom of the screen do not contain the names of standard disk files as with the other print-time options, but rather a list of installed PDFs. This list includes nine special-purpose ones (the DRAFT printer description file among them) discussed later in this chapter. Depending on which printers you installed for your system, the screen looks similar to the one shown in figure 7.3.

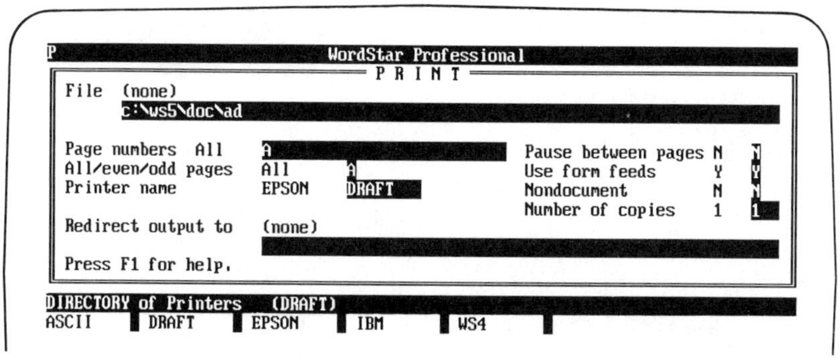
P WordStar Professional
PRINT
File (none)
c:\ws5\doc\ad
Page numbers All
All/even/odd pages All
Printer name EPSON DRAFT
Redirect output to (none)
Press F1 for help.
Pause between pages N
Use form feeds Y
Nondocument N
Number of copies 1
DIRECTORY of Printers (DRAFT)
ASCII DRAFT EPSON IBM WS4

Fig. 7.3.
WordStar's print-time options and directory of printer description files.

To use the default printer, press Enter to advance to the next print-time option, or press ^K or F10 to accept the remaining option defaults and immediately start the default printer.

You can select any of the alternative PDFs by typing the printer name at the prompt or by using the arrow keys to bring the cursor to the appropriate name. Press Enter, ^K, or F10, and the designated printer is used from the port set in the PDF. This port can be reset with the WSCHANGE program (see Chapter 11) or with a print-time option, as explained in the next section of this chapter.

Because WordStar Release 5 document files also retain the name of the PDF with the fonts and other print characteristics included in its text, you can change the designated printer at any time during editing. WordStar makes the conversion of font designations to those available on the printer. The command for doing so is a simple print control sequence.

At all help levels except 1 and 0, the classic Print Controls Menu (displayed by pressing ^P during editing) includes the command for changing the printer default. The listing is as follows:

```
? select printer
```

When you press ^P?, WordStar displays a dialog box titled CHANGE PRINTER, which lists the default printer to be used with the document. At the bottom of the screen, shown in figure 7.4, is a list of available PDFs similar to the one shown at the print-time option for selecting a printer.

As with the print-time option, you can accept the default printer by pressing Enter or you can select an alternative PDF. To choose a different PDF, type the printer name as indicated on the screen directory or move the cursor to the appropriate name. Press Enter. The designated PDF then becomes the default when printing is invoked again in this and subsequent editing sessions.

When changing printers, you do not need to reopen a document and change fonts and other printing characteristics. WordStar Release 5 automatically translates the fonts in your file to those that most closely resemble it among the new printer's

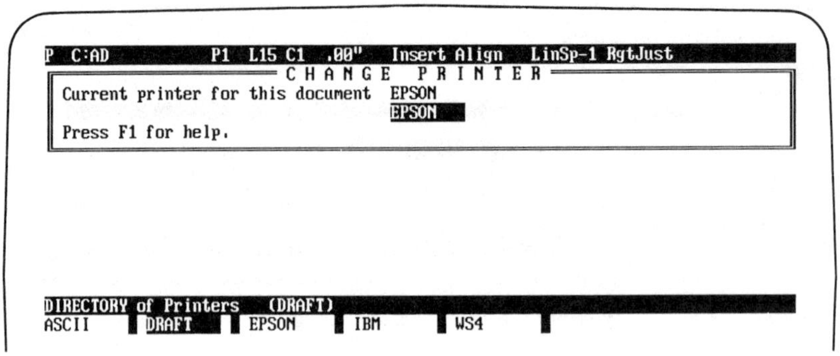
P C:AD P1 L15 C1 .00" Insert Align LinSp-1 RgtJust
C H A N G E P R I N T E R
Current printer for this document EPSON
EPSON
Press F1 for help.
DIRECTORY of Printers (DRAFT)
ASCII
DRAFT
EPSON
IBM
WS4

Fig. 7.4. *Designating a printer from within a document.*

functions. If sophisticated typestyles or colors are not supported by the new printer, simpler standard print characteristics are used.

Redirecting Printer Output

When a printer is installed with the WINSTALL program or with WSCHANGE, its PDF is set to send its output to a default system port, usually PRN or LPT1 for a parallel printer or COM1 for a serial printer. If you want to send output to a different port where the printer is currently connected, or to disk where printer output codes are to be stored as a separate file, use the last of the print-time options in the Print dialog box.

The prompt in the Print dialog box that lets you reset where printer output is sent appears as follows:

```
Redirect output to    (none)
```

If you press Enter, ^K, or F10, WordStar sends printer output to the default setting in the designated PDF. To send printer output to a different port, type *prn*, *lpt1*, *lpt2*, or *lpt3* for a parallel printer, or *com1* or *com2* for a serial printer port.

When you type a valid DOS file name (up to eight characters long) at the `Redirect output to` prompt, your printer output is saved on the default disk drive and directory as a disk file. To save this output to disk on a different drive or directory, type the appropriate file path before the file name. Saving printer output to disk is one of the useful functions available with WordStar's special-purpose PDFs. Printer output on disk is essential to the special purpose of PDFs—producing ASCII or WordStar Release 4-compatible files from WordStar documents.

Using Printer Description Files

In WordStar Release 5, the software instructions for running a printer properly are in one of four printer driver files: DRIVERN.OVR for most printers; DRIVERA.OVR for special-purpose printer drivers; DRIVERT.OVR for draft and generic printers, or DRIVERPS.OVR for PostScript-driven laser printers. Codes for modifying a driver and producing special types of output are stored as a PDF. When installed for a specific printer model, a PDF includes the proper codes to control features such as underlining, italic, font styles, size, spacing, and color. Other preinstalled PDFs are printer-independent, producing standardized output for special purposes such as translating WordStar Release 5 document files to formats readable by earlier versions of WordStar or by other word processing programs.

If you want to determine whether your working copy of WordStar has the correct PDF for your hardware, you can print the PRINT.TST file that is supplied with WordStar Release 5 on the Installation Disk. In its text, PRINT.TST includes nearly two dozen print effects that you can achieve with WordStar. To print the test file, make sure that the PRINT.TST file has been copied onto the disk with your working copy of WordStar, and invoke printing from the WordStar screen by pressing P (or FP). Designate the test file by typing *print.tst* or by pointing to the name with the cursor. Press ^K or F10 to begin printing immediately, or press Enter to go through the print-time options.

If any of the PRINT.TST file's features do not work properly with your printer, select a different printer driver and related PDF. (Check your printer manual for compatibility and functional specifications; also see Appendix B of this book.) At the print-time option for printer name, you may have to experiment with different installed printer description files. For example, one of the most common complaints about WordStar reported to MicroPro is that printers claiming compatibility with the popular Epson MX® and FX™ dot-matrix printer series do not respond to all of the Epson printer driver codes.

In addition to the more than 100 specific PDFs that can be installed with WordStar Release 5's WINSTALL or WSCHANGE programs, and the 100 more PDFs that can be ordered at no charge from MicroPro (see Appendix B), WordStar Release 5 has three generic printer drivers and two customizable ones, as well as four special drivers that are screen- or disk-oriented.

For specifics on printer drivers and printer description files supplied with WordStar Release 5, consult the chart in Appendix B.

Using Generic Printer Description Files

Among the preinstalled PDFs supplied with WordStar Release 5 are three generic ones. These printer description files, which have a minimum number of settings for the simplest of printer functions, can run most printers. All use the DRIVERT.OVR printer driver.

The most universally applicable of the generic PDFs is DRAFT, the default for an unmodified copy of WordStar. This PDF is for any nonbackspacing printer or line printer—the simplest of all models. Print effects such as boldface and overstrike are created by separate passes of the print head. More advanced features, such as variable character width, proportional spacing, or special fonts, are not supported. Because the DRAFT PDF can run a full range of models, from early units to the latest, you can select DRAFT as the PDF when you are in doubt. However, keep in mind that DRAFT requires many separate passes during printing and is, therefore, the slowest way to print a document.

The next most commonly used generic printer file is TYPEWR, for typewriter-like printers that can backspace a character at a time. Backspacing means that overprinting features such as boldface and double-strike can be produced more quickly. Although TYPEWR provides no support for advanced functions, this PDF is likely to run any common printer at its fastest print speed.

You can use the AUTOLF PDF for printers that automatically add a line feed—that is, they move the carriage up one line—when they receive a carriage return character. Such line feeds usually are issued by WordStar, but are suppressed in this case. The simple print functions supported by automatic line-feed printers are similar to those supported by typewriter-style printers. The AUTOLF PDF invokes backspacing to produce elementary print effects such as boldface and overstrike more quickly than DRAFT and TYPEWR drivers.

Customizing Printer Description Files

When none of the listed PDFs is right for your printer, you have the option of editing an existing printer-specific PDF or customizing either of two nonspecific PDFs to create your own PDF. With the WSCHANGE program described in Chapter 11, you can specify the control command sequences for boldface, underlining, and more advanced print features. You can use the strings of control commands shown in your printer manual for either of the customizable PDFs. These PDFs must be installed before they can be used with the DRIVERA.OVR printer driver.

The more straightforward of the customizable PDFs is the SIMPLE file. This PDF transmits all printer-control command codes directly as it encounters them in a document and prints each line of text in a single pass from left to right. Although the PDF may contain the correct codes for your printer, SIMPLE's transmission method may not work with more sophisticated printers. Also, the SIMPLE PDF does not compensate for failure to specify control character codes for all printer functions and therefore leaves some features inoperative.

The CUSTOM driver is the more accommodating of the customizable PDFs. CUSTOM prints a line in multiple passes and, using the printer's logic circuitry, can issue each control sequence as it is needed. CUSTOM also makes allowances for incomplete print-control code assignments. For instance, CUSTOM recognizes the control character code for underlining even if you haven't installed it.

The same strings of characters can be installed for both customizable PDFs. You can try your printer with both SIMPLE and CUSTOM PDFs to see which does the better job of activating printer features. Use the PRINT.TST file as a test document.

Because of greater standardization and sophistication among printer models, you may never need to create a customized PDF from scratch, as with SIMPLE and CUSTOM. An easier alternative is to customize a few settings for a model-specific PDF with WSCHANGE (see Chapter 11).

Printing to Disk with Special Printer Description Files

At times, you may want to reduce printer output to its simplest form, without any print enhancements. Such output would be useful not only when directed to a simple printer but also when stored to disk in a form compatible with other word processors. Such simplifying codes are included with WordStar Release 5 as special PDFs that are designed to modify the DRIVERA.OVR printer driver.

Four of the preinstalled PDFs in WordStar Release 5 are not meant to put text on paper directly, but are special PDFs that produce files to be stored on disk. These PDFs can be invoked just like other PDFs, either by typing their names at the print-time prompt `Printer name` or by installing one of them as a default PDF with the WSCHANGE program. Three of these special-function files will be familiar to veterans of the previous version of WordStar. A new PDF is used to convert WordStar Release 5 files into files readable by WordStar Release 4 and earlier program editions.

The PREVIEW PDF produces output to disk that is similar to the display you obtain with the ^OP advanced preview mode command (see Chapter 6). Selecting the PREVIEW PDF in response to the `Printer name` print-time prompt results in a disk file called PREVIEW.WS, unless you type a different name for the file at the

Redirect output prompt. When the resulting WS disk file is opened as a standard document file, you see what the document will look like when it is printed, complete with headers, footers, page breaks, and print controls displayed as on-screen attributes for underlining and boldface, for example. The file begins with a .PL command, which sets page length to the default of 66 lines, and each line ends with a hard carriage return.

You can use the XTRACT PDF to extract information from data files, as noted in Chapter 8. The output from the XTRACT driver is a disk file named XTRACT.WS, unless you type another name at the Redirect output prompt. The resulting file does not contain headers, footers, or page breaks, but can be used as a data file in its own right.

The output from the ASCII (American Standard Code for Information Interchange) PDF is similar to that from WordStar's nondocument mode. Selecting the ASCII PDF at print time produces a disk file named ASCII.WS (or a name you designate at the Redirect output prompt)—with no headers, footers, or print controls. WordStar's document-formatting peculiarities are converted to the "plain vanilla" file format, complete with hard carriage returns at the end of every line. This is the format readable by ASCII-compatible word processing programs and required by most electronic mail systems. Though printing to disk with the ASCII special driver can be a slow process, it is the only method of converting documents to ASCII format in WordStar Release 5 (the additional method available in WordStar Release 4, using ^QU in nondocument mode to strip out formatting high-bit codes, is no longer valid). For more information on using ASCII files, see Chapter 12.

The WS4 PDF can be specified at WordStar Release 5's Printer name option to produce a disk file readable by WordStar Release 4 and previous program editions. The new file should be given its own name at the Redirect output prompt. The resulting disk file replaces incompatible WordStar Release 5 commands with equivalent dot commands, or inserts comments where WordStar Release 5 commands have been entirely erased. You may have to reset tabs and margins after such a file conversion.

If you do not rename the output from one of the special PDFs at the print-time prompt, the creation of one of these files with a WS extension may erase an earlier disk file with the same name. You can rename files you want to save (with the E command on the classic Opening Menu) before your next use of a special PDF.

You also can create a disk file with output from a printer-specific PDF. Instead of transmitting the file's output control codes to the printer driver, WordStar sends the output into a file saved on disk. Later, without using a copy of WordStar, this file with machine-specific formatting codes can be used to run a similar printer model that is plugged into another computer system running MS-DOS or OS/2 operating system software.

To save a PDF's output on disk, at the Printer name prompt type the name of the printer driver, then at the Redirect output prompt type a name for the resulting disk file. Once you have this file on disk, you don't need to run WordStar on another computer system in order to send your PDF's output to the system's printer. Depending on which MS-DOS version is available, you can use one of two commands to print a disk file. If LPT1 is the parallel port to which the similar printer is attached, for example, type at the DOS prompt

copy filename lpt1

or

print filename lpt1

Either command prints text on the other system's printer with all active printer codes, resulting in an appropriately formatted document in hard copy.

Once you set print-time options to suit your needs and press ^K or F10, the printer goes into action. WordStar returns to the screen from which printing was invoked—either the Opening display or a document screen. The word `Printing` appears on the right of the status line. You can invoke other WordStar functions during the printer's operation, because printing is set to be done as a background task. (For greater printing speed, don't edit while printing; background printing can be turned off with the WSCHANGE program—see Chapter 11).

Pausing or Stopping the Printer

While printing goes on in the background, you can create or edit other documents. To invoke another printing-related command, you first must bring the Printing Menu to the screen. This menu displays printer-related messages and lists options for pausing or terminating printing. During printing, you can access the Printing Menu by pressing P from the Opening screen (press F first at help level 4) or ^KP from within a document file.

Invoking the print command again during printing displays one of WordStar's shortest menus (see fig. 7.5). The Printing Menu's listings are unchanged from WordStar Release 4, though additions above and below it in WordStar Release 5 increase the screen display's informational content. Prompt messages appear below the Printing Menu listings—making it easier to see that printing is paused, for example. While printing, WordStar Release 5's status line displays the number of the page currently being printed as well as the copy number.

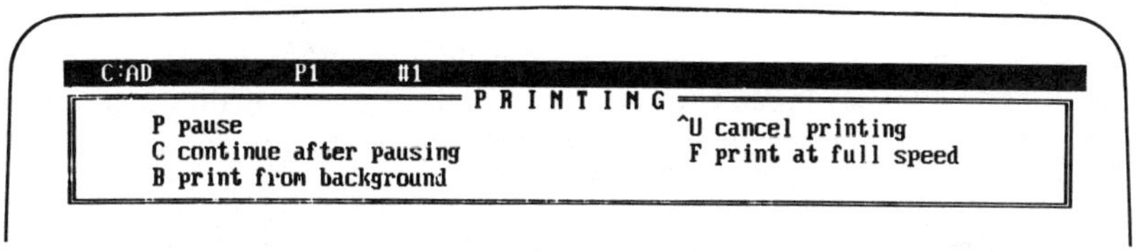
C:AD P1 #1
PRINTING
P pause
C continue after pausing
B print from background
^U cancel printing
F print at full speed

Fig. 7.5.
The Printing Menu for pausing or stopping printer operation.

The Printing Menu's five options are summarized in table 7.1. Discussed in the following sections, these options are crucial when printing must be halted or ended.

Table 7.1
Printing Menu Commands

Command	*Function*
P	Pauses printing
C	Continues printing after pause
^U	Cancels printing
B	Returns to Opening or Document screen with printing in background
F	Prints at full speed

Pausing and Resuming Printing

Being able to interrupt the printer during a print run is a vital function in any word processing program. For instance, you may need to realign paper in the printer or stop a noisy printer during an important telephone conversation. This command on the Printing Menu halts the stream of text sent to the printer:

```
P pause
```

Press PP from the Opening screen (FPP at help level 4) or ^KPP from the Document screen. When you invoke the command, your printer may not come to a stop right away. This delay is not a software malfunction, but a normal response of your system's hardware. Most printers have an internal memory that can store a half page or more of a document in a buffer. Such printers continue to print until their memory has been emptied.

To temporarily halt a printer with its own memory buffer, you can press the pause or on-line button located on the printer's front control panel. Before you resume printing, remember to press the printer's pause button again to complete printing of the contents in the printer's buffer. If you fail to print the rest of the buffer text before resuming printing, the text is lost.

When printing is paused, the message below the Printing Menu says `Printing Paused` instead of `Printing`. Press C to continue or P to pause again at the next page. To resume printing, you can invoke another command from the menu's listings:

```
C continue after pausing
```

This command is the equivalent of pressing N in early versions of WordStar (prior to Release 4) to resume printing after a pause. In WordStar Release 5, you have the additional option of pressing P (instead of C) to continue printing until the next page, where the printer will pause again.

To try pausing the printer, start to print any of the sample documents in this chapter. Invoke the Printing Menu by pressing P at the Opening screen and then pressing P again. You see how much text your printer continues to put on paper after you issue a pause command; the extra text is your printer's buffer capacity.

Canceling Printing

Occasionally, you need to discontinue a printing job. You can cancel printing in progress with one of the commands on the Printing Menu. Display the Printing Menu by pressing P at the Opening screen (FP at help level 4) or ^KP from within a document. The menu displays this command for ending printing:

```
^U cancel printing
```

In early releases of WordStar, after the P or ^KP commands were invoked during printing, pressing ^U paused printing. In WordStar Release 5, pressing ^U stops the printing operation and cancels all the printing options you selected. This use of ^U is in keeping with its usual undo function throughout WordStar Release 5. In this case, pressing ^U undoes all printing command information and returns you to the Opening screen or to your document page. Printing may continue for a while, depending on the capacity of your printer's buffer. To empty your printer's buffer, simply flick off the printer's power switch and then turn it on again a moment later.

To try canceling a print job, begin to print your sample AD document. When the printer starts, press P (or FP at help level 4) at the Opening screen to display the Printing Menu. Pressing ^U displays the Opening screen again. As soon as the contents of your printer's buffer are printed, the printer stops.

Printing as a Background Task

With WordStar Release 5 you can continue using other functions while printing. The command for WordStar to continue printing while you use other functions is listed on the Printing Menu as:

```
B print from background
```

While printing is in progress, pressing B is a simple way to leave the Printing screen and resume other tasks. After you are back at the Opening screen or within a document, you can continue to perform various tasks at normal speed, or close to it. If you make any changes to the document you are printing, however, you cannot save your altered file to disk until printing is completed.

Printing at Full Speed

With WordStar Release 5, you may be unnecessarily slowing down the printing process if you opted for a slower printing speed with the WSCHANGE program (see Chapter 11). WordStar's default setting is for the fastest printing speed. To be sure you are printing at full speed, press F at the Printing menu. If WordStar was sending text to the printer at a slower rate than necessary, you may detect a marked increase in speed in your printer's operation.

The speed at which signals are sent between computer and printer is one of the many variables and codes involved in "handshaking" between components. To send the proper handshaking codes, you must install the appropriate PDF.

To try the effects of the Printing Menu commands, print your AD document or another sample text. Start by pressing the appropriate print command. With printing in progress, display the Printing Menu by pressing P at the Opening screen. To be sure that WordStar is sending text as fast as possible to the printer, press F. To go on to another task while printing continues in the background, press B. After you are back at the Opening screen, open another file and proceed with editing.

Controlling Common Printer Functions

Now that you have acquired a working knowledge of WordStar's print-time options and PDFs, you can apply the features supported by WordStar Release 5 and your printer. WordStar provides nearly equal numbers of print-control commands and dot commands to produce effects that now are widely available on daisywheel, dot-matrix, and laser printers.

Attention-getting printing effects such as italics, color, or special fonts are readily produced with WordStar Release 5. Invoking these printer functions requires no more than including the proper commands in a document's text. Table 7.2 summarizes the printing commands that you issue from the Document screen. All these commands are discussed in this chapter.

Table 7.2
Commands for Controlling the Printer

Command(s)	*Function*
^PL	Sends form feed to printer
^PJ	Sends line feed to printer
^PY	Turns italic on or off
^PN	Selects standard pitch (default is 10 characters per inch)
^PA	Selects alternative pitch (default is 12 characters per inch)
^P0	Displays extended character set
^P@	Prints character at indicated column
^P!	Inserts one-time custom print control
^PQ, ^PW, ^PE, ^PR	Control user-defined custom printer functions
^PF, ^PG	Prints phantom character
^P =	Displays font choices
^P-	Displays color choices
^P*	Inserts pix tag for InSet graphics
.RPn	Repeats printing of file n times
.ULon/off	Toggles continuous underlining on or off
.SRn	Rolls printer carriage n/48 inch for subscripting or superscripting
.CWn	Sets spacing between characters at n/120 inch
.XQ, .XW, .XE, .XR	Define custom print-control commands ^PQ, ^PW, ^PE, ^PR
.XL	Redefines form-feed character code
.XX	Changes the strikeout character
.UJon/off	Turns microjustified printing on or off
.OJon/off	Turns justification on or off
.PSon/off	Turns proportional spacing on or off
.BPon/off	Turns bidirectional printing on or off
.LQon/off	Toggles near-letter-quality printing with a dot-matrix printer

Table 7.2—*Continued*

Command(s)	*Function*
.PR OR=P .PR OR=L	Sets laser printer for portrait or landscape mode
.BNn	Selects sheet feeder or ejects paper; n must be a number 0-4 that represents the number of different feeder bins or ejects

In recent years, the three major types of personal computer printers have become functionally similar. The daisywheel printer no longer holds a monopoly on letter-quality output, nor does its inability to print graphics prevent it from approximating the IBM extended character set by overprinting keyboard characters. Dot-matrix printers with fine 24-dot print heads now approximate letter-quality printing. Laser printers can produce near-typeset-quality documents or emulate the lower-quality output of a dot-matrix printer.

Still, the unique characteristics of daisywheel, dot-matrix, and laser printers are served by specific WordStar commands. No printer responds to all the commands described in the following sections. To see which features can be implemented on your printer, check its printout of the PRINT.TST file and review the information on its printer driver in the README file.

Invoking Italic

One of the first personal computer printer enhancements was the capability to differentiate italic from standard text, either as a slanted typeface or simply as underlined characters. WordStar did not include a direct way to invoke italic until Release 4; even then, this command was shared with an existing command for changing ribbon color. Because most printer models offer either italic or ribbon-color change (but not both), no conflict existed in how WordStar interpreted the command.

5 With WordStar Release 5, the print control command for invoking italic is dedicated solely to that function. Color printing now has a command of its own, as explained later in this chapter.

At all help levels except 1 and 0, the command to select italic is listed under the BEGIN & END heading of the Print Controls Menu. It is

```
Y  italics
```

Two ^PY commands are required to toggle the italic on and then off again. On-screen attributes for text to be printed in italic can be set with the WSCHANGE program.

As with most print-control effects, the italic selection should be used sparingly to preserve its impact in emphasizing a few words or phrases. This printing effect can be quite eye-catching on paper—or distracting if overused.

To try the italic command on your printer, open the sample AD document file, move the cursor to the first character of the memo's top line, press ^PY, and a `^Y` marker appears on-screen. Move the cursor to the end of the word `Communications` and press ^PY again. Another `^Y` marker is added to your file. At print time, the lines of text between markers are printed in italic, if your printer supports this function.

Using Continuous Underlining

One difference between WordStar Release 5 and early versions of WordStar is in the underlining function. When the ^PS underline command was invoked in versions prior to Release 4, WordStar omitted underlining between words. Such noncontinuous underlining is the correct form for citations of book titles in reports or manuscripts. Many WordStar users, however, prefer underlining the words and the spaces between words. In early versions of WordStar, continuous underlining required typing an underline character (_) between words to be underlined. In WordStar Release 5, you can choose between two more practical ways of invoking continuous underlining.

One method is to use the WSCHANGE program to alter the program's default setting of noncontinuous underlining. The other solution, listed on WordStar Release 5's fifth help screen of dot command listings, is to toggle continuous underlining on and off with a dot command. The command for turning on continuous underlining is listed as follows:

```
.ul on/off          Underline between words
```

Placing a .UL dot command near the top of a document guarantees that continuous underlining is in effect at print time—though underlining between words does not appear on-screen. You can place .UL Off and .UL On commands throughout a document where you want noncontinuous and continuous underlining to take effect.

To try continuous underlining, reopen your AD sample document. At the beginning, in column 1, type *.ul on* and press Enter. Press ^PS before text to be underlined and press ^PS again after that text to end the underlining. Print this file and you see that the copy you marked has underlining between words.

Changing Carriage Roll

WordStar always has had a feature that lets you control how much a printer's roller moves above or below the line to imprint a superscript or subscript. On some older printers, the carriage can roll only the space of a full line. In such cases, WordStar conforms to the limitation. On other printers, WordStar uses a default roll of 3/48 inch, which you can modify by placing a dot command in your document.

The dot command that controls carriage roll is listed on the fifth screen of WordStar Release 5's dot-command help listings. To display the screen at all help levels except 4, you can press ^J or F1, a period (.), and then Enter five times. The command is as follows:

```
.sr n        Set super-/subscript roll (n/48 inch). Default: 3
```

The default carriage-roll setting is 3/48 inch (which is equivalent to .SR3). A carriage roll of a full line space is usually equivalent to .SR8. Knowing these settings should make it easy to find the right in-between value for the best appearance of your document.

With some newer dot-matrix printers, a half-height font just for subscripts and superscripts is available. If this is the case with your printer, set carriage roll to 0 with a .SR0 command.

Note: Failure to set carriage roll to 0 results in special fonts being printed incorrectly above or below the line.

The report created in Chapter 3 has examples of subscripted and superscripted characters. To try an alternative setting for the carriage roll, open the report file and, near its beginning, type the dot command .SR6, and press Enter. Save and print this document. You see that the subscript and superscript in the text are printed with a carriage roll twice the size of the default.

Changing Character Width and Pitch

Setting the space between characters on a printed line is another important function that always has been part of WordStar. In unjustified printing of non-proportional fonts, most printers reproduce every character and blank space in horizontal intervals of equal width. For proportional fonts, which include characters of different widths, character width is expressed as an average. Character width is measured in units of 1/120 inch, with an associated value, called pitch, noted in characters per inch (cpi).

WordStar comes preset for a character width of 12/120 or 1/10 inch—that is, 10 cpi. This is the standard setting for pica type. If you prefer to use an elite type that allows more characters per inch, you should switch the character width to 10/120 inch for a pitch of 12 cpi. With other type sizes, you may have to modify the character width further at print time. To set any new character width, all you need to do is embed in your document a dot command with a suitable numerical value.

The dot command to reset character spacing is listed on the first screen of dot command help listings. It is as follows:

```
.cw n            Set character width to n/120 inch. Default: 12
```

After the .CW command, you can use any number through 255 for the character width. A practical range of values, however, is from 5 through 24. The larger the number that follows .CW, the greater the spacing between printed characters. Table 7.3 summarizes the common character-width settings, showing resulting pitch and maximum right-margin column settings for a standard 8 1/2-inch-wide sheet of paper. When you select a character width that fits many characters to the inch, text may be displayed beyond the right side of the screen, automatically scrolling so you can see what you are typing.

Table 7.3
Common Character-Width Settings

Dot command	*Pitch—cpi*	*Right margin*
.CW24	5	3.1″
.CW20	6	3.8″
.CW15	8	5.1″
.CW12	10	6.4″
.CW10	12	7.7″
.CW8	15	9.7″
.CW6	20	12.9″
.CW5	24	15.5″

The .CW character-width command is probably familiar to you if you have used early WordStar versions, although the command's results may seem different in a WordStar Release 5 printout. Since Release 4, WordStar's print instructions result in lines that are printed slightly wider, with more space between characters. In fact, to reproduce the standard printing width of early releases of WordStar, you may have to redefine your printer pitch with the dot command .CW10.

All releases of WordStar are supplied with an alternative default pitch setting of 12 characters per inch, corresponding to the dot command .CW10. To switch from a normal default pitch of 10 characters per inch to the more compressed, alternate pitch of 12 characters per inch, you can place a print-control command in the document. With another print-control command, you can change back quickly to a standard default pitch of 10 characters per inch.

5

In WordStar Release 5, the default pitch-control commands that apply to character width for all printers are listed on the classic Print Controls Menu according to their function with laser printers.

At all help levels but 1 or 0, both default pitch commands are listed in the second STYLE column of the classic Print Controls Menu, as follows:

```
N normal font
A alternate font
```

The command sequences are ^PN and ^PA. Their menu listings refer to the fact that character width or pitch determines font size (and style) on a laser printer. Using ^PN and ^PA provides an easy way to switch between two default fonts in a document to be printed on a laser printer. Shown later in this chapter is a more comprehensive command for selecting from among the whole range of fonts available on a laser printer. The default pitch commands provide a convenient though limited way of changing fonts.

By combining the .CW dot command with ^PA and ^PN pitch commands, you can alternate between a pair of character-width settings (and fonts) that are different from WordStar's defaults. For instance, the first time you insert a ^PA command in a document, at column 1 of the next line you can insert a .CW command and a new value for alternative pitch. Whenever ^PA is used in the document, this new alternative pitch (and the corresponding font on a laser printer) is invoked. The default normal pitch (and font) remains unchanged unless a .CW dot command is used after a ^PN normal-pitch command to establish a different value for this pitch. From that point on, when the normal pitch is restored, the new character width setting (and font) will be implemented. New normal and alternate pitch settings and fonts can be set as often as needed in a document. If you prefer, you can reset normal and alternate pitch values for ^PN and ^PA with WSCHANGE (see Chapter 11).

Putting character-width commands to work is easy. Open your sample AD document file and try it. At the top of the document, enter the command ^PA to use the alternative pitch of 12 cpi. Before the "INSIDE TRADER" outline, press ^PN for normal pitch. In column 1 of the next line, enter the dot command .CW8 and press Enter. This command defines a denser normal pitch. After the outline's last word, restore the normal pitch to 10 cpi by entering the .CW12 command. The resulting document is printed in pitches of 12, 15, and 10 cpi.

Using Custom Printer Functions

Your printer may have special functions such as double-width or compressed fonts that are not supported by the printer's description file in WordStar Release 5. You can access such features by issuing special character codes described in your printer manual. WordStar Release 5 improves on the four definable custom print controls in previous versions by adding a fifth print control command for one-time use.

The classic Print Controls Menu displays this listing of customizable print-control commands in the first OTHER column:

```
Q W E R ! custom
```

The first four letters chosen for these control commands are the far-left keys in the top row of the common QWERTY keyboard. Identical in all versions of WordStar, each of these commands—^PQ, ^PW, ^PE, and ^PR—can be assigned a string of up to 24 characters to be issued to your printer whenever invoked in a document. The fifth command, ^P!, is for codes used only once in a document.

In early releases of the program, custom print-control codes could be defined only by reinstalling your working copy of WordStar. In WordStar Release 5, you can assign special print codes permanently to ^PQ, ^PW, ^PE, and ^PR by using the WSCHANGE program. You also can designate these special print controls temporarily by using four dot commands.

In WordStar Release 5, the following commands for defining custom print functions in a document are on the fifth screen of dot command listings:

```
.xe        Redefine custom print ^PE
.xq        Redefine custom print ^PQ
.xr        Redefine custom print ^PR
.xw        Redefine custom print ^PW
```

You can remember each of these dot commands as "X marks the spot" for codes to be issued by each of the print-control commands: ^PQ, ^PW, ^PE, and ^PR. Each of the dot commands—.XQ, .XW, .XE, and .XR—must be followed by character codes expressed in hexadecimal (base-16) number pairs, totaling no more than 24 characters each as recommended in your printer manual. If no code is included with these dot commands, the corresponding print-control command does not function. Once set, the dot commands supersede codes installed with WSCHANGE.

The following example shows how to assign custom printer features with dot commands. According to the printer's documentation, on an Epson dot-matrix printer, a double-width typeface is invoked by sending to it the numerical equivalent of an Esc character followed by an SO character. Checking a list of ASCII codes, such as the one in Appendix C, you find the hexadecimal equivalents of these characters to be 1B and 0E. To set ^PW as the command for turning on double-width typeface at print-time, near the top of your document type the dot command

.XW 1B 0E

Turning off double-width printing requires a different code: the DC4 character—14 in hexadecimal notation. To make ^PQ the command for turning off double-width characters, at the beginning of your document, type

.XQ 14

In your document, press ^PW before text to be printed double-width and ^PQ after it to revert to normal type.

For one-time use of a printer code in a document, you can use the ^P! command, new in WordStar Release 5. When you press ^P! during editing, WordStar displays a dialog box labeled USER PRINT CONTROL (see fig. 7.6). This dialog box includes prompts for the characters to be sent to the printer, for any identifying characters you want displayed on-screen, and for the printed width (in inches) the resulting effect produces—so this new positioning can be reflected by WordStar's on-screen formatting.

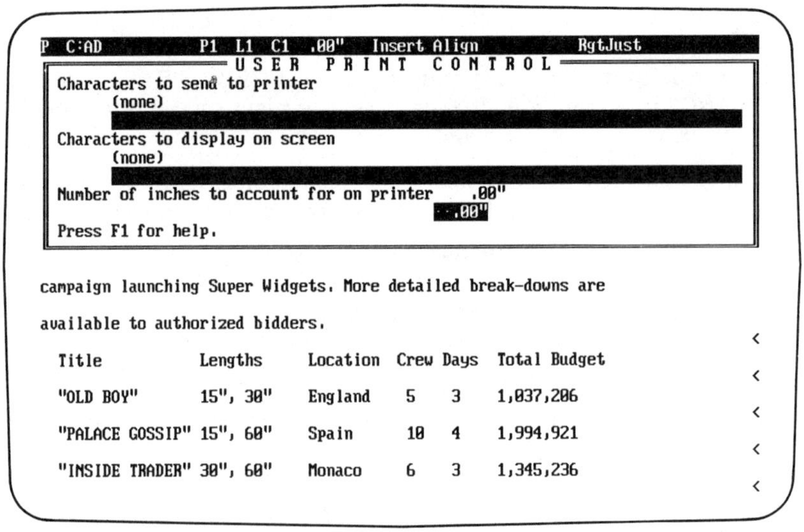
P C:AD P1 L1 C1 .00" Insert Align RgtJust
USER PRINT CONTROL
Characters to send to printer
(none)
Characters to display on screen
(none)
Number of inches to account for on printer .00"
.00"
Press F1 for help.
campaign launching Super Widgets. More detailed break-downs are
available to authorized bidders.
Title Lengths Location Crew Days Total Budget
"OLD BOY" 15", 30" England 5 3 1,037,206
"PALACE GOSSIP" 15", 60" Spain 10 4 1,994,921
"INSIDE TRADER" 30", 60" Monaco 6 3 1,345,236

Fig. 7.6. *Setting a one-time print control command.*

To send characters to the printer, you can type the desired print code at the User Print Control dialog box. This code acts as a control character when you enter a caret (^) before the character. If you want to include a caret in the printer code, you can type *%^*. For a percent symbol to be entered, type *%%*. For an Esc character, type ^[. To express the print code in hexadecimal numbers, you must type *%x* before the hexadecimal code.

When defining custom print controls, use only those codes indicated in your printer manual. Custom codes differ widely among printers. Don't try to use custom settings with a printer for which the codes were not intended. Avoid defining as custom features common functions such as double strike and subscript, which are already part of your PDF. Interaction between custom print controls and codes issued by the PDF could cause commands to be canceled or erroneously replaced.

Using Extended Characters

WordStar Release 5 is the first version of WordStar to reproduce the entire IBM extended character set of more than 150 marks. These extra characters, including foreign symbols, elementary graphics, and scientific notations, are stored in your computer's permanent ROM memory and can be seen on-screen after you enter them with WordStar. The extended character set can be printed accurately with dot-matrix or laser printers, or the symbols can be approximated by most daisy-wheel printers using multiple strikes to combine characters. For the first time with WordStar, Release 5 can access the lower range of extended characters from 0 to 31.

All characters transmitted from the keyboard to the screen and ultimately to the printer actually are numerical codes that adhere to standard definitions. Numbers ranging from 32 through 127 are used for keyboard symbols and special control codes, in keeping with the ASCII format. Values from 0 through 31 and from 128 through 255 produce the extended character set on-screen and in WordStar files. Because extended characters are not directly symbolized on the keyboard, you must enter them from the keyboard in one of two ways when using WordStar.

Still valid is the method introduced in the previous version of WordStar: entering numerical codes for extended characters directly at the Document screen by pressing the Alt key along with the appropriate number. (Your printer's manual should have a list of decimal values for various printer output characters; these extended characters are usually similar to the standard set listed in Appendix C of this book.) More convenient is WordStar Release 5's new print-control command, which displays all available extended characters in a dialog box on-screen.

The command for easy input of extended characters is listed on the classic Print Controls Menu. In the last OTHER column, you find this notation:

```
0 extended characters
```

When you press ^P0, WordStar Release 5 displays a dialog box titled EXTENDED CHARACTER MENU, which shows the entire set of extended characters arrayed beside columns and rows of numbers for quick reference. As shown in figure 7.7, the dialog box includes a space where you can type the number for the character you want inserted in your document.

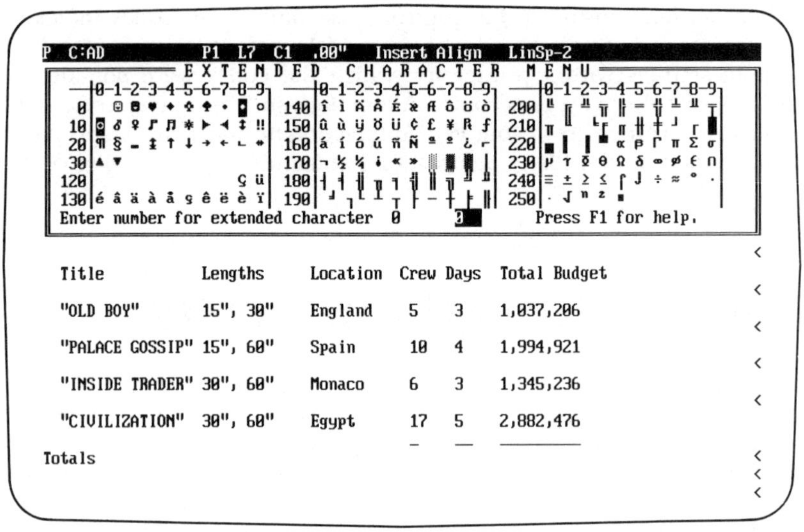
P C:AD P1 L7 C1 .00" Insert Align LinSp-2
EXTENDED CHARACTER MENU
Enter number for extended character 0
Press F1 for help.
Title Lengths Location Crew Days Total Budget
"OLD BOY" 15", 30" England 5 3 1,037,206
"PALACE GOSSIP" 15", 60" Spain 10 4 1,994,921
"INSIDE TRADER" 30", 60" Monaco 6 3 1,345,236
"CIVILIZATION" 30", 60" Egypt 17 5 2,882,476
Totals

***Fig.* 7.7.** *Selecting an extended character from WordStar Release 5's new menu.*

To find the number for a symbol on the Extended Character Menu, first look for the number to the left of the symbol on the same line and then add to this the number above the symbol in the same row. This is the number you should type at the cursor and then press Enter. For example, the Greek letter alpha is located on the line numbered 220 and in the row numbered 4—thus you type the numerical code 224 at the prompt and press Enter to insert an alpha in your document for later printing.

Try the procedure first described and insert an extended character code in a WordStar Release 5 document. While editing, hold down the Alt key and type one of the three-digit numbers, using the numeric keypad. When you release the Alt key, the extended character appears on-screen at the cursor and will later be transmitted to your printer. For instance, to enter a square root sign, you press Alt-251.

In general, the decimal values for extended characters from 1 through 31 invoke useful symbols, including musical notes, paragraph signs, and a variety of directional arrows. Most of the decimal values from 128 through 154 represent foreign language characters and accents, 155 through 157 refer to foreign currency marks, and 158 through 168 denote more foreign language symbols. A palette of border and line graphics elements are invoked with values 176 through 223. Values 224 through 235 invoke Greek letters, and the values through 254 enter mathematical and scientific notation symbols. The highest value, 255, sends out a form feed.

Even though the IBM extended character set has become standard, not all printers reproduce all the characters exactly as depicted in reference tables. You may want to experiment with your printer to find out how it prints specific characters you might need for your word processing requirements.

Using Bar Drawing

Among the extended characters produced with decimal values from 176 through 223 are the line- and box-drawing symbols explained in Chapter 4. The extended character set contains double-lined versions of these characters for creating borders. Eight other characters are useful for drawing bars and shading charts.

The extended characters numbered 219 through 223 are varying portions of a solid black bar. Extended characters numbered 176 through 178 provide bars of shading composed of lesser or greater density. By using combinations of these characters, you can compose bar charts to illustrate business figures or trends.

The example shown in figure 7.8 is a horizontal chart containing three trend lines: one composed entirely of solid black bars produced by pressing ^P0, typing *219*, and pressing Enter (or Alt-219); a second line of intermittent black bars created by pressing ^P0, typing *221*, and pressing Enter (or Alt-221); and a third trend line consisting of repeated shading bars created by pressing ^P0, typing *177*, and pressing Enter (or Alt-177). For each bar, you press Enter or the Alt-number combination as many times as necessary to fill the desired amount of space. The fourth example shows all three characters on one trend line.

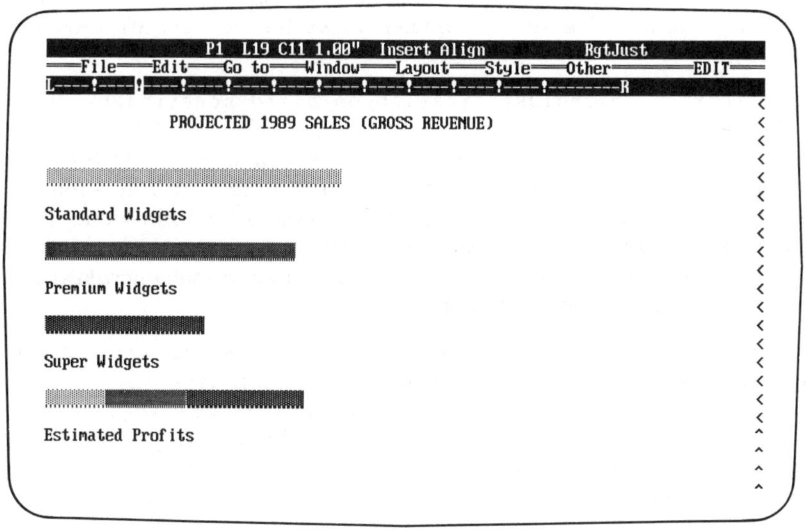
P1 L19 C11 1.00" Insert Align RgtJust
File Edit Go to Window Layout Style Other EDIT
PROJECTED 1989 SALES (GROSS REVENUE)
Standard Widgets
Premium Widgets
Super Widgets
Estimated Profits

Fig. 7.8.

A bar chart created with extended characters.

Bar characters can be printed correctly on a dot-matrix or laser printer, but may yield unsatisfactory results with a daisywheel unit. Bar drawing is recommended only for graphics-oriented printers. If you will be making extensive use of these graphics elements, you might want to program them as single keystroke shorthand macros (see Chapter 9).

Using Microjustification

Until now, this chapter has assumed that your printer spaces characters and words evenly on a line. Most printers, however, are capable of varying spacing to improve formatting and readability. This and the following section detail the two principal ways in which character spacing can be modified with functions controlled by WordStar from within a document.

Many printers can produce microjustification: while maintaining a flush-right margin in justified text, the printer inserts tiny blank spaces between words and letters to distribute the characters evenly on the line. Although these insertions improve the appearance of justified text, microjustification can disrupt the alignment of text columns and slow down printing noticeably as each line's formatting is automatically reset.

WordStar leaves implementation of microjustification to the PDF. Printers with slow microjustification capability rarely have this feature invoked by their drivers. Using WSCHANGE, you can reset your WordStar working copy to turn on or off microjustification permanently; or, as in previous program versions, you can use a dot command inserted in text to regulate whether or not microjustification is used.

WordStar Release 5's fifth screen of dot-command help listings (invoked by pressing ^J or F1, a period, and Enter five times) shows the microjustification dot command like this:

```
.uj on/off/dis    Microjustification on/off/discretionary
```

As in earlier versions of WordStar, the .UJ dot command can turn microjustification on or off with the proper modifier toggling this function at print time. You can keep inserting .UJ On and .UJ Off commands throughout a file to influence both print formatting and printer speed. After invoking one or the other of these settings, WordStar Release 5's PDF determines whether to continue microjustification if you type *.uj dis*—for a discretionary setting.

Try turning on and off microjustification. Open your sample AD document and type *.uj on* and then press Enter to turn on microjustification. Press ^OJ to turn on justification, and then press ^QU to realign the entire document with this new formatting. With the cursor moved to the middle of the document, type *.uj off* and press Enter to turn off microjustification. Save this file and print it. You see how microjustification changes your document's appearance and your printer's speed.

Using Proportional Spacing

Proportional spacing, a standard feature in typeset-quality documents, adjusts the spaces accorded to letters in proportion to the actual width of the letters. This adjustment, which is made to improve legibility, means that an "i" printed with proportional spacing is given less space on either side than the slightly wider "g" or the even wider "w". Simple monospacing (as on most typewriters) provides equal horizontal spacing to every character, regardless of width. Microjustification adjusts the spacing of characters and words on a justified line by roughly equal amounts.

WordStar Release 5 is the first version of WordStar to support proportional spacing accurately. To ensure correct intervals in proportional spacing, WordStar Release 5's PDFs include proportional character-width information for a printer's available fonts. Though this information takes effect only at print time, actual character positioning on a line is shown by the marker on the ruler line. Proportionally spaced characters may exceed the width of your on-screen margins because more proportional characters fit on a line (they usually take up less room than evenly spaced nonproportional characters), but they print properly within specified margins. Line breaks and page breaks are correctly displayed during editing, and WordStar Release 5's page preview function shows exactly how proportional fonts will look when printed.

Because proportional fonts are part of a printer's characteristics, in WordStar Release 5 the best way to invoke proportional spacing is with the PDF-oriented font selection command explained later in this chapter. However, WordStar also provides the option of turning proportional spacing on or off with a dot command typed in a document.

The following dot command for proportional spacing is on the fourth listing of dot commands:

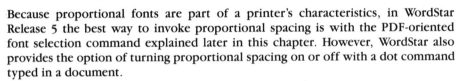

```
.ps on/off          Turn proportional spacing on/off
```

When you type *.ps*, you must add either *on* or *off*. Place the command on a line of its own starting at column 1. In dot-matrix printers with multiple built-in typefaces, the .PS On command selects the correct proportional typeface based on the character width (.CW) setting. For a daisywheel printer, you may need to have a proportional print element with characters arranged in a special sequence. Unless the PDF is properly set, your output may print incorrectly. Because different proportional fonts are most often used with laser printers, the font selection print control command is discussed in the section of this chapter relating to such models.

Note: When you turn justification off or on for proportionally spaced text in a document, use the dot commands .OJ Off and .OJ On instead of the equivalent ^OJ on-screen format control toggle; using the dot commands avoids disruption of the formatting.

When you invoke proportional spacing, column formatting that appears correct on-screen may be altered as spacing between characters on a line becomes relative. Because tabs can be set to absolute measurements (see Chapter 4), the best way to ensure left edge alignment of a column of proportional text is by using tabs set at the proper position for printing.

All the common printer features discussed up to this point in this chapter are available on a variety of printers. The following sections discuss specific features as they apply to daisywheel, dot-matrix, and laser printers, respectively.

Using a Daisywheel Printer

The operation of daisywheel printers has changed little in recent years. These printers have interchangeable, molded wheel-like printing elements to print the characters on paper with the same clarity as typewritten characters. Because the operation of daisywheel printers has not changed, WordStar Release 5 retains the same commands for these models as in previous versions of WordStar. One of these commands can limit the directions in which printing is performed. In addition, two print-control commands can print daisywheel characters that are not shown on the keyboard.

Setting Bidirectional Printing

Most printers produce text by moving the print head from left to right on one line and then from right to left on the next. On some daisywheel printers, such bidirectional printing can result in slightly off-register characters and poor print quality. WordStar is preset for bidirectional printing as a default. You can change this setting with the WSCHANGE program, or you can use a dot command to turn bidirectional printing off or on.

WordStar Release 5's first screen of dot-command help listings shows the following command for controlling bidirectional printing:

```
.bp on/off        Bidirectional printing on/off
```

When you enter this dot command, you must type a modifier, either *off* (or *0*) to discontinue bidirectional printing or *on* (or *1*) to turn on the feature.

If your daisywheel's bidirectional printing can be turned off and on, try printing your AD document with one half printed in a single direction (by typing *.bp off* at the beginning of the file) and the other half printed in bidirectional mode (by typing *.bp on* before the second half of your document). This example lets you compare the speed and accuracy of the two printing methods.

Using Phantom Characters

Occasionally, a daisywheel print wheel includes two extra characters that do not appear on your keyboard. These are known as phantom characters because they normally are not visible until print time. Phantom characters correspond to two specific hexadecimal character codes. The phantom space, invoked by hexadecimal code 20, is a space on some print wheels; on others, the phantom space can be a cent sign. The phantom rubout is the printer's response to hexadecimal code 7F: often a double underline; or, on a bilingual print wheel, a German umlaut. Access to these or reassigned characters for these codes is ensured by a couple of print-control commands.

Phantom print functions are listed on the Print Controls Menu as follows:

```
F   phantom space
G   phantom rubout
```

When you press ^PF or ^PG, ^F or ^G appears on-screen. Unlike other print-control commands, however, these symbols are counted as occupying a character position. When the document is printed, the correct phantom characters are substituted for ^F or ^G.

Some dot-matrix and laser printers also produce special characters when ^PF and ^PG are invoked. These phantom characters can be changed with the WSCHANGE program, as noted in Chapter 11.

If you don't know which characters your printer prints for phantom space and phantom rubout, you can try placing the ^PF and ^PG commands in a document to be printed. Open the sample AD file and press ^PF and ^PG right after the end of the first text line; on-screen, you see ^F and ^G. Print this file and check to see which characters, if any, are printed for the phantom characters.

Using a Dot-Matrix Printer

Dot-matrix printers have come a long way since the Epson MX-80 set the standard for such printers. Characters still are formed on paper by a moving print head that is composed of pins arrayed in a matrix of dots. But now that dot-matrix printers use a finer set of pins to form characters, the output of dot-matrix and daisywheel printers can be difficult to distinguish. And with multiple fonts included in newer models, some dot-matrix printers rival laser printers for versatility; the same font selection command described for laser printers later in this chapter can be used for such advanced dot-matrix units.

In many cases, one dot command suffices to get the best results from certain dot-matrix printers. WordStar Release 5 includes this command for achieving letter-quality printing on properly equipped dot-matrix printers. Assuming that fast, draft-quality printing is your dot-matrix printer's default mode, all you need to do to switch to letter-quality printing is to embed a dot command at the beginning of your document.

WordStar Release 5's third help screen of dot-command listings notes the letter-quality command as follows:

```
.lq on/off/dis    Near letter quality print on/off/discretionary
```

Like many other print-time dot commands, .LQ usually should be included at the beginning of a document, before any characters to be printed. When invoking the .LQ letter command, use the qualifier "on" or "off" according to whether you want the greater legibility of letter-quality printing or the speed of draft mode printing. WordStar Release 5 has an added third option: "dis" to leave the selection of print quality to the discretion of the fonts set in WordStar's PDF.

In general, letter-quality printing on a dot-matrix printer means true descenders (the tails on p's, q's, and y's), rounder contours, finer letter strokes, and barely noticeable constituent dots. The trade-off is slower printing—usually 25 to 50 percent slower than draft mode.

If you have a dot-matrix printer with a letter-quality typeface, try this feature by opening the AD document and inserting a .LQ command at the top of the screen. At print time, letter-quality print mode is activated.

Using a Laser Printer

One of the greatest changes in printing in recent years has been the emergence of laser printers from the laboratory onto desks and into offices everywhere. The laser printer, based on an electrostatic transfer system not unlike that of the office copier, and triggered by laser light, earns high marks for speed, silent operation, quality typefaces, and adaptable formatting.

Another WordStar first in Release 5 is full support for laser printers. Now accessible are a printer's complete array of font styles and sizes (up to 255 fonts per printer), downloadable fonts, and PostScript encoded fonts. Font selections with a particular printer are displayed in a document; if the document is printed on a different printer, similar fonts on that model are automatically substituted by WordStar.

To see whether your laser printer is compatible with the PDF you have chosen, try a test printing of the files LASER1.DOC and LASER2.DOC, which are provided on the WordStar Release 5 Program Disk. Invoke printing by pressing P at the Opening screen (FP at help level 4) or ^KP from within a document, and then designate which of the laser test documents is to be printed. At the print-time options, press Y in response to the `Use form feeds` prompt.

Laser printers always require the use of form feeds. If a laser unit is your primary printer, you will want to keep the form-feed print-time option default at Yes when exploring options in WSCHANGE (see Chapter 11). In addition to the common printer functions discussed earlier in this chapter, users of laser printers must concern themselves with two other matters: a special dot command for choosing paper orientation and the new command for selecting type fonts.

Setting Page Orientation

Among the features of many laser printers is the capability to print on a page positioned vertically or horizontally. In the vocabulary of painting, these positions are known as portrait and landscape orientation, respectively. WordStar Release 5 includes a dot command for selecting a laser printer's orientation. Portrait (vertical) orientation is the default.

The dot command for selecting printer orientation is not listed on any of WordStar's built-in help screens. The command works as a toggle for switching between printing modes. The command .PR OR=L sets the printer for landscape orientation, and the command .PR OR=P sets the printer for portrait orientation.

Because laser printers are usually calibrated to preselected margins, you may have to change the formatting of your documents for printing on these units. Table 7.4 lists the margin settings, dot commands, and recommended values for resetting margins. These settings, which assume the default of 6 lines per inch, leave 55 lines of text in portrait orientation and 40 lines of text in landscape mode. If you frequently use a laser printer with one of these page orientations, you may want to reset WordStar's margin defaults to the appropriate settings with WSCHANGE.

Table 7.4
Recommended Margin Settings for Laser Printers

Setting	*Dot command*	*Default value*	*Portrait orientation*	*Landscape orientation*
Page length	.PL	66 (11″)	62 (10.3″)	47 (7.8″)
Top margin	.MT	3 (.5″)	2 (.33″)	2 (.33″)
Bottom margin	.MB	8 (1.33″)	5 (.83″)	5 (.83″)
Header margin	.HM	2 (.33″)	1 (.16″)	1 (.16″)
Footer margin	.FM	2 (.33″)	2 (.33″)	2 (.33″)

You can change page orientation at the beginning of any page in a document, but you cannot invoke different modes on the same page.

Selecting Fonts

When you run a laser printer (or a dot-matrix printer with multiple typefaces), you can invoke appropriate typestyles and sizes for legible body copy, attention-grabbing headlines, or emphasized words and phrases. Each particular style and size of type constitutes a separate font. Choosing fonts by name and size is essential to controlling how your printed document looks. With Release 5, WordStar for the first time includes the capability to select specific fonts. 5

Font selection is accomplished with a print control command. At help level 4, this command can be found on the pull-down Style menu (displayed by pressing Alt-S during editing). The command is

```
Choose font...           ^P=
```

At help levels 4, 3, or 2, the classic Print Controls Menu (accessed by pressing ^P) includes the following listing:

```
= select font
```

The cursor should be at the place in your document where you want a new font to start when you invoke ^P=.

Pressing ^P= displays a dialog box titled FONT with a line indicating the font currently in effect. As shown in figure 7.9, the directory below the dialog box shows the names of all available fonts for a particular printer, according to what is included in its PDF. For a nonproportional font, a font name includes the font pitch (number of characters per inch). For a proportional font, its name indicates typestyle and size measured in points (indicating letter height). The font name may also refer to a plug-in font cartridge used with some printers.

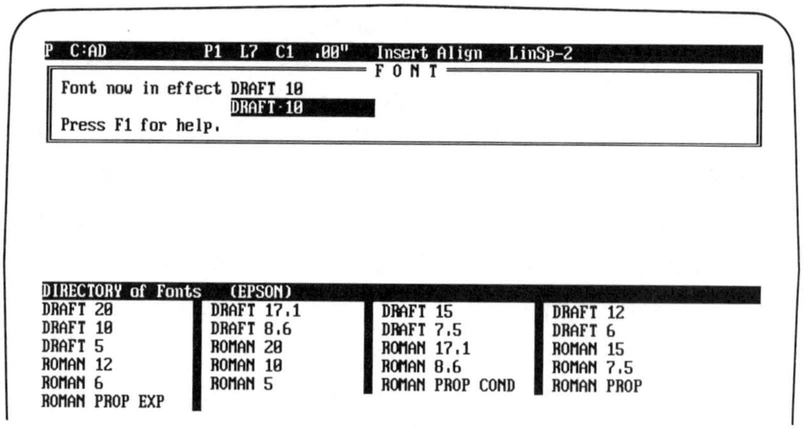
P C:AD P1 L7 C1 .00" Insert Align LinSp-2
F O N T
Font now in effect DRAFT 10
DRAFT 10
Press F1 for help.
DIRECTORY of Fonts (EPSON)
DRAFT 20
DRAFT 10
DRAFT 5
ROMAN 12
ROMAN 6
ROMAN PROP EXP
DRAFT 17.1
DRAFT 8.6
ROMAN 20
ROMAN 10
ROMAN 5
DRAFT 15
DRAFT 7.5
ROMAN 17.1
ROMAN 8.6
ROMAN PROP COND
DRAFT 12
DRAFT 6
ROMAN 15
ROMAN 7.5
ROMAN PROP

Fig. 7.9. *Selecting printer fonts with WordStar Release 5's new Font dialog box.*

To invoke a font when the Font dialog box is displayed, type the desired name at the prompt or use the arrow keys to highlight the font's name in the directory, then press Enter. With on-screen print controls displayed, WordStar inserts a command tag in your text that indicates the font name (for instance, <TIMES 12>). When on-screen display is toggled off with ^OD, the font tags are hidden. Whether a font tag is displayed or not, text following it prints in the new font until another font is chosen. Existing text is not reset in a new font until that text is changed or realigned with ^B or ^QU. When fonts are changed, line breaks and page breaks are adjusted accordingly. To eliminate a font from a document, you can simply remove its command tag with one of WordStar's deletion commands. If the file is printed on a printer other than the default printer for that document, WordStar chooses the most similar font based on character width, height, and typestyle.

To facilitate editing of fonts in a document, WordStar Release 5 includes a new command for locating the next font tag in your text. This command is a quick control sequence with the same final character as the font selection command.

At help level 4, the pull-down Go To menu (shown by pressing Alt-G while editing) includes this listing:

```
Go to the next font      ^Q=
```

At help level 4, 3, or 2, the following notation is located in the FIND column on the classic Quick Menu (displayed by pressing ^Q during editing):

```
= next font
```

To move the cursor to the location of the next font tag in your document, you press ^Q=.

For examples of the fonts available with your printer, open one of the sample documents created previously, and use ^P= commands to select in turn each of the fonts listed for your printer for a line of text. Remember to realign your text with ^QU so the font changes affect your text. After saving and printing this document, you see the range of typestyles and sizes that can be invoked with your printer.

Using a PostScript Printer

If your laser printer uses the PostScript page description language, you must follow a slightly different procedure for installing and using your printer.

The files for using a PostScript printer with WordStar Release 5 are contained on the PostScript Files/Font Utility disk. The files on this disk should be copied to the same disk and directory as your working copy of WordStar. On a dual floppy disk system with limited storage, copy just the files WSPROL.PS and DRIVERPS.OVR (the printer driver for PostScript printers). Because of the large memory overhead typical of PostScript printers, such models should be operated on systems with hard disks.

For a PostScript printer installation, with WINSTALL or WSCHANGE, choose one of two generic printer options on the Printer Selection Menu: PostScript Generic creates an all-purpose printer description file and adds PostScript to the printer possibilities at print-time; PostScript Generic Two-Up is the printer description file to choose for printing booklets or program listings. The PostScript Generic Two-Up PDF prints in landscape mode, two pages at a time, with fonts reduced in size by 65 percent.

Generic PostScript PDFs include default settings for the most commonly used PostScript fonts. These fonts are listed under the WordStar Font Menu. Additional fonts can be appended to the database for font information. The LSRFONTS program (also found on the PostScript Files/Font Utility disk) was designed for this task. Invoked by typing LSRFONTS at the DOS prompt, this program searches through the font disk files, compiling a database of available font options. Font file names for standard PostScript fonts are distinguished by AFM extensions (Adobe Font Metrics). After adding fonts to the current database, run the PRCHANGE program (see Chapter 11) to include these fonts in your PostScript PDF.

Any soft fonts must be downloaded from disk files according to printer manual instructions. When WordStar Release 5 is properly installed, the ^P= command provides full font control over PostScript files. With printers that support color, ^P also is valid (see following section). On a printer without color support, ^P invokes shades of gray; printing the PRINT.TST file reveals on paper how your printer responds to color choices.

Some PostScript printers are unable to print text at the edges of standard-sized paper. Margins should be set to avoid dropping characters off the paper's edge.

Using a Color Printer

The latest development in personal computer printers is an assortment of affordable models that can print text in as many as 16 different colors for greater impact, especially when presenting charts or tabular material. Though their technology is still exotic, with special inks and print heads, such printers are supported by WordStar for the first time with WordStar Release 5.

The WordStar Release 5 command for specifying text colors from within a document is listed on the classic Print Controls Menu (displayed by pressing ^P), in the first column of STYLE commands:

```
- select color
```

Before invoking ^P-, place the cursor in your text where you want a new print color to begin.

After you press ^P-, WordStar Release 5 shows a dialog box on-screen with the heading COLORS and a line indicating the color now in effect. In this case, the directory below the dialog box lists the names of 16 available text colors (see fig. 7.10).

To select a color from the Colors dialog box, type the desired color at the prompt or press the appropriate arrow keys to highlight a color in the directory, then press Enter. When on-screen print controls are displayed, WordStar puts a command tag in your text to indicate color (for example, <LIGHT BLUE>). If on-screen display is toggled off with ^OD, color tags are hidden. Whether a color tag is displayed or not, text following it prints in the new color until another color is specified. To remove a color selection, just erase its command tag with one of WordStar's deletion commands.

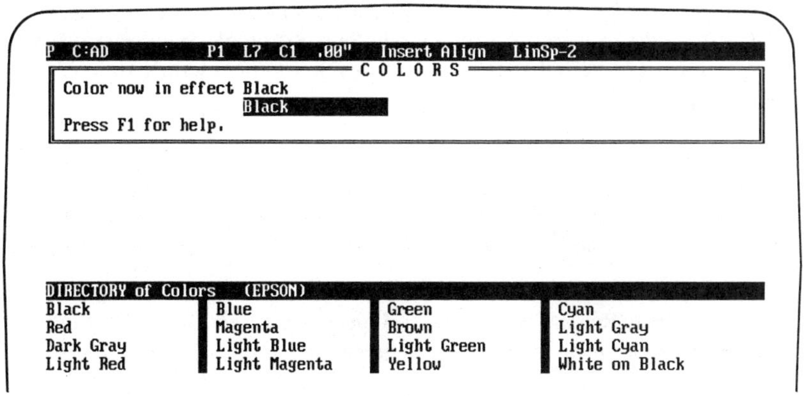
P C:AD P1 L7 C1 .00" Insert Align LinSp-2
COLORS
Color now in effect Black
Black
Press F1 for help.
DIRECTORY of Colors (EPSON)
Black
Red
Dark Gray
Light Red
Blue
Magenta
Light Blue
Light Magenta
Green
Brown
Light Green
Yellow
Cyan
Light Gray
Light Cyan
White on Black

Fig. 7.10. *Selecting print colors from 16 available colors.*

The color selection command also can apply to printers that alternate between two colored ribbons—thus ^P- replaces the ribbon color function of the ^PY command in earlier versions of WordStar. If your printer cannot print a color selected for text, that color tag is disregarded at print time. Some laser printers that cannot print colors may print tagged text in inverse characters or with a shaded gray background. Consult your printer manual to find out what colors are available for printing.

To see examples of color printing with your printer, open one of the sample documents created earlier, and with successive ^P- commands invoke each of the colors listed for a line of text. Save the document and print it to see exactly how color tags translate in hard copy.

Printing Graphics

Printing graphics images within text was a function pioneered by desktop publishing programs. Reports, newsletters, and documentation can benefit from incorporating charts, drawings, and scanned images, so merging graphics into documents is fast becoming a standard feature of word processing programs. WordStar Release 5 takes a first step toward graphics capability with a new print control command for printing, along with a document, images from the InSet graphics capture program.

Though INSET Systems' program is not officially part of the WordStar Professional package (as it is with WordStar 2000 Release 3), MicroPro International added a specific command for incorporating InSet graphics with documents from WordStar Release 5. The installation and use of InSet with WordStar are explained in Chapter 12. Of interest here is the procedure for inserting a command tag to print InSet graphics within a document.

InSet tags are easy to type into text, but WordStar Release 5 includes a handy command for this function, listed on the classic Print Controls Menu (accessed by pressing ^P when editing at help levels 4, 3, or 2). In the menu's first OTHER column, the listing is noted as:

```
* graphics tag
```

As with manual typing of such a tag, there should be a blank area in the text (created by properly adjusting margins) where the image is to appear when printed, and the cursor should be at the top left corner of that area when you invoke ^P*

Pressing ^P* in WordStar Release 5 displays a dialog box titled GRAPHICS INSERT with a line where you can indicate an image file to be inserted (see fig. 7.11).

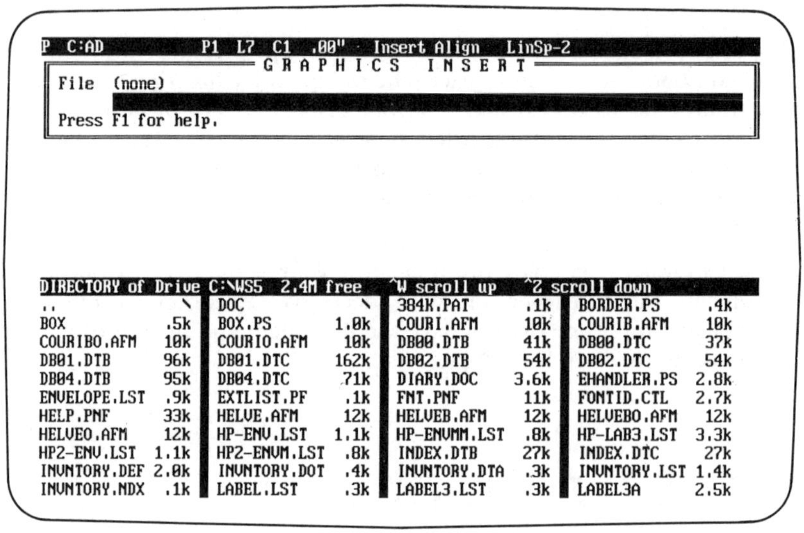
P C:AD P1 L7 C1 .00" Insert Align LinSp-2
GRAPHICS INSERT
File (none)
Press F1 for help.
DIRECTORY of Drive C:\WS5 2.4M free ^W scroll up ^Z scroll down
.. \ DOC \ 384K.PAT .1k BORDER.PS .4k
BOX .5k BOX.PS 1.0k COURI.AFM 10k COURIB.AFM 10k
COURIBO.AFM 10k COURIO.AFM 10k DB00.DTB 41k DB00.DTC 37k
DB01.DTB 96k DB01.DTC 162k DB02.DTB 54k DB02.DTC 54k
DB04.DTB 95k DB04.DTC 71k DIARY.DOC 3.6k EHANDLER.PS 2.8k
ENVELOPE.LST .9k EXTLIST.PF .1k FNT.PNF 11k FONTID.CTL 2.7k
HELP.PNF 33k HELVE.AFM 12k HELVEB.AFM 12k HELVEBO.AFM 12k
HELVEO.AFM 12k HP-ENV.LST 1.1k HP-ENVMM.LST .8k HP-LAB3.LST 3.3k
HP2-ENV.LST 1.1k HP2-ENVM.LST .8k INDEX.DTB 27k INDEX.DTC 27k
INVNTORY.DEF 2.0k INVNTORY.DOT .4k INVNTORY.DTA .3k INVNTORY.LST 1.4k
INVNTORY.NDX .1k LABEL.LST .3k LABEL3.LST .3k LABEL3A 2.5k

Fig. 7.11. *Inserting a graphics tag for printing images in text.*

To select a graphics image file for printing at this spot in your document, type its name at the prompt or use the arrow keys to highlight the image file's name in the directory below the Graphics Insert dialog box, then press Enter. All InSet image files are named with a PIX extension, making it easy to distinguish them among the directory file listings.

Once you have completed selection of an InSet file with ^P*, you see that WordStar inserts a command tag indicating the name of the file between square brackets in your text (for instance, [FIG7.PIX]). If on-screen display is toggled off with ^OD, the graphics tags are hidden. At print time, with InSet loaded as a memory-resident program, the corresponding image is printed in this space in graphics mode on a dot-matrix or laser printer. (InSet graphics cannot be reproduced on a daisywheel printer.) To eliminate a graphics tag from a document, delete it with one of WordStar's standard deletion commands. For more about InSet graphics capabilities, see Chapter 12.

Using Sheet Feeders

WordStar Release 5 can accommodate printers with automatic sheet feeders. This capability is useful, for example, when you print a continuous document on letterhead, second page stock, and colored paper, along with an envelope, each from different feeder bins.

To use an automatic sheet feeder with WordStar, first you must use the WSCHANGE program to install it along with the PDF for your printer (see Chapter 11). If a sheet feeder isn't listed for your printer model, you can add the feeder codes noted in your printer manual to the PDF.

Most sheet feeders require a form feed after every page. The form feed ejects a printed page and substitutes a new one. You ensure this function by pressing Y at the `Use form feeds` print-options prompt. Sheet feeders also may impose their own formatting requirements on your documents; you may have to change your document defaults with dot command settings for the top margin (.MT) to 2 lines (.33″), bottom margin (.MB) to 5 lines (.83″), and page length (.PL) to 62 lines (10.3″) to accommodate the most common margins for feeder handling. You may have to adjust these settings further to prevent text from advancing up or down the page.

For sheet feeders with more than one bin, a simple dot command at the top of a document page can switch bins to access different types of paper or envelopes. The command for activating sheet feeders is listed on WordStar Release 5's first help menu of command listings as follows:

```
.bn n              Use sheet feeder bin n (1-4)
```

You can remember this command as .BN for "bin." When typed, the command must be followed by a number from 1 through 4 to designate the bin from which you want to send paper to be printed. If you type *0* after a .BN command, the previously activated sheet feeder is disabled. Typing ***end*** after a .BN command clears the last page in a print run.

With most printers and feeders, putting a .BN command at the top of a document page, before the first printing character, causes paper to be loaded before that page begins to be printed. Placing a .BN command at the end of a document causes the last page to be ejected, and no new paper is loaded. Before invoking automatic sheet feeders, make sure that the bins are filled with stationery and are ready to operate.

Advanced Editing of Printer Description Files

Beyond the extensive adjustments to printer description files available with WSCHANGE and PRCHANGE programs (see Chapter 11), WordStar Release 5 provides additional customization for printer characteristics. The PDFEDIT program, supplied on the WordStar package's Advanced Customization Disk, is a new option for expert users of customized printers.

After being copied onto the same disk and directory as your program and PDF files, the PDFEDIT program can be run from the DOS prompt by typing *pdfedit*. As soon as the program is loaded, however, the following warning appears on-screen:

```
                    CAUTION

MicroPro does not provide telephone support for the PDF
Editor. This program is intended for use by original
equipment manufacturers (OEMs), value-added resellers
(VARs), printer manufacturers, or individuals with extensive
knowledge of printer technology.
```

As the README file on the Advanced Customization Disk explains, "This is a very technical program for advanced users. Any modifications are made entirely on your own." The README file should be read for late-breaking information concerning WordStar Release 5.

In keeping with MicroPro International's warnings, this author does not believe in, or condone, the use of PDFEDIT except under expert supervision.

Troubleshooting Printer Problems

If your printer fails to work properly with WordStar, the malfunction could be due to possible problems in three areas. Complications can occur in hardware (your computer or printer), in software (in WordStar and its settings), or in an area often overlooked: the computer-printer connection. By following simple diagnostic procedures, most common problems can be remedied easily.

Often a printer malfunction is due to an improperly set printer switch or incorrectly installed WordStar PDF. At other times, the situation may be beyond your ability to remedy; your computer or hardware may need repair by a competent technician. Unless you have the proper tools and knowledge, do not try to fix a computer or printer on your own. With delicate chips and electromechanical systems on the line, you could compound any damage sustained by your equipment.

Before searching for a serious malfunction, check the obvious. Are the computer and printer power switches turned on? Be sure that wall plugs are plugged in and that power is flowing, as confirmed by indicator lights on the hardware components. If you have not already done so, make sure that everything that should be connected, installed, and loaded has been correctly hooked up. The printer connection is a good place to start troubleshooting.

Testing the Printer Connection

Sometimes connector cables sold as "standard" for printers turn out to be configured for someone else's standard. Or maybe your cable is damaged. Signals sent to one of the 25 pins on the parallel cable connector may not be getting through to their destination. As a result, your printer either may not start printing, or it may print incorrect characters. After you have established that the computer-printer connection is the problem, the remedy may be as simple as changing cables.

To test your printer connection, press ^P at the DOS prompt to establish a direct connection between your computer's screen and printer. Now, whatever you type on-screen at the DOS prompt is reproduced by your printer—the rough equivalent of typewriter mode—provided your printer is properly connected.

The printed characters must be the same ones you typed, with no missed or substituted entries. Try all the character keys. If errors seem limited to certain keys or codes, you may have a problem with your keyboard or printer. If the errors are similar throughout, the problem may be the connection between the printer and keyboard. If you discover that the connection is not the problem, your next step should be to examine hardware settings as the possible source of the problem.

Checking Hardware Settings

Printer errors often are caused by improperly set switches inside computer and printer hardware. Frequently overlooked are the settings of the banks of tiny plastic controllers known as DIP switches. The size of these switches makes them inconvenient to set, but correct settings are essential for the proper functioning of your printer.

In your computer or on add-on interface circuit boards, a half dozen of these switches may allocate internal memory, set communications speed, and address printer connectors. If you have not set these switches, check your computer and board manuals' listings of DIP-switch settings. For printers, DIP switches can set character width, fonts, foreign characters, letter-quality printing, proportional spacing, and other print-time features. Check your printer's manual for instructions on selecting the proper switch settings.

If you use special batch file setups, complete with memory-resident programs loaded along with WordStar, you may find that the layers of software are resetting the hardware switches. Make sure that any DOS commands you are using to define your system assign the correct printer port addresses: PRN, LPT1, or LPT2 for a parallel printer; or COM1 or COM2 for a serial printer. These printing port designations also can be reset with the WSCHANGE program.

Checking WordStar Settings

If all else seems to be working properly, but your printer fails to respond, prints incorrect text characters, or formats the text improperly, a WordStar setting may be the problem. The most common problems are easily corrected by changing to a different PDF or modifying a PDF with the WSCHANGE program.

As mentioned earlier in this chapter, you can print the PRINT.TST file to see how well your printer reproduces special effects. If certain print functions in PRINT.TST are incorrectly implemented, try a different PDF for your printout. One common error is to use a PDF for a printer that is nearly identical to yours, but that issues extra line feeds. These extra line feeds can cause your printer to double-space single-spaced copy. To correct this problem, switch PDFs or change WordStar's default settings with the WSCHANGE program.

To see whether problems are specific to your working copy of WordStar, try using an unmodified copy of the program with the generic DRAFT printer driver installed. Sometimes the simplest settings are the best for WordStar's printer functions.

Part III

Advanced WordStar

This book's first two parts cover word processing essentials: entering, editing, formatting, and printing text, using approximately two-thirds of WordStar's commands. Beyond these core tasks, you may need advanced functions for your own applications.

The last part of this book describes productivity-enhancing features beyond those of standard word processing. These functions are part of the latest version of the WordStar program—or available with compatible software in the WordStar Release 5 package or purchased separately. WordStar's advanced features can help you communicate more efficiently, automate or customize major functions, check spelling or use specialized text database functions. The WordStar package also bundles advanced outlining, file handling, and useful add-on capabilities.

You may follow Part III of this book in order as it increases in complexity and separation from the core program. Or you may prefer using these pages as a reference for advanced WordStar functions. New with the WordStar Release 5 package are auxiliary programs for managing mailing lists, communicating text files to other computers, outlining a document's structure, and locating text within files. WordStar Release 5 also has improved spelling checker and thesaurus functions (which now include definitions) and expanded WordStar customization options.

Through the five chapters in Part III, you can explore the following advanced operations:

- Chapter 8 shows how to print form letters with WordStar, how to manage mailing lists with MailList, and how to telecommunicate with other computers with TelMerge.
- Chapter 9 analyzes WordStar's shorthand macro feature for automating repetitive keystrokes and complex functions. Creating your own special functions is detailed.
- Chapter 10 examines WordStar's spelling checker, electronic thesaurus, index, and table of contents functions. The ProFinder add-on program for text file location is also covered.

- Chapter 11 describes how to customize WordStar features and default settings with WSCHANGE. WordStar Release 5 includes a new customization program, PRCHANGE, specifically for modifying printer settings.
- Chapter 12 explains how to enhance WordStar with other programs—compatible add-ons, like PC-Outline for advanced outlining, and incompatible MS-DOS software for which files must be converted.

Part III provides shortcuts, cautionary notes, and helpful hints. You can master even the most advanced features with a little time, effort, and the advice in these pages.

8

Mailing and Communicating with WordStar

WordStar pioneered in widening the scope of word processing on personal computers by automating mass mailings. Merge printing was first implemented as a separate MailMerge file, but is now part of the main WordStar program. The WordStar Release 5 package also includes separate MailList software for manipulating mailing lists. WordStar's communications range has been significantly extended in the WordStar Release 5 package with the add-on TelMerge program for transmitting and receiving computerized information (including data from commercial services) via telephone line.

Merge printing itself goes beyond producing multiple mailings or personalizing word-processed letters. With merge printing, you can save keystrokes when you enter numerical data for invoices, customize boilerplate text for contracts, or print multiple versions of a report. When supplemented with the MailList program for editing and sorting address lists, WordStar's merge printing feature can facilitate billing, promotional mailings, and other uses of selectively addressed documents. To send files faster than by mail or even overnight delivery, you can run TelMerge communications functions to send files to another computer as fast as a dozen pages per minute—anywhere on earth.

This chapter covers about three dozen WordStar and associated program commands that you can use to do the following:

- Create a master document to be modified by merge printing
- Compose a file with data for insertion in the document
- Set up conditional functions for merge printing or mailing list management
- Transmit and receive documents or data via telephone line

If you are a veteran user of WordStar, you will find merge printing functions in WordStar Release 5 essentially unchanged from those in WordStar 4. Welcome additions in Release 5 include the sorting powers of the MailList program and automated communications with TelMerge (an option with WordStar Release 3.3). This chapter's Release 5 icons signal many ways of extending WordStar's value in your office and home.

In this chapter, the sample business letter created in Chapter 4 serves as an example for generating a form letter. Also featured are timesaving tips for printing envelopes and mailing labels. Even if your word processing applications currently don't require form-letter or telecommunications capabilities, learning about these features could spark your use of WordStar's advanced functions for increasing the reach of your documents.

Introducing Merge Printing

Ordinarily, when you invoke printing from the Opening screen by pressing P (or FP at help level 4) or from within a document with a ^KP command and typing *n*, WordStar treats the document as text to be sent unchanged to the printer. On the other hand, when you invoke merge printing by pressing M at the Opening screen or after pressing ^KP within a document and typing *y*, WordStar treats a document as a string of characters that can be uncoupled, combined with other strings that are stored on disk or typed at print time, and then sent to the printer. During merge printing, your computer's processor acts as a miniaturized switching yard, arranging words according to merge-print commands included in a master document or stored in a separate command file.

With merge-print commands, most of which are easy-to-use dot commands, you can program a whole series of text changes that result in dozens or even hundreds of documents being customized and printed without human intervention. Such sophisticated applications suggest an important corollary: the need for clearly annotating merge-print uses. Even if you are the only person who normally works with a particular master document or data file, you never know when you might want to swap files with a colleague. Including nonprinting comment lines in documents and data files so that anyone can understand their content and applications is a good practice. Also helpful are the screen messages WordStar lets you add to explain what should be done when a merge-print job is run.

Preparing the Master Document

No doubt you have received more than your share of computerized form letters. These letters are often obvious in their attempts to be "personal." They use variables or generic labels to "personalize" the text of a master letter with mailing list information. When the master document is fed incorrect data from the commercial lists used for such mailings, an erroneous spelling, personal reference, or company name reveals the machine-generated origins of the "personal" letter. Nevertheless, you can judiciously include data in a letter's variables to enhance, not detract from, its impact.

The most common use for WordStar's merge-printing feature is the creation of a simple form-letter mailing. For an example of such an application, you can create a one-page master letter, a brief mailing list, and a printout of the resulting personalized letters. You can also modify the promotional letter created and saved in Chapter 4. By the time you have finished making these modifications, the Widgets, Inc., sales promotion master letter will look like the one that follows. Sections of this chapter explain each of the merge-print commands in the letter and tell you how to use them.

```
.. Master letter for New Product Sales Promotion
.IG Version 3.1 - 10/23/88
.OP
.DF MAILLIST.DAT
.RV First-name,Last-name,Title,Company,Street-address,City,State
    ZIP,Business-category,Volume-87,Volume-88,Handedness.
.SV Product-line=office widgets
.CS Type the appropriate adjective after the question mark:
.AV "economical, expensive, adaptable, profitable ",Qualifier
.DM Thank you!
.MA Volume-87+88=&Volume-87& + &Volume-88&
.PF on
               Widgets Inc.

                          &#&



   &First-name& &Last-name&
   &Title/o&
   &Company&
   &Street-address&
   &City&, &State& &ZIP&

   Dear &First-name&:
```

```
    You are among the first &Business-category&s to know about
    plans for extending our &Product-line& with a new and more
    &Qualifier& Premium Widget and a high-end Super Widget.

    As someone whose business with Widgets, Inc., will total
    more than &Volume-87+88& in 1987 and 1988, you will
    share our enthusiasm for these models when you see the
    figures below. The margins between wholesale and suggested
    list prices should provide you with ample profits. By
    placing an advance order now, you will be guaranteed the
    following prices:

.AWoff
```

Price	1-999 units	1000 or more	Sug. List
Premium Widget	$9.75	$7.95	$19.99
Super Widget	$12.95	$10.25	$29.99

```
.AWon

    Our local sales rep will be calling you soon with details on
    our introductory pricing structure.

    Help us make the launch of these new Widgets the most
    mutually rewarding ever in our industry!

                                Sincerely,

.PA
```

Often, a master document is derived from an existing WordStar document, as in the example used here. How is a master document different from an ordinary WordStar document? It contains commands and symbols that are activated only when merge printing is invoked. In fact, if a master document is printed with a standard P print command, the mail-merge commands and symbols will be printed as plain text.

During merge printing, however, those special dot commands and characters invoke powerful functions. Odd-looking pairs of ampersands (&) in a master document turn generic text labels into variable names. The variables become insertion points for data items from the mailing list like address or ZIP code to individualize the form letter at print time. Other commands in the master letter let you chain together different files, combining them according to alphabetical or numerical conditions met by the data for any variable—for example, for accounts more than 90 days overdue or for a single category of supplier.

The actual content of variables, such as names and addresses, is inserted automatically from a separate data file during merge printing. Or, a user can specify the content by entering it at print time. Using variables correctly is essential to error-free insertion of information with merge printing.

A master document is always created and edited in document mode to retain the formatting features that distinguish WordStar document files. Print controls and dot commands that set the master document's format remain in force during merge printing.

Using Variables

Variables within a master document indicate information that changes from one copy to the next when the document is printed. In a form letter, variables would include such information as first name, last name, address, and ZIP code. When the master document and the data file are merge printed, individual items from the mailing list replace the variables in the letter.

You must assign a generic name to each variable you use in a master document. The information that is inserted in place of that variable name during merge printing is called *data*. A generic name for a variable must be a single word, which can be as long as 39 characters. Upper- and lowercase letters are interchangeable. The variable name must be bracketed by ampersands—as in &Name&. You may use spaces on either side of the name within ampersands, but WordStar ignores these spaces at print time. Therefore, the following two variables are equivalent:

&Company&

& Company &

On the other hand, within a variable name, you cannot have any spaces, commas, or ampersands. You can include hyphens or other punctuation marks in place of spaces.

When you choose variable names, select ones that are readily understandable, by you at some later time or by anyone else. For example, &Business-category& would be a better choice than &Type& for a variable name that identifies a prospect's kind of business. You can use the same data several times in a document by repeating the variable name.

WordStar has only two limitations to variable use: no data item can be more than 255 characters long and the total number of characters in all the variable data inserted into any copy of a master document cannot exceed 4,000 characters—about two typewritten pages of text. (The latter limit can be altered with WSCHANGE.)

To ensure proper placement of data at merge-printing time, each generic name—complete with ampersands—must be at the place in the master document's text where individualized information is to appear. When the document is merge printed, the ampersands and their generic names are replaced by data from another file or from typed input. If no data is available for a particular variable at printing time, WordStar inserts nothing. When an empty variable is the only text on a line—often the case with addresses—WordStar leaves a blank line. To avoid the blank line, which disrupts proper print formatting, you can make the variable optional. Typing the /o option (upper- or lowercase) just before the second ampersand in a variable name does the job. Any variable alone on a line can be made optional, meaning that it prints only when data is available. An example of an optional variable is &Title/o& for job titles in addresses.

WordStar Release 5 also includes four predefined variables, shown in table 8.1. The data for these variables is supplied by WordStar at merge-print time. These predefined variables can insert into printed documents current page and line numbers, or the current date or time from DOS.

Table 8.1
Predefined Merge-Printing Variables

Variable	*Function*
&#&	Inserts current page number
&_&	Inserts current line number
&@&	Inserts current date from DOS
&!&	Inserts current time from DOS

The format for the date in WordStar Release 5 is the name of the month, followed by day and year (July 4, 1990). The time format is the 12-hour format for hour and minute display (10:30). These default settings can be reset with the WSCHANGE program (see Chapter 11).

The predefined variables for inserting the current page or line number can be useful for setting merge-printing conditions, as explained later in this chapter. The date and time variables are a handy way of stamping business documents with current timing information. These preset variables are similar to their counterpart @ and ! shorthand commands, which are explained in Chapter 9.

To try including variables in a master document, you can type the variables into the sample master letter for a Widgets, Inc. mailing. At the top of the finished master letter, shown earlier in this chapter, are a number of dot command lines. These lines can be added later; for now, you would start by typing variable names into the document.

If you created the original letter according to instructions in Chapter 4, make a copy of its file from the opening screen by first pressing O (or FO at help level 4).

Then, designate the file by typing its name or pointing with the cursor, press Enter, and name the copy LETTER.MSR to indicate that the letter is to be used as a master document. After you press Enter again, the new file name should appear on the file directory and you can open the LETTER.MSR file for editing.

If you did not create the letter file earlier, simply open a new file called LETTER.MSR and type the text of the finished master letter as shown in this chapter. Whether you enter the sample letter for the first time or copy it from Chapter 4, you need to adjust the left and right margin settings to 0.7 inches and 5.9 inches. For this example, leave line spacing at the default for single-spacing. If you have already entered the letter, auto-align will reformat for single-spacing as text is entered.

With the cursor at the beginning of the date in the letter, delete the date and type &@& to signal WordStar to insert the current date automatically during merge printing. (If you do not have a clock card that sets the date and time in DOS, make sure to do so manually when you boot your system.) Next, with the cursor at the beginning of the address block for the master letter, deleting and retyping where necessary, change Richard Roe's four-line address block into the following five lines of generic variables:

&First-name&
&Last-name&
&Title/o&
&Company&
&Street-address&
&City&, &State& &ZIP&

Notice that the second line of the address block contains an optional variable. Also notice that first and last names are kept in separate variables so that either can be used independently of the other. This is the case in the salutation that follows. In place of `Mr. Roe`, which should be deleted, you type *&First-name&*. Now when printed the letter should begin with the greeting `Dear (first name here):`.

After you put all the variables in place in the first paragraph of the master document, move the cursor to the beginning of the second paragraph. With ^G, delete the uppercase `Y` in `You` and replace it with `y`; then, at the cursor, type the following:

As someone whose business with Widgets, Inc., will
total more than &Volume-87+88& in 1987 and 1988,

You now have entered all the variable names to be used in your master document. These variables are like the cutouts for a stencil. They are of little use without the data from a mailing list to fill in the spaces in the stencil. To access a file that contains such data, or to allow manual entry of data before or at print time, a master document requires special dot commands for merge-print functions.

Using Merge-Print Dot Commands

The merge-print commands in WordStar Release 5 are dot commands familiar to veteran users of MailMerge. When you insert these commands in existing text, the WordStar document screen displays a colon (:) in the flag column.

In a master document, every variable must be defined with a dot command inserted at the start of the document. If a dot command is mistyped, or if the data is unavailable, WordStar prints the variable name itself in place of the data.

The dot commands for merge printing must begin in column 1. The merge-print dot commands for simple form letters are detailed in table 8.2.

Table 8.2
Merge-Print Dot Commands

Dot Command	*Function*
.DF filename	Reads the named data file
.RV v1, v2, etc.	Inserts data from the named file into specified variable names in the master document
.RV*	Inserts data from dBASE® file
.RV* $x,$y	Inserts data from spreadsheet file
.SV v=text	Sets the value of a variable within a master document
.AV text,v	Displays text requesting the specified variable value be typed into the master document
.CS text	Clears the screen and displays text as a message
.DM text	Displays text as a message
.MA v=text	Inserts the value of a math equation into the specified variable in the master document
.PF on/off/dis	Reformats while merge printing

Along with these merge-print commands, one other dot command must always appear in every master document. A .PA page-break command followed by a carriage return must come at the end of the document to ensure that every additional copy begins printing at the top of a new page. Always be sure to type *.pa* at column 1 (0.0″) at the bottom of a master document and press Enter before you close and save the file. Also, be sure that the file ends immediately after the .PA command and the carriage return.

Before you insert merge-print dot commands in the Widgets master document, enter the necessary page-break command at the end of the letter. Move the cursor to the end of the open LETTER.MSR document and at the first column of the last line, type *.pa* and press Enter.

Reading Variables from a Data File

Merge-print operations most frequently draw on external data stored in a separate disk file (like an address or billing file) to replace variables in a master document. The dot commands for merging data files and master documents are paired. They cannot operate separately, and they must be entered in a set order.

In WordStar Release 5, all the available merge-print commands are displayed on a a single dot command help screen, the sixth screen of listings. Invoke this display with ^J. or F1. Then press Enter six times. The listings screen, labeled MERGE PRINT, is shown in figure 8.1.

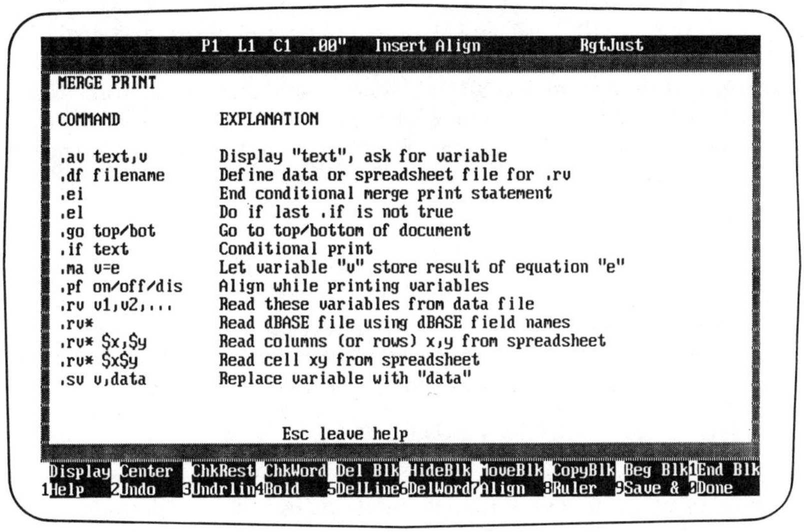
P1 L1 C1 .00" Insert Align RgtJust
MERGE PRINT
COMMAND EXPLANATION
.av text,v Display "text", ask for variable
.df filename Define data or spreadsheet file for .rv
.ei End conditional merge print statement
.el Do if last .if is not true
.go top/bot Go to top/bottom of document
.if text Conditional print
.ma v=e Let variable "v" store result of equation "e"
.pf on/off/dis Align while printing variables
.rv v1,v2,... Read these variables from data file
.rv* Read dBASE file using dBASE field names
.rv* $x,$y Read columns (or rows) x,y from spreadsheet
.rv* xy Read cell xy from spreadsheet
.sv v,data Replace variable with "data"
Esc leave help
Display Center ChkRest ChkWord Del Blk HideBlk MoveBlk CopyBlk Beg Blk End Blk
1Help 2Undo 3Undrlin 4Bold 5DelLine 6DelWord 7Align 8Ruler 9Save & 0Done

Fig. 8.1.
WordStar Release 5's help screen listing of merge printing dot commands.

Of the thirteen listings on the Merge Print screen of dot commands, five pertain to the two principal commands for merge printing:

```
.df filename        Define data or spreadsheet file for .rv
.rv v1,v2,...       Read these variables from data file
.rv*                Read dBASE using dBASE field names
.rv* $x,$y          Read columns (or rows) x,y from spreadsheet
.rv* $x$y           Read cell xy from spreadsheet
```

With WordStar Release 5, you have greater flexibility in designating data sources, which now can be selected portions of dBASE or spreadsheet files. In WordStar merge printing, specifying data from other programs' files requires a properly chosen combination of .DF and .RV commands. As always, you should take care to match data to variable names.

The .DF and .RV commands always are used together in a master document file, and .DF always comes first. The .DF command must specify the name of a data file before the .RV command can define the variable fields used by each record in that file.

In many cases, the .DF command is followed on the same line by the name of a data file on disk. If necessary, you can include a drive letter or subdirectory path, as in the following example:

.DF C:\WS5\FILES\LIST.DAT

5

In WordStar Release 5, you can designate a spreadsheet or database file as the data source for merge printing. In your master document, type the .DF command followed by the file name. Files from Lotus 1-2-3 (through Version 2.1), Symphony, Quattro, dBASE II®, III®, or III Plus®, and MailList can be read into a merge printing operation. WordStar accepts a spreadsheet file's rows of data as records, with each column in the spreadsheet treated as a field. When named, an entire spreadsheet file and window 1 (the MAIN window in Symphony) are used for WordStar merge printing. The command to incorporate data from the complete range of a spreadsheet file might look like this:

.DF C:\LOTUS\1988\BUDGET.WKS

You can modify the .DF command to limit the data source for merge printing to a range of spreadsheet cells or a window other than 1. After the dot command and file name, type the appropriate letter and number designations using commas as separator characters. For instance, you could draw data from the range E6 to N12 and from window 3 by entering this command in the master document:

.DF C:\LOTUS\1988\BUDGET.WKS,E6...N12,3

When limiting the range of data from a spreadsheet for merge printing, you can type range names or cell numbers. With cell numbers, use an asterisk to designate the last cell in a worksheet. With a Symphony spreadsheet file, if you don't specify a window, WordStar searches out the MAIN window; if this has been renamed, type the new window name. If you specify only a window with the .DF command, use two commas before the window number, as in

.DF C:\LOTUS\1988\BUDGET.WKS,,3

An option with the .DF command is the addition of `change` or `c` to display to the user a prompt at print time that floppy disks must be swapped in order to read in the data file. For example, you might type the following to indicate that this hypothetical data file disk must be placed in drive B to complete a merge:

.DF B:SHRTLIST.DAT change

The .RV command indicates the variable names that correspond to data in the data file. The .RV command must be followed by the variable names of all the fields in the data file in the order in which the fields are listed in each record. Even if data from a field is not used to replace a variable in the master document, the field must be indicated in the proper position after the .RV command. Typically a .RV command would be typed as follows:

```
.RV name,street,city,state,ZIP,amount-due,due-date
```


With WordStar Release 5, if a dBASE database file is your data source (as specified with the .DF command), simply type .RV without any variable names. The dBASE names for fields are entered automatically as merge printing data. (For a listing of field names from a dBASE file, from within your master document press ^KR and, when prompted for the file to read, type its name followed by */f*. This procedure brings in all the names of the dBASE data fields without the data.) One of the features in dBASE III Plus is the creation of memo fields of unlimited length. Any such memo field can be designated as a variable, so you can include notations from your dBASE file.

If a spreadsheet file is your data source for merge printing, you can use variable names as you would with a regular .RV command—or indicate selected columns, rows, or cells within the worksheet file. For columns, enter a dollar sign ($) before each column letter. Thus, data from columns B, D, and F would be designated with a command like this

```
.RV $B,$D,$F
```

On a vertically based (column-major) worksheet, rows can be specified with a dollar sign before row numbers in this manner

```
.RV $2,$4,$8,$9,$10
```

Row and column designations cannot be used with the same .RV command, but you can mix in specific cell designations by putting dollar signs before appropriate coordinates and omitting commas, like the following example:

```
.RV $B,$D,$F,$G$6,$I$10
```

When typing variable names for spreadsheet data in the master document, remember to include the dollar sign before rows and columns or cells, as in &$F& or &$G$6&.

When .RV is used with spreadsheet vocations, WordStar goes to a new record at the end of each .RV command. If more than one .RV command is needed for all the variable names in a worksheet, follow all but the last .RV with a plus sign (+) continuation character, as in this example

```
.RV + $A,$C,$D
.RV + $E,$G,$H
.RV $I
```

During merge printing, the .RV command tells WordStar to continue inserting data as indicated until each record (all the information pertaining to a person's name or a billing number, for example) is read from the data file. WordStar keeps track of the number of variable names listed after the .RV command and reads in an identical number of fields (items of information, such as address, amount due, and so on) for each record.

If the variable names listed after the .RV command don't fit the data file listings, incorrectly ordered information will be inserted throughout copies of the master document. On the other hand, if a record doesn't have enough fields to fit the variables in a master document, WordStar reads fields from the next line or record, resulting in confusion for the merge-print operation's inserts.

Incidentally, as with other merge-print dot commands, you can repeat the .RV command so that it applies to different lines of data in the same data record. For example, the two dot command expressions that follow are equivalent:

```
.RV First-name,Last-name,Title,Company,Street-address,City,State
    ZIP,Business-category,Volume-87,Volume-88,Handedness
```

```
.RV First-name,Last-name,Title,Company,Street-address,City,State
.RV ZIP,Business-category,Volume-87,Volume-88,Handedness
```

If you use the first format shown here, be sure to press Enter after the first line is typed.

In the Widgets sample form letter, begin entering merge printing dot commands by first entering the familiar .IG and .OP commands. Then type either of the preceding pairs of lines. With the master document file LETTER.MSR open, move the cursor to the top of the file and type the following dot commands:

```
.IG Master letter for New Product Sales Promotion
.IG Version 3.1 – 10/23/88
.OP
.DF MAILLIST.DAT
.RV First-name,Last-name,Title,Company,Street-address,City,State
.RV ZIP,Business-category,Volume-87,Volume-88,Handedness
```

By entering the .DF and .RV commands into the master letter, you are defining the data to be merged with the document. In this case, you indicate the mailing list file MAILLIST.DAT as the data file and set the exact order in which data is to be read.

If a mailing list doesn't have all the data to be inserted into the form letter, you can use two merge-printing dot commands that permit the manual insertion of data not included in a data file. These commands are discussed in the next section.

Entering Variable Data Manually at Print Time

On occasion, you will want to add data to form letters manually, either before or as they are printed. You can avoid mistakes that can occur using unchecked data files by doing this. If there's any chance of variable data being misread, you can specify a data entry for all instances of a variable or pause printing to request input from an operator.

On the sixth screen of dot command help listings, all merge-print commands, you see the following at the top and bottom of the list:

```
.av text,v    Display "text", ask for variable
.sv v,data    Replace variable with "data"
```

The .AV and .SV dot commands can be best described, respectively, by the simple mnemonics "ask for variable" and "set variable."

The .SV command substitutes a string of characters for a variable name—not unlike the search-and-replace function during editing. This feature is useful for contracts and court documents where a few .SV commands can substitute real names for terms such as "first party" and "second party."

A .SV dot command should be followed by the name of a variable in the document, a comma or equal sign, and the data to be substituted for that variable. Both these .SV commands are similar in effect:

.SV Name,Smith

.SV Name=Smith

When WordStar merge prints, spaces after the comma or equal sign are omitted. If spaces are to be included in a variable name, the data must be enclosed in quotation marks or apostrophes. During execution of merge printing, the data specified by .SV commands is inserted in place of the corresponding variable names throughout the master document.

The .AV command doesn't preset a variable in a master document. Rather, the command halts merge printing so that a variable can be typed at the prompt and inserted separately in each copy of a form letter. The simplest format for this command consists of the .AV command followed by the name of a variable.

When merge printing occurs, the .AV command displays a prompt with the variable name and a question mark. For example, the command line `.AV Age` at merge-print time results in the prompt `Age?`. Typing a response and pressing Enter inserts this data into the new copy of the document as printing resumes.

You also can use the .AV command if you want your own prompt text or message to appear on-screen when merge printing is paused for data entry. The command sequence is .AV followed by the text of the prompt in quotation marks or apostrophes, a comma, and the name of the variable. Any prompt or question and its answer must fit into a line of text on-screen. If long answers are necessary, you may prefer to keep the text of the .AV prompt as short as possible to leave room for answers. Additional merge-print dot commands explained in the next section of this chapter let you display messages on-screen during merge printing.

With the sample letter to be merge printed, place the cursor at the beginning of the line below the .RV command and type the following set-variable command line:

.SV Product-line = office widgets

At merge print time, this command substitutes the words `office widgets` for the variable `Product-line` throughout the master document. For an application of the .AV command, you can type this text at column 1 of the line below the .SV command:

.AV "economical, expensive, adaptable, profitable ",Qualifier

During merge printing, each time the master document reaches the variable `Qualifier`, the merge-print operation would then pause and the following prompt would appear:

```
economical, expensive, adaptable, profitable?
```

Only after a typed response does printing resume. To make the prompt more understandable, you can display messages during merge printing.

Displaying Messages during Printing

To make merge-printing applications easier to use, you can add your own messages to offer instructions, explain operations, or provide additional information at prompts.

In WordStar Release 5, the first screen of dot-command help listings includes these two lines of entries:

```
.cs         Clear screen for messages while printing

.dm text    Display "text" while printing
```

Although the feature is not noted in the help listing, .CS also can display a message based on text typed after it. Both these commands can display a message on-screen during merge printing; the .CS command clears the screen and .DM does not. Messages are displayed on the printing screen, not on the editing screen, during background printing.

To use dot commands for messages during merge printing in the Widgets, Inc. master document, first move the cursor to the line above the .AV command and type this line:

.CS Type the appropriate adjective after the question mark:

During merge printing, this .CS dot command clears the screen and displays an explanatory message that clarifies the input needed by the .AV command. To improve this message even more, move the cursor to the line below the .AV dot command and insert a line with this dot command:

.DM Thank you!

After you enter the data requested by the .AV command and press Enter while printing, this line rewards you with a little courtesy.

Setting Variables with Math Results

Among WordStar's useful merge-printing commands is the one for performing calculations on variables. You can use this function to define a variable as an equation that operates on data from a separate file. An obvious application would be to total purchases in an account and include the sum in a form letter for billing.

In the middle of the sixth help screen of dot command listings notice the following command description:

```
.ma v=e    Let variable "v" store result of equation "e"
```

The dot command for storing math results during merge printing is therefore .MA. Usually, it's expressed in this form:

.MA variable = equation

When you use the .MA command, you compose equations as you do with the on-screen calculator—with the handy option of treating merge-print variables as terms that can be calculated. In the example of totaling billing data for insertion in a form letter, a .MA command line might read:

.MA total-outstanding = &itemA& + &itemB& – &itemC&

When using variables in a math command, include ampersands for variable names to the right of the equal sign. Omit ampersands to the left of the equal sign.

In the master document for the Widgets, Inc. form letter, for example, type the following dot command line. As with all dot commands, start at the first column. The cursor should be on the line below the .DM command.

.MA Volume-87+88 = &Volume-87& + &Volume-88&

During merge printing, the total of the data fields Volume-87 and Volume-88 are computed and inserted at the Volume-87+88 variable position in the master document.

Because of all the insertions to be made during merge printing, formatting is often disrupted. The following section explains automatic realigning and prestored formats, features for controlling the appearance of merge-printed form documents.

Formatting Merge-Printed Documents

Data items read into merge-printed documents are likely to vary in length from the variable names the data replaces. The lengths of data items also can vary from copy to copy of the personalized master letter. As a default setting, the WordStar merge-print function automatically realigns paragraphs of text where insertions have been made.

Dot commands allow you to override or reset the automatic realigning function to preserve existing formats. Variable formatting also can be controlled by defining special formats for text or numbers in order to preserve their positions in tables and other structured applications.

Toggling Print-Time Formatting

During merge-printing operations, WordStar's realignment of paragraphs where insertions have been made is said to be discretionary. In other words, realigning of text at print time is limited—at WordStar's discretion—to those portions of a document where data has been substituted for a variable name.

At times, as a quality-assurance measure, you may want to have print-time reformatting turned on for all paragraphs. At other times, you may want to turn off print-time formatting to maintain a table or some page design element in a report. You can use a special dot command to control such different formatting situations.

In WordStar Release 5, you can find this special dot command toward the bottom of the sixth screen of dot-command help listings, as follows:

```
.pf on/off/dis   Align while printing variables
```

In effect, WordStar is preset with a .PF Dis (discretionary) command, whether or not the command is actually typed into a master document. When you type *.pf on*, every paragraph is realigned during printing, whether or not merge-print substitutions were made. Typing a *.pf off* command turns off print-time reformatting so that special formats can be preserved.

Alternatively, you can designate sections of text with a dot command so that realignment skips them. The command for this is on the first line of the first screen of dot command listings:

```
.aw on/off        Word wrap and aligning on/off
```

The command .AW Off preserves existing formatting of text (including line spacing), even if formatting dot commands are added in the document. Embedding the command .AW On puts formatting dot commands into effect again.

When reformatting text at merge-print time, WordStar conforms to current margins and line spacing, as modified by dot commands. If formatting is specified with dot commands in a document, that formatting remains in effect during merge-print realignment.

In the Widgets mailing, to realign text during merge printing at the start of the file you would type:

.pf on

or

.aw on

To preserve the formatting of the tabular section of the document, bring the cursor to the line before the pricing table in the letter and type:

.pf off

or

.aw off

Now that the necessary changes for using the master document in merge printing are complete, you could save the LETTER.MSR file.

For highly formatted text applications—such as columns and rows of numbers—WordStar merge printing includes provisions for setting special formats. These are explained in the next section.

Using Variable Formats

When data is inserted into specially formatted columns of text (as in a table) or in limited space (as in a boilerplate document), defining specific formats for variables can save on revisions and other annoyances. You can control the appearance of text inserted at variables with WordStar's merge-printing variable-formatting feature.

After variable format definitions are set with the .SV dot command followed by special code characters, you can limit the length of data entries and align them with other text or number formats in a master document.

To use variable formatting, you must start by defining the possible formats for variables. These are inserted as .SV dot commands at the top of a document. Once in a document, these formats can be set to work with different variables.

Typically, variable formats are set as follows, depending on whether data is text or numbers:

.SV B = LLLLLLLLLLLLLLLLLL

or

.SV 7 = $$,$$$.99

In the master document text, a format can be attached to a variable name by typing a slash (/) after the name, then its letter or number, before the closing ampersand, like this:

&Name/B&

or

&Rent/7&

For text formats, the definitions are based on left-justified (L), right-justified (R), or centered (C) characters, repeated to represent the actual number of letters to fit in the space. Data entries that exceed the formatted length limits are truncated.

For numeric formats, definitions include various wild-card characters describing whether missing digits should be replaced by 0 (using the 9 option), a space (using Z as a wild card), or an asterisk (using the * character). Decimal points, commas, and negative number formatting in form documents are also set with appropriate symbols: a period (.), comma (,), or a set of parentheses [()]. The code characters that define special number formats are summarized in table 8.3.

Table 8.3
Merge-Print Number Format Character Codes

Character	*Function*
9	Inserts a digit. If no digit in data, places a 0 at character.
Z	Inserts a digit. If no digit in data, or a lead 0, places a space at character.
*	Inserts a digit. If no digit in data, or a lead 0, places an asterisk at character.
$	Inserts a dollar sign before first digit. Places a digit if not 0, otherwise a space.
-	Inserts a digit, if not a lead 0. If negative, places a minus sign before character.
( )	Inserts parentheses around a number if negative, substitutes spaces if positive.
.	Inserts a decimal point. If more data than length of format, digits truncated.
,	Inserts a comma.

All these number formats can be combined.

To flag an error when an item of data is longer than the format designated for it (not including extra digits after a decimal point), the merge printing function inserts a string of question marks the length of the format indicated in the master document.

Creating a Data File

A data file contains the information to be substituted during merge printing in place of the variables in a master document. A data file might be an address list, an inventory manifest, or a set of billing information. Such a file is composed of a series of records—information associated with individual names, item numbers, or accounts. Each record consists of several fields—elements such as name, address, financial information, part numbers, and the like. Individual fields in a data file correspond to data to be inserted in place of a variable.

Any merge-print data file must conform to the following data management conventions:

1. The file must be in ASCII format—the format that is produced when you edit in WordStar's nondocument mode.
2. Commas must separate fields of data.
3. Quotation marks must set off fields when a comma is used within data.
4. Each record must end with a hard carriage return.

Creating a data file can be an exacting task with numerous records. As noted, WordStar merge printing can be accomplished with data files created by data management or spreadsheet programs that adhere to this "delimited" ASCII file format for information. The MailList program included in the WordStar Release 5 package can also facilitate creation of data files for mailings (see middle sections of this chapter). If you use only small data files, with a page of two of information, you may prefer to type these files using WordStar's nondocument mode.

For the Widgets' mailing list, each record can follow the data field pattern that qualifies the .RV command in the master document:

First-name,Last-name,Title,Company,Street-address,City,State
ZIP,Business-category,Volume-87,Volume-88,Handedness

This order of data fields must be followed throughout the mailing list. To create a mailing-list data file in this example, begin by opening a nondocument file with the file name MAILLIST.DAT, using the DAT extension to identify a merge-print data file.

When the Nondocument editing screen appears, carefully begin typing the formatted data records to be merged into the form letter.

Formatting a Data File

The rules for formatting a data file are stringent and must be observed for information to be inserted flawlessly within a master document. In addition to being in plain ASCII characters, all data fields must be in the same order in all records.

Data in one field must be separated from data in the next field by a comma or a carriage return. If a field's contents include a comma, the field should be enclosed in quotation marks. For a field that contains quotation marks, apostrophes (') can be used to enclose the field. The following sample entries illustrate these rules:

Bill,Adams,"Vice-President, Purchasing"

Anne, Garvey, Controller, 'New "Antiques"'

Unlike the variable names they replace, fields can have spaces around words, although such spaces are ignored at merge-print time. If a field remains empty because information is missing for that part of the record, the blank field should be indicated by a space and a comma. Here is an example:

Richard, Roe, ,Western Fastmart Co.

If you need to use a separator character other than a comma, as you might with a nonstandard data file format, you can substitute any other keyboard character by running the WSCHANGE program. Instead of changing the data separator character with WSCHANGE, you can add an optional notation to a .DF command when you designate a data file from within the master document. A noncomma separator character that is used in the data file can be read during merge printing if you add to the .DF command the name of the file, a comma, and the character. For example, to read a MAILLIST.DAT file that uses an asterisk as the separator character, you type the following in the master document:

.DF MAILLIST.DAT,*

In early versions of WordStar's merge print function, data records had to be numbered but in Release 5 numbering is optional. Still, you may want to consider numbering as an aid in finding and structuring your records. Simply enter a number at the start of each record to indicate the numerical order and type a comma. When referring to a data file, the .RV command should list variable N (for the data record numbers) first, though this data won't be entered into the master letter.

Entering Data

Because the items in a merge print data file may be reused for subsequent mailings, inventory lists, and so on, they represent a valuable resource—well worth the investment of time and attention to detail in entering data. When you enter data, you must remember to maintain correct formatting and be sure to include all required fields of information. If something is not in your data file, it won't be in your merge printed documents.

In the Widgets, Inc. promotional mailing, the data file includes all necessary address information, account figures, and business categories for individualizing the form letters. One field of data that may not seem standard is the one indicating whether an addressee is right- or left-handed. This is included so that a mailing can be limited to left-handed Californians on the mailing list—a use of conditional merge printing explained later in this chapter.

The sample data file is short but very detailed. The data to be typed is as follows:

Bill, Adams,"Vice-President, Purchasing",ZIPCO,1 ZIPCO Plaza
Zipco, MA, 01999,national account,"3,298,371","4,728,976"
right-hander

Richard,Roe, ,Western Fastmart Co.,1313 Blueview Terrace
San Francisco, CA, 94107,wholesaler,"9,871,382","10,120,918"
right-hander
Anne, Garvey, , 'Anne's New "Antiques"' , 178361 Suncoast Dr.
San Hombre, CA, 90099, retailer, "35,298", "41,728"
left-hander

If you type this file, you start with the first record in the mailing list: the record for Bill Adams. In nondocument mode, there is no word wrap, so you can type all the information for an individual record on a single line of text up to 255 characters long. Because a carriage return can also be used as a field delimiter, here simply press Enter at the end of each line of data shown, and then type the next line. These line lengths allow you to view your data files on the document screen yet maintain the proper delimiters between fields.

Each line in the mailing list ends with a carriage return, which serves as a field separator. The result of using carriage returns to separate records is that the .RV command correctly counts the fields in a record and reads all the data into a personalized letter before proceeding to the next record on the mailing list. Make sure that lines of data that terminate in a carriage return do not have a redundant comma as well.

For this example, continue typing the data fields, paying attention to inserting commas as field separators and using adjoining commas to signal empty fields. When you finish typing data, check for possible errors, particularly in the order of entries, comma placement, and paired quotation marks. You should also make sure that you have included a carriage return at the end of the last line. If typed correctly, your data file should look like the one shown in figure 8.2.

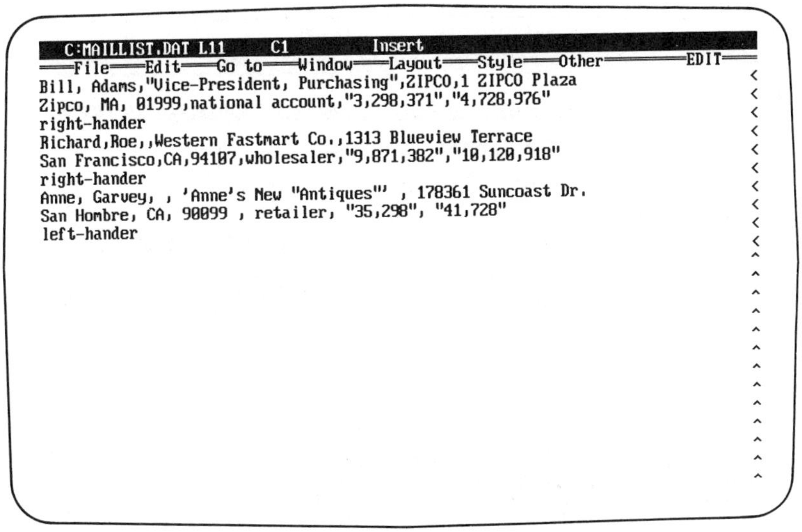
C:MAILLIST.DAT L11 C1 Insert
File Edit Go to Window Layout Style Other EDIT
Bill, Adams,"Vice-President, Purchasing",ZIPCO,1 ZIPCO Plaza
Zipco, MA, 01999,national account,"3,298,371","4,728,976"
right-hander
Richard,Roe,,Western Fastmart Co.,1313 Blueview Terrace
San Francisco,CA,94107,wholesaler,"9,871,382","10,120,918"
right-hander
Anne, Garvey, , 'Anne's New "Antiques"' , 178361 Suncoast Dr.
San Hombre, CA, 90099 , retailer, "35,298", "41,728"
left-hander

Fig. 8.2.
A WordStar merge-print data file.

After you type the data file, close and save it. With both a master document and a data file on your disk, you can now start a merge-printing session to produce copies of your sample form letter.

Printing Merged Documents

As noted earlier in this chapter, the merge-printing process in WordStar Release 5 is a variation of simple printing with WordStar. Commands and options are similar, but the potential for multiple mayhem makes care and planning essential when merge printing.

Before you start a merge-printing session, make sure that all disk files referred to in dot commands are readily accessible, that dot commands and variables in the master document are in the correct order and location, and that data files are properly typed and formatted. On the hardware side, make sure that all printer connections are in place and that all power switches are turned on.

To start the merge-printing operation, select M from the opening screen (FM when at help level 4), or press ^KP from inside a document and press M at the `Print or Merge print (P/M)?` prompt. Regardless of how you invoke merge printing, WordStar displays the dialog screen for merge print options.

In WordStar Release 5, the dialog screen headed MERGE PRINT is similar to the dialog screen for print-time options. The merge print options, as illustrated in figure 8.3, are identical to the standard print options explained in the previous chapter.

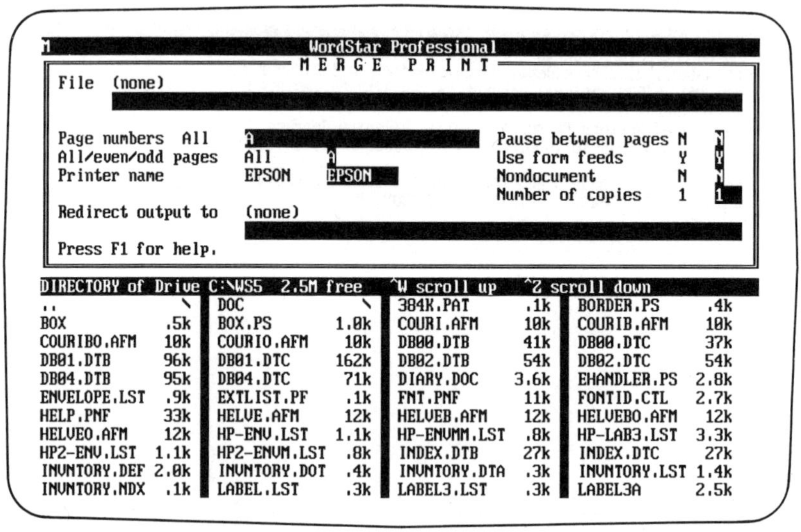
WordStar Professional
M E R G E P R I N T
File (none)
Page numbers All
All/even/odd pages All
Printer name EPSON EPSON
Pause between pages N
Use form feeds Y
Nondocument N
Number of copies 1
Redirect output to (none)
Press F1 for help.
DIRECTORY of Drive C:\WS5 2.5M free ^W scroll up ^Z scroll down
.. \ DOC \ 384K.PAT .1k BORDER.PS .4k
BOX .5k BOX.PS 1.0k COURI.AFM 10k COURIB.AFM 10k
COURIBO.AFM 10k COURIO.AFM 10k DB00.DTB 41k DB00.DTC 37k
DB01.DTB 96k DB01.DTC 162k DB02.DTB 54k DB02.DTC 54k
DB04.DTB 95k DB04.DTC 71k DIARY.DOC 3.6k EHANDLER.PS 2.8k
ENVELOPE.LST .9k EXTLIST.PF .1k FNT.PNF 11k FONTID.CTL 2.7k
HELP.PNF 33k HELVE.AFM 12k HELVEB.AFM 12k HELVEBO.AFM 12k
HELVEO.AFM 12k HP-ENV.LST 1.1k HP-ENVMM.LST .8k HP-LAB3.LST 3.3k
HP2-ENV.LST 1.1k HP2-ENVM.LST .8k INDEX.DTB 27k INDEX.DTC 27k
INVNTORY.DEF 2.0k INVNTORY.DOT .4k INVNTORY.DTA .3k INVNTORY.LST 1.4k
INVNTORY.NDX .1k LABEL.LST .3k LABEL3.LST .3k LABEL3A 2.5k

Fig. 8.3.
Merge printing options in WordStar Release 5.

At the dialog screen's first prompt, indicate the name of the master document file to be merge printed. You can type the name or use the arrow keys to select one of the files in the directory listing. Pressing Enter leads through the options on-screen. To avoid mistakes in merging data, you should print all pages of the master document. Depending on your printer hardware, you may need to invoke another printer description file, or indicate an alternative to the defaults for pausing between pages and using form feeds. When all default settings are acceptable, press ^K or the F10 key. Merge printing begins.

For the Widgets, Inc. mailing example, you would type the name of the master document, LETTER.MSR, at the Merge Print dialog box prompt. Then press Enter if you want to access any of the print-time options. Your choices for these options are similar to those you give in a standard printing session. Pressing ^K or F10 then starts merge printing. The printer should produce three personalized copies of the master letter. When the screen display pauses for the entry of the Qualifier variable, you type an appropriate choice: *economical*, *expensive*, *adaptable*, or *profitable*.

As with Release 5's regular printing, once the printer goes into action, you can interrupt or terminate merge printing from the Printing Menu by pressing P or ^KP; this menu is shown in figure 8.4. The menu choices are as follows: P to pause merge printing; C to resume merge printing after a pause (including one for a paper change); B to return to the Opening Menu or to the document screen with merge printing continuing in the background (although you will be interrupted for variable entry prompts); ^U to cancel merge printing entirely; and F to print at full speed.

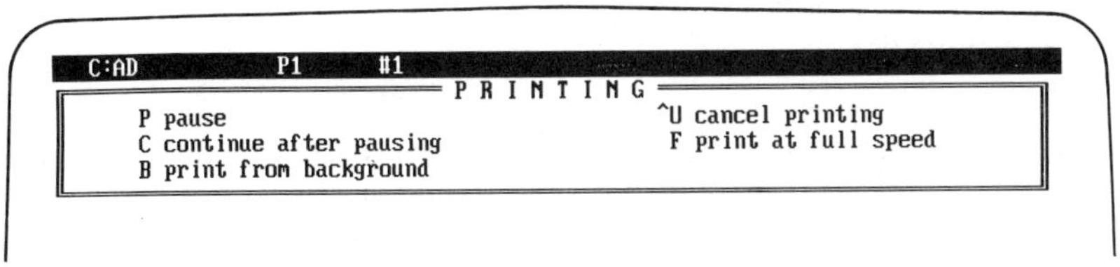
C:AD P1 #1
P R I N T I N G
P pause
C continue after pausing
B print from background
^U cancel printing
F print at full speed

Fig. 8.4.
The Printing Menu for pausing or stopping printer operation.

Previewing the Merge-Print Operation

Though WordStar Release 5's Advanced Page Preview function does not display merge printing results, you can test the output of a merge-print operation without wasting paper. To do so, simply run the master document through a special driver that creates a facsimile of the results of merge printing in a disk file. You can then open that file and review it on-screen.

Selecting the PRVIEW special printer description file at the Printer name prompt creates a disk file named PRVIEW.WS that has the same content and formatting as the output of a merge-print operation. Mistakes in merging data are apparent on-screen when you review the file.

Another special printer description file, XTRACT, produces a disk file with data extracted from merge-printing functions. Once selected at the `Printer name` prompt and printing is started, XTRACT creates a file called XTRACT.WS, which includes soft carriage returns but no headers, footers, or page breaks.

XTRACT makes it easy to report data contained in one or more variable fields. For example, a set of dot commands and variable names can produce a disk file with only the names and corresponding business categories from the data in a mailing list file.

For the Widgets mailing list example, you open a document file that contains the following commands:

```
.OP
.DF MAILLIST.DAT
.RV First-name,Last-name,Title,Company,Street-address,City,State
.RV ZIP,Business-category,Volume-87,Volume-88,Handedness
&First-name& &Last-name&, &Business-category&
```

These commands omit page numbers, designate the MAILLIST.DAT file as the data file to read, note the variable fields in each record, and signal WordStar to insert data for the variables First-name, Last-name, and Business-category.

Merge printing this type of document with the XTRACT printer description file produces a disk file named XTRACT.WS that contains the desired information:

Bill Adams, national account
Richard Roe, wholesaler
Anne Garvey, retailer

You can give the XTRACT output file a name other than the default name XTRACT.WS. At the `Redirect output to` prompt, you can type a file name with the extension XTR; here you store extracted data, the output of the XTRACT driver, in a named file of your choosing. By merge printing with the XTRACT driver, you can create a variety of data listings, all stored in files noted with XTR name extensions.

Although producing a simple form letter with inserted data from a mailing list is probably the most common application for merge printing, this task hardly uses the full versatility of WordStar's special merge print dot commands. The following section discusses how to alter text to suit your conditions.

Customizing a Form Letter's Text

In generating personalized copies of your sales letter, you have kept the main text intact. With another set of merge-printing commands, you can alter the basic text and manipulate files according to certain logical conditions, customizing form letters with text for California left-handers, for example.

In WordStar, special merge-print dot commands can directly merge text from separate files and impose conditions on merge printing. These dot commands are shown in table 8.4.

Table 8.4
Merge-Printing and Conditional Merge-Printing Commands

Command	*Function*
.FI filename	Inserts the named file at a specified location in a master document or command file
.GO top/bottom	Moves to the beginning or end of the .FI file
.IF text	Defines a conditional merge-print statement
.EL	Changes a conditional merge-print statement to its opposite (ELSE)
.EI	Ends a conditional merge-print statement

You can use these dot commands to modify the contents of a document generated with merge printing. The commands range in applicability from chaining together printing of any available files to restricting narrowly the conditions under which a file is to be merge-printed. These dot commands can provide control over complex print jobs and increase productivity by automating tasks with WordStar's conditional "intelligence."

Inserting Files for Chained or Nested Printing

Being able to invoke printing of a series of files—whether successive paragraphs of boilerplate text, sections in a report, or chapters of a book—relieves the tedium of constantly invoking printing for large jobs. Instead of hovering around the keyboard to type separate file names, you can run merge printing in response to dot commands that automatically link files at print time.

In WordStar Release 5, the file insertion command has been omitted from dot command help screens. The dot command is .FI—the merge-print equivalent of a ^KR command for importing a file into an open document. An inserted file starts printing wherever the .FI command is placed in a document (with the command beginning at column 1). Using this command, you can import text at any line within a document file.

When you want to insert a file, the .FI FILENAME command must be followed by the name of the disk file to be read. If that file is on a different drive or directory, the directory path must precede the name of the file. If a floppy disk has to be swapped, add the `change` or `c` option after the name of the file in the .FI command. The following examples show typical .FI command sequences:

.FI B:CHAP3.REP c

.FI C:\SPECS\FORMS\STYLE1

You can invoke the .FI command by chaining or nesting. Placing the .FI command at the end of one file to call up printing of another file is known as chaining. You can chain files on a single page, or you can insert a page break with a .PA command to chain a file starting on a new page. The page-break command should immediately precede the .FI command line.

Files also may be merge-printed within other files. That is, the text of a file may be inserted somewhere in the text of another file in a process known as nesting. As many as eight files can be nested inside each other.

To begin printing either chained or nested files with .FI commands, designate the first file in the series. WordStar does the rest, following chained or nested .FI command lines and printing text accordingly. All printed pages, whether chained or nested, are numbered consecutively as if part of a single file.

Using Conditional Printing

Conditional merge-printing commands, which were first offered in MailMerge Release 3.3, have changed only slightly since then. By defining the conditions to be met for file merging and printing, you can literally instruct WordStar to compose special versions of a master letter for particular audiences—for example, left-handed retailers in California. The procedure involves defining the criteria by which files are chosen.

In WordStar Release 5, the merge-printing conditional commands are shown on the sixth screen of dot command help listings. Among the listings are the following notations:

```
.ei            End conditional merge print statement
.el            Do if last .if is not true
.go top/bot    Go to top/bottom of document
.if text       Conditional print
```

(Veterans of MailMerge Release 3.3 will find the conditional commands changed: the old .EX command has been replaced by the new .EL command. The .IF command can contain only one comparison per line, eliminating AND and OR operators. To achieve the same result, you must use several .IF commands.)

When WordStar evaluates conditions for merge printing, the program compares one item to another. Typically, WordStar compares a constant with an item of variable data. WordStar can determine whether two text or numerical items are the same and, if not, which comes first in alphabetical or numerical order.

To set WordStar's merge-printing conditional logic for comparisons, the .IF dot command is qualified by one of the special symbols known as operators. Separate operators set conditions for text or numbers. The operators to which the .IF command responds when making comparisons are shown in table 8.5.

Table 8.5
Operators for Conditional Merge Printing

Operator	*Definition*
=	Is the same as (for all text)
<	Comes before (alphabetically)
< =	Comes before (alphabetically) or is the same as
>	Comes after (alphabetically)
> =	Comes after (alphabetically) or is the same as
< >	Is not the same as (alphabetically)
#=	Is equal to (numerically)
#<	Is less than (numerically)
#< =	Is less than or equal to (numerically)
#>	Is greater than (numerically)
#> =	Is greater than or equal to (numerically)
#< >	Is not the same as (numerically)

The simplest format for the .IF command is to follow the command with an item and no operator. If the data for the variable is not zero, the condition is met. For example, if WordStar is testing for data on the variable Handedness for the Widgets mailing, the following command is met if any data for this variable is in the record:

```
.IF &Handedness&
```

The most frequently used format for the .IF command consists of the .IF command, followed by the name of an item, a conditional operator, and a second item. For two items of text to be the same (=), they must have identical characters (case notwithstanding). For example, to establish the condition for sending a version of the Widgets promotion letter to left-handers, you type this command:

```
.IF &Handedness& = left-hander
```

Several .IF commands can be stacked to narrow a condition. To limit the criteria for customized text for the example letter to left-handers from California, type into your master document (after the first paragraph of body text) the following dot commands:

```
.IF &Handedness& = left-hander
.IF &State& = CA
```

When the .IF command is used with an operator preceded by #, only numerical amounts are compared. As an application of this, you can use this feature to confine certain letters to clients with a Volume-88 figure higher than $1,000,000. The dot command line reads as follows:

```
.IF &Volume-88& #> 1000000
```

The item that follows the .IF command is the action to be followed when the condition is true. If the item is a block of text, that conditional text is printed. In the case of the sample letter to California left-handers, you might type a sentence like the following:

> As a fellow California left-hander, you can appreciate
> how much the new Widgets will mean to eradicating the menace
> of sinister Med flies.

If the item after an .IF condition is a dot command, its actions are invoked when the .IF proviso is met. After you list selected conditional text or dot commands, the action to be taken must be ended in the master document with a .EI command (for END IF). In the sample letter, for instance, you type *.ei* at the left edge of the screen on the line following the text to be inserted for left-handed Californians.

Two other dot commands can modify conditional actions. The ELSE command, .EL, is used to branch between .IF conditions, usually triggering the action opposite to the one specified. In the sample letter, you send a different paragraph to right-handed non-Californians by adding an .EL command, followed by the text to be appended.

The .GO command, as in `.GO top` or `.GO bottom`, terminates a conditional sequence by resuming merge printing at the top or bottom of the current master document file. This command gives you the option of printing another file or terminating printing.

Conditional merge-print commands and simple merge-print features can enhance your applications when used outside a master document. In the next section, you learn how to include these commands in a special command file.

Merging Tasks with Command Files

Instead of scattering merge-print commands throughout master documents and subsidiary text files, all the dot commands you need can be stored and edited in a separate disk file known as a *command file*. A command file is a document file that contains only dot commands (no text), whether for merge printing or for other tasks, including reformatting documents during regular printing.

At print time, a command file can be started like a master document, although a command file's commands refer to text that is stored in other files. With combinations of merge-print and formatting commands, you can rearrange text for special purposes. Such uses might include printing envelopes or labels from mailing-list data files.

A command file is created in document mode, where flag characters are activated by dot commands. From the Opening Menu, you simply open a file with the D command and enter your dot commands text, always being careful to begin dot commands at column 1 and to end lines with a carriage return.

As an example of a command file, you can extract addresses from the Widgets mailing list for printing on envelopes. Start by opening a document file and naming it ENVELOPE.FRM or some appropriate name. Then type the dot commands that follow, complete with annotations. The commands omit automatic page numbering, set up merge-printing and formatting for a business envelope, list fields to be inserted, and provide a prompt to press Enter when an envelope is ready to print:

```
.OP
.DF  MAILLIST.DAT
.RV  First-name,Last-name,Title,Company,Street-address,City,State
.RV  ZIP,Business-category,Volume-87,Volume-88,Handedness
.AV  "Place an envelope in the printer. Press Enter when ready.",X
.CS
.PL  4.2"
.MT  2"
.MB  0
.PO  4"
&First-name& &Last-name&
&Street-address&
&City&, &State& &ZIP&
.PA
```

After you have typed the command file, you can save it to disk. Then you invoke merge printing of this file to address automatically the envelopes for the Widgets mailing. Of course, you can edit this example to address envelopes for your own mailings.

To create mailing labels drawn from the sample data file, you would type the command file that follows:

```
.OP
.PF  off
.PO  2
.PL  6
.MT  2
.MB  2
.DF  MAILLIST.DAT
.RV  First-name,Last-name,Title,Company,Street-address,City,State
.RV  ZIP,Business-category,Volume-87,Volume-88,Handedness
&First-name& &Last-name&
&Street-address&
&City&, &State& &ZIP&
.PA
```

To run a command file, you invoke merge printing by pressing M at the Opening screen and specifying the name of the file. In the case of the command file for envelopes, type *envelope.frm*, press Enter and continue as for other merge-print operations. By placing an envelope in the printer and responding to the screen prompt, you produce envelopes for the Widgets mailing.

Keep in mind that merge-print commands can be invoked independently through a command file, creating greater possibilities for word processing automation.

Using MailList

With WordStar Release 5, MicroPro's MailList program becomes a standard component of the WordStar Professional package. Offered as an option with Release 3.3 and omitted from Release 4, MailList now provides WordStar users an easy-to-use alternative to the exacting entry of names and addresses in a mailing list or items in an inventory list. Files produced with MailList can be used as data files with WordStar's merge print function. MailList also has auxiliary files for extracting information from its data files and printing this on envelopes, labels, and in reports.

The advantage of MailList is the availability of its two handy preset formats: one for names, addresses, phone numbers and other useful mailing list information, and one for information to be used in an inventory listing. Individual records can be quickly viewed, sorted, and retrieved with MailList functions. This makes data much easier to consult than in raw data files generated with WordStar. The disadvantage to MailList formats is their inflexibility; though well-designed with ample room for data, they cannot be altered, nor are they suitable for merge printing applications other than mailings and inventories.

You can run MailList from the WordStar Release 5 Opening screen. Supplied on the MailList/TelMerge/PC-Outline disk, the principal MailList program files are WSLIST.COM and WSLIST.OVR. These and other files starting with the names WSLIST and INVNTORY should be on the same disk as the WordStar program. Other files with the extension LST are used for special purposes, as noted later.

If you are using a hard disk system, the MailList files should be in the same directory as the WordStar program (usually \WS5).

If you are using a two floppy disk system, you may save on limited disk space by keeping MailList and auxiliary files on a separate disk and running MailList as a stand-alone program. Data files can always be copied to your document disk for use with WordStar merge print functions.

Starting MailList

You can start MailList three different ways, depending on whether you are running MailList from the WordStar Opening screen with pull-down menus or classic menus or as a stand-alone program.

To start MailList from WordStar at help level 4, you should press A at the Opening screen. This displays the Additional Menu, shown in figure 8.5. Pressing Enter with the highlight on MailList or pressing M starts the MailList program.

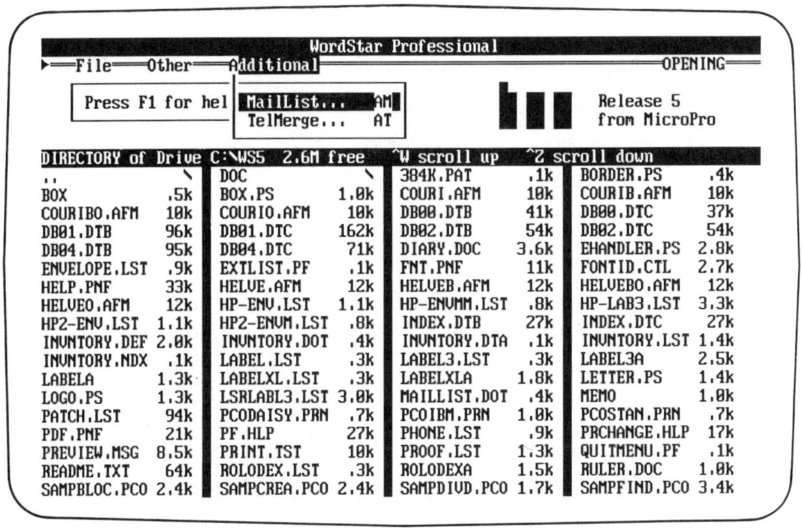

WordStar Professional
File Other Additional OPENING
Press F1 for hel
MailList... ^M
TelMerge... ^T
Release 5
from MicroPro
DIRECTORY of Drive C:\WS5 2.6M free ^W scroll up ^Z scroll down
.. \ DOC \ 384K.PAT .1k BORDER.PS .4k
BOX .5k BOX.PS 1.0k COURI.AFM 10k COURIB.AFM 10k
COURIBO.AFM 10k COURIO.AFM 10k DB00.DTB 41k DB00.DTC 37k
DB01.DTB 96k DB01.DTC 162k DB02.DTB 54k DB02.DTC 54k
DB04.DTB 95k DB04.DTC 71k DIARY.DOC 3.6k EHANDLER.PS 2.8k
ENVELOPE.LST .9k EXTLIST.PF .1k FNT.PNF 11k FONTID.CTL 2.7k
HELP.PNF 33k HELVE.AFM 12k HELVEB.AFM 12k HELVEBO.AFM 12k
HELVEO.AFM 12k HP-ENV.LST 1.1k HP-ENVMM.LST .8k HP-LAB3.LST 3.3k
HP2-ENV.LST 1.1k HP2-ENVM.LST .8k INDEX.DTB 27k INDEX.DTC 27k
INVNTORY.DEF 2.0k INVNTORY.DOT .4k INVNTORY.DTA .1k INVNTORY.LST 1.4k
INVNTORY.NDX .1k LABEL.LST .3k LABEL3.LST .3k LABEL3A 2.5k
LABELA 1.3k LABELXL.LST .3k LABELXLA 1.8k LETTER.PS 1.4k
LOGO.PS 1.3k LSRLABL3.LST 3.0k MAILLIST.DOT .4k MEMO 1.0k
PATCH.LST 94k PCODAISY.PRN .7k PCOIBM.PRN 1.0k PCOSTAN.PRN .7k
PDF.PNF 21k PF.HLP 27k PHONE.LST .9k PRCHANGE.HLP 17k
PREVIEW.MSG 8.5k PRINT.TST 10k PROOF.LST 1.3k QUITMENU.PF .1k
README.TXT 64k ROLODEX.LST .3k ROLODEXA 1.5k RULER.DOC 1.0k
SAMPBLOC.PCO 2.4k SAMPCREA.PCO 2.4k SAMPDIVD.PCO 1.7k SAMPFIND.PCO 3.4k

Fig. 8.5. *The WordStar Release 5 pull-down Additional menu.*

When starting MailList from WordStar at help level 3, 2, 1, or 0, press A at the Opening screen. This displays an Additional Menu, with the same content as at level 4 though shown differently, as in figure 8.6. Pressing M starts the MailList program.

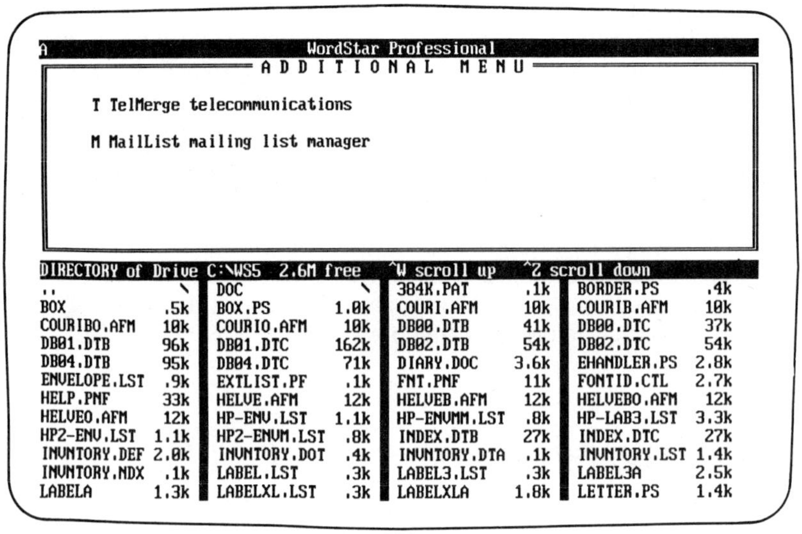
WordStar Professional
A D D I T I O N A L M E N U
T TelMerge telecommunications
M MailList mailing list manager
DIRECTORY of Drive C:\WS5 2.6M free ^W scroll up ^Z scroll down
.. \ DOC \ 384K.PAT .1k BORDER.PS .4k
BOX .5k BOX.PS 1.0k COURI.AFM 10k COURIB.AFM 10k
COURIBO.AFM 10k COURIO.AFM 10k DB00.DTB 41k DB00.DTC 37k
DB01.DTB 96k DB01.DTC 162k DB02.DTB 54k DB02.DTC 54k
DB04.DTB 95k DB04.DTC 71k DIARY.DOC 3.6k EHANDLER.PS 2.8k
ENVELOPE.LST .9k EXTLIST.PF .1k FNT.PNF 11k FONTID.CTL 2.7k
HELP.PNF 33k HELVE.AFM 12k HELVEB.AFM 12k HELVEBO.AFM 12k
HELVEO.AFM 12k HP-ENV.LST 1.1k HP-ENVMM.LST .8k HP-LAB3.LST 3.3k
HP2-ENV.LST 1.1k HP2-ENVM.LST .8k INDEX.DTB 27k INDEX.DTC 27k
INVNTORY.DEF 2.0k INVNTORY.DOT .4k INVNTORY.DTA .1k INVNTORY.LST 1.4k
INVNTORY.NDX .1k LABEL.LST .3k LABEL3.LST .3k LABEL3A 2.5k
LABELA 1.3k LABELXL.LST .3k LABELXLA 1.8k LETTER.PS 1.4k

Fig. 8.6. *The WordStar Release 5 classic-style Additional Menu.*

If you are using MailList as a stand-alone program, at the DOS prompt for the disk and directory containing MailList files, type *wslist* and press Enter.

No matter how you start MailList, the screen displays the MailList Menu, illustrated in figure 8.7, as soon as the program is loaded.

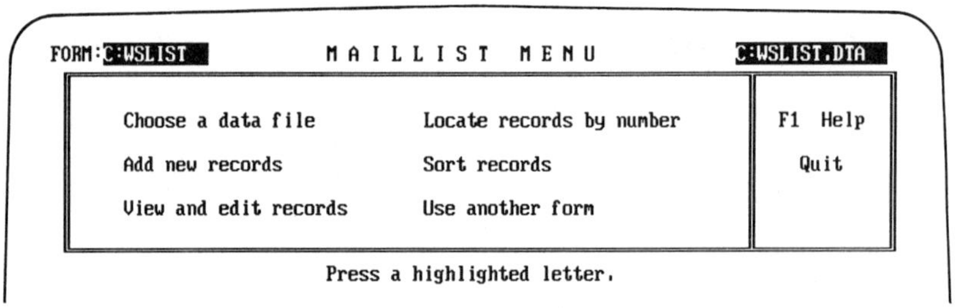
FORM:C:WSLIST
M A I L L I S T M E N U
C:WSLIST.DTA
Choose a data file
Locate records by number
F1 Help
Add new records
Sort records
Quit
View and edit records
Use another form
Press a highlighted letter.

Fig. 8.7. *The MailList Menu.*

In addition to commands for choosing a data file, adding or viewing data, locating or sorting records, or changing formats, the MailList Menu shows the current data format and file.

Selecting a Mailing List Data File

When MailList starts up, its default setting is for the mailing list format with name, address, and other information fields. It also starts up with the specific file WSLIST.DTA as the one to be used. The first time it is started, the WSLIST.DTA file is empty; you can use this as your principal mailing list file by filling in data following instructions in this chapter's next section.

If you want to use a mailing list data file other than WSLIST.DTA, you should press C for `Choose a data file` at the MailList Menu. This displays a screen headed CHOOSE A DATA FILE, indicating current form and data file at the top and a prompt asking for the name of the file or directory to use, along with the current directory and data files (with a DTA extension) available in that directory.

When you have data files stored on another disk or directory, type the letter of the drive and press Enter to show a directory of data files on that disk. For a listing of directories, press \ and press Enter; then use the arrow keys to highlight a desired directory and press Enter.

To select an existing data file for updating, type its name or use the arrow keys to move the highlight to its name on-screen; then press Enter. To create a new data file using the current format shown at the top of the screen, simply type a file name (without the DTA extension because MailList adds this automatically) and press Enter. When a new data file has been selected, the MailList Menu returns with the name of the file indicated in the top right corner.

To select a file in the inventory list format, you must first invoke the U command at the MailList Menu, as indicated later in this chapter. If you designate a data file created with the inventory form while still using the MailList format, you see an error message.

Filling In MailList Data

Enter information into a data file by filling appropriate spaces in an on-screen form—either a mailing list or inventory format. The form for an individual person or unit in the list is called a *record*. Each item in a record—address, phone number, price, remark, and so on—is called a *field*.

To enter information into the data file designated at the top of the MailList screen, press A for `Add new records`. This displays an empty data entry form for the current file, with the Add New Records Menu above it on-screen. With the WSLIST.DEF format for mailing list records, the screen appears as shown in figure 8.8. If you are using a file in the inventory list format, an empty data entry form shows up.

Each record in a data file is numbered sequentially. When a data file is opened for the first time, the cursor appears at the Record Number field. You should type the number for the first record—usually 1—and press Enter. If the data file has been used previously, the Record Number field shows the next available number for an empty record and the cursor appears in the first field for data to be entered.

When filling in information, type the data appropriate to each labeled field and press Enter to go on to the next field. Data should include a character in the first space of a field; with a blank space at the beginning of a field, data cannot be sorted correctly. Each field in a form is optional, except for the Record Number. If

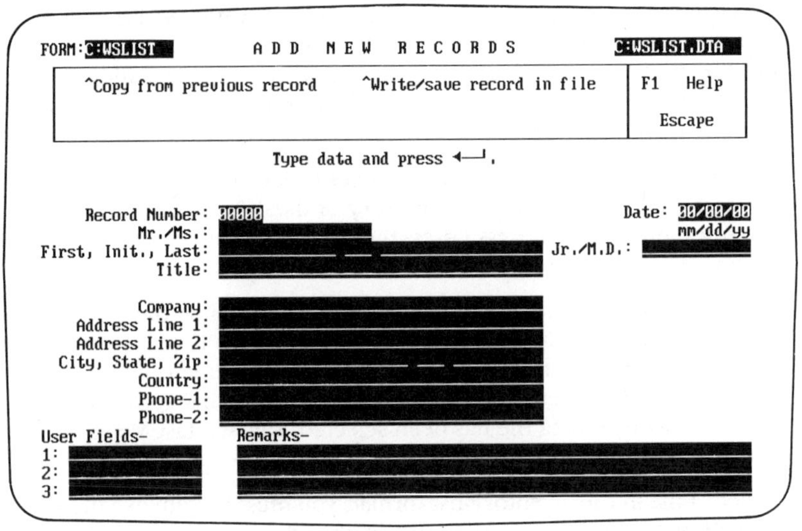
FORM: C:WSLIST
A D D N E W R E C O R D S
C:WSLIST.DTA
^Copy from previous record
^Write/save record in file
F1 Help
Escape
Type data and press ←┘.
Record Number: 00000
Date: 00/00/00
mm/dd/yy
Mr./Ms.:
First, Init., Last:
Jr./M.D.:
Title:
Company:
Address Line 1:
Address Line 2:
City, State, Zip:
Country:
Phone-1:
Phone-2:
User Fields-
Remarks-
1:
2:
3:

Fig. 8.8.
The MailList Add New Records Menu for mailing list formatted data files.

you do not want to fill a particular field, press Enter to leave it blank and the cursor moves to the next field. To copy information typed in the same field in the previous record you filled out—for instance, a date, company name, or street address—press ^C and the same information appears in that space.

In a mailing list form, consider the line for First, Init., Last name information as three separate fields, each requiring that Enter be pressed after its completion. The data in each field of a record is limited in length, with maximums of 13 characters for the first name, 18 characters for the last name, 21 characters for the city and 36 characters for other major fields. Any characters beyond these limits are truncated and do not appear in the data file. Incidentally, each record in either mail list or inventory list format includes three user fields for data up to 15 characters long and associated remarks up to 57 characters long; you can use these to include information not categorized elsewhere on a data entry form.

Deletion and cursor movement commands in MailList are not identical to WordStar's. If you make a typing error while filling in a field, use the Backspace key to erase characters one at a time. WordStar's other deletion commands are not valid. To change erroneous text anywhere but beside the cursor, you must move the cursor (with MailList commands) to the incorrect text and type it over. The MailList cursor movement commands are indicated in table 8.6.

Table 8.6
MailList Cursor Movement Commands

Command	*Function*
^S or ←	Moves left one character
^D or →	Moves right one character

Table 8.6—*Continued*

Command	*Function*
^A or ^←	Moves to previous field
^F or ^→	Moves to next field
^T or Home	Moves to first field
^L or End	Moves to last field

When you have finished filling in a record, press ^W from any field or Enter from the last field. You must press Enter again to save the record to disk. If you have pressed ^W and change your mind about saving this information, press the space bar to return to the record without saving it.

After completing data entry in a record and saving it, you see another empty form on-screen. The Record Number field indicates the number of this new record. You can type information into each record in turn, saving each with ^W and Enter.

Once you have filled out all the records needed during a work session, press Esc to return to the MailList Menu.

Viewing and Updating Records

Bringing the records in an existing data file on-screen for viewing and updating can be done in several ways: you can display all the records in a file, narrow the selection to a group of records within the file, or choose a specific record by number.

To display all the records in a file, at the MailList Menu press V for `View and edit records`. This displays the first record in your file, along with the View and Edit Records Menu above it. Records are usually arranged in order of their record number, but if you have sorted your data file according to other criteria, the records appear in the sorted order (see the section on *Sorting Data Lists*).

Once a record is displayed on-screen, you can update it by changing appropriate data fields, using the cursor movement commands in table 8.6. When you have finished modifying a record you can press ^W and Enter to save its contents. The next record in the file is then displayed.

To browse through records without changing them, press ^N to show the next record or ^P to put the previous record on-screen.

Once you have finished viewing and editing records, you can press Esc to return to the MailList Menu.

If you wish to view a specific group of records, like those for a particular state or telephone area code, MailList includes a feature for creating a “record filter” to select only those records that match the criteria you determine. To filter out all but the records you want, press V at the MailList Menu and then ^C for Create/Change record filter on the View and Edit Records Menu. This displays a version of the data entry form with asterisks in every field and the Record Filter Menu above it, as illustrated in figure 8.9.

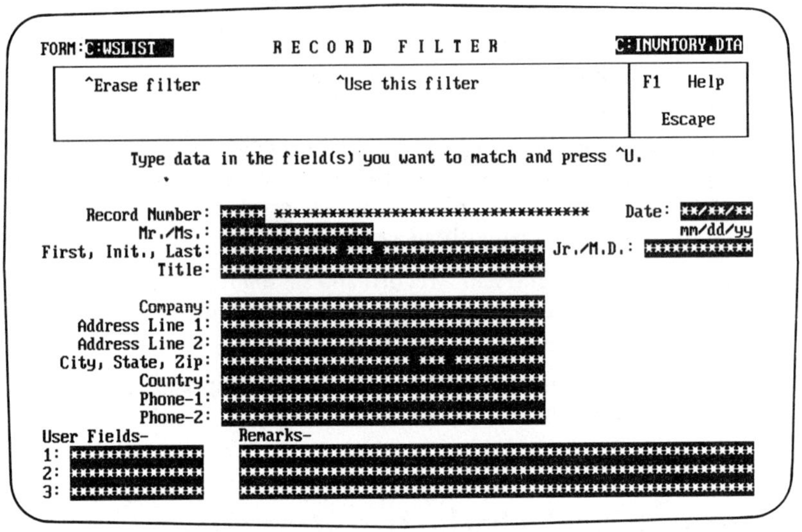
FORM: C:WSLIST
R E C O R D F I L T E R
C:INVNTORY.DTA
^Erase filter
^Use this filter
F1 Help
Escape
Type data in the field(s) you want to match and press ^U.
Record Number: ***** ***********************************
Date: **/**/**
mm/dd/yy
Mr./Ms.: ****************
First, Init., Last: ************ *** *****************
Jr./M.D.: ***********
Title: **********************************
Company: **********************************
Address Line 1: **********************************
Address Line 2: **********************************
City, State, Zip: ******************** *** **********
Country: **********************************
Phone-1: **********************************
Phone-2: **********************************
User Fields-
Remarks-
1: **************
2: **************
3: **************

Fig. 8.9.
MailList's Record Filter Menu and filter form.

With the record filter on-screen, move the cursor to the field where you want to type data or partial data to be matched in the records you are seeking. For instance, you move to the ZIP code field and type *100*** to limit records to those with ZIP codes in the New York City area. If you want to narrow the search further, you can type filter information in several fields. If you are looking for a specific record relating to a person by name, you can simply fill in the First, Init., Last field to filter out all but that record.

To activate the record filter, press ^U. This displays the first record that matches the data in the filter, with the View and Edit Records Menu on-screen—allowing you to continue viewing and modifying the records you want. To change a filter during a viewing session, just press ^C at the View and Edit Records Menu and type new data in the filter. To stop using a filter, press ^E at the Record Filter Menu.

When you want to find a single numbered record for viewing or editing, from the MailList Menu press L for `Locate Records by number`. MailList then displays an empty form with the cursor in the Record Number field; above the record is the Locate Records by Number Menu. Type the desired record number and press Enter. The data in the corresponding record appears on-screen. You can edit this record and save the changes by pressing ^W and Enter. MailList displays an empty record again with the cursor at the Record Number field, where you can type another number for a designated record.

Erasing Records

In MailList, a record can only be erased from a data file when the record is on-screen.

To erase a record, from the MailList Menu, press V or L to put the record you wish to eliminate on-screen. Then press ^E. At the resulting prompt, press R to confirm your decision to eliminate the record. MailList erases all the information in the record from your data list. The record number is then available for reuse with new data.

Sorting Data Lists

MailList stores the records in a data file according to the order in which they were created. In other words, the records are ordinarily arranged in ascending order of their Record Number fields. Another MailList feature makes it easy to sort the records in a data list according to various fields within each record. Up to 32 different sort orders can be defined and saved for varied criteria, permitting sorts alphabetically by name, or chronologically by date, for example. Sorting records can be useful for rearranging data files after they have been updated or modified and helpful in saving disk storage space.

To sort a data file, from the MailList Menu press S for `Sort records`. The MailList program displays a data entry form with asterisks in the various fields and the Sort Records Menu above it, as shown in figure 8.10. If this is the first time you are creating a sort order, the screen shows the default sort order `RECORDNO` in the upper left corner, with `1111A` in the Record Number field to indicate that the data file is to be sorted in the order of record numbers.

If you want to choose a different sort order or create a new one, at the Sort Records Menu press ^C. You see a list of sort orders available to you. With the arrow keys, move the highlight to the desired sort order and press Enter to display the data entry form and order you select. If this is the first time that you are creating sort orders, the only listing is for RECORDNO.

When you want to create a new sort order, at the list of sort orders type the name of the order you are using (a maximum of eight characters is allowed). When you press Enter, MailList displays a data entry form with asterisks in all the fields. A sort order can be invoked according to fields called keys—up to nine keys per sort. Each numbered key is checked in turn as the sort is performed. For instance, if the first key is the State field and the second key is the Company field, all the records are sorted alphabetically by state first. Then within each state the records are grouped in alphabetical order by company name.

Within the data entry form to be used for sorting, you can use the left- or right-arrow keys (or ^F or ^A) to move the cursor to the field intended as the first key and press ^K. The asterisks in the field are replaced by a string of ones, except for the

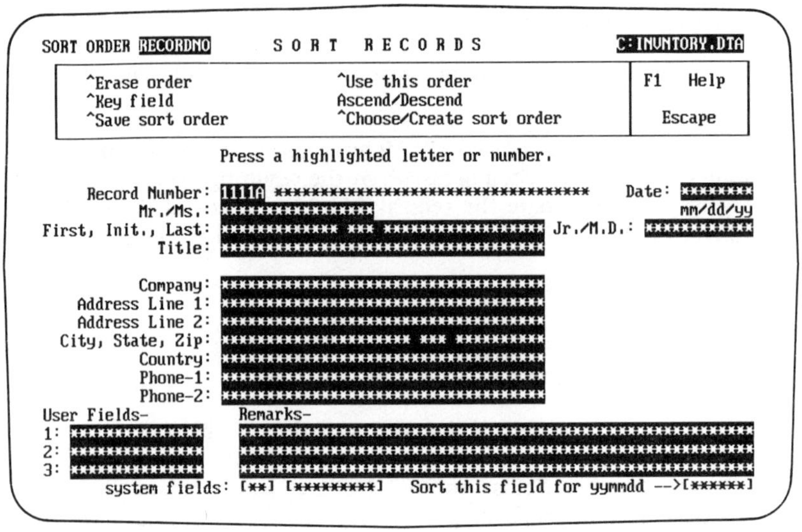
SORT ORDER RECORDNO
S O R T R E C O R D S
C:INVNTORY.DTA
^Erase order
^Key field
^Save sort order
^Use this order
Ascend/Descend
^Choose/Create sort order
F1 Help
Escape
Press a highlighted letter or number.
Record Number: 1111A
Date:
mm/dd/yy
Mr./Ms.:
First, Init., Last:
Jr./M.D.:
Title:
Company:
Address Line 1:
Address Line 2:
City, State, Zip:
Country:
Phone-1:
Phone-2:
User Fields-
Remarks-
1:
2:
3:
system fields:
Sort this field for yymmdd -->

Fig. 8.10.

The MailList Sort Records Menu and sort form.

last character, which is an A—for ascending order (sorting upward according to numbers, followed by letters starting with A with lowercase following uppercase). Pressing D with the cursor in the key field makes D the last character in the field and designates descending order (downward with Z as the first letter and A as the last, and so on). Pressing A restores ascending order. You should move the cursor to the second key field and press ^K, filling up the field with the number 2 and A as the last character. When you have completed designating the key fields for the sort order you want, press ^S to save the sort order without sorting or ^U to save the sort order and perform a sort on your data file.

When you choose a sort order, at the Sort Records Menu press ^U for `Use this order` to start the sort. The following message replaces the commands listed in the menu box:

```
Now sorting the file by the field(s) marked below. Please wait.
```

Depending on the number of records to be sorted and the key fields chosen for the sort, the operation may take from a few seconds to several minutes. When sorting is done, a message like the following appears:

```
The file sort is completed. 27 records were sorted.
```

Once the sort is done, pressing Esc returns the MailList Menu to the screen.

Using an Inventory Data File

Besides the mailing list format for data files, MailList also includes a data entry form for inventory information. Instead of name, address, and phone data, the inventory data entry form has fields for item number, description, quantity, price and other information relevant to keeping track of goods of all kinds. In all other respects, data entry, editing, viewing, and sorting are identical to operations on mailing list forms.

To select the inventory data format instead of the default mailing list format, at the MailList Menu press U for `Use another form`. This choice displays a screen headed CHOOSE A FORM, with a prompt asking for the form to use; also shown are listings of the current disk and directory and the two available data formats. Because the highlight is on the INVNTORY.DEF format, choose the inventory form by pressing Enter. MailList continues to use this data format until you change it by typing *u* at the MailList Menu or exit from the MailList program.

Once you have selected the inventory list format, you can open the default file INVNTORY.DTA from the MailList Menu by pressing A for `Add new records`. You can also open a different data file using the same format by pressing C for `Choose a data file`, naming the desired file, pressing Enter and finally pressing A at the MailList Menu. The inventory data entry form appears on-screen as illustrated in figure 8.11.

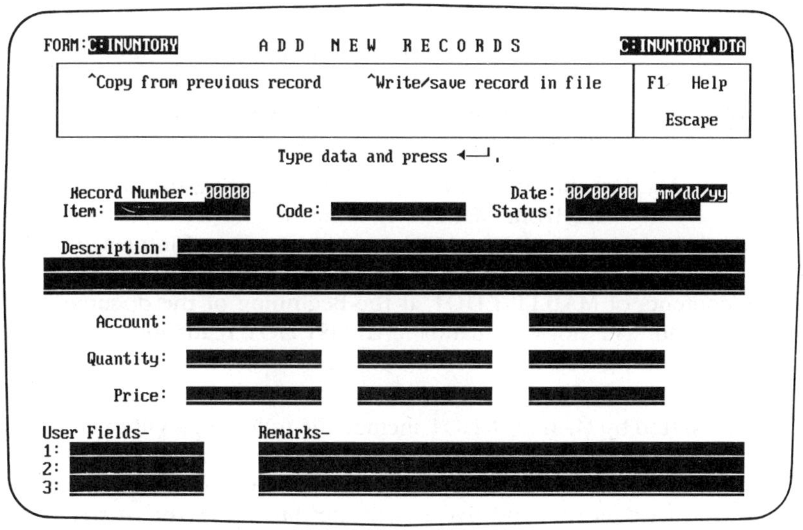
FORM: C:INVNTORY
A D D N E W R E C O R D S
C:INVNTORY.DTA
^Copy from previous record
^Write/save record in file
F1 Help
Escape
Type data and press ↵.
Record Number: 00000
Date: 00/00/00 mm/dd/yy
Item:
Code:
Status:
Description:
Account:
Quantity:
Price:
User Fields-
Remarks-
1:
2:
3:

Fig. 8.11.
The MailList Add New Records Menu for inventory list formatted data files.

To add records, view and edit records, locate a record by number, or sort records in the inventory list format, follow the procedures explained in the previous sections about the mailing list data format.

Exiting MailList

After completing a work session with MailList, you can exit the program from the MailList Menu by pressing Q for `Quit`. If you started MailList from within WordStar, the WordStar opening screen returns. If you started MailList as a stand-alone program, the screen displays the DOS prompt.

Incidentally, whenever a MailList data file is created or updated, the program also produces a corresponding index file with the same file name and the NDX extension. Both data file and index file must be present for MailList to access a data list for updating. If you have erased an index file, when you try to work on the corresponding data file a message appears prompting you to press R to reconstitute the index file.

Merge Printing with MailList Data Files

Using information from MailList data files for merge printing is similar to using information from manually entered data files. As indicated earlier in this chapter, you must create a master document that includes the name of the data file, its fields of information, and any variables to be inserted in text.

Files supplied with MailList include a useful file for expediting the creation of a master document with data from MailList mailing list format data files. The MAILLIST.DOT file contains the .DF and .RV dot commands and information that you must type into the master document. When you open a master document, you can insert the contents of MAILLIST.DOT at the beginning of the document file with a ^KR command. The dot commands MAILLIST.DOT reads into the master document are shown in figure 8.12.

Dot commands inserted by MAILLIST.DOT include the following: .OP to eliminate page numbering (can be deleted); .DF to designate the data file WSLIST.DTA (substitute the correct name if necessary); .RV to name fields of data contained in the mailing list format data file; and .PA to indicate the end of the master document. A reminder to type text and variable names is also inserted but you should delete it when typing the document.

You can insert in the master document variable names corresponding to the fields in the MailList mailing list data format. These variable names are the same as those in the .RV commands inserted with the MAILLIST.DOT file. Variable names and the fields in the MailList data file to which they refer are listed in table 8.7.

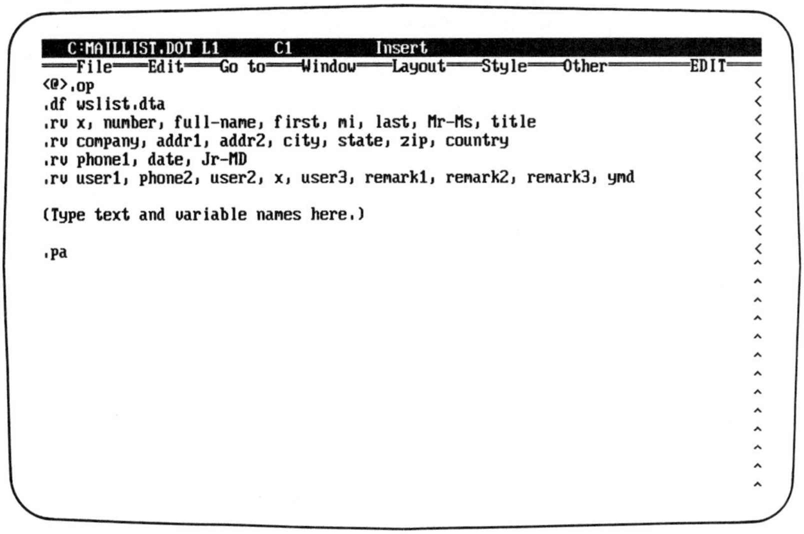
C:MAILLIST.DOT L1 C1 Insert
File Edit Go to Window Layout Style Other EDIT
<@>.op
.df wslist.dta
.rv x, number, full-name, first, mi, last, Mr-Ms, title
.rv company, addr1, addr2, city, state, zip, country
.rv phone1, date, Jr-MD
.rv user1, phone2, user2, x, user3, remark1, remark2, remark3, ymd
(Type text and variable names here.)
.pa

Fig. 8.12.
Dot commands for a master document in the MAILLIST.DOT file.

Table 8.7
Variables for MailList Mailing List Format Data Files

Variable	*MailList Field*
x	
&number&	Record Number
&full-name&	First, Initial, and Last
&first&	First
&mi&	Initial
&last&	Last
&Mr-Ms&	Mr./Mrs.
&title&	Title
&company&	Company
&addr1&	Address Line 1
&addr2&	Address Line 2
&city&	City
&state&	State
&zip&	ZIP
&country&	Country

Table 8.7—*Continued*

Variable	*MailList Field*
&phone1&	Phone-1
&date&	Date
&Jr-MD&	Jr./M.D.
&user1&	User Field 1
&phone2&	Phone-2
&user2&	User Field 2
x	
&user3&	User Field 3
&remark1&	Remark 1
&remark2&	Remark 2
&remark3&	Remark 3
&ymd&	(year, month, date)

To use a MailList inventory list format data file for merge printing, enter appropriate .DF and .RV dot commands in your master document. In your text, type variable names, where appropriate, corresponding to the data fields in the MailList's inventory list format, as indicated in table 8.8.

Table 8.8
Variables for MailList Inventory Format Data Files

Variable	*Description*
x	
&number&	Record Number
&date&	Date
&item&	Item
&code&	Code
&status&	Status
&desc1&	Description Line 1
&desc2&	Description Line 2
&desc3&	Description Line 3

Table 8.8—*Continued*

Variable	*Description*
&acct1&	Account 1
&qty1&	Quantity 1
&price1&	Price 1
&acct2&	Account 2
&qty2&	Quantity 2
&price2&	Price 2
&acct3&	Account 3
&qty3&	Quantity 3
&price3&	Price 3
&user1&	User Field 1
&remark1&	Remark 1
&user2&	User Field 2
&remark2&	Remark 2
&user3&	User Field 3
&remark3&	Remark 3
&ymd&	(year, month, date)

When you have completed your master document incorporating variables from MailList data files, merge printing can proceed as with as any other data files.

Printing Envelopes, Labels, and Reports from MailList Data

Provided with MailList are command files for merge printing information from MailList data files on standard business envelopes, mailing labels, Rolodex cards, or as reports, phone lists, or inventory lists. With additional steps to ensure correct positioning at print time, these files can be merge printed like any other master documents.

You can use the ENVELOPE.LST file to print standard-sized business envelopes (4 1/8-by-9 1/2 inches) with names and addresses from a MailList mailing list format data file. For the formatting required by Hewlett-Packard LaserJet printers, you can use one of two other files: HP-ENVMM.LST for LaserJet or LaserJet+ models, or HP2-ENVM.LST for LaserJet Series II printers. Each of these files specifies WSLIST.DTA as the name of the MailList data file to be used; if you want a different data file name, open the file and substitute that name at the .DF command.

When the appropriate command file for envelopes is merge printed, it starts the process with print paused. Once an envelope is positioned in the printer, press C to start printing. After the first envelope, printing pauses once more until the next envelope is in the printer and C is pressed again. This process continues until all addresses in the data list are printed.

You can print three different sizes of labels with names and addresses from MailList-generated mailing list data files. For 3 1/2-by-1-inch labels, one across on a sheet, use the LABEL.LST file. For 5-by-3-inch labels, one across, use the LABELXL.LST file. To print 3 1/2-by-1-inch labels, three across, use one of two files: LABEL3.LST for most printers or LSRLABEL3.LST with a laser printer. When using LABEL.LST, LABELXL.LST, or LABEL3.LST files for merge printing, you must respond by typing *y* at the `Use form feed` print-time option. Another file, ROLODEX.LST, prints 2 1/2-by-4-inch continuous strip Rolodex cards. Again, each of these files specifies WSLIST.DTA as the MailList data file to be used; for a different data file name, open the file and substitute at the .DF command.

Two label files exist for use with laser printers. HP-PAB3.LST is used to print 27 labels when they are three across the page. (The top and bottom rows of labels are not printed because most laser printers cannot print at the extreme top and bottom of the page.) LSRLABL3.LST prints 30 labels when they are three across the page. This label file is intended for label stock with half-high labels on the top and bottom rows.

When you merge print any of the label command files, they begin with printing paused. Press C to start printing. The first label printed is a sample, with printing paused again to allow positioning of labels. Each time you press C, two more samples are printed. Then printing is continuous until all addresses in the data list are printed.

You can also use MailList files to merge print reports with information from MailList data files. The PROOF.LST file lists all the data in a mailing list file. The PHONE.LST file prints a directory of telephone numbers in a mailing list file. For a report of inventory data from an inventory format file, choose INVNTORY.LST. All of these files refer to WSLIST.DTA as the data file; change this for other file names.

Using TelMerge

MicroPro's telecommunications program, TelMerge, returns to the WordStar Professional package with Release 5. Like MailList, TelMerge was an option with Release 3.3 and dropped from Release 4. As one of the valuable extras in the Release 5 package, TelMerge affords basic communications abilities via computer modem and telephone lines to computerized information services, electronic mail systems, mainframe computers and other personal computers (whether equipped with TelMerge or not).

Although TelMerge does not compare in flexibility with more sophisticated stand-alone communications software, it does provide the basics for exchanging data with other computer systems at transmission rates from 300 and 1200 baud up to 9600 baud. TelMerge also provides error checking protocols like XMODEM, emulation of VT100 or VT52 terminals, and scripting of phone numbers, passwords, and user ID to automate log-on procedures. TelMerge's emphasis on communicating with commercial information services is both its strength and its weakness. Though it is easy to set up for such purposes, the emphasis of MicroPro's documentation obscures TelMerge's usefulness in accessing mainframe computers, electronic bulletin boards, and other personal computers.

To run TelMerge, in addition to the system requirements for Release 5, your computer should be equipped with a Hayes-compatible modem connected to a serial port or to a communications interface card, and a single-line telephone connection. TelMerge may not work properly with other RAM-resident programs loaded in memory, a printer and modem on the same port, a telephone line with "call waiting," or a multiline phone system.

TelMerge is meant to operate with the default switch settings of a Hayes-compatible modem. If these have been changed, you may have to reset them to conform to the original factory settings, described in table 8.9. For TelMerge to place a call, your modem must be turned on, as indicated by its display lights. If the modem is off, you see an error message.

Table 8.9
Hayes-Compatible Modem Switch Settings

Switch Number	*Setting*	*Function*
External modem		
1	Down	Turns off Data Terminal Ready Signal
2	Up	Puts result codes (RING, and so on) into words
3	Down	Sends result codes to computer
4	Up	Shows commands on-screen when dialing

Table 8.9—*Continued*

Switch Number	*Setting*	*Function*
5	Down	Turns off automatic call answering
6	Down	Ignores the carrier signal
7	Up	Sets modem for single-line telephone
8	Down	Sets modem command recognition
Internal modem		
1	On	Specifies communications port (On = COM1, Off = COM2)
2	Off	Sets modem for single-line telephone
3	Off	Ignores the carrier signal

You can run TelMerge directly from the Release 5 Opening screen. The essential TelMerge program files, TELMERGE.EXE and TELMERGE.SYS, are supplied on the MailList/TelMerge/PC-Outline disk. If you are using a hard disk system, the TelMerge files should be in the same directory as the WordStar program (usually \WS5). If you are using a two floppy disk system, you can save disk space by keeping TelMerge files apart from your WordStar program files on a separate disk. When you start TelMerge from WordStar, a prompt reminds you to change disks. You also can run TelMerge as a stand-alone program.

Starting TelMerge

TelMerge is started in one of three different ways, according to whether you are running the program from the WordStar Opening screen with pull-down menus or classic menus, or as a stand-alone program.

If you start TelMerge from WordStar at help level 4, press A at the Opening screen to display the Additional Menu (see figure 8.5). Then press T to start the TelMerge program. To start TelMerge from the Opening screen at help level 3, 2, 1, or 0, press A. WordStar displays the classic Additional Menu, shown in figure 8.6. Pressing T starts TelMerge.

When you use TelMerge as a stand-alone program, first access the disk and directory containing TelMerge files. At the DOS prompt, type *telmerge* and press Enter.

As soon as TelMerge is loaded, no matter how you started it, the screen displays the TelMerge Communications Menu, shown in figure 8.13.

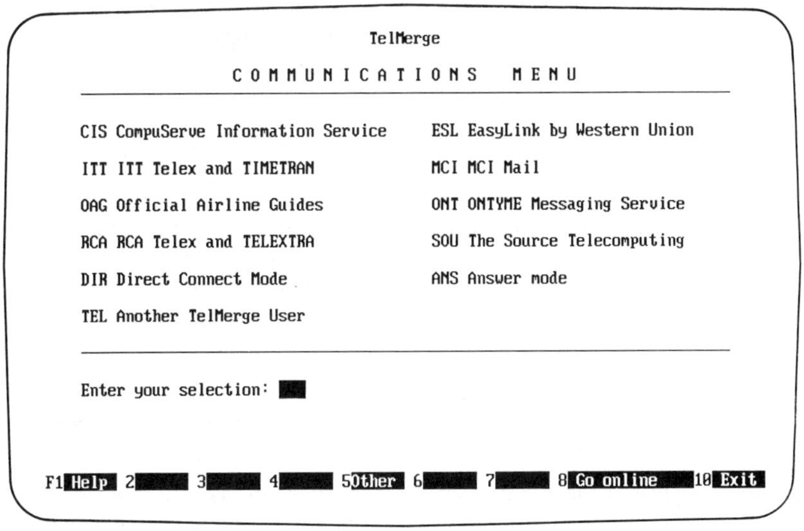
TelMerge
COMMUNICATIONS MENU
CIS CompuServe Information Service
ESL EasyLink by Western Union
ITT ITT Telex and TIMETRAN
MCI MCI Mail
OAG Official Airline Guides
ONT ONTYME Messaging Service
RCA RCA Telex and TELEXTRA
SOU The Source Telecomputing
DIR Direct Connect Mode
ANS Answer mode
TEL Another TelMerge User
Enter your selection:
F1 Help 2 3 4 5 Other 6 7 8 Go online 10 Exit

Fig. 8.13.
The TelMerge Communications Menu.

The Communications Menu lists three-letter abbreviations and corresponding names for commercial information services or communications modes. All of these listings and accompanying instructions for automating a communications session are stored in a special system file, TELMERGE.SYS, which the user should modify to include phone numbers, IDs, passwords, and other essential information to establish contact.

TelMerge provides for an alternative method of entering phone numbers and other information in individual control files, ending with a TEL extension, that can be invoked to initiate a call. Creating a TEL file gives you an opportunity to learn about the necessary information that can later be entered into the TELMERGE.SYS file.

Placing a Call

Most communications programs provide a way to place a call to another computer by typing the phone number and other information, but TelMerge requires that these keystrokes be saved in either the system file TELMERGE.SYS or in a control file identified by the extension TEL—even for a one-time call. If you create a TEL file, TelMerge helps you by asking for essential information the first time a call is placed and saving the information on disk for easy reuse. However, once you enter erroneous information, the entire TEL file must be deleted or edited as a nondocument with WordStar before you can try placing the call again.

To place a call with a TEL control file, press the F5 key on the Communications Menu. This displays a screen headed CHOOSE/CREATE CONTROL FILE with instructions for invoking an existing TEL control file or creating a new one. Below this is a list of available files. If you have already created an appropriate control file, type its name (you can omit its TEL extension) and press Enter. TelMerge places a call using the information in that control file.

If no control file exists for a call you wish to place or if you are using TelMerge for the first time, press Enter at the `Choose/Create Control File` screen. You see a series of screens with prompts for entering the information necessary for placing a call. The first such prompt has room for the name of the new control file; type a name up to eight characters long (the TEL extension is not necessary) and press Enter. The next prompt asks for the phone number to dial; type any prefix and area code you might need followed by the number (use hyphens as separator characters) and press Enter.

The subsequent prompts are optional, to be filled in if required by the computer or service to be contacted. To skip a prompt, press Enter. To skip the remaining prompts, press the Escape key.

The next prompt requests a three-letter service abbreviation, like those used in the Communications Menu. Pressing Enter displays a prompt for the user ID—a code consisting of letters and/or numbers. User ID codes are issued by communications services or computer networks to limit access to authorized users. Type your ID, if needed. Pressing Enter brings up the prompt for the password, assigned to or chosen by the user. Type your password, if needed.

Pressing Enter again shows a prompt for setting the baud rate—the rate at which your modem transmits and receives information. The default rate of 1200 is most common, while older systems may use a rate of 300 baud and more state-of-the-art systems transmit at 2400, 4800, or 9600 baud. Another press of the Enter key produces the prompt for changing the default serial port, COM1. Pressing Enter once more displays a prompt for the name of a network you may be using as an intermediary in accessing commercial information systems. One more press of Enter brings up a prompt for the host ID, a code used by a network to identify the service you are trying to access. Pressing Enter finally displays the same screen you see if you press Escape at any point after typing the phone number to dial.

All the information entered at the prompts is stored in the file you named (with a TEL extension). This file can be designated at the `Choose/Create Control File` screen the next time you press F5 from the Communications Menu. If you want to change a control file, edit it as a nondocument with WordStar.

When you are done entering information for initiating a call or have selected an existing command file, the top of the screen indicates that a start-up string of instructions is being sent to the modem, along with the port it is attached to and the modem's transmission rate. Prompts exist for any special characters to be sent to the modem at start-up. The modem dials the phone number you designated and if the other computer responds, transmits the user ID, password, and network information indicated in the command file.

Receiving and Preserving Files

Once communications are established with another computer, your system is "logged on" and TelMerge displays its on-line screen, shown in figure 8.14. This screen has a status line at the top indicating the computer or information service to which you are connected, the time elapsed since making the connection, whether what appears on-screen is being saved to a disk file and whether what you see is also being saved as hard copy on your printer.

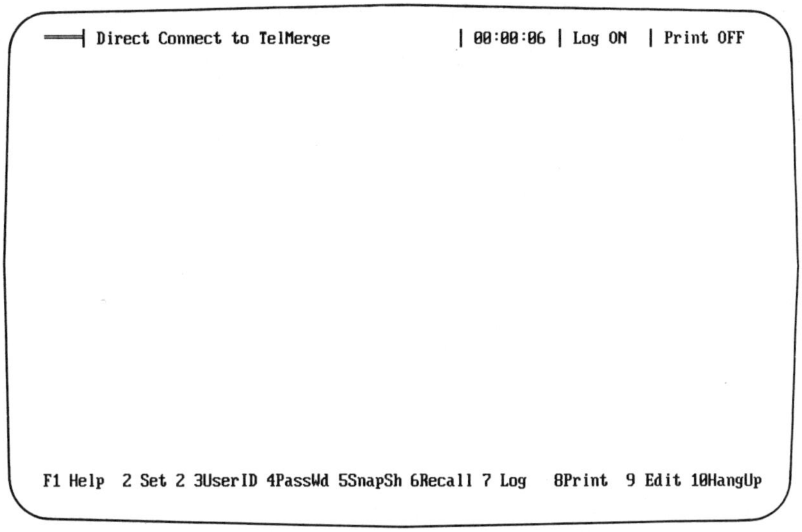
Direct Connect to TelMerge | 00:00:06 | Log ON | Print OFF
F1 Help 2 Set 2 3UserID 4PassWd 5SnapSh 6Recall 7 Log 8Print 9 Edit 10HangUp

Fig. 8.14.
The TelMerge screen while on-line.

At the bottom of the on-line screen are abbreviations for 10 function key commands. Pressing F2 shows a second set of 10 commands; pressing F2 again restores the first set to the screen. Pressing F1 lists all function key commands, summarized here in table 8.10.

Table 8.10
TelMerge On-Line Function Key Commands

Key	*Command*	*Function*
Set 1		
F1	Help	Displays a listing of all function keys
F2	Set2	Toggles on Set 2 function keys
F3	UserID/Hereis	Transmits User ID code from TelMerge file
F4	Password/Mail	Transmits password (telex: gets messages)
F5	SnapShot	Saves screen on disk or memory (up to 5 screens)

Table 8.10—*Continued*

Key	*Command*	*Function*
F6	Recall	Displays screens saved with F5
F7	Log/WRU	Turns logging on/off (telex: WHO ARE YOU command)
F8	Print	Turns printing on/off
F9	Edit	Exits TelMerge, stays connected (return with F8)
F10	Hangup	Disconnects phone line, exits TelMerge
Set 2		
F1	ShowFile	Displays any file, including current log file
F2	Set1	Toggles on Set 2 function keys
F3	DOS	Goes to DOS, stays connected (type *exit* to return)
F4	Send	Transmits a WordStar or ASCII file
F5	XM Receive	Receives file with XMODEM protocol (chksum or CRC)
F6	XM Send	Transmits file with XMODEM protocol
F7	User 1	Can be programmed for a command (use keyword FK1)
F8	User 2	Can be programmed for a command (use keyword FK2)
F9	Break	Interrupts other computer with break command
F10	Hangup	Disconnects phone line, exits TelMerge

While at the on-line screen, TelMerge displays all the information sent by the computer with which you are communicating, and under most circumstances, what is sent when you press the keys on your computer keyboard. Depending on the speed at which your modem is transmitting, text appears as received at a rapid but readable pace on your screen (at 1200 baud), at a less hurried gait (at 300 baud), or at speeds too fast to read comfortably (at 2400 baud and beyond).

To facilitate examination and use of the information you receive with TelMerge—whether stock quotes from a service, electronic mail from a mainframe, file listings from a bulletin board, or a real-time written dialogue with another personal computer user—four of the twenty on-line function key commands save or print what appears on-screen during a communications session. TelMerge's logging feature automatically saves all the text from a session in a disk file with the extension LOG. Unless otherwise specified, the log file is called TELMERGE.LOG. (Log files for commercial services named on the TelMerge Communications Menu are saved in their own specially named files with a LOG extension.) The default setting for TelMerge is for logging on, as indicated at the top of the on-line screen. Logging can be toggled Off or On by pressing the F7 key of the Set 1 function keys.

There must be enough room on disk for a log file or else TelMerge automatically disconnects a call. Log files are saved as nondocuments and can be edited with WordStar. Whenever you begin a new on-line session, the log file for the previous session is renamed with the extension SAV, writing over the previous SAV file. To keep an earlier log file from being overwritten, you should rename it with a different file extension.

If you prefer, the contents of a new session can be added to a previous log file without creating a new one by adding the keyword APPEND to the TELMERGE.SYS file, as explained later in the section on *Automating Communications Sessions*. The current log file can be viewed at any time during a communications session, just like any file, by pressing the F1 key when the Set 2 function keys are on-screen.

Another handy TelMerge function saves on-line information a screen at a time, in effect taking a snapshot of the screen. This Snap Shot feature can be invoked by pressing the F5 key from among the Set 1 function keys. When you invoke this function, the brief Snap Shot Menu appears on-screen, indicating that pressing any key from 1 to 5 saves current screen information in one of five memory locations to be recalled later, or that pressing Enter adds the snapshot of screen text to the current log file (pressing the Escape key exits from this function without saving). When you want to view a Snap Shot screen saved in memory during the current session, press the F6 key (Set 1) and press the appropriate number to designate the screen you want.

If you prefer, you can keep track of the information communicated during a session by printing it while on-line. Set 1's F8 function key toggles printing On or Off, as indicated at the top of the on-line screen. (The TelMerge default is for printing Off.) If you have a slow printer, it should have a large enough memory buffer to retain text transmitted at a fast baud rate; otherwise you may lose information from a session. When printing is invoked, make sure that your printer is on or the TelMerge screen may freeze up. Incidentally, when printing out a WordStar file, you may not see enhancements such as underlining or bold face. For the sake of compatibility with other computer programs, TelMerge strips out such printing information.

While on-line, you can examine or edit files on disk. To see a disk file without having to go off line, press the F1 key in Set 2. At the prompt, type the name of the file to display, including file path if necessary, and press Enter. For the current log file, just press Enter. To see a file directory, press the key that accesses DOS while staying on-line: F3 from function key Set 2. Once at the DOS prompt, you can type *dir* for a directory or any other DOS command or program to be run. To return to the on-line screen, type *exit* at the DOS prompt.

If you want to edit a file to transmit, you can exit to WordStar while staying connected on-line (if you started TelMerge from WordStar): press Set 1's F9 function key for the WordStar Opening Menu. When done editing, restart TelMerge and press the F8 key from the TelMerge Communications Menu to return to the on-line screen.

Transmitting Files

Transmitting files is an essential feature for any communications program, whether you use it to send and receive word processing documents, program files, electronic mail or telexes. Three on-line function key commands relate to file transfer.

The simplest way to send files is as straight WordStar or ASCII text by pressing the F4 key from Set 2; a prompt appears asking for the name of the file to send. As noted on-screen, you don't have to type the full name of the file if you use the DOS wild card characters * or ?. With these characters, you can designate several files at a time with the same extension or part of a name and the rest of the name replaced by wild card characters. After typing the file name, press Enter. Receiving a file is automatic and it becomes part of the log file, from which you can write it out to disk as a separate file with WordStar.

To avoid transmission errors when transferring files (increasingly rare with improved modems and telephone lines), you can use an error-checking "protocol" to encode and decode your files. The protocol most used by personal computers or with electronic bulletin boards is called XMODEM. To receive a file with the XMODEM protocol (either checksum or CRC), press the F5 key from function key Set 2. At the prompt, type a name for the file to be saved on disk. To send a file with the XMODEM protocol, press F6 from Set 2. At the resulting prompt, type the name of the file to send (wild cards are not accepted). If you designate TelMerge as the service on the Communications Menu, the CompuServe® A protocol is used automatically when the F4 (Send) command is invoked.

Incidentally, several function keys have special meanings when logged onto a telex service. Because logging is automatically on during a telex session, F7 in Set 1 of the function key commands does not affect logging, but rather sends out a WHO ARE YOU telex command when pressed. The F3 key of Set 1 issues a HERE IS identification code during a telex session, while the F4 key of Set 1 automatically requests messages when communicating telexes.

To save keystrokes while on-line, you can use four function keys to issue often-used character strings. During standard transmission, the previously mentioned F3 key in Set 1 automatically issues the user ID stored in a TEL file or in TELMERGE.SYS. F4 of the same set sends out the password for a logged service. In addition, keys F7 and F8 of Set 2 can be programmed to issue a command or character string of your choice by adding the TelMerge keywords FK1 and FK2, respectively, followed by the desired characters, to the appropriate TEL file or TELMERGE.SYS section.

An extra step is involved if you want to send a document that contains footnotes, endnotes, line numbers, or paragraph numbers. Print the document to disk in ASCII format first, then send the ASCII file.

When a communications session is finished, you can disconnect the modem from the phone line by pressing F10 in either function key set. This displays a message informing you that the session has been saved in a log file and indicates its name. According to the on-screen prompt: pressing F1 restarts TelMerge, returning you to the Communications Menu; pressing F10 again exits TelMerge, returning you to the WordStar Opening screen or the DOS prompt, depending on how you started TelMerge.

Using the Communications Menu

For greater convenience with TelMerge, typing a three-letter selection at the Communications Menu is the fastest and most efficient way to initiate a call and log on to another computer or information service. To do this, you must edit and complete the TELMERGE.SYS file containing the necessary connection information for the listed menu options and any you wish to add. If you need to change system defaults, modify program settings in the TELMERGE.SYS file.

You can make other changes within TELMERGE.SYS if you want to automate communications beyond logging on, with command scripts to automatically execute sending and receiving of information.

Once you have customized TELMERGE.SYS—as explained in succeeding sections—you may not have to press any more keys after you invoke a particular telecommunications connection; TelMerge can issue all other necessary responses to retrieve information. This is especially desirable if you regularly need to be in contact with an information service—for instance to download daily closing stock prices or electronic mail messages.

The default Communications Menu, illustrated in figure 8.13, includes options for eight of the most widely used communications services and networks. To access any of these computerized systems, you must first register with the service and receive an authorized ID code, password, and telephone number. No one is likely to register with all eight of the listed services on the Communications Menu: CompuServe and the Source™ virtually duplicate each other's functions, as do ITT Telex and RCA Telex. EasyLink™, MCI Mail®, and ONTYME® Messaging Service also cover similar ground. The Official Airline Guide can be accessed from within several other services, including the Dow-Jones News Retrieval Service®, which is not listed on the Communications Menu. You probably will want to edit the TELMERGE.SYS file to list only those services to which you subscribe.

To invoke a valid service from the Communications Menu, simply type its three-letter code and press Enter. TelMerge dials the phone number and sends the log-on information for the desired service, as you list them in the TELMERGE.SYS file.

There are three other useful listings on the Communications Menu. The Direct Connect Mode, invoked by typing the three-letter code *dir*, can be used to communicate directly between computers linked by a cable between their serial ports—without requiring a telephone line. In Answer mode, set by typing *ans*, TelMerge turns your computer into a receiver for incoming calls via modem, automatically adding information from all calls into a single log file for later reference. By invoking TEL for `Another TelMerge User`, you ensure that the CompuServe A protocol is used for error-checking when communicating with another personal computer running TelMerge.

Editing the TELMERGE.SYS File

You must edit the TELMERGE.SYS file to customize TelMerge's default settings, Communications Menu listings, accompanying phone numbers, log on codes and other information for automating telecommunications. This is a nondocument file, six pages long, including complete explanations and instructions for modifying and filling in information within its three main areas: the System Section, Menu Section, and Service Section. To preserve TELMERGE.SYS in nondocument ASCII format, edit the file in WordStar's nondocument mode, invoked from the WordStar Opening screen at help level 4 by pressing F for the `File pull-down` menu and N for a `non-document`. At other help levels, simply press N at the Opening Menu. Typing *telmerge.sys* and pressing Enter opens the file's informative introductory section, shown in figure 8.15.

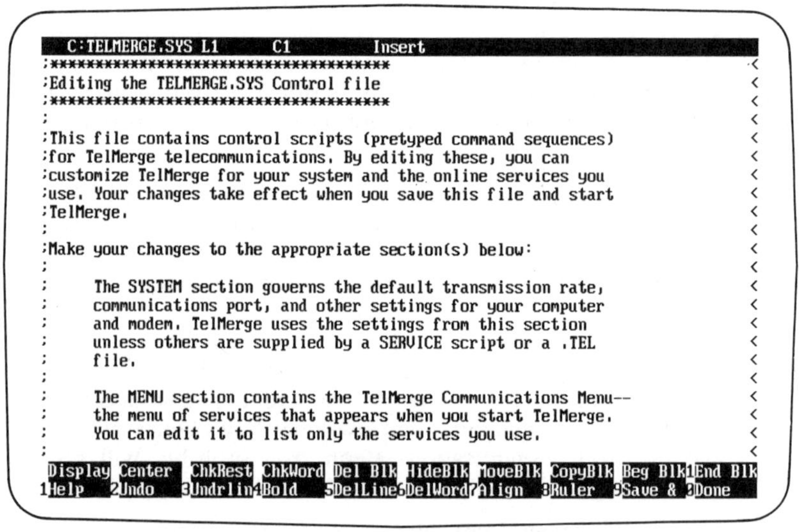
C:TELMERGE.SYS L1 C1 Insert
;*************************************
;Editing the TELMERGE.SYS Control file
;*************************************
;This file contains control scripts (pretyped command sequences)
;for TelMerge telecommunications. By editing these, you can
;customize TelMerge for your system and the online services you
;use. Your changes take effect when you save this file and start
;TelMerge.
;Make your changes to the appropriate section(s) below:
The SYSTEM section governs the default transmission rate,
communications port, and other settings for your computer
and modem. TelMerge uses the settings from this section
unless others are supplied by a SERVICE script or a .TEL
file.
The MENU section contains the TelMerge Communications Menu--
the menu of services that appears when you start TelMerge.
You can edit it to list only the services you use.
Display Center ChkRest ChkWord Del Blk HideBlk MoveBlk CopyBlk Beg Blk End Blk
1Help 2Undo 3Undrlin 4Bold 5DelLine 6DelWord 7Align 8Ruler 9Save & 0Done

Fig. 8.15.

The TELMERGE.SYS introductory section.

As with other nondocuments, any of WordStar's cursor movement and text deletion commands can be invoked. To advance to the TELMERGE.SYS file sections to be edited, you can press ^C or the PgDn key.

Within the TELMERGE.SYS file, comment text is preceded by a semicolon (;) or a left bracket ({); these characters indicate that the text is to be ignored by TelMerge. Information to be read by TelMerge consists of a keyword command or label tag followed by an appropriate setting. Keywords and settings can be upper- and lowercase or all caps.

Resetting TelMerge System Defaults

The communications defaults set by TelMerge for your computer system are listed in the System Section of TELMERGE.SYS, depicted in figure 8.16. These defaults are meant to work with most computers and modems, but can be reset for your on-line sessions. Settings required by particular services or destination computers can be entered at the appropriate place in the Service Section of TELMERGE.SYS; settings in a service script or in a TEL file override those in the System Section.

```
   C:TELMERGE.SYS L59      C2          Insert
Modem    HAYES    {Specifies a Hayes Smartmodem.                              <
                  {Other  choices: HAYES2400, DIRECT, ANSWER, ACOUSTIC.       <
Port     COM1     {Indicates that the modem is connected to serial port COM1  <
                  {Other choice:  COM2.                                       <
Baud     1200     {Specifies a baud rate of 1200                              <
                  {Other choices:  110, 300, 2400, 4800, 9600.                <
Logging ON        {Opens a logfile as soon as you connect to the remote       <
                  {service.  Both sides of the session are saved in that file. <
                  {Other choice:  OFF.                                        <
Print    YES      {Prints incoming information from a session to your         <
                  {default printer, alternate printer, or a disk file.        <
                  {YES prints to your default printer.                        <
                  {NO turns printing off.                                     <
                  {COM2 or LPT2 direct printing to a different device.        <
                  {<filename> prints to a disk file.                          <
LineDelay 2       {Delays specified number of tenths of a second              <
                  {after sending a line of text.                              <
                  {Current setting is 2/10 second.                            <
Emulate VT100     {Emulates a mainframe terminal.                             <
                  {Other choices: NONE, VIDTEX (VT52).                        <
Graphic NO        {Will not display graphics characters from remote.          <
                  {Other choice: YES                                          <
 Display Center  ChkRest ChkWord Del Blk HideBlk MoveBlk CopyBlk Beg Blk1End Blk
1Help   2Undo   3Undrlin4Bold   5DelLine6DelWord7Align  8Ruler  9Save & 0Done
```

Fig. 8.16. *The TELMERGE.SYS file listing of system defaults.*

The listing in the System Section shows eight default settings in an unmodified version of TelMerge. Other settings are optional, with four preceded by semicolons to show that they are ignored by TelMerge unless reset. Additional settings can be invoked by including appropriate keywords. System setting keywords and their functions are summarized in table 8.11.

Table 8.11
TelMerge System Settings

Keyword	*Function*
Default settings	
INIT ATE1	AT prepares modem for a command; E1 echoes input to the screen
MODEM HAYES	Specifies type of modem used
PORT COM1	Specifies communications port for system
BAUD 1200	Sets transmission rate
LOGGING ON	Sets status of logging function
PRINT YES	Turns printing On during session
LINEDELAY 2	Pauses after line sent with F4 (SEND) key
EMULATE VT100	Designates VT100 terminal to be emulated
GRAPHIC NO	Extended graphic set not used for display
Optional settings	
USEDTR YES	Speeds modem hang up with DTR signal
APPEND YES	Adds information from session to named log file
NETWORK name	Specifies network for contacting service
PROTOCOL name	Specifies error-checking protocol
PARITY	Specifies error-checking mode
BITS number	Sets number of bits transmitted per character
STOPS 1 or 2	Sets number of stop bits
DUPLEX FULL or HALF	Sets computer control of character display
TRY number 1-99	Sets times to redial after busy signal

Default system settings changes depend on the modem you have. HAYES-compatible modems are most common, and you can specify a high-speed Hayes Smartmodem 2400™, or a more primitive ACOUSTIC modem. For direct-communications, the correct modem setting is DIRECT, but for answer mode it should be ANSWER. The only valid alternative to Port COM1 is COM2. If a baud rate of 1200 is not suitable, the other choices are 110, 300, 2400, 4800, or 9600. If you do not want to save the contents of a communications session in a log file on disk, you can change logging from On to Off. Printing of a session can also be turned off by changing Yes to No, or printer output can be redirected to COM2, LPT2, or a disk file name.

A brief delay of 0.2 seconds is inserted after every line of text sent by your system; you can change this number (in units of a tenth of a second). Currently, TelMerge emulates the performance of a VT100 terminal when connected to a mainframe computer; you can change this to a VIDTEX™ or VT52 terminal or NONE at all. Graphic characters are not recognized when sent by another computer; the alternative is Yes to recognize these.

Optional settings can be added to the system setting listings. (Remember to omit the initial semicolon if invoking the ones already in the unmodified TELMERGE.SYS file.) These additional settings affect modem performance, error checking, and on-line display.

To speed up phone line hang up, you can invoke the modem data terminal ready signal by typing *usedtr yes* (Hayes switch 1 should be On). For the contents of a new communications session to be added to the previous log file instead of starting a new one, type ***append yes***; a log file name other than TELMERGE.LOG can be specified by typing the keyword *logfile* and the new file name. When using a commercial network as an intermediary to connect with an information service, specify ***network tymnet, telenet***, or ***uninet***. If invoking on-line function key Set 2 commands F5 or F6, the error-checking protocol is XMODEM checksum; typing *protocol xmcrc* specifies the XMODEM CRC protocol.

Depending on the computer with which you are communicating, you may have to reset error-checking PARITY (NONE is the default; other possibilities are ODD, EVEN, ZERO, or ONE), the number of character BITS (8 is the default; 7 the usual alternative) and bits for STOPS (1 is the default; 2 is the other possibility). Usually, the characters you type are echoed by the computer to which you are transmitting and shown on your screen in `DUPLEX FULL` mode (the TelMerge default); some systems, however, require that you be in DUPLEX HALF mode. If TelMerge reaches a busy signal, it can be set to keep placing the call with *try* and a number from 1 to 99 for the number of times to retry (the default is 2).

Incidentally, while at the TelMerge on-line screen, you can display default settings by pressing the Set 1 function key F1 twice. The resulting screen, headed CURRENT TELMERGE SETTINGS, is illustrated in figure 8.17.

Editing Communications Menu Settings

The TelMerge Communications Menu is the only menu that can be fully edited and customized among all the programs included in the WordStar Release 5 package. Every listing can be changed and new ones added, provided a control script is also modified or added for each listing. The text for the Communications Menu is located in the Menu Section of the TELMERGE.SYS file, as shown in figure 8.18.

The Communications Menu listings format is simple: typing the word *say* preceding a line in TELMERGE.SYS invokes text to be displayed by TelMerge. The symbol ¦

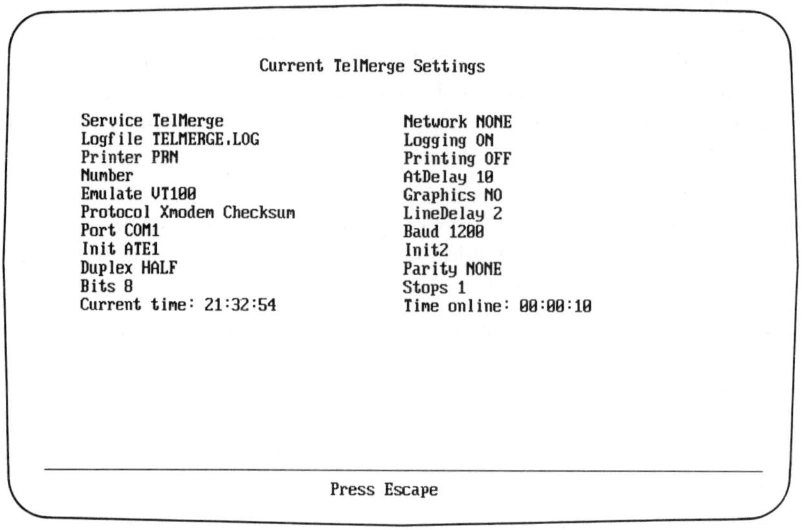

```
                Current TelMerge Settings

Service TelMerge                  Network NONE
Logfile TELMERGE.LOG              Logging ON
Printer PRN                       Printing OFF
Number                            AtDelay 10
Emulate VT100                     Graphics NO
Protocol Xmodem Checksum          LineDelay 2
Port COM1                         Baud 1200
Init ATE1                         Init2
Duplex HALF                       Parity NONE
Bits 8                            Stops 1
Current time: 21:32:54            Time online: 00:00:10

                      Press Escape
```

Fig. 8.17.

The TelMerge on-line help screen of system defaults.

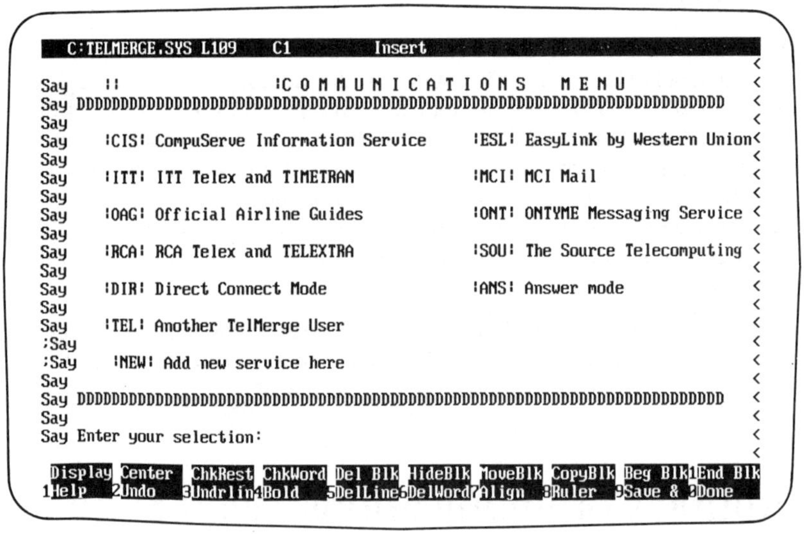

```
 C:TELMERGE.SYS L109    C1          Insert
                                                                    <
Say  ¦¦              ¦C O M M U N I C A T I O N S   M E N U         <
Say DDDDDDDDDDDDDDDDDDDDDDDDDDDDDDDDDDDDDDDDDDDDDDDDDDDDDDDDDDDDDDD <
Say                                                                 <
Say    ¦CIS¦ CompuServe Information Service    ¦ESL¦ EasyLink by Western Union<
Say                                                                 <
Say    ¦ITT¦ ITT Telex and TIMETRAN            ¦MCI¦ MCI Mail       <
Say                                                                 <
Say    ¦OAG¦ Official Airline Guides           ¦ONT¦ ONTYME Messaging Service <
Say                                                                 <
Say    ¦RCA¦ RCA Telex and TELEXTRA            ¦SOU¦ The Source Telecomputing <
Say                                                                 <
Say    ¦DIR¦ Direct Connect Mode               ¦ANS¦ Answer mode    <
Say                                                                 <
Say    ¦TEL¦ Another TelMerge User                                  <
;Say                                                                <
;Say    ¦NEW¦ Add new service here                                  <
Say                                                                 <
Say DDDDDDDDDDDDDDDDDDDDDDDDDDDDDDDDDDDDDDDDDDDDDDDDDDDDDDDDDDDDDDD <
Say                                                                 <
Say Enter your selection:                                           <
                                                                    <
 Display Center  ChkRest ChkWord Del Blk HideBlk MoveBlk CopyBlk Beg Blk End Blk
1Help   2Undo   3Undrlin4Bold   5DelLine6DelWord7Align  8Ruler  9Save & 0Done
```

Fig. 8.18.

Communications Menu listings in TELMERGE.SYS.

(typed with a Shift-backslash keystroke) turns on-screen highlighting on or off; a three-letter service label is placed between two such symbols, followed by the name of the service or computer to be called. At the bottom of the menu listings, the line `Say |NEW| Add new service here` indicates the format for adding a new selection to the Communications Menu (omit the initial semicolon). You should delete from the Menu Section any services to which you do not subscribe and add listings for those services and remote computers you do call. If you add a new service, remember to delete the semicolon from the beginning of the line when you replace `NEW` with the name of the new service.

Below the Communications Menu listings is the following command line:

```
Goto !          {Go to the Label that matches selection
```

This line directs TelMerge to find within TELMERGE.SYS the three-letter label entered at the Communications Menu prompt. The label and the phone number and other log-on information associated with it are located in an individual script within the Service Section of the system file. The information in a designated script is sent out by TelMerge to initiate a call. Each Communications Menu listing must have a valid script with all essential information included. Examples of the scripts contained in an unmodified copy of TELMERGE.SYS are illustrated in figure 8.19.

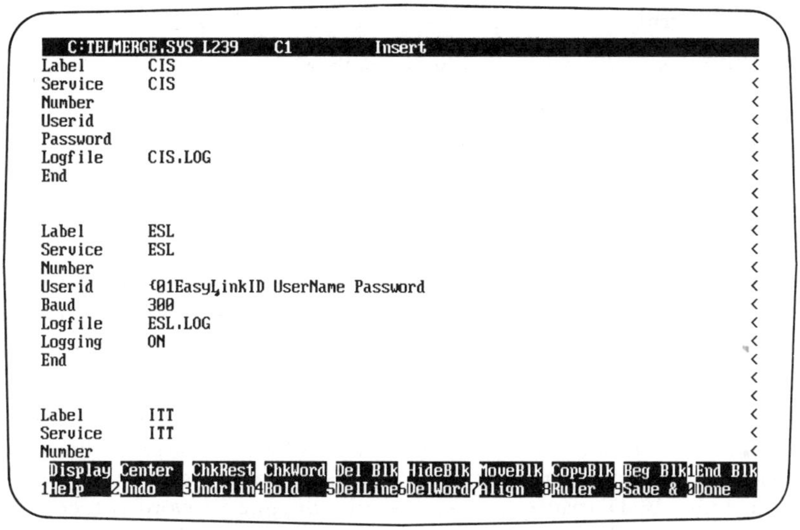
C:TELMERGE.SYS L239 C1 Insert
Label CIS
Service CIS
Number
Userid
Password
Logfile CIS.LOG
End
Label ESL
Service ESL
Number
Userid {01EasyLinkID UserName Password
Baud 300
Logfile ESL.LOG
Logging ON
End
Label ITT
Service ITT
Number
Display Center ChkRest ChkWord Del Blk HideBlk MoveBlk CopyBlk Beg Blk End Blk
1Help 2Undo 3Undrlin 4Bold 5DelLine 6DelWord 7Align 8Ruler 9Save & 0Done

Fig. 8.19. *Service information in the TELMERGE.SYS file.*

Keywords used in TELMERGE.SYS scripts are summarized in table 8.12.

To complete scripts in TELMERGE.SYS for existing Communications Menu listings, type the appropriate telephone numbers, user IDs, and passwords where indicated.

For a new Communications Menu listing, type a script similar to the ones already in TELMERGE.SYS, specifying the label, accompanying name, phone number, and other information essential to initiating a call and logging on to another computer.

Beyond the information for calling a service or computer listed on the Communications Menu, you can add to a script keywords to automate what is sent and received during an on-line session. These useful keywords are noted in the next section.

Table 8.12
Common TelMerge Script Keywords

Keyword	*Function*
LABEL label name	Sets destination in control file for GOTO
SERVICE abbr name	Designates name of service being contacted
NUMBER phone #	Designates phone number to dial
USERID string	Sends ID code required by service
PASSWORD string	Sends password required by service
ANSWERBACK string	Sends personal ID at a telex WHO ARE YOU code
INTERACTIVE phone #	Specifies phone number of telex real-time service
END	Starts call, ignores subsequent display

Automating Communications Sessions

Any command script in TELMERGE.SYS can be augmented to automate a TelMerge session once communications with another computer have been established. Keywords typed into the script can specify information to be transmitted and when to terminate a call.

Each keyword and its accompanying information should occupy a separate line in the script. Among the most commonly used keywords for automating a communications session are self-evident ones like CALL (starts a call and then invokes further commands), WAIT (pauses a session until a designated word is received), SEND (transmits specified text), FILESEND (transmits a named file), and HANGUP (terminates the call, readies another call). For a complete list of keywords to use for automating TelMerge Communications, see table 8.13.

Table 8.13
TelMerge Keywords for Automating On-Line Sessions

Keyword	*Function*
ATDELAY 10ths of second	Pauses before sending first character
ATTENTION character	Sends character required by a service
AUTOLOG YES or NO	Turns automatic log on or off
CALL	Starts call and invokes further commands
CLS	Clears the screen

Table 8.13—*Continued*

Keyword	*Function*
ELSE string	Sets action if opposite of designated condition
ENDIF string	Starts call if condition is satisfied
EXIT	Stops session and returns to WordStar
FILESEND filename	Sends specified file
FIRST character	Waits for transmitted character before displaying
FK, label string	Programs function key F7 or F8 of key set 2
GOTO label	Goes to a LABEL in control file
HANGCOM string	Sets hangup command for modem
HANGUP	Hangs up on phone line
HOLD ?	Stores keyboard input in memory buffer
HOSTID string	Issues host ID on network
IF string	Tests for designated condition, invokes action
IFNOT string	Tests for designated condition, invokes action
INCLUDE filename	Runs another script in midst of current script
INIT string	Initializes modem before making call
LOGON string string string	Issues user ID, password, terminal, host ID
PAUSE seconds	Pauses transmission to allow response
POSTMODEM string	Sends characters to electronic switch
PREFIX string	Specifies condition before dialing number
PREMODEM string	Sends string to port before modem initialization
PROMPT character	Specifies extra service prompts in TelMerge
QUIET seconds	Specifies time to wait after receiving
SAY string	Displays string during session
CALL	Starts call, ignores subsequent commands
WAIT string	Waits for particular string from service

Table 8.13—*Continued*

Keyword	*Function*
SEND string	Sends character string and carriage return
SUFFIX string	Sends command to modem after dialing
TERMINAL string	Specifies terminal type

Keywords and their information should be entered in the order in which they are to be executed, keeping in mind that TelMerge follows the following order when sending these keywords during a call: PREMODEM, INIT, PREFIX, NUMBER, ATTENTION, ATDELAY, TERMINAL, HOSTID, USERID, PASSWORD, LOGON, FILESEND, HANGCOM, POSTMODEM.

When you have completed editing the TELMERGE.SYS file, close and save it as you do any nondocument or document. The next time you run TelMerge, the new settings are invoked.

9

Using Shorthand Macros

You can greatly enhance word processing efficiency with WordStar's "shorthand" macro feature, simplifying complicated or repetitious tasks. Macros are two-key commands, starting with Esc, that invoke longer sequences of keystrokes and save typing time. WordStar permits the definition of as many as 36 keyboard macros, each of which can contain up to 64 keystrokes. All macros are contained in a WSSHORT.OVR file, which must be on the same disk and directory as the WordStar program.

Shorthand macros were not available in early releases of WordStar, making their debut in Release 4. Before the shorthand feature was available, many users added macros with memory-resident programs such as ProKey™ and SuperKey®. WordStar's built-in macro capability is not the equal of separate macro programs, which are more flexible and powerful. Nonetheless, your word processor's shorthand feature adds to the power of WordStar without the penalties of expense, memory consumption, and unreliability caused by memory-resident programs.

All the features introduced in previous chapters, including commands for starting WordStar, editing and formatting documents, and printing hard copy, can be automated with macros. This chapter shows you how to increase your productivity—not to mention the quality of your documents—by using WordStar's shorthand capabilities.

With the macro procedures in this chapter you will be able to do the following:

- Insert the date, time, or result of a calculation into a text
- Plan, write, and save macros for custom functions
- Move, delete, and format text with macros
- Automate insertion of often-used text in documents

Veterans of Release 4 will find WordStar's macro function essentially unchanged. One of the predefined WordStar macros has been omitted, but you can easily restore it. The method for creating and invoking shorthand macros remains the same.

Of all the advanced features in WordStar, shorthand macros are among the most neglected. Experienced users who could benefit from automating frequent operations often miss the advantages of macros. Beginners can also enjoy improved efficiency with shorthand macros, both preassigned and customized. Consider using macros, no matter what your level of expertise.

What Are Macros?

With the WordStar macro feature, while at the editing screen, you can issue multiple keystrokes, either text or commands, by pressing Esc followed by a keystroke from the central keyboard. Such macro commands are especially useful for automating routine tasks requiring multiple keystrokes. You could, for example, invoke a two-key macro to print your name, address, and the date at the top of all your letters. Complex command sequences can also be invoked in this way.

The word *macro* is derived from the Greek word *makron*, meaning *big*. When you create a macro, you assign a sequence of many keystrokes to a single key. A macro keystroke is a "big" keystroke because pressing Esc and one more key can produce the same effect as entering a greater number of individual keystrokes.

Using Permanent Shorthand Macros

The WordStar program comes preset with several permanent shorthand commands, which cannot be altered, and other preset macros that can be redefined or extended. All shorthand macros conform to the same two-keystroke structure: Esc followed by a character typed from the central keyboard.

From within a document, pressing Esc once displays WordStar's Shorthand Menu, shown in figure 9.1. To exit the Shorthand Menu, press Esc again or press ^U.

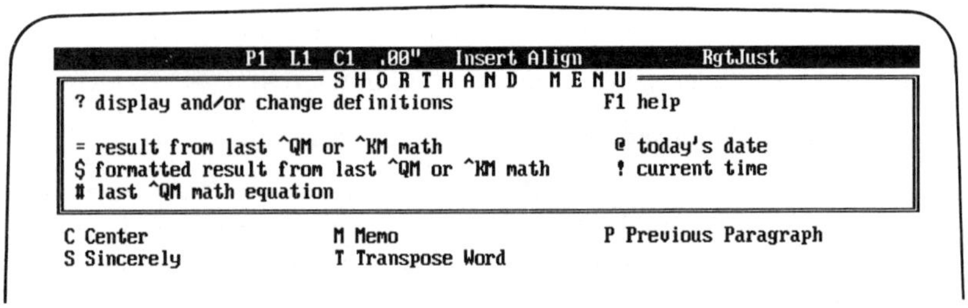
P1 L1 C1 .00" Insert Align RgtJust
S H O R T H A N D M E N U
? display and/or change definitions
F1 help
= result from last ^QM or ^KM math
@ today's date
$ formatted result from last ^QM or ^KM math
! current time
last ^QM math equation
C Center
M Memo
P Previous Paragraph
S Sincerely
T Transpose Word

Fig. 9.1.

WordStar's Shorthand Menu, listing built-in macro commands.

The options on the Shorthand Menu, which are discussed in the following sections, are straightforward. Permanent macros for math, date, and time functions are within the menu box. Below the box are definable macros for format and text applications.

WordStar's on-line help is readily available with the Shorthand Menu. If you need help, press F1 or ^J to display the brief help screen shown in figure 9.2. As the help screen indicates, press Esc to return to the Shorthand Menu.

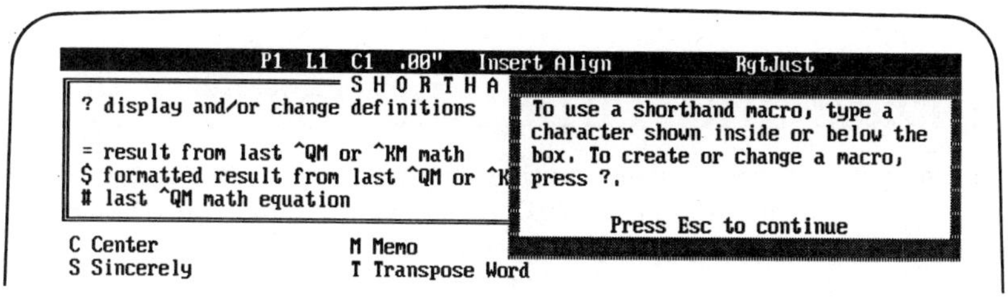
P1 L1 C1 .00" Insert Align RgtJust
S H O R T H A
? display and/or change definitions
= result from last ^QM or ^KM math
$ formatted result from last ^QM or ^K
# last ^QM math equation
To use a shorthand macro, type a character shown inside or below the box. To create or change a macro, press ?.
Press Esc to continue
C Center
S Sincerely
M Memo
T Transpose Word

Fig. 9.2.
The Shorthand Menu's on-line help screen.

Using Math Macros

WordStar includes two built-in facilities for performing mathematical calculations, both introduced in Chapter 6. One is the column-math capability, and the other is the built-in calculator.

Three of WordStar's permanent macros enable you to insert in a document the result of the last math operation performed or the equation used to produce that result. After pressing Esc to display the Shorthand Menu, you can execute either of these actions by pressing a single symbol key. Table 9.1 summarizes the math shorthand commands and their effects.

Table 9.1
Math Macro Commands

Command	*Function*
=	Inserts the result of the last shorthand or column-math operation
$	Inserts in currency format the result of the last shorthand operation
#	Inserts the last math equation

To use math shorthand for inserting a result or an equation in your document, first position the cursor where you want the result or equation to appear. Then press Esc to access the Shorthand Menu and press =, $, or # to insert the result in simple number form, as a dollar amount, or to insert the equation itself in your text. If you have not previously performed a math operation in the current WordStar session, = enters a 0, $ enters .00, and # enters nothing. The program returns to the editing screen, and the first character of the result or equation aligns with the cursor position.

When inserting math results or equations into existing text, make sure that insert mode is on (indicated by the presence of the word `Insert` on the status line). If insert mode is off, the results overwrite the existing text.

Using Date and Time Macros

WordStar's permanent macros for date and time functions are as easy to use as the shorthand math macros. First press Esc to call up the Shorthand Menu. Then press @ to insert the current date or press ! to insert the current time at the cursor. Commands for date and time are summarized in table 9.2.

Table 9.2
Date and Time Shorthand Commands

Command	*Function*
@	Inserts the current date from DOS
!	Inserts the current time from DOS

By default, the format for the date is *Month DD, YYYY*, as in May 22, 1988. The default format for the time is *HH:MM AM/PM*, as in 4:47 AM. You can change these defaults with the WSCHANGE program (see Chapter 11).

Date and time information are drawn from the current DOS settings. If your system does not keep track of these automatically with a clock circuit board, be sure to enter date and time manually any time you start WordStar.

Using Definable Macros

Defining and using macros is a simple matter, as you will learn from the examples presented in this chapter. In the sections that follow, you become acquainted with macros as applied in a sample letter that the credit department of Widgets, Inc. might send to a slow-paying customer. Even if you don't plan to use a particular macro presented here, read the discussion so you can learn techniques that are useful in designing your own macros.

Four predefined modifiable macros are provided with WordStar Release 5. One macro available in Release 4, for moving the cursor to the beginning of a paragraph, has been omitted, but you can restore it by following instructions later in this chapter. Keys used to activate predefined macros and brief descriptions of their effects are shown below the Shorthand Menu box in figure 9.1. They include two formatting functions: centering text on a line and transposing two words. The other two "ready-made" macros are for inserting text: a memo heading and the ending of a business letter.

Ready-made macros and others you can define demonstrate the use of shorthand functions. By comparing the macro definitions with already familiar WordStar commands, you learn that defining and using macros is not at all complicated.

As an introduction to macro use, you can create the "reminder" letter for Widgets, Inc. shown here. (Note: Errors in the letter are intentional; you will make corrections later in this chapter.)

```
                    Widgets, Inc.
                 2323 Burroughs Road
                San Andreas, CA 93939

                   (408) 555-5555

                                  November 3, 1988

Mr. Richard Dodgson
Universal Gadget Co.
49373 Gibson Blvd.
Elk's Tooth, NV 81192

Dear Mr. Dodgson:

Our records show your that account balance of $4,969.83 is 145
days past due. If this account is not paid in full within 15
days, we shall be forced to turn it over to our collections
agency. If payment has already been sent, please disregard this
letter.

                                  Sincerely,


                                  Norma Jean Baker
                                  Credit Manager
```

Fig. 9.3.

The reminder letter for Widgets, Inc.

The first of the predefined macros below the Shorthand Menu box is `C` for Center. Press Esc to access the Shorthand Menu, and then type *?* to display the sequence of keystrokes invoked by this macro. This displays a screen headed SHORTHAND, as shown in figure 9.4.

The definable macro keys, descriptions, and definitions are shown in the lower part of the screen. The information for the C macro is the following:

```
C  Center
   ^OC
```

Fig. 9.4.
WordStar's listing of macro descriptions and definitions.

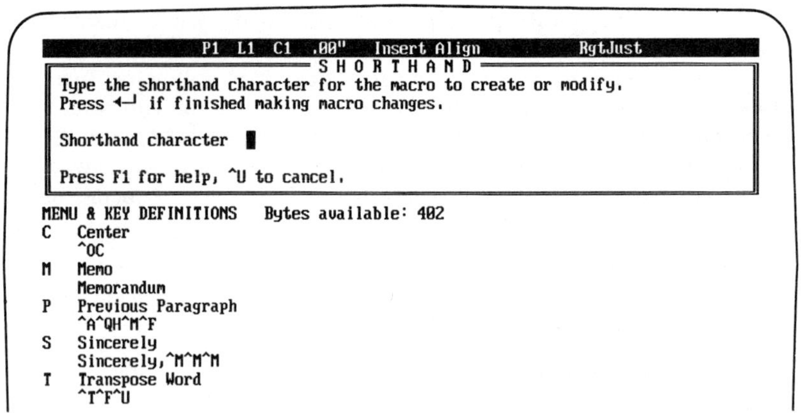
P1 L1 C1 .00" Insert Align RgtJust
SHORTHAND
Type the shorthand character for the macro to create or modify.
Press ←┘ if finished making macro changes.
Shorthand character
Press F1 for help, ^U to cancel.
MENU & KEY DEFINITIONS Bytes available: 402
C Center
^OC
M Memo
Memorandum
P Previous Paragraph
^A^QH^M^F
S Sincerely
Sincerely,^M^M^M
T Transpose Word
^T^F^U

The macro definition and a manual keyboard entry are identical. The first keystroke of the manual keyboard command—and the first part of the macro definition—is *^o*. The second keystroke is *c*, which, when entered after *^o*, causes WordStar to center the current line of text. Thus pressing Esc and C is equivalent to typing the *^oc* text-centering command within a document.

To try this macro in the sample letter, you could begin by opening a document file named PAYLTR. When the editing screen appears, enter the first line of text:

Widgets, Inc.

This is the first line of Widgets, Inc.'s letterhead. Press Esc to call up the Shorthand Menu, and C for centering text. (You can enter the C in upper- or lowercase.) As soon as you press C, the Shorthand Menu disappears, and the line of text is centered between the margins of the editing screen, as shown in figure 9.5.

Fig. 9.5.
WordStar's built-in Center macro used to center a heading.

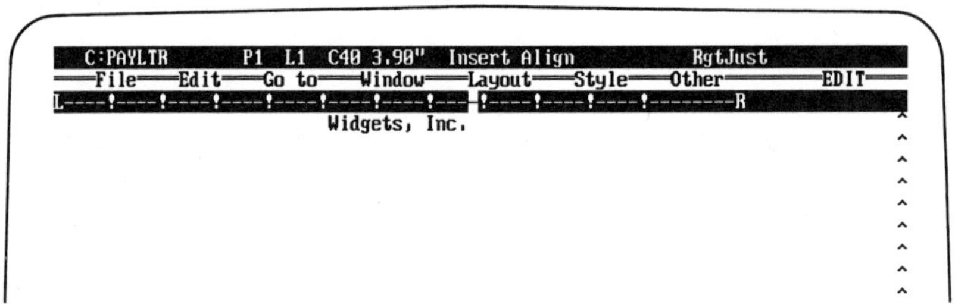
C:PAYLTR P1 L1 C40 3.90" Insert Align RgtJust
File Edit Go to Window Layout Style Other EDIT
Widgets, Inc.

Next type the rest of the letterhead:

2323 Burroughs Road
San Andreas, CA 93939

(408) 555-5555

As you complete each line, press Esc and then C to center it.

To create another blank line, press Enter. On the next line, enter the date. In most business-letter layouts, the date is "tabbed over" toward the right margin. In this example, the date is positioned with the first character in column 46 (or 4.50"), which is the ninth tab stop in WordStar's default ruler-line definition. Pressing the Tab key nine times is the kind of repetitious keypunching to avoid. Furthermore, unless you pay close attention, you're likely to press the key eight times or overshoot the mark and end up on tab 10. This operation is a perfect candidate for a macro. Because such a shorthand command is not preset in WordStar, you need to create it.

Creating a Simple Macro

The procedure for creating a shorthand macro is straightforward. First press Esc from the document screen to display the Shorthand Menu; then type *?* for the shorthand definition screen. At the prompt for the shorthand character, you can assign the macro you are going to create to any of 36 keys: the 26 letter keys plus the 10 numeric keys. (Note: WordStar does not distinguish the number keys on the numeric keypad from those at the top of the main keyboard.) If you want, you can overwrite another macro by assigning a new macro to a previously assigned key.

In WordStar Release 5, once you type a character, a second dialog box titled SHORTHAND appears on-screen. This box includes lines for a brief description of the command you are about to create and a line for the command or text it is to invoke (see fig. 9.6).

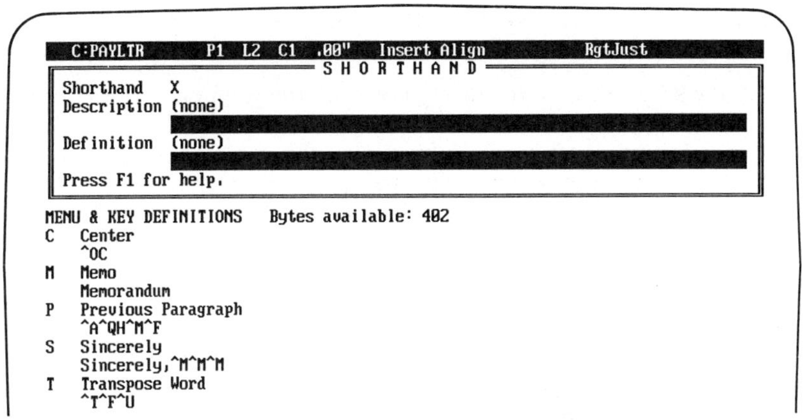
C:PAYLTR P1 L2 C1 .00" Insert Align RgtJust
SHORTHAND
Shorthand X
Description (none)
Definition (none)
Press F1 for help.
MENU & KEY DEFINITIONS Bytes available: 402
C Center
^OC
M Memo
Memorandum
P Previous Paragraph
^A^QH^M^F
S Sincerely
Sincerely,^M^M
T Transpose Word
^T^F^U

Fig. 9.6.
WordStar's dialog box for typing macro key definitions and their functions.

At the prompt for Description, type a brief description of the command you are about to program. This description appears on-screen whenever the Shorthand Menu is invoked with the Esc key. You can enter up to 50 characters for each description, but keep them concise. WordStar allocates a fixed amount of memory for macros. The default amount, which can be altered with WSCHANGE, is 512 bytes. The characters used for macro descriptions are counted as part of that total. The remaining bytes for macro descriptions and definitions are indicated below the Shorthand dialog box.

Once you have typed your macro's description, press Enter to move the cursor to the Definition prompt, where you should type the WordStar command sequence or text to be invoked with the selected macro command. To enter Ctrl-letter commands, you must press ^P followed by the letter(s). You can press F10 or ^K or Enter to return the first Shorthand dialog box to the screen; then you can either press another key to begin another macro definition or press Enter to indicate that you have finished.

When you finish defining macros, you see a prompt asking whether to `Store macro changes on disk (Y/N)?` To save the macro you have just defined, press Y. This records the macro to disk and makes it available every time you start WordStar. Once you have entered a macro, it is added under the Shorthand Menu in alphabetical order, with numbers appearing before letters.

If you make a mistake while defining a macro, use the Backspace and Del keys to correct the error. You can press ^U to return the cursor to the Shorthand character prompt. You can reenter the character or type another one if you change your mind. To quit the process entirely, press ^U once more.

As an example of creating a simple macro, try defining one to automatically issue the tabs for placing a date at the proper position on the line in a business letter. Start by pressing Esc to call up the Shorthand Menu, and press ? to display the Shorthand character prompt. A logical key choice for the new macro is the 9 key (for ninth tab). Choosing keys with an easily remembered connection to their macro functions is a good idea. For example, notice that the ready-made macros use C for Center, M for Memo.

After you press the 9 key, you see the dialog box with the prompts for description and definition. For this macro, enter the description *9th Tab*, and press Enter. Then enter the definition of your macro by issuing the commands equivalent to pressing the Tab key nine times. Each time you press the combination ^P^I, `^I` appears on the definition line. When you have completed the definition by pressing ^P^I nine times, your screen should look similar to the one in figure 9.7. Press F10 or ^K, and then press Enter to bring up the prompt for saving the macro. Press Y to save it.

To use this macro, at the document screen press Esc to display the Shorthand Menu. This time, the 9 character and the macro's description appear at the top of the left column of macros below the Shorthand Menu.

Pressing the 9 key activates the macro. You can press either the 9 key at the top of the main keyboard or on the numeric keypad. If you use the numeric keypad, remember to press the Shift key first to switch the keypad to numeric mode temporarily. As soon as you press 9, the cursor moves to the ninth tab position, and you can enter the date. Instead of entering the date used in the example, you can use the shorthand feature to enter the current date by pressing Esc and the @ key.

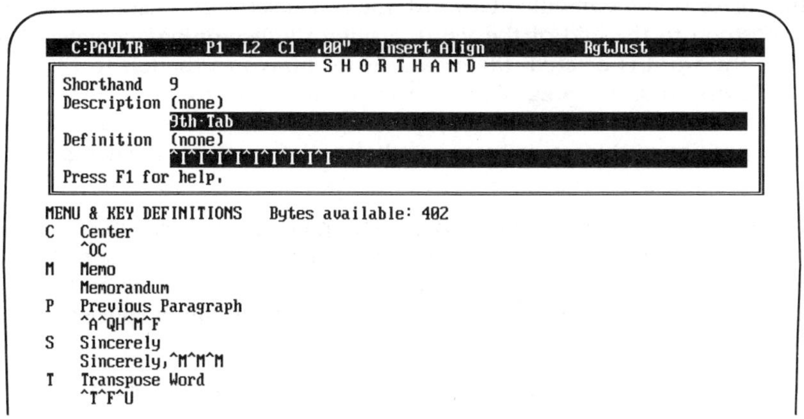
C:PAYLTR P1 L2 C1 .00" Insert Align RgtJust
S H O R T H A N D
Shorthand 9
Description (none)
9th Tab
Definition (none)
^I^I^I^I^I^I^I^I^I
Press F1 for help.
MENU & KEY DEFINITIONS Bytes available: 402
C Center
^OC
M Memo
Memorandum
P Previous Paragraph
^A^QH^M^F
S Sincerely
Sincerely,^M^M^M
T Transpose Word
^T^F^U

Fig. 9.7.
A simple tab-stop macro defined on the Shorthand Menu.

If you want to continue practicing macro applications in the sample letter, enter the rest of the document. You should type the letter exactly as shown previously, without correcting the errors you might notice: the transposition of `your` and `that` in the first sentence or the misspelling of `to` in the last sentence. These intentional errors are to be corrected with macros explained later in this section.

Remember that you have two macros to help you type the letter's closing. You can use the 9 macro to move the cursor to the ninth tab position, and the S macro to enter the word *Sincerely*. If you examine the definition of the S macro (see fig. 9.7), you see that the word `Sincerely` is followed by a comma (,) and three repetitions of the ^M character, each of which is the equivalent of the Enter keystroke. Those last three keystrokes move the cursor down three lines, leaving room for the signature between the closing and the name of the sender.

Using a Macro To Transpose Words

Among the more common errors during typing is the accidental reversal of two words in text. The T macro, which is supplied ready-made with WordStar 5, is the shorthand command you need to correct this error quickly and efficiently.

To understand how the Transpose Word macro works, look up its definition by pressing Esc and then ?. The T macro definition contains three keystrokes: ^T, ^F, and ^U, described below:

^T	Deletes a word forward from the cursor
^F	Moves the cursor forward to the next word
^U	"Undeletes" the last word deletion

If you place the cursor at the beginning of the first word to be transposed and press ^T, the entire word is deleted. (Note that the cursor must be at the beginning of the word; if the cursor is in the middle of a word, then ^T deletes the characters from the cursor position to the end of the word, leaving the beginning characters in place.) When the word is deleted, the second word moves to the left to fill the space vacated by the first. Pressing ^F then advances the cursor to the beginning of the following word in the sentence. Finally, pressing ^U undeletes the erased word at the current position of the cursor, reversing the previous order of the designated words.

To try out this predefined macro in the sample letter, correct the transposition of the words `your` and `that` in the first sentence. First position the cursor at the beginning of `your`, press Esc to call up the Shorthand Menu, and press T. The Shorthand Menu disappears, the macro goes to work, and within a split second, the sentence should read as follows:

```
Our records show that your account balance of $4,969.83 is
145 days past due.
```

"Walking through" the commands you plan to implement in a macro is always a good idea. In the next section, you will use this technique to design a macro for transposing characters. This can then be used to correct the second error in the sample document.

Creating a Macro To Transpose Characters

Reversing the order of two letters in a word is another of the most common typing errors. Deleting and retyping erroneous letters can be time-consuming, so a macro for correcting such errors is a great convenience.

A few word processing programs have a command for transposing two letters. In the absence of such a function in WordStar, you can create a custom macro, combining several manual commands in a single keystroke. A character-transposing macro might reflect a strategy similar to that of the word-transposing macro, but that strategy is not the best.

The problem is that, by default, WordStar's undelete feature does not work for single characters. Although you can use the WSCHANGE program to reset WordStar so that single characters are undeleted, doing so is not recommended. As you become familiar with WordStar, you may use the undelete feature as an easy way to move text: delete the text, move the cursor, and press F2 or ^U to undelete the text at the new cursor location. But the deletion of single characters—with the Backspace key, the Del key, or ^G—is so common that, without thinking about it, you are likely to delete a single character while preparing to undelete a block of text in its new position.

When text is deleted, it is copied into an internal memory buffer maintained by WordStar; when text is undeleted, the contents of the buffer are copied into the document. Each deletion overwrites the previous contents of the buffer. Single characters, however, are not copied into the buffer (and the previous buffer contents are unchanged) unless WSCHANGE has been used to enable undeletion of single characters. Then deletion of just a single character can wipe out a whole paragraph of text stored in the internal buffer. You're better off, therefore, if you do not use the option for undeleting single characters.

Another strategy must be substituted for transposing characters. The alternative is to use a block move: mark a block consisting of the second of the two transposed characters, move the cursor to the preceding character, and then move the block.

Planning the Macro

Before writing a macro command, it is best to break the sequence into individual functions that lead to the desired effect. Observe how you apply a series of commands manually to resolve an editing or formatting situation; then decide the best way to automate it as a single shorthand macro.

In the case of transposed characters, starting with the second character is logical because you are likely to catch a transposition error right after you've made it. At that time, the cursor is immediately after the second of the two characters—the proper position for entering ^KK to mark the end of the block.

You should manually work through the operations that a macro is to perform. Re-create the condition in which you will most often use the macro. For correcting the transposition error, you would note these keystrokes as you enter them:

1. Press ^KK to mark the end of the block.
2. Press ^S to move the cursor one column to the left.
3. Press ^KB to mark the beginning of the block. The misplaced character is highlighted.
4. Press ^S to move the cursor another column to the left.
5. Press ^KV to move the marked block to the cursor position.
6. Press ^KH to clear the marked block. The error is now corrected.
7. Press ^D twice to return the cursor to its original position so that you can continue typing.

You may want to try alternate strategies when planning a macro, but the sequence of commands you choose to automate should always be the most generally applicable and efficient to use.

Writing the Macro

To write your character-transposing macro, press Esc to display the Shorthand Menu, and then press ? for the macro definitions. Now you need to decide to which key this macro will be assigned.

For the character transposition macro, a likely candidate is the C key (C for character). The macro already assigned to that key— ^OC, for centering a line—is a useful example for studying how macros work, but it only saves you one keystroke. Using the macro requires two keystrokes, Esc and C, but three keys are required to enter the command manually. Furthermore, centering also can be performed by pressing Shift-F2. Because only 36 macro keys are available, you're better off reserving them for macros that save you more effort—such as this macro for transposing characters.

Press C to indicate that you are assigning a macro to that key. At the Description prompt, enter a brief description, such as *Transpose Chars*, and press Enter.

At the definition prompt, the keystrokes listed previously must appear as follows:

^KK^S^KB^S^KV^KH^D^D

But to indicate control-key combinations, you must enter ^P before the control character. You also must hold down the Ctrl key as you enter the control character itself. To enter the first ^K of this definition, for example, you press ^P^K.

Note: When you write macros, you don't need to enter the keystroke commands in uppercase letters, just as you don't need to use uppercase letters when you enter commands manually.

After you enter the remaining keystrokes for the definition and press Enter, your screen should resemble figure 9.8.

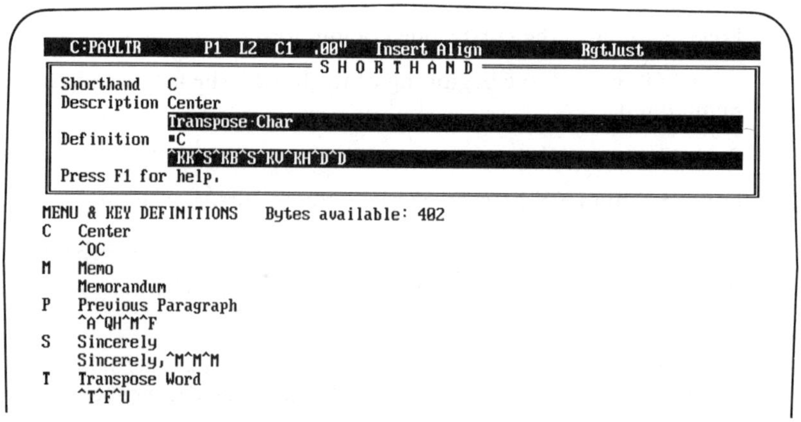
C:PAYLTR P1 L2 C1 .00" Insert Align RgtJust
SHORTHAND
Shorthand C
Description Center
Transpose Char
Definition ▪C
^KK^S^KB^S^KV^KH^D^D
Press F1 for help.
MENU & KEY DEFINITIONS Bytes available: 402
C Center
^OC
M Memo
Memorandum
P Previous Paragraph
^A^QH^M^F
S Sincerely
Sincerely,^M^M
T Transpose Word
^T^F^U

Fig. 9.8.

The definition entered for the character-transposition macro.

Once the definition is complete, press Enter again. At the prompt `Store changes on disk (Y/N)?`, press Y.

Testing the Macro

You should test a new macro to make sure that it works properly. If it does not yield the appropriate results, you can correct the macro by following the definition procedure again and substituting the appropriate WordStar commands.

To test the character-transposition macro defined previously, try it out on the second error in the sample document. In the second sentence, the word *to* is misspelled as `ot`. Now you can use the C macro to correct the spelling. With the cursor at the space following `ot`, activate the macro by pressing Esc followed by C. The macro should change `ot` to `to`. If not, carefully compare your macro definition to the one shown in figure 9.8, and make any necessary corrections.

The steps for describing, defining, and saving any shorthand macro are similar to the ones used to create the macro for transposing characters. More powerful macros may require special procedures to enhance their usefulness, as discussed in the next section of this chapter.

Techniques for Writing Command Macros

Macros are most useful when they can be applied in a wide variety of situations and when they exploit WordStar's command capabilities to the fullest. This section discusses techniques that can add power to your macros: including commands in macros, automating cursor movements, and combining macros.

Including WordStar Commands in Macros

To get the most out of your macros, you should be able to invoke any WordStar function. To do so, you often must include special WordStar commands in shorthand macro definitions. You may wonder, however, how some keystrokes are included in macros. How, for instance, do you include the Enter keystroke? Pressing Enter at the `Definition` prompt indicates the end of the definition. What do you do?

Most of the command keys have Ctrl-key equivalents; use these to include WordStar commands in macros. In the previous discussion of the S macro for ending a letter, for example, the ^M command, the equivalent of the Enter key, was used to insert a blank line in the text. This Ctrl-key equivalent also can be used wherever a

WordStar command requires pressing Enter to terminate a command. Table 9.3 summarizes Ctrl-key equivalents of important WordStar command keys and how these equivalents can be entered in macro definitions.

Table 9.3
Ctrl-Key Equivalents of Commands

Key	*Equivalent*	*Macro Definition*
Enter	^M	^P^M
Esc	^[	^P^[
Ins	^V	^P^V
Del	^G	^P^G
Backspace	^H	^P^H
Home	^QE	^P^QE
PgUp	^R	^P^R
End	^QX	^P^QX
PgDn	^C	^P^C
↑	^E	^P^E
→	^D	^P^D
↓	^X	^P^X
←	^S	^P^S

WordStar does not offer a way to include function keys in macro definitions. However, all the function keys also have Ctrl-key equivalents. For example, the equivalent of F7, which aligns text starting at the current cursor position and then returns the cursor to that position, is ^B^QP.

Options for functions like find or find-and-replace can also be included in macros. Suppose, for example, that you are working on a document in which each subheading begins with a distinctive string of text, such as the word `Section` followed by a number. You want to find each subheading so that you can prepare the document for automatic generation of a table of contents. This macro definition can be used:

^QFSection^MU^M

The first portion of this definition, ^QFSection^M, instructs WordStar to search for the string `Section`. Pressing ^P^M serves as an equivalent of pressing Enter. Because major headings may begin with the word `SECTION` in uppercase, the definition specifies that WordStar is to use the U (ignore case) option in searching for the specified text. The second ^P^M signals the end of your options entry and begins the search.

As command sequences included in a macro become more complex, they often require moving the cursor to another location within a document to complete a useful task. Including cursor movement in a macro may require special techniques to invoke a desired increment of movement, as discussed in the following section.

Automating Cursor Movement

Powerful macros often involve automation of cursor movement. For instance, consider two of the macros discussed earlier in this chapter. The T (transpose words) macro deletes a word, moves the cursor, and undeletes the word. The C (transpose characters) macro gains much of its usefulness by eliminating the need for you to move the cursor in order to correct a common typing mistake.

To make a macro generally applicable to any document, you should think about "landmarks" in the text that can be used in automating cursor movement. These landmarks should be characteristic places in text that can be located by means of a WordStar cursor-movement command or a search operation. In the example of an outline format, the macro for converting it to a table of contents takes advantage of the fact that every subheading begins with `Section` or `SECTION`. Specific strings of text (such as `Section`) are convenient landmarks; so are points that can be located regardless of the text, such as the beginnings and ends of words or lines. For example, the T macro (for transposing words) uses the beginning of the next word as a landmark. Such a landmark is often useful, and you always can use the ^F to move the cursor to it.

Because all the cursor-movement commands can be included in macros (as shown in table 9.3), you can use macros to perform any cursor movement otherwise done manually. The real challenge is in finding ways to automate the process, but this chapter should give you good ideas.

Using Cursor Movement Commands

When you plan automatic cursor movements to be invoked with a shorthand macro, you should try to sequence them to minimize inconsistencies in WordStar commands. The ^A command, for example, is ambiguous. If it is issued when the cursor is within a word (not at the beginning of the word), then the cursor moves to the beginning of that word. But when issued with the cursor at the beginning of the word, the ^A command moves the cursor to the beginning of the preceding word.

The ^F command, on the other hand, does not have such an ambiguity. ^F always moves the cursor to the beginning of the next word.

Sometimes planning requires tracking a task backward from its result to the initial cursor position. If your shorthand macro highlights a block, for instance, your natural impulse is to design the macro so that the cursor moves first to the point that is to be marked as the beginning of the block. That approach, however, isn't always the best one.

Working around WordStar's inconsistencies can make your macros easier to use. Clearly, a macro that has the same effect, regardless of the cursor's position within a word, is more useful than one whose effect depends on the cursor position. You can use the former without preparation; to use the latter, however, you first need to position the cursor.

A Macro that Highlights a Word

The following macro applies the principle of working around the ambiguities of WordStar's cursor movement commands to produce a consistent result. This macro always highlights a whole word with block definition commands so that you can easily delete, move, or copy it, regardless of where the cursor is located in the word when the shorthand command is invoked:

^F^KK^A^KB

The ^F command is used first. This command moves the cursor to the beginning of the next word. Because the cursor is now at the beginning of a word, ^A always moves the cursor to the beginning of the preceding word—that is, to the word the cursor was on when the macro was issued. Therefore, this macro highlights the word at the cursor, even if the cursor does not start out at the beginning of the word.

This macro can be used by itself to define a block for a word or in combination with other commands or macros for powerful applications. As useful as this macro is, you probably will want to enter and save it by following the procedure for defining a macro. A logical key assignment is W (for word).

A Macro that Highlights a Line

For longer expanses of text, other useful landmarks are the beginnings and ends of lines. You can use a macro to send the cursor automatically to these landmarks (using the ^QS and ^QD quick movement commands, respectively). This capability is handy for highlighting lines of text as blocks to be copied, deleted, or moved.

A macro for highlighting a line of text is defined as follows:

^QS^KB^QD^KK^QB

The first command in this macro, ^QS, moves the cursor to the beginning of the line. The next command, ^KB, marks this cursor position as the beginning of a block. Similarly, ^QD and ^KK are used to go to and mark the end of the line. The last command, ^QB, moves the cursor to the beginning of the marked block, which is at the beginning of the line; ^QS would have the same effect here.

The last command in the sequence is optional for the macro to achieve its effect—namely, highlighting the line as a block. However, the ^QB command makes the macro easier to use. If you are highlighting the line so that you can move it (with ^KV), for example, you usually will want to move the cursor to the first column before moving the line. The macro, therefore, positions the cursor so that you need only move it up or down before moving the block.

This macro does not highlight the carriage return at the end of the line. Sometimes, not highlighting the carriage return is advantageous: when you move the line, it blends in easily with other text when auto-align is activated. The disadvantage is that when you move the line, the carriage return is left in its original position, creating an extra blank line in your document.

A macro to highlight an entire line, including the final carriage return, can be created in two ways. One is to insert the command ^D between ^QD and ^KK in the preceding definition. Such a definition is inefficient, however. Notice that it moves the cursor first to the beginning of the current line, then to the end of the line, and finally (with ^D) to the beginning of the next line.

A more efficient definition for highlighting a line plus its final carriage return is the following:

```
^QS^KB^X^KK^E
```

This macro uses two bytes less than the one just mentioned and acts more quickly on text. If you will be copying or moving lines of text, you may want to enter this macro on the Shorthand Menu, assigning it an appropriate key like L (for line). Use the definition procedure to create such a macro.

Using Search Commands in a Macro

Search operations also are useful for moving the cursor to landmarks within the text. A macro using a search command was part of WordStar Release 4, but has been left out of WordStar Release 5. To restore this Previous Paragraph macro to WordStar, create a macro for the P key, defining it with the following commands to move the cursor to the beginning of a paragraph:

5

```
^A^QH^M^F
```

The sequence of commands starts with ^A to bring the cursor to the beginning of a word. The next command, ^QH, invokes a search backward for the next character, ^M, a carriage return. The last command, ^F, advances the cursor to the first character of the paragraph following the carriage return.

The result of this macro is that the cursor moves to the beginning of the current paragraph when the cursor is within the paragraph, or to the beginning of the previous paragraph when the cursor is at the beginning of the current paragraph.

The definition assumes that you do not insert extra blank lines between paragraphs. If you do, you must insert additional ^A commands at the beginning of the definition.

A Macro that Highlights a Paragraph

A macro for highlighting a paragraph has many uses. Because paragraphs are fundamental units of information, often you need to manipulate a paragraph as a unit. For example, when you revise a document, you frequently need to move or delete paragraphs. Other "paragraph-like" blocks of text—blocks that are preceded and followed by hard carriage returns and one or more blank lines—are frequently treated as units.

The macro for highlighting a paragraph as a text block is defined as follows:

^KB^QF^N^K^D^D^KK

The ^KB command marks the beginning of the block. Then the ^QF command begins the search for the end of the paragraph. Entering ^N at the `Find what?` prompt instructs WordStar to find the carriage return that marks the end of the paragraph. The ^K command, which is equivalent to the F10 key, bypasses the `Option(s)?` prompt. Then two ^D commands move the cursor two characters forward to the beginning of the next paragraph, and the ^KK command marks the end of the block. The blank line that follows the paragraph is made part of the marked block so that if you move or delete the paragraph, the blank line is also moved or deleted. (If you do not insert blank lines between paragraphs, use only one ^D command.)

If you decide to include this macro for paragraph highlighting in your working copy of WordStar, you may want to assign it to the H key (for highlight paragraph).

A Macro that Highlights a Sentence

Punctuation marks and other features that appear at key points in the structure of your text are useful landmarks for automating cursor movement. For instance, consider this sequence of commands for highlighting a sentence:

^QH.^D^D^KB^QG.^D^D^KK

The macro's first command, ^QH., searches backward for the period at the end of the sentence preceding the sentence within which the cursor is located. Then the macro uses ^D to move the cursor forward to the beginning of the next sentence. After the beginning of the block is marked with ^KB, the command ^QG is used to find the period at the end of the sentence, and again ^D is used to move the cursor to the beginning of the next sentence. Finally ^KK marks the end of the block.

Note: This definition assumes that you customarily include one space after a period. If you include two spaces, use three ^D commands in the macro where two ^D commands are shown. Note also that this macro works only for "internal" sentences—those other than the first and last ones in the paragraph.

Using Place Markers in a Macro

WordStar's capability to insert place markers in text can serve to automate cursor movement in macros. Place markers are especially useful when a macro must move the cursor to a previous position before the macro was activated.

Extensive editing of a paragraph, for example, can render the text difficult to read. Auto-align always proceeds with reformatting from the cursor position downward. If you are like most people, you revise documents and paragraphs from the top down; moving the cursor backward is extra work.

With a macro, however, you can reformat a paragraph from the very beginning. This macro definition for reformatting a paragraph should be effective:

```
^K1^QH^M^F^B^Q1^K1^KH
```

First the macro uses ^K1 to place a marker at the current cursor position. Then the ^QH command is used to search backward for a hard carriage return, which always immediately precedes the first character of a paragraph. The ^F command then moves the cursor to the beginning of the next word, which is the first word of the paragraph. After issuing the ^B command to reformat the paragraph, the macro uses ^Q1 to return to the original position. Then ^K1 is used again to remove the marker.

The command ^KH is used at the end of the macro because WordStar has an interesting quirk: if a block has been marked and then "hidden" (with ^KH), the marker commands (^K followed by a number from 0 through 9) cause the marked block to appear again. Because that effect can be distracting, the macro uses ^KH to hide the block again. If no block has been defined, the command has no effect.

Even if you haven't entered some of the other macros demonstrated in this section of the chapter, you probably should enter and save this one. This macro is used as a component of some powerful macros presented later in this chapter. A logical choice of a key for this macro is B. You can associate the macro key with ^B, the manual keystroke for reformatting a paragraph. Think of the sequence for executing the macro—Esc and B—as the more powerful version of ^B.

Nesting Macros

By including the equivalent of the Esc key in a macro definition, you can "nest" one macro in another. Nesting enables you to assemble powerful macros by combining other macros. You then save memory by not having to repeat identical sections of macro definitions in several shorthand definitions.

Nesting gives you a way around the limit of 64 keystrokes per shorthand macro. With several macro keys nested within a master macro, one macro can invoke many more than the 64 keystroke maximum for a single macro.

Moving Text and Reformatting a Paragraph

A convenient way to have a marked block and reformat it in its new location, the following macro definition applies the technique of assembling and nesting macros. The macro uses as a component the B macro for aligning text (see the *Using Place Markers in a Macro* section of this chapter). The larger macro uses ^KV to move a marked block of text to the cursor position, reformats the paragraph, and returns the cursor to the beginning of the moved block:

^KV^[B

The sequence ^[B in this macro activates the B macro, exactly as if you had called up the Shorthand Menu with the Esc key and manually selected the B macro.

Without using nested macros, the definition would be the following:

^KV^K1^QH^M^F^B^Q1^K1^KH

The shorter form of the macro saves 11 bytes of memory.

A natural choice of a key for the macro that moves and aligns text is V, which you can associate with the block command ^KV.

Positioning the Cursor and Inserting the Date

You can use the nesting technique in a number of ways to build larger macros from combinations of smaller ones. Suppose, for example, that you want to create a macro to "tab over" to a certain column of your document and insert the date there. The following macro achieves this purpose:

^[9^[@^M^M

The first part of this macro, ^[9, activates the 9 macro, which was defined earlier in this chapter. That macro moves the cursor to the ninth tab position. The second part of the macro, ^[@, issues the shorthand command for inserting the date. The third part, ^M^M, ends the line with a hard return and inserts one blank line after the date.

If this macro seems useful for your WordStar applications, you should define it in your working copy of the program—designating the D key, for date.

Using Macros To Insert Text

Typically, certain blocks of text recur in WordStar users' documents. Such text can be defined as a macro in the same way as a command macro. For proper formatting, text and WordStar commands can be combined in a shorthand macro. Invoking the text macro inserts the defined text at the cursor in a document.

A good example of often-used text is the return address inserted at the top of letters written on non-letterhead paper. You can eliminate drudgery and impart a uniform appearance to such letters with a macro to read your letterhead into your document.

The most efficient way to insert blocks of recurring text into documents is to write the text directly into a macro definition. A macro to insert your name and address, for instance, is defined in a form similar to the following:

```
Name^OC^MStreet Address^OC^MCity, State ZIP^OC
```

Substituting your own name, street address, city, and ZIP code in this format produces centered text, on separate lines, as your letterhead. If such text entry is useful for your applications, you may want to define a macro with your letterhead, assigning it to the A key—for address.

Reading In Boilerplate Files

If often-used text is long, writing it into macro definitions is not practical. Macro definitions that contain lengthy text can quickly consume the shorthand buffer space. You can't include more than 64 characters in a macro unless you use nested macros. For all but the shortest pieces of text, therefore, you should use macros to read in text from separate disk files. Recurring text stored as separate files is often referred to as "boilerplate," from the term used for standard components in legal contracts. Such boilerplate files can easily be inserted in a document with a macro using the ^KR command to read in a file.

Assume that you have created a file that consists of Widgets, Inc.'s address and telephone number as they appear in the billing reminder letter. The letterhead text can be stored in a file called LH (for letterhead). A macro to read this file into the current document is defined as follows:

```
^KRlh^M
```

(Remember that you use ^P^K to enter the ^K command in the definition, and ^P^M to enter the ^M command.) This macro saves you more keystrokes than the letterhead macro for entering your name and address, yet it consumes much less space in the shorthand buffer. However, it also requires that the LH file be present on your disk.

You might assign this macro to a number key. You will probably use this macro less often than macros for editing text, so you can reserve the letter keys, which are more easily remembered, for macros used more frequently. Because number-key macros appear first on the shorthand menu, you can select digits for less-used functions even though they are more difficult to remember.

Combining Boilerplate Macros with Other Macros

A macro like the preceding boilerplate-file inserter can be linked easily with another macro to fill in more of a standard letter like the heading, including the date.

Suppose, for instance, that you have assigned to the D key (for date) the following macro definition:

```
^[9^[@^M^M
```

This macro for entering the date is discussed in the *Nesting Macros* section earlier in this chapter.

The following macro reads into your document the contents of the LH file and then activates the D macro to insert the date at the ninth tab stop:

```
^KRlh^M^QC^[D
```

The definition of this macro assumes that you use the macro when the file is initially created. The command ^QC is used after the command for reading in the boilerplate file, because ^KR causes the specified text file to be read in after the cursor position. In other words, after ^KR is executed, the cursor is on the first character of the text contained in the file. The ^QC command moves the cursor to the end of the file before the date macro is activated. If the macro is used after other text has been typed into the current document, the date is inserted at the very end of the file. That may not be the result you desire.

If you modify the macro, you can use it at any time during the creation of your letter. Here is the modified definition:

```
^QR^M^K1^QR^KRlh^M^Q1^K1^[D
```

The commands and their effects are as follows:

^QR	Moves the cursor to the top of the file
^M	Inserts a blank line (the cursor moves down)
^K1	Inserts a place marker on the second line
^QR	Moves the cursor to the top of the file again
^KRlh^M	Reads in the LH file
^Q1	Moves the cursor to place marker 1
^K1	Removes the place marker
^[D	Inserts the date
^KH	Toggles off block display (to avoid accidental block delete)

The trick to this macro is the use of a place marker. An extra line is created at the top of the file, and marker 1 is placed on the second line. Then the cursor is moved to the top of the file again, and the boilerplate file is read in. Next the cursor is moved to place marker 1. Because the boilerplate text is read in on the line before the one that contains place marker 1, the ^K1 command moves the cursor to the line following the boilerplate text.

The boilerplate file should end with a carriage return. To ensure that a file ends with a carriage return, press Enter at the end of the last line if you create the file in a separate operation. If you create the file by writing a marked block to disk, make sure that the end of the block is at the beginning of the line following the last line of text in the block. Remember that a K is displayed at the right edge of the screen on the line containing the block-end marker.

Removing Carriage Returns

As discussed in Chapter 12, ASCII files are often used to transfer information between computers or between word processing programs. Each line in an ASCII file ends with a hard carriage return. (ASCII stands for American Standard Code for Information Interchange; ASCII files are so called because they use the standard characters of the ASCII character set.)

The hard carriage returns in an ASCII file prevent you from reformatting the text because WordStar treats a hard return as the end of a paragraph. A macro to remove hard returns should be simple:

^QD^G

When invoked, this macro moves the cursor to the end of the line and then deletes the hard return. An alternative definition is the following:

^QG^M^G

Both macros remove a hard return: the first by moving to the end of a line and deleting a character, the second by searching for a hard return and deleting a character.

Note: Both macros require a space after the letter G in order to avoid merging words.

Either of these macros can be further refined by adding commands to reformat the text after the carriage returns are removed. Reformatting is convenient because when the carriage return is deleted from the end of a line, the next line moves up and is "grafted" to the end of the current line.

A macro that reformats the text after deleting the hard return is defined as follows:

^QG^M^G ^B^QP

The added commands, ^B^QP, reformat the paragraph and then return the cursor to its position prior to the realignment with ^B. This last step is needed because after the ^B command is issued, the cursor is positioned on the line that follows the last hard return.

Though the previous macro removes carriage returns and reformats text, it does not turn ASCII files into correctly formatted WordStar document files. The macro reduces all text into a single block, because it does not take into account the ^J line feeds issued at the end of paragraphs. Properly converting ASCII files into WordStar document files with paragraph breaks requires two search-and-replace operations, one of which can be invoked only manually. For more on this procedure, see Chapter 12.

Automating DOS Commands

WordStar has expanded on a capability that was available in early releases: issuing commands to run other programs without exiting WordStar. In early versions of WordStar, external programs could be run only from the Main Menu. Furthermore, the programs could be run only if they were on the logged disk drive. Internal DOS commands, such as COPY and MD (or MKDIR), which are not stored in separate files, could not be run at all from within WordStar. Since Release 4, however, you can issue any DOS command either from the Opening Menu or from within a document and then return to WordStar with the press of any key on the keyboard.

This section presents a macro for writing a block of text from the current document into a file and appending that file to another file. The method used is adaptable for other applications, such as saving notes in a separate disk file while you work on a document.

Suppose that you store on a disk a file called PASTDUES containing a list of the names, companies, and addresses of people to whom you've sent past due "reminder" letters. With all this information contained in the destination address for each letter, the address block is a convenient source for copying the information to your PASTDUES file. The contents of a sample PASTDUES file could be as follows:

Mr. Alphonso D'Abruzzo
Personal Systems, Inc.
1400 Old Orchard Road
Armonk, NY 10509

Ms. Joan Sandra Molinsky
Hilarity Stores Ltd.
33 Rodeo Dr.
Beverly Hills, CA 90055

Mr. Milton Hines
Auto Parts 'R' Us
16780 Dearborn Street
Detroit, MI 48223

The macro for adding information to the PASTDUES file performs the following tasks:

1. Highlights the address block
2. Writes the paragraph to a temporary disk file
3. Appends the new disk file to the existing file

Although WordStar Release 5 includes an option with the ^KW command for appending the contents of one file to another, this macro uses WordStar's DOS "gateway." This shorthand macro invokes a DOS command for combining files so you can see an example of how DOS functions can be used in macros.

Here is the complete macro definition:

^KB^QF^N^N^[^D^D^KK^KWp^My^KH^KFcopy b:pastdues+b:p b:pastdues^M

Note: You should write the definition on a single line.

The first part of the macro,

^KB^QF^N^N^[^D^D^KK

highlights the block of text (in this case to the carriage returns at the end of the address block). The command ^KB marks the block beginning. Then the command ^QF^N^N^[searches for the two consecutive hard returns at the end of the block. The ^D^D commands move the cursor forward two spaces so that the cursor is positioned below the blank lines under the address block. Then the ^KK command marks the end of the block.

The next part of the macro,

^KWp^My^KH

writes the marked block to a temporary file called P. Because you are likely to use this macro (or one like it) frequently, the macro assumes that a file named P already is present in the current directory. Including the letter *y* provides a Yes answer to the prompt

```
That file already exists. Overwrite (Y/N)?
```

The last command in the macro, ^KH, hides the block.

Before using this macro for the first time, create a file named P. Its contents are of no consequence because your macro will overwrite the file. You also should make sure that your disk contains a file called PASTDUES before you use the macro for the first time.

The next part of the macro,

^KFcopy pastdues+b:p pastdues^M

issues a DOS command that appends the file P to the file PASTDUES. The command says, in effect, "Copy the file PASTDUES plus the file P to the file PASTDUES." DOS permits you to join together (or "concatenate") two files' contents by means of the plus sign (+). If you want to experiment with concatenating files, consult your DOS manual first; you can lose a file if you are not careful in using this option. Rest assured, however, that this macro works as stated—provided that you enter it exactly as shown and follow the instructions for use.

To use the macro in the sample letter, place the cursor on the first character of the address block, the `M` in `Mr. Richard Dodgson`. Then all you need to do is press Esc and the key to which you've assigned the macro. WordStar does the rest. Figure 9.9 shows the contents of the PASTDUES file after you use this macro to add Richard Dodgson's name, company, and address.

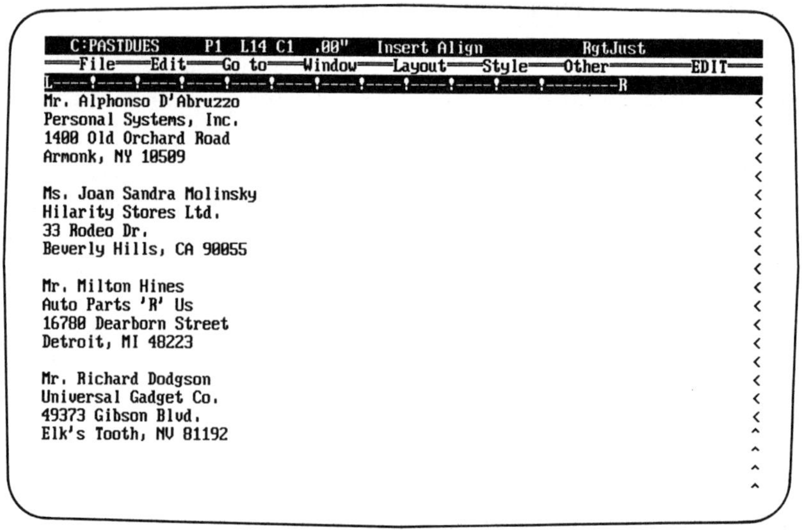
C:PASTDUES P1 L14 C1 .00" Insert Align RgtJust
File Edit Go to Window Layout Style Other EDIT
Mr. Alphonso D'Abruzzo
Personal Systems, Inc.
1400 Old Orchard Road
Armonk, NY 10509
Ms. Joan Sandra Molinsky
Hilarity Stores Ltd.
33 Rodeo Dr.
Beverly Hills, CA 90055
Mr. Milton Hines
Auto Parts 'R' Us
16780 Dearborn Street
Detroit, MI 48223
Mr. Richard Dodgson
Universal Gadget Co.
49373 Gibson Blvd.
Elk's Tooth, NV 81192

Fig. 9.9.
The contents of the PASTDUES file after using a macro to add information.

After you use the macro, you see the following prompt:

`Press any key to return to WordStar.`

Unfortunately, you cannot include that keystroke in the macro. Keystrokes that follow a DOS command in a macro definition are ignored. Tapping the space bar is a small effort, however, compared to the amount of work this macro saves you from performing manually—about 60 keystrokes!

The method used in this macro can be applied to other tasks, like saving notes in an external file without interrupting your work on a document. All you do is type the note as a separate paragraph, position the cursor on the first character of the note, and activate the macro. If you use a macro for this purpose, remember to enter

^KH to show the marked block again, and then enter ^KY to delete the note from the file you are working on.

If you use this macro for such a purpose, note that it does not work on the last paragraph of a file unless the paragraph ends with two hard returns. Similarly, you should enter two hard returns after the address block if you use this macro as you compose the letter (rather than extracting the block after you've written the letter).

Automatic Printing

One of the most vexing of word processing tasks is addressing envelopes. Unless you have a printer that enables you to insert an envelope without removing the fanfold paper, getting the envelope into position can be problem enough. In many offices, typewriters for typing envelopes are still found beside personal computers. The macro presented in this section won't help you load and align envelopes in your printer, but it does help automate the rest of the process.

Part of the problem is positioning the text on the front of the envelope. An address with lines of average length looks good indented 4 inches from the left edge of the envelope—a margin offset of 4.0″ if you are printing 10 characters per inch. As for positioning the address from the top of the envelope, note that a standard envelope is a little more than 24 lines high (6 lines per inch). A 4-line address—name, company, street address, and city and state—begins at 1.66″ from the top. WordStar's dot commands simplify the positioning of the text; the following macro uses three margin commands.

The macro in this section enables you to print an address on an envelope, using the address information that appears in your letter. You don't have to create a separate file for the address. The macro extracts the information and writes it to a file, using a method similar to that described in this chapter's *Automating DOS Commands* section. Before writing the file to disk and issuing the print command, the macro inserts appropriate dot commands to position the text on the envelope.

The dot commands are the following:

```
.PO 4.0″
.OP
.PL 4.0″
.MT 1.66″
```

These dot commands specify a page offset of 40 columns, no page number, a page length of 24 lines, and a top margin of 10 lines.

Because of the length of this macro, you can use the nesting technique. Before creating your main macro, then, you need to create a macro that contains the dot commands:

```
.po 4.0"^M.op^M.pl 4.0"^M.mt 1.66"^M
```

The main macro, shown in the next paragraph, assumes that this definition is assigned to the 7 key. The main macro is defined below:

```
^K1^KB^[7^QF^N^N^K^KK^KWadrs^My^KH^KPnadrs^K^Q1^K1
```

Again, this macro definition should appear on one line of the macro definition screen.

The commands in the macro and their effects are as follows:

^K1^KB	Sets marker 1 and marks the beginning of the block
^[7	Invokes the 7 macro to insert dot commands
^QF^N^N^K	Finds the end of the address block
^KK	Marks the end of the block
^KWadrs^My	Writes the block to a disk file called ADRS and overwrites the existing file of that name
^KH	Hides the marked block
^KPn	Prints a file, answering No to the `Merge print` prompt
adrs^K	Enters the name of the file to be printed and Esc to skip the options menu
^Q1^K1	Goes to marker 1 and clears the marker

Like the macro for adding names to the list of slow-paying customers, this macro assumes that your disk already has a file named ADRS. Before you use this macro for the first time, you should create such a file. Again, its content doesn't matter; the file will be overwritten.

To use this macro, insert an envelope in your printer, aligning the left edge at the point where you normally position the left edge of the paper, and advancing the envelope through the printer until the top edge is even with the top of the print head. After you position the cursor on the first character of the address block of your letter, the `R` in `Richard Dodgson` in this example, invoke the macro.

Some printers have a "paper out" sensor that may misread a short envelope for a lack of paper and must be disabled for printing envelopes. If your printer has this feature, consult your printer manual for details on how to disable the sensor.

Marking Your Place

If you work with long documents and do a lot of revisions, finding your previous stopping point when you reopen a document may be difficult. This section presents macros to mark your place in a document and find that place when you open the document again.

The macro to mark your place is defined as follows:

```
^QH^M^M..PLACE
```

This macro moves to the beginning of the current paragraph, inserts an extra line, and writes on that line the following nonprinting comment:

```
..PLACE
```

Because this comment line does not print, the insertion of an extra line doesn't disrupt the pagination of your document.

The corresponding place-finder macro is defined as follows:

```
^QF..PLACE^K
```

Instead of the relatively prosaic PLACE, you can use any string of text. Just make sure that you don't use the string as a comment anywhere else in the document. Otherwise, you find the wrong place when you invoke the place-finder macro. Of course, you can create a boilerplate file containing the dot command and have the macro read it into your document. As mentioned earlier, using boilerplate files is to your advantage (see this chapter's *Reading In Boilerplate Files* section).

If you want, you can add to the place-finder macro a command to delete the place marker after it has been located:

```
^QF..PLACE^K^Y
```

Bear in mind, however, that macros that delete text—especially without giving you a chance to confirm the deletion—can cause problems. For example, suppose that your document has the following comment line:

```
.. PLACE DISCLAIMER HERE! THE BOSS WILL FIRE US IF WE OMIT IT.
```

You wouldn't want to delete such an important reminder, but that would happen if your macro included a ^Y command. One way to eliminate this danger is to use for your marker a string that never appears elsewhere, such as $@$ or >>>>HERE<<<<.

Some Shorthand Macro Tips

If you've studied or worked through the macros presented in this chapter, you should have a good idea of how you can use macros for a variety of purposes. Here are a few tips you might bear in mind as you use WordStar Release 5's shorthand macro capabilities.

***Tip**: Update macros when you change WordStar's default settings.*

Many WordStar features can be altered with the WSCHANGE program, discussed in Chapter 11. For instance, you might use WSCHANGE to reset your WordStar working copy to require pressing Enter after an entry of Y or N in response to a prompt such as `That file already exists. Overwrite (Y/N)?` If you modify the program in this way, remember to add ^M after the Y or N in macros that answer such questions for you.

***Tip**: Use a common name for temporary files.*

Some macros write temporary files that are of no use to you after the macro has done its job. Examples are the macros for adding names to the PASTDUES file and for printing envelopes. As you become more expert in using macros, you may write other macros that create such files.

You can simplify management of your macro library and avoid cluttering your disk with useless files if you always use the same name for temporary files. The letter T, for temporary, is a logical choice. You aren't likely to assign this name to a working file that you want to keep.

If you adopt this strategy, you can nest the following macro in any other macro that writes a marked block to disk:

^KWt^My

This macro issues the ^KW (block write) command, enters the file name T, and answers Yes to the prompt `That file already exists. Overwrite (Y/N)?`. If you assign this macro to an easily remembered key, such as W (for write), you can nest the macro in any other macro that writes a temporary file to disk.

***Tip**: Use nesting as often as possible.*

Because the shorthand feature's memory space is limited, always consider ways to make a single macro definition do extra duty. For instance, many macros need to find the beginning of a paragraph (like macros to highlight a paragraph, to move to the beginning of a paragraph, and so on). Instead of including the command string ^QH^M in several macros, make a macro of that string and invoke it from any other macro that needs to find the beginning of a paragraph.

Nesting also simplifies modification of your macro library. Suppose, for example, that you have a number of macros that create temporary files. All of them answer Y to the `Overwrite (Y/N)?` prompt. Suppose also that, after writing these macros, you change WordStar so that Enter is required after an answer of Y or N. If you don't use a nested macro to write a block to disk, then you must modify each of the macros that do so, after you change the WordStar default. If all of the macros use the nested macro, however, you need to change only one definition.

***Tip**: Create separate macro files for different tasks.*

WordStar's macro definitions are stored in a file called WSSHORT.OVR, which WordStar reads when you start it. You may find that the 36 keys available for macros are not enough for all the macros you want to use. The solution is to create different versions of WSSHORT.OVR for different tasks. Suppose, for example, that you regularly create budget reports and compile billing information; for each task, you want a different set of macros.

Assume that you already have accumulated a set of macros for your most frequent application, writing reports, and those macros are in the file WSSHORT.OVR. (This file is updated whenever you answer Y to the prompt `Store changes on disk (Y/N)?` on the shorthand definition screen.) To create a second macro file, first move to the directory containing the WordStar program files. Then enter the following command:

copy wsshort.ovr wsshort.rpt

Now you have a copy of your file with the report macros. The extension RPT is your reminder of the file's contents. Because the extension is different, WordStar does not read this file when you start the program.

The next step is to enter WordStar and create the macros for billing; the macros given in the *Automating DOS Commands* section of this chapter will get you started. Answer Y at the prompt `Store changes on disk (Y/N)?` each time you create or change a macro.

After you've created your macros, exit WordStar and return to the directory containing the WordStar program files. Enter the following commands:

ren wsshort.ovr wsshort.bil
ren wsshort.rpt wsshort.ovr

Now the macros you use most frequently are stored in the file WSSHORT.OVR, and WordStar reads that file whenever you start the program.

You also have the set of billing macros in the file WSSHORT.BIL. When you are ready to create a bill, issue the following commands at the DOS prompt:

ren wsshort.ovr wsshort.rpt
ren wsshort.bil wsshort.ovr

The file extensions RPT and BIL are to remind you, of course, what each WSSHORT file is for. The extension RPT stands for report, and BIL stands for billing. By examining your WordStar directory, you can tell which set of macros is in effect at the current time. However, you need to think backward: the existence of the RPT file signifies that the billing macros are read when you start WordStar. If, on the other hand, you see a file called WSSHORT.BIL, then you know that the report macros are in effect when you start WordStar.

You can use the following batch file to make this change automatically:

```
echo off
if exist c:\ws5\wsshort.bil goto bill
```

```
rem Change to report setup
ren c:\ws5\wsshort.ovr wsshort.bil
ren c:\ws5\wsshort.rpt wsshort.ovr
echo Ready for writing reports
goto done
rem Change to billing setup
:bill
ren c:\ws5\wsshort.ovr wsshort.rpt
ren c:\ws5\wsshort.bil wsshort.ovr
echo Ready for writing bills
:done
```

You can create this batch file by using WordStar in nondocument mode. Assign the file any name you like, as long as the file has the extension BAT. The name CHNGMAC (for change macros) is a logical choice. The listing shown here assumes that WordStar files are in the directory C:\WS5. You should change the path names if your system is set up differently.

Each time you enter the command CHNGMAC, the batch file changes from one setup to another: if the report macro file is currently named WSSHORT.OVR, then that file is renamed WSSHORT.RPT and the file WSSHORT.BIL is renamed WSSHORT.OVR. The batch file also sends a message to the screen, telling you what setup has been activated.

Because the batch file works as a toggle, you simply can issue the CHNGMAC command again if you find, for instance, that the report setup, which you wanted to use, was in effect the first time you issued the command. If you enter CHNGMAC and see the message `Ready for writing bills`, you need only enter CHNGMAC again to revert to the report-writing setup.

Bear in mind that you cannot change macro setups by issuing this command from within WordStar because the file WSSHORT.OVR is read only when WordStar is started. If you need to change setups, you should exit WordStar, issue the CHNGMAC command, and start WordStar again.

WordStar Shorthand versus Memory-Resident Macro Programs

As mentioned at the beginning of this chapter, WordStar's macro capabilities are limited in comparison to those of memory-resident programs. This section is included to help you decide whether you want to invest time and money in a separate macro program.

WordStar permits only 36 macros: one for each alphabetical key and one for each of the 10 number keys. Each macro can contain a maximum of 64 characters. But the leading memory-resident macro programs—ProKey, from RoseSoft, Inc., and SuperKey, from Borland International—place a much higher limit on the number of macros you can create, and each macro can contain thousands of keystrokes. The only limits are imposed by such physical constraints as the amount of memory available.

The memory-resident macro programs have many features that are not available with WordStar's macro facility. Both ProKey and SuperKey, for example, support macros that pause for user input. Both programs also allow you to "record" keystrokes as they are entered, whereas WordStar requires you to define your macro as a separate operation. And there's no need to press ^P every time you want to put a Ctrl character into a macro. SuperKey even enables you to create custom menus for macros.

Another disadvantage of WordStar's shorthand feature is that macros are available only when you're running WordStar. With a memory-resident program, on the other hand, you can design a macro to perform some operation in WordStar (or in another program), exit the program, perform one or more DOS commands, and then load and execute another program. For example, such a macro could extract a block of data from a WordStar file, write the data to disk, exit to DOS, copy the file of extracted data to another subdirectory, load 1-2-3, read in the file of extracted data, perform calculations on it, write the calculated data to disk, and finally return to WordStar to read the results of the calculation into the original document. And you enter just two keystrokes to start the whole process!

Still, WordStar's macro capabilities are well worth learning. They are included in the program at no extra cost, whereas most macro programs cost $35 to $100 or so. By not using a separate macro program, you avoid the problems that sometimes plague users of memory-resident programs. DOS was not designed to support memory-resident programs, so using them sometimes leads to problems, particularly when more than one such program is in use. Also, memory-resident programs can consume impractical amounts of RAM. ProKey and SuperKey each use a minimum of about 40K, for example.

WordStar's shorthand macros may well fulfill your word processing requirements. The principles you've learned in creating and using WordStar macros also come in handy if you later decide to purchase ProKey, SuperKey, or some other keyboard macro program. You are likely to find that WordStar's macro capabilities are adequate for your needs, especially after you've mastered the techniques presented in this chapter.

10

Using WordStar's Spelling, Thesaurus, and Other Text-Retrieval Functions

In recent years, professional-level word processing programs have included advanced functions based on personal computers' capacity for storing and retrieving text. These features use the same principle as WordStar's find function, but instead of locating a phrase within a single document, these features search out words in computerized dictionaries for checking spelling, supplying synonyms, creating indexes, and creating tables of contents. Or software can search through disk files to locate text in a number of documents.

These functions are considered advanced because they go beyond the word processing essentials of editing, formatting, and printing. But these functions can be crucial to WordStar beginners and veterans alike. The most carefully composed document can be marred if you fail to catch spelling errors or to replace inexact or redundant words. Indexes and tables of contents make long reports or book-length manuscripts more accessible to the reader; creating these lists is often a tedious task without a computer. And as you amass more and more documents on disk, finding the one concerning a specific topic or containing a desired phrase can be time-consuming—unless you let your computer do the work for you.

The yield in clearer written communications and greater efficiency will more than justify the time you spend learning the WordStar package's text-retrieval functions. With these functions, you can do the following:

- Detect misspellings in a document and correct them
- Find synonyms for a word and replace it with a better choice
- Compile document text to create an index or table of contents
- Improve file handling by quickly locating needed information

Release 5's text-retrieval functions have had many upgrades. MicroPro's spelling checker, used in previous WordStar releases, has been replaced by software from Microlytics, Inc.—the company responsible for WordStar's thesaurus. The speller's vocabulary has been increased from 87,000 words to more than 100,000 words, and the speller now can detect repeated words. The thesaurus no longer requires separate installation. A new dictionary file provides word definitions for both the speller and thesaurus. Indexing has been enhanced; it has been made a note function. With the inclusion of the ProFinder program, locating text within files and file handling are now a breeze.

The spelling checker, thesaurus, index compiler, table of contents generator, and ProFinder all involve separate text-retrieval operations. These features can be applied as needed, but you should take time to discover their capabilities, which is the focus of this chapter.

Using WordStar's Spelling Checker

The idea of a computer that checks for misspelled words and offers corrections used to be the stuff of science fiction. In the last few years, spelling checker software has become commonplace. By pressing a few keys, you can have your computer indicate whether a word in a document is misspelled and, if so, which is the most likely correct spelling.

Any electronic spelling checker is based on software called an *engine* that scans document text and compares that text to a database of correctly spelled words stored on disk or in internal memory. The engine must not only accurately read the characters on-screen but also take into account such variations in words as capitalization, plurals, and conjugation. In WordStar, the spelling checker engine is contained in the WSSPELL.OVR file, which should be located on the same disk and directory as the WordStar program file.

The spelling checker engine considers as misspellings any words in a document that have no match in the database. The checker engine flags these words, searches for approximate matches as alternative correct spellings, and displays these near matches on-screen. You can choose one of the suggested spellings, or you can enter another spelling from the keyboard. When the same mistake recurs in the document, WordStar automatically substitutes the correct spelling.

WordStar Release 5's spelling checker now features a dictionary of more than 100,000 words, compiled by computerized text-retrieval specialists: Microlytics, Inc. The spelling checker incorporates phonetic and linguistic rules that pinpoint suggested corrections with greater accuracy than most such programs. Incidentally, the most frequently misspelled word in contemporary usage is *from*, but none of today's spelling checkers spot *from*'s usual misspelling—*form*—because *form* is valid in any dictionary.

The WordStar spelling checker's principal dictionary is stored on disk in the MAIN.DCT file. Many words the spelling checker considers to be misspelled may, in fact, be correct but are not included in the precompiled dictionary; these words may be proper nouns, technical terms, or vocabulary particular to your word processing applications. Whenever the spelling checker flags such a word, you can tell the engine to add the word to a personal dictionary file (PERSONAL.DCT). Afterward, the word will not be flagged again unless it actually is misspelled.

Even if you have used the spelling checker in earlier versions of WordStar, read the following sections carefully. The spelling checker's screen and options have been revised in Release 5 to make its operation more consistent. If you are familiar with versions prior to Release 4, you will find that WordStar's spelling checker is greatly improved.

Configuring the Spelling Checker for Your System

The WordStar program, spelling checker dictionary, software engine, and messages can fit in less than 360K, provided that you don't intend to use WordStar's help messages (on WSHELP.OVR) or additional word processing features. Otherwise, you will require more disk space than is available on a standard 5 1/4-inch disk. In any case, the file WSSPELL.OVR must be on the same disk and directory as the WS.EXE main WordStar program file. If you have a two floppy drive system with such disks, you must swap your working copy of WordStar with a dictionary disk every time you check spelling in a document. If you have internal memory of 640K, however, with an adjustment available in WSCHANGE (see Chapter 11), you need to swap disks only the first time you run the spelling checker during a work session. You can find this option by pressing D at the WSCHANGE program's Main Installation Menu, followed by C for Other features and A for Spelling Check. At the resulting Spelling Check Menu, press E for Dictionary usage, A for Swap dictionary/program disk, and then Y to turn on this feature. Press C for Personal dict. on work disk and then press Y. Press D for loading memory in RAM and press Y to toggle on this feature. Also set E for the Main spelling dict. buffer to *130* (kilobytes). Make sure that options B and G are off. Other spelling checker disk configurations can be set at this menu, as well as in WINSTALL.

After you have finished at the Spelling Check screen, keep pressing X until you are back at the WSCHANGE Main Installation Menu. Press C for Computer, followed by C for Memory usage. Then press C for Speller, thesaurus, hyphenator memory usage. Ordinarily, these three functions share memory space, but to put the spelling dictionary in memory, you must press B for separate memory allocation. Follow the usual procedure for saving WSCHANGE alterations (see Chapter 11).

With WordStar Release 5, you also can access definitions for words you type when checking spelling. To do so, you will need to have available the definitions file DEFN.DCT (supplied on the Definitions disk in the Release 5 package); with standard 5 1/4-inch floppy disk drives, you must have a separate Definitions disk with a copy of this file on it. In addition, you will have to use the WSCHANGE program (see Chapter 11) to allocate internal memory. From the main WSCHANGE Menu, you must press C for Computer options, C for Memory usage, and C for Speller, thesaurus, hyphenator memory usage. These three functions share memory unless reset. At the Speller, Thesaurus, Hyphenator Memory Usage Menu, you must press D for the definitions capability to be properly installed with separate memory allocations.

To turn on use of definitions during a spelling check, do the following procedure: from the WSCHANGE Main Installation Menu, press D for WordStar, C for Other features, and A for Spelling check. Press E for Dictionary usage and then press G and Y for the proper setting. Save your WSCHANGE alterations according to the procedure in Chapter 11.

If you have a floppy disk system with higher capacity 3 1/2-inch disks or high-capacity 5 1/4-inch disks, you will be able to fit word processing program files and the dictionaries (including definitions) for the spelling checker on a single disk. On a computer with a hard disk, you will have ample room for all these files.

Using the Spelling Checker on a Standard 5 1/4-Inch Floppy Disk System

The files you need for conducting a spelling check total at least 150K. When you add this figure to the requirements for WordStar's main program and other useful files, the total easily surpasses the capacity of a 360K standard 5 1/4-inch disk.

If you have less than than 640K of internal memory in your computer, you will have to maintain the main spelling dictionary file on a separate dictionary disk, which you must swap with your working copy disk every time you need to check spelling.

On a floppy disk system with 640K of memory, you can do away with disk swapping after you invoke the spelling checker during a work session. Properly configured with the WSCHANGE program, the spelling checker will load the main dictionary file into internal memory, leaving just the personal dictionary to be maintained on your WordStar working copy disk. This procedure eliminates time-consuming disk swapping and allows your spelling checker to operate much more quickly because most of the dictionary information is in fast-access RAM. For such a configuration, see this chapter's preceding section, which discusses using the spelling checker on systems that have at least 640K of RAM.

Regardless of the memory capacity, for definitions during a spelling check on a standard two floppy disk system, you also will need a Definitions disk to swap into a disk drive when prompted.

Two Floppy Disk Systems with Less Than 640K of RAM

If your computer system's internal-memory capacity is less than 640K, your separate dictionary disk should contain the dictionary files MAIN.DCT and PERSONAL.DCT. If you have not already done so, use the WINSTALL program's Dictionaries Menu to indicate to WordStar that program and dictionary files are stored on separate disks (see Chapter 2). Another disk can store the DEFN.DCT file if you will be using the definitions feature. Be sure to adjust Speller, thesaurus, hyphenator memory usage, as explained in the section *Configuring the Spelling Checker for Your System*.

Each time the spelling checker is invoked, you see the following message at the top of the document screen:

```
Please replace WordStar program diskette with dictionary
diskette.

Press Esc to continue.
```

After you swap disks and press Esc, the spelling checker proceeds according to the command you used. When this function has been completed, another message is displayed:

```
Please replace dictionary diskette with WordStar program
diskette.

Press Esc to continue.
```

After you exchange disks and reinsert your working copy of WordStar, press Esc to resume editing.

Because disk swapping is not only tedious but also interrupts your work flow as you create or edit a document, you will want to reserve a spelling check for when an entire document is near completion. This procedure does eliminate the flexibility of WordStar Release 5's implementation of the spelling checker. If you will be using your spelling checker often, think about expanding your computer's internal memory to 640K so that you can limit disk swapping to just one cycle per work session.

Two Floppy Disk Systems with at Least 640K of RAM

If your computer system has 640K of internal memory, you can configure WordStar to load the contents of Release 5's precompiled dictionary files into memory—provided that the extra space is not already used up with other memory-resident programs. This setup is similar to the one discussed in the preceding section, with two major exceptions:

- The PERSONAL.DCT file should be on your working copy disk. (The MAIN.DCT file should remain on the dictionary disk. Run WINSTALL or WSCHANGE to indicate that program and dictionary files are stored on separate disks.)
- The WSCHANGE program must be used to specify loading the main dictionary into internal memory (see this chapter's section called *Configuring the Spelling Checker for Your System*).

When a spelling check is invoked for the first time during a work session, you see the screen prompts for swapping disks. After completing this procedure, you will not have to repeat it again as long as you don't turn off your computer's power. The contents of your dictionary disk will reside in internal RAM, quickly checking spelling whenever you invoke this feature.

Using the Spelling Checker on a 3 1/2-Inch Disk System

On a computer system equipped with 3 1/2-inch disks, program and dictionary files can fit easily on one disk. To run the spelling checker, make sure that the files MAIN.DCT and PERSONAL.DCT as well as WSSPELL.OVR all are on your working copy of WordStar. You even can include the definitions file DEFN.DCT or the thesaurus dictionary file THES.DCT on the same disk (see the next part of this chapter for how to use the thesaurus).

Don't forget to run WINSTALL and specify the selection on the Dictionaries Menu to indicate that dictionary files are on the same disk as program files. Choose `B Hard disk` from the Dictionaries Menu. In this way, you avoid prompts asking for disk swaps. If you have less than 640K of internal memory, this setup is the best you can do in configuring the spelling checker. To speed this spelling checker function, you may want to increase your system's RAM.

If your system has 640K of internal memory, WordStar Release 5's main dictionary file can be stored automatically in memory. To do so, don't give up this extra storage to memory-resident programs. To take advantage of the full array of internal memory or to use the definitions dictionary when checking spelling, you must run the WSCHANGE program to invoke loading of the main dictionary into internal memory (see the section *Configuring the Spelling Checker for Your System*).

Using the Spelling Checker on a Hard Disk System

A hard disk system has ample room for program and dictionary files, including definitions (as well as the thesaurus dictionary). As noted in Chapter 2, these files should be in the same directory: \WS5. For the spelling checker to find its dictionary files, you must indicate to WordStar that you are using a hard disk by running the WINSTALL program and selecting the proper option on the Dictionaries Menu. Disk access on a hard disk is quicker than with floppy disks, so spelling checks will be faster. However, neither setup is speedier than loading dictionaries in internal memory on a system with 640K of RAM.

On a 640K system that is not overloaded with memory-resident software, WordStar Release 5's main dictionary file can be stored automatically in memory the first time you use the spelling checker in a work session. To reconfigure WordStar for this method or to use the definitions dictionary when checking spelling, run the WSCHANGE program to set loading of the main dictionary into RAM (see the section *Configuring the Spelling Checker for Your System*).

Correcting Spelling as You Edit

In WordStar Release 5, spelling correction is triggered by any of four control-command sequences that are accessible from the document screen. These different commands give you the choice of checking a word you type, verifying a single word during editing, and correcting all remaining misspellings in a document or in its notes. This last function is new in Release 5. Table 10.1 lists the spelling checker commands covered in the following sections.

Table 10.1
Spelling Checker Commands

Command	*Function*
From the document screen:	
^QL	Checks spelling throughout a document from the cursor
^QN	Checks spelling of a word at the cursor
^QO	Checks spelling of a typed word
^ONL	Checks spelling of text in notes
From the Spelling Check Menu:	
I	Ignores a word throughout a document; continues spelling check

Table 10.1—*Continued*

Command	*Function*
A	Adds a word to the personal dictionary
B	Bypasses a word once only
E	Enters a typed replacement word
G	Toggles global replacement on/off
M	Displays more spelling suggestions

In WordStar Release 5 at help level 4, the Other pull-down menu (displayed when you press Alt-O) lists these spelling commands:

```
Check document spelling...    ^QL
Check word spelling...        ^QN
```

At help level 3, 2, or 1, WordStar Release 5's classic Quick Menu (displayed with a ^Q keystroke) contains these commands for checking spelling from the document screen:

```
L check rest
N check word
O enter word
```

The complete sequences for these commands are ^QL, ^QN, and ^QO.

In addition, the Notes Menu, which you call up with a ^ON command, includes this command listing:

```
L spell check rest
  of notes
```

Each of these commands is examined in detail in this chapter, in the most common order of use when you draft or edit a document.

Checking Spelling of a Word To Be Typed

To experiment with checking spelling, you can type a brief note with misspellings. Enter the text in stages, according to the instructions in the following sections, so you can see different spelling checker functions. When printed, the text of the note appears as shown in figure 10.1.

Note that the last part of this sample text is an annotation, one of the notes that can be entered with WordStar Release 5 (see Chapter 6).

```
                    From the Office of the President

      I apreciate your acomplishments in launching the new WIDGET
product line, superceding our status as a one-product firm. It
would be a serious ommission not to ofer thanks for the most
succesful quater in the companys history. Therefore, I am
recomending our first bonus ever. I couldn't embarass you with
money--any amount would be too minascule. So instead, you will be
be given your choice of refurbished WIDGETS from our service
department--at a special discount!*
                                            Your C.E.O.
--------------------
* This offer velid for employees with ten years' service or more.
```

Fig. 10.1.

A note with misspellings.

When you first compose a document, you may want to invoke the spelling checker to verify the spelling of a word you are about to type. In WordStar Release 5, the command sequence for checking spelling of a word you want to type is ^QO.

When you press ^QO from within a document, a dialog box labeled SPELL CHECK appears and you are prompted to type the word to be checked (see fig. 10.2).

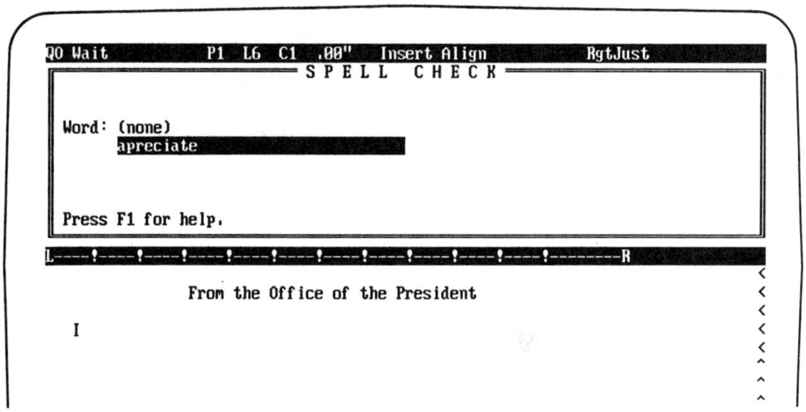
QO Wait P1 L6 C1 .00" Insert Align RgtJust
SPELL CHECK
Word: (none)
apreciate
Press F1 for help.
From the Office of the President
I

Fig. 10.2.

A word typed at the prompt for a spelling check.

After you type a word at the prompt and press Enter, WordStar displays the word in the Spelling Check Menu, along with suggested spellings and a list of options (see fig. 10.3).

If a word is spelled incorrectly, the spelling checker suggests possible spellings—including plurals, conjugated forms of verbs, or homonyms. In WordStar Release 5, consecutively duplicated words are flagged, with a single occurrence as the suggested alternative. If you request a single-word or enter-word check (^QO) and the

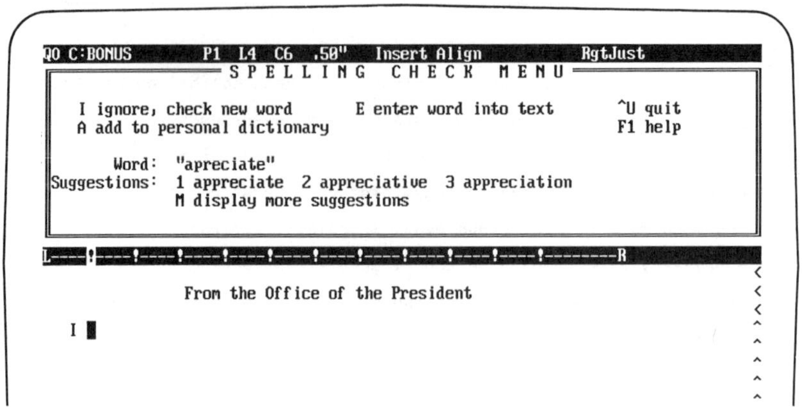
QO C:BONUS P1 L4 C6 .50" Insert Align RgtJust
S P E L L I N G C H E C K M E N U
I ignore, check new word
E enter word into text
^U quit
A add to personal dictionary
F1 help
Word: "apreciate"
Suggestions: 1 appreciate 2 appreciative 3 appreciation
M display more suggestions
L----!----!----!----!----!----!----!----!----!----!----!--------R
From the Office of the President
I

Fig. 10.3. *WordStar's Spelling Check Menu for a word typed at the prompt.*

typed word is spelled correctly, the screen displays the word's definition—if the definition file is on disk and you allocated memory for it with WSCHANGE. At any time, you can press ^U to quit the spelling check.

For an example of a spelling check, you can start entering some sample text from the BONUS memo shown in the preceding section. You open a document file called BONUS and then type and center the first line of the memo: *From the Office of the President*. On the first line of body copy, the second word's spelling is questionable, so that's a perfect place to invoke a check of the word to be typed. Press ^QO. At the prompt, type *apreciate*. To start the checking process, press Enter. After the spelling checker consults its dictionaries, the word you typed is displayed within quotation marks on the Spelling Check Menu (see fig. 10.3).

Because the spelling checker cannot find *apreciate* in its dictionaries, you have several suggested spellings and options from which to choose. Each option, which you invoke by pressing a letter, is explained in the following sections.

Ignoring a Word

When the word you type is correctly spelled but among those words not in the spelling checker's dictionaries, you can issue a command to disregard the word. On the Spelling Check Menu, this option is indicated in the left column:

```
I ignore, check new word
```

By ignoring a word at this point, you are overriding the spelling checker. When you invoke a spelling check with ^QO and press I at the Spelling Check Menu, the prompt requesting a word to be typed and checked returns to the screen.

Adding a Word to Your Personal Dictionary

If the word you type is correct but unknown to the spelling checker, you can add the word to your personal dictionary. After you add the word to the dictionary, the word continues to be considered properly spelled by the spelling checker.

To add a word to your personal dictionary, you can select the second option on the Spelling Check Menu:

```
A add to personal dictionary
```

When you press A for this option, the new word is saved permanently to the PERSONAL.DCT file on disk. The screen continues to display the Spelling Check Menu until you select another option or press ^U to quit the spelling function.

As you begin to use the spelling checker function, you probably will make frequent additions to your personal dictionary in order to include proper nouns, technical terms, and terminology that is specific to your business or areas of personal interest. In effect, you are customizing the spelling checker for your needs.

The PERSONAL.DCT file into which these additions are inserted is the only spelling checker dictionary file that can be altered. It is a simple nondocument file. Although the file's name does not appear in your WordStar directory (files with the extension DCT are omitted), the file can be edited like any other nondocument file.

To save time in increasing your spelling checker's vocabulary, you can open the PERSONAL.DCT file with an N command at the Opening Menu and type all the uncommon words that are part of your everyday writing. The form to observe is simple: each word must begin in column 1 and must be followed by a carriage return.

In WordStar Release 5, personal dictionaries must be sorted in ascending order. When you finish adding words manually, use the ^KZ Sort command to rearrange your list. If you are upgrading from an earlier version of WordStar, you can use personal dictionaries from your working copy after opening them as nondocuments, sorting them in alphabetical order, and saving.

When a personal dictionary file is more than a few pages long, it may slow down a spelling check. If you have sufficient disk space and need to add more words, or if you share your copy of WordStar with other users on the same computer, you may want to create multiple personal dictionaries. By running the WSCHANGE program, you can set WordStar to request the name of a personal dictionary to be accessed for a spelling check. With different file names, you can maintain dictionaries for specialized vocabularies. Individual users can choose the appropriate dictionary as needed.

Accepting a Suggested Spelling

In early releases of WordStar, the spelling checker displayed one suggested spelling at a time and required you to press a key for each suggestion if the first one was not correct. In WordStar Release 5, as many as eight suggestions at a time are shown on a line directly below the word you type. If additional words are available, the following prompt appears below the `Suggestions` line:

```
M display more suggestions
```

When you press M, other words appear on the `Suggestions` line. When you reach the end of the list of additional suggestions (three screens can appear), the prompt changes to the following:

```
M redisplay first suggestions
```

Each suggested spelling has a number beside it. To select a spelling, simply type the number of your choice. The selected word is then entered into your text at the cursor, and the Spelling Check Menu disappears from the screen.

Entering a Correct Spelling

What if the spelling of the word you typed is incorrect but isn't contained in the WordStar Release 5 dictionary? To enter the correct spelling into your document, you choose the E option from the Spelling Check Menu:

```
E enter word into text
```

Pressing E displays a box labeled CORRECTION. Type the correct spelling and press Enter. WordStar Release 5 enters the word into your document. You use this same command to enter an incorrectly spelled word into text, if you want to do so for a stylistic effect.

When you use the spelling checker to insert a word into existing text, your document's formatting may be disrupted. With the auto-align feature on, WordStar Release 5 automatically realigns the text of a paragraph in which a checked word has been inserted.

Having reviewed the Spelling Check Menu options, you now can choose one for the misspelled word *apreciate*: pressing 1 inserts the correctly spelled word *appreciate* into your document.

In addition to verifying the spelling of a word to be typed, the spelling checker offers three ways of checking the spelling of existing text. Before you learn about any of those methods, you can start by typing the main body copy of the BONUS memo shown earlier in this chapter. If you enter the text exactly, complete with spelling errors, you can use the spelling checker to rid this document of all misspellings.

Checking Spelling in a Document a Word at a Time

When in doubt about the spelling of a single word, rather than interrupt your typing, you can verify the word's spelling after the text is on-screen. Among WordStar Release 5's commands for invoking a spelling check is one dedicated to examining a single word in a document. The complete command sequence is ^QN. Note that the cursor can be positioned anywhere in the word for this spelling check. The cursor also can be between words; in that case, WordStar checks the next word on the document screen.

Typing the complete command sequence invokes a function similar to the one for checking a word to be typed—with a few exceptions. Because the word is already on-screen at the cursor, the prompt asking you to type a word does not appear. The Spelling Check Menu appears with the word to be checked in quotation marks. Suggestions are displayed beneath the word. This menu now has a couple of additional options, and two of the previous options are modified slightly.

To see the check-word function at work, you can try checking the BONUS memo you just typed. Using the appropriate cursor-movement command keys, move the cursor anywhere within the word *acomplishments* in the first line of the memo's body. Press ^QN to check the spelling of this word. The Spelling Check Menu displays `"acomplishments"`; the menu also lists five options (not counting `^U quit`) and suggests correct spellings (see fig. 10.4). To enter a suggested spelling in your text, simply press the number beside it.

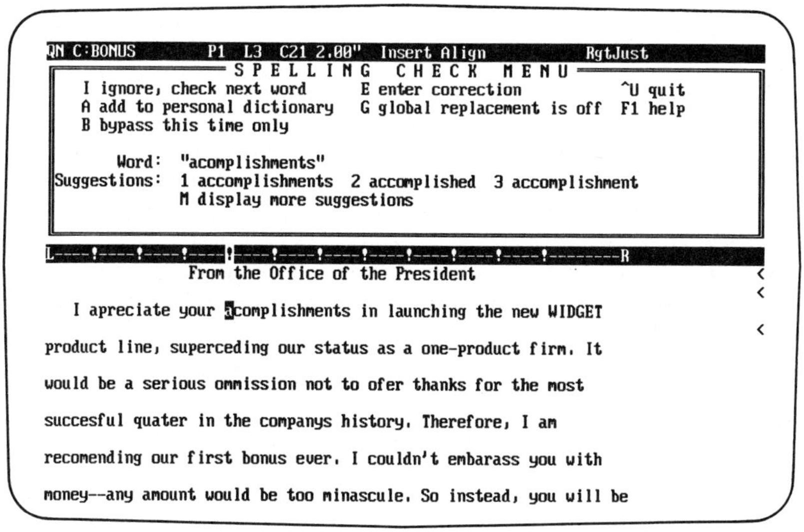
QN C:BONUS P1 L3 C21 2.00" Insert Align RgtJust
S P E L L I N G C H E C K M E N U
I ignore, check next word E enter correction ^U quit
A add to personal dictionary G global replacement is off F1 help
B bypass this time only
Word: "acomplishments"
Suggestions: 1 accomplishments 2 accomplished 3 accomplishment
M display more suggestions
From the Office of the President
I apreciate your acomplishments in launching the new WIDGET
product line, superceding our status as a one-product firm. It
would be a serious ommission not to ofer thanks for the most
succesful quater in the companys history. Therefore, I am
recomending our first bonus ever. I couldn't embarass you with
money--any amount would be too minascule. So instead, you will be

Fig. 10.4. *WordStar's Spelling Check Menu for checking existing text.*

Notice that the listings on the Spelling Check Menu differ slightly from the listings on the menu shown in figure 10.3. The first command in the left column is now the following:

```
I ignore, check next word
```

If you choose to ignore the current word, the next word in the document is checked automatically. The next word appears on the menu even if the spelling is correct.

The top listing in the second column is now this:

```
E enter correction
```

This command permits you to type into your document a spelling of the word that is different from the spelling checker's suggestions. When you press E, the Spelling Check Menu is replaced by a dialog box labeled CORRECTION, which has a prompt that displays the current word. A second prompt, `Replace with`, also appears. After you type the correction you want and press Enter, the new word replaces the word at the cursor.

On occasion, you will want to override the spelling check function for a word but check that word where it reoccurs in a document. The `I ignore` option excludes any further consideration of a word. To neglect a word only once in a document, you must use a different command, listed in the left column of the Spelling Check Menu:

```
B bypass this time only
```

When you press B, the spelling check continues. If the bypassed word occurs later in your document, the word is displayed in the Spelling Check Menu again.

Checking Spelling throughout a Document

Checking the spelling of *every* word in a document and stopping at each, whether correct or not, would be tedious. Instead, you can invoke the spelling checker to stop at only those words that it finds to be misspelled. In WordStar Release 5, you can check spelling from the cursor forward throughout a document as you edit by using the command sequence ^QL. If you want to check spelling for an entire document from start to finish, you need to move the cursor to the beginning of your file before you invoke ^QL.

After you begin a spelling check with ^QL, the Spelling Check Menu appears only for those words the spelling checker does not find in its dictionaries. The options on the menu for these words are the same as the options for the ^QN command, but pressing I for ignore omits the word from consideration for the rest of the document. Also, when ^QL is used, words on dot-command lines are not checked for spelling.

If you consistently misspelled a word throughout a document, you can select a correct spelling and have the spelling checker replace the word throughout the document. This automatic replacement function for spelling correction is similar in principle to a global find-and-replace operation (see Chapter 5). The option letter for ordering replacement spelling throughout a document is G. The command is listed on the Spelling Check Menu as follows:

```
G global replacement is off
```

Pressing G turns on global replacement for the current word being corrected. (WordStar reverts to the default setting of `global replacement is off` for the next word you check.) After you choose a correct spelling, the global replace feature substitutes the correct spelling for the misspelled word every time the word occurs in the document. The actual replacement is performed during the off-screen check. When the cursor scans through the text during correction, the words already are substituted.

On completion of a spelling check throughout a document, WordStar displays the number of words checked and prompts you to press the Escape key to resume WordStar operations.

In the BONUS memo example, check the spelling in the rest of the sample document by pressing ^QL. Note that the spelling checker has no problem recognizing conjugated verbs and plural nouns as correctly spelled; the spelling checker even recognizes the capitalized word *WIDGET*. Each time a word in the memo is displayed on the Spelling Check Menu, you will find that the first suggested spelling is usually the correct one. In fact, in this example, the only word for which the spelling checker will fail completely to provide a correct spelling is *C.E.O.*

After you run the spelling check for the main part of the sample document—choosing proper spellings along the way by pressing the appropriate numbers—the corrected text should look like the text in figure 10.5.

```
                  From the Office of the President
      I appreciate your accomplishments in launching the new
WIDGET product line, superseding our status as a one-product
firm. It would be a serious omission not to offer thanks for the
most successful quarter in the company's history. Therefore, I am
recommending out first bonus ever. I couldn't embarrass you with
money--any amount would be too miniscule. So instead, you will be
given your choice of refurbished WIDGETS from our service
department--at a special discount!
                                          Your C.E.O.
```

Fig. 10.5.
The note's corrected text.

Still to be typed and checked is the annotation at the bottom of the sample document. Notes often containing proper nouns or technical words are excluded from a standard spelling check in WordStar Release 5. To verify the spelling of note text, you use a separate command. Before trying this command, place the cursor after the exclamation point in the memo; using the ^ONA command, select an asterisk as the marker and type the annotation's text as shown previously.

Checking Spelling in Notes

In WordStar Release 5, text in footnotes, endnotes, annotations, and comments is maintained separately from the main text in a document. As a result, a spelling check of a document ignores misspellings contained in notes. To invoke a spelling check of note text, use a command on the Notes Menu (displayed when you press ^ON). The complete command sequence for checking spelling of the notes in a document is ^ONL.

The procedure invoked when you press ^ONL is similar to the procedure for checking text in a document with ^QL. The spelling check is done from the cursor position forward; options and their effects for note text are identical to those for document text.

For the sample memo's annotation, you can catch misspellings by typing ^ONL. In this case, the incorrectly spelled *velid* will show up in the Spelling Check Menu, and you can correct it by designating the correct alternative: *valid*.

Now that you have explored the use of WordStar's spelling checker, you can apply another dictionary-based feature—the electronic thesaurus—to further polish your text.

Finding Synonyms with the Word Finder Thesaurus

An electronic thesaurus is a significant improvement over Roget's and successors' compilations of synonyms on paper. Instead of reaching for a weighty tome for inspiration, you can move the cursor to a desired word on the document screen. With a keystroke, you can immediately fill a portion of the screen with synonyms drawn from a file on disk. Pressing another key will enter into your document a fitting replacement for the word you designated.

Like an electronic spelling checker, a computerized thesaurus is a specialized database program with a software engine that scans a word on-screen and searches for the word in a list on disk. If the word is found in this *key word* dictionary, links are made to synonyms in a larger word list, called the thesaurus' *word base*. Synonyms listed in the word base should be suitable for common usage. Many electronic thesaurus programs, however, include unedited reference works' lists, containing archaic words.

Word Finder, the thesaurus software included with WordStar Release 5, uses a word base meant for contemporary business and colloquial communications. Using special compression techniques, the thesaurus now includes more than 220,000 words in a 100K file called THES.DCT. This file requires less than one-third of the disk space of its counterpart in Release 4; you no longer need to install a less complete dictionary for a floppy disk system. The program's key word dictionary still contains more than 15,000 entries—more than enough to recognize most commonly used words.

The Word Finder thesaurus engine is no longer deployed as a memory-resident program but as an auxiliary program file called WSTHES.OVR, which must be on the same disk and directory as your WordStar program files. The Word Finder program overlay occupies 17K on disk, and you now can access its functions directly from within WordStar by using a simple command sequence starting with ^Q. (The Word Finder program is no longer loaded separately, as in WordStar Release 4.)

The WordStar Release 5 thesaurus can display definitions on-screen for a word you indicate. To implement this function, the definitions file DEFN.DCT (supplied on the Definitions disk in the Release 5 package) must be available to the Word Finder program. If your system uses standard 5 1/4-inch disks, you will need a separate Definitions disk with a copy of this file on it; with a hard disk system, the DEFN.DCT file should be in the same directory as the WordStar program and WSTHES.OVR thesaurus files. In addition, you will need to use WSCHANGE to set the default memory allocation setting for speller, thesaurus, and hyphenator programs in memory: from the main WSCHANGE Menu, press C for Computer options; then press C for memory usage and C for Speller, thesaurus, hyphenator memory usage; finally, press D on the Speller, Thesaurus, Hyphenator Memory Usage Menu.

Configuring Word Finder for Your System

Because of the Word Finder synonym and definition files' disk-storage demands, you must choose from several options when using the thesaurus with a low-capacity floppy disk drive—especially if you want to use the spelling checker as well. A larger capacity floppy disk or a hard disk's ample storage allow a simpler configuration.

After you have properly placed Word Finder's files (supplied with WordStar Release 5 on the disks labeled Spelling Dictionary/Thesaurus and Definitions), the thesaurus program will be ready to put a wide assortment (collection, mixture, selection, spectrum, or variety) of synonyms on your computer screen.

Using Word Finder on a 5 1/4-Inch Floppy Disk System

If your computer uses standard 5 1/4-inch floppy disks, you can fit the Word Finder file WSTHES.OVR and the synonym file THES.DCT on your working copy of WordStar—with no need to swap disks if you are not using WordStar help, the spelling checker, or other add-on functions.

On a floppy disk system with 640K of internal memory, you can use any of the other thesaurus configurations discussed in this section along with WordStar's spelling checker. All you must do is load the spelling checker's main dictionary into memory as explained earlier in this chapter.

Depending on how often you will invoke your electronic thesaurus and whether you are using your spelling checker, you can opt for one of two other setups involving separate dictionary file disks from your main Program disk. For these configurations, you must put both thesaurus and spelling checker dictionaries on one disk (with definitions on a separate disk) or thesaurus dictionary and definitions files on one disk. Both of these setups require that the thesaurus engine WF.OVR be on the same disk as your WordStar program file.

Using Word Finder with a Spelling Dictionary/Thesaurus Disk

One straightforward configuration uses a working copy of the Spelling Dictionary/Thesaurus disk supplied with the WordStar Release 5 package. When you use such a setup, you are prompted to insert this disk rather than the Program disk into drive A when you invoke a thesaurus or spelling check operation. This setup is convenient because only one disk is required for both operations.

If you load the spelling checker dictionary into memory after its first use, this setup becomes even more efficient—requiring disk swapping for only thesaurus operations. You still will need an extra disk for definitions (a copy of the Definitions disk in the Release 5 package), if you choose to invoke the definitions function as well. For users who do not need the spelling checker or who maintain the speller dictionary on another disk (from where the speller file can be loaded into memory), an alternate configuration is available, with thesaurus dictionary and definitions files on one disk.

Using Word Finder with a Dictionary/Definitions Working Disk

Thanks to the greater compression of Word Finder synonyms on disk, you can put both the synonym file WS.DCT (from the Spelling Dictionary/Thesaurus disk) and the definitions file DEFN.DCT (from the Definitions disk) on a single 5 1/4-inch disk. The total disk space of 350K occupied by these files fits into the 360K capacity of standard-formatted disks.

The advantage to using this configuration is that both thesaurus synonyms and definitions are available after a single disk swap.

In either setup, with the synonym file separate from the WordStar Program disk, you will want to keep disk swapping to a minimum by invoking the thesaurus for several words, one after another, before resuming editing—a precaution you don't need on a hard disk system or with higher capacity disks.

Using Word Finder on High-Capacity 3 1/2-Inch or 5 1/4-Inch Disks

With the larger capacity of 3 1/2-inch disks or high-density 5 1/4-inch disks, you can incorporate the files for the electronic thesaurus (WSTHES.OVR, THES.DCT, and DEFN.DCT) on your working copy of WordStar. Depending on what other program functions you include on disk, you also may have enough space for the files necessary for the spelling checker.

Using Word Finder on a Hard Disk System

As noted previously, a hard disk has enough storage capacity to hold the thesaurus files supplied with WordStar Release 5—including definitions and synonyms—as well as all the other files in the WordStar package. Following the instructions in Chapter 2, you should copy your electronic thesaurus files from both the Spelling Dictionary/Thesaurus disk and the Definitions disk into the \WS5 directory with the other WordStar files.

Using the Electronic Thesaurus during Editing

With thesaurus files on disk and the WordStar editing screen displayed, you are ready to use the Word Finder thesaurus to present synonyms and definitions for a word on-screen or one that you type at a prompt. The commands you can apply are covered in the following sections and summarized in table 10.2.

Table 10.2
Thesaurus Commands for Finding Synonyms

Command	*Function*
^QJ	Displays synonym list for word at cursor
PgDn	Displays next synonym screen
PgUp	Displays preceding synonym screen
Cursor-movement keys	Selects synonym
Enter	Substitutes word at cursor for word in document
Esc or ^U	Leaves Word Finder
L	Searches for synonyms of a synonym
P	Returns to previous searched synonym screen
I	Displays synonyms for word typed at prompt
K	Displays definition for word at cursor
N	Displays next definition for word
P	Displays preceding definition for word

Users of WordStar Release 4 will note that in Release 5, the synonyms displayed are identical to those available with the WFBG.SYN file of the earlier program; but the command for accessing the electronic thesaurus is different, and several commands have been added to enhance the thesaurus' versatility.

With the Word Finder electronic thesaurus integrated within WordStar Release 5, you now can evoke synonyms for any word on-screen by using a command similar to the ones for a spelling check. The sequence for invoking the thesaurus also begins with ^Q—for a "quick" function.

At help level 4, the Other pull-down menu (displayed when you press Alt-O) includes the following command on the third line of listings:

```
Thesaurus...  ^QJ
```

At all help levels but 1 and 0, pressing ^Q shows the classic Quick Menu, with the following listing in the column of OTHER functions:

```
J thesaurus
```

The complete command for the thesaurus in this case is ^QJ.

When invoked, the Thesaurus command searches within its dictionary for the word at the cursor. The cursor can be located anywhere within the word or in the space before the word.

Invoking the thesaurus highlights the chosen word and displays the Thesaurus Menu, with the word for which you want synonyms and with commands that apply to the thesaurus function. If you are using a floppy disk system, you will be prompted to swap disks. When the definitions file DEFN.DCT is not available, the screen indicates this and instructs you to press the Escape key to continue. Otherwise, you may see a blank area below the menu until the appropriate synonyms are found on disk. Then the blank area of the screen will fill up with listings of alternative words grouped by part of speech and by nuance, similar to the example in figure 10.6.

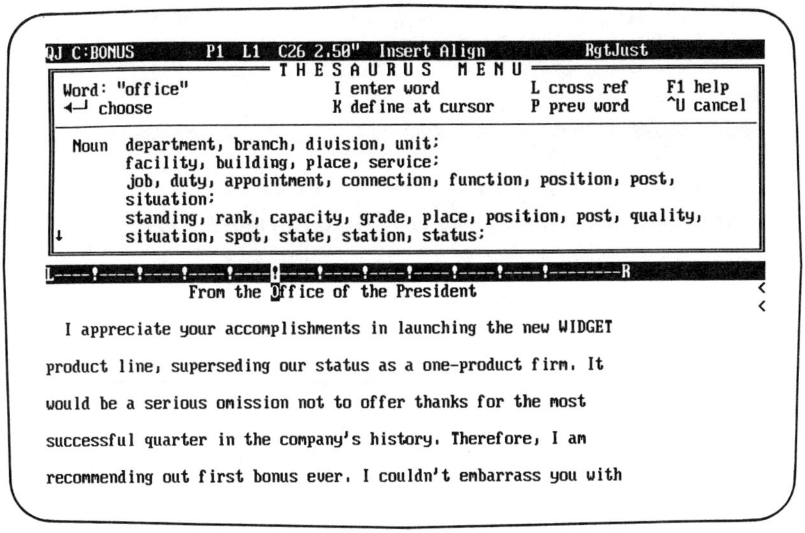
QJ C:BONUS P1 L1 C26 2.50" Insert Align RgtJust
THESAURUS MENU
Word: "office" I enter word L cross ref F1 help
choose K define at cursor P prev word ^U cancel
Noun department, branch, division, unit;
facility, building, place, service;
job, duty, appointment, connection, function, position, post,
situation;
standing, rank, capacity, grade, place, position, post, quality,
situation, spot, state, station, status;
From the Office of the President
I appreciate your accomplishments in launching the new WIDGET
product line, superseding our status as a one-product firm. It
would be a serious omission not to offer thanks for the most
successful quarter in the company's history. Therefore, I am
recommending out first bonus ever. I couldn't embarrass you with

Fig. 10.6.

The Word Finder synonym window for the word office.

If more synonyms are available than can be displayed on a single screen, a semicolon appears after the last word in the synonyms list and a down arrow appears at the bottom left corner of the synonym window. Pressing the PgDn key displays additional synonyms. Pressing PgUp returns the display to the preceding synonym set. If a period is displayed after a word, no more synonyms or definitions are available.

In WordStar Release 5, the Thesaurus Menu initially displays six possible actions in addition to accessing help: choosing a synonym to replace the word in your document, typing a word to be checked for synonyms, defining the word at the cursor, looking up synonyms of a synonym, accessing the preceding synonym checked, and exiting from the thesaurus without replacing a word.

To better understand the possibilities with the thesaurus, you can look up a word in the BONUS memo used previously to demonstrate the spelling checker, as explained in the first part of this chapter. With the BONUS memo on-screen, move the cursor to the word `Office` in the first line of text and press ^QJ. In half of the screen, you will see a window full of synonyms, as illustrated in figure 10.6.

To display another window of synonyms—indicated by the down arrow at the bottom left of the synonym window—press the PgDn key. The second screen of synonyms for the word *Office* is shown in figure 10.7. Pressing PgUp restores the first set of synonyms.

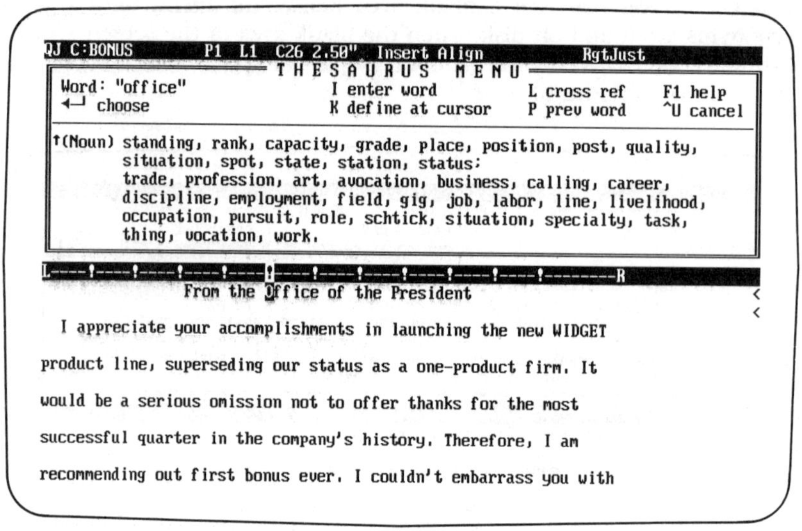
QJ C:BONUS P1 L1 C26 2.50" Insert Align RgtJust
THESAURUS MENU
Word: "office"
choose
I enter word
K define at cursor
L cross ref
P prev word
F1 help
^U cancel
↑(Noun) standing, rank, capacity, grade, place, position, post, quality, situation, spot, state, station, status;
trade, profession, art, avocation, business, calling, career, discipline, employment, field, gig, job, labor, line, livelihood, occupation, pursuit, role, schtick, situation, specialty, task, thing, vocation, work.
From the Office of the President
I appreciate your accomplishments in launching the new WIDGET
product line, superseding our status as a one-product firm. It
would be a serious omission not to offer thanks for the most
successful quarter in the company's history. Therefore, I am
recommending out first bonus ever. I couldn't embarrass you with

Fig. 10.7. *Additional synonyms for the word* office.

With a large assortment of synonyms from which to choose, you can follow any of several courses of action. The options are described in the sections that follow.

Choosing a Displayed Synonym

Often you will want to substitute one of the words shown in the thesaurus window in place of a word in your text. Doing so requires a simple two-step process: highlighting the desired synonym with the cursor and issuing the command to transfer the synonym to your document.

You can use the arrow keys to move the cursor to the synonym you want to select from the window. You also can use the commands in the cursor-control diamond (^S, ^E, ^D, and ^X) to point to the proper word with the cursor.

Without retyping, you can replace the original word in text with the synonym you select. Press the Enter key, as indicated on the Thesaurus Menu. When you do so, the highlighted word in your document disappears, the designated synonym is inserted, and the thesaurus window is removed from the screen. Capitalization and punctuation are maintained for the new word. If WordStar's auto-align feature is turned on, text is reformatted automatically after word replacement.

In the example memo, any replacement for the word *Office* will automatically begin with a capital letter, and text will be realigned to restore correct formatting.

If none of the alternatives displayed in the thesaurus window is suitable, you can cancel the synonym display, leaving your original word intact in the document. The screen lists `^U cancel`, but you also can press the Esc key to exit from the thesaurus. Either command eliminates the Thesaurus Menu and synonym window and returns you to the screen displayed before you invoked Word Finder.

Displaying Synonyms of a Synonym

What if you want to display synonyms for one of the words in the synonym window? The thesaurus' cross-reference function lets you search for synonyms of synonyms without having to return to the document screen. In WordStar Release 5, the command for this feature is listed in the Thesaurus Menu as `L cross ref`.

To use this function, you highlight with the cursor a synonym for which you want to display more synonyms. Then you press L to bring up another synonym window that replaces the current window. With the new window, the designated synonym is listed in the Thesaurus Menu. In the synonym window, you can see alternative words. As before, pressing Enter replaces the word in your document with a synonym, and pressing Esc or ^U cancels the Thesaurus Menu and synonym window.

Another command related to looking up synonyms of synonyms is shown on the WordStar Release 5 Thesaurus Menu: `P prev word`. Pressing P restores the preceding synonym listings. The WordStar thesaurus can keep track of as many as 10 lists of synonyms of synonyms, restoring each one's preceding set of synonyms in turn when the P command is invoked. Thus, you can retrace your "synonym trail" while you search for the exact word you need.

To try the cross-reference feature with the sample document, move the cursor in the thesaurus window to `department` and press L. A set of synonyms appears for *department* (see fig. 10.8). Pressing P brings back the synonyms set for *office*.

Typing a Key Word

While the Thesaurus Menu is on-screen, you can look up synonyms for another word without returning to the document screen. The command in WordStar Release 5 is indicated as `I enter word`.

When you press I, the Thesaurus Menu is replaced by a dialog box labeled SYNONYM LOOKUP, which has a prompt for the word to be typed. When you

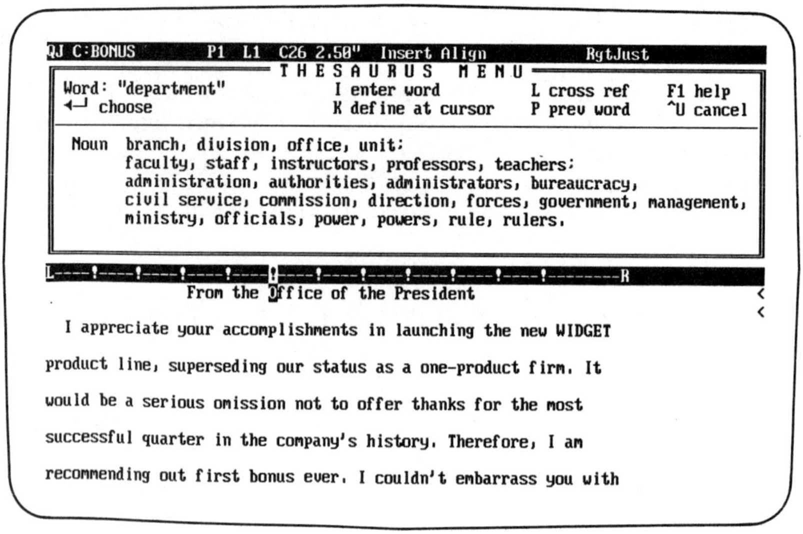
QJ C:BONUS P1 L1 C26 2.50" Insert Align RgtJust
THESAURUS MENU
Word: "department"
↵ choose
I enter word
K define at cursor
L cross ref
P prev word
F1 help
^U cancel
Noun branch, division, office, unit;
faculty, staff, instructors, professors, teachers;
administration, authorities, administrators, bureaucracy,
civil service, commission, direction, forces, government, management,
ministry, officials, power, powers, rule, rulers.
From the Office of the President
I appreciate your accomplishments in launching the new WIDGET
product line, superseding our status as a one-product firm. It
would be a serious omission not to offer thanks for the most
successful quarter in the company's history. Therefore, I am
recommending out first bonus ever. I couldn't embarrass you with

Fig. 10.8.

A Word Finder window showing synonyms for a synonym.

type the desired word and press Enter, the thesaurus window displays the synonyms for the word you typed, and the Thesaurus Menu is restored to the screen. Pressing P displays the synonyms for the word preceding the one you typed.

You can observe this enter-word feature by pressing I while synonyms for the word *office* are displayed. The Synonym Lookup window will appear. Typing the word *staff* and pressing Enter shows the synonyms for this word in the synonym window (see fig. 10.9).

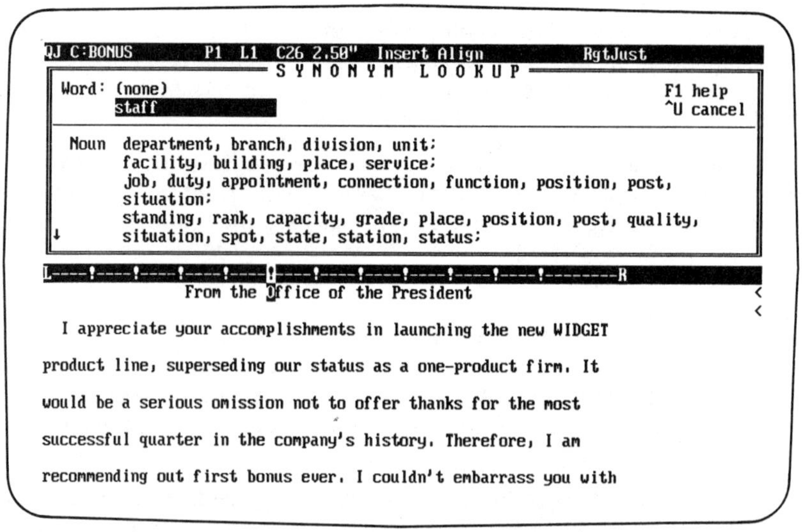
QJ C:BONUS P1 L1 C26 2.50" Insert Align RgtJust
SYNONYM LOOKUP
Word: (none)
staff
F1 help
^U cancel
Noun department, branch, division, unit;
facility, building, place, service;
job, duty, appointment, connection, function, position, post,
situation;
standing, rank, capacity, grade, place, position, post, quality,
situation, spot, state, station, status;
From the Office of the President
I appreciate your accomplishments in launching the new WIDGET
product line, superseding our status as a one-product firm. It
would be a serious omission not to offer thanks for the most
successful quarter in the company's history. Therefore, I am
recommending out first bonus ever. I couldn't embarrass you with

Fig. 10.9.

A new word typed in the thesaurus window.

Finding a Key Word in Alphabetical Listings

On occasion, the thesaurus does not recognize a word for which you request synonyms—either because the word is misspelled or because it is not included in Word Finder's dictionary of key words. When the electronic thesaurus does not find your exact word in its word listings, the Word Finder engine searches for the root word. If Word Finder still cannot find the word, it displays the prompt `Word not found-near alphabet guesses`, along with the words alphabetically closest to the word the program did not recognize.

To find synonyms for a word in this list of alternatives, move the cursor to the word you want. Invoking the L command generates a list of synonyms for the word. Pressing Enter at the cursor inserts the word into your text.

The provision for showing close likenesses for a word allows you to quickly spot-check spellings with the thesaurus (without using the spelling checker). If a word is spelled correctly, a synonym window is displayed and you can press Esc to return to your document. If the word is misspelled, the thesaurus produces the closest correctly spelled words. Moving the cursor to one of these words and pressing Enter replaces the incorrect word in your document with one that is spelled correctly.

Displaying a Definition

5

In Release 5, the WordStar thesaurus can display definitions for a key word or one of its synonyms. The command listed on the second line of the Thesaurus Menu is `K define at cursor`. The cursor usually appears within the synonym window, where you can seek definitions for a synonym. If you prefer to find the definition for the key word originally designated for the synonym search, you can move the highlight (using an upward cursor-movement key) to the key word in the Thesaurus Menu.

Once you have highlighted the word for which you want definitions, pressing K starts the search. On a floppy disk system, you will be prompted to swap disks so the file DEFN.DCT will be accessible; on a hard disk system, the DEFN.DCT file should be in the same directory as the WordStar program and thesaurus overlay files. When a definition is found, it is displayed on the second line of the Thesaurus Menu, directly below the word it defines.

With a definition on-screen, the second line of commands on the Thesaurus Menu is eliminated, and the first line is reduced to four options for definitions. These options include `^U` (or Esc) to cancel the definition and return to synonym mode and `I enter word` to be invoked if you want to type a word to be defined. Often, a word will have more than one definition, so two other options are available: `N next def` and `P prev def`. Pressing N displays the next available definition, and pressing P brings up the preceding definition.

Try an example to see how the definitions function works. While synonyms for the word *office* are shown, as in previous demonstrations in this section, move the highlight cursor to `office` in the Thesaurus Menu and press K to display the one available definition (see fig. 10.10).

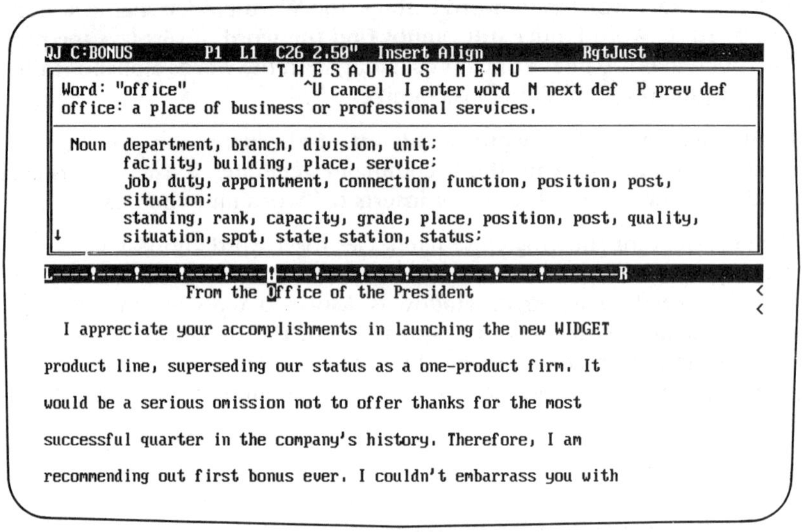
QJ C:BONUS P1 L1 C26 2.50" Insert Align RgtJust
THESAURUS MENU
Word: "office" ^U cancel I enter word N next def P prev def
office: a place of business or professional services.
Noun department, branch, division, unit;
facility, building, place, service;
job, duty, appointment, connection, function, position, post,
situation;
standing, rank, capacity, grade, place, position, post, quality,
situation, spot, state, station, status;
From the Office of the President
I appreciate your accomplishments in launching the new WIDGET
product line, superseding our status as a one-product firm. It
would be a serious omission not to offer thanks for the most
successful quarter in the company's history. Therefore, I am
recommending out first bonus ever. I couldn't embarrass you with

Fig. 10.10.
Displaying a definition for a thesaurus key word.

Since its introduction in WordStar, the electronic thesaurus has become one of the most appreciated auxiliary functions in the package. Even if you do not normally use a thesaurus when writing and editing, the convenience of this feature, especially as it is enhanced in WordStar Release 5, can make the thesaurus indispensable for anyone who learns how to invoke it.

Creating an Index

Indexing can be one of the most cumbersome tasks in producing a long report or manuscript. The process requires painstaking effort in marking, compiling, and sorting listings of key words and phrases in a document. Indexing is the kind of job for which a computer's text-retrieval capacity can come in handy.

WordStar's indexing function is a specialized text-retrieval application in which marked portions of text and associated page numbers are turned into a text database. Their alphabetized listing is the resulting report. The speed with which the indexing function sorts and formats an index renders archaic any other way of indexing.

Early versions of WordStar offered an optional indexing program whose seldom-used formatting options made the process seem daunting. With Release 4, indexing became fully integrated into the WordStar program; the words and phrases to be included in the index were marked in a document, and you compiled these words and phrases with a command invoked from the program's Opening screen.

In WordStar Release 5, indexing has been made even more versatile with the addition of a note function for creating index entries and a convenient way of boldfacing page numbers. The commands available for indexing a document are listed in table 10.3.

Table 10.3
WordStar's Indexing Commands

Command	*Function*
From the document screen:	
^PK	Marks text to be indexed
^ONI	Adds an entry to be indexed
.IX	Adds an entry to be indexed
From the Opening Screen:	
I or OI	Compiles an index

Marking Index Entries in Text

To create an index, you can start within a document by indicating the specific entries to be included in your finished listing. To be sure that your index is complete, you will have to mark each occurrence of the word or phrase intended for inclusion in your listing. In your text, the marker for index entries is a special print-control command sequence.

The indexing command must be used in pairs to delimit text. Therefore, the command is listed in the BEGIN & END column of WordStar's classic Print Controls Menu (displayed when you press ^P from the document screen at all help levels but 1 or 0):

```
K indexing
```

The complete command for marking an index entry in text is ^PK. The ^PK command must be placed before and after the text to be included in your index. On-screen, the command produces markers that appear as ^K at the beginning and end of your designated text. The limit for any single index entry is no more than 50 characters. Excess characters are omitted from the index.

To mark every occurrence of a word or phrase to be indexed in a document, you can use the find-and-replace function, ^QA. When invoking ^QA for indexing, type at the `Find` prompt the text for an index entry. At the `Replace with` prompt, type the same text preceded and followed by ^PK. At the `Option(s)` prompt, enter *ng* to replace throughout your document without confirmation.

For an example of WordStar's indexing function, you can index the combined CEO document created in Chapter 4. After opening the file, mark for indexing the following words and phrases throughout the text:

marketing

New Products Committee

Premium Widget

sales

Super Widget

To mark the words quickly, you can use the find-and-replace command for each word to be indexed. When you finish, the CEO document will be seeded with ^K markers.

Adding Index Entries to Text

In addition to indexing text already in a document, you can use one of two procedures to embed topic headings as well as words and phrases that may not appear as desired for indexing in your text.

One of the indexing commands, new in WordStar Release 5, is listed at help level 4 on the Other pull-down menu:

```
Index entry...   ^ONI
```

At all help levels but 1 and 0, the classic Notes Menu (displayed when ^ON is pressed) also lists this command:

```
I index entry
```

Thus, the complete sequence for adding a note for indexing in text is ^ONI. Invoking this command displays a dialog box with the label INDEX; in this dialog box is a prompt titled `Entry`. At this prompt, you can type the desired index entry. Then press Enter. You will see the first 15 characters of the entry in your document within brackets at the cursor position where ^ONI was invoked. To see the full text of the index notation, position the cursor at the bracketed text and press ^OND.

The alternate command for adding an index entry in a document is a dot command listed on the third screen of WordStar Release 5's dot-command help listings. At any help level but 4, you can get help with dot commands by pressing ^J or F1 and then a period (.). To display the appropriate screen, you press Enter three times. The top of the screen lists this indexing command:

```
.ix text  Use "text" as index entry
```

As with other dot commands, this one must begin at column 1. Any text on the dot-command line will not be reproduced in the document at print time.

When adding an entry with either the ^ONI or .IX command, place your cursor on the line before the paragraph that contains the topic to be indexed. To place a subreference in the index one line below the main entry, follow this form:

Phrase to index, subreference

When printed, the index will be formatted automatically with a subreference indented two spaces below the main reference, along with the page number. Here is an example:

Phrase to index
  subreference, 10

Release 5 has a handy embellishment to index formatting: for the page number to be in boldface when printed, type a plus sign (+) before the text in an entry, as in this example:

+ Phrase to index

As with the ^PK command, the maximum length of an index entry is 50 characters.

Either the ^ONI or .IX command also can be used to insert a cross-reference if you precede the text with a hyphen. The cross-reference will not be accompanied by a page number when the index is compiled. Here is the correct form:

- Phrase to cross-reference, see reference

For an example, you can try using the two formats for the .IX command in the sample CEO document. On the first page of the report, above the memo's address line, type the two entries that follow:

.IX Executive memo, new products

.IX - New products, see Premium Widget, Super Widget

The beginning of your document, which now is ready for index compilation, is shown in figure 10.11. You save the revised CEO file by pressing ^KD.

Compiling an Index

In WordStar Release 5, the function for compiling an index is part of the main program. You invoke indexing from the Opening screen, just like you open a document or print.

At help level 4, the Other pull-down menu includes this command at the top of the listings:

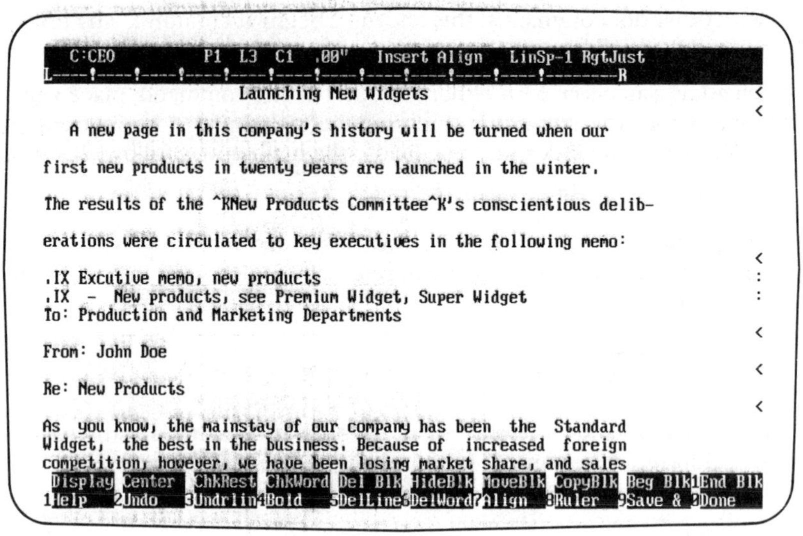
C:CEO P1 L3 C1 .00" Insert Align LinSp-1 RytJust
Launching New Widgets
A new page in this company's history will be turned when our
first new products in twenty years are launched in the winter.
The results of the ^KNew Products Committee^K's conscientious delib-
erations were circulated to key executives in the following memo:
.IX Excutive memo, new products
.IX - New products, see Premium Widget, Super Widget
To: Production and Marketing Departments
From: John Doe
Re: New Products
As you know, the mainstay of our company has been the Standard
Widget, the best in the business. Because of increased foreign
competition, however, we have been losing market share, and sales
Display Center ChkRest ChkWord Del Blk HideBlk MoveBlk CopyBlk Beg Blk End Blk
1Help 2Undo 3Undrlin 4Bold 5DelLine 6DelWord 7Align 8Ruler 9Save & 0Done

Fig. 10.11.

Text marked for indexing.

```
Index...   I
```

Pressing Enter with the highlight on the top line or pressing I invokes the indexing process.

At all help levels but 4, the classic Opening Menu displays the following listing:

```
I index a document
```

When you press I (or OI at help level 4) at the Opening screen, WordStar shows the Index dialog box, which has a prompt for the name of the document to index and three options for compiling the index (see fig. 10.12).

At the Index dialog box, type the name of the document you want indexed. If you press ^K or F10 at this point, the options are ignored and the indexing procedure begins for those words and phrases you marked in the file you specified.

Pressing Enter after typing the name of the document moves the cursor through the three option prompts. Pressing ^K or F10 at any of these prompts lets you bypass further options and begin indexing. The nondocument file created during the indexing process will have the same name as the document you indexed, with the addition of an IDX extension. You can edit or print this index file as you would any other.

The first indexing option prompt is `Index every word` with a default of `N` (unless you change the setting with the WSCHANGE program). If you keep the `N` default, only text marked with the ^PK, ^ONI, and .IX commands in the document will be indexed.

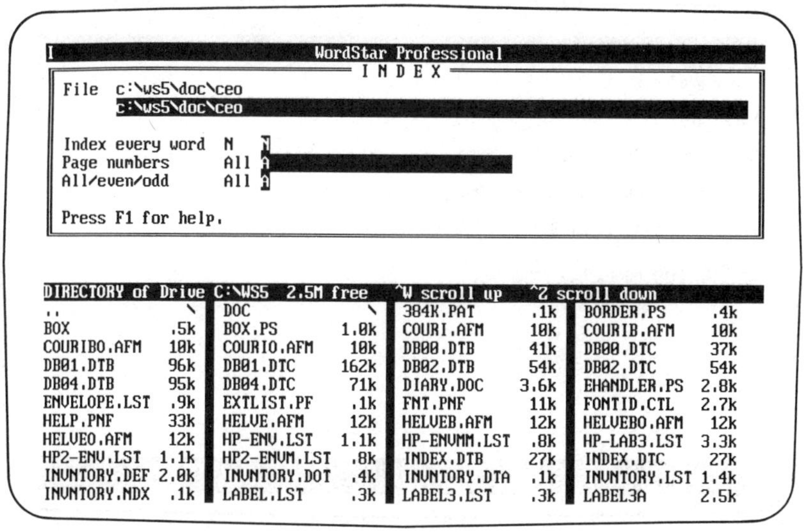
WordStar Professional
I N D E X
File c:\ws5\doc\ceo
c:\ws5\doc\ceo
Index every word N
Page numbers All
All/even/odd All
Press F1 for help.
DIRECTORY of Drive C:\WS5 2.5M free ^W scroll up ^Z scroll down
.. \ DOC \ 384K.PAT .1k BORDER.PS .4k
BOX .5k BOX.PS 1.0k COURI.AFM 10k COURIB.AFM 10k
COURIBO.AFM 10k COURIO.AFM 10k DB00.DTB 41k DB00.DTC 37k
DB01.DTB 96k DB01.DTC 162k DB02.DTB 54k DB02.DTC 54k
DB04.DTB 95k DB04.DTC 71k DIARY.DOC 3.6k EHANDLER.PS 2.8k
ENVELOPE.LST .9k EXTLIST.PF .1k FNT.PNF 11k FONTID.CTL 2.7k
HELP.PNF 33k HELVE.AFM 12k HELVEB.AFM 12k HELVEBO.AFM 12k
HELVEO.AFM 12k HP-ENV.LST 1.1k HP-ENVMM.LST .8k HP-LAB3.LST 3.3k
HP2-ENV.LST 1.1k HP2-ENVM.LST .8k INDEX.DTB 27k INDEX.DTC 27k
INVNTORY.DEF 2.0k INVNTORY.DOT .4k INVNTORY.DTA .1k INVNTORY.LST 1.4k
INVNTORY.NDX .1k LABEL.LST .3k LABEL3.LST .3k LABEL3A 2.5k

Fig. 10.12.
The screen for invoking an indexing operation.

Pressing Y at the `Index every word` prompt will compile every word in the document file minus the words in the WSINDEX.XCL exception file. The exception file, part of WordStar Release 5, lists articles, pronouns, prepositions, and other common parts of speech. The exception file is a nondocument file to which you can add your own words. You also can create a separate exception dictionary specific to your document. You do so by listing in a nondocument file the words you do not want indexed. You name the nondocument file after the document you are indexing by adding to the document file name the extension XCL.

The last two prompts ask for `Page numbers` and `All/even/odd` pages to be indexed. The default settings are for all pages to be included in the index, although you easily can modify this setting by entering the page numbers (as a range with beginning and ending pages separated by a hyphen or with specific page numbers set off by commas) and even (E) or odd (O) indicators at the appropriate prompts. Pressing ^K or F10 starts the indexing operation.

To compile an index for your sample document, press I (or OI at help level 4) at the Opening screen and type *ceo* at the prompt. Pressing F10 accepts the indexing defaults. While the index is being compiled, a screen message will indicate that pressing ^U will end indexing in the middle (without saving anything to disk). The Opening screen soon will reappear. Notice that the disk directory now lists a new file name: CEO.IDX. If you open that file as a nondocument, you will see the index listing shown in figure 10.13.

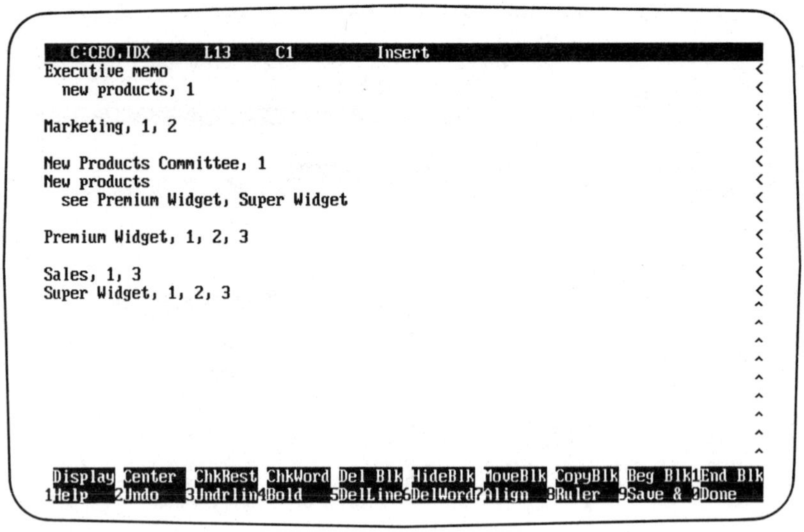
C:CEO.IDX L13 C1 Insert
Executive memo
new products, 1
Marketing, 1, 2
New Products Committee, 1
New products
see Premium Widget, Super Widget
Premium Widget, 1, 2, 3
Sales, 1, 3
Super Widget, 1, 2, 3
Display Center ChkRest ChkWord Del Blk HideBlk MoveBlk CopyBlk Beg Blk End Blk
1Help 2Undo 3Undrlin 4Bold 5DelLine 6DelWord 7Align 8Ruler 9Save & 0Done

Fig. 10.13.

An index compiled by WordStar.

Generating a Table of Contents

Like indexing, creating a table of contents for a long document can be tedious and time-consuming. Although a table of contents is compiled in the order in which topics and their pages appear rather than in alphabetical order like an index, creating a table of contents requires the same kind of painstaking work and attentiveness as an index. And, again, a computer's text-retrieval capability can streamline the process considerably.

Frequently, the same specialized data management software that turns marked text and associated page numbers into an index also can produce a report in table of contents format. The commands involved may be different, but the principles are similar. In fact, in early releases of WordStar, the optional StarIndex program was used to generate table of contents listings as well as indexes.

In WordStar Release 5, table of contents creation is simple. Topics can be marked easily, and you don't have to worry about proper form or presentation options. When the time comes to compile the table of contents, all you have to do is choose the appropriate command on the Opening screen and specify the document for which you want to create a listing. As with indexing, generating a table of contents is a fully integrated part of WordStar that requires no ancillary files for proper functioning. The commands you need for creating a table of contents are listed in table 10.4.

Table 10.4
WordStar's Commands for Creating a Table of Contents

Command	*Function*
From the document screen:	
.TCn	Marks a table of contents entry
From the Opening Screen:	
T or OT	Compiles a table of contents

Entering Table of Contents Notations

Any table of contents for a document is based on compiling title or topic entries you specify within your text. The nine different dot commands that were used in early WordStar table of contents functions have been reduced to a single easy-to-use command.

At help level 4, WordStar Release 5's Other pull-down menu includes the following command near the bottom of its listings:

5

```
Table of contents entry...    .tc
```

When set at any help level except 4, WordStar Release 5's fifth dot-command help screen displays these table of contents listings:

```
.tc text       Use "text" in table of contents

.tc n text     Use "text" in table of contents 1-9
```

The .TC command must appear at column 1 of a line. Text on that line will not be printed with the rest of the document. The *n* after the command is an option you can use to create more than one table of contents at the same time. This option is explained later in this section.

Enter the .TC command on a line before any paragraph whose heading is to be included in the table of contents. The full text to appear in the table of contents entry should follow, along with punctuation, indentation, and any print effects. Here is the proper form:

```
.TC    HEADING......................#
.TC        Subheading.................#
```

When the table of contents is compiled, the number sign (#) on the line with the .TC command is replaced by the actual number of the page where the entry appears. If you need to include an actual number sign in your text, you must precede the sign with a backslash character (\).

As mentioned previously, you can use the *n* option with the .TC command to create more than one table of contents at the same time. To do so, you follow the command with a number from 1 through 9. All similarly numbered entries will be compiled in a like-numbered table of contents file. This feature lets you compile as many as nine different tables of contents at the same time from the same document.

WordStar Release 5 includes a new print-control command designed specifically to facilitate typing of table of contents entries. The command is listed on the classic Print Controls Menu (at help levels 4 through 2 when ^P is pressed):

```
. dot leader
```

When you press ^P. you insert periods into a document from the cursor position up to the next tab stop—avoiding the repetitious entry of periods in table of contents listings.

To create a table of contents for the sample CEO document, open the file and type the following dot-command line at the beginning of the document. You can use ^P. to fill in periods quickly. Note that any spaces inserted after the .TC dot command and an optional space will be turned into indents in the index. The number of trailing dots is adjusted in this example for the page number to appear at column 35 in the index.

```
.TC    LAUNCHING NEW WIDGETS................................#
```

On the same page, directly above the address line, type this table of contents entry:

```
.TC        New Products Memo ...................................#
```

Further down in the document, just before the marketing section of the report, enter this line:

```
.TC        Marketing Report .......................................#
```

On the second page of the document, above the citation to the marketing report, add this line:

```
.TC            Fetzer Citation.........................................#
```

With the cursor on the next page, at the line prior to the sales solicitation line, type this text:

```
.TC        Sales Letter.............................................#
```

Finally, on the same page, just above the pricing section of the letter, enter this information:

```
.TC            Pricing Table .........................................#
```

After entering these table of contents entries, save your document by pressing ^KD.

Compiling a Table of Contents

In WordStar Release 5, unlike early versions of the program, the function for compiling the table of contents is integrated into the word processing program. This feature is invoked directly from the Opening screen.

At help level 4, pressing O for the Other pull-down menu shows the following command listing near the top of the menu:

```
Table of contents...      T
```

At all help levels except 4, the classic Opening Menu includes this notation just below the indexing command in the left column:

```
T table of contents
```

In WordStar Release 5, pressing T (or OT at help level 4) at the Opening screen displays a dialog box labeled TABLE OF CONTENTS, which has a prompt for the name of the document for which to generate a table of contents along with two options (see fig. 10.14).

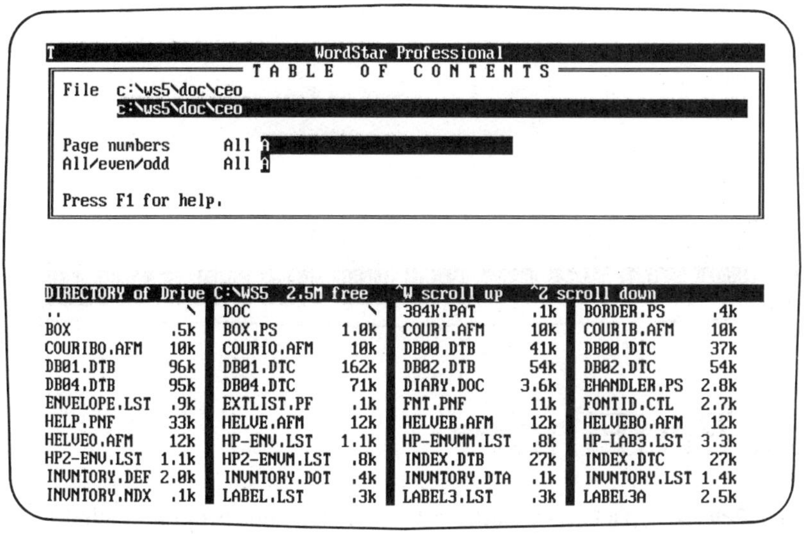
T WordStar Professional
TABLE OF CONTENTS
File c:\ws5\doc\ceo
c:\ws5\doc\ceo
Page numbers All A
All/even/odd All A
Press F1 for help.
DIRECTORY of Drive C:\WS5 2.5M free ^W scroll up ^Z scroll down
.. \ DOC \ 384K.PAT .1k BORDER.PS .4k
BOX .5k BOX.PS 1.0k COURI.AFM 10k COURIB.AFM 10k
COURIBO.AFM 10k COURIO.AFM 10k DB00.DTB 41k DB00.DTC 37k
DB01.DTB 96k DB01.DTC 162k DB02.DTB 54k DB02.DTC 54k
DB04.DTB 95k DB04.DTC 71k DIARY.DOC 3.6k EHANDLER.PS 2.8k
ENVELOPE.LST .9k EXTLIST.PF .1k FNT.PNF 11k FONTID.CTL 2.7k
HELP.PNF 33k HELVE.AFM 12k HELVEB.AFM 12k HELVEBO.AFM 12k
HELVEO.AFM 12k HP-ENV.LST 1.1k HP-ENVMM.LST .8k HP-LAB3.LST 3.3k
HP2-ENV.LST 1.1k HP2-ENVM.LST .8k INDEX.DTB 27k INDEX.DTC 27k
INVNTORY.DEF 2.0k INVNTORY.DOT .4k INVNTORY.DTA .1k INVNTORY.LST 1.4k
INVNTORY.NDX .1k LABEL.LST .3k LABEL3.LST .3k LABEL3A 2.5k

Fig. 10.14.

The screen for invoking table of contents compilation.

At the prompt, type the name of the document for which you want to compile a table of contents. Pressing ^K or F10 here begins the compilation of a table of contents for the entire document you designated. Pressing Enter moves the cursor to the option prompts for selecting page numbers and even or odd page designations for the document. The default for both options is `All`—producing a table of contents covering the entire document, unless otherwise designated.

The table of contents created by WordStar will be contained in a nondocument file that has the same name as your document file but with a TOC extension. If you include numbers after the .TC dot commands in your document, you will obtain different tables of contents with the numbered extensions TO1, TO2, TO3, and so forth.

To compile the table of contents prepared for your sample report, press T (or OT) at the Opening screen, enter *ceo* at the prompt, and press F10. The program displays a message telling you that the table of contents is being compiled and that you can stop the table of contents in the middle of compilation by pressing ^U. Soon the Opening Menu will return to the screen. After pressing N to open the new file CEO.TOC as a nondocument, you see your table of contents (see fig. 10.15).

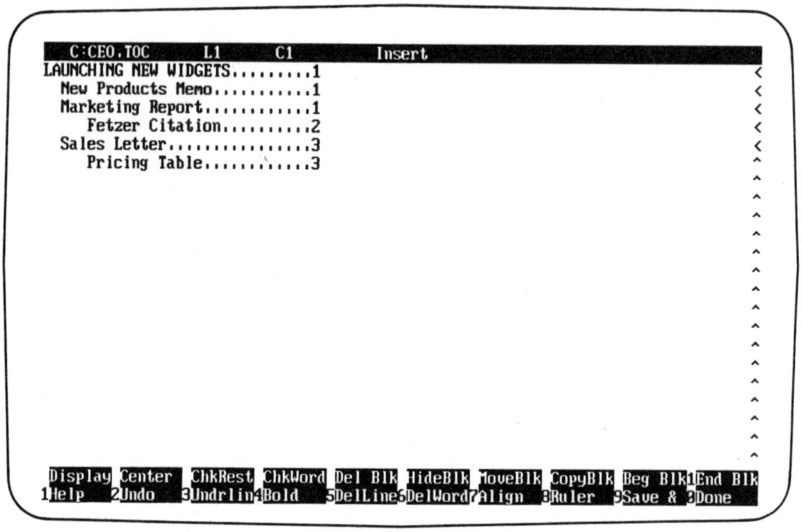
C:CEO.TOC L1 C1 Insert
LAUNCHING NEW WIDGETS.........1
New Products Memo...........1
Marketing Report............1
Fetzer Citation..........2
Sales Letter................3
Pricing Table............3
Display Center ChkRest ChkWord Del Blk HideBlk MoveBlk CopyBlk Beg Blk End Blk
1Help 2Undo 3Undrlin 4Bold 5DelLine 6DelWord 7Align 8Ruler 9Save & 0Done

Fig. 10.15.

A table of contents compiled by WordStar.

Using ProFinder

The WordStar Release 5 package includes a file management program called ProFinder, developed by Jetson Industries, Inc. Meant to supplement the file-handling capability of MS-DOS, ProFinder includes such handy features as locating text in files, viewing the contents of documents on disk, and sorting file names in a directory listing.

Sometimes described as a "DOS shell," in keeping with the type of software that puts a new face on your computer's operating software, the ProFinder program is most useful on computer systems with hard disks containing numerous files. The program also can be used on high-capacity floppy disk drives, although ProFinder's main program file of more than 160K and help messages that occupy another 26K of disk space make the program too onerous for use on standard 5 1/4-inch disks.

In addition, ProFinder should be used only on systems with 640K of memory when it is run as a memory-resident program—if you use "hot keys" to keep the program in the background as WordStar operates. ProFinder's substantial memory requirements also preclude it from being run at the same time as WordStar Release 5's Advanced Page Preview function, TelMerge, or other large memory-resident programs. You can run ProFinder from the DOS prompt displayed within WordStar by using the R or ^KF command. But to avoid memory complications, you should invoke ProFinder from DOS before WordStar or separately from WordStar.

Before starting to use ProFinder, copy the files on the ProFinder disk (included with the WordStar Release 5 package) to the same disk and directory as your working copy of WordStar. The principal ProFinder files are the PF.EXE program and PF.HLP help message files. Also useful on computers that aren't 100 percent IBM compatible is the PFINST.EXE file for modifying monitor and other system settings. (To use this file, type *pfinst* and press Enter; then select the appropriate system options to be modified on the Installation Options Menu.)

Starting ProFinder

To run the ProFinder program, type *pf* at the DOS prompt and press Enter. ProFinder displays a screen of file listings for the current directory (see fig. 10.16).

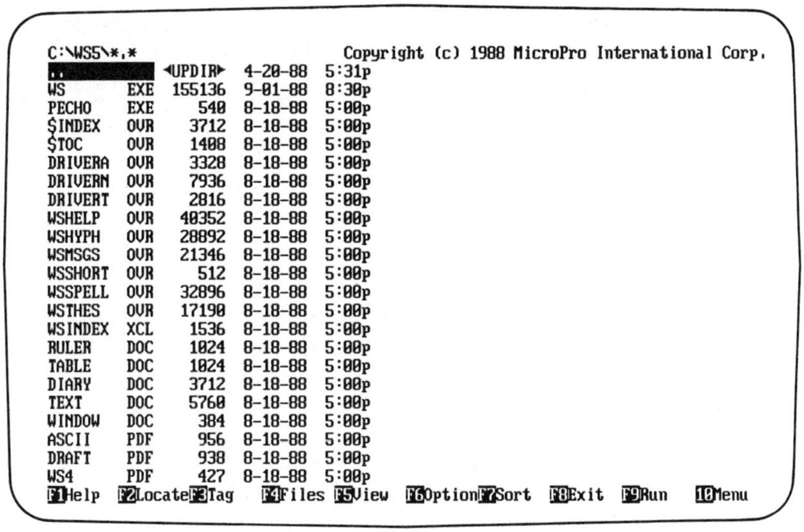

```
C:\WS5\*.*                               Copyright (c) 1988 MicroPro International Corp.
..             ◄UPDIR►   4-20-88  5:31p
WS       EXE   155136   9-01-88  8:30p
PECHO    EXE      540   8-18-88  5:00p
$INDEX   OVR     3712   8-18-88  5:00p
$TOC     OVR     1400   8-18-88  5:00p
DRIVERA  OVR     3328   8-18-88  5:00p
DRIVERN  OVR     7936   8-18-88  5:00p
DRIVERT  OVR     2816   8-18-88  5:00p
WSHELP   OVR    40352   8-18-88  5:00p
WSHYPH   OVR    28892   8-18-88  5:00p
WSMSGS   OVR    21346   8-18-88  5:00p
WSSHORT  OVR      512   8-18-88  5:00p
WSSPELL  OVR    32896   8-18-88  5:00p
WSTHES   OVR    17190   8-18-88  5:00p
WSINDEX  XCL     1536   8-18-88  5:00p
RULER    DOC     1024   8-18-88  5:00p
TABLE    DOC     1024   8-18-88  5:00p
DIARY    DOC     3712   8-18-88  5:00p
TEXT     DOC     5760   8-18-88  5:00p
WINDOW   DOC      384   8-18-88  5:00p
ASCII    PDF      956   8-18-88  5:00p
DRAFT    PDF      930   8-18-88  5:00p
WS4      PDF      427   8-18-88  5:00p
F1Help  F2LocateF3Tag   F4Files F5View  F6OptionF7Sort  F8Exit  F9Run   10Menu
```

Fig. 10.16.

A ProFinder file directory listing.

A ProFinder file list resembles the one you would obtain with a DOS DIR command, with the addition of a top line that indicates the current directory path and a copyright message as well as a bottom line that shows function key tags for the 10 principal ProFinder commands. These commands are summarized in table 10.5.

Table 10.5
Principal ProFinder Commands

Function Key	*Command*	*Function*
F1	Help	Displays window with help message
F2	Locate	Locates files containing specified text
F3	Tag	Tags file at cursor
F4	Files	Displays menu of operations on tagged files
F5	View	Displays contents of highlighted file
F6	Option	Displays menu of ProFinder options
F7	Sort	Sorts file names in directory
F8	Exit	Exits from ProFinder
F9	Run	Runs highlighted program
F10	Menu	Displays customizable menu of programs

You invoke ProFinder commands by pressing the appropriate function key, its equivalent number key at the top of the keyboard (the 0 key corresponds to F10), or the Alt key and the first letter of the command (Alt-L for Locate, for example).

Many ProFinder functions require that you designate file names by moving the highlight in the file list on-screen. The standard WordStar up- and down-arrow keys (or ^E and ^X) move a line at a time; PgUp and PgDn (or ^R and ^C) move a screen at a time; Home or End (or ^QE or ^QX) moves to the top or bottom of the screen; ^Home or ^End (or ^QR or ^QC) moves the highlight to the top or bottom of the directory list; and ^Z or ^W scrolls the screen up or down one line.

Like DOS, ProFinder only lists the files in a directory or subdirectory. But unlike DOS, ProFinder indicates that you are in a subdirectory by displaying the word `UPDIR` in the first line of the file listing. The commands for changing from one directory to another are variations on DOS commands: typing a backslash (\) and the name of another directory and then pressing Enter changes the listing to the one for that directory; typing a colon (:) and the name of the disk drive and pressing Enter switches to that drive; pressing Ctrl-backslash (^\) moves to the root directory; and typing a period and pressing Enter moves to a parent directory from a subdirectory.

The area to the right of a file name can display up to 38 characters in a "title," used to describe a file at greater length than the eight-character name and three-character extension allowed by MS-DOS. To access the title area beside a file name, press the Tab key, the right-arrow key, ^D, or ^F. Once the title area is highlighted, you can type your descriptive message and then press Enter or Esc to save it. Titles are saved in files named TITLES.PF, which ProFinder stores along with the files in each subdirectory. When ProFinder is used to copy, move, or delete files, the files' titles are copied, moved, or deleted, too.

Locating Text in Files

Among the most convenient of ProFinder's features is the one that locates disk files containing text you specify (without you having to open those files individually). You can type text to be located, using up to three separate strings as much as 20 characters long, so multiple searches can be done simultaneously. Here, again, is an application of how efficient computers are at retrieving text. In this case, the entire contents of a directory's files constitute the text database. Text may be found in a file itself or in its ProFinder title, adding to the versatility of this function.

You can invoke the function for locating text in files by pressing the F2 key (or 2 or Alt-F) from the main display. Regardless of how you issue this command, ProFinder opens the small Locate window, which has four options (see fig. 10.17).

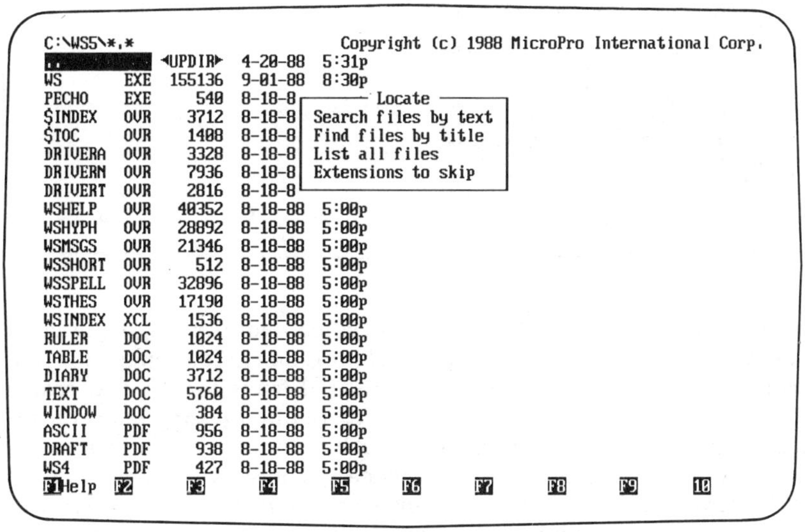
C:\WS5*.*
Copyright (c) 1988 MicroPro International Corp.
.. ◄UPDIR► 4-20-88 5:31p
WS EXE 155136 9-01-88 8:30p
PECHO EXE 540 8-18-8
$INDEX OVR 3712 8-18-8
$TOC OVR 1408 8-18-8
DRIVERA OVR 3328 8-18-8
DRIVERN OVR 7936 8-18-8
DRIVERT OVR 2816 8-18-8
Locate
Search files by text
Find files by title
List all files
Extensions to skip
WSHELP OVR 40352 8-18-88 5:00p
WSHYPH OVR 20892 8-18-88 5:00p
WSMSGS OVR 21346 8-18-88 5:00p
WSSHORT OVR 512 8-18-88 5:00p
WSSPELL OVR 32896 8-18-88 5:00p
WSTHES OVR 17190 8-18-88 5:00p
WSINDEX XCL 1536 8-18-88 5:00p
RULER DOC 1024 8-18-88 5:00p
TABLE DOC 1024 8-18-88 5:00p
DIARY DOC 3712 8-18-88 5:00p
TEXT DOC 5760 8-18-88 5:00p
WINDOW DOC 384 8-18-88 5:00p
ASCII PDF 956 8-18-88 5:00p
DRAFT PDF 938 8-18-88 5:00p
WS4 PDF 427 8-18-88 5:00p
F1Help F2 F3 F4 F5 F6 F7 F8 F9 10

Fig. 10.17.
ProFinder's Locate window, for finding files containing specified text.

To locate text within files, make sure that the first Locate window option (Search files by text) is highlighted and then press Enter. When looking for text in ProFinder file titles, use the down-arrow key to highlight Find files by title; then press Enter.

ProFinder displays two small windows partially obscuring the preceding one. The Locate Text window is partially obscured by the Text To Locate window. This window has room for three strings of text to be typed and searched out in your files or file titles. Fill in the text you want and press Enter after each string of up to 20 characters or press Esc when done with less than three text strings.

After indicating the text to be searched, ProFinder returns you to the Locate Text window. This window, with six different listings, is shown in figure 10.18. The highlight appears at the Begin search option; pressing Enter with the highlight at this choice starts the search operation.

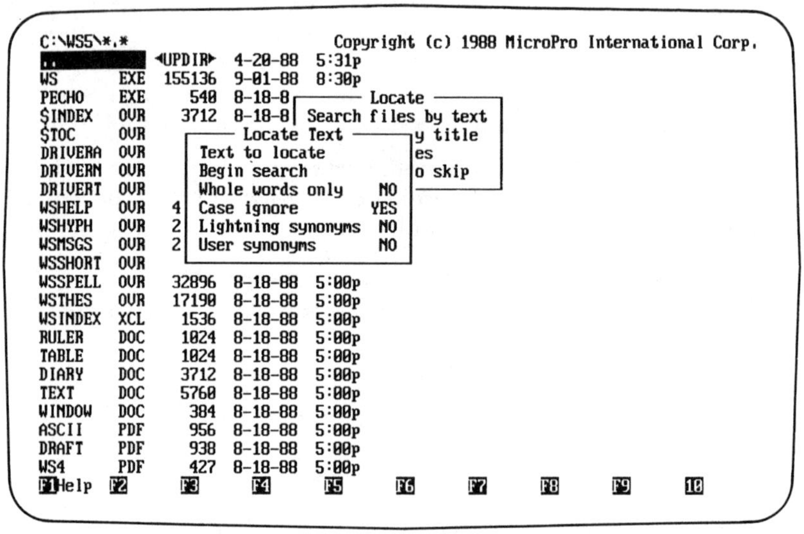

C:\WS5*.* Copyright (c) 1988 MicroPro International Corp.
.. ◄UPDIR► 4-20-88 5:31p
WS EXE 155136 9-01-88 8:30p
PECHO EXE 540 8-18-8
$INDEX OVR 3712 8-18-8
$TOC OVR
DRIVERA OVR
DRIVERN OVR
DRIVERT OVR
WSHELP OVR 4
WSHYPH OVR 2
WSMSGS OVR 2
WSSHORT OVR
WSSPELL OVR 32896 8-18-88 5:00p
WSTHES OVR 17190 8-18-88 5:00p
WSINDEX XCL 1536 8-18-88 5:00p
RULER DOC 1024 8-18-88 5:00p
TABLE DOC 1024 8-18-88 5:00p
DIARY DOC 3712 8-18-88 5:00p
TEXT DOC 5760 8-18-88 5:00p
WINDOW DOC 384 8-18-88 5:00p
ASCII PDF 956 8-18-88 5:00p
DRAFT PDF 938 8-18-88 5:00p
WS4 PDF 427 8-18-88 5:00p
Locate
Search files by text
y title
es
o skip
Locate Text
Text to locate
Begin search
Whole words only NO
Case ignore YES
Lightning synonyms NO
User synonyms NO
F1Help F2 F3 F4 F5 F6 F7 F8 F9 10

Fig. 10.18.
ProFinder's Locate Text window, with options for searching out specified text in a disk directory's stored files.

If you want to review or change the text you specified, move the highlight up to the first line of the window, Text to locate, and press Enter. You can use the four lower options in the Locate Text window to reset defaults for the text search operation: Toggling Whole words only from NO to YES by pressing Enter on the option specifies that words in the string should not be considered as parts of longer words in text; moving the highlight to Case ignore and pressing Enter changes this default to NO, narrowing the search to exact matches of upper- and lowercase text; pressing Enter at the Lightning synonyms option enables the use of synonym files from the Borland International program Turbo Lightning; pressing Enter with the highlight on User synonyms lets you use other synonym files with ProFinder.

Once the `Begin search` option is invoked, ProFinder displays a screen showing the strings of text you specified and a prompt indicating the number of search items. As files are searched, their names and paths are shown at the top of the screen. When files containing the text are located, their names appear in a list on-screen, along with Xs that indicate which of the text strings they contain. After the search is completed, the number of files located, the total disk space the files occupy, and the remaining space on disk are shown at the bottom of the screen.

Any of the located files can be opened and viewed: move the highlight to the appropriate file name on the list and press Enter. The screen will show the contents of the file, open at the first occurrence of the specified text, which is now highlighted. A bar at the top of the screen indicates your relative position within the file. To return to the located files list, press the Escape key.

After seeing the list of files containing specified text, you can redisplay the main ProFinder listing: type an asterisk (*); or press F2 and, at the Locate window, select `List all files` and then press Enter. Incidentally, if you had pressed Enter on the `Extensions to skip` option before you searched, you would have seen a list of 13 file name extensions, including those for program and special-purpose files that can be excluded from a search to speed up the operation. (To exclude the extensions, highlight and press Enter.)

Viewing Files

While at the main ProFinder screen, you can open a file and view its contents without restarting WordStar or having to contend with the format incompatibilities revealed with the TYPE command.

After moving the highlight to a file name on the ProFinder list, you can view the file's contents by pressing F5, 5, or Alt-V and then pressing Enter. A screenful of text will be displayed, along with the file's name and directory path at the top of the screen and the ProFinder function key command line at the bottom of the screen. You can use WordStar's cursor-movement keys to view different sections of the file's text.

ProFinder comes preset for showing files in WordStar format. This setting is usually valid for text in ASCII format, although such files' graphics characters may not be displayed correctly, so you will have to change ProFinder's format setting. WordStar 2000 files also require a different text format. To change formats, press ^QG. This sequence acts as a three-way toggle, from WordStar to ASCII to WordStar 2000 formats and through the same cycle again.

With a file's contents on-screen, you can move quickly to specific text within the file by pressing the WordStar Find command, ^QF, or a ProFinder command, F2. Within the window displayed, type the text to locate—one line up to 20 characters long. Press Enter to display a window of options similar to those available when you're locating a file. Options include finding whole words only, ignoring case, or invoking Turbo Lightning or user synonyms. You can use an additional option to specify the direction of a search; the default is for a global search through an entire file, but you can select a search forward or backward from your current position. Moving the highlight to `Begin search` and pressing Enter sends the cursor to the text you typed.

After finding the desired text, you can search for the next occurrence of text in the file by pressing the equivalent command in WordStar, ^L, or ProFinder's command, F4. If you want to find the preceding occurrence of designated text, press ^QV or F3.

While viewing a file, you can mark off a text block for writing to another file or to print out separately. The commands for marking a block are WordStar's ^KB (for a beginning marker) and ^KK (for an end marker). Or you can use the ProFinder commands F7 and F8 for beginning and end markers. You can use another useful ProFinder command, F10, to mark the current line as a block; repeating this command marks successive lines as part of the same block. To write a block to a file, press ^KW (in WordStar) or F5; then type the name of the new file at the prompt and press Enter. If this is an existing file, press O to overwrite the file, A to add the block to the end of the file, or Escape to exit.

To print a marked block, press ^KP or F6. At the `Left margin` prompt, specify the number of columns for a page offset from the left edge of the paper or press Enter for a default margin of 0.

When viewing a file with ProFinder, you can open another file for viewing (without returning to the main file listing): press ^OK or F9. In a displayed window, you then can type the name of the second file and press Enter to view it. If the cursor in your first document is on a word that occurs in any of the names of files in that directory, that second file is opened automatically. Both file names are shown at the top of the screen when one file is opened from within another. You can open a third file for viewing in this same way. To back out of one file and view the preceding one, press Escape or a period (.).

Tagging Files

ProFinder can enhance your efficiency when a task requires multiple file operations. Clearing a hard disk of obsolete files, copying dozens of files to a floppy disk for archival purposes, or just moving a few documents from one directory to another can be relatively quick and easy procedures. By selectively "tagging" files—marking them for inclusion in a multiple file operation— you can use a single command sequence to manipulate as many files as you want at a time, saving yourself from a lot of repetitious typing of DOS commands.

To tag a file, just move the highlight cursor to the file name you want to designate and press F3 or ^K. Once tagged, the name of the file is indicated in boldface. When a tagged name is highlighted with the cursor, the name's background color or intensity changes to indicate the tag. You can tag as many files as exist in a directory. Do not try to tag a file title—pressing F3 erases a title from the screen.

You can tag an entire group of files by name: press the F4 key. When ProFinder displays the Files window (see fig. 10.19), press F or the cursor-movement keys to move the highlight to the listing `File tag by wild card`. Press Enter.

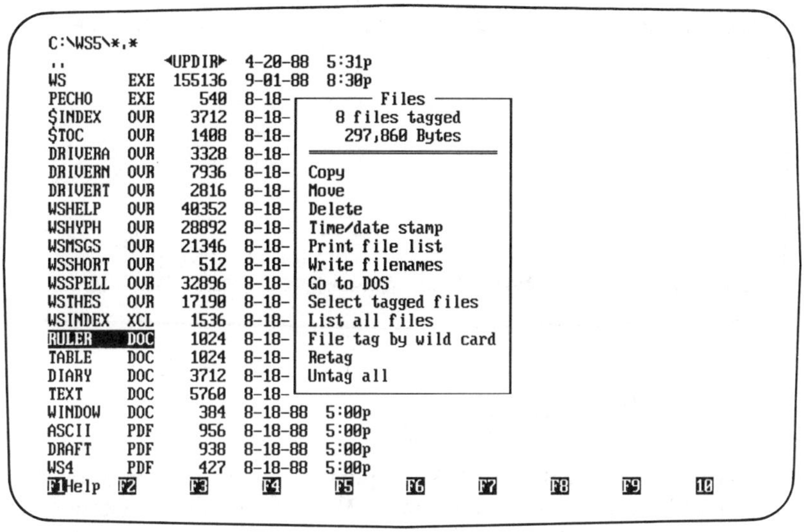
C:\WS5*.*
..   ◄UPDIR► 4-20-88 5:31p
WS EXE 155136 9-01-88 8:30p
PECHO EXE 540 8-18-
$INDEX OVR 3712 8-18-
$TOC OVR 1408 8-18-
DRIVERA OVR 3328 8-18-
DRIVERN OVR 7936 8-18-
DRIVERT OVR 2816 8-18-
WSHELP OVR 40352 8-18-
WSHYPH OVR 28892 8-18-
WSMSGS OVR 21346 8-18-
WSSHORT OVR 512 8-18-
WSSPELL OVR 32896 8-18-
WSTHES OVR 17190 8-18-
WSINDEX XCL 1536 8-18-
RULER DOC 1024 8-18-
TABLE DOC 1024 8-18-
DIARY DOC 3712 8-18-
TEXT DOC 5760 8-18-
WINDOW DOC 384 8-18-88 5:00p
ASCII PDF 956 8-18-88 5:00p
DRAFT PDF 938 8-18-88 5:00p
WS4 PDF 427 8-18-88 5:00p
Files
8 files tagged
297,860 Bytes
Copy
Move
Delete
Time/date stamp
Print file list
Write filenames
Go to DOS
Select tagged files
List all files
File tag by wild card
Retag
Untag all
F1Help F2 F3 F4 F5 F6 F7 F8 F9 10

Fig. 10.19.
ProFinder's window of efficient file operations.

A window just one line high appears at the bottom of the screen with the prompt `Tag the files: *.*`. Here you can type a file name, using DOS wild card characters (see Chapter 2) where appropriate. For instance, you can tag all major program files associated with WordStar by typing *ws**.* and then pressing Enter. The appropriate file names will be tagged.

For a separate display of file names that have been tagged, press F4 to show the Files window. Highlight the `Select tagged files` option and press Enter. The on-screen summary of tagged file names, disk space used, etc., is illustrated in figure 10.20.

You can return to the full listing of files in the directory by typing an asterisk (*). Another way you can display a full directory is to press F4 or F6; then move the highlight in the window that appears to the `List all files` option and press Enter. The ProFinder main file listing returns to the screen. Don't press Esc or you will be dumped to DOS.

To remove the tags from the files you designated, press F4 for the Files window and select `Untag all`. Press Enter and all the boldface file names on-screen revert to standard intensity. The tags are no longer active, but you can restore them to the screen by pressing F4 again; then at the Files window, move the cursor to `Retag` and press Enter. Tagged files' names are in boldface once again.

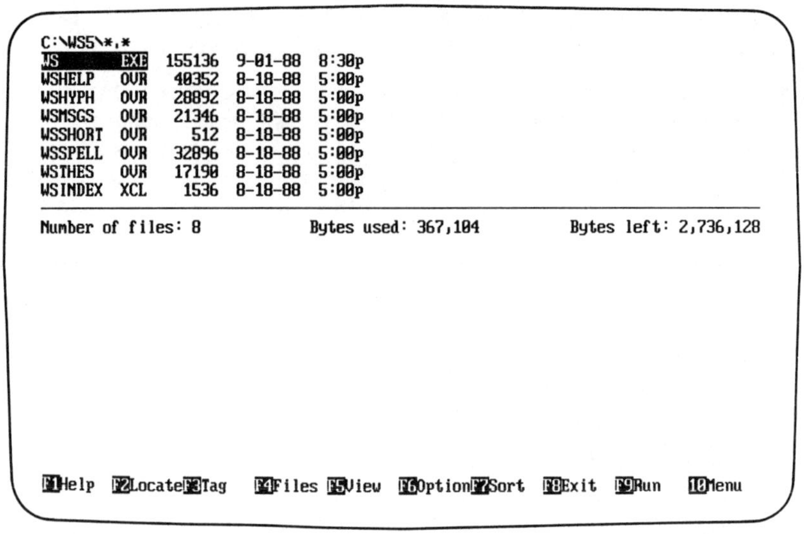
C:\WS5*.*
WS EXE 155136 9-01-88 8:30p
WSHELP OVR 40352 8-18-88 5:00p
WSHYPH OVR 28892 8-18-88 5:00p
WSMSGS OVR 21346 8-18-88 5:00p
WSSHORT OVR 512 8-18-88 5:00p
WSSPELL OVR 32896 8-18-88 5:00p
WSTHES OVR 17190 8-18-88 5:00p
WSINDEX XCL 1536 8-18-88 5:00p
Number of files: 8
Bytes used: 367,104
Bytes left: 2,736,128
F1Help F2Locate F3Tag F4Files F5View F6Option F7Sort F8Exit F9Run 10Menu

Fig. 10.20.
A ProFinder on-screen summary of tagged files' names and other characteristics.

Using File Operations

After tagging files, you can invoke a variety of operations to be performed on these marked files or on files that you specify by name. Most of ProFinder's file functions are listed in the Files window. Such useful operations as copying, moving, and deleting files are as easy to actuate as moving the highlight cursor and pressing Enter.

When you press F4 from ProFinder's main screen, the Files window appears with the top option, `Copy`, highlighted. If you press Enter, all tagged files are copied to another disk or directory. If you haven't tagged any files, a prompt window requests the name of the file(s) to be copied; with wild card characters typed in the appropriate places, you can apply the copying operation to an entire category of files. Pressing Enter produces another prompt window, Copy To, in which room is available for you to type the disk and directory to store copies of the designated files.

Copying files produces copies of files while originals remain on disk. A related ProFinder operation, moving files, makes copies and eliminates the originals. Moving files is similar to copying files: you press F4 for the Files window, move the highlight to `Move`, and press Enter. At the `Move to` prompt, you type the disk and directory to which files are to be moved.

Pressing Enter after specifying the target disk and directory for copy or move functions brings up the Options window (see fig. 10.21). To accept the default settings, valid for most operations, press Enter with the highlight at `Begin`. ProFinder lists file names as they are copied or moved. The main directory listing returns to the screen on completion of the operation.

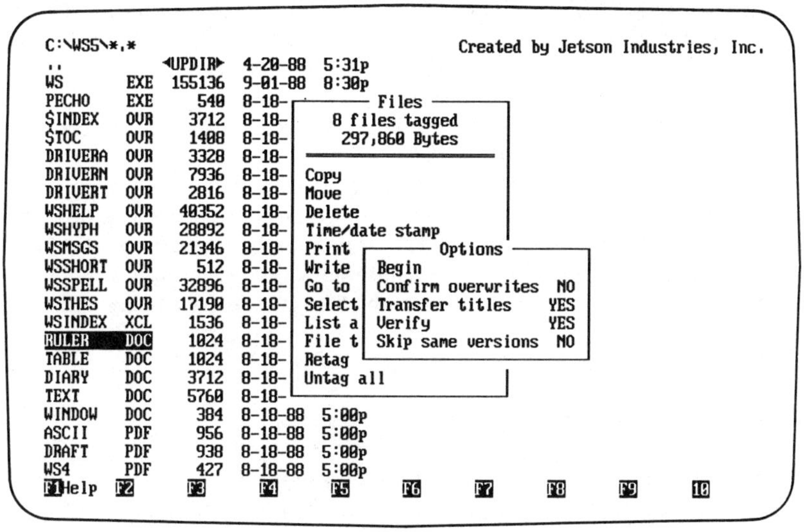
C:\WS5*.*
Created by Jetson Industries, Inc.
.. ◄UPDIR► 4-20-88 5:31p
WS EXE 155136 9-01-88 8:30p
PECHO EXE 540 8-18-
$INDEX OVR 3712 8-18-
$TOC OVR 1408 8-18-
DRIVERA OVR 3328 8-18-
DRIVERN OVR 7936 8-18-
DRIVERT OVR 2816 8-18-
WSHELP OVR 40352 8-18-
WSHYPH OVR 28892 8-18-
WSMSGS OVR 21346 8-18-
WSSHORT OVR 512 8-18-
WSSPELL OVR 32896 8-18-
WSTHES OVR 17190 8-18-
WSINDEX XCL 1536 8-18-
RULER DOC 1024 8-18-
TABLE DOC 1024 8-18-
DIARY DOC 3712 8-18-
TEXT DOC 5760 8-18-
WINDOW DOC 384 8-18-88 5:00p
ASCII PDF 956 8-18-88 5:00p
DRAFT PDF 930 8-18-88 5:00p
WS4 PDF 427 8-18-88 5:00p
Files
8 files tagged
297,860 Bytes
Copy
Move
Delete
Time/date stamp
Print
Write
Go to
Select
List a
File t
Retag
Untag all
Options
Begin
Confirm overwrites NO
Transfer titles YES
Verify YES
Skip same versions NO
F1Help F2 F3 F4 F5 F6 F7 F8 F9 10

Fig. 10.21. *ProFinder's Options window for modifying file copy or move operations.*

The options for file operations presented in the Options window can be reset for special needs when you're copying or moving files. Highlighting `Confirm overwrites` and pressing Enter toggles to `YES` a valuable safeguard: whenever you are about to overwrite a file, ProFinder will display a prompt asking for confirmation before overwriting. By selecting the `Transfer titles` option and pressing Enter, you can toggle to `NO` the usual practice of transferring descriptive titles along with the files to which they apply (you usually will want to keep this function at `YES`). The equivalent of the /v verify option in DOS, ProFinder's `Verify` option automatically checks the integrity of data transfer during copy or move operations. The option at the bottom of the list, `Skip same versions`, has a default setting of `NO`; when toggled to `YES`, this function saves time by not copying or moving files for which a copy exists with identical size, time, and date information.

You can remove files from your disk with another option in the Files window: `Delete`. If you have tagged files, they will be deleted after you press Enter, as indicated by the prompt that appears on-screen. If no files have been specified, another prompt has a space for you to type the file name with wild card characters in the appropriate places.

You can access one more useful file operation from the Files window. Highlighting the `Time/date stamp` option and pressing Enter provides a simple way for you to reset the DOS date and time information stored when files are saved—a handy operation for correcting such information or adding it when it is missing. At the prompt, you can correct the current date and, by pressing Enter, the time as well. Just type the correct date or time abbreviation for the setting you desire. Pressing Enter again displays the new date and time with the designated files.

From the main ProFinder display, pressing another function key, F7, invokes a sort of file names in the directory list. The window that appears has three options.

Pressing Enter with the highlight at the default, `Begin sort`, puts a sort into operation with the current default settings in ascending alphabetical order of file extensions, followed by file names. To change the sorting order for file names, move the highlight to `Order of sort` and press Enter. Another prompt offers sort choices by name, extension, date/time, and size. You can highlight any combination of these choices in the order in which they will be invoked. Press Enter to designate a sort order. Then indicate ascending or descending order and press Enter again to select more sort keys. Sorts will progress in the order you designate once you select the Resume key, press Enter, and press Enter again at the `Begin sort` prompt. To have file names sorted automatically whenever you change directories on-screen, highlight `Auto sort` in the Sort window and press Enter.

Invoking Other Programs

Running other programs from ProFinder provides a unified way for you to invoke software applications, always returning to the main file display as a reference point. Several ways are available for you to run a program, with enough styles of invocation to suit any user.

For DOS traditionalists, pressing F4 for the Files screen, highlighting `Go to DOS`, and pressing Enter yields a DOS prompt on-screen within a window. Type any DOS command, including a program name, and press Enter; the command will be executed in DOS. When the DOS prompt returns, type *exit* and press Enter to display the ProFinder main screen.

Do you prefer the simpler point-and-shoot invocation of a program? At the main ProFinder display, you can highlight the name of a program file to run on the list of files and press F9. ProFinder exits to DOS and starts the program file. Only programs with the file extensions COM, EXE, or BAT can be run (this is modified by including valid extensions in a file called EXTLIST.PF). You can tag a text file along with a program file; for example, pressing F9 for WordStar's WS.EXE program file and a document file opens the designated document when started. If you use this function, when you run a program, you leave ProFinder. To enter ProFinder again, you must type *pf* and press Enter at the DOS prompt.

If you want your own customizable menu of programs to run, press F10 from the main ProFinder screen. The Sample Menu window provides a typical configuration on which you can select from options to show documents, run Inset or remove Inset from memory, run PC-Outline in its normal or small version, or run 1-2-3. The contents of this menu are stored in the file USERMENU.PF. Edit this file as a nondocument, and you can substitute the names of the programs you use most often. Notice that WordStar is not included in the Sample Menu; ProFinder includes a special single-stroke "hot key" for running WordStar.

Using Hot Keys

The ProFinder program features two handy keys for invoking complex functions at a single stroke. These hot keys are the *flip key* for moving back and forth between ProFinder and WordStar and the *copy key* for copying a text block marked with ProFinder in a document to another disk file. Using the hot keys provides an elegant way for you to work within WordStar, exit occasionally to ProFinder to locate text in files, bring into a WordStar document a block marked with ProFinder in another file, and resume editing in WordStar. With access to other files' contents, ProFinder provides the equivalent of a third window to WordStar Release 5.

In an unmodified copy of ProFinder, the flip hot key is assigned to the plus (+) key on the numeric keypad. After you move the highlight on the main ProFinder screen to a document file name, pressing the plus key starts WordStar and opens that document.

Once WordStar has been started from within ProFinder, pressing the plus key again during editing exits to ProFinder and then flips again to where you were in WordStar. You cannot exit from ProFinder unless you exit from WordStar first.

If you have marked a block of text while viewing a file with ProFinder, you can flip to WordStar Release 5 by using the plus (+) key. Move the cursor to the area you want the text to be copied to and then press the copy hot key—the minus (−) key on the numeric keypad. To enter multiple copies of the marked block, press the minus key several times. If no block has been marked with ProFinder, the plus key copies a highlighted file name on the main file display.

For users who need the numeric keypad for numerical entry, the plus and minus hot key assignments can be changed. From the main ProFinder display, press F6 to display the Options window, move the highlight to the `Configure` option, and press Enter. The Configuration window appears (see fig. 10.22).

If you move the cursor to `Hot key settings` and press Enter, you will see a Hot Key Settings window with four options. To change any of these settings, move the cursor to the setting and press Enter once more. If you are changing the `Flip hotkey` or `Copy hotkey` option, you will see a window that prompts you to press a key to be designated as a hot key (see fig. 10.23).

You can reset other settings for ProFinder, including print margins and file format during viewing, in a similar manner by highlighting a selection and following the prompts after pressing Enter.

Fig. 10.22.

The ProFinder Configuration window for program settings.

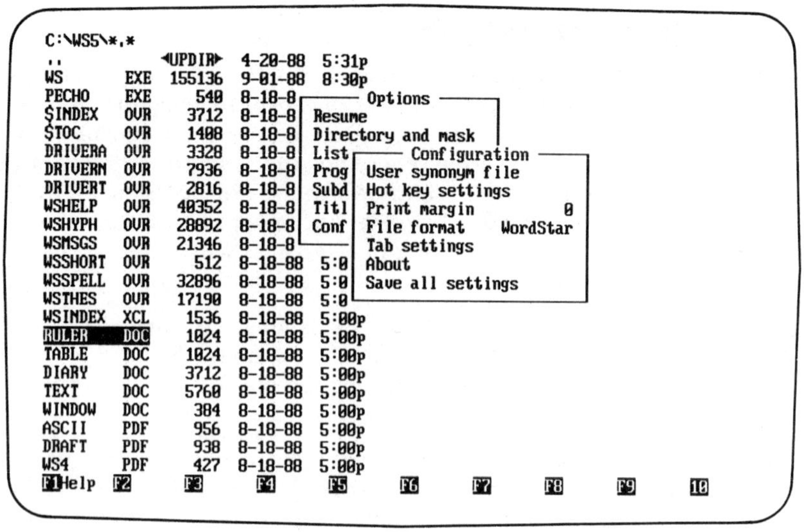
C:\WS5*.*
.. ◄UPDIR► 4-20-88 5:31p
WS EXE 155136 9-01-88 8:30p
PECHO EXE 540 8-18-8
$INDEX OVR 3712 8-18-8
$TOC OVR 1408 8-18-8
DRIVERA OVR 3328 8-18-8
DRIVERN OVR 7936 8-18-8
DRIVERT OVR 2816 8-18-8
WSHELP OVR 40352 8-18-8
WSHYPH OVR 28892 8-18-8
WSMSGS OVR 21346 8-18-8
WSSHORT OVR 512 8-18-88 5:0
WSSPELL OVR 32896 8-18-88 5:0
WSTHES OVR 17190 8-18-88 5:0
WSINDEX XCL 1536 8-18-88 5:00p
RULER DOC 1024 8-18-88 5:00p
TABLE DOC 1024 8-18-88 5:00p
DIARY DOC 3712 8-18-88 5:00p
TEXT DOC 5760 8-18-88 5:00p
WINDOW DOC 384 8-18-88 5:00p
ASCII PDF 956 8-18-88 5:00p
DRAFT PDF 938 8-18-88 5:00p
WS4 PDF 427 8-18-88 5:00p
Options
Resume
Directory and mask
List
Prog
Subd
Titl
Conf
Configuration
User synonym file
Hot key settings
Print margin 0
File format WordStar
Tab settings
About
Save all settings
F1Help F2 F3 F4 F5 F6 F7 F8 F9 10

Fig. 10.23.

Changing a ProFinder hot key assignment: follow the windows.

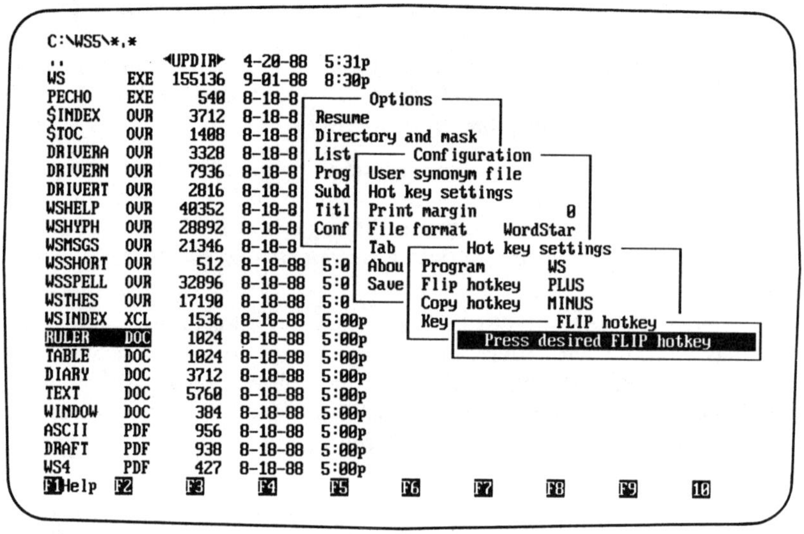
C:\WS5*.*
.. ◄UPDIR► 4-20-88 5:31p
WS EXE 155136 9-01-88 8:30p
PECHO EXE 540 8-18-8
$INDEX OVR 3712 8-18-8
$TOC OVR 1408 8-18-8
DRIVERA OVR 3328 8-18-8
DRIVERN OVR 7936 8-18-8
DRIVERT OVR 2816 8-18-8
WSHELP OVR 40352 8-18-8
WSHYPH OVR 28892 8-18-8
WSMSGS OVR 21346 8-18-8
WSSHORT OVR 512 8-18-88 5:0
WSSPELL OVR 32896 8-18-88 5:0
WSTHES OVR 17190 8-18-88 5:0
WSINDEX XCL 1536 8-18-88 5:00p
RULER DOC 1024 8-18-88 5:00p
TABLE DOC 1024 8-18-88 5:00p
DIARY DOC 3712 8-18-88 5:00p
TEXT DOC 5760 8-18-88 5:00p
WINDOW DOC 384 8-18-88 5:00p
ASCII PDF 956 8-18-88 5:00p
DRAFT PDF 938 8-18-88 5:00p
WS4 PDF 427 8-18-88 5:00p
Options
Resume
Directory and mask
List
Prog
Subd
Titl
Conf
Configuration
User synonym file
Hot key settings
Print margin 0
File format WordStar
Tab
Abou
Save
Hot key settings
Program WS
Flip hotkey PLUS
Copy hotkey MINUS
Key
FLIP hotkey
Press desired FLIP hotkey
F1Help F2 F3 F4 F5 F6 F7 F8 F9 10

Exiting from ProFinder

As with most of its functions, ProFinder includes a choice of ways to exit from the program. With the options available, you easily can reemerge from ProFinder to where you can resume a work session conveniently.

The easiest way for you to exit from ProFinder is with one of two keys: the F8 function key, which returns the DOS prompt at the current ProFinder directory, or the Escape key, which exits to the original directory where ProFinder was started. If you are running WordStar (or another program) from ProFinder, you must exit the other program first.

You also can exit from ProFinder by pressing the F10 key for a menu, highlighting the `Quit` option, and pressing Enter. Then choose `Current directory`, `Initial directory`, or `Resume`.

11

Customizing WordStar

However well designed it is, no word processing program as configured by its publisher is right for all users. Every default, from margins and line spacing to laser printer support, should be easily altered to suit your needs. Instead of resetting features for every work session, you should be able to make permanent alterations to meet your word processing requirements.

Since its creation, WordStar has been more open to customization than other word processors. WordStar was the first major applications software with program codes revealed in documentation for users. This feature encouraged otherwise non-technical users to learn base-16 hexadecimal numbering and to use DEBUG, the editor supplied with CP/M and MS-DOS, to "patch" the software's default settings. Adjusting WordStar was made easier by the improved WINSTALL program, which provided menus of settings that users could customize without using hexadecimal code. The WSCHANGE utility program in WordStar Release 4 further extended the range of easy modifications for WordStar.

In WordStar Release 5, WSCHANGE Menu listings include more than 250 WordStar settings that can be reset without programming hexadecimal code. This edition of WordStar introduces another utility program, PRCHANGE, for altering the printer description file. Although you can run PRCHANGE by itself, the program is more conveniently run from within WSCHANGE. To make further modifications, you can use the WSCHANGE patcher to edit WordStar's program code. (*Using WordStar*, 2nd Edition, does not detail how to patch WordStar program addresses, because the subject is beyond the scope of this book.)

With customization options in WSCHANGE, you can

- Turn off right-justification, pull-down menus, or hyphen help
- Set double-spacing, new margins, page length, or cursor shape
- Select colors for text and/or various on-screen print attributes
- Reassign function key commands, printer fonts, and memory usage

With more than 50 customization options not available in the last version of WordStar, Release 5 is the most versatile edition of the program to date. Most users will continually fine-tune the WSCHANGE settings to adjust the program for their needs. Advanced users probably will find undocumented WordStar features to patch—as many have done for previous versions of the program. Whether you're a novice or veteran, you will find WSCHANGE essential to getting the most from WordStar.

Starting the WSCHANGE Program

The WSCHANGE program functions similarly to the WINSTALL program you used when preparing to use your copy of WordStar Release 5 (see Chapter 2). The two utilities use similar program codes. Both programs are invoked from the DOS prompt and present menus that show current settings you can change. Only the programs' text and range of choices differ. WINSTALL is far less extensive than WSCHANGE. The latter includes every major WordStar setting—altered by changing a simple Yes/No toggle or by filling in a number for a new setting.

To run the WSCHANGE program with its full range of options, in WordStar Release 5 you must have copies of six files that are supplied on the package's Installation Customization Disk plus those on Printer Disks 1 and 2. If you have a two floppy disk system, these files are on separate copies of the Installation Customization Disk and the Printer Disks. On a hard disk system, you would store the files in the \WS5 directory, the same directory for your other WordStar program files. The WSCHANGE files necessary for running the program are WSCHANGE.EXE, the principal executable program code; WSCHANGE.OVR; and CHANGE.OVR, the program's on-screen text and help information overlays. You also need PRCHANGE.EXE, the program code for printer customization, and PRCHANGE.OVR, the text and help overlays relating to printers. A formatting file, TABLE2.OVR, also must be available on the same disk and directory.

Loading the WSCHANGE program is nearly identical to loading WINSTALL. The instructions that follow are for two floppy disk systems and hard disk systems. If your computer has different drive designations, substitute the appropriate letters.

1. Turn on your computer and load DOS.
2. For two floppy disk systems:

    Put into drive A the Installation Disk copy that contains the WSCHANGE files and put your working copy of WordStar into drive B.

    For hard disk systems:

    Change to the directory that contains your WordStar program files (including those for WSCHANGE). For most installations, you type *cd \ws5*.

3. Type *wschange* and press Enter to load the WSCHANGE program.

   The screen displays a brief copyright notice and a prompt that asks for the name of the file to install.

4. For two floppy disk systems:

   Type *b:ws* and press Enter.

   For hard disk systems:

   Type *ws* and press Enter.

   Another screen message requests the name of the file to store the changed version of WordStar. You normally would give the file the name WS. Answering the prompt by pressing Enter inserts WS as the target name and starts the program. You may prefer to type a different name for a version of WordStar adapted to a specific application. A version called WSLETTER, for example, might be for correspondence, and WSLEGAL might start with defaults set for legal document format. Versions of WordStar generated with WSCHANGE are stored on disk with the extension EXE appended to their names. (On two floppy disk systems, make sure that the disk has space for multiple versions of the program.)

5. For two floppy disk systems:

   Type *b:ws* (or the name that you prefer for an alternative customized version of WordStar). Then press Enter to start program execution.

   For hard disk systems:

   Type *ws* (or a file name to store another, customized version of WordStar). Then press Enter to start program execution (see fig. 11.1).

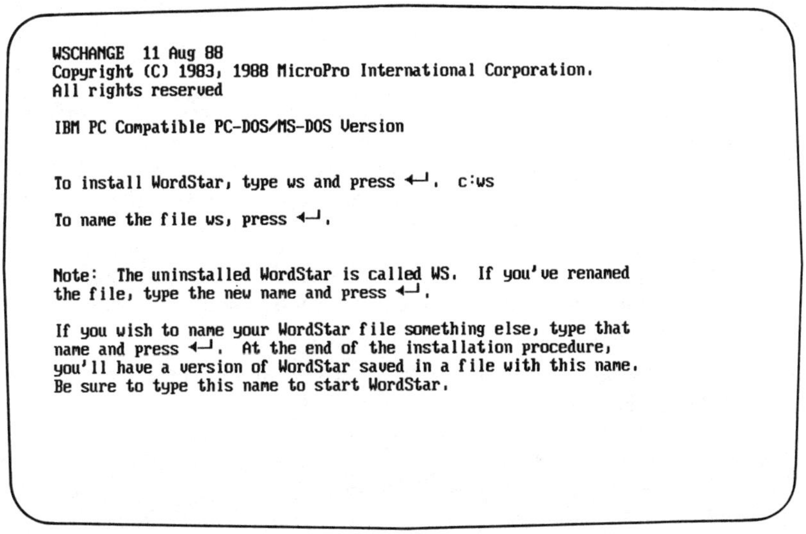
WSCHANGE 11 Aug 88
Copyright (C) 1983, 1988 MicroPro International Corporation.
All rights reserved
IBM PC Compatible PC-DOS/MS-DOS Version
To install WordStar, type ws and press ↵. c:ws
To name the file ws, press ↵.
Note: The uninstalled WordStar is called WS. If you've renamed the file, type the new name and press ↵.
If you wish to name your WordStar file something else, type that name and press ↵. At the end of the installation procedure, you'll have a version of WordStar saved in a file with this name. Be sure to type this name to start WordStar.

Fig. 11.1.

The screen for naming the WordStar file to be customized.

Using the Main Installation Menu

As soon as WSCHANGE reads the WordStar program file to be modified, the Main Installation Menu is displayed (see fig. 11.2). You will return to this screen as you complete changes in the four main modification areas of WSCHANGE: the Console (changing keyboard and display settings), the Printer (adjusting the printer and printing defaults with the PRCHANGE program), the Computer (making alterations that involve disks, files, and memory usage), and WordStar itself (modifying editing, formatting, spelling checks, and other word processing features).

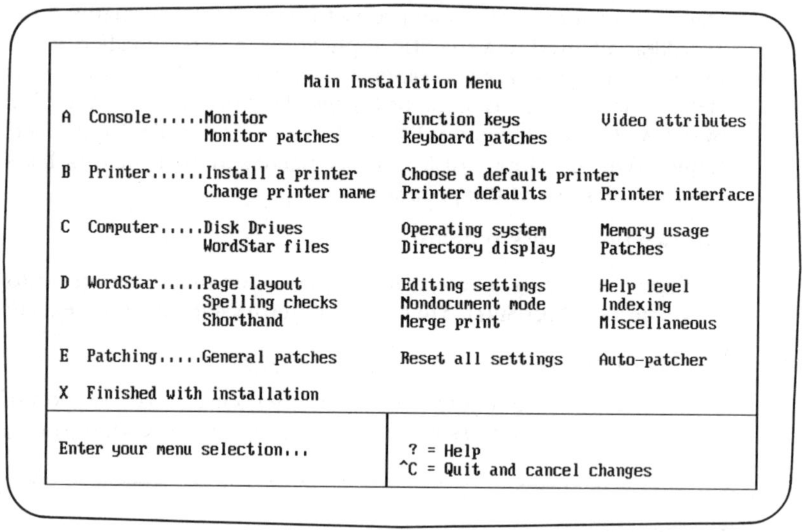
Main Installation Menu
A Console......Monitor
Monitor patches
Function keys
Keyboard patches
Video attributes
B Printer......Install a printer
Change printer name
Choose a default printer
Printer defaults
Printer interface
C Computer.....Disk Drives
WordStar files
Operating system
Directory display
Memory usage
Patches
D WordStar.....Page layout
Spelling checks
Shorthand
Editing settings
Nondocument mode
Merge print
Help level
Indexing
Miscellaneous
E Patching.....General patches
Reset all settings
Auto-patcher
X Finished with installation
Enter your menu selection...
? = Help
^C = Quit and cancel changes

Fig. 11.2.
The WSCHANGE program's Main Installation Menu.

To select an item from the Main Installation Menu or from most other menus in WSCHANGE, type the letter that appears to the left of the option you want. This step generates one or more submenus that offer more selections. A series of choices leads to a list of specific settings. Picking one of these options displays prompts that ask for changes you want to make.

If you are unsure of a technical term or how to proceed, you can summon help at any point in WSCHANGE. Each screen includes a `? Help` prompt. To display a help screen, just press the ? key.

To help you navigate through the levels of WSCHANGE menus, table 11.1 provides an overview of the program's organization.

Table 11.1
The WSCHANGE Program's Menu Structure

Main Installation Menu	*Area menus*	*Function submenus*
A Console	A Monitor	A Monitor Selection
		B Monitor Name
		C Screen Sizing
	B Function keys	
	C Video attributes	
	D Monitor patches	
	E Keyboard patches	
B Printer	A Printer Install	(Printer Selection)
	(Starts PRCHANGE)	(Change Fonts)
		(Printer Port)
		(Sheet Feeder)
		(Printer Information)
	B Default Printer	
	C Printer Name	
	D Printer Defaults	
	E Printer Interface	A Printer Busy Handshaking
		B Printer Subroutines
		C Background Printing
C Computer	A Disk Drives	
	B Operating System	
	C Memory Usage	
	D WordStar Files	
	E Directory Display	
	F Check System Files	
	G Computer Patches	
D WordStar	A Page Layout	A Page Size & Margins
		B Headers & Footers
		C Tabs
		D Footnotes and Endnotes
		E Stored Ruler Lines
		F Paragraph Numbering
	B Editing Settings	A Edit Screen, Help Level
		B Typing
		C Paragraph Alignment
		D Blocks
		E Erase & Unerase
		F Lines & Characters
		G Find & Replace

Table 11.1—*Continued*

Main Installation Menu	*Area menus*	*Function submenus*
		H WordStar Compatibility
		I Printing Defaults
		J Line Numbering
	C Other Features	A Spelling Checks
		B Nondocument Mode
		C Indexing
		D Shorthand
		E Merge Printing
		F Character Conversion Patches
		F Miscellaneous
E Patching	A Auto Patcher	
	B Save Settings	
	C Reset All Settings	

If you are familiar with WSCHANGE in the previous edition of WordStar, you will notice several modifications in menu formats as you work through WordStar Release 5's version of WSCHANGE. For instance, many function menus, like the Printing Defaults Menu, are now split into submenus because of WordStar Release 5's many additions. With the inclusion of PRCHANGE, the printer-related options no longer conform to the letter-driven selection procedure used throughout the rest of WSCHANGE. When you modify printer settings, the point-and-shoot method of highlighting a selection and pressing Enter leads to the desired function. For more on PRCHANGE and its options, see the section on printer settings later in this chapter.

To make changes in most of WSCHANGE, you can simply type the letters indicated on area menus and function menus. After you save your customized version of WordStar by pressing X at the Main Installation Menu and then Y, the program reflects the adjustments you made through WSCHANGE. Any mistakes you make in resetting items can be corrected before you save the file. If you would rather start over, you can cancel the entire WSCHANGE procedure by pressing Ctrl-C. (If you get lost in WSCHANGE's submenus, pressing Ctrl-X moves the display back to the Main Installation Menu.)

The Main Installation Menu and many submenus often refer to patching and patches. Detailed discussion of patching is beyond the bounds of this book. However, WSCHANGE includes menu selections for customizing most of the features that required program-code patches in early WordStar releases. Auto patching, the technique for resetting other WordStar Release 5 copies to your copy's customizations, is discussed at the end of this chapter.

With one exception (printer description file patching), the only patching indications on menus are the user area labels—the six-character acronyms beside many setting listings in WSCHANGE. You will also see the Ctrl commands or dot commands that invoke or modify a listed setting on the menu.

Customizing Console Options: Display and Keyboard Defaults

By selecting the Console option from the Main Installation Menu, you can make major changes in WordStar's display and keyboard functions. For example, you can reassign the commands for WordStar Release 5's 40 function key combinations, change the height or width of your monitor display, or create a more readable color scheme for text and on-screen attributes. Changing the display and changing the keyboard are among the easiest ways to customize WordStar with WSCHANGE.

When you press A at the Main Installation Menu, WSCHANGE displays the Console Menu screen, (see fig. 11.3). Options A, B, and C lead, respectively, to essential changes in monitor selection, function keys, and on-screen color. Options D and E provide ways to enhance save settings made with the preceding options; in addition, options D and E contain patch information for functions that don't apply to IBM PC-compatible systems. The first time you use the Console Menu, select options A, B, and C in turn to become familiar with changes to make in your WordStar working copy.

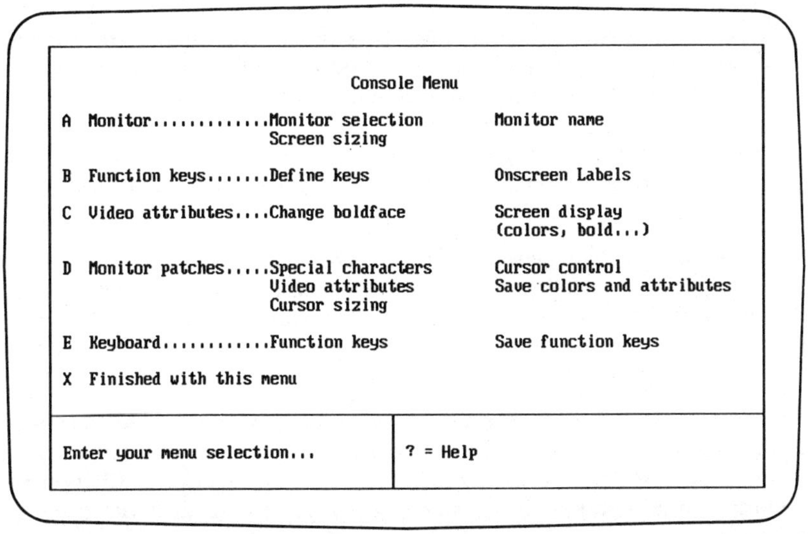
Console Menu
A Monitor.............Monitor selection Screen sizing
Monitor name
B Function keys.......Define keys
Onscreen Labels
C Video attributes....Change boldface
Screen display (colors, bold...)
D Monitor patches.....Special characters Video attributes Cursor sizing
Cursor control Save colors and attributes
E Keyboard............Function keys
Save function keys
X Finished with this menu
Enter your menu selection...
? = Help

Fig. 11.3.

The WSCHANGE Console Menu.

Resetting Monitor Characteristics

Pressing A on the Console Menu selects the menu's Monitor option. The Monitor Menu, which shows the name of the monitor for which WordStar is currently installed, lists three primary functions:

```
A    Monitor selection
B    Monitor name
C    Screen sizing
```

5

If you press A again, the WSCHANGE program displays Monitor Selection Menu #1. Monitor Selection Menus #1 and #2 are the same as the Monitor Selection Menus in the WINSTALL program (see fig. 11.4). To revise a choice made when you installed WordStar, press A for 100 percent IBM-compatible video display, B or C for a less than 100 percent IBM-compatible display, or D to display 43 lines of text (instead of 25) on an IBM Enhanced Graphics Adapter setup. Pressing 2 for Monitor Selection Menu #2 adds two choices: A for an IBM VGA display to show 50 lines of text on-screen; B to restore all screen and function key settings to their original default values (as shipped by MicroPro). Once you press any of these settings or X (to retain the previously specified monitor choice), the Monitor Menu returns.

Pressing B at the Monitor Menu leads to a screen that shows the current monitor name and a prompt that asks whether you want to make a change. If you answer Y for yes, you then can enter the name of the monitor you want to install. Answering N for no returns the Monitor Menu to the screen.

Choosing the Monitor Menu's C option for screen sizing can be essential for matching WordStar's output to a special monitor's characteristics. After you press C, a menu displaying the five principal screen-sizing settings appears (see fig. 11.5).

From the Screen Sizing Menu, pressing A for `Height` lets you change the current default of 25, the number of text lines on a standard monitor. (The screen choices on the Monitor Selection Menu include an option for a 43-line display only with an enhanced graphics board and 50 lines with a VGA.) If you are using a full-page monitor, such as the ones for desktop publishing, you can reset the screen height to 66 lines or another appropriate setting. Pressing Enter shows the new value on the Screen Sizing Menu.

Pressing B at the Screen Sizing Menu can alter the screen-width setting of 80 columns. You may want to make this change if you are using a wide-screen monitor intended for spreadsheets. Pressing Y to change the setting and typing *132* let you make full use of such a monitor. Pressing Enter brings you back to the Screen Sizing Menu.

The Screen Sizing Menu's C option resets the horizontal scroll width. This setting is the default increment of 20 columns by which WordStar scrolls from left to right and back on an oversized line (see the *Scrolling Horizontally* section in Chapter 5). If your monitor works better with a different setting, this menu is the place to make the change.

```
                     Monitor Selection Menu #1

A  IBM Compatible using video RAM directly.  (Fastest way to display
   characters on 100% IBM compatible machines.)

B  IBM Compatible using CGA video RAM directly.  (Removes most "snow" from
   screen but is slower.  Used for 100% IBM compatible machines only.)

C  IBM Compatible using ROM BIOS calls only.  (Removes all "snow" from screen
   but is slowest.  Also used for less than 100% IBM compatible machines.)

D  Use IBM EGA to display 43 lines in WordStar.  Restore to 25 lines
   when finished with WordStar.

2  Monitor Selection Menu #2
X  Finished with this menu

Enter your menu selection...          ? = Help
                                      For detailed changes, run WSCHANGE.
```

```
                     Monitor Selection Menu #2

A  Use IBM VGA to display 50 lines of WordStar.  Restore to 25 lines
   when finished with WordStar.

1  Monitor Selection Menu #1
X  Finished with this menu

Enter your menu selection...          ? = Help
                                      For detailed changes, run WSCHANGE.
```

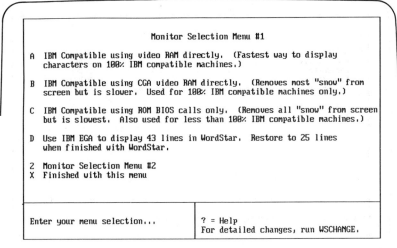

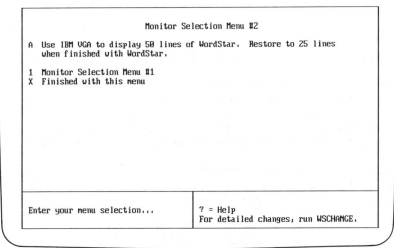

Fig. 11.4.
The Monitor Selection Menus.

The next Screen Sizing Menu option—`D Directory size`—presents the default setting for the number of lines of file directory listings that are to be displayed on-screen. When prompts are short, the default setting is 11 lines of directory listings. If prompt messages on-screen are longer, the default setting is 5 lines and can be reset here to as few as 1 or 2 lines. When you are installing a full-page monitor screen, adjust this setting upward accordingly.

The last screen-sizing option, `E Cursor wrap at right edge`, doesn't apply to IBM PC-compatible computers.

After you finish with the settings on the Screen Sizing Menu, press X to bring back the Monitor Menu. Press X again to return to the Console Menu.

Fig. 11.5.

The Screen Sizing Menu.

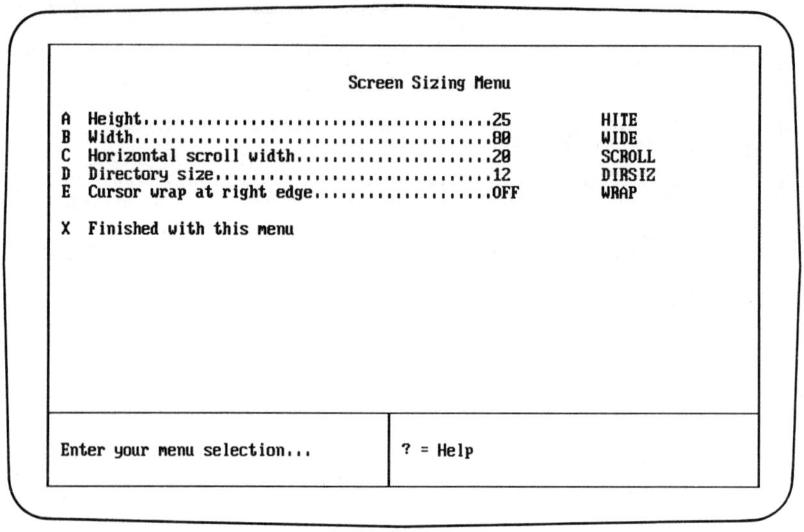

```
                    Screen Sizing Menu
A  Height..................................25        HITE
B  Width...................................80        WIDE
C  Horizontal scroll width.................20        SCROLL
D  Directory size..........................12        DIRSIZ
E  Cursor wrap at right edge...............OFF       WRAP

X  Finished with this menu

Enter your menu selection...        ? = Help
```

Reconfiguring Function Key Settings

If you want to reassign the commands invoked by function key combinations, you press B on the Console Menu. This is also the option to select if you want to free up two lines of text on the editing screen by eliminating the function key labels displayed at help levels 3, 2, and 1. After you select B, you see a screen with instructions and four columns of function key commands, as shown in figure 11.6.

Fig. 11.6.

The screen for customizing function key commands.

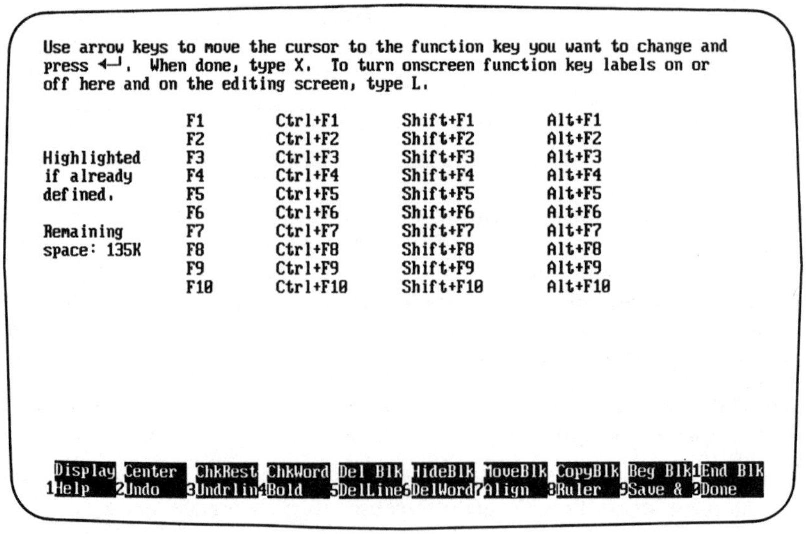

```
Use arrow keys to move the cursor to the function key you want to change and
press ←┘. When done, type X. To turn onscreen function key labels on or
off here and on the editing screen, type L.

                     F1      Ctrl+F1     Shift+F1     Alt+F1
                     F2      Ctrl+F2     Shift+F2     Alt+F2
Highlighted          F3      Ctrl+F3     Shift+F3     Alt+F3
 if already          F4      Ctrl+F4     Shift+F4     Alt+F4
defined.             F5      Ctrl+F5     Shift+F5     Alt+F5
                     F6      Ctrl+F6     Shift+F6     Alt+F6
Remaining            F7      Ctrl+F7     Shift+F7     Alt+F7
space: 135K          F8      Ctrl+F8     Shift+F8     Alt+F8
                     F9      Ctrl+F9     Shift+F9     Alt+F9
                     F10     Ctrl+F10    Shift+F10    Alt+F10

 Display  Center  ChkRest  ChkWord  Del Blk  HideBlk  MoveBlk  CopyBlk  Beg Blk  End Blk
1Help    2Undo   3Undrlin 4Bold    5DelLine 6DelWord 7Align   8Ruler   9Save &  0Done
```

The default commands for the 40 function key combinations in WordStar Release 5 may seem arbitrary. No doubt, you will prefer some function key assignments other than those chosen by MicroPro.

Here are some possible alternatives to current function key assignments:

- Adding back WordStar 3.3's function key commands for restoring margins (if you do a great deal of reformatting)
- Adding back WordStar 3.3's function key commands for restoring margins (if you do a lot of reformatting)
- Including ^KN and ^KI column mode toggles (for tables and columns)
- Reclustering delete and block-command keystrokes

Reassigning function keys requires some planning. Observe your use of WordStar in typical applications. Which keyboard commands, either Ctrl sequences or dot commands, do you use most? Would your word processing be easier if you assigned certain keystroke combinations to function keys?

What about using Alt-, Shift-, and Ctrl-function key combinations to reflect the way you conceptualize WordStar functions—perhaps assigning deletion and editing commands to Shift-function keys and assigning formatting commands to Ctrl-function key combinations. The most frequently used commands should occupy the single-stroke function key assignments. If you won't be using the box-drawing features, reassign the Alt-function key commands, too.

Plot on a keyboard overlay the commands you want to ascribe to each function key and function key combination. The overlay supplied has color-coded lines on the back for entry of custom function key assignments. Be sure that your placement of commands on the function keys is logical and promotes ease of use.

To change a function key assignment, move the cursor to the desired function key designation and press Enter. The program displays a prompt that lists the function key, the number of characters used for the key assignment, the definition (the keystrokes the function key invokes), and a query that asks whether you want to change the definition (see fig. 11.6). Press Y, and a prompt asks for your WordStar keystrokes. Type the keystrokes you normally would enter for a command or a series of commands. Pressing the Del key erases any mistakes you make. When you are finished making changes, press the End key.

After you type the keystrokes to be assigned to a function key or key combination, WSCHANGE prompts you to redefine the corresponding label at the bottom of the screen. With the cursor at the correct spot for the function key, enter a label of no more than seven characters, that sums up the key's new action. Again, use the Del key if you need to delete what you have typed. After you have finished typing, press the End key.

Notice that after you finish typing, parts of the prompt change. For example, the prompt at the left of the screen (which originally read `Remaining space: 135`) now shows less remaining space. This prompt is a reminder that the number of keystrokes you can add to the WordStar Release 5 function keys is limited. At the default setting, only 135 more characters (or Ctrl-letter combinations) can be added to the 40 current function key assignments. Although hackers have ways around this limitation, any lengthy combination of commands or characters (including boilerplate text) would be better programmed as a keyboard shorthand macro or series of macros to be played back by a reassigned function key (see Chapter 9).

The function key screen is also useful if you want to eliminate the two lines of function key labels from the bottom of the screen. To reclaim for your documents the two lines occupied by those labels, press L. The labels disappear from the function key screen and from the document screen, as seen when you use your customized WordStar. Pressing L a second time toggles back on the display of the function key label display.

After you complete your changes on the function key screen, press X to return to the Console Menu. When you save all modifications at the end of a WSCHANGE session, function key changes become part of your customized WordStar program file.

You can also save the new function key settings as a separate file to customize this and other copies of WordStar Release 5. To save your changes to function key assignments in a separate file, press E at the Console Menu and, at the resulting Keyboard Menu, press C. This step displays the following screen message:

```
                 Save Function Keys

You can save the current function key settings in a
nondocument file that can later be used by the auto patcher.

Enter file name to hold settings (or press Enter to quit)...
```

When you create a file for your function key settings, follow DOS conventions for naming files. Use as many as eight characters, followed in this case by a PAT (patch file) extension. Files with this extension are usable with WSCHANGE's auto patcher feature. To save your WordStar Release 5 function key assignments, for example, you could type *ws5keys.pat* and press Enter. The resulting file is of the same type as WS3KEYS.PAT (supplied on the Installation Disk of WordStar Release 5). The WS3KEYS.PAT file installs WordStar 3 function key and label assignments to WordStar Release 5—with help from the auto patcher function. To return to the Console Menu from the Save Function Keys Menu, press Enter and then X.

Selecting Screen Colors

Choosing C from among the Console Menu's options is a must if you have a color adapter board and monitor. (Monochrome setups can also benefit from some settings.) With this menu option, you access the Video Attributes Menu, an addition to WSCHANGE with WordStar Release 5. Option A is a holdover from Release 4, leading to the screen for resetting each of WordStar's color attributes. The three new options—B, C, and D—are similar to selections on the Console Menu in WINSTALL (see Chapter 2).

Pressing A at the Video Attributes Menu displays the screen for assigning color settings to 17 types of WordStar text or screen messages (more than in WordStar Release 4); each type can be represented on the document screen by a distinctive color combination. WSCHANGE includes instructions for regulating color and intensity settings by pressing designated function keys. These settings affect the display of characters and background, strikeout, underline, and boldface, as well as error messages, menu text, key labels, and the ruler line. Among the attributes assigned color selections in WordStar Release 5 are directory and warning listings—the two kinds of WordStar error messages (see fig. 11.7).

```
Use the arrow keys to move the cursor to the feature you wish to change
and press a function key to select a color or turn bold and blink on/off:
        F1 black       F2 blue        F3 green       F4 cyan
        F5 red         F6 magenta     F7 yellow      F8 white
        F9 bold        F10 blink

               Character           Background          Example
   Normal text white               black               Abcde 12345
   Strike-out  white+bold          black               Abcde 12345
   Underline   blue                black               Abcde 12345
   Subscript   white+bold          black               Abcde 12345
   Superscript white+bold          black               Abcde 12345
   Bold & double white+bold        black               Abcde 12345
   Italics     white+bold          black               Abcde 12345
   Status line black               white               Abcde 12345
   Menus       white               black               Abcde 12345
   Menu highlight white+bold       black               Abcde 12345
   Key highlight white             black               Abcde 12345
   Key labels  black               white               Abcde 12345
   Directory   white               black               Abcde 12345
   Dir heading black               white               Abcde 12345
   Ruler line  black               white               Abcde 12345
   Warning     white               black               Abcde 12345
   Warning high white+bold         black               Abcde 12345
Press the Esc key to quit without making changes, or X when done.
```

Fig. 11.7.

The video attributes screen.

You have three considerations to keep in mind when you assign colors to video attributes: how to make standard document text most readable against a particular background, how to make text attributes distinctive while not clashing with regular text, and how to coordinate WordStar's menu and message colors with the other settings. Note that you won't be able to make a final judgment about colors until you run your customized WordStar and see an actual display. You may have to run WSCHANGE several times and view the results on your WordStar files before finding the optimum color scheme.

Everyone has an opinion about which colors look best on-screen, but most users settle on standard combinations of white text on black, green on black, yellow on black, or white on blue. Another possibility worth considering is black text on a white background (like a typewritten page or an original Macintosh® screen) for normal text, status line, ruler line, and key labels. With proper brightness and good resolution, this combination is less fatiguing than other colors. If you consistently use white in the background, you can assign different colors to underline, bold, italics, and other attributes, and soothing green or blue to menus. (If you have a monochrome monitor, you should consider using the black text on white background settings, as well as using bold and flashing characters.)

To change the color of a particular type of on-screen text, move the cursor to the character or background color to be changed and look at the list of function keys that invoke various colors. Press the function key for the color you want to substitute at the cursor. For example, selecting F1 produces black; F8, white; and F9 or F10 turns on or off bold or blink, respectively.

A sample of your new color scheme appears in the `Example` column to the right of the cursor position. Use this to avoid color clashes. Remember that color schemes may look different with a full screen of text. Do not invoke the same color for characters and background, or text will be invisible.

5

After you have finished assigning colors, press X, and the screen again displays the Video Attributes Menu. By pressing B at the Video Attributes Menu, you can accept WordStar Release 5's default color settings: normal text in white on a black background and decorative attributes in variations on red, white, and blue. Pressing C at the Video Attributes Menu resets the WordStar display to monochrome settings (with text in white on black, highlighting, and one gray setting for attributes). Typing *d* restores the original monochrome display default setting. Press X to return to the WSCHANGE Console Menu.

As with monitor settings, color settings can be stored in a separate nondocument file for later use in customizing this and other copies of WordStar Release 5 with WSCHANGE. If you want to save your color assignments in a separate file, press D at the Console Menu. When the Monitor Patches Menu appears, press D for `Save colors`. The following message is displayed on-screen:

```
          Save Colors and Video Attributes Menu

  You can save the current screen color settings in a
  nondocument file that can later be used by the auto patcher.

  Enter file name to hold settings (or Press ↵ to quit)...
```

To create a file for WordStar color settings, type a name up to eight characters long, followed by the extension PAT. To save your WordStar Release 5 color scheme, you can type *ws5color.pat* and press Enter. This returns the display to the Monitor Patches Menu.

Of the five principal options on the Monitor Patches Menu, only two, D for `Save colors` (just described) and E for `Cursor sizing`, do not require hex code programming.

Changing Cursor Settings

The cursor sizing option is new in WordStar Release 5; with it you can change cursor style to differentiate three kinds of text entry.

After typing *e* at the Monitor Patches Menu, you see the Cursor Sizes for CGA Menu (see fig. 11.8). Choose this menu for CGA or EGA displays. For a system with another kind of monitor, you should choose F at the Monitor Patches Menu to display the Cursor Sizes for all Other Monitors Menu (see fig. 11.9) with listings identical to the Monitor Patches for CGA Menu. The six choices on either menu are actually three sets of toggles: between a thin cursor at the bottom of a character or a character-sized rectangular block that flashes on screen—during text insertion, overtype mode, or after a return to DOS. The thin cursor for all three text modes is WordStar's default setting.

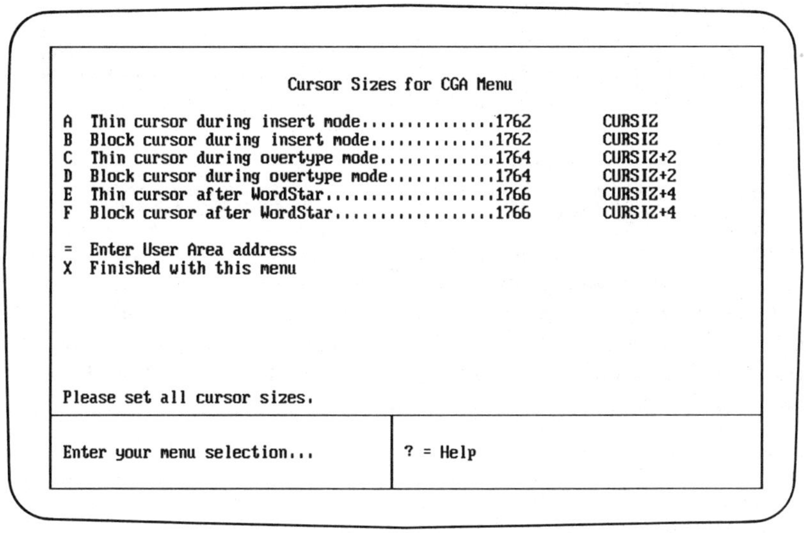
Cursor Sizes for CGA Menu
A Thin cursor during insert mode...............1762 CURSIZ
B Block cursor during insert mode..............1762 CURSIZ
C Thin cursor during overtype mode.............1764 CURSIZ+2
D Block cursor during overtype mode............1764 CURSIZ+2
E Thin cursor after WordStar...................1766 CURSIZ+4
F Block cursor after WordStar..................1766 CURSIZ+4
= Enter User Area address
X Finished with this menu
Please set all cursor sizes.
Enter your menu selection...
? = Help

Fig. 11.8.
The WSCHANGE Cursor Sizes Menu.

Users of EGA monitors with 43-line displays may want to substitute an easier-to-see block cursor during insert mode by pressing B. To distinguish text entry during overtype mode with a block cursor, users of any text display may choose to press D. Pressing F at the Cursor Sizes Menu, shows that you have exited to DOS with a block cursor. Press X to return to the Monitor Patches Menu.

Pressing X twice from the Monitor Patches Menu displays the Main Installation Menu.

Fig. 11.9.

The Cursor Sizes for all Other Monitors Menu.

```
                    Cursor Sizes for all other Monitors Menu

A  Thin cursor during insert mode..............1762        CURSIZ
B  Block cursor during insert mode.............1762        CURSIZ
C  Thin cursor during overtype mode............1764        CURSIZ+2
D  Block cursor during overtype mode...........1764        CURSIZ+2
E  Thin cursor after WordStar..................1766        CURSIZ+4
F  Block cursor after WordStar.................1766        CURSIZ+4

=  Enter User Area address
X  Finished with this menu

Please set all cursor sizes.

Enter your menu selection...          ? = Help
```

Customizing Printer Defaults

From the Main Installation Menu, selecting option B opens the way for adjusting printer features: installing and modifying printer description files, customizing printer output, and resetting printing defaults. Many of these settings may be temporarily reset with procedures described in Chapter 7. For more permanent modifications to WordStar's print functions, you should proceed through WSCHANGE's Printer area.

Pressing B at the Main Installation Menu displays the Printer Menu shown in figure 11.10. In WordStar Release 5 this menu includes five choices for modifying printer selection and performance. The first option issues the command to start the PRCHANGE.EXE program, WordStar Release 5's utility software for altering printer description files. The other four options on the Printer Menu change printer-related settings within the WordStar program code. Before you modify any settings to optimize your printer's output, be sure to examine all the Printer Menu choices you might otherwise overlook.

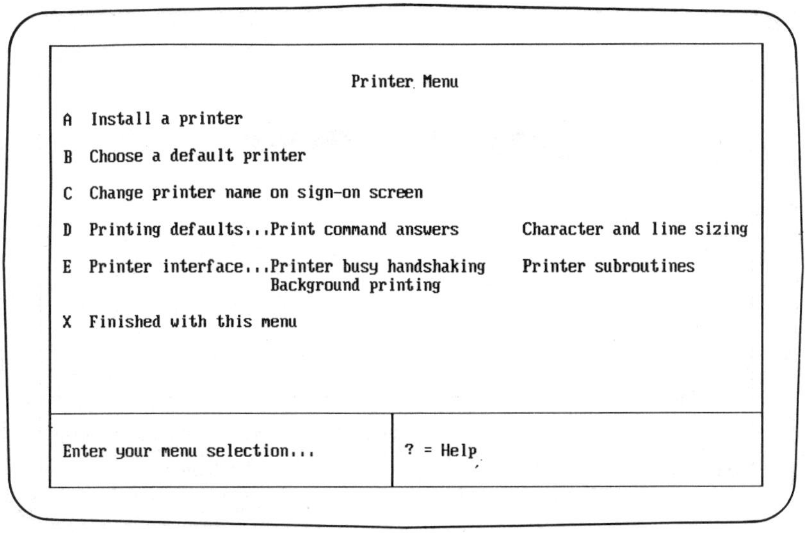
Printer Menu
A Install a printer
B Choose a default printer
C Change printer name on sign-on screen
D Printing defaults...Print command answers
Character and line sizing
E Printer interface...Printer busy handshaking
Background printing
Printer subroutines
X Finished with this menu
Enter your menu selection...
? = Help

Fig. 11.10. *The Printer Menu.*

Installing and Modifying Printer Description Files

Selecting the Printer Menu's A option starts the PRCHANGE program from within WSCHANGE. The Printer Menu stays on-screen for several seconds while the Printer alteration program loads into memory. The display returns with the PRCHANGE Printer Type Menu, from which you can select the appropriate listing, laser or nonlaser printer, by moving the cursor and pressing Enter.

If you want to customize printer description files and don't care to access other areas of WSCHANGE, you can run PRCHANGE directly from the DOS prompt. Simply type *prchange* and press Enter and the program loads from disk into working memory. The first display you see is a copyright screen for the WordStar Professional Printer Installation Program. This is quickly followed by a Main Menu similar to the one in figure 11.11.

When started directly from DOS, PRCHANGE exits back to DOS after changes have been completed and saved. When you start PRCHANGE from within WSCHANGE, you can continue to exercise options within the principal WordStar customization program.

Essentially, two parallel sets of functions can be followed when accessing the printer settings in PRCHANGE: installing a printer description file or modifying the

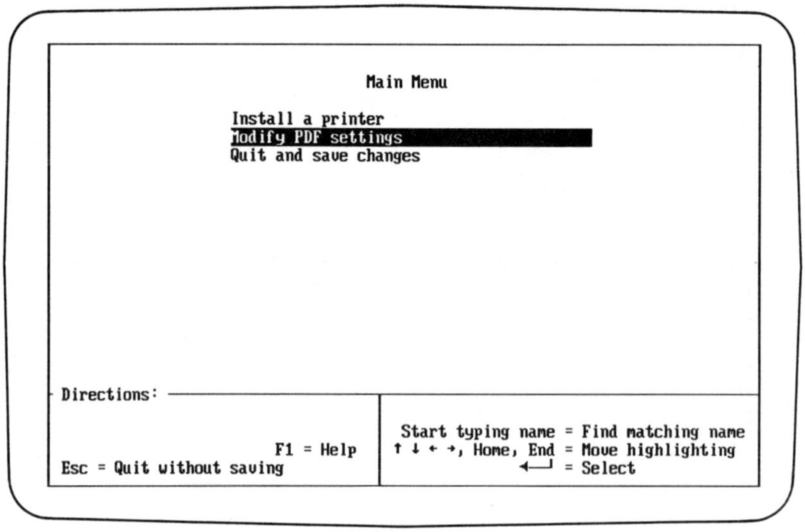
Main Menu
Install a printer
Modify PDF settings
Quit and save changes
Directions:
F1 = Help
Esc = Quit without saving
Start typing name = Find matching name
↑ ↓ ← →, Home, End = Move highlighting
↵ = Select

Fig. 11.11.
The PRCHANGE Main Menu.

settings of an already installed printer description file. Remember that you must first install a PDF and save it before you can start modifying its contents.

To install a new printer description file, you should leave the highlighting on the PRCHANGE Main Menu at the first selection: `Install a printer`. When running WSCHANGE, the same is accomplished by pressing A at the Printer Menu. Press Enter and the screen displays the Printer Type Menu, from which you should select the correct type and press Enter. For either selection, you see a Printer Selection Menu, also seen during printer installation in WINSTALL. For laser printer models, one screen of options is available, and for other models, five screens of choices are available, the first of which is shown in figure 11.12. If you are using a two floppy disk system, follow on-screen instructions for placing Printer Data Base disks in your system's disk drives.

When at the Printer Selection Menu for nonlaser printers, use the arrow keys to highlight a model on the current list of printer names, use the PgDn/PgUp keys to view one of the four other screens of printer listings, or simply type the first letter of the intended printer's brand name and press Enter to match it to a model's name contained in WordStar's database. As explained in Chapter 7, if your printer is not among the more than 100 models included in WordStar Release 5's printer listings, nor any of the additional 100 printer definition files available upon request from MicroPro International, you can choose one of WordStar's preinstalled generic printer description files and modify it to fit your printer's needs.

Once you select a printer name from the Printer Selection Menu and press Enter, the next screen displayed is the Installed Printer Menu, also previously seen from within WINSTALL. This menu shows the name of the printer selected and a list of already installed printer description files. You can type a new file name up to eight

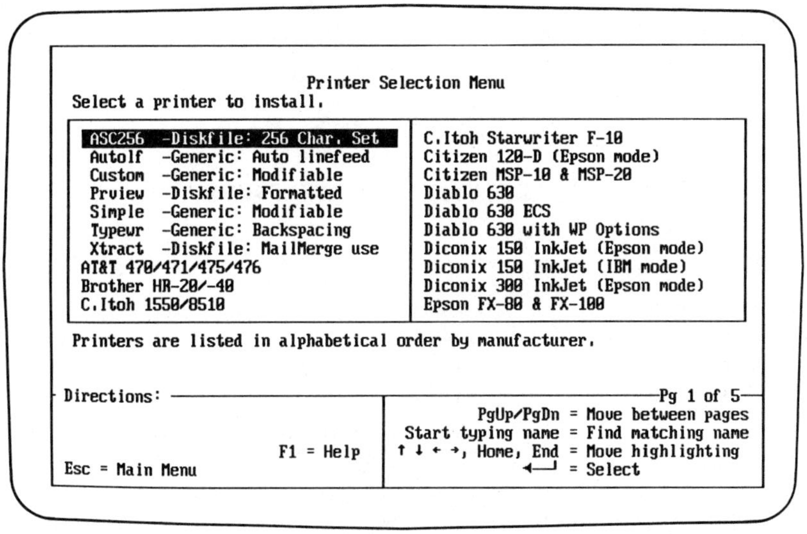
Printer Selection Menu
Select a printer to install.
ASC256 -Diskfile: 256 Char. Set
Autolf -Generic: Auto linefeed
Custom -Generic: Modifiable
Prview -Diskfile: Formatted
Simple -Generic: Modifiable
Typewr -Generic: Backspacing
Xtract -Diskfile: MailMerge use
AT&T 470/471/475/476
Brother HR-20/-40
C.Itoh 1550/8510
C.Itoh Starwriter F-10
Citizen 120-D (Epson mode)
Citizen MSP-10 & MSP-20
Diablo 630
Diablo 630 ECS
Diablo 630 with WP Options
Diconix 150 InkJet (Epson mode)
Diconix 150 InkJet (IBM mode)
Diconix 300 InkJet (Epson mode)
Epson FX-80 & FX-100
Printers are listed in alphabetical order by manufacturer.
Directions:
Pg 1 of 5
PgUp/PgDn = Move between pages
Start typing name = Find matching name
F1 = Help
↑ ↓ ← →, Home, End = Move highlighting
Esc = Main Menu
↵ = Select

Fig. 11.12.
The first Printer Selection Menu.

characters long or select an existing one to be replaced by moving the highlight with the arrow keys and then pressing Enter. PRCHANGE begins to assemble the elements of the Printer Definition File. You may see a message in a box indicating that you should wait while the installation program finds the appropriate font listings.

At the PRCHANGE Main Menu, if you select `Modify PDF settings` by highlighting this line and pressing Enter, the screen displays the Installed Printer Menu, listing the names of installed printer description files. Instructions prompt you to select the PDF to modify: move the highlight to the desired PDF and press Enter.

If you are installing a printer description file or modifying one, the screen following the Installed Printer Menu is similar: the WSCHANGE-accessed Additional Installation Menu, including four options for fonts, printer port, sheet feeder, and access to a submenu of information about the printer description file selected; or the more extensive PRCHANGE-accessed PDF Modification Menu with a total of seven primary options, including three from the other menu. The Additional Installation Menu is illustrated in figure 11.13.

With the highlight on the first line of the Additional Installation Menu or the PDF Modification Menu, pressing Enter leads you through a series of screens for selecting fonts in the current printer description file—a convenient addition for laser printers.

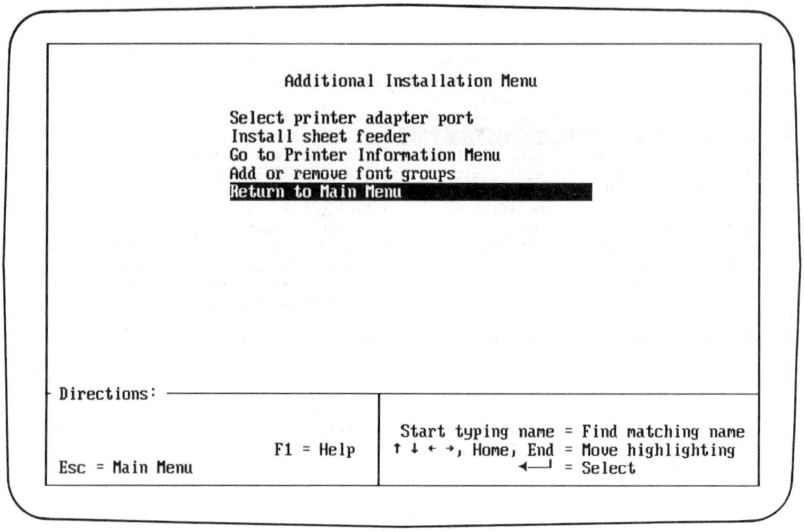
Additional Installation Menu
Select printer adapter port
Install sheet feeder
Go to Printer Information Menu
Add or remove font groups
Return to Main Menu
Directions:
F1 = Help
Esc = Main Menu
Start typing name = Find matching name
↑ ↓ ← →, Home, End = Move highlighting
↵ = Select

Fig. 11.13. *The Additional Installation Menu.*

Modifying Printer Font Sets

When you select the `Add or remove font groups` option on the Additional Installation Menu or the PDF Modification Menu, the first screen displays the principal fonts and their characteristics as they are currently listed in your printer description file. The Current Fonts in PDF Menu provides information on listed font groups' type style, size, width, orientation, bold, italic, super- and subscript types, graphics characters, and symbol set (see fig. 11.14).

According to the instructions on-screen, you can delete a font by highlighting its name and pressing the minus (−) key. To add a font, press the plus (+) key; this displays a screen instructing you to select the type of font to install and four sources for fonts. The choices for fonts are cartridge fonts, internal fonts, soft fonts, and third-party laser fonts.

Selecting any of the four font sources by highlighting it and pressing Enter calls up one of three screens with font choices: Available Cartridges, Available Internal Groups, Available Fonts, and, if accessible, Available Third-Party Laser fonts. At each font listing, you can designate any font by highlighting a choice and pressing Enter. All designated fonts are noted with a square marker on-screen. When all choices on a font list have been made, save your selections by pressing F10, which also returns you to the menu for choosing the type of font.

To display the Additional Installation Menu again or PRCHANGE's PDF Modification Menu, you can highlight that selection on the menu and press Enter.

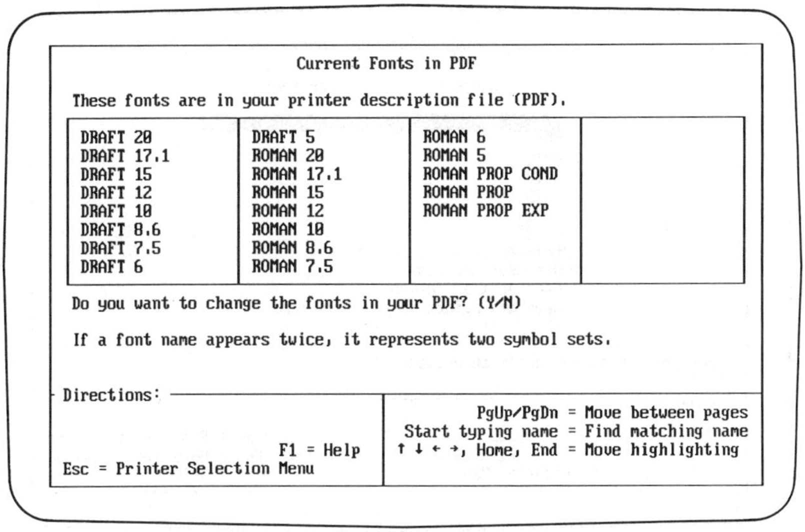
Current Fonts in PDF

These fonts are in your printer description file (PDF).

DRAFT 20	DRAFT 5	ROMAN 6	
DRAFT 17.1	ROMAN 20	ROMAN 5	
DRAFT 15	ROMAN 17.1	ROMAN PROP COND	
DRAFT 12	ROMAN 15	ROMAN PROP	
DRAFT 10	ROMAN 12	ROMAN PROP EXP	
DRAFT 8.6	ROMAN 10		
DRAFT 7.5	ROMAN 8.6		
DRAFT 6	ROMAN 7.5		

Do you want to change the fonts in your PDF? (Y/N)

If a font name appears twice, it represents two symbol sets.

Directions:

F1 = Help
Esc = Printer Selection Menu

PgUp/PgDn = Move between pages
Start typing name = Find matching name
↑ ↓ ← →, Home, End = Move highlighting

Fig. 11.14.
Specifying font files for the current printer description file.

Specifying the Printer Port

The Additional Installation Menu or PRCHANGE's PDF Modification Menu has a selection for changing the printer adapter port assigned to the current printer description file. Highlighting this line and pressing Enter displays a screen titled Change Printer Adapter Port, also accessed with WINSTALL and shown in figure 11.15.

As in WINSTALL, the possible port selections are five designations for parallel ports (PRN, LPT1, LPT2, LPT3, and AUX) and two for serial ports (COM1 or COM2). You also have options for Printer Protocol selection (this choice produces a menu with settings for Printer protocol, Number of characters between ETX printer control characters and Background Print Speed—none of which need to be modified with most IBM PC-compatible systems); User-defined disk (enter the correct letter at the prompt); or User-defined device (enter the correct DOS device designation at the prompt).

A reminder: If you use a serial printer, you still may have to create a nondocument BAT file that includes a MODE command to tell DOS the communications speed between your computer and printer. For more on this topic, consult your printer and DOS manuals.

When you have selected and highlighted your printer port selection, press Enter. This returns you to the Additional Installation Menu or the PDF Modification Menu.

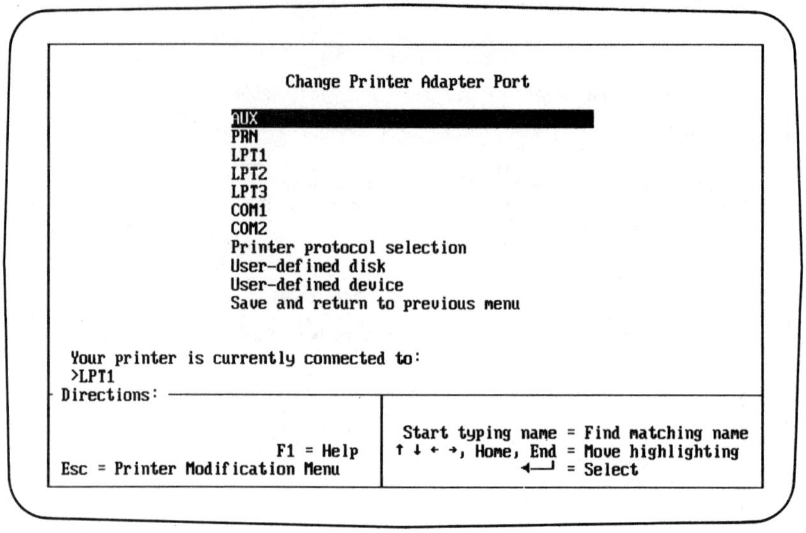
Change Printer Adapter Port
AUX
PRN
LPT1
LPT2
LPT3
COM1
COM2
Printer protocol selection
User-defined disk
User-defined device
Save and return to previous menu
Your printer is currently connected to:
>LPT1
Directions:
F1 = Help
Esc = Printer Modification Menu
Start typing name = Find matching name
↑ ↓ ← →, Home, End = Move highlighting
↵ = Select

Fig. 11.15.
The Change Printer Adapter Port Menu.

Selecting Sheet Feeder

The Additional Installation Menu (also the PRCHANGE-accessed PDF Modification Menu) has an option relating to sheet feeders: `Install sheet feeder`, (and `Modify sheet feeder` on the PDF Modification Menu.) Setting these selections is imperative if you are using a sheet feeder with your printer. Choosing either of the sheet feeder options with the highlight cursor and pressing Enter displays a Sheet Feeder Menu for your printer model. An example of this menu is shown in figure 11.16.

The Sheet Feeder Menu lists available sheet feeders; to select the appropriate one(s) you can move the highlight and press the plus (+) key. After you have made your sheet-feeder selection, press F10 to save your choices and return to the Additional Installation Menu or the PDF Modification Menu.

If you select the sheet feeder option on the menu and your printer is not equipped to use sheet feeders, you see this error message:

```
The printer you selected does not currently support feeders.

Press any key to continue.
```

Press any key to return to the appropriate printer description file menu.

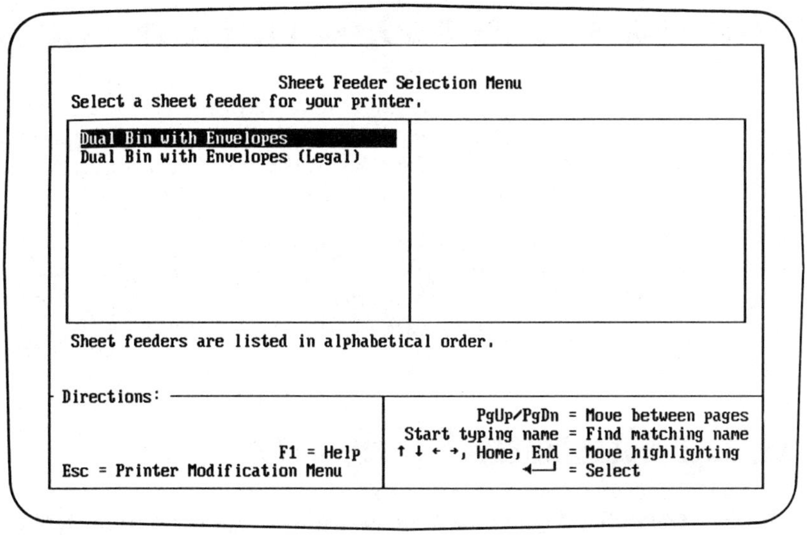
Sheet Feeder Selection Menu
Select a sheet feeder for your printer.
Dual Bin with Envelopes
Dual Bin with Envelopes (Legal)
Sheet feeders are listed in alphabetical order.
Directions:
F1 = Help
Esc = Printer Modification Menu
PgUp/PgDn = Move between pages
Start typing name = Find matching name
↑ ↓ ← →, Home, End = Move highlighting
↵ = Select

Fig. 11.16.
A Sheet Feeder Selection Menu.

Displaying Printer Information

The WSCHANGE-accessed Additional Installation Menu has one more principal option, `Go to Printer Information Menu`. By highlighting this selection and pressing Enter, you display the Printer Information Menu. This menu has four options relating to printer information for the printer description file you are installing.

Selecting the last command line on the Printer Information Menu by moving the highlight and pressing Enter merely returns the display to the Additional Installation Menu—without displaying printer information.

Most users highlight the top Printer Information Menu selection, `View printer information`. After this selection is entered, information about the designated printer's special attributes is displayed.

To print a copy of this printer information, highlight the second choice on the Printer Information Menu, `Print printer information`. When you press the Enter key (with printer power turned on), this information becomes output to the printer.

The third menu choice, `Save printer information to a disk file`, saves your printer data to disk for later use. After this option is selected with the Enter key, a prompt requests a name for the file. Type a new name up to eight characters long and press Enter. The resulting file can be read as a document file.

Renaming a Printer Description File

Among the PRCHANGE-accessed PDF Modification Menu options, note the second listing, which renames a PDF. When you select this option with the highlight and the Enter key, PRCHANGE displays a screen similar to the Installed Printer Menu, accessed when you install a printer file or use WINSTALL.

The Rename PDF screen shows the name of the current printer description file and a list of installed PDFs. You can type a new file name up to eight characters long or select an existing one to be replaced by moving the highlight and pressing Enter. Either procedure returns the display to the PDF Modification Menu.

Changing Custom Print Control

The PRCHANGE-accessed PDF Modification Menu also has a selection for assigning codes for the custom printer functions prompted with the commands ^PQ, ^PW, ^PE, and ^PR.

These useful printer command options are described in detail in Chapter 7. Instead of having to reset custom print controls with dot commands in every document, you can more permanently assign default codes to the custom print controls here in PRCHANGE.

When you designate the `Change custom print control line` on the PDF Modification Menu by highlighting it and pressing Enter, the next display is the Custom Print Control Modification Menu (see fig. 11.17).

To set a custom print control, type its command sequence, *^pq*, *^pw*, *^pe*, or *^pr*, and press Enter. At the next prompt, type the corresponding hex code, as explained in the *Using Custom Printer Functions* section of Chapter 7. When you finish assigning custom print control commands, press F10 to save these settings.

Creating A Font Download Batch File

The last option on the PRCHANGE-accessed PDF Modification Menu creates a DOS batch file to load laser printer soft fonts from disk into memory. You can include the commands for accessing such fonts in your AUTOEXEC.BAT file (see Chapter 4) at start-up or in a separate BAT file. Run the separate file by typing its name at the DOS prompt or by automatically invoking it from AUTOEXEC.BAT.

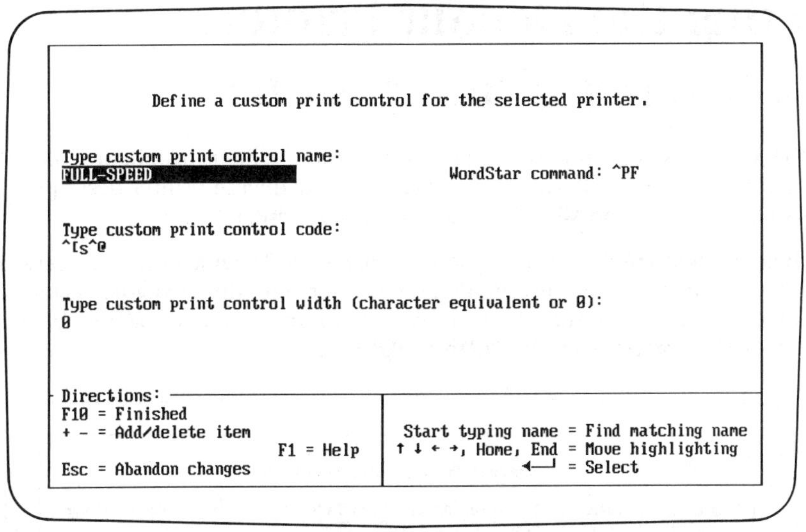
Define a custom print control for the selected printer.
Type custom print control name:
FULL-SPEED
WordStar command: ^PF
Type custom print control code:
^[s^@
Type custom print control width (character equivalent or 0):
0
Directions:
F10 = Finished
+ - = Add/delete item
F1 = Help
Esc = Abandon changes
Start typing name = Find matching name
↑ ↓ ← →, Home, End = Move highlighting
↵ = Select

Fig. 11.17.

The Change Custom Print Control Menu.

If you highlight `Create download batch file` on the PDF Modification Menu and press Enter, the next screen shows a menu of existing batch file names on the logged drive and directory. Figure 11.18 shows the Batch File Menu.

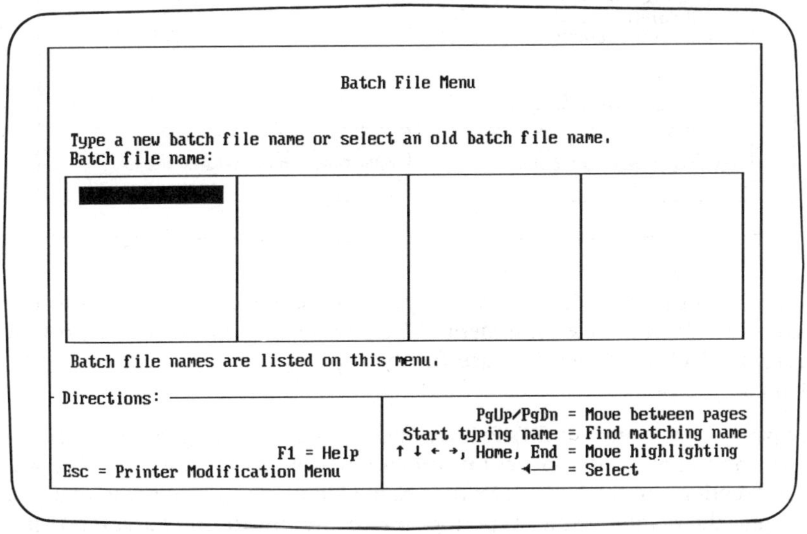
Batch File Menu
Type a new batch file name or select an old batch file name.
Batch file name:
Batch file names are listed on this menu.
Directions:
F1 = Help
Esc = Printer Modification Menu
PgUp/PgDn = Move between pages
Start typing name = Find matching name
↑ ↓ ← →, Home, End = Move highlighting
↵ = Select

Fig. 11.18.

A Batch File Menu.

According to instructions on the Available Batch Files Menu, you can type the name of a new file with a BAT extension or select an existing file by highlighting the selection and pressing Enter. The next series of prompts leads you through typing the commands for fonts to be downloaded. When the batch file is complete, you can save it by pressing the F10 function key.

Selecting the Default Printer and Changing Printer Name

Also on the WSCHANGE Printer Menu (accessed from the Main Installation Menu) are two options in WordStar Release 5 that deal with the default printer description file and its name as listed on WordStar's initial sign-on screen.

Pressing B at the WSCHANGE Printer Menu displays the Default Printer Selection Menu with the name of the current default printer and the available installed printer description files (see fig. 11.19). If more than one menu is available, move between the listings by pressing the PgDn or PgUp keys.

Fig. 11.19.
The Default Printer Selection Menu.

```
                     Default Printer Selection Menu

Choose the printer (and printer description file) to use if no other printer
is specified at print time.  Current PDF:  DRAFT

Menu 1  of 1

Printer Name                                                  PDF Name
A  ASCII                                                      ASCII.PDF
B  Draft                                                      DRAFT.PDF
C  Epson FX86e/286e/EX800/1000(Epson)                         EPSON1.PDF
D  Epson LQ-800/1000                                          EPSON.PDF
E  IBM Quietwriter III                                        IBM.PDF
F  PostScript Generic                                         POSTSCRI.PDF
G  WS4                                                        WS4.PDF

X  Finished with this menu

Enter your menu selection...          PgUp/PgDn = Move between menus
```

To select the default printer definition file, press the letter corresponding to the name listed on the Printer Selection Menu. The new name appears at the prompt for the current selection. When you are finished, press any key to return to the Printer Menu.

Choosing option C on WSCHANGE's Printer Menu brings up a display for changing the default printer name as it appears on-screen when WordStar starts up. According to the instructions on the Default Printer Name Menu, press Y to show that you want to change the printer name, type the new name (up to 40 characters), and press Enter. To accept the current default printer name, just press N at the `Change this?` prompt. Pressing X displays the Printer Menu again.

Changing Printing Defaults

Selecting option D from the WSCHANGE Printer Menu begins the process of resetting printing defaults in the WordStar program. These default settings include some print-time options (see Chapter 7) and basic printing settings.

In WordStar Release 5 choosing the printing defaults option (pressing D) calls up a submenu full of printing defaults with 12 major settings to regulate print output (see fig. 11.20).

```
                    Printing Defaults Menu

A  Print nondocument as default.................OFF          PNODOC
B  Bidirectional printing.......................ON           .bp
C  Letter quality printing (NLQ)................DIS          .lq
D  Microjustification...........................DIS          .uj
E  Underline blanks.............................OFF          .ul
F  Proportional spacing.........................DIS          .ps
G  Normal character font........................No font name
H  Alternate character font.....................No font name
I  Strikeout character..........................""-"         STKCHR
J  Line height (1440ths/inch)...................240          INIEDT+40
K  Sub/superscript roll (1440ths/inch)..........80           .sr
L  Print page numbers...........................ON           .op

X  Finished with this menu

Enter your menu selection...          ? = Help
```

Fig. 11.20.
The Printing Defaults Menu.

Option A on the Printing Defaults Menu lets you reset the print-time option for treating nondocument printing as standard. The default is Off and should remain that way, unless you are using WordStar mainly as an editor program.

The setting for bidirectional printing, B on the Printing Defaults Menu, should be On for the way most printers move the print head. For some daisywheel printers, turning bidirectional printing off can improve print quality as well as speed. Press B and Y to reset this. (From within a document, you can use the .BP command to turn on or off bidirectional printing; see Chapter 7.)

If you have a dot-matrix printer with both near-letter-quality and draft-quality modes, you can make letter-quality printing the default setting with option C on the Printing Defaults Menu. The default setting for WordStar Release 5 is for near-letter-quality printing to be discretionary (DIS) according to the printer description file. To change the setting, press Y. The default setting can be set to On (keeping letter-quality on throughout a document) or Off (toggling on draft mode). From within a document, you can change print modes by embedding the .LQ command.

On the Printing Defaults Menu, the D option is set at DIS for discretionary, leaving the decision to invoke microjustification to the printer description file. At times, however, you may want to make this decision yourself. For example, on an Epson MX-80, microjustified printing can be noticeably slow. If you press D followed by Y at the Change this? (Y/N) prompt, you can turn microjustification definitely on, definitely off, or leave the decision to the printer description file. (From within a document, microjustification can be turned on or off with the .UJ dot command.)

If you prefer that the blanks between underlined words be underlined, select E from the Printing Defaults Menu. The current default setting is Off, as in standard manuscript form. By pressing Y at the change prompt, you can opt for the On setting—ensuring that everything between ^PS markers is underlined.

5 To toggle proportional spacing on or off, choose the F option on the Printing Defaults Menu. WordStar Release 5 is supplied with the default setting at DIS, for discretionary according to settings in the printer description file. Pressing F displays a prompt for setting proportional spacing on or off. (From within a document, you can control proportional spacing with the .PS command.)

5 In WordStar Release 5 the Printing Defaults Menu includes settings for default normal and alternate fonts to be invoked by ^PN and ^PA commands (see Chapter 7). The WordStar Release 5 default settings are for character widths of 0.10 inches and 0.8 inches, respectively. You can change font names by pressing H or I and responding with a new name at the prompt.

The strikeout character invoked by the ^PX command is currently a hyphen (-). You can choose another character by selecting G from Printing Defaults Menu #1. At the change prompt, press Y, and then type the strikeout character you prefer. You might want to choose a slash (/), an asterisk (*), or a vertical bar (¦) for your strikeout application.

The next two items on the Printing Defaults Menu are related. The J setting is for line height, and the K option is for subscript and superscript roll choices. Possible settings for these options are discussed in Chapters 6 and 7, respectively.

With the L option on the Printing Defaults Menu you can turn off page numbering as a default setting—without resorting to a dot command at the top of every document to omit page numbers. Pressing L and responding with *y* at the prompt switches the default for printing page numbers from on to off.

When you have finished customizing the settings on either Printing Defaults Menu, pressing X redisplays the WSCHANGE Printer Menu.

Changing Printer Interface Settings

An era of standardized printers and 100 percent IBM PC- or PS/2-compatible computers has rendered superfluous many of the printer interface options available with option E on the Printer Menu. The Printer Interface Menu includes three functions crucial to communications between computer and printer. A quick tour may suggest remedies to printing problems.

Choosing A on the Printer Interface Menu displays the Printer Busy Handshaking Menu with just two listings. As the menu heading implies, these functions are necessary when your system checks the connection between printer and computer. Option A toggles off a "busy" test signal. You are unlikely to reset this option unless your computer is less than 100 percent IBM-compatible.

With selection B you can insert a time-out pause during signaling between computer and printer. A value of 100 instead of the default may be the answer to timing problems between printers and COMPAQ® computer models based on the Intel 80386 processor running at 20 MHz. To return to the Printer Interface Menu, press X.

Option B on the Printer Interface Menu displays the Printer Subroutines Menu. Each of the seven selections relating to special codes for older printer models leads to patching areas of WordStar's program code. If you must enter special printer codes (check your printer manual), you must use a numerical system different from the standard ten-digit numbering: hexadecimal. Patching involves directly changing strings of hexadecimal values within WordStar.

Because hexadecimal numbers convert easily to computers' internal binary scheme, the base-16 numbering system (digits 0–9 and A–F) is used for programming codes. When you alter WSCHANGE Menu settings, you are changing hexadecimal values within WordStar program instructions. The hex numbers often represent a character coded according to the ASCII standard, with each symbol assigned a different value from decimal 0 through 128 (see Appendix C).

Pressing the letter next to any of the Printer Subroutines Menu options displays a patching screen similar to the one shown in figure 11.21.

The last line on the preceding screen shows the program address in hexadecimal code for a specific setting, followed by pairs of digits expressing the bytes of data for that setting. At the right of this line is the hexadecimal digits' equivalent in ASCII characters. With the cursor at the first data byte, you can begin changing these values either in hexadecimal or, after you type a single quotation mark ('), in ASCII. To leave a byte as is, type a period (.). When you have finished making changes, press X.

Fig. 11.21.
A WSCHANGE patching screen.

```
While patching:

        X - Return to Patch Menu
        , - End of changes, redisplay
    Enter - Leave current byte unchanged; advance to next location
        ' - Enter the next character in ASCII

0-9, A-F - Enter the hex digit

0904 90 90 C3 90 90 C3 00 08 2C 26 2D 42 6C 61 63 6B .........,&-Black
```

Here is an example of patching a printer setting. To change the initialization subroutine—the command to start printing—select A from the menu of Printer Subroutines. For a draft printer, the program code line displayed would be as follows:

```
08F0 90 90 C3 90 90 C3 00 04 2C 26 2D 42 6C 61 63 6B.........
```

For a printer that requires an initialization string of Escape (ESCAPE), a carriage return (CR), and P, you replace the values shown on-screen. The first value after the address shows the number of characters to follow. In this case, you type *03* (3 in decimal). Looking up the ASCII values in Appendix C, you would find the hexadecimal equivalents of ESCAPE, CR, and P: 1B, 0D, and 50. The setting you type is therefore *03 1b 0d 50*.

Instead of typing the hexadecimal equivalent, you can type single ASCII characters after a single quotation mark. In this case, the string you type is *03 1b 0d 'p*. After you have finished with either method, press X to return to the Printer Interface Menu.

The Printer Interface Menu's option C displays a Background Printing Menu with just two functions displayed—again for vintage printers. The A selection on the Background Printing Menu turns off concurrent printing; you may have to do this if you are having problems with a non-IBM PC-compatible system. The B option seldom needs to be reset to Off.

Pressing X at the Printer Interface Menu displays the WSCHANGE Printer Menu. When you have completed all your printer settings, press X to return to the Main Installation Menu.

Changing Computer Defaults

The C option on the WSCHANGE Main Installation Menu leads to changing hardware-related WordStar settings. These settings affect essential operations such as disk drive allocations, memory usage, file names, and directory search paths.

When you type *c* at the Main Installation Menu, you see the Computer Menu, shown in figure 11.22. This menu lists seven major system options, three of which include screens seen in the WINSTALL program.

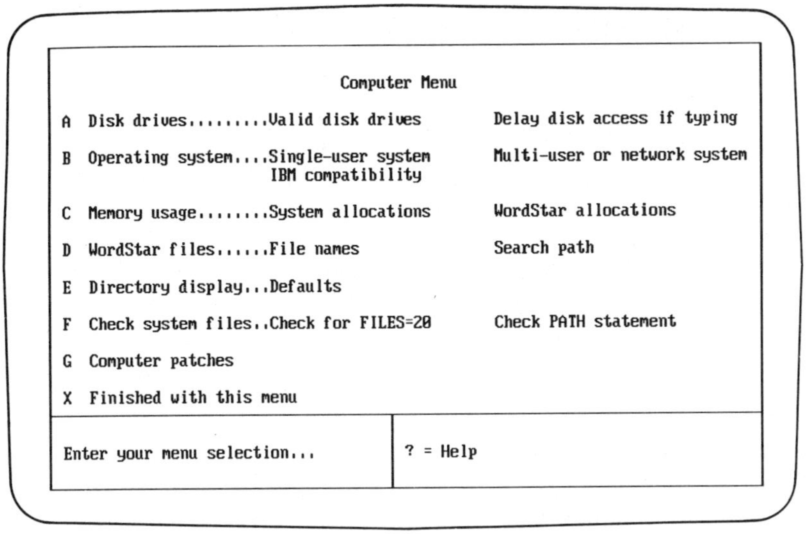
Computer Menu
A Disk drives.........Valid disk drives
Delay disk access if typing
B Operating system....Single-user system
IBM compatibility
Multi-user or network system
C Memory usage........System allocations
WordStar allocations
D WordStar files......File names
Search path
E Directory display...Defaults
F Check system files..Check for FILES=20
Check PATH statement
G Computer patches
X Finished with this menu
Enter your menu selection...
? = Help

Fig. 11.22.
The WSCHANGE Computer Menu.

Pressing A at the Computer Menu calls up a brief menu of selections regarding disk drives:

```
A Valid disk drives
B Delay disk access if typing
```

Option A on the Disk Drives Menu displays a screen titled `Disk Drives on Your Computer`. Reset drive settings here if you did not properly specify disk drives (path and type) with WINSTALL, or if you are changing your system configuration. First, press Y at the change prompt. Then type the letter designating the default drive and type the letters for any other drives, noting whether the drive is a floppy or hard drive. When you finish, press Enter, N, and X to return to the Computer Menu.

Option B on the Disk Drives Menu is unnecessary with IBM-compatible systems.

Selecting B from the Computer Menu takes you to an Operating System Menu with three selections:

```
A Single user system
B Multi-user or network system
C IBM compatibility
```

The first two selections lead to screens that are identical to screens in the WINSTALL program (see Chapter 2). The third choice brings up a menu of settings that are adjusted automatically when you make in the WSCHANGE area changes related to IBM compatibility for monitors.

Regulating Memory Usage

In WordStar Release 5, choosing option C (Memory Usage) from the Computer Menu leads to a pair of submenus listing default settings for internal memory allocation. The default settings are relatively modest and can be changed for greater storage capacity. If your computer has RAM totaling 512K (or better yet, 640K), you can increase WordStar's performance significantly by loading its program files, printer description file, and spelling checker dictionary into internal memory. With these menu options, you can eliminate time-consuming disk reading operations and increase the size of memory partitions to expand the capacity of WordStar features such as shorthand.

In WordStar Release 5, Memory Usage Menus #1 and #2, shown in figures 11.23 and 11.24, list a total of 19 settings (up from 12 settings on one menu in WordStar Release 4). Everyone should consider the first 5 settings on Memory Usage Menu #1 for loading more of WordStar into fast internal memory from slower disk storage. Users who have room for more memory chips in their computers owe it to themselves to increase their systems' internal storage to take fuller advantage of WordStar Release 5.

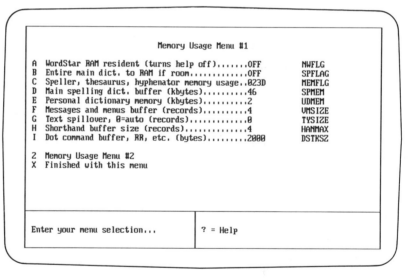

Fig. 11.23.

Memory Usage Menu #1.

```
                         Memory Usage Menu #1

A  WordStar RAM resident (turns help off).......OFF          NWFLG
B  Entire main dict. to RAM if room.............OFF          SPFLAG
C  Speller, thesaurus, hyphenator memory usage..023D         MEMFLG
D  Main spelling dict. buffer (kbytes)..........46           SPMEM
E  Personal dictionary memory (kbytes)..........2            UDMEM
F  Messages and menus buffer (records)..........4            VMSIZE
G  Text spillover, 0=auto (records).............0            TYSIZE
H  Shorthand buffer size (records)..............4            HANMAX
I  Dot command buffer, RR, etc. (bytes).........2000         DSTKSZ

2  Memory Usage Menu #2
X  Finished with this menu

Enter your menu selection...          ? = Help
```

Choosing the A option on Memory Usage Menu #1 does the most to accelerate WordStar's performance. Press Y at the change prompt to toggle the default setting to On and to load WordStar's essential program files and overlays into internal memory. Making WordStar RAM-resident requires about 150K of internal memory. This is the most important use you can make of a full complement of 650K.

```
                    Memory Usage Menu #2

A  Memory allocated for unerase buffer (bytes)..500      UNSIZE
B  Memory allocated for editor (kbytes).........64       EDTMEM
C  Header and footer size (bytes)..............2048      HFSIZE
D  Memory for merge print (kbytes).............4         MRGMEM
E  Number of menu font definitions.............100       MFDSIZ
F  Number of font family member definitions.....20       FAMSIZ
G  Number of proportional space data tables.....2        PSTSIZ
H  PDF buffer size (records)...................16        LRUSIZ
I  Footnote buffer size (records)..............8         FNSIZE
J  Endnote buffer size (records)...............2         ENSIZE

1  Memory Usage Menu #1
X  Finished with this menu

Enter your menu selection...        ? = Help
```

Fig. 11.24.

Memory Usage Menu #2.

Note: While speeding WordStar's performance, option A on Memory Usage Menu #1 also eliminates the `Wait` messages that WordStar produces as it accesses the disk for program components. The sole drawback: Help messages are not loaded into memory, so you must be well acquainted with WordStar before you opt for this setting.

If your computer has 512K of RAM or more, you can speed spelling and thesaurus checks with the B option on Memory Usage Menu #1. Pressing Y to change the Off setting to On sets WordStar to load the entire main spelling/thesaurus dictionary file MAIN.DCT automatically into internal memory the first time you use the spelling checker or thesaurus. As a result, all subsequent word checks are also accelerated.

In WordStar Release 5 the availability of more compact configurations of spelling checker, thesaurus, and automated hyphenation features makes it possible to load all or any combination of these into memory. Selecting the C option on Memory Usage Menu #1 accesses a menu with four different combinations of spelling checker, thesaurus, hyphenator, and memory usage (see fig. 11.25). Choose the functions you want to have loaded in memory, but remember the limit imposed by your total internal memory. The default setting is for all to share memory. If you use the hyphenator often, choose B. To load the thesaurus in memory, select option C to load definitions with either the spelling checker or thesaurus.

The next four options on Memory Usage Menu #1—D, E, F, and G—regulate memory buffer settings that are best left unchanged for current spelling checker software. If WordStar's spelling function is upgraded, these defaults can be reset to accommodate the new version.

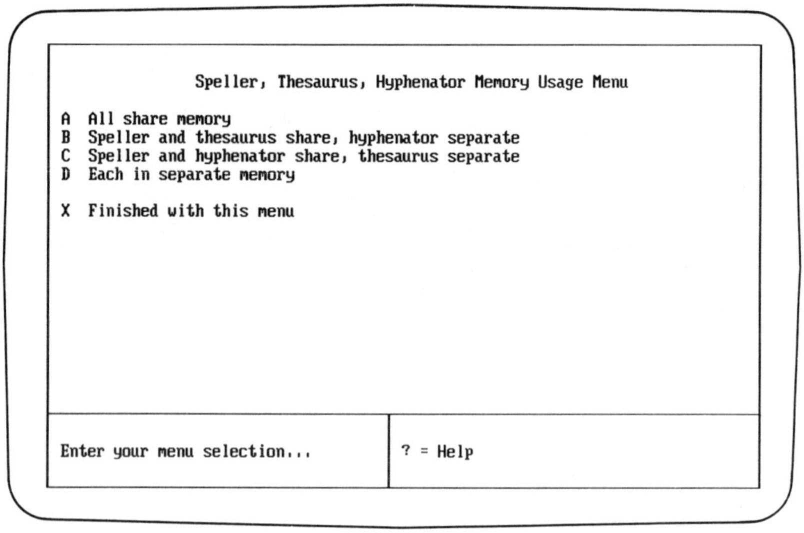
Speller, Thesaurus, Hyphenator Memory Usage Menu
A All share memory
B Speller and thesaurus share, hyphenator separate
C Speller and hyphenator share, thesaurus separate
D Each in separate memory
X Finished with this menu
Enter your menu selection...
? = Help

Fig. 11.25.
The Speller, Thesaurus, Hyphenator Memory Usage Menu.

Option H on Memory Usage Menu #1 lets you increase the space allocated to WordStar Release 5's shorthand function for storing command sequences or keyboard macros. The default setting of `4 records` means that assigned shorthand keys can represent a total of 512 characters (at 128 characters—or bytes—per record). To increase to 1 page of text the maximum number of characters available, enter a new value. At the prompt, change the number of records to 16. If you want to store paragraphs of boilerplate text, try a setting of 32 or 64.

Memory Usage Menu #1's I option lets you make extensive use of dot commands in formatting long documents. As a document is scrolled, WordStar keeps track of the number of dot command settings. The WordStar Release 5 default setting of 2,000 (four times as large as in the previous version of WordStar) can be used up quickly when stored ruler line commands are included (see Chapter 7). For longer documents, enter a new setting of 4,000 or more at the prompt.

At any time while in Memory Usage Menu #1, you can press 2 to display Memory Usage Menu #2 (see fig. 11.25). In the same way, pressing 1 switches from Memory Usage Menu #2 to Memory Usage Menu #1.

The A option on Memory Usage Menu #2 can invoke another useful modification by raising the default limit of the unerase function. WordStar is preset to unerase a maximum of 500 characters. This limit effectively means that you can undo text blocks no longer than a quarter-page of text. To increase the limit to a full page, enter a new value of 2,000 at the prompt. If you will be doing considerable editing with erase and unerase to move blocks of text, raise the limit to 4,000 or even 8,000.

Most of the remaining options on Memory Usage Menu #2 can remain unchanged. Selections B and D are set for memory allocation of editor and merge printing functions and need no resetting. The C setting is for header and footer buffers. Options C, E, F, and G on Memory Usage Menu #2 are for font-related memory functions, all of which can remain at their current defaults. The H option is for memory allocation when using a printer description file. The default setting of 16 is adequate.

With the inclusion of footnotes and endnotes, WordStar Release 5 also keeps track of citations in special memory buffers. Indicated as selections I and J on Memory Usage Menu #2, the default settings for footnote and endnote buffers are adequate for business documents and reports. If you are writing a thesis-length document, you could press I or J and reset the buffer size to a setting of 16. 5

When you have finished with Memory Usage Menus #1 and #2, pressing X returns you to the Computer Menu.

Resetting WordStar File Path and Name Defaults

Option D on the Computer Menu is useful if you are maintaining customized versions of WordStar under different file names for specialized applications. With the settings on WordStar Files Menus #1, #2, and #3, which the D option displays in WordStar Release 5, other file names can be substituted for the default designations of files that contain messages, printer drivers, and spelling checker dictionaries. Options for renaming other files round out the 23 selections (16 in Release 4) on the WordStar Release 5 WordStar Files Menus (see figs. 11.26, 11.27, and 11.28). Although you probably will want to keep most of the settings on the menus as they are, you should be familiar with their effects. 5

If you have a hard disk system, the A option on WordStar Files Menu #1 opens the way to resetting the file search path for WordStar Release 5 program files stored in a directory other than \WS5. Pressing A brings up the Default Search Path for WordStar Files screen. Pressing A again displays the Search Path for WordStar Files Menu and the prompt asks whether you want to change the current setting (see fig. 11.29). You can press Y and type a new search path for your WordStar files. For example, if you are storing WordStar program files in a subdirectory called \WS that is part of a special word-processing directory called \WP, you might type *c:\wp\ws* for the search path. You can select two other optional paths from the Default Search Path Menu: B and C.

The B option on WordStar Files Menu #1 provides an opportunity to reset the drive and path for all WordStar files. Items C through J on WordStar Files Menu #1 and selections A through D on WordStar Files Menu #2 show default names for essential program and auxiliary files. You can assign a different name for any of these files

```
                    WordStar Files Menu #1

A  Define default search path..................@B1A        DEFPTH
B  Reassign drive and path for all WordStar files
C  Messages and menus file.....................WSMSGS.OVR
D  Indexer exclusion list file.................WSINDEX.XCL
E  Shorthand storage file......................WSSHORT.OVR
F  Help overlay................................WSHELP.OVR
G  Hyphenation overlay.........................WSHYPH.OVR
H  Printer description files...................????????.PDF
I  Spelling checker overlay....................WSSPELL.OVR
J  Main spelling dictionary file...............MAIN.DCT
K  Personal spelling dictionary file...........PERSONAL.DCT

2  WordStar files menu #2
3  WordStar files menu #3
X  Finished with this menu

Enter your menu selection...          ? = Help
```

Fig. 11.26.

WordStar Files Menu #1.

```
                    WordStar Files Menu #2

A  Thesaurus overlay file......................WSTHES.OVR
B  Thesaurus dictionary........................THES.DCT
C  Thesaurus definitions overlay...............DEFN.DCT
D  Advanced page preview file..................PREVIEW.OVR
E  Backup file type............................BAK          BAKTYP
F  Temporary text file type....................$A$          AFTYPE
G  Temporary text file type....................$B$          BFTYPE
H  Temporary block file type...................$C$          BLKTYP
I  Footnote file type..........................$F$          FNOTYP
J  Endnote file type...........................$E$          ENOTYP
K  Newspaper column file type..................$D$          NCLTYP

1  WordStar files menu #1
3  WordStar files menu #3
X  Finished with this menu

Enter your menu selection...          ? = Help
```

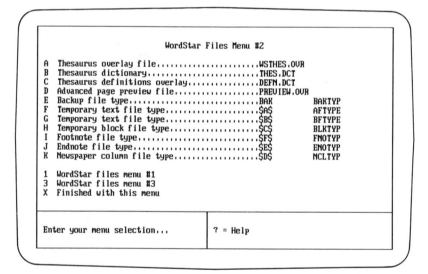

Fig. 11.27.

WordStar Files Menu #2.

by selecting the appropriate letter on the menu, pressing Y at the prompt, and entering the name you want to use. Such file name changes are necessary when you maintain multiple versions of these files for use in special word processing applications.

```
                  WordStar Files Menu #3

A  Make backup files when saving................ON          INIBAK
B  Messages buffer size (records)...............4           VMSIZE

1  WordStar files menu #1
2  WordStar files menu #2
X  Finished with this menu

Enter your menu selection...          ? = Help
```

Fig. 11.28.
WordStar Files Menu #3.

```
                 Search Path for WordStar Files Menu

WordStar looks for its files using a search path.

To leave the current path unchanged, press N.  To change the search path,
press Y and type the location of your program files (don't include the
drive letter.)

For search path 1, for example, you might type \WS5 to indicate where all
your WordStar files are located.  For search path 2, you might type the
location of your printer files, \WS5\PRINTER, and so on.

Currently: \WS5

Do you want to change this? (Y/N)
```

Fig. 11.29.
The WSCHANGE Search Path for WordStar Files Menu.

From WordStar Files Menu #1, pressing 2 displays WordStar Files Menu #2 (see fig. 11.27) and pressing 3 brings up WordStar Files Menu #3 (see fig. 11.28). Likewise, when WordStar Files Menu #2 or WordStar Files Menu #3 is displayed, you can press the appropriate number to display another WordStar Files Menu.

Options E through J on WordStar Files Menu #2 can change the file name extensions identifying files created by your program's operations: BAK for backup files,

A, B, or C for temporary files, and—new with WordStar Release 5's note functions—F or E for footnote and endnote temporary files and—also new in WordStar Release 5—D for newspaper-style column temporary files. Although there is no need to tamper with these extensions, any three-letter extension can replace them.

On WordStar Files Menu #3, item A can be essential when disk storage capacity is at a premium. This setting gives you the choice of turning off one of WordStar's characteristic functions: the automatic storage of a backup file when you save edited text. To save only the latest version of a file, press Y at the change prompt, toggling the setting to off. ***Caution:*** In general, backing up files can turn out to be too valuable a function to turn off.

The other selection on WordStar Files Menu #3, B, regarding memory-buffer allocation settings for program messages, is best left unchanged.

After you have finished resetting WordStar files on any of the WordStar Files Menus, press X to bring back the WSCHANGE Computer Menu screen.

Changing File Directory Defaults

Option E on the WSCHANGE Computer Menu brings up the Directory Usage Menu (see fig. 11.30), from which you can change defaults for the WordStar logged drive file directory. The Directory Usage Menu includes seven settings for the file directory listings.

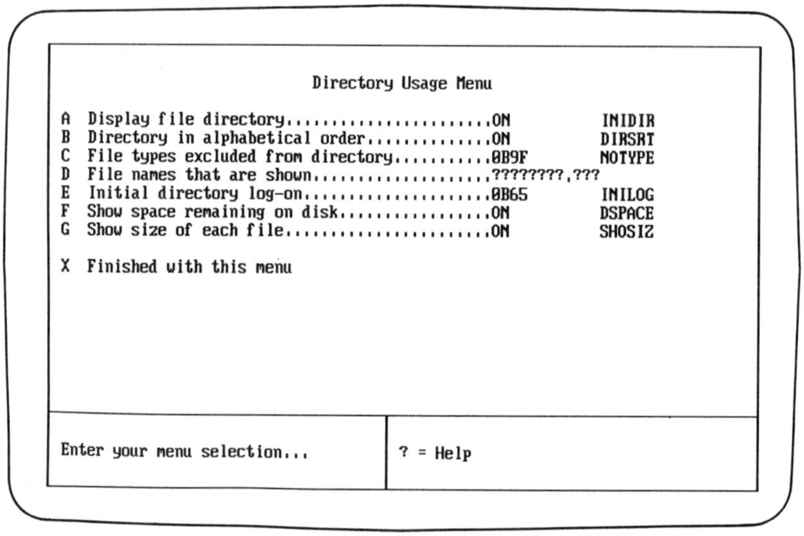
Directory Usage Menu
A Display file directory........................ON INIDIR
B Directory in alphabetical order..............ON DIRSRT
C File types excluded from directory...........0B9F NOTYPE
D File names that are shown....................????????.???
E Initial directory log-on.....................0B65 INILOG
F Show space remaining on disk.................ON DSPACE
G Show size of each file.......................ON SHOSIZ
X Finished with this menu
Enter your menu selection...
? = Help

Fig. 11.30.
The Directory Usage Menu.

Select item A on the Directory Usage Menu if you don't want to have the file directory displayed when you are using WordStar. Although few users prefer this option, you can, nonetheless, toggle from the default setting of On to Off by pressing Y at the `Change ON to OFF? (Y/N)` prompt.

Option B on the Directory Usage Menu lets you turn on and off the alphabetical order of WordStar's file directory listings. The current default setting is On. With the default Off, files are listed in order according to when they were saved to disk. If you prefer that setting, press B, followed by Y at the `Change ON to OFF? (Y/N)` prompt.

With the Directory Usage Menu's C option, you can include on the logged disk drive's current directory certain file names not ordinarily shown by WordStar Release 5. The default setting excludes all file names ending with extensions of COM, EXE, OVR, $?$, $?W, SYS, DCT, CRT, and LCF. All these file extensions are used in WordStar, so none of them should be assigned to document files. If you want to see the names and lengths of some or all of these program and utility files, press Y at the `Change the file types? (Y/N)` prompt. This step displays a message explaining that all file name exceptions have been cleared, meaning that every file is to be displayed. Press Enter if you no longer want to exclude any file names from the directories. Or type the extensions for as many as 12 file types that you want to omit from the directory. Press Enter when you have finished with this menu.

The D option on the Directory Usage Menu limits the file names to be listed on the directory of the logged disk drive according to a wild-card file specification. A question mark in the exclusion specification matches any character at that position in the file name. The default file specification is ????????.???. You can type a new specification at the prompt. For example, typing *b???????.???* would exclude from the directory all file names except those that begin with B. This feature is similar to the one you encountered when you toggled the directory display with F at the Opening Menu (see Chapter 4).

The E option on the Directory Usage Menu lets you reset the program's logged drive and directory as soon as WordStar starts. This feature is useful when storing data files apart from the disk or directory that contains program files. If you select this option, a message appears below the Directory Usage Menu and informs you that the default is `None`, which means that the logged drive and directory are the same as the drive and directory that hold the WordStar program files. To change this, press Y at the change prompt. For a two floppy disk system, enter the new value as *b:*. For hard disk systems, type the file path to your document files.

The F and G items on the Directory Usage Menu toggle the directory notations for the amount of space remaining on disk and file sizes, respectively. Because this information is essential to most WordStar users, you probably will want to retain the current On setting for both.

When you have finished with the settings on the Directory Usage screen, press X to return to the Computer Menu.

Checking System Files

The F option on the Computer Menu brings up a screen that is similar to one encountered in the WINSTALL program. The System Files Menu screen here includes two system file test functions: for the CONFIG.SYS memory allocation file and for the AUTOEXEC.BAT file to include the current PATH for the WS.EXE main program file.

If you did not request creation of a CONFIG.SYS file with the statement FILES=20 during installation, you should do so now. Press A from the System Files Menu and at the prompt that asks whether you would like CONFIG.SYS to be checked, press Y. You are prompted for the letter of the disk drive used to load DOS. Type the appropriate letter and press Enter. A message indicates that a CONFIG.SYS file has been added or that one already existed. Type any key to redisplay the System Files Menu. Incidentally, the FILES=20 statement may be insufficient on some IBM PC/AT-compatible systems; a setting of FILES=30 is recommended. To change this, open CONFIG.SYS as a nondocument file and type *files=30*. Then save to disk.

Locating the WordStar program file WS.EXE is easier if you check your AUTOEXEC.BAT automatic start-up file for a DOS PATH statement. Press B and then Y when prompted about checking AUTOEXEC.BAT. Pressing any key after this operation returns you to the System Files Menu. This step of verifying the AUTOEXEC file is not needed if you followed the instructions in Chapter 4 for creating a sign-on batch file including the PATH statement with disk and directory location for WordStar.

Pressing X at the System Files Menu returns the Computer Menu to the screen.

The Computer patches listing, option G on the Computer Menu, is of little importance on IBM PC-compatible computers. The nine initialization and control settings accessed as computer patches have no use on standardized systems.

After you complete WSCHANGE alterations for computer settings, press the X key to redisplay the Main Installation Menu.

Changing WordStar Program Defaults

On the Main Installation Menu, the D option (WordStar) makes available a wide variety of WordStar program settings you can alter with WSCHANGE. Menu entries here lead to default settings for items such as screen appearance, margins, and tabs as well as page formatting, line spacing, help level, and spelling functions. If you want to customize your working copy of WordStar thoroughly, this area merits your attention.

The WordStar Menu, which appears when you select the Main Installation Menu's D option, is divided into three major sections: page layout, editing settings, and other features, as illustrated in figure 11.31.

```
                         WordStar Menu

A  Page layout.........Page size and margins     Headers and footers
                       Tabs                      Footnotes and endnotes
                       Stored ruler lines        Paragraph numbering

B  Editing settings....Edit screen, help level   Typing
                       Paragraph alignment       Blocks
                       Erase and unerase         Lines and characters
                       Find and replace          WordStar compatibility
                       Printing defaults         Line numbering

C  Other features......Spelling checks           Nondocument mode
                       Indexing                  Shorthand (key macros)
                       Merge printing            Miscellaneous
                       Char conversion patches

X  Finished with this menu

Enter your menu selection...        ? = Help
```

Fig. 11.31.
The WordStar default settings you can modify with WSCHANGE.

Altering Page Layout Settings

The A option on the WordStar Menu provides access to setting page formatting with WSCHANGE. In WordStar Release 5 the Page Layout Menu includes six choices, shown in figure 11.32. New in this release are the menu's last three options: regulating footnoting, stored ruler lines, and paragraph numbering.

Choosing item A on the Page Layout Menu displays the Page Sizing and Margins Menu, which lists default settings for a document page (see fig. 11.33). In WordStar Release 5 these defaults are expressed in inches, instead of in lines and columns as in Release 4. To the right of the default settings and their program tags for patching, the menu lists corresponding dot commands for changing defaults in a document. (See Chapter 6 for a discussion of dot commands.)

Press A at the Page Sizing and Margins Menu if you need to change WordStar's default page length. Page length is currently set for a standard 11.00" page; you may want to change this, for example, to 14.00" for legal paper or to 4.12" for standard business envelopes. Type the new value at the prompt after picking A and press Enter. Note that the .PL dot command still resets page length from within a document.

When you press this letter or any Page Sizing and Margins Menu selection, the following prompt appears at the bottom of the screen:

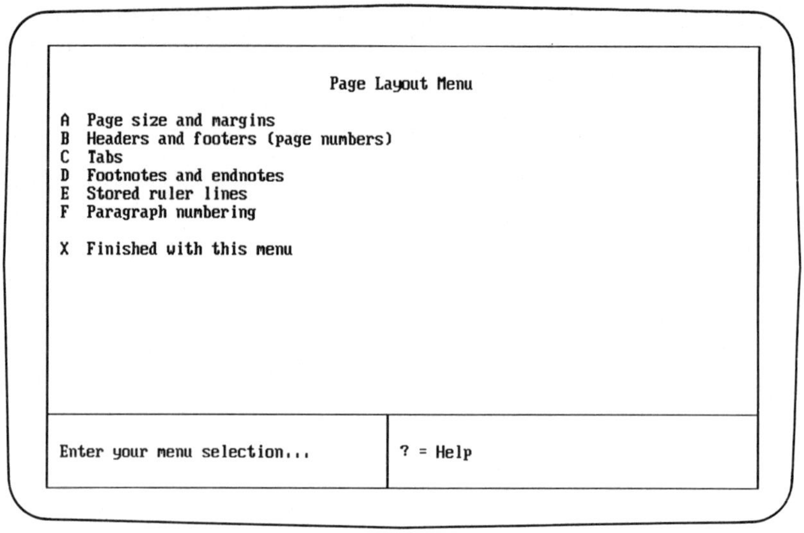
Page Layout Menu
A Page size and margins
B Headers and footers (page numbers)
C Tabs
D Footnotes and endnotes
E Stored ruler lines
F Paragraph numbering
X Finished with this menu
Enter your menu selection...
? = Help

Fig. 11.32.
The Page Layout Menu.

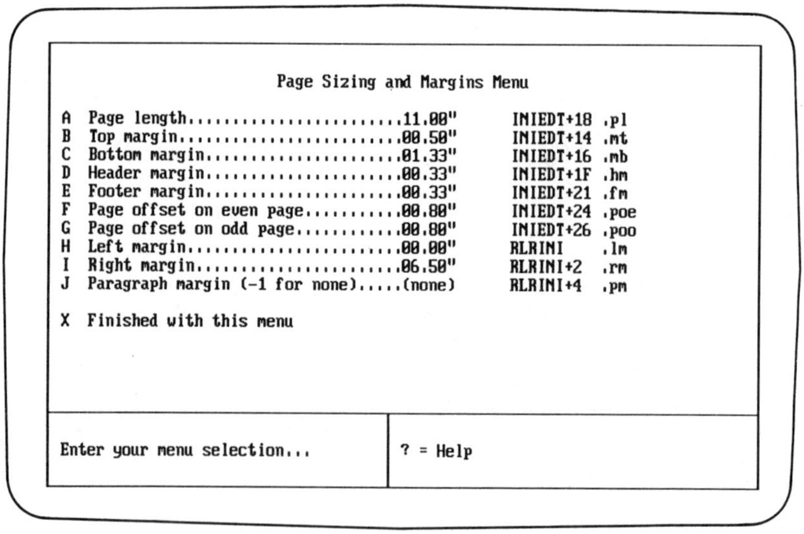
Page Sizing and Margins Menu
A Page length.......................11.00" INIEDT+18 .pl
B Top margin........................00.50" INIEDT+14 .mt
C Bottom margin.....................01.33" INIEDT+16 .mb
D Header margin.....................00.33" INIEDT+1F .hm
E Footer margin.....................00.33" INIEDT+21 .fm
F Page offset on even page..........00.80" INIEDT+24 .poe
G Page offset on odd page...........00.80" INIEDT+26 .poo
H Left margin.......................00.00" RLRINI .lm
I Right margin......................06.50" RLRINI+2 .rm
J Paragraph margin (-1 for none).....(none) RLRINI+4 .pm
X Finished with this menu
Enter your menu selection...
? = Help

Fig. 11.33.
The Page Sizing and Margins Menu.

```
(Press ↵ if no change)
Enter new value...
```

You can type the appropriate setting number at the prompt. WSCHANGE automatically adds the inch sign ("). When you are satisfied with the setting, press Enter to see it included as the new default on the Page Sizing and Margins Menu.

To adjust default settings for top or bottom margins in WordStar, select option B or C on the Page Sizing and Margins Menu. If you need space for more than one header line, you must increase the top margin setting to .83″ or more (instead of the current top margin default of .50″). From within a document, top and bottom margins are overridden by .MT and .MB commands.

You can alter the default setting of 2 lines each (.33″) for header and footer margins by selecting D or E on the Page Sizing and Margins Menu. At the prompt, type a new setting of *0.5″* for 3 lines of header or footer. Caution: The total of header or footer lines and the corresponding margin settings must be equal to or less than the top or bottom margin setting. (In a document, .HM and .FM still alter header and footer margin settings.)

The Page Sizing and Margins Menu offers options for four other margin settings: F for page offset of even-numbered pages, G for page offset of odd-numbered pages, H for the left margin, and I for the right margin. You can adjust the current default settings of .80″, .80″, .00″, and 6.50″, respectively, by pressing the key for the appropriate option and entering a new value. When you open a document with your customized WordStar, the new left and right margins are reflected on the ruler line. (From within a document, you can change page offset and margin settings with the .PO, .LM, and .RM commands.)

If you would like WordStar to indent the first line of a paragraph automatically, select option J on the Page Sizing and Margins Menu. The default setting of 0 withholds paragraph indentation. To create an automatic indentation, enter the value (in inches) of the indentation—usually .30″ or .50″. (From within a document, you also can indent a paragraph with the .PM command.)

When you finish making changes at the Page Sizing and Margins Menu, press X to return to the Page Layout Menu.

The second selection on the WSCHANGE Page Layout Menu—`B Headers and footers`—brings up the following Header and Footers Menus, with three settings, including the following page numbering specifications:

```
A Print page numbers............................ON      .op
B Position of page number (-1 = center)....(center)    .pc
C Initial page number............................1     .pn
```

By selecting item A on the Header and Footer Menu, you can turn off the default printing of page numbers. If you change this default, you don't have to use the .OP dot command within a document. If you want to omit page numbers, press A and then press Y at the `Change ON to OFF? (Y/N)` prompt.

You can use the B option on the Header and Footer Menu to adjust the column position where page numbers are printed. You can alter the current default setting of a centered position by pressing B and entering a new value in inches. From within a document, you can adjust the location of page numbering with the .PC command.

Pressing option C on the Header and Footer Menu resets page numbering to begin with a number other than the default setting of 1. At the prompt, type the new beginning page number, and press Enter. Page numbering within a document is regulated by the .PN command.

When you have finished with the Header and Footer Menu, press X to bring back the Page Layout Menu.

The Page Layout Menu's option C leads to another menu with two selections for tab settings:

```
A Regular tab stops
B Decimal tab stops
```

The procedure for setting the default values for both kinds of tab stops is similar. In WordStar Release 5, pressing A displays the following information for regular tab stops (expressed in inches, instead of in column numbers as in WordStar Release 4):

```
Tab stops:
00.50", 01.00", 01.50", 02.00", 02.50", 03.00", 03.50", 04.00",
04.50", 05.00", 05.50"

Do you want to change this? (Y/N)
```

To change these default tab settings, press Y. Another message appears on-screen:

```
The current tab stops have been cleared. Enter the new tab
stops one at a time below.

Type tab settings in inches (press ↵ when done):
```

On this screen, you can type each new tab column setting, one at a time, pressing Enter after each. After you have entered all the settings, press Enter once more to redisplay the Tabs Menu.

Counting both regular and decimal tabs, you can designate a total of 32 tab settings. If you choose the Tabs Menu's B option for decimal tab stops, the procedure for creating new settings is similar, except that WordStar Release 5 has no defaults for decimal tabs. To create new settings, press Y at the change prompt, type each new decimal tab setting, and press Enter. After you have entered all the settings, press Enter once again.

At the Tabs screen, press X to return to the Page Layout Menu.

Changing Footnote and Endnote Settings

At the Page Layout Menu, press D to adjust settings for footnotes and endnotes, features introduced in WordStar Release 5. Among the new menus in WSCHANGE are Footnotes and Endnotes Menu #1 and Footnotes and Endnotes Menu #2 (see figs. 11.34 and 11.35), with 18 different settings. All the options on Footnotes and Endnotes Menu #1 are for footnote settings. Similar settings for endnotes are found on Footnotes and Endnotes Menu #2.

The A option on both Footnotes and Endnotes Menus allows font and display styles to be set with three useful defaults for font name, default ruler (from 1 to 9 among preset rulers), or default color (from 1 to 16 for different colors).

Pressing B on Footnotes and Endnotes Menu #1 displays a screen for changing the default repeating characters * and ~ as optional designators for footnotes (see Chapter 6). To substitute other characters, press Y at the prompt on-screen and type your two choices from those available on the keyboard.

The C and D selections on Footnotes and Endnotes Menu #1 can be used to reset the character style of footnote attributes in text and in the note itself. Pressing C or D displays similar screens with three selections, the first of which is for `Attribute`, with a default setting of 32. Numbers represent typestyles according to the following code: 8 for underline, 16 for subscript, 32 for superscript, 64 for bold, or 128 for italic. You can change from the default superscript setting to one of the other code numbers by pressing A at the specific Reference Mark Menu and entering the new value at the prompt.

```
                    Footnotes and Endnotes Menu #1

A  Footnote font and style......................158A        FNFONT
B  Footnote repeating character table...........159C        FNRCH
C  Footnote reference mark in text..............15AF        FNTXT
D  Footnote reference mark in note..............15B9        FNTXT+0A
E  Footnote tag type............................159A        FNTYP
F  Footnote separator...........................15BF        FNSEP
G  Footnote continuation text...................1688        FNCNTU
H  Footnote position............................0           FNPOSN
I  Running footnote format......................8           FNRUN
J  Footnote VMI lines...........................174E        FNVMI
K  Footnote file type...........................$F$         FNOTYP
L  Footnote buffer size (records)...............8           FNSIZE

2  Footnote and Endnote Menu #2
X  Finished with this menu

Enter your menu selection...          ? = Help
```

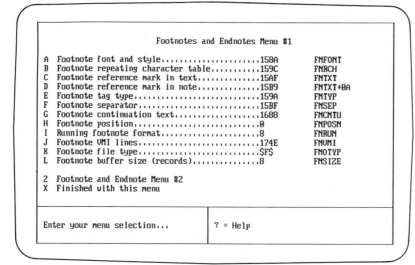

Fig. 11.34.

Footnotes and Endnotes Menu #1.

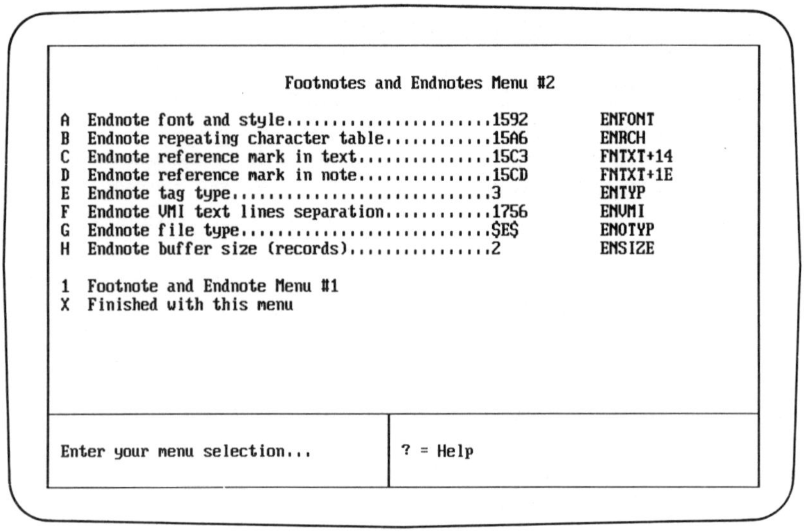
Footnotes and Endnotes Menu #2
A Endnote font and style.......................1592 ENFONT
B Endnote repeating character table............15A6 ENRCH
C Endnote reference mark in text...............15C3 FNTXT+14
D Endnote reference mark in note...............15CD FNTXT+1E
E Endnote tag type.............................3 ENTYP
F Endnote VMI text lines separation............1756 ENVMI
G Endnote file type............................E ENOTYP
H Endnote buffer size (records)................2 ENSIZE
1 Footnote and Endnote Menu #1
X Finished with this menu
Enter your menu selection...
? = Help

Fig. 11.35.
Footnotes and Endnotes Menu #2.

You can choose the E option on Footnotes and Endnotes Menu #1 if you want to alter the tags used for footnotes. Pressing E produces the Footnote Tag Type Menu, with two listings. The A option is for the type of reference mark, currently 3 for alphabetical tags. Set this to 1 to invoke repeating character tags or to 2 for number tags. With the B selection at the Footnote Tag Type Menu you can change the default setting (0) of tags increasing in value throughout a document; the alternative is 1 for resetting tag values with each new page.

Pressing F at Footnotes and Endnotes Menu #1 is the way to change the string of characters used to set footnotes apart from text. Currently set for a default of 20 hyphens, you can substitute your own line of characters by pressing Y at the prompt on the Footnote Separator Menu and typing in your preference. Press Enter to return to Footnotes and Endnotes Menu #1.

When you choose option G on Footnotes and Endnotes Menu #1, you see a screen titled Footnote Continuation Text Menu, indicating that you can change the text to show that a footnote continues to the next page. Currently this text is: `Continued`. To alter this, press Y at the prompt and type your own continuation message. Press Enter to return to Footnotes and Endnotes Menu #1.

The H selection on the Footnotes and Endnotes Menu #1 is for altering the position of a footnote on the page. The default of 0 formats footnote text to be centered on the page. If you want to set a specific left margin position for the footnote, press H at the Footnotes and Endnotes Menu, type the position in inches, and press Enter.

Footnotes and Endnotes Menu #1's I selection indicates the number of lines of a footnote that appear on a page before it continues to the next page. The current default of 8 lines is sufficient for most applications, although you may want to change this to as few as 2 lines or as many as 20 lines.

Selection J on Footnotes and Endnotes Menu #1 can be invoked to reset the spacing between footnotes, lines, text, and separator line. When you press I, WSCHANGE displays a screen headed `Footnote VMI Settings`. The Vertical Motion Increment (VMI) is a fine measurement of carriage movement in units of 1,440 to the inch. The four options on the Footnote VMI Settings Menu are for single line (.16″) spaces between various footnote format features—expressed as 240 VMI. For double-spacing, you would reset the appropriate option to 480. For finer-tuned spacing, you can experiment with intermediate settings.

The last two options on Footnotes and Endnotes Menu #1, K and L, can remain unchanged. They include the extension designating the temporary file for footnotes, `$F$`, and the WordStar memory buffer for footnotes. As mentioned earlier in this chapter (in *Setting Memory Usage*), you may want to reset the K option for the footnote buffer to 16 for longer documents like theses or reports with many footnotes.

Pressing 2 at Footnotes and Endnotes Menu #1 produces Footnotes and Endnotes Menu #2 (see fig 11.36). Pressing 1 at Footnotes and Endnotes Menu #2 displays Footnotes and Endnotes Menu #1.

The eight listings on Footnotes and Endnotes Menu #2 concern endnote settings similar to footnote settings on Footnotes and Endnotes Menu #1. When you finish with settings on either Footnotes or Endnotes Menu, press X to display the Page Layout Menu.

Setting Stored Ruler Lines

Another new feature in WordStar Release 5, stored ruler lines (see Chapter 6), is accorded a selection on the Page Layout Menu. Pressing E displays the Stored Ruler Lines Menu, illustrated in figure 11.36, from which you can set up to 10 different ruler lines to be invoked in a document with an .RR command.

Pressing any letter from A to J on the Stored Ruler Lines Menu leads to defining the margins and tab settings for the corresponding preset ruler line. Three ruler lines, including the default ruler line, are preset in WordStar Release 5; the remaining ruler lines start out undefined. All ten ruler lines can be set from this menu. Pressing any of the letters produces a numbered Ruler Line Menu with five settings like the following for ruler line #1:

```
A  Left margin.......................00.50"     RLRINI+74
B  Right margin......................06.00"     RLRINI+74+2
C  Paragraph margin.(-1 for none).....(none)    RLRINI+74+4
D  Regular tab stops.................10         RLRINI+74+8
E  Decimal tab stops.................0          RLRINI+74+9
```

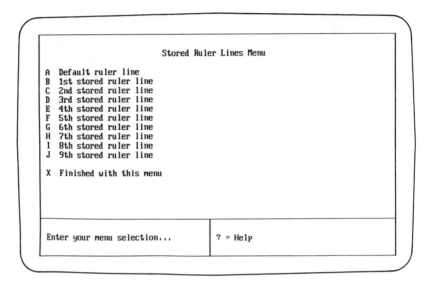

Fig. 11.36.
The Stored Ruler Lines Menu.

```
                     Stored Ruler Lines Menu

A  Default ruler line
B  1st stored ruler line
C  2nd stored ruler line
D  3rd stored ruler line
E  4th stored ruler line
F  5th stored ruler line
G  6th stored ruler line
H  7th stored ruler line
I  8th stored ruler line
J  9th stored ruler line

X  Finished with this menu

Enter your menu selection...          ? = Help
```

After you press A, B, or C, you can type a new setting for left, right, or paragraph margin. Pressing D or E displays a tab setting screen similar to the one accessed from option C on the Page Layout Menu, described earlier in this chapter. When you are finished setting margins and tabs at the Ruler Line Menu, press X to display the WSCHANGE Page Layout Menu again.

Resetting Paragraph Numbering

The last principal option on the Page Layout Menu treats paragraph numbering, another new WordStar Release 5 feature. Pressing F displays the Paragraph Numbering Menu, with these three main selections:

```
A  Paragraph numbering style...................1559     IPFRMT
B  Paragraph numbering separator at end........OFF      PPRSEP
C  Show preceding numbers......................OFF      PROUTL
```

Press A at the Paragraph Numbering Menu in order to reset the numbering or lettering of paragraphs. WSCHANGE displays the Paragraph Numbering Menu, shown in figure 11.37.

At the Paragraph Numbering Style screen, you can change from WordStar's pre-set paragraph numbering in Arabic numerals starting with 1. First, press Y at the prompt and then type any of the six character codes similar to the ones used with .P# (see Chapter 6). The style codes are 9 for Arabic numerals from 0 up, 1 for Arabic numerals from 1 up, Z for uppercase letters, z for lowercase letters, I for uppercase roman numerals, and i for lowercase Roman numerals. Styles can be

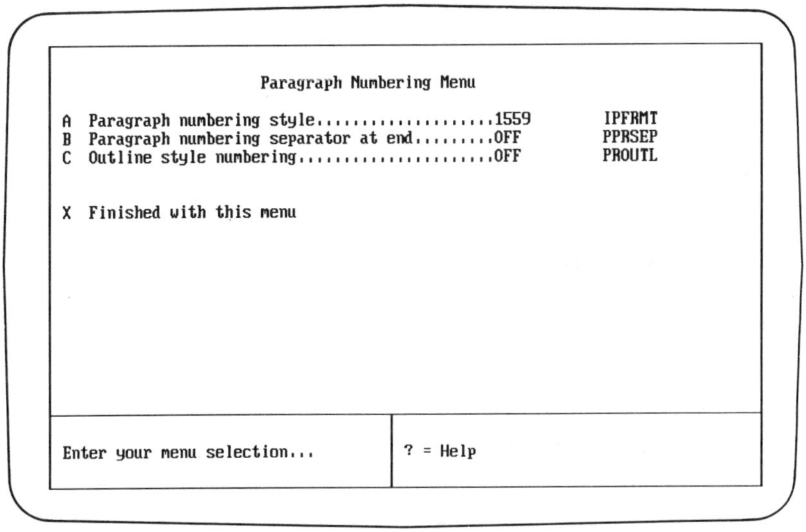
Paragraph Numbering Menu
A Paragraph numbering style....................1559 IPFRMT
B Paragraph numbering separator at end.........OFF PPRSEP
C Outline style numbering......................OFF PROUTL
X Finished with this menu
Enter your menu selection...
? = Help

Fig. 11.37.
The Paragraph Numbering Menu.

combined. For example, to invoke standard outline-style paragraph numbering, you can type *Z.1.z* and press Enter.

If you prefer a different separator character instead of the default periods, type the appropriate symbol between paragraph numbering codes. At the Paragraph Numbering Menu, the B option provides the opportunity to add a period (or other symbol) as a separator character after paragraph numbers. WordStar's default is for no character after paragraph numbers; to change this, press B, and at the prompt for `Change OFF to ON`, press Y. For outline-style paragraph numbering, you should set this choice to On.

Choosing C at the Paragraph Numbering Menu lets you change the number at the paragraph numbering prompt when you use the ^OZ command. The WordStar default is for the currently available level number to be shown (known as "outline" style). Pressing C and changing the default from Off to On by pressing Y produces "double numerator" style paragraph numbering, with the last available number indicated when ^OZ is used.

When you finish with the Paragraph Numbering Menu, press X twice to bring back the WSCHANGE WordStar Menu.

Changing Editing Settings

The WSCHANGE WordStar Menu's B option leads to default settings for the document screen, text entry, editing, and correction. The major features that are adjustable from option B are listed on the Editing Settings Menu, shown in figure 11.38.

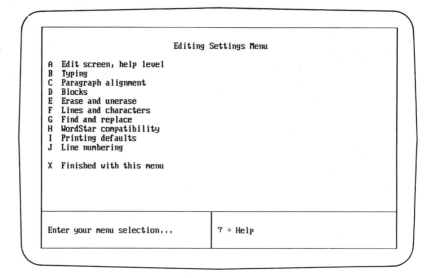

Fig. 11.38.
The Editing Settings Menu.

```
                    Editing Settings Menu

A  Edit screen, help level
B  Typing
C  Paragraph alignment
D  Blocks
E  Erase and unerase
F  Lines and characters
G  Find and replace
H  WordStar compatibility
I  Printing defaults
J  Line numbering

X  Finished with this menu

Enter your menu selection...        ? = Help
```

The Editing Settings Menu in WordStar Release 5 is almost unchanged from Release 4, with the exception of an added menu for line numbering settings. Although not all the selections on the Editing Settings Menu are important to you, each is worth examining.

The A option on the Editing Settings Menu brings up three full submenus headed `Edit Screen, Help Level Menu #1`, `#2`, and `#3` (see figs. 11.39, 11.40, and 11.41). These menus include 29 separate screen parameters instead of the 10 available in the previous version of WSCHANGE. You can use screen-display options on these menus to customize WordStar's document screen to your needs.

Fig. 11.39.
Edit Screen, Help Level Menu #1.

```
                Edit Screen, Help Level Menu #1

A  Help level.................................4          INIHLP   ^jj
B  Status line................................ON         INISTA
C  Status line filler character..............." "        STFILL
D  Soft space display.........................OFF        INIEDT+0D
E  Soft space character......................· FA        SOFTSP
F  Page break character......................– C4        SOFTSP+1
G  Binding space character...................■ FE        SOFTSP+2
H  Snaking column character..................≡ F0        SOFTSP+3
I  Column break character....................= CD        SOFTSP+4
J  Dot leader character.......................".'"       SOFTSP+5
K  Print control display......................ON         INIEDT+3 ^od

2  Edit Screen Menu #2
3  Edit Screen Menu #3
X  Finished with this menu

Enter your menu selection...        ? = Help
```

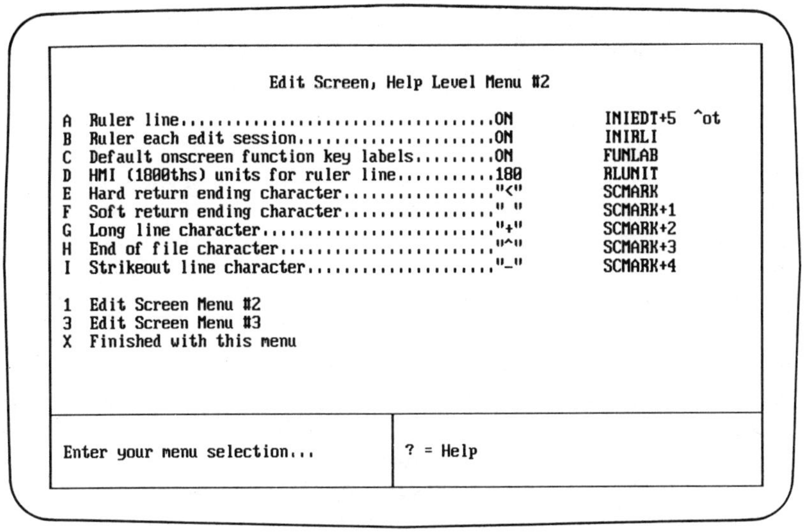
Edit Screen, Help Level Menu #2
A Ruler line.................................ON
B Ruler each edit session.....................ON
C Default onscreen function key labels.........ON
D HMI (1800ths) units for ruler line...........180
E Hard return ending character................"<"
F Soft return ending character................" "
G Long line character.........................."+"
H End of file character......................"^"
I Strikeout line character...................."-"
INIEDT+5 ^ot
INIRLI
FUNLAB
RLUNIT
SCMARK
SCMARK+1
SCMARK+2
SCMARK+3
SCMARK+4
1 Edit Screen Menu #2
3 Edit Screen Menu #3
X Finished with this menu
Enter your menu selection...
? = Help

Fig. 11.40.
Edit Screen, Help Level Menu #2.

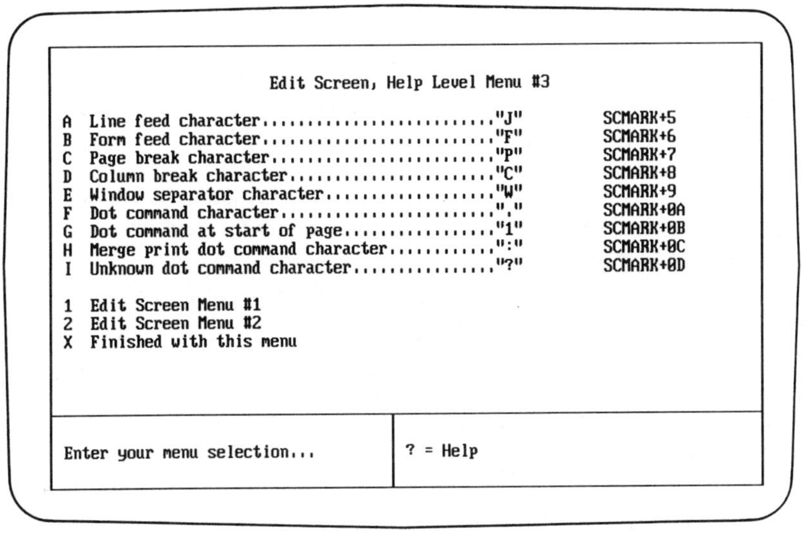
Edit Screen, Help Level Menu #3
A Line feed character.........................."J"
B Form feed character.........................."F"
C Page break character........................"P"
D Column break character......................"C"
E Window separator character.................."W"
F Dot command character......................"."
G Dot command at start of page................"1"
H Merge print dot command character..........":"
I Unknown dot command character..............."?"
SCMARK+5
SCMARK+6
SCMARK+7
SCMARK+8
SCMARK+9
SCMARK+0A
SCMARK+0B
SCMARK+0C
SCMARK+0D
1 Edit Screen Menu #1
2 Edit Screen Menu #2
X Finished with this menu
Enter your menu selection...
? = Help

Fig. 11.41.
Edit Screen, Help Level Menu #3.

Setting Help Level

Choose the A option on the Edit Screen, Help Level Menu #1, to avoid changing WordStar's help level with each work session. To speed up editing, you should reset the default help level setting as soon as you advance beyond beginner level 4, with its pull-down menus. At the prompt, change the default by entering 3 or 2 to display all or most of WordStar's classic menus. Then press Enter. If you are an advanced user, select level 1 or 0 (to display few help menus) and press Enter. (From within WordStar, you can change the help level with J at the Opening Menu or with ^JJ or by pressing F1 twice while you are editing.)

Two options for WordStar's status line are next on Edit Screen, Help Level Menu #1. Option B toggles the display of the status line—from a default of On to Off. ***Note:*** For most purposes, status line information is too important to turn off. If you press C, you can set something other than blank spaces between the letters and numbers on the status line. You can alter this arrangement by typing another character, such as a hyphen or asterisk. (Use this option sparingly; it could clutter your status line display.)

Options D and E on Edit Screen, Help Level Menu #1 deal with soft space display, WordStar's insertion of marker characters where text is indented or differs in some other way from standard formatting. When you installed WordStar with the WINSTALL program, you had the option of turning on soft character display. If you did not do so then, you can do it now by pressing D, and at the change prompt, press Y to toggle the default setting from Off to On. The character displayed for each soft space is a dot. Pressing E, typing a different character, and then pressing Enter causes the new character to be displayed for soft spaces.

Extending customization of screen appearance during editing, WordStar Release 5 includes a variety of on-screen attribute characters that can be reset with WSCHANGE. Options F through J on Edit Screen, Help Level Menu #1 are settings for the characters used by WordStar to show page breaks, binding spaces, snaking columns, column breaks, and dot leaders. To change an indicator character, press the appropriate on-screen letter, type the new character, and press Enter. Ordinarily, you wouldn't need to change any characters except to avoid confusion with special characters in your documents.

If you use many print-control commands for formatting documents, option K on Edit Screen, Help Level Menu #1 merits attention. This choice governs on-screen print-control display. WordStar Release 5 is preset for all print-control commands to be shown on the document screen. Pressing K followed by Y changes the print-control display from a default of On to Off. Some effects of print-control command sequences, not the control commands themselves, appear on-screen as you edit.

If you are working with Edit Screen, Help Level Menu #1, press 2 to switch to Edit Screen, Help Level Menu #2 (see fig. 11.41) or 3 to bring up Edit Screen, Help Level Menu #3 (see fig. 11.42). Similarly, while at Edit Screen, Help Level Menu #2 or #3, pressing the appropriate number displays another Edit Screen, Help Level Menu.

The ruler line is the subject of options A and B on Edit Screen, Help Level Menu #2. Choose A and press Y at the change prompt if you want to toggle the ruler line display from the default of On to Off, freeing an extra line for text on-screen. (From within a document, the ^OT command toggles the ruler line.)

Each time you open a document, the ruler line is reset anew according to margin defaults. If you prefer to retain the ruler line from the last document edited during the same work session, press B at Edit Screen, Help Level Menu #2 and then Y to change the setting to Off. When you exit WordStar or reboot your system, the default ruler line reappears.

The C option on Edit Screen, Help Level Menu #2 provides you with another chance to toggle the display of the function key labels at the bottom of WordStar Release 5's editing screen. (Pressing L at the Function Key screen from the Console Menu does the same thing.) If you want to alter the current setting on-screen, press Y at the `Change ON to OFF? (Y/N)` prompt.

Selecting D on Edit Screen, Help Level Menu #2 is the way to reset units of length for the ruler line and horizontal formatting. Horizontal Motion Increment (HMI), measured in 1800ths of an inch, can be fine tuned for character and spacing widths in WordStar Release 5. The default setting of 180 is equivalent to a column unit width of .1", a practical setting with which to work. Other settings may accommodate system or printer needs.

In WordStar Release 5, WSCHANGE also provides settings for characters used in the flag column on the right of the screen. These are reset with options E through I on Edit Screen, Help Level Menu #2 and all of Edit Screen, Help Level Menu #3. Though these symbols for various formatting and dot command situations have long been standard with WordStar, they are also now open to customization.

Choices E through I on Edit Screen, Help Level Menu #2 reset the symbols for text line characteristics in the flag column on the right of the document screen. Option E can be used to change the hard carriage return character (<). Picking F is the way to include a character for the blanks now used to note soft carriage returns. The G and H selection are to replace the current long line and end of file characters: + and ^. Press I to change the strikeout line character. In all of these cases, after you press the appropriate letter key, type a new character at the prompt. Then press Enter.

The A through E options on Edit Screen, Help Level Menu #3 can reset the letters currently indicating special characters in the flag column on-screen. In order, these include line feeds (J), form feeds (F), page breaks (P), column breaks (C), and Window separators (W). Any of these can be changed to avoid confusion or to conform to personal preferences.

For altering dot command symbols in the flag column, you can pick selections F through I on Edit Screen, Help Level Menu #3. The symbols subject to change are for: dot command (.), dot command at start of page (1), merge print dot command (:), and unknown dot command (?).

When you are done with making changes on any of the Edit Screen, Help Level Menus, press X to return to the Editing Settings Menu.

Setting Typing Defaults

The B option on the Editing Settings Menu displays the Typing Menu, depicted in figure 11.42. This menu includes seven items that deal with text entry. Of these items, C, D, and E are incidental to proper use of WordStar with IBM PC-compatible computers. The other four items, A, B, F, and G, merit consideration for customizing default settings.

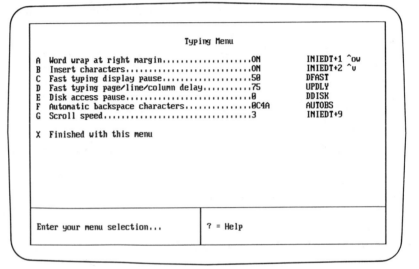

Fig. 11.42.
The WSCHANGE Typing Menu.

```
                         Typing Menu

A  Word wrap at right margin....................ON        INIEDT+1 ^OW
B  Insert characters............................ON        INIEDT+2 ^V
C  Fast typing display pause....................50        DFAST
D  Fast typing page/line/column delay...........75        UPDLY
E  Disk access pause............................0         DDISK
F  Automatic backspace characters...............0C4A      AUTOBS
G  Scroll speed.................................3         INIEDT+9

X  Finished with this menu

Enter your menu selection...              ? = Help
```

For WordStar applications that involve columnar material or lines that extend past the right margin, option A on the Typing Menu can make text entry easier by toggling off word wrap. At the change prompt, press Y to toggle the wrapping of text from the default setting of On to Off. (From within a document, word wrap can be toggled with ^OW.)

If you learned word processing on another system, you may prefer typing in overtype mode—the setting for many early text-editing programs. To change WordStar's default setting, press B at the Typing Menu, and then press Y. This procedure toggles text entry into overtype mode. (Within a document, ^V is the toggle for insert/overtype mode.)

5 Option F on the Typing Menu invokes a useful setting for a character to be preceded automatically by a ^PH backspace command while typing. This makes it easy to insert a tilde (˜), umlaut (¨) or accent (ˆ) in foreign language applications. To establish one of these characters, press F, press Y at the prompt on the Automatic BackSpace Character Menu, type the character to be recognized, and press Enter.

You can press G from the Typing Menu to add another new customized element to your working copy of WordStar: the default scroll speed when you use ^QW or ^QX. The current default is for a moderately fast setting of 3. To reset scroll speed anywhere from 0 (fastest) to 9 (slowest), press G, type a new single-digit value at the prompt, and press Enter.

Pressing X after you finish with the Typing Menu brings back the Editing Settings screen.

Resetting Justification, Spacing, and Hyphen Defaults

The C option on the Editing Settings Menu accesses the Paragraph Alignment Menu (see fig. 11.43). This menu shows six major default settings related to text formatting that you may vary for particular word processing applications.

```
                    Paragraph Alignment Menu

A  Right-justification.........................ON        INIEDT ^oj
B  Line spacing................................1         INIEDT+8 ^os
C  Auto-hyphenation............................ON        INIEDT+4 ^oh
D  Characters before auto-hyphenation..........5         HYMAX
E  Auto-align..................................ON        INIEDT+0E
F  Delay value for auto-alignment..............500       DALIGN

X  Finished with this menu

Enter your menu selection...           ? = Help
```

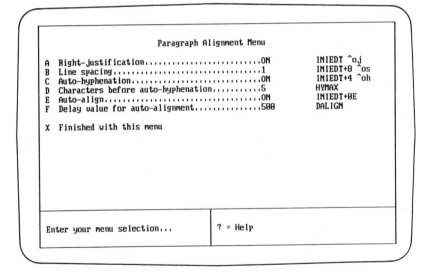

Fig. 11.43.

The Paragraph Alignment Menu.

One of the first changes you may want to make when you customize WordStar is to toggle off right-justification. To switch the default from On to Off, select option A at the Paragraph Alignment Menu, press Y at the change prompt, and press Enter. (You can toggle right-justification with ^OJ from within a document.)

If you frequently type double- or triple-spaced text, you should use the B option on the Paragraph Alignment Menu to change the default setting for line spacing. At the prompt, press 2 (for double-spacing) or 3 (for triple-spacing) and press Enter. (To change line spacing from the editing screen, use ^OS.)

With option C on the Paragraph Alignment screen, you can turn off WordStar's auto-hyphen function for displaying suggested word breaks during editing (see Chapter 5). Simply press N at the change prompt to toggle the default from On to Off. (The ^OH command toggles auto-hyphen within the document screen.) To reset the hyphenation limit—the number of characters overhanging the right margin before auto-hyphen is invoked—press D on the Paragraph Alignment Menu, and then press Y. To avoid frequent interruptions by the auto-hyphen feature, you may want to raise the default setting from 5 characters to 8 or even 10.

The last two major options on the Paragraph Alignment Menu customize the auto-alignment function, new in WordStar Release 5. You may want to turn off auto-align if you're working extensively with columnar text that could be accidentally reformatted. After you press E, press Y at the prompt and the default for auto-align is then Off. The current delay for invoking auto-align after a pause in typing is a half-second—or 500 milliseconds, according to the default for F on the Paragraph Alignment Menu. Press F if you want to reset the delay to a second with a setting of 1000, or several seconds, in multiples of 1000. Simply press Y at the prompt and type the desired default value. Press Enter to redisplay the Paragraph Alignment Menu. Auto-alignment may be toggled off within the document by pressing ^OA.

When you have finished with the Paragraph Alignment Menu, press X to return to the Editing Settings Menu.

Setting Column and Block Defaults

The D option (`Blocks`) on the Editing Setting Menu displays four default settings, any of which you may want to change if you work with large amounts of text or tabular information. These are the options:

```
A Column mode......................OFF   INIEDT+6   ^kn
B Column replace mode..............OFF   INIEDT+7   ^ki
C Beginning block marker...........04B3  BBLOCK
D Ending block marker..............04B8  KBLOCK
```

The first two choices on the Blocks Menu let you toggle default settings for a pair of related column-mode features. To have WordStar always start in column mode, press A and then Y at the prompt, toggling Off to On. If you also want to begin editing sessions with column replace in effect, press B on the Blocks Menu, followed by Y to toggle the column-replace default setting from Off to On. (You can toggle column mode and column replace from within a document with ^KN and ^KI.)

With the C and D options on the Blocks Menu, you can change the beginning block marker (<B>) or the end block marker (<K>) to any characters you prefer. Although the option may seem unnecessary, it indicates the thoroughness of

WSCHANGE. If you choose to change a block marker, select the appropriate option and press Y. Then type the characters you prefer as markers and press Enter.

Pressing X at the Blocks Menu restores the Editing Settings Menu.

Resetting Unerase Defaults

Selecting the E option on the Editing Settings Menu brings up the Erase and Unerase Menu, with three default settings, A to C, that could mean the difference between an accidental erasure that is permanent or one that is easily restored. (The fourth setting, D, may be important if you run memory-resident programs along with WordStar.) These are the menu's options:

```
A Max characters that can be unerased...500 UNSIZE
B Unerase single character erasures.....OFF UNONE
C DEL erases to left (not at cursor)....OFF DELFLG
D Erasing and cursor type ahead.........OFF AHEAD
```

The A option on the Erase and Unerase Menu is the same as one on the Memory Usage Menu in the WSCHANGE Computer section. This option sets the amount of text that the unerase function can restore to the screen. The default setting of 500 characters is for text approximately one-quarter page long. To increase this limit, press A and enter at the prompt 2000 (for a page of text) or more.

You should maintain the B setting on the Erase and Unerase Menu at its current default value, Off. This means that single-character erasures, which you can restore simply by retyping the character, do not replace a much longer deletion you might want to unerase. If for some reason you want to unerase single characters, press the key for this option, followed by Y at the change prompt.

The C option on the Erase and Unerase Menu can change the Del key's function so that it erases the character to the left of the cursor rather than the one at the cursor. Pressing Y at the change prompt toggles this WordStar Release 5 default from Off to On.

If you plan to use a text-intensive memory resident program along with WordStar, you may need to select option D at the Erase and Unerase Menu. This default is usually left unactivated, but you may need to turn it on to insert characters or erase them in your document. In such a case, to speed up the program's text erasure functions you may have to toggle the D setting to On by pressing Y at the prompt and then pressing Enter.

After you have finished with the Erase and Unerase Menu options, press X to go back to the Editing Settings Menu.

Resetting Line and Character Defaults

From the Editing Settings Menu in WordStar Release 5, pressing F displays a series of three submenus for resetting line and character defaults. Altogether, Lines and Characters Menus #1, #2, and #3 present 25 different setting options—nearly twice as many as on the corresponding menu in the previous edition of WordStar. Nonetheless, all but four of these selections merely duplicate ones encountered on the Edit Screen, Help Level Menus displayed by pressing A at the Editing Settings Menu (see figs. 11.39, 11.40, and 11.41).

The four unique listings here are the first two and last two principal options on Lines and Characters Menu #1, selections A, B, J, and K, as shown in figure 11.44.

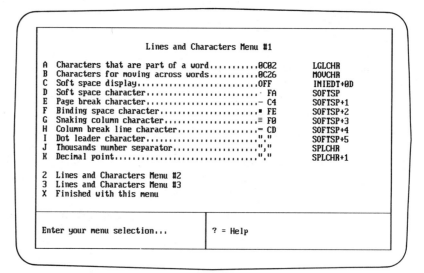

Fig. 11.44.

Lines and Characters Menu #1.

```
                    Lines and Characters Menu #1

A  Characters that are part of a word..........0C02      LGLCHR
B  Characters for moving across words..........0C26      MOVCHR
C  Soft space display..........................OFF       INIEDT+0D
D  Soft space character.......................· FA       SOFTSP
E  Page break character.......................- C4       SOFTSP+1
F  Binding space character....................▪ FE       SOFTSP+2
G  Snaking column character...................≡ F0       SOFTSP+3
H  Column break line character................= CD       SOFTSP+4
I  Dot leader character.......................".."       SOFTSP+5
J  Thousands number separator.................","       SPLCHR
K  Decimal point..............................".."       SPLCHR+1

2  Lines and Characters Menu #2
3  Lines and Characters Menu #3
X  Finished with this menu

Enter your menu selection...          ? = Help
```

To reset the boundaries of erasures within words (^T) or of movement across them (^S, ^D), select A or B on Lines and Characters Menu #1. The program displays two screens of tables that include all standard text, punctuation, and control characters; items that are considered part of a word for purposes of erasure are marked by an asterisk (*). To change any of these settings, type the 2-digit hex code that is beside the character and press Enter. A prompt indicates the character's current status and asks whether you want to make a change. Pressing Y or N produces the desired result.

The J and K options on Lines and Characters Menu #1 can be pressed to reset default characters separating thousands in numbers and indicating decimal points, respectively. The WordStar defaults are for U.S. style characters: a comma to separate thousands and a period for decimals. If you prefer European notations (for example a period for thousands or a comma for decimals), press the appropriate letter on the menu, type the preferred character at the prompt, and press Enter.

Pressing X from any of the Lines and Characters Menus restores the Editing Settings screen.

Changing Find and Replace Defaults

To reset default values for the options available with find-and-replace functions, select option G from the Editing Settings Menu. This step brings up a menu with one option:

```
A Default find and replace options
```

Pressing A displays the Find and Replace Options Menu (see fig. 11.45), listing the options available for a find and replace operation. For details on these options, see Chapter 5. A notation indicates that none of these options is currently set as a default, to be invoked automatically when a find or find-and-replace operation is specified. To change this situation, press Y and type the appropriate letters.

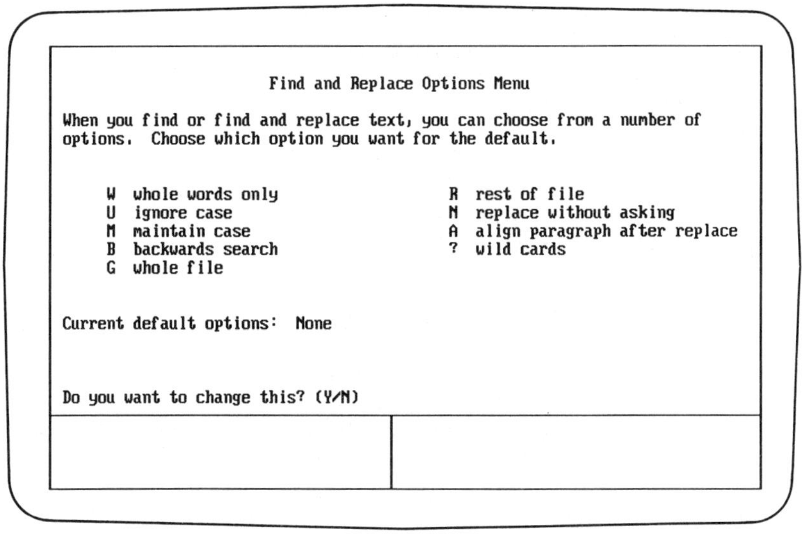
Find and Replace Options Menu
When you find or find and replace text, you can choose from a number of options. Choose which option you want for the default.
W whole words only
U ignore case
M maintain case
B backwards search
G whole file
R rest of file
N replace without asking
A align paragraph after replace
? wild cards
Current default options: None
Do you want to change this? (Y/N)

Fig. 11.45. *The Find and Replace Options Menu.*

After you make your changes at the Find and Replace Options Menu, press Enter. Then press X to get back to the Editing Settings Menu.

Configuring WordStar Release 5 to Resemble Previous Editions

At the Editing Settings Menu, pressing H leads to the WordStar Compatibility Menu, illustrated in figure 11.46. This menu lists ten settings that define some of the major functional differences between WordStar Release 5 and previous WordStar editions. If you prefer the look and feel of WordStar Release 4 or Release 3 while using the improvements in Release 5, here is where you can make adjustments.

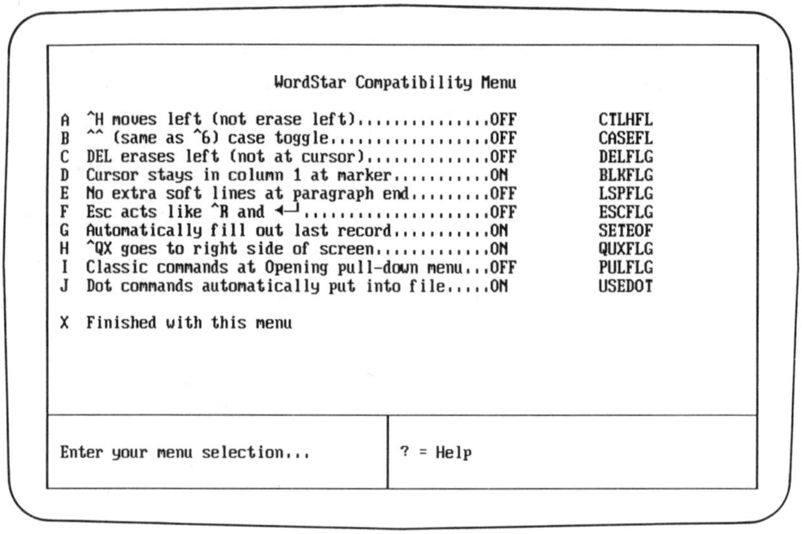
WordStar Compatibility Menu
A ^H moves left (not erase left)..............OFF CTLHFL
B ^^ (same as ^6) case toggle.................OFF CASEFL
C DEL erases left (not at cursor).............OFF DELFLG
D Cursor stays in column 1 at marker..........ON BLKFLG
E No extra soft lines at paragraph end........OFF LSPFLG
F Esc acts like ^R and ◄┘.....................OFF ESCFLG
G Automatically fill out last record..........ON SETEOF
H ^QX goes to right side of screen............ON QUXFLG
I Classic commands at Opening pull-down menu...OFF PULFLG
J Dot commands automatically put into file.....ON USEDOT
X Finished with this menu
Enter your menu selection...
? = Help

Fig. 11.46. *The WordStar Compatibility Menu.*

You can reset your working copy of WordStar Release 5 to resemble Release 4's appearance and keystroke responses by selecting options D through I in turn and toggling the default settings to their opposites: with cursor staying in column 1 Off, extra soft lines with multiple line spacing On, Esc acting like ^K turned On, automatically filling out last record Off, ^QX to right of screen Off, and classic commands at opening screen On.

To recreate the WordStar Release 3.3 interface, in addition to the settings for Release 4, press A, B, and C at the WordStar Compatibility Menu—in effect reversing all of the preset defaults at this menu. Press each key in turn and answer Y at the prompts to toggle On or Off keystroke actions characteristic of previous versions of WordStar. These functions also can be restored to their earlier versions when you auto-patch the WS3KEYS.PAT or WS4KEYS.PAT files.

When you finish with the WordStar Compatibility Menu, press X to restore the Editing Settings screen.

The I option on the WSCHANGE Editing Settings Menu leads to three submenus identical to Printing Defaults Menus #1, #2, and #3, previously invoked from the Printer Menu. You can make any changes here that you didn't make earlier.

The last major option on the Editing Settings Menu, J, displays the Line Numbering Menu, depicted in figure 11.47. This menu includes eight different settings for line numbering, another new feature in WordStar Release 5.

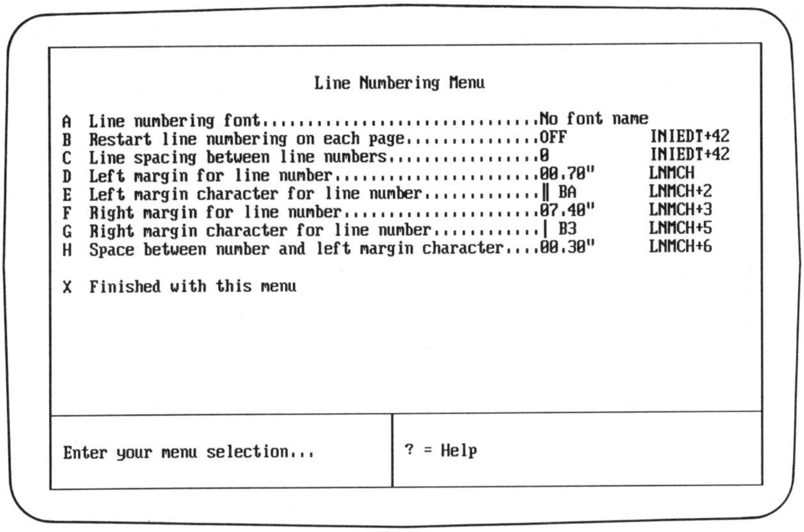
Line Numbering Menu
A Line numbering font..............................No font name
B Restart line numbering on each page..............OFF INIEDT+42
C Line spacing between line numbers................0 INIEDT+42
D Left margin for line number......................00.70" LNMCH
E Left margin character for line number............‖ BA LNMCH+2
F Right margin for line number.....................07.40" LNMCH+3
G Right margin character for line number...........| B3 LNMCH+5
H Space between number and left margin character...00.30" LNMCH+6
X Finished with this menu
Enter your menu selection...
? = Help

Fig. 11.47.
The Line Numbering Menu.

By pressing A, you can specify the font invoked for numbering. Option B of the Line Numbering Menu can be used to change the numbering of lines in a document. The current default increases line numbers from the beginning to the end of a file. If you press Y at the prompt, you can toggle Off to On and cause line numbering to restart with each page of a document.

Choose C at the Line Numbering Menu if you want to increase spacing between line numbers. The 0 setting is for no line spaces to be added to the default single-spacing. You can add line spaces to the default text line spacing by pressing C, typing your choice at the prompt, and pressing Enter.

The Line Numbering Menu's D, E, F, G, and H options are for positioning line numbers and specifying characters at the left and right to frame them on the page. The defaults set line number positioning and framing characters in accord with the appearance of a legal pleading paper. To change positioning of left or right margins for line numbers, press D or F, type a new margin value at the prompt, and press Enter. For different left and right margin characters, press E or G, specify new default characters, and press Enter. The H option on the Line Numbering Menu sets the space between line number and left margin character—a setting you can also change.

Pressing X from the Line Numbering Menu returns the display to the Editing Settings Menu.

After you complete your changes at the Editing Settings Menu, press the X key to display the WordStar Menu again.

Modifying Spelling Checker Settings

The C option on the WordStar Menu allows you to modify a variety of other WordStar features, as shown on the Other Features Menu in figure 11.48.

Fig. 11.48.
The WSCHANGE Other Features Menu.

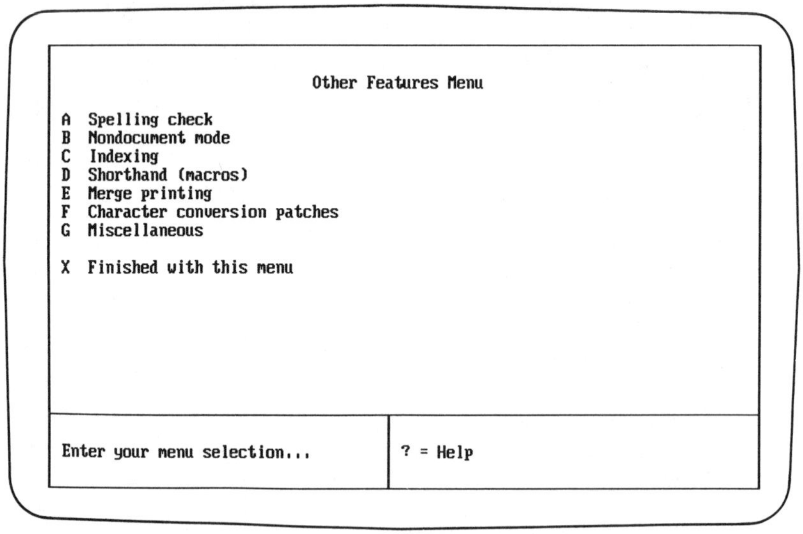
Other Features Menu
A Spelling check
B Nondocument mode
C Indexing
D Shorthand (macros)
E Merge printing
F Character conversion patches
G Miscellaneous
X Finished with this menu
Enter your menu selection...
? = Help

The first items on the Other Features Menu affect spelling and thesaurus functions. Press A to see the Spelling Check Menu (see fig. 11.49), with possible adjustments to the spelling-checker/thesaurus features.

Options A through D on the Spelling Check Menu are the same as the options on the WordStar Files Menu in the WSCHANGE Computer area. If you want to use different names for your spelling and thesaurus files, press the appropriate letter. At the prompt, type a new name and press Enter.

The E option on the Spelling Check Menu displays the Dictionary Usage Menu options that follow. Depending on your computer's disk or internal memory configuration, you may want to change these settings. Many of these items for

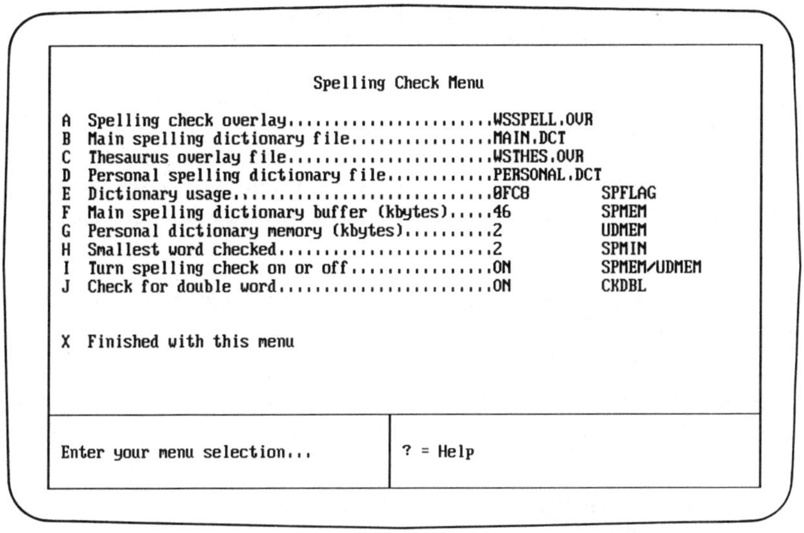
Spelling Check Menu
A Spelling check overlay......................WSSPELL.OVR
B Main spelling dictionary file...............MAIN.DCT
C Thesaurus overlay file......................WSTHES.OVR
D Personal spelling dictionary file...........PERSONAL.DCT
E Dictionary usage............................0FC8 SPFLAG
F Main spelling dictionary buffer (kbytes).....46 SPMEM
G Personal dictionary memory (kbytes)..........2 UDMEM
H Smallest word checked.......................2 SPMIN
I Turn spelling check on or off...............ON SPMEM/UDMEM
J Check for double word.......................ON CKDBL
X Finished with this menu
Enter your menu selection...
? = Help

Fig. 11.49.
The Spelling Check Menu.

spelling changes also are on other WSCHANGE screens, but are grouped more conveniently here.

```
A Swap dictionary/program disk...............OFF
B Personal dict on dictionary disk...........OFF
C Personal dict on program disk..............ON
D Entire main dict to RAM if room............OFF
E Main spelling dict buffer (kbytes).........46
F Always ask for personal dictionary.........OFF
G Definitions during spelling session........OFF
```

The first three options are needed only on floppy disk systems. If you are using standard 5 1/4-inch floppy disks, press A to set WordStar so that the program will prompt you to swap the program and dictionary disks when a spelling check is run. Press Y at the change prompt, and the default is toggled from Off to On. Depending on where you store your personal dictionary, you also should toggle item B (for the personal dictionary on the dictionary disk) or C (for the personal dictionary on the program disk). Press the proper letter key followed by Y to reset Off to On.

If your computer has 512K or more of internal memory, you can eliminate multiple disk swaps and accelerate spelling checks by loading the main spelling dictionary into RAM the first time you invoke a spelling check. To set WordStar for this function, first press D on the Dictionary Usage Menu and Y to toggle the setting to On. Then press E to change the main dictionary memory buffer, type *130*, and press Enter to replace the default setting.

Are you using several personal dictionaries or sharing your workstation and WordStar with others who have their own spelling dictionaries? Press F at the Dictionary

Usage Menu, and then press Y to toggle to On the default setting that asks for the name of the personal dictionary file to be used with any particular spelling check.

Another new feature in WordStar Release 5, dictionary definitions (see Chapter 10), is accorded a Dictionary Usage Menu option (see Chapter 10). On a hard disk system with room for the definitions file, you can ensure that these definitions are shown during a spelling session by pressing G at the Dictionary Usage Menu and toggling the default setting to On by pressing Y at the prompt and then the Enter key.

When you are satisfied with the settings on the Dictionary Usage screen, press X to display the Spelling Check Menu again.

On the Spelling Check Menu, the F option allocates space for the main spelling dictionary buffer. This option should have been reset, if needed, at the Dictionary Usage screen. The G default setting should not be changed for the current version of the spelling checker.

You can speed spelling checks significantly by limiting the words the speller checks to longer ones. Of course, you then must spot shorter misspelled words on your own. To make this change, press H on the Spelling Check Menu. At the prompt, press 4 or 5 and then press Enter.

If you decide to forgo the use of your spelling checker, you can save the amounts of internal memory that options F and G on the Spelling Checks Menu would otherwise allocate. Press I and answer Y at the prompt to toggle the default from On to Off.

Another toggle setting, J on the Spelling Check Menu, regulates whether the spelling checker's filter for double words (a new feature in WordStar Release 5) should be active. The default is for this function to be On, adding to the usefulness of the spelling checker. You toggle this Off only if your documents deliberately contain double words.

After you finish with the spelling-check options, press X to get back to the Other Features Menu.

Resetting Nondocument Mode

The B option on the Other Features Menu brings up a screen of settings that you may want to change if you frequently use nondocument mode (see fig. 11.50).

The first two choices on the Nondocument Mode Menu are toggles that substitute nondocument mode for document mode. Press A and then Y to toggle the first setting from Off to On. The On setting ensures that when you invoke WordStar from DOS along with the name of a file to be edited, the program comes up in nondocument mode. Pressing B and Y toggles from Off to On the print-time option default setting for printing in nondocument mode.

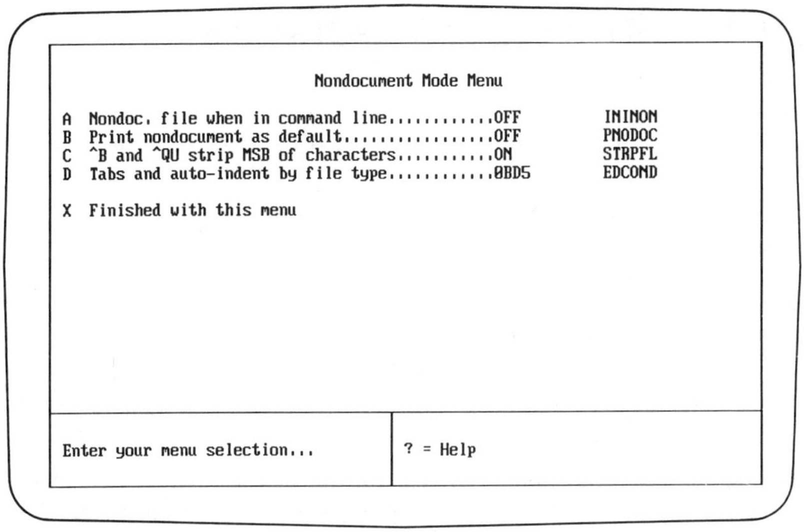
Nondocument Mode Menu
A Nondoc. file when in command line...........OFF INIMON
B Print nondocument as default................OFF PNODOC
C ^B and ^QU strip MSB of characters..........ON STRPFL
D Tabs and auto-indent by file type...........0BD5 EDCOND
X Finished with this menu
Enter your menu selection...
? = Help

Fig. 11.50.
Default settings for WordStar's nondocument mode.

In WordStar Release 5, you can no longer use nondocument mode to strip WordStar files of their characteristic high-bit marker to turn them into pure ASCII files. If you prefer a nondocument mode resembling that of WordStar Release 4, where ^B and ^QU strip out high bits, select C at the Nondocument Mode Menu, and then press Y to change the default setting from Off to On.

The Nondocument Mode Menu's choice D regulates automatic tab settings by file type and total number. Changes to these settings are primarily of interest to programmers. Appropriate settings can be selected after invoking this option.

To return to the Other Features Menu from the Nondocument Mode Menu, press X.

Choosing option C from the Other Features Menu displays a screen with two options related to indexing settings:

```
A Indexer exclusion list file..........WSINDEX.XCL
B Normally index every word............OFF
```

Option A on the Indexing Menu lets you type a new name for the exclusion file WordStar recognizes. This feature is handy if you use multiple exclusion files for indexing. To complete the change, type a new name at the prompt and press Enter.

The B option on the Indexing Menu lets you set WordStar to index every word in a document automatically. Press Y at the change prompt to toggle the default from Off to On.

Press X at the Indexing Menu to display the Other Features Menu.

Resetting Shorthand Defaults

When you select the D option on the Other Features Menu, you are given five options regarding the WordStar shorthand feature's operation and default formats (see Chapter 9). The choices on the Shorthand (Key Macros) Menu are the following:

```
A Shorthand storage file
B Storage buffer size (records)
C Format for today's date
D Format for current time
E Dollar format for numbers
```

If you want to use a shorthand storage file that has a different name than the WSSHORT.OVR default, press A on the Shorthand (Key Macros) Menu, enter the new file name, and press Enter.

The B option on the Shorthand Menu is the same as one on the Memory Usage Menu in the Computer area of WSCHANGE. This option lets you increase substantially the number of keystrokes the WordStar shorthand function can store. The default setting of 4 allows a maximum of 512 characters. Press Y at the change prompt and press 1, 32, or even 64, followed by Enter.

To revise the default date or time formats invoked by the shorthand commands Esc @ and Esc !, select option C or D on the Shorthand (Key Macros) Menu. These choices display the Date Format and Time Format Menus (see figs. 11.51 and 11.52).

Fig. 11.51.
The Date Format Menu.

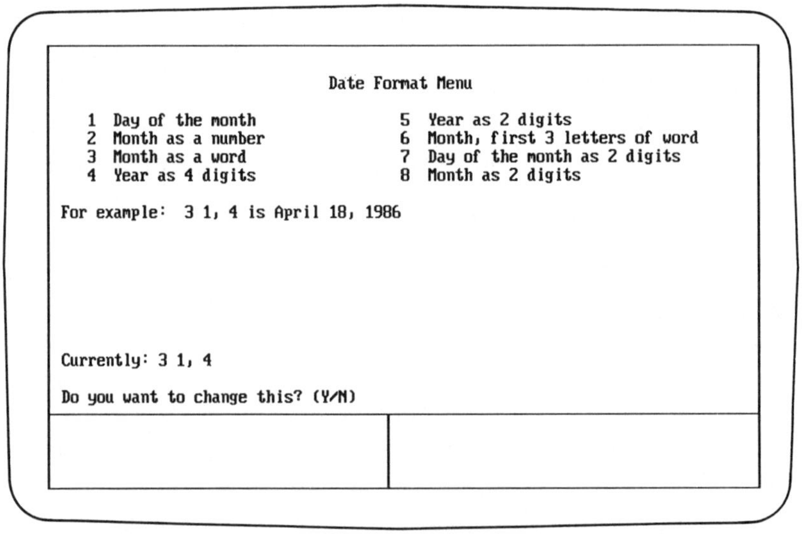
Date Format Menu
1 Day of the month
2 Month as a number
3 Month as a word
4 Year as 4 digits
5 Year as 2 digits
6 Month, first 3 letters of word
7 Day of the month as 2 digits
8 Month as 2 digits
For example: 3 1, 4 is April 18, 1986
Currently: 3 1, 4
Do you want to change this? (Y/N)

On the Date Format Menu, options 1 through 8 relate to date components.

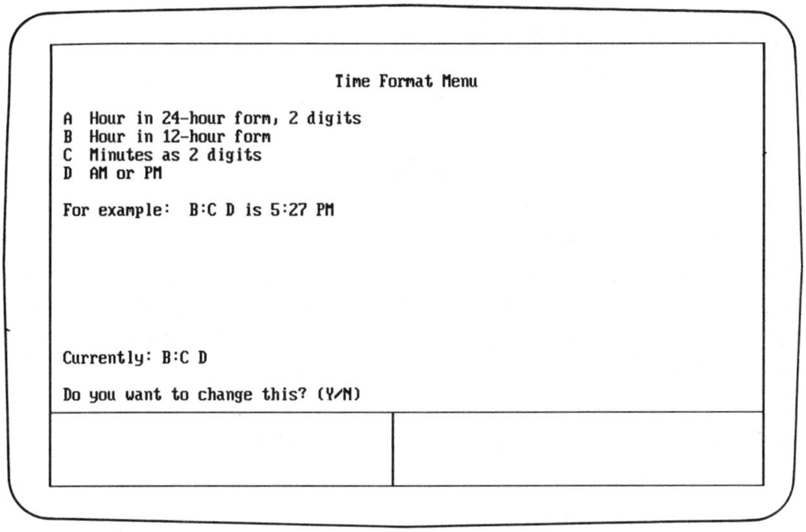
Time Format Menu
A Hour in 24-hour form, 2 digits
B Hour in 12-hour form
C Minutes as 2 digits
D AM or PM
For example: B:C D is 5:27 PM
Currently: B:C D
Do you want to change this? (Y/N)

Fig. 11.52.
The Time Format Menu.

On the Time Format Menu, items A through E indicate different time formats.

On Date or Time Format menus, a prompt notes the current combination of options used to express date or time. To change the default, first press Y at the change prompt. Then type the new choices by number or letter (uppercase only), separating the characters with the desired punctuation marks. Press Enter to return to the Shorthand (Key Macros) Menu.

If you want to alter the number format invoked by the shorthand command Esc $, press E at the Shorthand (Key Macros) Menu. This action displays the Dollar Formatting Menu, showing the default number format as follows:

```
--,---,---,---.99
```

To change this, press Y at the prompt; then type a different format, using hyphens where numbers go and appropriate symbols for separator characters. Then press Enter.

When you have finished with the settings on the Shorthand (Key Macros) Menu, press X to bring back the Other Features Menu.

Resetting Merge Printing Defaults

The Other Features Menu's E option changes default settings for merge printing. Here are the four Merge Printing Menu options:

```
A Separator between data items
B Variable name indicator
C Date format for &@& variable
D Time format for &!& variable
```

The first two choices on the Merge Printing Menu, A and B, let you change the separator character and variable name indicator in merge-print data files from the default comma (,) and ampersand (&), respectively. If you are so inclined, type replacement characters, and press Enter.

Options C and D on the Merge Printing Menu are for changing the date and time formats invoked by the commands &@& and &!&. The screens displayed by these options are similar to the screens for changing date and time formats for corresponding shorthand commands (see figs. 11.51 and 11.52).

To change date and time formats for merge printing, follow the procedure used to alter date and time default settings for the shorthand feature.

When you have completed your changes on the Merge Printing Menu, press X to return to the Other Features Menu.

Pressing F at the Other Features Menu displays the Character Conversion Patches Menu for character substitutions—an advanced feature beyond the scope of this book.

Resetting Miscellaneous Defaults

The G option on the Other Features screen displays a Miscellaneous Menu, illustrated in figure 11.53. This menu includes various WordStar timing functions and three added settings for new features in WordStar Release 5.

With option A on the Miscellaneous Menu, you can create a brief message to be displayed below the system hardware indicators on the copyright screen that appears when WordStar is first started. The message could be a reminder of the date on which you made changes and a brief description of these for later reference. To create a message, press Y at the change prompt, type your message (limit the text to four lines), and press Enter. This message also appears each time the console and printer installation defaults are indicated in WSCHANGE or WINSTALL.

Options B, C, and D on the Miscellaneous Menu provide delays during WordStar sign-on, menu display, and document-alignment operations. You should reset all three of these delays. Press each letter in turn, enter 100 as each setting's default, and press Enter after each change. These changes reduce the delays from the current values of 2,000, 1,000, and 200 milliseconds, respectively to 100 milliseconds.

Do not reset setting E (`Erasing & cursor type ahead`) on the Miscellaneous Menu, if you already reset it elsewhere in WSCHANGE.

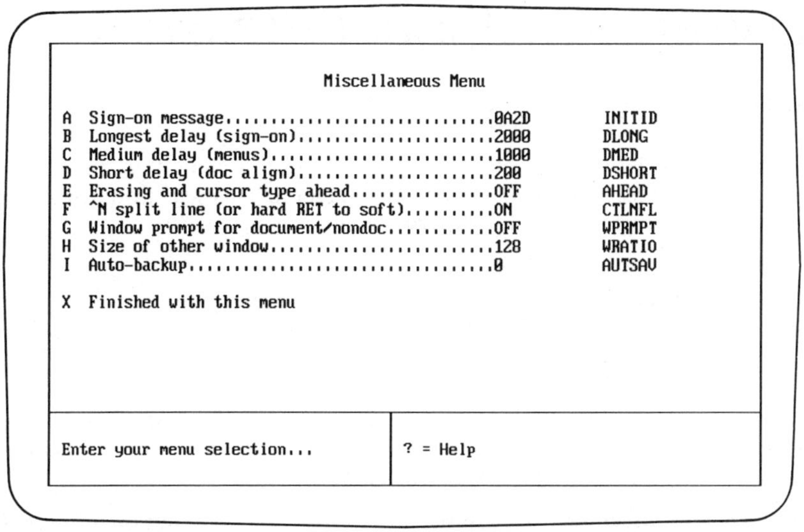
Miscellaneous Menu
A Sign-on message.............................0A2D INITID
B Longest delay (sign-on).....................2000 DLONG
C Medium delay (menus)........................1000 DMED
D Short delay (doc align).....................200 DSHORT
E Erasing and cursor type ahead...............OFF AHEAD
F ^N split line (or hard RET to soft).........ON CTLNFL
G Window prompt for document/nondoc...........OFF WPRMPT
H Size of other window........................128 WRATIO
I Auto-backup.................................0 AUTSAV
X Finished with this menu
Enter your menu selection...
? = Help

Fig. 11.53.
Default values for miscellaneous WordStar features.

The F choice on the Miscellaneous Menu lets you toggle off the ^N command in WordStar Release 5—another change you may find unnecessary.

With the inclusion of windows in WordStar Release 5, the new H selection on the Miscellaneous Menu can be used to include a prompt for specifying either document or nondocument mode in the window opened by pressing ^OK. Press Y at the prompt.

The Miscellaneous Menu's A option lets you reset the initial size of a text window opened in WordStar Release 5. The current default is for 128, or half of a text screen. Pressing 0 at the prompt sets full screens of text "paged" back and forth onscreen, while typing *64* creates a window one quarter the size of a full text screen.

The last selection on the Miscellaneous Menu, I, provides a useful new option in WordStar Release 5: automatic saving to disk of a document file during editing, at preset time intervals. The current default of 0 has this function turned off. After pressing J, type a new interval value (in seconds) at the prompt to ensure automatic backups at the interval you set. A setting of 1200 for 20-minute intervals is recommended. (This feature only applies to IBM PC/AT- or PS/2-compatible computers manufactured after November 15, 1985.)

After you have finished with the Miscellaneous Menu, press X three times, and the WSCHANGE Main Installation Menu returns.

Patching WordStar Release 5 Program Code

To make changes to WordStar Release 5 that are not included in the other WSCHANGE menus, press E at the Main Installation Menu. This selection displays a screen with four options for patching WordStar code:

```
A Auto patcher...........Patch from file
B Save settings..........Make file for auto patcher
C Reset all settings.....Original settings

= Enter User Area address
```

The first three options on the Patching Menu can be used without any knowledge of hex or patching addresses. If you do know specific addresses to change, however, you can make more thorough use of these options.

The various user area addresses that can be altered directly are listed on a file that is included with every WordStar Release 5 package: the PATCH.LST (98K) file on the Advanced Customization Disk. A WordStar-formatted file, PATCH.LST can be printed like any other file—with one important proviso. Because the lines in the file are wider than standard paper, you must set the character width to 30 by placing the command .CW 30 at the top of the file. Then press P to print at the WordStar Opening Menu.

The listings in the PATCH.LST file are given by address and label name, and these items are followed by default settings. All numerical values are in hexadecimal code. Brief explanations at the start of each entry give information on new settings. After you decipher a listing in PATCH.LST, you can access that data in WordStar with either the hex address or the six-letter label.

Using the Auto Patcher

To read in a file that contains patching changes for the copy of WordStar you are customizing with WSCHANGE, you can use the Patching Menu's A option. Selecting that option displays the Auto-Patcher Menu (see fig. 11.54).

A patch file must be a nondocument file with address listings in a standard format. The file can include operations on addresses and data values. Fortunately for nonprogrammers, knowledge of hexadecimal codes is not necessary for patching WordStar Release 5. You can read in existing files, either files supplied with the WordStar package or files from other users who have saved their settings on an auto-patcher readable file. An example of a file supplied with WordStar is the WS3KEYS.PAT file, which is located on the WordStar Release 5 Advanced Customization Disk.

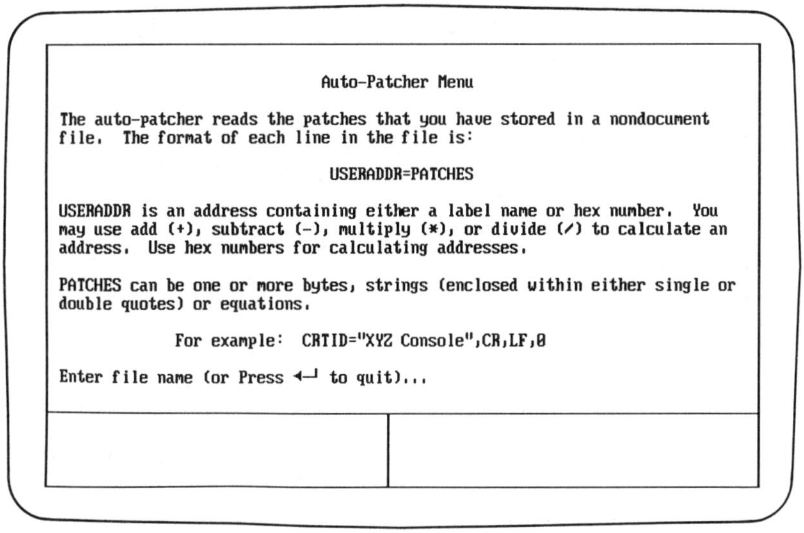
Auto-Patcher Menu
The auto-patcher reads the patches that you have stored in a nondocument file. The format of each line in the file is:
USERADDR=PATCHES
USERADDR is an address containing either a label name or hex number. You may use add (+), subtract (-), multiply (*), or divide (/) to calculate an address. Use hex numbers for calculating addresses.
PATCHES can be one or more bytes, strings (enclosed within either single or double quotes) or equations.
For example: CRTID="XYZ Console",CR,LF,0
Enter file name (or Press ←┘ to quit)...

Fig. 11.54.
The WSCHANGE Auto-Patcher screen.

To read in changes from a patch file with the auto-patcher is simple. Type the name of the file at the prompt on the Auto-Patcher Menu and press Enter.

Using the WS3KEYS.PAT file as an example, you would type WS3KEYS.PAT and press Enter. This procedure gives WordStar Release 5 the same keyboard and function key assignments as early WordStar versions. The customized copy of WordStar that results from this session with WSCHANGE would have a familiar interface for veterans of WordStar Release 3.3.

You also can save your own WSCHANGE settings in a patch file to modify other copies of WordStar Release 5 or to restore a particular customization to your own copy. Just choose another option on the Patching Menu. Pressing Enter brings back the Patching Menu.

Saving WordStar Release 5 Patches

If you want to create a patch file to save one or a range of WordStar Release 5 custom settings, select the B option on the Patching Menu. The resulting Save Settings Menu includes the message shown in figure 11.55.

To save WSCHANGE settings, type the name of a disk file on which to store the settings and press Enter. A prompt asks `Save entire user area? (Y/N)`. To store all custom settings, press Y. If you prefer to keep one or a few specific settings, press N, and another prompt asks for the User Area label for the data to be saved. (This label is indicated on WSCHANGE listings and in the PATCH.LST file.) Type the label name and press Enter. Press any key to return to the Patching Menu.

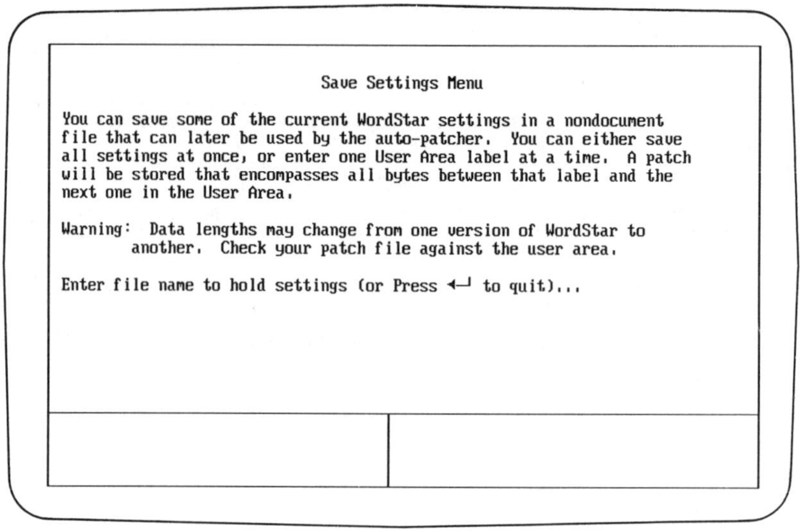
Save Settings Menu
You can save some of the current WordStar settings in a nondocument file that can later be used by the auto-patcher. You can either save all settings at once, or enter one User Area label at a time. A patch will be stored that encompasses all bytes between that label and the next one in the User Area.
Warning: Data lengths may change from one version of WordStar to another. Check your patch file against the user area.
Enter file name to hold settings (or Press ←┘ to quit)...

Fig. 11.55.
A message on the Save Settings screen.

Restoring WordStar Release 5 Settings

Choose the C option on the Patching Menu if you make a mistake or get confused amidst all the changes available with WSCHANGE and want to return to the original program configuration. The Reset All Settings message shown in figure 11.56 confirms your decision to go back to the original settings for WordStar as the program came from the manufacturer.

If you want to wipe out all the modifications you've made to WordStar, just press Y. This action returns you to the Patching Menu. Press X to return to the Main Installation Menu. You now have completed the review of all alterable menu settings in WordStar WSCHANGE.

Patching WordStar Directly

If you want to alter program data directly in WordStar Release 5, press the equal sign (=) at the Patching Menu. The following prompt appears:

```
Enter User Area address (label or hex)...
```

To further customize a WordStar default, find its address and proper setting in the PATCH.LST file and access this area by typing its address at the prompt. You see a

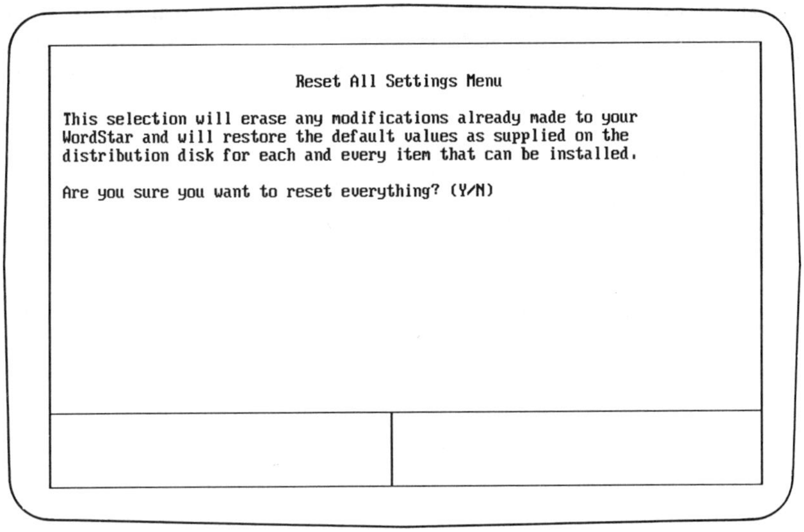
Reset All Settings Menu
This selection will erase any modifications already made to your WordStar and will restore the default values as supplied on the distribution disk for each and every item that can be installed.
Are you sure you want to reset everything? (Y/N)

Fig. 11.56.
A message on the Reset All Settings screen.

line of code that includes the address in hex, 16 bytes of code expressed in hex, and the ASCII equivalent at the far right. To edit this code, use the procedure outlined in the *Changing Printer Interface Settings* section of this chapter.

Saving Your Customized WordStar

After you have made all your adjustments to WordStar with WSCHANGE, you can save the resulting modified WordStar files by choosing this option from the Main Installation Menu:

```
X Finished with installation
```

Press X at the Main Installation Menu or ^X from anywhere within WSCHANGE, and you see a confirmation screen that displays information similar to the following (console and printer settings differ according to the changes you've made):

```
All changes have been made.

WS.EXE is now installed for...

IBM PC Compatible
Draft Printer

Are you through making changes? (Y/N)
```

If you want another chance to make modifications, press N. If you are ready to save your customized WordStar and exit to DOS, press Y. The DOS prompt appears on-screen. You now can run your customized WordStar by typing its name at the DOS prompt.

12

Using WordStar with Other Programs

WordStar Release 5, one of the most complete word processing packages available, can be made still more versatile by using it with other programs. After you try WordStar and then hear about rival programs' features, you may want additional capabilities not included in even the newest release of WordStar. Fortunately, you can enhance this popular word processor with compatible software. Functions easily added with other programs include outlining, restoring files that have been erased accidentally, displaying more text windows, and adding graphics to WordStar documents.

Many users put WordStar in their software libraries after starting with spreadsheet, database, or communications applications on a personal computer. In some cases, people purchase WordStar after realizing the limitations of slower or less powerful word processors. These new users run into problems because most business applications programs, including word processors, produce data files that are incompatible with WordStar's special file format. You do not have to abandon files created by incompatible programs, however. By converting data to an intermediate format with WordStar or by performing a direct conversion with an optional program, you can transfer files from other programs into WordStar documents and vice versa.

In this chapter you will learn about

- Outlining with the PC-Outline program included in WordStar Release 5
- Augmenting WordStar with add-on programs
- Converting document files for use with other word processors
- Reading WordStar files into spreadsheets and databases

Because you may not have all the software described in this chapter, tutorial examples have been omitted in favor of more general explanations of features and procedures for using WordStar with other programs. Programs that are fully compatible and programs that can be made compatible are covered in this chapter.

As you read about WordStar and auxiliary programs, you probably will find at least one application that is worth adding to your system. If you already are using several programs other than WordStar, you will understand how WordStar can be placed at the center of all the reporting and data integration you do with your computer system.

Enhancing WordStar with Compatible Programs

Soon after WordStar was introduced, other publishers began producing add-on software. The lack of important features in early versions of WordStar encouraged enterprising software firms to release products for enhancing the best-selling word processor. Many of these products ran separately from WordStar, but used similar menus and Ctrl-letter combinations so that they were command-compatible with WordStar.

Although critics thought that WordStar's distinctive formatting of document files was a drawback, this distinction turned out to be an advantage. WordStar's popularity forced programmers to consider its file format when they created new utility or text-enhancement software for general use on personal computers. The commands and user interfaces for the more generic programs differed from WordStar's, but the programs were often file compatible with the best-seller.

As more internal memory became available on personal computers, programmers began creating software that could be loaded in RAM along with WordStar. Known as terminate, stay resident (TSR) software, or simply as memory-resident programs, these add-ons can operate during the WordStar editing process. Often, text from the memory-resident program can be substituted within a document, as in the case of the PC-Outline program included with WordStar Release 5.

Many add-on programs are available to enhance the functions of WordStar. These programs may be file compatible, command compatible, or memory-resident compatible with WordStar. Representative packages are discussed in this chapter. For a discussion of two other memory-resident programs—ProKey and SuperKey, see Chapter 9; these programs can be used to enhance WordStar's macro capabilities.

Outlining with Memory-Resident PC-Outline

You can outline a document with the WordStar commands discussed in Chapter 6, but they don't have the flexibility of programs designed specifically for outlining. Instead of merely differentiating heading levels, specialized software can create an outline that displays only main headings or uncovers selected subheads. Other useful functions include moving quickly to headings on similar levels, sorting headings alphabetically, and isolating a section of an outline for insertion into a WordStar document.

Several rival word processors include outlining functions that let you move directly from sketching a document's outline with a full range of display and editing options to filling in its text. For word processing programs that do not have strong outlining functions, certain stand-alone software packages provide commands for producing outline files that can be read as text files. As part of the Release 5 package, WordStar Professional now includes the PC-Outline program, which can be run separately or as a memory-resident program for use at the same time as WordStar.

PC-Outline is a versatile outlining program from Brown Bag Software®. One advantage of PC-Outline is its capability to insert an outline in WordStar or read text from a WordStar document window directly into an outline. With nearly as many commands and options as WordStar itself, PC-Outline is easily mastered, thanks to its logically organized pull-down menus.

Running PC-Outline as a memory-resident program requires 128K of internal memory in addition to the amount used by WordStar and other memory-resident software you have loaded. To invoke PC-Outline, PCO.EXE (PC-Outline's program file—supplied on the TelMerge/MailList/PC-Outline Disk in the WordStar Release 5 package) must be in the same directory as the main WordStar program file—along with one of three outline printer drivers (also on the TelMerge/MailList/PC-Outline Disk: PCODAISY.PRN [for daisywheel printers], PCOIBM.PRN [for IBM Graphics printers, Epson MX-80™ dot matrix printers, or compatibles], or PCOSTAN.PRN [for other printers, including laser printers]). If your system has a Hewlett-Packard LaserJet printer, use the printer driver PCOLASER.PRN, supplied on the PostScript Files/Font Utility Disk.

Because the necessary PC-Outline files occupy a substantial amount of disk space, many users of floppy disk systems load READY.EXE separately from the programs on their working disks. When running PC-Outline as a stand-alone program, you start the program directly from the DOS prompt by typing *pco* and pressing Enter. The outliner loads from disk and the screen displays the PC-Outline Opening Menu—the same one displayed when running PC-Outline as a memory-resident program.

To load PC-Outline as a memory-resident program, type *pco/r* at the DOS prompt, then press Enter. PC-Outline does not place any restrictions on the order in which it is loaded along with other memory-resident software, as long as you place the program in memory before you run WordStar. If starting WordStar from an AUTOEXEC.BAT batch file, type *pco/r* at the appropriate place in the list of commands in your file.

After PC-Outline loads into memory, a three-line message on-screen indicates that the program is loaded and gives version and copyright information. The DOS prompt reappears on-screen below this information. You can then type the name of any other memory-resident programs you want to run, followed by *ws* for starting WordStar.

Once loaded as a memory-resident program, PC-Outline is called up from the WordStar document screen when you press ^\. This displays the PC-Outline Opening Menu, with choices for opening a new outline, loading an existing outline, or changing the drive/directory for the logged directory where program and outline files are stored.

The procedure for opening a new outline or loading an existing outline are similar. After the highlight on the PC-Outline Opening Menu is positioned on the appropriate line, pressing Enter displays a prompt for the name of the new or existing file. Any file created with PC-Outline is saved to disk with a DOS file name followed by the extension PCO to distinguish it as an outline file. When typing the name, you can use the first eight letters only. Pressing Enter then displays the PC-Outline Working screen.

The PC-Outline Working screen is an uncluttered display with a menu bar and status line similar to those on the WordStar editing screen with pull-down menus. When you open a new outline, the screen appears like the one in figure 12.1; the `A.` on-screen denotes the first heading in the new outline.

Fig. 12.1.

The PC-Outline Working screen.

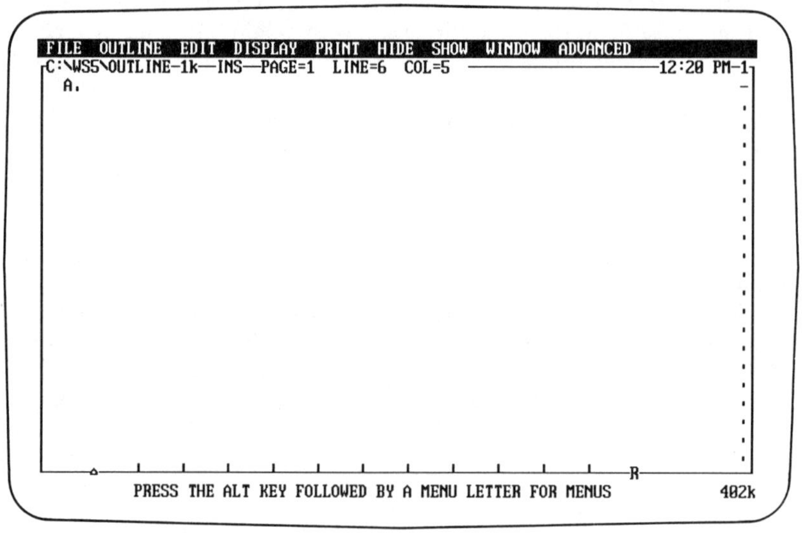
FILE OUTLINE EDIT DISPLAY PRINT HIDE SHOW WINDOW ADVANCED
C:\WS5\OUTLINE-1k—INS—PAGE=1 LINE=6 COL=5
12:20 PM-1
A.
PRESS THE ALT KEY FOLLOWED BY A MENU LETTER FOR MENUS
402k

Text for the first outline heading is typed at the cursor. Other headings and subheads can be added, displayed, hidden, or rearranged by choosing from the nearly 200 different commands available in PC-Outline.

As with WordStar Release 5 at help level 4, PC-Outline's pull-down menus are displayed by pressing the Alt key and the first letter of a listed menu. The menu bar on the PC-Outline Working screen lists the following menu possibilities:

```
FILE  OUTLINE  EDIT  DISPLAY  PRINT  HIDE  SHOW  WINDOW  ADVANCED
```

From the PC-Outline Working screen, pressing Alt-F (or F10) displays the pull-down File Menu, including seven options for file-related functions and the option to quit the menu (Q, also Esc). Any option on a PC-Outline pull-down menu can be invoked by moving the highlight with the up- and down-arrow keys and pressing Enter—or by pressing the indicated letter for a single-keystroke shortcut. As shown in figure 12.2, the File menu includes options for saving the current outline, loading an existing outline, starting a new outline, renaming the current outline, changing the current drive directory, choosing among file options (picking a subdirectory, parent directory, creating a new subdirectory, erasing an outline), or entering other file types (ASCII, WordStar Release 4, WordStar Release 5, structured outline, or WordStar 2000). As with other pull-down menus in PC-Outline, you can move to other pull-down menus by pressing left- or right-arrow keys.

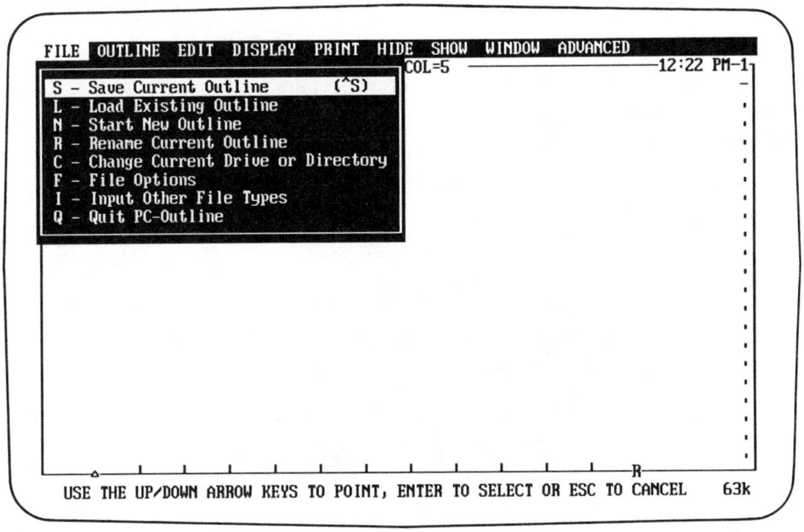
FILE OUTLINE EDIT DISPLAY PRINT HIDE SHOW WINDOW ADVANCED
COL=5
12:22 PM-1
S - Save Current Outline (^S)
L - Load Existing Outline
N - Start New Outline
R - Rename Current Outline
C - Change Current Drive or Directory
F - File Options
I - Input Other File Types
Q - Quit PC-Outline
USE THE UP/DOWN ARROW KEYS TO POINT, ENTER TO SELECT OR ESC TO CANCEL
63k

Fig. 12.2.

PC-Outline's pull-down File menu.

Pressing Alt-O from the PC-Outline Working screen (or the left-arrow key from the pull-down File menu) accesses the Outline menu, which lists the principal functions for manipulating outline text. Outline entries usually include subheadings (called *children*). The options on the pull-down Outline menu (see fig. 12.3) cover moving, deleting, or creating outline entries; marking entries for moving one level to the left (promoting) or right (indenting); dividing or joining outline entries; and sorting outline elements at the same level by letter or number.

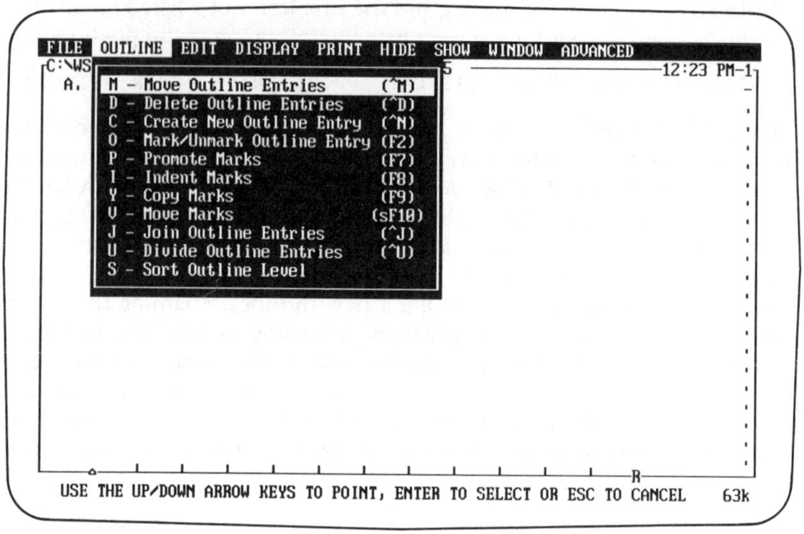
FILE OUTLINE EDIT DISPLAY PRINT HIDE SHOW WINDOW ADVANCED
C:\WS
12:23 PM-1
A.
M - Move Outline Entries (^M)
D - Delete Outline Entries (^D)
C - Create New Outline Entry (^N)
O - Mark/Unmark Outline Entry (F2)
P - Promote Marks (F7)
I - Indent Marks (F8)
Y - Copy Marks (F9)
V - Move Marks (sF10)
J - Join Outline Entries (^J)
U - Divide Outline Entries (^U)
S - Sort Outline Level
USE THE UP/DOWN ARROW KEYS TO POINT, ENTER TO SELECT OR ESC TO CANCEL 63k

Fig. 12.3.
The Outline menu for controlling outline text created with PC-Outline.

The pull-down Edit menu (press Alt-E from the Working screen) exhibits commands for editing strings and blocks of text. The functions seen on this menu, shown in figure 12.4, include unerase; find and replace; block move, copy, and delete; and rudimentary printer formatting.

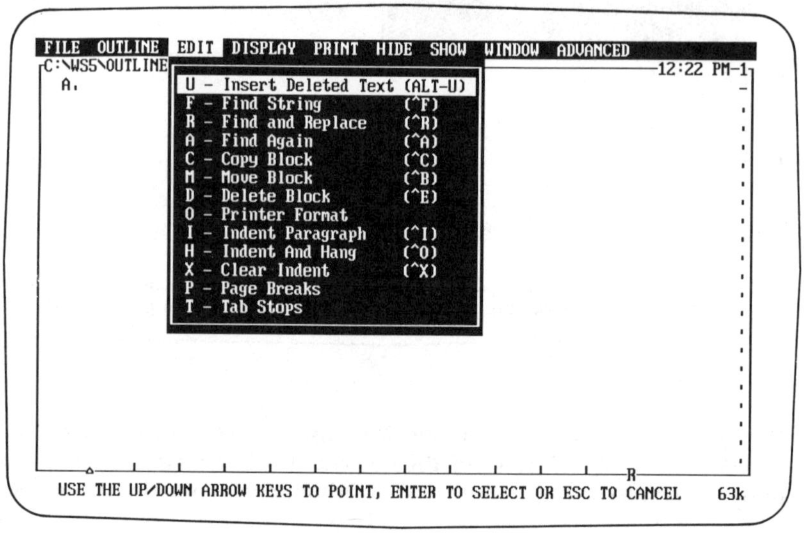
FILE OUTLINE EDIT DISPLAY PRINT HIDE SHOW WINDOW ADVANCED
C:\WS5\OUTLINE
12:22 PM-1
A.
U - Insert Deleted Text (ALT-U)
F - Find String (^F)
R - Find and Replace (^R)
A - Find Again (^A)
C - Copy Block (^C)
M - Move Block (^B)
D - Delete Block (^E)
O - Printer Format
I - Indent Paragraph (^I)
H - Indent And Hang (^O)
X - Clear Indent (^X)
P - Page Breaks
T - Tab Stops
USE THE UP/DOWN ARROW KEYS TO POINT, ENTER TO SELECT OR ESC TO CANCEL 63k

Fig. 12.4.
The PC-Outline pull-down Edit menu.

Outline format style, placement of entries, and numbering options are covered by the commands listed on the PC-Outline pull-down Display menu (press Alt-D—see fig. 12.5). Outline formatting style parameters include paragraph alignment, first line alignment, and left and right margin settings. By selecting appropriate options on the Display menu, outline numbering can be restarted, omitted, or reset to other numbers.

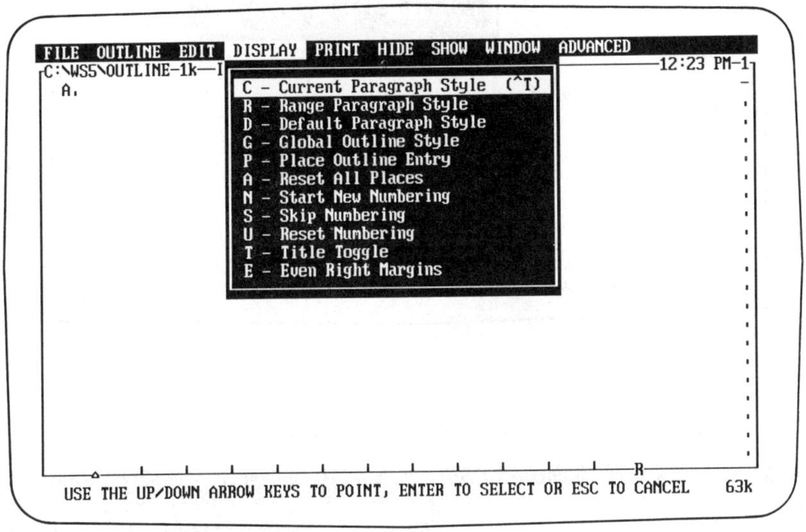
FILE OUTLINE EDIT DISPLAY PRINT HIDE SHOW WINDOW ADVANCED
C:\WS5\OUTLINE-1k—I
12:23 PM-1
A.
C - Current Paragraph Style (^T)
R - Range Paragraph Style
D - Default Paragraph Style
G - Global Outline Style
P - Place Outline Entry
A - Reset All Places
N - Start New Numbering
S - Skip Numbering
U - Reset Numbering
T - Title Toggle
E - Even Right Margins
USE THE UP/DOWN ARROW KEYS TO POINT, ENTER TO SELECT OR ESC TO CANCEL
63k

Fig. 12.5.
Formatting for PC-Outline text is controlled with Display menu options.

Printing options are grouped on the pull-down Print menu (see fig. 12.6). Shown on-screen when you press Alt-P, this menu provides the way to invoke printing of an entire outline or a limited range of the outline, including page formatting, font selection, and printer code insertion.

The pull-down Hide and Show menus offer great versatility in selecting portions of the outline to appear on-screen. The Hide menu (press Alt-H—see fig. 12.7) has five options for hiding entries, children, or other text in the outline. The pull-down Show menu (press Alt-S—see fig. 12.8) has a greater variety of options—nine in all—extending the range of possibilities for showing outline text beyond entries and children of entries to entire families of text.

PC-Outline can show more than one file (outline) at a time. The Window commands are grouped together on the pull-down Window menu (press Alt-W). As seen in figure 12.9, it contains a variety of commands for opening new windows, and moving, sizing, and arranging windows—up to nine separate windows at a time.

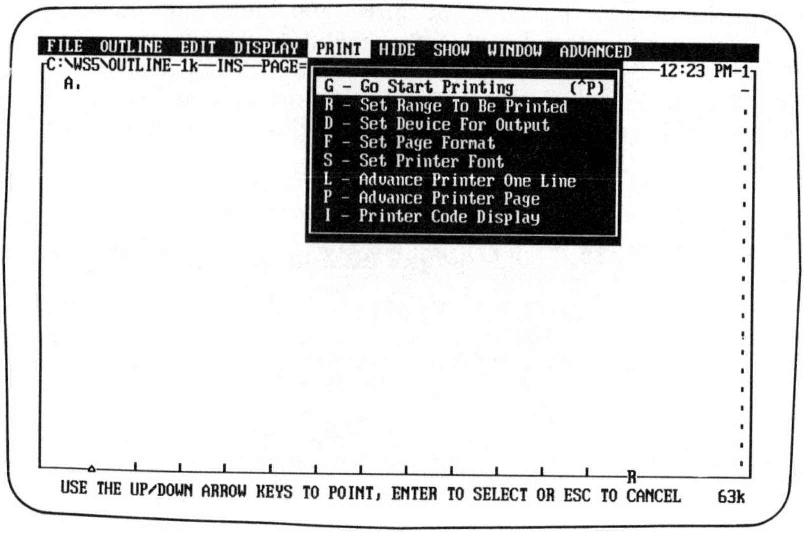
FILE OUTLINE EDIT DISPLAY PRINT HIDE SHOW WINDOW ADVANCED
C:\WS5\OUTLINE-1k—INS—PAGE=
12:23 PM-1
A.
G - Go Start Printing (^P)
R - Set Range To Be Printed
D - Set Device For Output
F - Set Page Format
S - Set Printer Font
L - Advance Printer One Line
P - Advance Printer Page
I - Printer Code Display
USE THE UP/DOWN ARROW KEYS TO POINT, ENTER TO SELECT OR ESC TO CANCEL 63k

Fig. 12.6.
Printing options displayed on the PC-Outline Print menu.

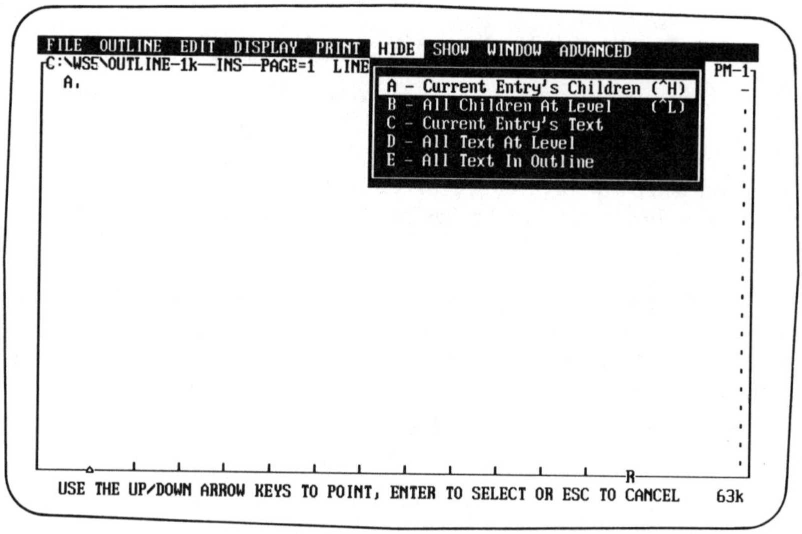
FILE OUTLINE EDIT DISPLAY PRINT HIDE SHOW WINDOW ADVANCED
C:\WS5\OUTLINE-1k—INS—PAGE=1 LINE
PM-1
A.
A - Current Entry's Children (^H)
B - All Children At Level (^L)
C - Current Entry's Text
D - All Text At Level
E - All Text In Outline
USE THE UP/DOWN ARROW KEYS TO POINT, ENTER TO SELECT OR ESC TO CANCEL 63k

Fig. 12.7.
PC-Outline's pull-down Hide menu.

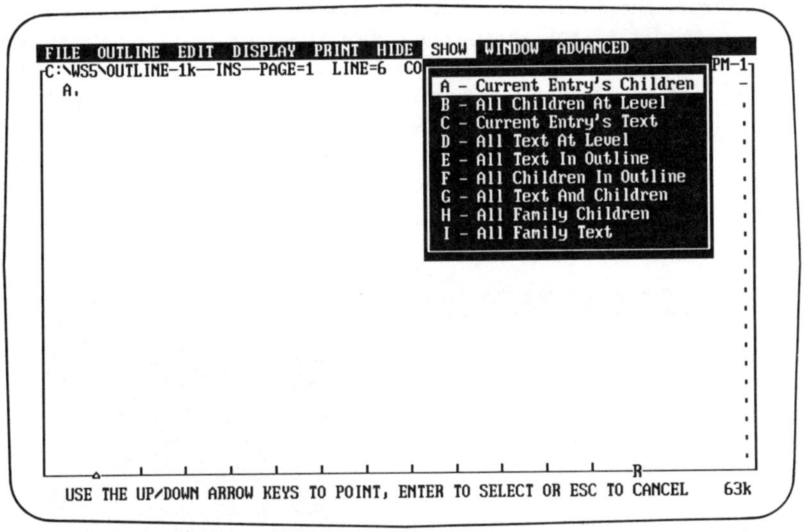
FILE OUTLINE EDIT DISPLAY PRINT HIDE SHOW WINDOW ADVANCED
C:\WS5\OUTLINE-1k—INS—PAGE=1 LINE=6 CO
PM-1
A.
A - Current Entry's Children
B - All Children At Level
C - Current Entry's Text
D - All Text At Level
E - All Text In Outline
F - All Children In Outline
G - All Text And Children
H - All Family Children
I - All Family Text
USE THE UP/DOWN ARROW KEYS TO POINT, ENTER TO SELECT OR ESC TO CANCEL 63k

Fig. 12.8. *PC-Outline's pull-down Show menu.*

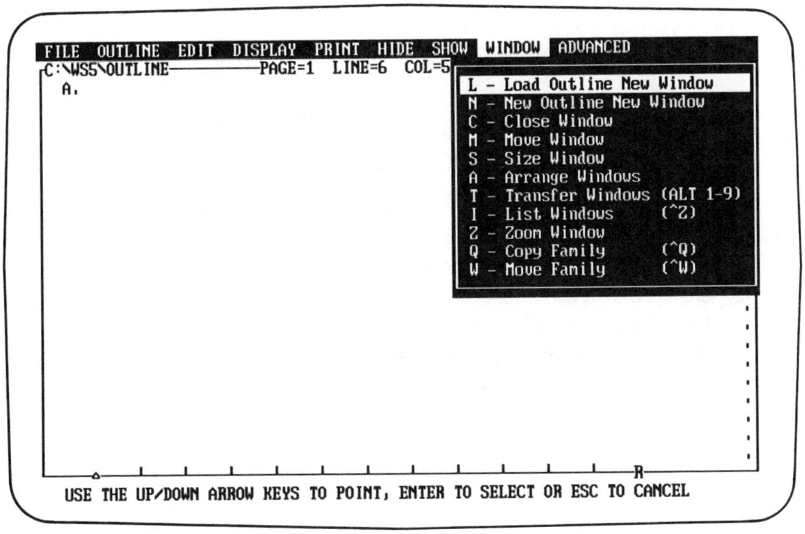
FILE OUTLINE EDIT DISPLAY PRINT HIDE SHOW WINDOW ADVANCED
C:\WS5\OUTLINE—PAGE=1 LINE=6 COL=5
A.
L - Load Outline New Window
N - New Outline New Window
C - Close Window
M - Move Window
S - Size Window
A - Arrange Windows
T - Transfer Windows (ALT 1-9)
I - List Windows (^Z)
Z - Zoom Window
Q - Copy Family (^Q)
W - Move Family (^W)
USE THE UP/DOWN ARROW KEYS TO POINT, ENTER TO SELECT OR ESC TO CANCEL

Fig. 12.9. *Window commands in PC-Outline.*

Pressing Alt-A from the PC-Outline Working screen produces the pull-down Advanced menu (see fig. 12.10). Among the options here are two crucial ones for exporting or importing a block of text from PC-Outline to or from a WordStar document. To export PC-Outline text to WordStar, the procedure is simple. Start with the cursor in the WordStar document where the block is to appear and invoke PC-Outline by pressing ^\. Next, position the cursor at the beginning of the block to export, press Alt-A, then E for Export Block, move the cursor to the block end, and press Enter.

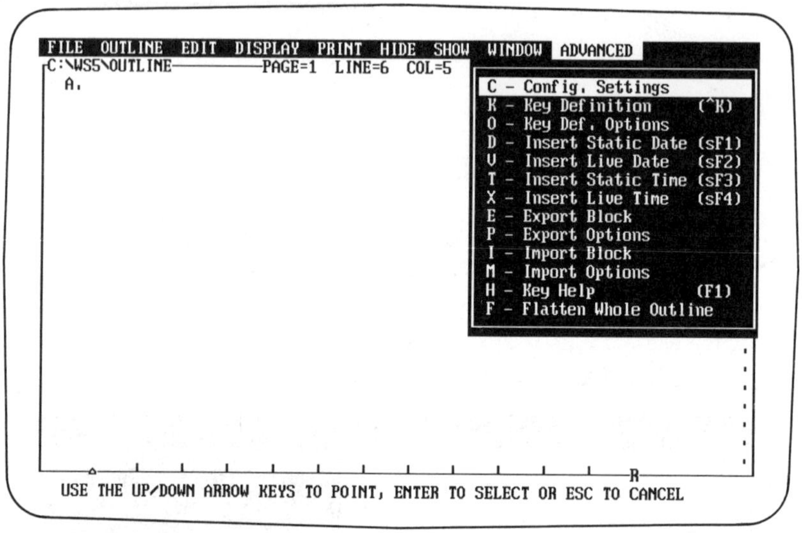
FILE OUTLINE EDIT DISPLAY PRINT HIDE SHOW WINDOW ADVANCED
C:\WS5\OUTLINE PAGE=1 LINE=6 COL=5
A.
C - Config. Settings
K - Key Definition (^K)
O - Key Def. Options
D - Insert Static Date (sF1)
V - Insert Live Date (sF2)
T - Insert Static Time (sF3)
X - Insert Live Time (sF4)
E - Export Block
P - Export Options
I - Import Block
M - Import Options
H - Key Help (F1)
F - Flatten Whole Outline
USE THE UP/DOWN ARROW KEYS TO POINT, ENTER TO SELECT OR ESC TO CANCEL

Fig. 12.10.

The PC-Outline pull-down Advanced menu.

To import a block of text from WordStar to PC-Outline, the procedure is slightly different. Start with the WordStar editing screen showing the text to be imported (as much as a screenful), and invoke PC-Outline by pressing ^\. Next, position the cursor in the PC-Outline Working screen where you want the block to appear, and press Alt-A, then I for Import Block. On the redisplayed WordStar screen, move the cursor to the upper left-hand corner of the block to be moved and press Enter, then move the cursor to the lower right-hand corner of the text to be imported. Press Enter to start importing.

Import and export formatting options can be reset from their own options on the Advanced menu, as can important defaults listed when the `Config. Settings` option is selected on this menu.

This brief overview of PC-Outline only hints at its versatility for outlining, especially when loaded as a memory-resident program. In addition to including instructive examples in outlining applications, the WordStar Release 5 manual explains how PC-Outline's usefulness extends beyond outlining. For example, you can use PC-Outline as a free-form organizer for appointments, business plans, and meeting agendas.

Although PC-Outline uses a pull-down menu structure similar to WordStar's, very few of their commands are identical. Programs can be compatible with WordStar, then, to the point of directly exchanging text, without being command compatible. Some programs that can enhance WordStar may be even less similar in command structure than PC-Outline, while others may be far more command compatible. Each kind of compatible program may have its place alongside WordStar in your software collection.

Enhancing WordStar with Other Compatible Software

Full compatibility with WordStar, from text files to commands, is rare and unnecessary. Programs with different degrees of compatibility can be equally useful in enhancing WordStar.

The bare minimum for compatibility with WordStar Release 5 is that the other program can be run by an IBM PC or PS/2 or compatible computer. This kind of program is simply DOS-compatible, though no less helpful than more compatible software. Among DOS-compatible programs are a wealth of *utility* programs for adding to the file-handling capabilities of WordStar.

The most valuable DOS-compatible program you can buy may also be among the least expensive (about $100 or less). This kind of program can pay for itself quickly by restoring important files accidentally erased from disk with a hasty WordStar Y delete command from the Opening screen or ^KJ from within a document. If no backup file is left on disk, you can lose hours of work with a keystroke or two. In a worst-case scenario, you could lose the only copy of a file containing irreplaceable data.

Several different programs can *unerase* a deleted file if no other files have been saved to disk in the meantime. If other data has been saved, some of the disk sectors occupied by the deleted file may be overwritten. In that case, the restoration of the file's remaining contents is more difficult. With the help of a recovery program, you can examine the data in each sector. (You can also restore files when a disk is partially damaged.)

Unerase programs are usually included in a package of DOS utilities, like the Mace Utilities, or the package that popularized such software, the Norton Utilities from Peter Norton Computing. Norton's Quick Unerase (QU.EXE), or a program like it, can easily restore a deleted file. You start the program from the DOS prompt, select the name of the partially erased file you want to restore to the directory, add a missing first letter to the file name (a deleted file is not erased from a disk; only the first letter of its file name is erased to keep it from being read), and press Enter. The file is restored to the directory listing on disk within seconds.

The Norton Utilities package, like its counterparts, includes more than a dozen other programs that perform useful functions, such as restoring accidentally reformatted hard disks or removed directories, reorganizing disk files for faster retrieval, testing disks for physical flaws, or even permanently erasing files without a trace so that they cannot be restored by any recovery program. The Norton Utilities are partially command compatible with WordStar: editing of text entries can be done with cursor movement and text deletion commands that are the same as WordStar's.

The familiar WordStar S-E-D-X cursor movement diamond and other Ctrl-letter combinations are also recognized in a number of memory-resident compatible programs, like SideKick Plus. Meant to be run in background memory at the same time as WordStar, SideKick Plus is a type of program known as a desktop accessory.

As the name indicates, desktop-accessory programs provide the computer equivalent of common business tools found on many office desks, including an appointment calendar, telephone book, and a notepad that can appear on-screen while you use WordStar. Like memory-resident PC-Outline, most desktop-accessory programs include the capability to import text from an open WordStar file or export it from the notepad into WordStar.

SideKick Plus is the successor to Borland International's SideKick, the top-selling desktop accessory package. With up to nine separate windows available in SideKick Plus, bringing the program's Notepad on-screen during a WordStar work session opens the way for writing notes into several different files, viewing up to a total of 10 different documents in separate windows, or cutting and pasting text between an open WordStar file and Notepad windows.

With only one window of its own, WordStar Release 5 lags behind rival word processors such as XyWrite and Sprint®—which are able to put as many as nine windows on-screen simultaneously. SideKick Plus is the logical choice for ending the WordStar "window gap," provided you can accommodate this memory-resident program's hardware and memory requirements.

Improvements in SideKick Plus, including its nine windows, have taken their toll in program size and convenience. Installing SideKick Plus requires a hard disk with at least 1.5M of free memory. Running all of SideKick Plus requires extra RAM memory conforming to the extended memory standard beyond 640K. A minimal installation of SideKick Plus with just Notepad functions can fit into a little over 100K of internal memory.

SideKick Plus always must be loaded last among memory-resident programs before loading WordStar. Because of possible memory conflicts, SideKick Plus should not be run along with WordStar's Advanced Page Preview or TelMerge. To load SideKick Plus, type ***skplus*** at the DOS prompt.

From within WordStar, SideKick Plus can be invoked by pressing Ctrl and Alt keys at the same time. Once SideKick Plus is on-screen, the Notepad selection is activated with one of several Alt-letter or Alt-number key combinations. A pop-up menu offers a selection of Notepad windows numbered from 1 to 9; each of these can store up to 54K of text—roughly 25 pages. Within any Notepad window, text can be edited with WordStar commands. Compatible find-and-replace and block functions are also available in SideKick Plus.

Copying and exporting text from and to WordStar only requires placing the cursor at the destination for a text block, marking the block in SideKick Plus, and selecting the appropriate variation on the command series Services Quick Paste.

When text is transferred from SideKick Plus to a WordStar document, it has a carriage return at the end of each line. To align the text properly with the rest of the document, replace extra carriage returns with soft returns, as explained later in *Converting Files to and from ASCII Format.*

In addition to the Notepad windows, SideKick Plus can simultaneously display windows with a phone directory, a monthly calendar, a date book, and a full-function calculator. Whether you use any of these functions or limit yourself to the program's text window features, SideKick Plus should prove to be a handy complement to WordStar.

Though far less command-compatible than SideKick Plus, another memory-resident program is the only add-on program outside of the WordStar package to have its own command in WordStar Release 5. The InSet program, from INSET Systems, Inc., is the object of the ^P* command, which inserts a special tag noting where InSet graphics files are to be inserted when printing a WordStar document.

InSet is the best known of a type of program known as *screen capture* software. Originally a means for reproducing the contents of a computer screen, including graphics, such programs evolved to include graphics editors and the capability to integrate text and graphics on properly equipped printers.

The lack of integrated graphics along with text is one of the great failings of WordStar Release 5. The ability to lay out and print documents with charts, scanned images, or clip art within text is included in so-called desktop publishing programs and some rival word processors like WordPerfect 5. Graphics capability was actually part of the program that eventually became WordStar's Advanced Page Preview function, but the final version of WordStar Release 5 has no internal commands for either displaying or directly printing graphics.

Running InSet as a memory-resident program along with WordStar can offer a viable alternative for printing graphics and text. InSet requires 132K or 115K of internal memory, depending on how it is installed. All necessary InSet files can be loaded from a separate working copy on dual floppy systems, or from a directory named INSET on a hard disk. InSet requires no special order in loading, though it should be loaded before WordStar. To load InSet, type *inset*. After pressing Enter, you will see InSet load and return the DOS prompt to the screen. (If this is a first use, you must follow on-screen instructions to supply system information for a correct installation of the program).

Once WordStar is loaded, you can invoke InSet from background memory by pressing the left-Shift and Ctrl keys at the same time. If you want InSet to insert graphics images into a WordStar document at print time, once the program is set for Output Merge, the steps are simple. Start by creating the necessary images as InSet graphics files, using the file name extension PIX (images can be sized and edited with InSet's editing commands). Clear appropriate amounts of space within the WordStar document to accommodate illustrations, and tag each one with a unique PIX tag (using ^P*). Then, with InSet in background (pressing Esc returns the computer display to the WordStar editing screen), invoke printing in WordStar. InSet automatically prints PIX files where indicated by their tags in the document (on dot-matrix or laser printers only).

As a screen capture program alone, InSet still sets the standard. All Que Corporation books, including this one, use InSet to reproduce screens for illustrations. Add to this the ability to simulate rudimentary desktop publishing with WordStar Release 5 and you have a valuable addition to any software library. Don't be surprised if something like InSet is added to a future release of WordStar to give it built-in graphics capability.

The Norton Utilities, SideKick Plus, and InSet provide excellent examples of roughly compatible programs that can augment WordStar so that it becomes the equal of any rival word processor's combination of functions.

Using WordStar with Other Word Processing Software

With the exception of the NewWord program (which preceded WordStar Release 4 and was discontinued) and MicroPro's Easy, no other major word processing program has ordinarily produced a file format similar to WordStar's. Whether programmers were convinced that they could produce something new and better or were simply falling back on the "not invented here" syndrome that often impedes the establishment of standards, designers of word processors have avoided creating anything resembling the WordStar file format. The result has been incompatibility between other word processors' document files and WordStar's files. And to make things worse, Release 5's format is partially incompatible with the classic document format in Release 4 and earlier versions of WordStar.

What has always distinguished a WordStar file is the way the program encodes characters and formatting commands in a document. The keyboard input of personal computers in the United States must conform to the American Standard Code for Information Interchange (ASCII). This code represents each letter, number, punctuation mark, and special function command as a string of seven binary data bits followed by an optional eighth bit to test for transmission errors. (See Appendix C for ASCII binary values translated to the base-10 number system.) WordStar, however, encodes the eighth bit in a nonstandard manner in order to indicate character placement on a line. Even if WordStar conformed to the ASCII code (as it does when producing a nondocument file), WordStar's distinctive Ctrl-letter and dot commands for formatting cannot be recognized by other word processors.

For the first time, the WordStar document format produced by Release 5 includes a "header"—information inserted into the file ahead of text. Of the 128 byte header, Release 5 uses only a few bytes to record the name of the default PDF to be used to print the document. Presumably, the remaining header space is being reserved for more advanced features in a subsequent WordStar release. Header information and codes for note functions further separate WordStar Release 5 files from their ASCII counterparts, as well as from earlier WordStar versions.

On the other hand, few other major word processing programs observe the ASCII standard. Document files from the programs that adhere to the established seven-bit code for text characters can be read by WordStar, but those programs' schemes for recording formatting information are foreign to it. Other programs use techniques more complicated than WordStar's for representing characters and for formatting. If WordStar can read these programs' files at all, their text may look like gibberish when displayed.

One solution to incompatibility between word processor files is transforming everything to "plain vanilla" ASCII files, in which characters are expressed in the recognized seven-bit binary code and formatting information is removed. As a print option, WordStar can produce unformatted ASCII files—just like most major word processors for MS-DOS computers. The output of these ASCII files, however, sacrifices underlining, boldface, italic, subscripts, and other useful text attributes.

WordStar Release 5 converts document files to ASCII files or to Release 4-compatible files with a similar procedure: you invoke printing of the document and at the resulting dialog box designate as printer a special-purpose PDF—either `ASCII` for ASCII output or `WS4` for WordStar classic-style files (these should be among the PDF files on your working copy disk directory). Output is a disk file called ASCII.WS in one case, or the name of the document with the extension WS4 for WordStar format in the other case. As with converting to ASCII, there is a loss of information when converting Release 5 to an earlier WordStar format: fonts, color designations, footnotes, endnotes, annotations, and comments are not retained.

In attempts to preserve full formatting information, creators of a few word processing packages have included utility programs for converting the programs' files directly to WordStar text and back, although with uneven results. Not even file conversion programs created as stand-alone products, as in the case of Systems Compatibility Corporation's Star Exchange (included as the file conversion utility in WordStar 2000 Release 3), can produce 100 percent equivalence between incompatible text files.

Alternative procedures for sharing files between WordStar and incompatible word processors are examined in this chapter because the capability to transfer document content quickly and easily (with only minor limitations) may prove invaluable.

Converting Files to and from ASCII Format

WordStar Release 5 continues with Release 4's reliable method for converting document files to ASCII format by invoking a special printer file. In this case, the printer file is the ASCII PDF, and invoking it is made simpler with the appearance of the Print dialog box with prompts for printer name and the disk file name to which output should be redirected.

To create an ASCII version of a document, after pressing P for print or M for merge print, type the document's name in the Print dialog box and then press Enter three times to get to the `Printer name` prompt. Designate the ASCII PDF and move the cursor to the `Redirect output to:` prompt and type the name for the new ASCII file, or accept the default ASCII.WS. Press ^K or F10 to complete the conversion.

After the disk operations are completed, press Enter. The name of your new ASCII file is shown in the file directory below the Opening screen, as is the name of the original file, which is not erased. If you open the ASCII file in nondocument mode, you can see that all print-control and dot commands have been removed and that hard carriage returns have been placed at the end of each line, according to the ASCII standard. (Remember that conversion from Release 5 document file format to older WordStar format files is accomplished by substituting the WS4 special PDF file for ASCII in the previous procedure.)

To read and edit in WordStar an ASCII file produced by another program, press D at the Opening Menu, type the file name, and press Enter. As you can see on the Document screen, ASCII text differs from typical WordStar document formatting in one important respect: each line ends with a hard carriage return, indicated by the < symbols at the right edge of your screen. You must remove the hard carriage returns within the paragraphs if you want to use realignment commands after you edit the text.

You can remove the hard carriage returns manually with deletion commands, or you can use a Release 5 command to change all hard carriage returns to soft returns quickly. Pressing ^6 from anywhere on a line of text in document mode converts a hard return to a soft one on the line at the cursor and advances the cursor to the beginning of the next line. You can keep pressing ^6, or you can issue the command sequence ^QQ^6 once to delete the hard returns in an entire document file. The latter method, however, will also eliminate hard returns that mark the ends of paragraphs.

A better method involves WordStar's find-and-replace function. You invoke find-and-replace twice, with a carriage return conversion in-between. The following steps mark paragraph ends, remove all hard carriage returns, and reinsert hard carriage returns at the ends of paragraphs only.

1. Position the cursor at the beginning of the file and press ^QA for find-and-replace.
2. At the `Find` prompt, enter ^P^M^P^J and a space to search for hard carriage returns that precede paragraph indents. If your paragraphs are not indented, try entering the following to indicate two successive carriage returns:

   ^P^M^P^J^P^M^P^J

   On-screen, you see `^M^J` (or `^M^J^M^J`).
3. Press Enter and at the `Replace with` prompt, type a marker string of characters not used in the file (such as ***).
4. Press Enter again and type *ng* at the options prompt to replace without confirmation throughout the file.
5. Press ^K or F10 and then the space bar to start the operation and to speed the process.
6. Move the cursor back to the beginning of the file by pressing Esc and ^QR.
7. Press ^QQ^6 to convert all remaining hard carriage returns to soft returns. You then can press 1 to speed the process.
8. Move the cursor back to the top of the file by pressing ^QR.
9. Press ^QA for the final find-and-replace procedure.
10. To locate the paragraph limits, enter the marker characters (in this example, ***) at the `Find` prompt.
11. After pressing Enter at the `Replace with` prompt, enter ^P^M^P^J to reinsert the carriage returns in their proper places.
12. Press Enter and type *ng* at the `Find and replace` options prompt on-screen.
13. Press F10 and the space bar.
14. Move the cursor back to the beginning of the file by pressing Esc and ^QR.
15. Realign the resulting extended single-line paragraphs by pressing ^QU.

You now should have a conventionally formatted WordStar document file that is ready for editing.

Note: Do not use this procedure for ASCII files that are not word processing files. You may need to retain the positions of numbers from a spreadsheet or fields from a database program.

Converting Files with Star Exchange™

Traditionally, WordStar releases have ignored the existence of competing programs and excluded software for converting files to other formats. Any direct translations relied on rival publishers who recognized the importance of WordStar and provided their own conversion programs.

Some conversion software, such as the utility program in some versions of the best-selling MultiMate, often failed to work. (The WordStar conversion utility has been dropped from the latest MultiMate Advantage packages.) Other programs, such as Microsoft Word's utility for transferring WordStar documents to Word's structured file scheme, offered only one-way conversion.

As part of Release 3 of WordStar 2000, MicroPro included one of the most complete conversion facilities for any word processor by bundling the independently developed Star Exchange program from Systems Compatibility Corporation. Unfortunately, MicroPro omitted Star Exchange from the WordStar Release 5 package. If you need to convert files from WordStar to other popular word processor file formats and back again, you can purchase Star Exchange as a separate program.

The Star Exchange program can convert files from DEC® WPS PLUS, IBM DisplayWrite 2, 3, and 4, Microsoft Word (through version 4.0), Ashton-Tate's MultiMate, SAMNA Word, Wang® PC, WordPerfect, WordStar 2000, and Volkswriter 3® to WordStar Release 5 format and vice versa. Supplied on four separate 5 1/4-inch floppy disks with files for each conversion, Star Exchange can be installed on a two floppy disk system by being selective about needed conversion files. A hard disk system can accommodate the full array of possible conversions.

Once installed on disk, Star Exchange can be run by typing *convert* at the DOS prompt and pressing Enter. The Star Exchange Main Menu has options for conversions from and to preset word processors or for system setup (the choice to make during a first use; system setup options include names of word processors for conversions and formatting, as well as filters for eliminating incompatible commands or typefaces).

When a conversion from one format to another is selected, Star Exchange prompts you with its `Input Queue` screen with room for the names of up to five document files to be converted. Once you indicate the names of files to translate, pressing F1 begins conversion of each specified document in turn. On-screen a box shows the name of each new file version on disk as it is converted (the original files also remain on disk). Unless reset, Star Exchange automatically names conversions with the file name of the original document and an extension in accordance with the new file format. (The extension consists of the characters after the period in the file name.) The extensions are as follows: ASC for ASCII, DX for DEC WPS PLUS, TXT for DisplayWrite, MSW for Microsoft Word, SAM for SAMNA, VW for Volkswriter, WPF for WordPerfect, WS for WordStar, or WS2 for WordStar 2000.

Even with the proper use of filters for trapping incompatibilities, converted files should be scanned for any disruptions in formatting or untranslatable characters—indicated in an unmodified copy of Star Exchange by the @ symbol in documents. Such conversion exceptions should be replaced or edited out before using the converted file.

According to the Star Exchange manual, formatting features completely supported in conversions include tabs, boldface, headers and footers, hard carriage returns, subscripts and superscripts, line spacing, underscore, footnotes, and columns. Nonetheless, the documentation lists anywhere from a half-dozen to nearly two dozen conversion exceptions for each conversion it can produce.

For all the exceptions to its powers, Star Exchange is surely worth the investment if you need to convert WordStar Release 5 files to any other popular word processing format—except ASCII. Incidentally, an ASCII conversion can also serve as the gateway to business software not oriented toward word processing.

Using WordStar Files with Other Business Software

Business programs other than word processors have their own file data structures that render them directly incompatible with WordStar's document file format. Their content, however, can be read by WordStar and used in WordStar text. As in transfers from other word processors, the ASCII file format can serve as a common denominator for transferring information from and to other programs. In fact, most business applications programs have provisions for creating and importing ASCII files, but with some limitations.

Because of the special requirements for spreadsheets, database managers, and other applications programs, certain internal formatting conditions must be met to make data from these programs intelligible to WordStar. Usually, WordStar's margins, character placement in lines or columns, special symbol conventions, and so on, should be consistent with the programs' settings. In most cases, these conditions are met easily when you move text in and out of ASCII files.

Exporting and Importing Spreadsheet Data with Lotus 1-2-3

Manipulating financial data with spreadsheet software remains the primary use for many computers on office desktops. Budget calculations, economic forecasts, project bids, and other numerical applications are facilitated within the row-and-column environment of the electronic worksheet. Executives, managers, and support staff depend on their spreadsheets for day-to-day operations as well as for speculative "what if" calculations.

In addition to this "number crunching," many spreadsheet programs integrate functions for data management, graphics, and text editing. Yet, for full-powered word processing, no current integrated software program can match WordStar's speed or efficiency. Increasingly, spreadsheets and WordStar are coexisting in software libraries and on hard disks. This development makes data transfer from worksheets to documents and vice versa a necessity.

5 Lotus Development Corporation's 1-2-3, which is by far the biggest-selling spreadsheet package for MS-DOS computers, has inspired several competing programs with identical command structures. Other rival programs also have analogous commands. With Release 5, WordStar now includes a built-in conversion for importing 1-2-3 or similar spreadsheet data with a variation on the ^KR command. Nonetheless, there is another simple procedure for exporting figures and labels from 1-2-3 spreadsheet files to reports prepared with WordStar, as well as a unique procedure for bringing WordStar text into 1-2-3 worksheets. These operations can be adapted readily to any spreadsheet program with the capability to produce and read plain ASCII files.

A standard 1-2-3 worksheet file, which bears a WKS or WK1 file name extension, has a structured format that cannot be used directly in WordStar. Lotus has included in its own program a series of commands for producing ASCII text in a 1-2-3 print file, which is denoted by the extension PRN. With 1-2-3 running and the worksheet data to be transferred on-screen, you press the slash key (/) to call up the 1-2-3 menu bar (for Release 2) at the top of the screen:

```
Worksheet  Range  Copy  Move  File  Print  Graph  Data  System  Quit
```

Use the left-arrow key to move the highlighter to `Print` and press Enter, or simply press P to display the `Printer` and `File` choices on the menu bar. Select the second option by moving the highlighter to `File` and pressing Enter, or simply by pressing F. A prompt requests that you `Enter print file name:`. Be sure to use the correct form when you indicate the name: include the drive letter and the extension PRN. Type a file name for storing the data that you are transferring and press Enter. (Or you can indicate an existing file name with the highlighter and then press Enter.)

The 1-2-3 menu bar displays the following choices:

```
Range  Line  Page  Options  Clear  Align  Go  Quit
```

Choosing the `Range` function by pressing Enter or pressing R allows you to select a block of the worksheet to be transferred to the print file. This block should fit the margins of the WordStar document into which it is to be read.

To mark the block of cells and labels, with the arrow keys move the cell pointer to the top left corner of the desired cell range and then type a period. Move the cell pointer to the bottom right corner of the block and press Enter to return the menu bar. Select `Go` with the left-arrow key and press Enter, or simply press G, to begin processing the designated range. To save the resulting print file to disk, you press Q or move the highlighter to `Quit` and press Enter.

Importing text and numbers from a WordStar file to a 1-2-3 worksheet can be a straightforward process if the file is in plain ASCII and has a file name with the extension PRN. An imported file can be 240 characters wide and 8,192 characters long in 1-2-3 Release 2 (or 2,048 characters long in Release 1A).

Within the 1-2-3 screen, move the cell pointer to the position where text should be entered. The designated cell becomes the top left corner of the range that will contain the file's text. Press / to call up the main menu bar, and then use the left-arrow key to move the highlighter to `File` and press Enter, or simply press F. The menu bar then displays the following:

```
Retrieve  Save  Combine  Xtract  Erase  List  Import  Directory
```

From this menu, select `Import` with the highlighter and press Enter, or simply press I. Two choices are displayed on the menu bar: `Text` and `Numbers`. The Text option reads in each line of the file to be imported as a left-aligned label, which produces a column of long labels. The Numbers option reads in only numbers and any character strings enclosed in quotation marks; this option ignores the rest of the file contents. Each number is assigned to a separate number cell and each quoted label to a left-aligned label, with succeeding numbers and labels in corresponding column and row positions.

After you designate Text or Numbers, a prompt instructs you to `Enter name of file to import:`. A directory listing of files with the extension PRN appears below this prompt. Use the highlighter to indicate the file to be read and press Enter, or type the file name preceded by the drive and path designations and then press Enter. Text and numbers appear in your worksheet.

Using WordStar and dBASE Data Management Files

After word processors and electronic spreadsheets, the most widely used business applications software is in the data management category. Some programs, like WordStar's own MailList function, are limited in scope and features. These simple data management programs maintain address files, inventory lists, and so on. Other programs, however, have powerful commands for sorting, searching, and merging information that spans literally thousands of records.

Most data management programs supplement their data-handling capabilities with some functions for generating and printing tables, summaries, and other formatted reports. These text-based functions are limited, however, and don't match WordStar's versatility in producing documents that incorporate database information. Fortunately, most data management programs include the capability to create and read ASCII files if they are properly formatted.

As noted in Chapter 8, WordStar's merge print function can now read in dBASE data files. The most widely used data management program is dBASE, which was available originally as dBASE II®, and is now in the easy-to-use dBASE III Plus™. dBASE has always included a text editor with WordStar-like Ctrl commands for editing data files. One peculiarity of a dBASE file, however, renders it directly incompatible with WordStar. It is a "preamble" that begins the file with coded information about the number of records the file contains, when the records were created, their field names, and so on.

To read a dBASE file into a WordStar document, all you have to do is press ^KR and type the path and name of the file. WordStar recognizes the dBASE file format and converts the file to WordStar format.

A WordStar merge file can be read by dBASE provided that each field is enclosed in double quotation marks before appending into dBASE. Otherwise, dBASE considers all the data as one field—disregarding the commas as field delimiters.

A WordStar merge file can be read by dBASE provided that each field is enclosed in double quotation marks before appending into dBASE. Otherwise, dBASE considers all the data as one field— disregarding the commas as field delimiters.

To use a WordStar merge-print file that has been converted to an ASCII file in dBASE, you first must open an appropriate dBASE file and define the file structure with such field commands as NAME = 15 and ADDRESS = 20 (the number represents characters). The fields must be defined in the same order as the fields in the WordStar file, where a record ends with a hard carriage return.

After these conditions have been met, you choose the APPEND FROM command, followed by the WordStar file name and the DELIMITED option. This step brings in the WordStar file's data in the same order as the data appears on the data lines. After reading the first field, this function looks to the next comma-delimited field and inserts its contents into the next available field in the dBASE file.

The complexities of dBASE programming are beyond the scope of this book. Starting from the procedure described in this section, however, you can go on to try your own applications for exporting and importing dBASE data for use in WordStar.

Conclusion

If your business applications software or specific program has not been mentioned in this chapter, the procedures discussed here should give you some ideas about bridging the gap between WordStar and incompatible programs by means of ASCII and other formats or with special file conversion programs. As this chapter suggests, WordStar can continue to be an integral part of your computer use as your expertise and your system's capabilities evolve.

Improved computer hardware and operating environments eventually will eliminate incompatible files. New software designed to take advantage of the IBM PS/2—the next generation of MS-DOS personal computers—holds the promise of even greater productivity and efficiency in computer applications. You can bet that WordStar will not be left behind. Continuing research and development at MicroPro International guarantee that WordStar will adapt to the latest developments. The odds are that this classic word processor will remain a standard for many years.

A

WordStar Professional Release 5: New or Altered Commands

MicroPro International, publisher of WordStar Professional Release 5, claims that the new program has more than 300 major improvements. This appendix lists the WordStar commands that have been altered for Release 5 as well as the commands that are new to the upgraded package. New commands are noted by a 5 to the left of the command.

	Command	Function
	From the DOS prompt	
	WS /S	Starts WordStar and opens a Speed Write file.
	WS /[shorthand	Starts WordStar and executes the shorthand sequence at the Opening Menu.
	WS Filename/en	Opens file and runs macro n.
	From the Opening screen (help level 4)	
5	F	Displays pull-down File menu.
5	O	Displays pull-down Other menu.
5	A	Displays pull-down Additional menu.
	From the Opening Menu (help level 3, 2, 1, 0)	
5	S	Opens a Speed Write document file. Displays the editing screen without requiring naming of a file.

5	A	Displays the Additional Menu for invoking MailList and TelMerge.
	From the Edit screen (help level 4)	
5	Alt-F	Displays pull-down File menu.
5	Alt-E	Displays pull-down Edit menu.
5	Alt-G	Displays pull-down Go To menu.
5	Alt-W	Displays pull-down Window menu.
5	Alt-L	Displays pull-down Layout menu.
5	Alt-S	Displays pull-down Style menu.
5	Alt-O	Displays pull-down Other menu.

Block & Save Menu Commands

5	^K?	Counts words and characters in block or document.
5	^K.	Converts block text to upper- and lowercase.
5	^KA	Copies marked block to other window.
	^KC	Copies marked block of text within same window.
	^KD	Closes window and saves file.
5	^KG	Moves marked block to other window.
	^KR	Copies worksheet into file.
5	^KT	Saves document with new name.
	^KV	Moves marked block of text within same window.
	^KW	Adds marked block of text to end of existing disk file.
5	^KZ	Sorts lines in marked block.

Onscreen Format Menu Commands

5	^OA	Sets auto-align Off or On.
	^OE	Stops hyphenation of word.
	^OI	Sets multiple tabs, inserts .TB in text.

	^OJ	Inserts .OJ in text.
5	^OK	Opens, switches cursor in window.
	^OL	Inserts .LM in text.
5	^OM	Resets window size.
5	^ON	Displays Notes Menu.
5	^ONA	Creates annotation.
5	^ONC	Creates comment.
5	^OND	Displays full text of note.
5	^ONE	Creates endnote.
5	^ONF	Creates footnote.
5	^ONG	Finds note in document.
5	^ONI	Creates index entry.
5	^ONL	Checks spelling in notes.
5	^ONU	Aligns text in notes.
5	^ONV	Converts one note type to another.
	^OP	Starts Advanced Page Preview.
	^OR	Inserts .RM in text.
	^OS	Inserts .LS in text.
5	^OV	Centers text vertically on page.
5	^OZ	Starts paragraph numbering.

Print Controls Menu Commands

	^PY	Invokes italic only (not color).
5	^P0	Displays extended character menu.
5	^P?	Displays printer choices.
5	^P!	Inserts one-time custom print control.
5	^P.	Inserts dots to the next tab stop.
5	^P-	Displays color choices.
5	^P=	Displays font choices.
5	^P*	Inserts pix tag for InSet graphics file.

Quick Menu Commands

5	^QI	Moves cursor forward or backward specified number of pages with + or –.
5	^QJ	Starts thesaurus synonym search.
5	^Q=	Moves cursor to next font tag in document.

Commands for Responding to Prompts

	^K or F10	Signals that a response is complete.

Dot Commands

5	.CB	Forces column break.
5	.CB n	Conditional column break (n for number of lines to be kept together).
5	.CO n,w	Invokes snaking columns (n for number of columns, w for width between columns).
5	.CO 1	Turns off snaking columns while printing if .PF is on.
5	.CV	Converts notes from one type to another when printing.
	.CW	Sets character width in fractions or inches.
	.DF	Accepts dBASE, Lotus 1-2-3, Symphony, and Quattro files as data files.
5	.E#	Sets endnotes' starting value.
5	.F#	Sets footnotes' starting value.
	.FO o/e	Sets odd or even pages for footer.
	.HO o/e	Sets odd or even pages for header.
5	.L#	Sets line numbering On or Off.
	.LH	Sets line height in fractions or inches.
	.LM	Sets left margin in fractions or inches, relative values with + or –.
	.LQ dis	Set near-letter-quality print at WordStar's discretion.
5	.OC	Sets line centering On and Off for a section of text.
5	.P#	Sets starting number for paragraph numbering.

	.PC0	Centers page number between current margins.
5	.PE	Indicates where to print endnotes.
	.PM	Sets paragraph margins in fractions or inches, relative values with + or −.
	.PO	Sets page offset in fractions or inches.
	.PO o/e	Sets odd or even pages for page offset.
	.RM	Sets right margin in fractions or inches, relative values with + or −.
	.RR#	Specifies predefined ruler line, by number (0–9).
	.RV*	Selects first fields in data file, uses field names as variables with dBASE file.
5	.TB	Saves tabs with file.
5	.XX	Redefines strikeout character.

B

Printers Compatible with WordStar

Printers on the WordStar® Printer Selection Menu

PRINTER	DRIVER	UND[1]	PS[2]	NLQ[3]	ECS[4]	COLOR[5]
Draft Printer (nonbackspacing)	DRIVERT	B	N	N	BS	N
Typewriter Printer (backspacing)	DRIVERT	B	N	N	BS	N
Auto Line Feed Printer	DRIVERT	B	N	N	BS	N
Custom	DRIVERN		*(Depends on printer)*			
Simple	DRIVERT		*(Depends on printer)*			
AT&T 470	DRIVERN	B	J	A	PI	N
Brother HR-20	DRIVERN	C	J	A	PI	Y
Brother HR-40	DRIVERN	C	J	A	PI	Y
C. Itoh 1550/8510	DRIVERN	B	J	A	PI	N
C. Itoh Starwriter	DRIVERN	C	J	A	BS	N
Canon LBP-8 A1/A2	DRIVERN	C	J	A	BS	N
Canon Series II	DRIVERN	C	J	A	DF	N
Citizen 120D	DRIVERN	C	U	Y	BS	N
Citizen MSP 10/20	DRIVERN	C	N	Y	BS	N
Cordata LP-300	DRIVERN	C	J	A	DF	N
Diablo Daisy Wheel	DRIVERN	B	J	A	BS	N
Diablo 630 ECS	DRIVERN	C	J	A	DF	N
Diablo 630 w/WP option	DRIVERN	C	J	A	BS	Y
Diconix 150	DRIVERN	C	U	Y	BS	N

1. **UND** *(Underscore between words)*: **C**=Continuous underscore **B**=Broken underscore
2. **PS** *(Proportional spacing)*: **J**=Justified proportional **U**=Unjustified proportional **N**=Not available
3. **NLQ** *(Near letter quality)*: **A**=Always on **Y**=Available **N**=Not available
4. **ECS** *(Extended character set)*: **FI**=Full IBM **PI**=Partial IBM **BS**=Foreign characters created by backspacing **DF**=Depends on font or print wheel
5. **Color**: **Y**=Supports color **N**=Not available

PRINTER	DRIVER	UND[1]	PS[2]	NLQ[3]	ECS[4]	COLOR[5]
Diconix 150 (IBM Mode)	DRIVERN	C	N	Y	BS	N
Diconix 300	DRIVERN	B	J	Y	BS	N
Epson FX-80/100	DRIVERN	C	N	N	BS	N
Epson FX-85/185/286	DRIVERN	C	N	Y	BS	N
Epson FX-86e/286e/EX800/EX1000	DRIVERN	B	J	Y	BS	N
Epson GQ-3500	DRIVERN	C	J	A	BS	N
Epson LQ-800/1000	DRIVERN	C	J	Y	PI	N
Epson LQ-800/1000 w/ESC P	DRIVERN	C	J	Y	FI	N
Epson LQ-1500	DRIVERN	C	J	Y	PI	N
Epson LQ-2500	DRIVERN	C	J	Y	FI	Y
Epson LX-80	DRIVERN	C	N	Y	BS	N
Epson MX-80/100 w/Graftrax+	DRIVERN	B	N	N	BS	N
Epson RX-80/100	DRIVERN	C	N	N	BS	N
HP DeskJet	DRIVERN	C	J	A	FI	N
HP LaserJet	DRIVERN	C	J	A	DF	N
HP LaserJet+	DRIVERN	C	J	A	DF	N
HP LaserJet Series II	DRIVERN	C	J	A	DF	N
HP QuietJet	DRIVERN	C	J	Y	FI	N
HP ThinkJet (HP Mode)	DRIVERN	C	U	N	DF	N
HP ThinkJet (IBM Mode)	DRIVERN	C	U	N	FI	N
IBM Color Graphics	DRIVERN	C	U	Y	FI	Y
IBM Graphics	DRIVERN	C	N	N	FI	N
IBM Proprinter	DRIVERN	C	N	Y	FI	N
IBM Proprinter II and XL	DRIVERN	C	U	Y	FI	N
IBM Proprinter XL24	DRIVERN	C	J	Y	FI	N
IBM QuickWriter	DRIVERN	C	J	Y	FI	N
IBM QuietWriter	DRIVERN	C	U	Y	FI	N
IBM QuietWriter II	DRIVERN	C	J	Y	FI	N
IBM QuietWriter III	DRIVERN	C	J	Y	FI	N
IBM WheelPrinter	DRIVERN	C	J	A	BS	N
IBM WheelPrinter E	DRIVERN	C	J	A	BS	N
Mannesmann Tally MT-160	DRIVERN	B	N	Y	BS	N
NEC 8023A	DRIVERN	B	J	A	PI	N
NEC Pinwriter P2/P3	DRIVERN	C	U	Y	FI	N
NEC Pinwriter P5/6/7	DRIVERN	C	J	Y	FI	Y
NEC Pinwriter P2200	DRIVERN	C	J	Y	FI	N
NEC Spinwriter 2010/2030	DRIVERN	B	J	A	BS	N
NEC Spinwriter 2015	DRIVERN	B	J	A	BS	N
NEC Spinwriter 2050/3550/8850	DRIVERN	C	J	A	BS	N
Okidata LaserLine 6	DRIVERN	C	J	A	DF	N
Okidata ML84 Step 2	DRIVERN	C	N	Y	BS	N
Okidata ML92/93	DRIVERN	C	N	Y	BS	N
Okidata ML84/92/93 (IBM Mode)	DRIVERN	C	N	Y	PI	N
Okidata ML182/183	DRIVERN	C	N	N	FI	N
Okidata ML182/183 (IBM Mode)	DRIVERN	C	N	N	FI	N
Okidata ML192/193	DRIVERN	C	J	Y	FI	N
Okidata ML192/193 (IBM Mode)	DRIVERN	C	J	Y	FI	N
Okidata ML292/293	DRIVERN	C	J	Y	FI	Y
Okidata ML292/293 (IBM Mode)	DRIVERN	C	J	Y	FI	Y
Okidata ML393	DRIVERN	B	J	Y	FI	N
Okidata Okimate 20	DRIVERN	C	N	Y	FI	N
Okidata Pacemark 2410	DRIVERN	C	N	Y	BS	N
Olivetti PG108 Laser	DRIVERN	C	J	A	DF	N
Olympia Laserstar 6	DRIVERN	C	J	A	BS	N
Panasonic P1080i	DRIVERN	C	U	Y	BS	N
Panasonic P1090	DRIVERN	C	N	N	BS	N

Reprinted with permission of MicroPro International Corporation.

PRINTER	DRIVER	UND	PS	NLQ	ECS	COLOR
Panasonic P1091	DRIVERN	C	N	Y	BS	N
Panasonic P1091 (IBM Mode)	DRIVERN	C	N	Y	BS	N
Panasonic P1091i	DRIVERN	C	U	Y	BS	N
Panasonic P1091i (IBM Mode)	DRIVERN	C	N	Y	BS	N
Panasonic P4450 Laser Partner	DRIVERN	C	J	A	DF	N
PostScript Generic	DRIVERPS	C	J	A	DF	Y
PostScript Generic Two-Page	DRIVERPS	C	J	A	DF	Y
Qume Sprint 11+	DRIVERN	C	J	A	BS	N
Qume Sprint w/WP Option	DRIVERN	C	J	A	BS	N
Ricoh LP4080C	DRIVERN	C	J	A	BS	N
Silver Reed EXP 550	DRIVERN	B	J	N	BS	N
Star Gemini 10X	DRIVERN	B	N	N	BS	N
Star NB-10/15	DRIVERN	C	J	A	FI	N
Star Radix 10/15	DRIVERN	B	N	Y	BS	N
Star NB-24/10-15	DRIVERN	C	J	A	FI	N
Star ND-10/15	DRIVERN	C	J	A	FI	N
Star NX-10	DRIVERN	B	U	Y	BS	N
Star SB-10	DRIVERN	B	U	Y	BS	N
Star SD/SG/SR 10/15	DRIVERN	B	N	Y	BS	N
Star SD/SG/SR 10/15 (IBM Mode)	DRIVERN	B	N	Y	BS	N
Tandy DMP-130	DRIVERN	C	J	Y	PI	N
Tandy DMP-2100P	DRIVERN	C	J	Y	PI	N
Tandy DMP-2110I	DRIVERN	C	J	Y	PI	N
Tandy DMP-2110	DRIVERN	C	J	Y	PI	N
Tandy DWP-210	DRIVERN	C	J	A	BS	N
Tandy DWP-230	DRIVERN	C	J	A	BS	N
Tandy DWP-520	DRIVERN	C	J	A	BS	N
TI 855/865	DRIVERN	C	J	Y	BS	N
Toshiba P351	DRIVERN	C	J	Y	PI	N
Toshiba P1340	DRIVERN	C	N	Y	PI	N
Toshiba P1351	DRIVERN	C	J	Y	PI	N

C

ASCII Character Codes and Extended Character Set

This chart shows decimal, hexadecimal, and ASCII values for all characters. The characters with decimal values above 127 are the extended character set.

Dec	Hex	CHR	Dec	Hex	CHR	Dec	Hex	CHR
000	00	NUL	024	18	↑	048	30	0
001	01	☺	025	19	↓	049	31	1
002	02	☻	026	1A	→	050	32	2
003	03	♥	027	1B	←	051	33	3
004	04	♦	028	1C	∟	052	34	4
005	05	♣	029	1D	↔	053	35	5
006	06	♠	030	1E	▲	054	36	6
007	07	•	031	1F	▼	055	37	7
008	08	◘	032	20	SPACE	056	38	8
009	09	○	033	21	!	057	39	9
010	0A	◙	034	22	"	058	3A	:
011	0B	♂	035	23	#	059	3B	;
012	0C	♀	036	24	$	060	3C	<
013	0D	♪	037	25	%	061	3D	=
014	0E	♫	038	26	&	062	3E	>
015	0F	☼	039	27	'	063	3F	?
016	10	►	040	28	(	064	40	@
017	11	◄	041	29	)	065	41	A
018	12	↕	042	2A	*	066	42	B
019	13	‼	043	2B	+	067	43	C
020	14	¶	044	2C	,	068	44	D
021	15	§	045	2D	−	069	45	E
022	16	▬	046	2E	.	070	46	F
023	17	↨	047	2F	/	071	47	G
072	48	H	134	86	å	196	C4	─
073	49	I	135	87	ç	197	C5	┼
074	4A	J	136	88	ê	198	C6	╞
075	4B	K	137	89	e	199	C7	╟
076	4C	L	138	8A	è	200	C8	╚
077	4D	M	139	8B	i	201	C9	╔
078	4E	N	140	8C	î	202	CA	╩
079	4F	O	141	8D	i	203	CB	╦
080	50	P	142	8E	A	204	CC	╠
081	51	Q	143	8F	Å	205	CD	═
082	52	R	144	90	É	206	CE	╬
083	53	S	145	91	æ	207	CF	╧
084	54	T	146	92	Æ	208	D0	╨
085	55	U	147	93	ô	209	D1	╤
086	56	V	148	94	ö	210	D2	╥

Dec	Hex	CHR	Dec	Hex	CHR	Dec	Hex	CHR
087	57	W	149	95	ò	211	D3	╙
088	58	X	150	96	û	212	D4	╘
089	59	Y	151	97	ù	213	D5	╒
090	5A	Z	152	98	ÿ	214	D6	╓
091	5B	[	153	99	Ö	215	D7	╫
092	5C	\	154	9A	Ü	216	D8	╪
093	5D	]	155	9B	¢	217	D9	┘
094	5E	^	156	9C	£	218	DA	┌
095	5F	_	157	9D	¥	219	DB	█
096	60	`	158	9E	Pt	220	DC	▄
097	61	a	159	9F	ƒ	221	DD	▌
098	62	b	160	A0	á	222	DE	▐
099	63	c	161	A1	í	223	DF	▀
100	64	d	162	A2	ó	224	E0	α
101	65	e	163	A3	ú	225	E1	β
102	66	f	164	A4	ñ	226	E2	Γ
103	67	g	165	A5	Ñ	227	E3	π
104	68	h	166	A6	ª	228	E4	Σ
105	69	i	167	A7	º	229	E5	σ
106	6A	j	168	A8	¿	230	E6	µ
107	6B	k	169	A9	⌐	231	E7	τ
108	6C	l	170	AA	¬	232	E8	Φ
109	6D	m	171	AB	½	233	E9	Θ
110	6E	n	172	AC	¼	234	EA	Ω
111	6F	o	173	AD	¡	235	EB	δ
112	70	p	174	AE	«	236	EC	∞
113	71	q	175	AF	»	237	ED	∅
114	72	r	176	B0	░	238	EE	∈
115	73	s	177	B1	▒	239	EF	∩
116	74	t	178	B2	▓	240	F0	≡
117	75	u	179	B3	│	241	F1	±
118	76	v	180	B4	┤	242	F2	≥
119	77	w	181	B5	╡	243	F3	≤
120	78	x	182	B6	╢	244	F4	⌠
121	79	y	183	B7	╖	245	F5	⌡
122	7A	z	184	B8	╕	246	F6	÷
123	7B	{	185	B9	╣	247	F7	≈
124	7C	¦	186	BA	║	248	F8	°
125	7D	}	187	BB	╗	249	F9	●
126	7E	~	188	BC	╝	250	FA	·
127	7F	DEL	189	BD	╜	251	FB	√
128	80	Ç	190	BE	╛	252	FC	n
129	81	ü	191	BF	┐	253	FD	²
130	82	é	192	C0	└	254	FE	■
131	83	â	193	C1	┴	255	FF	blank 'FF'
132	84	ä	194	C2	┬			
133	85	à	195	C3	├			

Reprinted with permission of MicroPro International Corporation.

Index

A

D

E

F

I

J

K

L

M

N

O

P

Q

R

S

T

U

V

W

X-Z

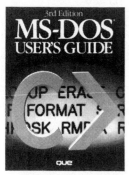

ORDER FROM QUE TODAY

Item	Title	Price	Quantity	Extension
837	Managing Your Hard Disk, 2nd Edition	$22.95		
838	MS-DOS User's Guide, 3rd Edition	22.95		
805	Using 1-2-3, Special Edition	24.95		
807	Using PC DOS, 2nd Edition	22.95		

Book Subtotal ____________

Shipping & Handling ($2.50 per item) ____________

Indiana Residents Add 5% Sales Tax ____________

GRAND TOTAL ____________

Method of Payment

☐ Check ☐ VISA ☐ MasterCard ☐ American Express

Card Number ______________________ Exp. Date ______________________

Cardholder's Name ____

Ship to ____

Address ____

City ______________________ State ______________ ZIP ______________

If you can't wait, call **1-800-428-5331** and order TODAY.

All prices subject to change without notice.

FOLD HERE

Place
Stamp
Here

Que Corporation
P.O. Box 90
Carmel, IN 46032

REGISTRATION CARD

Register your copy of *Using Wordstar*, 2nd Edition, and receive information about Que's newest products. Complete this registration card and return it to Que Corporation, P.O. Box 90, Carmel, IN 46032.

Name ____________________ Phone __________

Company ____________________ Title __________

Address ______________________________

City ______________ State _______ ZIP _______

Please check the appropriate answers:

Where did you buy *Using Wordstar*, 2nd Edition?

- ☐ Bookstore (name: ____________________)
- ☐ Computer store (name: ____________________)
- ☐ Catalog (name: ____________________)
- ☐ Direct from Que ____________________
- ☐ Other: ____________________

How many computer books do you buy a year?

- ☐ 1 or less
- ☐ 2–5
- ☐ 6–10
- ☐ More than 10

How many Que books do you own?

- ☐ 1
- ☐ 2–5
- ☐ 6–10
- ☐ More than 10

How long have you been using WordStar?

- ☐ Less than 6 months
- ☐ 6 months to 1 year
- ☐ 1–3 years
- ☐ More than 3 years

What influenced your purchase of *Using Wordstar*, 2nd Edition?

- ☐ Personal recommendation
- ☐ Advertisement
- ☐ In-store display
- ☐ Price
- ☐ Que catalog
- ☐ Que mailing
- ☐ Que's reputation
- ☐ Other: ____________________

How would you rate the overall content of *Using Wordstar*, 2nd Edition?

- ☐ Very good
- ☐ Good
- ☐ Satisfactory
- ☐ Poor

How would you rate the *Command Reference card*?

- ☐ Very good
- ☐ Good
- ☐ Satisfactory
- ☐ Poor

How would you rate the *Quick Tour through WordStar 5 in Chapter 1*?

- ☐ Very good
- ☐ Good
- ☐ Satisfactory
- ☐ Poor

How would you rate the *summary of new commands in Appendix A*?

- ☐ Very good
- ☐ Good
- ☐ Satisfactory
- ☐ Poor

What do you like *best* about *Using Wordstar*, 2nd Edition?

What do you like *least* about *Using Wordstar*, 2nd Edition?

How do you use *Using Wordstar*, 2nd Edition?

What other Que products do you own?

For what other programs would a Que book be helpful?

Please feel free to list any other comments you may have about *Using Wordstar*, 2nd Edition.

____

____

____

____

____

____

FOLD HERE

Place
Stamp
Here

Que Corporation
P.O. Box 90
Carmel, IN 46032